# ANIMALS, PROPERTY, *and the Law*

In the series
ETHICS AND ACTION,
*edited by Tom Regan*

# ANIMALS, PROPERTY,
## and the Law

### Gary L. Francione

*With a foreword by William M. Kunstler, Esq.*

TEMPLE UNIVERSITY PRESS

*Philadelphia*

Temple University Press, Philadelphia 19122
Copyright © 1995 by Temple University. All rights reserved
Published 1995
Reprinted 2005 with corrections
Printed in the United States of America

Text design by Gore Studio, Inc.

**Library of Congress Cataloging-in-Publication Data**
Francione, Gary L. (Gary Lawrence), 1954–
    Animals, property, and the law / Gary L. Francione ; with a foreword by William M. Kunstler.
        p.   cm.—(Ethics and action)
    Includes bibliographical references and index.
    ISBN 1-56639-283-7 (c : alk. paper).—ISBN 1-56639-284-5 (p : alk. paper)
    1. Animal welfare—Law and legislation—United States.   2. Animals—Law and legislation—United States.   3. Animal rights.   I. Title.
II. Series.
KF3841.F73   1995
346.7304'6954—dc20
[347.30646954]                                                               94-26263

468975

*For my family*

# Contents

vii

# *Foreword*

## William M. Kunstler, Esq.
### *Cofounder, Center for Constitutional Rights*

Although I have spent almost a half century in the field of civil rights and liberties, my efforts have been exclusively limited to attempting to secure them for human beings. For most of my professional life, I have been remarkably oblivious to the plight of animals used in experiments, in food and clothing production, and for human entertainment. Only recently, I have begun to notice the weekend antivivisection tables in my Greenwich Village neighborhood, and I have learned from my daughter, who refuses to eat veal, that calves are separated from their mothers as soon as they are born, and, in order to keep their meat white and tender, are reared in crates too cramped to permit them to move.

And as I have learned more, I have become more disturbed. The Draize irritancy tests on the unanesthetized eyes or genitalia of rabbits, the LD50 acute toxicity tests on rats and mice, the subjection of rhesus monkeys to lethal doses of gamma neutron radiation, and the removal of significant portions of the brains of cats to document the effect on the senses are but four of the supposedly scientific uses of animals. The situation of farm animals is arguably worse. In addition to keeping veal calves anemic and isolated in order to enhance the value of their flesh, we take piglets from their mothers a week after birth and then confine them in wire-mesh cages the conditions of which would put the Marquis de Sade to shame. Laying hens are jammed together in such a fashion that there is scarcely room for them to turn around, while broiler chickens, doomed to exist for less than 2 percent of their normal life cycle and imprisoned in mammoth flocks in darkened sheds, are cruelly debeaked in order to prevent the pecking and cannibalism engendered by such an unnatural environment.

In addition to using animals in experiments and for food, we use them for purposes of mere fashion or entertainment. Millions of animals lose their lives every year, caught in the deadly jaws of the steel leghold trap or raised in confined conditions in wire-mesh cages on fur farms, so that we can adorn ourselves with the latest fashions. Wild animals, captured violently and removed from their natural habitats, are crated and transported from city to city so that we can enjoy the circus. The abuses go on and on, and there is, I fear, little justification for any of it.

ix

It may surprise many who are familiar with my work that I have become interested in the plight of animals at a time in which there seems to be more human misery and injustice than ever before. I have given considerable thought to this question, and I have resolved any doubts in favor of speaking against the exploitation of nonhuman animals. It seems to me that there are at least two important reasons for taking animal rights seriously.

First, I cannot help thinking that our exploitation of animals has a direct link to our exploitation of our perennial human victims: African-Americans, poor whites, Latinos, women, lesbians and gays, social activists, Native Americans, and Asians, to name a few disempowered groups. As Tom Regan, Peter Singer, and other philosophers have argued so persuasively, speciesism, or the use of species to determine membership in the moral community, is no more morally justifiable than using race, sex, or age to determine who has rights and who does not. If we are speciesist and feel that we may exploit nonhumans simply because we are more powerful, and we judge that we will benefit from that exploitation, then discrimination against other disadvantaged groups becomes that much easier.

Second, and perhaps more important, is that it is unjust *to the animals themselves* to deny them their rights, irrespective of any salutary effect that it may have on relations among humans. Like us, animals are individuals with interests. Their value does not depend on their use *to us* any more than does the inherent value of a human being depend on that person's use to others. Justice for nonhumans requires that we recognize that all sentient beings have inherent worth that does not depend on our humanocentric and patriarchal valuation of that worth.

Lack of progress in ameliorating our treatment of nonhumans is attributable to several causes, many of which may be traced to people's ignorance about the animal abuse that they themselves indirectly support. The ultimate consumer of the veal, pork, chicken, and eggs simply has no more conception of what went on before these neatly packaged farm products arrived at the retail level than the purchasers of Civil War clothing had of the conditions under which enslaved black hands planted and picked the cotton from which its threads were made. We all need to educate ourselves about the ways in which we support animal exploitation in our daily lives.

There is another explanation, however, and that is the subject of this fascinating book by Professor Gary Francione. Francione argues—correctly, in my view—that although most of us are woefully ignorant of the massive animal suffering that we cause indirectly through our consumption of animal products, most of us reject the imposition of unnecessary suffering on animals and agree that animals ought to be treated humanely. Although these sentiments are broadly held, the law has lagged behind, and instead of evolving principles of animal protection that reflect our growing moral awareness, the law has continued to protect virtually every form of animal exploitation.

Francione proposes a thesis to explain why the law has failed to protect animals. Our legal system seeks to resolve human/animal conflicts by balancing human and animal interests. Although this appears to be appropriate in theory, in reality the balancing almost always comes out in favor of the human. The reason is that when we balance human and animal interests, we seek to compare the incomparable. Human interests are protected by claims of right; animals are regarded as *property* under the law and are not regarded as capable of having rights at all. When human interests, supported by claims of right and especially by the right to own and use property, are balanced against the unprotected interests of animals, who are the property of their human owners, the outcome is already determined. Francione explores how laws regulating cruelty to animals and experiments with animals delegate virtually plenary authority to animal owners to determine what level of care—or lack thereof—is appropriate.

Although much has been written on the technical legal aspects of animal ownership and veterinary malpractice, Francione's book is the first sustained effort to analyze our treatment of animals from a jurisprudential point of view. Despite its theoretical orientation, however, Francione's analysis also reflects his practical experience as a lawyer who has been at the cutting edge of litigating animal rights cases for over a decade. He has seen firsthand that the law is more interested in serving the interests of the powerful than it is in providing justice to the disempowered, and his analysis often draws upon his own cases.

Although Francione's analysis focuses on animals, his conclusions are applicable whenever the law allows sentient beings—human or nonhuman—to be treated solely as means to the ends determined by others. Although there were laws that supposedly protected slaves from abuse by their masters, the law very rarely punished any slave owner—regardless of the severity of the mistreatment—because slaves were regarded as property. Similarly, to the extent that our legal system has treated women or children as property, the interests of members of those groups have invariably been compromised.

We must come to understand that pain is pain, irrespective of the race, sex, *or species* of the victim. The animal rights movement is important precisely because it seeks liberation for *all* beings. The raising of consciousness about the plight of nonhumans must be accompanied by a correlative elevation about that of the millions of human beings who inhabit the ghettos, the barrios, or the streets of our inner cities. When we decry hens confined in precarious cramped spaces, we cannot be indifferent to the horribly overcrowded jails and penitentiaries of this land. Our concern for experimentation with toxic substances on rats and mice must not make us oblivious to the poisoning of entire urban communities with drugs that turn their residents into zombies, homicidal maniacs, or premature corpses.

We owe it to ourselves and to nonhuman animals to create not merely a body of rules and regulations to govern our conduct but a level of sensibility that makes us care, deeply and constructively, about the entire planet and all of its varied inhabitants. If we can accomplish this, then perhaps, some far-off day, those who follow us down the track of the generations will be able to dwell in relative harmony with all of the creatures of the earth, human and nonhuman.

This book presents an analysis that is meticulously researched and rigorously argued but is written with a level of clarity often lacking in books about legal subjects. It is my expectation that this book will provoke our rethinking about the status of animals as property and the consequent denial of justice that they suffer under the law.

May 25, 1994

# Preface and Acknowledgments

EVERY YEAR on Labor Day—for the past sixty years—the residents of Hegins, a small town near Harrisburg, Pennsylvania, have celebrated the holiday at the Fred Coleman Memorial Pigeon Shoot. The Hegins shoot is one of many live-bird shoots that occur every year throughout the Commonwealth of Pennsylvania. At Hegins alone, approximately eight thousand birds are slaughtered each year on Labor Day. And it is a gruesome ritual indeed.

At about 6:00 A.M., most of the town gathers for a festive breakfast. Afterward, everyone sings the national anthem. And then the killing begins. From approximately 9:00 A.M. until dusk, the shooters—men, women, and children—aim their shotguns and yell, "Pull." Trap boxes, which contain live pigeons, are opened at the same time that a device in the box either delivers an electric shock to the pigeons or propels them out with a moving wooden platform. The pigeons fly out of the boxes only to be shot by the shooters, who have paid approximately $80 each to participate in this "sport."

The pigeons are kept at an undisclosed location for several days prior to the shoot, and necropsy reports indicate that the birds are dehydrated and emaciated at the time that they are shot. Perhaps this explains why many of the pigeons cannot fly more than a few feet in the air, or why they beat their wings so furiously just to achieve that altitude. Most of the time, the pigeons are injured but not killed. The town employs young boys—called "trapper boys"—to reload the traps and collect the injured and dead pigeons. After each round of shooting, the trapper boys run out onto the field and reload the traps, often taking several minutes until they get around to collecting the wounded pigeons. The trapper boys place the dead and injured pigeons in a large barrel. If a pigeon is still obviously alive (even if the pigeon appears to be dead, the bird may still be alive), the trapper boys either rip the neck off or smash the pigeon repeatedly against the side of the barrel or against the wall of a small nearby shed until the pigeon dies. Sometimes the trapper boys just toss the struggling, dying birds into the barrel to bleed to death or to suffocate as more pigeons are added to the barrel. Trapper boys often "play" to protesters by smashing wounded pigeons together, carrying wounded pigeons by their broken wings, or swinging live, injured pigeons around in circles, obvi-

xiii

ously causing the pigeons great pain and distress. Birds who are wounded but who crash down in the woods immediately adjacent to the several shooting fields are simply left to die. The organizers of the event will not reveal the final destination of the dead and injured birds.

There is a law in Pennsylvania that prohibits the "wanton" or "cruel" treatment of animals and the withholding of "necessary" care to the animals. So far, no court in Pennsylvania has determined that the state anticruelty statute has any application to the pigeon shoot.

Several hundred Pennsylvania state troopers stand by and watch the carnage year after year. Their job is only to ensure that protesters and locals stay away from each other, but for the most part, they do nothing if a local person assaults, batters, or harasses protesters. One year, one shoot supporter sprayed urine on protesters. The state troopers did nothing. If a protester so much as tries to assist an injured pigeon that is lying somewhere on the grounds, however, the troopers arrest the protester and subject her to demeaning treatment. In 1992, female protesters who were arrested for trying to help the birds were subjected to body cavity searches — one police officer forced an arrested protester to remove her tampon. In my capacity as an attorney who has represented shoot protesters, I have asked the troopers why they do not enforce the Pennsylvania anticruelty statute when the organizers leave wounded pigeons to die slow and painful deaths. The troopers either shrug or tell me that I am risking being arrested, but they have thus far refused to reveal what law I am breaking by asking my question.

There is a carnival-like atmosphere as local people show up in hundreds to taunt protesters or just to enjoy the killing, which occurs continuously and simultaneously on seven different killing fields. Parents bring young children, teens bring their dates, and everyone cheers as the shooters kill or cripple pigeon after pigeon. By the afternoon, the killing fields are covered in feathers and drenched in blood, and the barrels are filled with thousands of dead and dying bodies. Locals wear T-shirts with messages such as "Hegins — Where the Flag and Feathers Fly" or "Kill at Will." One design features a colored drawing of a bleeding pigeon with a message to "Kill All the Pigeons — and Let God Sort Them Out." Beer is sold and consumed in astonishing quantities; the price of admission even includes three beers. Minors drink with complete impunity, and by 12:00 noon, there is hardly a sober person to be found. Shooters who are clearly drunk are nevertheless permitted to use their guns, which probably accounts for the fact that so many birds are merely wounded by shotguns fired only yards away from the birds. Again, the troopers turn their heads.

Wounded pigeons who fly out of the shooting area are often captured by locals, who then rip their heads off to taunt animal rights protesters. The state troopers stand by and watch, or turn their heads and then claim they saw nothing. On at least one occasion, members from the Pennsylvania chapter of the Ku Klux Klan showed up in full dress to support the right of the shooters to slaughter the pigeons.

Protesters who run out onto the field or otherwise protest the slaughter are routinely arrested and taken before one of three district judges, all of whom come from the area and are so hostile to the protesters that they can scarcely pass up any opportunity to treat them as though they were murderers or rapists. As each defendant is brought before the judge, I routinely make my speech that the pigeon shoot violates the anticruelty law of the Commonwealth of Pennsylvania and that my client was only trying to ensure that the pigeons were treated humanely. The judge just as routinely ignores me and fixes bail or, if my client does not have the several hundred dollars required for bail, orders that she be put in jail pending trial.

Every year, protesters set up a veterinary station to provide care for the injured birds who manage to fly out of the killing area. A small group of dedicated volunteers aids the veterinarians in treating dozens of injured birds. Locals surround the area and taunt the group mercilessly, but the troopers stand with their arms folded and refuse to intervene.

My discussion with one local shoot participant was instructive:

"How long have you participated in these pigeon shoots?"

"Since when I was a kid."

"Don't you think it's cruel to the pigeons?"

"Look, you're from the city. You don't understand. This is how we enjoy ourselves. And besides, pigeons are dirty animals anyway and don't deserve any better."

"But is it necessary to shoot and kill or wound them?

"It's necessary for us."

"Why?"

"It's a tradition. We've been doing it for sixty years."

"Just because it's a tradition doesn't mean it's right, does it? After all, racism is a tradition."

"It's different; these are pigeons. They're dirty, like flying rats."

"If the birds are dirty, why do you let these young children, the 'trapper boys,' handle the birds, especially when they're bleeding?"

"Well, we think it's okay. And it generates money for the town."

By this time, a crowd was gathering to listen to our discussion. The state troopers, ever vigilant, came over and told me that if I continued with the conversation, I would be charged with disorderly conduct.

Writing a book about animals and the law presented a rather interesting challenge. Previous scholarship on the subject has been restricted largely to descriptions of various areas of law with little attention to the theoretical analysis of basic issues concerning the purported justification of legally sanctioned animal exploitation. For example, in *The Law of Animals,* a treatise written in 1900, J. H. Ingham discusses at great length all types of legal transactions involving animals but very deliberately avoids issues concerning the rights of animals. Similarly, in the more recent *Animal Law,* David Favre and Murray Loring describe the various consequences of animal ownership, but, apart from describing types of anti-cruelty laws, the authors do not discuss the jurisprudential issues raised by the legal status of animals as property. Indeed, apart from a few scattered materials—including Christopher Stone's excellent and historically important essay "Should Trees Have Standing? Toward Legal Rights for Natural Objects"—there have been very few jurisprudential treatments of the subject.

Most legal scholarship—older and more modern alike—has tended to accept uncritically the basic normative assumptions underlying the law that governs our treatment of animals. For example, although many scholars have written about statutes that regulate the use of animals in medical experiments, few, if any, have attempted to analyze these statutes from the perspective of the basic but unarticulated moral positions used to justify animal use in the first place. Part of the problem is that early in our legal history, animals were relegated to the status of the property of their human owners. Consequently, the law developed doctrines that were responsive directly to this property status and that failed to reflect the moral reality that animals, even if property, constituted a unique form of property. The result is a body of law that accords animals very little protection.

Recently the controversy about our treatment of animals has reached a rather fevered pitch as more people have recognized that animal exploitation is morally questionable because it requires that we use species—just as we have used race, sex, age, and sexual orientation—to determine membership in the moral community. This moral recognition necessitates that we examine the legal system as it affects animals, in order to assess whether the current legal standards reflect these emerging and evolving moral concerns and, if not, why. This book is an attempt at such an examination.

There are many people to whom I owe significant debts of appreciation for their role in helping this project see the light of day. I want first to thank the thousands of animal advocates with whom I have worked over the past decade. Their courage in the face of insurmountable odds has not only been an important source of motivation for my legal efforts on behalf of animals but has also assisted my thinking about what the concept of animal rights means in a practical sense. I am most grateful to my colleagues at the Rutgers Law School, and, in particular, to my dean—and friend—Roger I. Abrams, and to Provost Norman Samuels, all of whom have defended my academic freedom in the face of occasional, but significant, threats, and who have supported my work in every possible way.

I want to acknowledge the many people with whom I have discussed these issues and whose input has been important in the completion of this book. The debt I owe to Professor Tom Regan is clear. It was Regan's work that first alerted me to issues concerning the gap between defensible moral theory and the law that actually regulated human/animal conflicts. Moreover, Regan's theory of animal rights provided a framework against which I could evaluate my claim that current laws that regulate our treatment of animals do not result in respect-based rights for animals. Others with whom I discussed the ideas and from whom I received valuable insights were Professor Alan Watson of the University of Georgia Law School; Professor Drucilla Cornell of the Cardozo Law School; Professors Howard McGary and Doug Husak of the Rutgers Department of Philosophy; Professor Priscilla N. Cohn of Pennsylvania State University; Professor Michael Fox of Queen's University; and Professors William Bratton, Ronald Chen, Howard Latin, and George Thomas of the Rutgers Law School. I am also grateful to Professors Cora Diamond and A. D. Woozley, who, many years ago, got me interested in the philosophical issues concerning animals.

The book started originally as an essay that I delivered at the 1991 summer session at the University of Madrid. That session was chaired by the late Professor José Ferrater Mora of Bryn Mawr College and Professor Priscilla N. Cohn, whose comments on the essay and personal encouragement caused me to develop the project in the first place. I presented the essay at a number of places as it developed into a book. These included Oxford University, the University of Minnesota, Duke University, the University of North Carolina at Chapel Hill, North Carolina State University, the University of Georgia, Pennsylvania State University, Osgoode Hall Law School, and Queen's University. At all of these places, I received excellent comments and criticism.

The research for the book itself took over a year and involved sources that dealt with animals, animal law in particular, law and jurisprudence, philosophy, and slavery. I am deeply grateful to our excellent library staff, including Paul Axel-Lute, Glen Bencivengo, Nina Ford, Martha Lewis, Ronnie Mark, Ernie Nardone, Evelyn P. Ramones, and Robert Shriek, all of whom helped in various ways to assemble the mountains of materials that literally filled two rooms. Our library supervisor, Margorie Crawford, borrowed hundreds of books and articles for me from libraries around the world and never complained, despite the sometimes esoteric nature of my requests. The manuscript, which was over nine hundred pages long, was prepared with very great care (and cheer) by Gwen Ausby, Roselene Correia, and Roseann Raniere. Our computer specialist, Jeff Katz, provided excellent support. Linda Garbaccio cheered me through various disasters. I received excellent research support from Brenda McDonough, Rutgers Law School, class of 1994, and John E. Clark, Rutgers Law School, class of 1996. The final manuscript was sent off on April 23, 1994. I did not attempt to update after that point except to edit the text to reflect major cases that had been reversed while the book was in production.

There is a direct link between my academic work and my professional work as a lawyer specializing in animal rights litigation. Indeed, one need only work on these cases for a short time to recognize the inherent limitations of the legal doctrines that supposedly protect animals. Despite the limitations of the legal system, I have continued to gain insights into the problem of animal exploitation as a direct result of my legal work. In an effort to continue this work and to train others to handle animal cases, I established the Rutgers Animal Rights Law Center at Rutgers Law School in 1990. At the Center, which is the only one of its kind in the country, law students earn academic credit and learn practical lawyering skills while they help to litigate actual cases involving animal exploitation. The Center also produces educational materials to help lawyers and nonlawyers better understand how they can use the law to help animals. I am grateful to a number of friends, including Patty Shenker and Doug Stoll, William E. Crockett, Esq., Dr. Priscilla N. Cohn, and Jim and Stephanie Schueler, for their support of the activities of the Rutgers Animal Rights Law Center. I am also grateful to the wonderful students whom I have had the pleasure to teach at the Center over the past five years.

The people at Temple University Press were nothing short of marvelous throughout the entire publication process. Many, many thanks to Doris Braendel and Keith Monley, who provided excellent editorial support; to Joan Vidal, who, with consistent equanimity, walked me through the production process; and to Jane Cullen, who originally acquired the book for Temple. I am very grateful to Bill Kunstler for the very kind words in his foreword, and to Sue Coe for permission to use the art that is on the jacket and papercover of the book.

Finally, I owe a very great debt of gratitude to my family. I acknowledge the considerable and constant support that I have received from my parents, brother, and sister-in-law. My life partner, Anna Charlton, Esq., who is also the cofounder and codirector of the Center, has been the single most important influence in my life. She has been with me through every animal case I worked on, and she has always provided creative and valuable insights. She is truly my comrade in the struggle for animal rights.

And then there are our alternative children, past and present—including Chelsea, The Bandit, Stratton, Emma, and Hamidallah—from whom I have learned that the line between human and nonhuman is, like all lines, one that should be drawn in pencil, so that it can be moved to accommodate moral evolution and the realization of moral reality.

April 23, 1994

# INTRODUCTION

# Legal Welfarism: The Consequences of the Property Status of Animals

FOR THE PAST DECADE, I have lectured, both in this country and abroad, at high schools, colleges, universities, professional schools, community groups, and animal protection groups about the topic of animal rights. I have debated research scientists in public forums. I have represented over a dozen of the major animal protection organizations in this country in connection with some of their most controversial cases. In 1985 I represented over one hundred animal advocates who, for the first time in the history of the National Institutes of Health, occupied that institution illegally for four days in order to force the closure of a federally funded animal laboratory at the University of Pennsylvania. The sit-in, which attracted attention worldwide and caused an avalanche of mail and phone calls to pour into congressional offices, ended when then Secretary of Health and Human Services Margaret Heckler ordered the lab closed for violating federal law. Since 1990 I have served with Anna Charlton as codirector of the Rutgers Animal Rights Law Center. The Center is part of the curriculum of the Rutgers University Law School, and law students earn academic credit as they learn litigation skills through working on animal rights cases. The Center has been involved in dozens of legal cases involving such matters as grand jury investigations into the activities of those who allegedly remove animals illegally from laboratories, the right of a student to refuse to dissect or vivisect an animal as part of her required coursework, the right of religious groups to perform animal sacrifices, the question whether pigeon shoots constitute cruelty to animals, the constitutionality of hunter harassment statutes, and the propriety of wild-horse "management" by the federal government.

In sum, I am well aware of what is at stake in the debate about animal rights and how acrimonious that debate may become on all sides.

It is clear to me that despite the sharp disagreement within our society over various issues of animal protection, almost everyone—including those who directly or indirectly support various forms of animal exploitation—agrees that nonhuman animals ought not to be subjected to "unnecessary" pain and that nonhuman animals ought to be treated "humanely." Indeed, I have yet to find a

3

single person in the course of my work, including the people who defend the pigeon massacre that I discussed in the Preface, who does not enthusiastically embrace the principle that we ought to treat animals "humanely." The law purports to reflect this concern in that there are laws that require that we accord such humane treatment to animals in every context in which we use animals. Despite this seemingly broad moral agreement and its supposed reflection in the law, no one can dispute that animals are routinely subjected to treatment that may be considered barbaric. The law in practice does little, if anything, to protect animals, even if there is absolutely no justification for their exploitation other than human amusement. On the one hand, it appears clear that most people strongly condemn, on moral grounds, the mistreatment of animals. On the other hand, although our written laws ostensibly reflect this concern, the legal system in practice seems to be completely unresponsive to that moral sentiment and permits any use of animals, however abhorrent.

The purpose of this book is to propose and to defend a thesis that explains why this is the case. The thesis is straightforward and simple. In our legal system, animals do not have rights as that term is normally used. Although there are restrictions on the use of animals (as there are on the use of all property), such restrictions, such as anticruelty laws or laws governing the use of animals in experiments, do not establish any rights for animals or impose any duties on humans that are directed ultimately to the well-being of the animal. Rather, these laws require that in determining whether suffering is "unnecessary" or treatment is "inhumane," we balance the interests of animals against the interests of human beings. The problem is that human interests are protected by rights in general and by the right to own property in particular. As far as the law is concerned, an animal is the personal property, or *chattel,* of the animal's owner and cannot possess rights. Indeed, it is a fundamental premise of our property law that property cannot itself have rights as against human owners and that, as property, animals are objects of the exercise of human property rights.[1] I emphasize that property rights are not the only rights relevant to this balancing process, but they are clearly the most important. There are other rights, however, such as the right of personal liberty or the right of expression, that also weigh in the "balance" against animal interests. Consequently, when we are faced with a human/animal conflict and use the prescribed "balancing" method to determine whose interests should prevail, the answer is determined from the outset. In such a system, animals almost never prevail, irrespective of what might be the relatively trivial human interest at stake and the relatively weighty animal interest involved in the particular case.

Throughout this book, I describe the prevailing legal theory concerning animals as *legal welfarism.* Legal welfarism is a normative theory implicit in the law and whose foundational assumptions are hardly ever recognized, much less discussed, in case law or academic comment. That is, although the law prohibits the infliction of "unnecessary" pain and suffering on animals and requires that they be treated "humanely," these terms are interpreted in light of the legal status of animals as property, the importance of property in our culture, and the general tendency of legal doctrine to protect and to maximize the value of property. Consequently, what is considered "humane" treatment or "unnecessary" suffering may, under the law, differ considerably from the ordinary-language interpretations of those terms. We recognize that animals are different from inanimate property, so we enact laws to protect this peculiar species of property; yet these laws are interpreted against a background that effectively obscures the difference between animal property and other forms of property. The result is that regulation of animal use does not, as a general rule, transcend that level of protection that facilitates the most economically efficient exploitation of the animal.

Many legal theorists subscribe to the view that the development of the common law may be explained largely by reference to the notion of wealth maximization—that is, that legal doctrines have the effect of maximizing overall social wealth.[2] Legal welfarism is the doctrine that developed to maximize the use of animal property. The doctrine of legal welfarism tends to proscribe only those uses of animals that are not "efficient" or that decrease overall social wealth. If an "unnecessary" infliction of pain is nevertheless part of an institutionalized or accepted exploitation of animals, then the activity is permitted. The property owner must not inflict gratuitous pain on the animal, since this would generate no social benefit and would decrease overall social wealth.

In addition, legal welfarism is characterized by the notion that the law can best assure the "welfare" of animals (understood as the level of care that maximizes the value of animal property) by allowing the property owner to determine what will maximize the value of the property to the property owner. Accordingly, the doctrine of legal welfarism tends to defer to owner determinations about animal welfare. For example, under the federal Animal Welfare Act, the primary source of regulation of laboratory animals is by those who own and use the animals. It is they who have the greatest interest in the integrity of scientific data, and they who presumably will be motivated the strongest to ensure that the appropriate level of animal welfare is provided. The approach to animal treatment embodied in legal welfarism is a logical consequence of the possession of rights by humans and the status of animals as property.

Our legal system is quite adept at making it appear as though disenfranchised groups receive legal protection. By directing our attention to issues that are often quite tangential, legal discourse steers clear of the more important fundamental moral and economic assumptions upon which the legal system ultimately rests. One need only read cases from the eighteenth and nineteenth centuries concerning slavery; these cases read with the same formality as cases decided just yesterday by the United States Supreme Court and solemnly discuss the same issues of due process and rights. Nevertheless, these slave cases avoid completely the issue of the justice of the institution of slavery and assume that the legal system functioned to provide adequate legal protection to those who were enslaved.

The same is true with nonhuman animals. We have numerous laws that purport to protect animals, and laws that ostensibly give rights to animals. These laws, however, focus our attention on matters of "unnecessary" suffering, "humane" treatment, and the "welfare" of animals. Never does the law examine the fundamental assumptions that are the basis of the various institutions of animal exploitation. Rather, the law creates the illusion that a vulnerable group that is, as a matter of law, treated primarily, if not exclusively, as means to human ends is provided with adequate protection through laws that provide for "humane" treatment.

## Animal Welfare as a General Theory

Legal welfarism is a version of the general moral theory of animal welfare. Animal welfare, understood in a very broad sense, is the view that it is morally acceptable, at least under some circumstances, to kill animals or subject them to suffering as long as precautions are taken to ensure that the animal is treated as "humanely" as possible. That is, an animal welfare position generally holds that there is *no* animal interest that cannot be overridden if the consequences of the overriding are sufficiently "beneficial" to human beings. Legal welfarism establishes a strong presumption in favor of letting animal owners determine what uses of animals best maximize the value of animal property. The presumption is that a benefit exists unless a use can be shown to be gratuitous.

Although a welfarist may base her theory ultimately on any one of a number of moral theories or on some combination of theories, most welfarists subscribe to some version of utilitarian moral theory. The details of utilitarian thought are complicated; it will suffice, however, for present purposes to say that utilitarian moral theory holds that the rightness or wrongness of an act is determined by reference to the consequences of an act understood in terms of "happiness," "pleasure," the "greatest good," and so on. A utilitarian will look at the available options, weigh the "pluses and minuses" of each option, or its "costs and benefits,"[3] and then choose to perform that act, or that type of act, that will maximize the desirable consequences however understood.

The connection between utilitarian theory and animal welfare is made explicit in the writings of nineteenth-century philosopher Jeremy Bentham. Bentham argued that although the state could create legal rights, the notion of rights made no sense apart from this purely positivist use, and that the moral worth of actions was to be determined by their consequences. Bentham rejected the position that only consequences *to humans* should matter when we weigh the results of actions. According to Bentham, as long as a being could suffer, the consequences to that being must be weighed in determining the propriety of action.[4]

There are many versions of animal welfare depending, for the most part, on the weight that is assigned to animal interests in performing the utilitarian balance, and to a lesser, but still important degree, on what is viewed as the intrinsic value (pleasure, happiness, preference satisfaction, and so on) that is sought to be maximized. For example, philosopher Peter Singer, who holds that the intrinsic value to be maximized is the furtherance of interests of those affected, argues that equal interests of nonhumans and humans should be given equal consideration.[5] Singer's more progressive version of animal welfare would require a drastic reduction in animal suffering but would permit animal exploitation when the consequences, properly characterized and considered, outweighed the animal's interest in not being exploited.[6] Other welfarists purport to take animal interests seriously in determining the propriety of animal use, but then merely endorse the status quo as it concerns animal use.[7] Still other animal advocates argue that the law should incorporate "improved" welfarist notions, such as additional layers of review, to ameliorate the treatment accorded to laboratory animals.[8]

I think it uncontroversial to say that *all* versions of welfarism involve some type of balancing. To the extent that animal advocates suggest that legal welfarism be replaced with some other, ostensibly more protective, theory of animal welfare, the replacement theory may very well still encounter the problem of trying to balance the interests of a human rightholder with property rights against the interests of property that is without any claim of right. In all but the most unusual circumstances, such a framework would probably employ the analytical approach of legal welfarism because animal interests, unprotected by rights, are balanced against competing claims of human right, including the right to exercise control over (animal) property and to determine what best maximizes the value of that property to the owner of the property.

In the Epilogue, I discuss some alternatives to legal welfarism in order to examine whether arguably more "humane" versions of animal welfare can ameliorate the deficiencies that I hope to identify with legal welfarism. Any consideration of the ways in which legal welfarism might be altered is, however, secondary to my more limited goal of demonstrating the systematic features of legal welfarism and thereby explaining the gap that exists between what I intuitively regard as our social concern for the "humane" treatment of animals and the extreme animal abuse that is currently sanctioned by the law.

It is, however, necessary that I introduce at the outset some notion of animal rights. As a practical matter, many of those who oppose legal welfarism are not seeking to improve animal welfare, but are, instead, looking to replace the paradigm that we use to understand human/animal relations in the first place. The replacement theory involves the notion of extending rights to animals. There are two reasons the reader should have at least a basic understanding of rights theory, especially as it applies to nonhuman animals. First, legal welfarism is a theory that treats animals solely as means to ends; rights theory requires that we see animals not merely as means to ends but as beings with value and with interests that should be respected. Rights theory, then, provides a contrast to legal welfarism. Second, I argue that despite some claims to the contrary, animals possess no rights under legal welfarism. In order to test that claim, I need some notion of rights against which to measure the supposed rights protection that some regard as existing under the current welfarist paradigm.

## Regan and Rights Theory

The primary alternative to the welfarist approach is found in rights theory. The reason that I label the rights approach as the "primary" alternative to welfarism is that there are other nonrights approaches that are nevertheless critical of welfarism. For example, certain feminist theorists are critical of rights talk but nevertheless reject welfarist theory and have very strong notions of animal protection.[9] Similarly, Marxists are critical of rights, but at least some theorists working in that tradition reject animal exploitation.[10] In any event, rights are important normative notions that we use to discuss the level of both moral and legal protection provided in particular circumstances, and it is to rights theory that I now turn. In addition to describing rights as an alternative to welfare, I want to examine a rights theory that embraces nonhumans. Although there may be criticisms of this theory, I believe that it represents a plausible account of animal rights against which we can compare legal efforts to protect animals, in order to see whether these laws create animal rights.

Generally speaking, when we say that someone has a right, we mean that the person has some value that requires our respect, whether or not our exploitation of that person would be beneficial to others. The point of having a right is to have something that stands as a sort of barrier between the holder of the right and everyone else. A right generally cannot be taken away simply because it would be beneficial for someone else if the rightholder lost the right. Rights theorists argue that at least some animals possess at least some of the same rights enjoyed by humans. Although they acknowledge that there may be conflicts between rights and that these conflicts may require accommodation of some sort, they reject out of hand the position that animals lose their rights whenever, or just because, humans stand to benefit by exploiting animals.

Although there has been a great deal of excellent philosophical scholarship concerning our treatment of animals,[11] the theory of animal rights that is regarded as most influential may be found in Professor Tom Regan's *The Case for Animal Rights.*[12] Regan begins by exploring the Cartesian claim that nonhuman animals are not conscious and, therefore, not sentient. Descartes, who is largely responsible for our current attitudes about animals, argued that the use of language by humans demonstrated consciousness and that since nonhuman animals did not exhibit linguistic behavior, they could not be regarded as conscious beings.[13] Regan effectively demonstrates that as an empirical matter, Descartes was wrong: at least some nonhuman animals exhibit linguistic behavior. More important, Regan also shows that Descartes was wrong as a logical matter; that is, Regan argues that humans have to be conscious *before* they learn to use language.

Regan then goes on to argue that evolutionary theory, common sense, and ordinary language all point to the possession of consciousness—indeed, of a complex mental life—by nonhuman animals. Normal mammals aged one year or more all (human and nonhuman) share mind states such as perception, memory, desire, belief, self-consciousness, intention, a sense of the future, emotion, and

sentience. Most of us regard these features—as they are exhibited by human beings—as necessary and sufficient for the status of personhood. Although a more
progressive utilitarian, such as Singer, might agree that these features as exhibited by nonhumans require that their equal interests be given equal consideration
in terms of determining the consequences of certain actions, Regan, as a *deontologist,* treats these similarities as erecting rights barriers that are impervious to
mere consequential considerations. As a deontologist, Regan argues that what is
right, wrong, good, or bad cannot be determined by an appeal to consequences or
contractarian social theory.[14] Accordingly, Regan rejects the utilitarian and animal welfare approaches, which do rely on an appeal to consequences, and argues
that human and nonhuman animals possess equal inherent value precisely because they share a crucial similarity: almost every mammal—human or nonhuman—is the subject-of-a-life that is meaningful to that being, irrespective of the
value of that being to anyone else. Indeed, Regan distills clearly the concept of a
right as it is used in modern law and philosophy: a right acts as a barrier of sorts
between the rightholder and everyone else, and the barrier cannot be breached
solely because that breach will be of utility to someone else.

Regan argues that the basic moral right possessed by all moral agents and patients is the right to respectful treatment. This right is based on the "respect principle," which precludes treating the rightholder merely as a means to an end.
Rather, the rightholder must be treated in a manner consistent with the recognition that she possesses an inherent value that is the same as any other holder of
such a right. Regan interprets the notions of inherent value and respect to support
the "harm principle," which holds that we have a prima facie duty not to harm individuals and that we owe this duty directly to the beneficiaries of the duty.[15] Regan recognizes, of course, that to say that animals (or humans) have rights is not
to say that those rights can never be overridden. Indeed, the reason that the harm
principle imposes a prima facie obligation—as opposed to an absolute obligation—is that the obligation may be overridden, but anyone who wishes to override the harm principle must present valid moral reasons for doing so and may not
simply appeal to consequences that would result were the right to be overridden.
For example, Regan accepts that rights can conflict and argues that in certain circumstances "numbers count" and that in those circumstances it is better to override the rights of the few rather than the rights of the many. In other circumstances, such as when overriding the rights of the few will leave the few worse
off than any of the many, then we should override the rights of the many. Regan
is clear, however, that "we must never harm individuals who have inherent value
on the grounds that all those affected by the outcome will thereby secure 'the best'
aggregate balance of intrinsic values (e.g., pleasures) over intrinsic disvalues
(e.g., pain)."[16]

After presenting his basic argument, Regan asks what implications arise from
accepting that nonhuman animals share with human animals this basic right to respectful treatment. He concludes that most forms of animal exploitation are
morally indefensible and that animal exploitation should be *abolished* and not

merely regulated. He rejects vivisection, animal agriculture, sport hunting, and other practices condoned by a Cartesian dualism that sees nonhuman animals as fundamentally different from humans.[17] Regan considers the major forms of animal exploitation as resulting from a general failure to regard animals as subjects-of-a-life. This failure is the direct result of the status of animals as property.

Accepting a rights position does not lead to the absurd result—as it is often asserted by those who exploit animals—that animals enjoy the exact same rights that humans enjoy or that humans and animals are the same for legal purposes.[18] Unfortunately, this misunderstanding about the nature of rights theory is endorsed by at least some academic commentators as well. For example, sociologists James Jasper and Dorothy Nelkin state that the animal rights position as a general matter maintains that animals "[h]ave absolute moral rights to full lives without human interference."[19] Neither Regan nor any other deontological theorist argues for "absolute" or "equal" rights for animals. Rather, rights are prima facie reasons for eliminating recourse to consequences, but these reasons may be overridden by appropriate moral considerations. Animal rights are no more "absolute" than human rights. Moreover, no one argues that nonhuman animals should be given a right to drive vehicles or to vote in national elections. Although all rightholders have equal inherent value, that does not mean that they have the same rights.

In addition, accepting a rights position does not mean that there can never be a conflict between rights. That is, the fact that animals may have certain rights does not mean that those rights will always trump other rights that may be held by humans or other nonhumans. This is another way of saying that rights are not absolute. For example, the First Amendment to the United States Constitution gives us the right of free speech. But even though the actual language of the First Amendment seems quite unequivocal—"Congress shall make *no* law" prohibiting speech—the right of free speech is not, and cannot be, absolute. If, for instance, we are sitting in a crowded movie theater, we cannot yell "fire" just for the fun of seeing everyone stampede out of the theater. Our speech rights are limited by the rights of others in the movie theater to their bodily safety; and their right is unnecessarily jeopardized by our "joke" of yelling "fire" when, in fact, there is no fire. So, too, if animals have rights, those rights cannot be absolute. There will be times when animal rights will conflict with human rights. There is no certain way to resolve such conflict, but then, our legal system must struggle with such conflict every day in the context of conflicts between human rights.

Although Regan's theory is important for many reasons, one of his primary contributions is to have presented a plausible account of how a central notion of rights theory—the notion that the rightholder is entitled to be treated as an end and not solely as a means to an end—applies to animals. That is, the concepts of animal rights and human rights are similar in at least this crucial respect, and anything that we call a right—whether human or animal—should exhibit this normative characteristic. As I argue, however, animals do not have rights in the sense that Regan uses that term, which is the way that the term is normally used in rights theory. Indeed, the law at present regards animals as the property of their owners and institutionally regards animals only as means to human ends. Legal welfarism recognizes only one animal interest—the interest of the animal in not being used "improperly" as property. According to the normative assumptions that are at the foundation of legal welfarism, animals *cannot* be regarded as subjects-of-a-life, or as carriers of interests, because to characterize animals as property is, from the outset, to treat animals as a legal entity that cannot, as a matter of law, truly have rights.

As far as animal interests are concerned, and in contrast with rights theory, legal welfarism reflects a particularly severe form of utilitarian thought in at least two respects. First, legal welfarism generally requires that when we determine the consequences of an act involving an animal, we should, for all intents and purposes, ignore any interests that the animal may have, because it is appropriate to regard animals solely as means to human ends.

Second, although legal welfarism does not seriously consider animal interests as "consequences" that need to be balanced, it does count as a "consequence" the violation of any possible legal or moral *human rights*. For example, some argue that humans have the *right* to knowledge that may (or may not) facilitate medical cures; scientists argue that they have the *right* to gather knowledge, whether or not it is ultimately useful. So although legal welfarism appears to be based on considerations of the consequences of actions, those consequences almost always implicate the supposed violation of human rights, and often of human rights to exercise control over property. As I just discussed in the context of explaining Regan's theory, a right is a prima facie reason to protect the rightholder's interest in the absence of a compelling reason to do otherwise. Since an animal is regarded solely as a means to an end as the property of human owners, and since the animal's interests are evaluated against this status as property, the outcome is almost certain: people win and animals lose.

In an important sense, then, legal welfarism is partly a theory about human rights and partly a theory of animal welfare; although it purports to balance the consequences, in its actual implementation in the legal system it provides virtually complete protection to human property rights except when doing otherwise would result in the gratuitous (i.e., economically unproductive) infliction of animal suffering or death.

It should come as no surprise that such a system does not work particularly well to provide meaningful protection to nonhuman animals.

## The Organization of the Book

The book is divided into three parts. In Part I, I examine in a general way the paradigm of property that pervades our treatment of animals, and I provide an extended discussion of legal welfarism. As part of this exploration of the status of animals as property, I present a brief historical sketch of our treatment of animals as property and discuss the effect that this categorization has had on selected legal doctrines that concern our treatment of animals. In this context, I explore the concept of "standing," a jurisdictional concept that has often been used to keep human/animal conflicts out of the courts. The concept of "standing" requires that the entity before the court be the entity properly empowered by the law to bring the particular claim. By treating animals as property, animals are simply excluded as unable to raise legal claims. This is true even though nonhuman entities, such as corporations, have standing to raise legal claims. I also explore how the characterization of animals as property often conflicts with the nonlegal status of at least certain animals as members of human families.

I argue that our way of resolving human/animal conflicts is facilitated by what may be called the "normativity" of legal regulation, or the notion that fundamental normative assumptions of legal welfarism are obscured by certain *other* normative notions. For example, the assumptions of legal welfarism that animals exist only as means to human ends and that animals have no interests that trump human property rights (themselves normative notions) are obscured by the normative principle that animal exploitation is perfectly permissible as long as it is done as "humanely" as possible.

Finally, in Part I, I consider the general theoretical claim that current laws regulating the use of animals do not give rise to animal rights. It is important for me to establish this claim as part of my argument that we balance considerations of human rights against animal interests that are unprotected by rights. If the current regulation of animal exploitation per se creates meaningful rights in animals, then my criticism of legal welfarism becomes far more difficult and far less interesting as a mere clash of rights. In any event, I explore the regulation/ rights question in general in Part I and then pursue the matter in Parts II and III in order to test the thesis, and its general theoretical formulation in terms of normative analysis and rights theory, in particular contexts.

In Part II, I examine how the paradigm of property applies in the context of anticruelty laws. Although "humane" laws provide an opportunity to test the thesis in a specific context, these statutes actually apply to a wide variety of conduct concerning animals, and in this sense, the context is more general than that provided in Part III. I argue that although anticruelty statutes supposedly represent a "regulation" of or restriction on our use of animals as property, these statutes are, for the most part, completely ineffective in protecting animals, although these laws probably do a very good job of protecting human property rights in animals.

In Part III, I examine the use of animals in an even more specific context — the use of animals in experiments. The use of animals in experiments is ostensibly the most heavily regulated use of animals in the United States. The primary regulatory structure, the federal Animal Welfare Act, and its various amendments and implementing regulations represent what at least appears to be a pervasive regulatory scheme. Further, this regulation occurs against a backdrop of certain assumptions that militate against governmental regulation of research and serve to inform how the "balancing" framework is applied in the case of animals used in experiments.

The propriety of using live animals in medical experiments is currently a most controversial social issue that has engendered highly charged responses from all sides. Although the issue is certainly not a new one, the debate has recently taken a marked turn. In the early 1980s an aggressive and highly organized animal rights movement emerged that was aimed directly at the use of animals in science. Some who adopt the animal rights position argue for the abolition of all vivisection on the ground that animals have rights that are violated by using them in experiments.[20] This position rejects efforts to apply the welfarist theory through federal laws, such as the Animal Welfare Act, and maintains that even if regulation were effective, it would be morally unacceptable to treat animals as means to human ends. Researchers obviously reject the animal rights position and instead claim to adopt a conservative animal welfare position, according to which "the responsible use of animals in scientific research for the benefit of humans is morally sound."[21] "Responsible" use, I argue, is any use that produces a "benefit," which is so measured that virtually *any* use of animals may be said to produce the requisite "benefit."

A discussion of the use of animals in experiments also serves to illustrate vividly issues of the normativity of law. Reliance on normative concepts such as the "humaneness" of research or the "necessity" of pain is problematic because such concepts are defined within a legal framework that from the outset is highly prejudicial to animal interests and that is inclined to consider any use "humane" or any level of pain "necessary" as long as there is some human benefit to be gained. This benefit may be only the satisfaction of some curiosity on the part of scientists. Moreover, these normative concepts miss the boat in the most crucial sense: they obscure the fundamental question whether such use of animals is morally acceptable in the first place, and assume that such use *must* be acceptable as long as there are benefits for human beings.

## Some Preliminary Observations

I offer four preliminary observations. First, I do not discuss at any length the current philosophical controversies concerning the nature of property.[22] That is, I do not discuss the justification of property or evaluate the institution of property. I discuss various conceptions of private property only to demonstrate that whatever restrictions are placed on an animal owner in terms of what use she may make of her property, such restrictions are unlikely to have any positive effect on the treatment of animals. Moreover, my discussion of property is restricted primarily to American law, with occasional references to British law. Property is, in essence, a bundle of rights that can differ considerably from place to place. Accordingly, I do not attempt a comparative analysis, although it is not disputed that animals are regarded as property in the law of virtually every legal system in the world.

Second, although I argue that the status of animals as property facilitates their exclusion from the scope of our legal (and moral) concern, I do not maintain that characterizing sentient beings as property *necessarily* means that those beings will be treated exactly the same as inanimate objects or that property can never have rights as a matter of formal jurisprudential theory. For example, although slaves were, for some purposes, considered "persons" who technically held certain rights, those rights were not particularly effective in providing any real protection for slaves. We *could* decide to grant certain rights to animals while continuing to regard them as property. The problem is that as long as property is, as a matter of legal theory, regarded as that which cannot have interests or cannot have interests that transcend the rights of property owners to use their property, then there will probably always be a gap between what the law permits people to do with animals and what any acceptable moral theory and basic decency tell us is appropriate. It is my tentative conclusion that animal rights (as we commonly understand the notion of "rights") are extremely difficult to achieve within a system in which animals are regarded as property, although this precise issue transcends the scope of the present work.

Third, and related to the foregoing consideration, I emphasize that I am only concerned with laws that attempt to regulate our treatment of animals through the requirement that we treat them "humanely" or that we not impose on them "unnecessary" suffering. I do not discuss—except where indicated—laws that regulate our treatment of animals through the imposition of *prohibitions* on particular conduct. The reason such prohibitory laws are important is that they arguably recognize that animals have at least some interests that may not be sacrificed; legal welfarism, by contrast, accepts that all animal interests may be sacrificed in favor of human interests. The vast majority of the laws in this country that affect our treatment of animals do not involve prohibitions, and my analysis will accordingly be focused on those types of laws that do presently characterize the legal treatment of animals in this country. In any event, it is clear that more work needs to be done on the role of prohibitions (as opposed to nonprohibitory regulation) in creating rights.

Fourth, although I will discuss various philosophical issues and doctrines, the reader should not regard these discussions as exhaustive in any sense. My discussions will be limited to those portions of philosophical doctrines that directly concern the legal issues under consideration.

# PART I

*The Status of Animals as Property*

By allowing [animals] to be owned by those who would raise them for food, as a source of various byproducts (e.g. wool), as objects to be entered into competitions, or even as pets, we show that we are willing to treat animals as mere means to human ends. All of this is, of course, perfectly compatible with insisting that unnecessary animal suffering should be eliminated.

Baruch A. Brody, "An Evaluation of the Ethical Arguments Commonly Raised Against the Patenting of Transgenic Animals"

# CHAPTER ONE

## *The Problem: "Unnecessary" Suffering and the "Humane" Treatment of Property*

### "Necessary" Suffering: Three Examples

THERE IS increasing social concern about our use of nonhumans for experiments,[1] food,[2] clothing,[3] and entertainment.[4] This concern about animals reflects both our own moral development as a civilization and our recognition that the differences between humans and animals are, for the most part, differences of degree and not of kind. For example, recent work in animal behavior and psychology has confirmed that many animals possess highly developed cognitive abilities.[5] A popular magazine had a front-cover feature on the implication of our recognition of animals' cognitive abilities and concluded that "it is one thing to treat animals as mere resources if they are presumed to be little more than living robots, but it is entirely different if they are recognized as fellow sentient beings."[6] Philosophical writings, such as *The Case for Animal Rights* by Tom Regan and *Animal Liberation* by Peter Singer, have presented and developed sophisticated and persuasive arguments in favor of increased moral consideration for animals. According to Regan and Singer, prevailing social attitudes toward animals are characterized by "speciesism," which, like racism, sexism, or homophobia, uses a morally irrelevant criterion—species membership—to determine membership in the moral community. Regan and Singer argue that speciesism is no more logically or morally defensible than is any other form of prejudice against the other or bias in favor of those who are like the self.

Although animal rights may be a remote goal in a nation that still disregards the rights of the poor, of women, of people of color, and of children and the elderly, there can be little, if any, doubt that conventional morality strongly proscribes the infliction of any "unnecessary" pain on animals and imposes an obligation of all humans to treat nonhumans "humanely."[7] Despite ubiquitous agreement on these points, there is also widespread acknowledgment that animal abuse does continue unabated in our society. What accounts for this ostensible irony is that animals do not have rights under the law. There are, of course, many laws on the federal and state levels that purport to protect animals from "inhumane" treatment, but these laws do not really confer rights in the sense that we usually use that term. Indeed, the vast majority of these laws do not even prohibit certain types of conduct that adversely affects animals. To the extent that the law does contain any types of prohibitions, such as the illegality of dogfighting or cockfighting, these prohibitions are usually more concerned with class issues or other moral issues than with animal protection. Similarly, aggressive efforts by police to prohibit the use of animals in religious "sacrifices" may have more to do with racist attitudes about the religion involved than with concern about animals. Both dogfighting and cockfighting are activities that are ostensibly more common among members of disempowered minority communities. Although these prohibitions also appear to be related to a general social disapproval of gambling, other animal wagering activities (e.g., horseracing) are more common among the middle and upper classes; indeed, several such events, such as the Kentucky Derby, are quite celebrated. Prohibitions (e.g., no animal can be used in burn experiments) *may* imply that there are some interests possessed by the animal that may not be traded away simply because of consequential considerations (e.g., the animal has an interest in not being used in burn experiments even where it can be plausibly argued that humans will benefit). Animals are the property of people, and property owners usually react rather strongly against any measure that threatens their autonomy concerning the use of their property.

I refer to the current regulatory structure in this country as it pertains to animals as *legal welfarism,* or the notion, represented by and in various legal doctrines, that animals, which are the property of people, may be treated solely as means to ends by humans as long as this exploitation does not result in the infliction of "unnecessary" pain, suffering, or death. I use this expression to distinguish current legal doctrine from other consequentialist moral theories that may advocate greater protection for animals and from the moral notion of animal rights, which, as I discussed in the Introduction, seeks to shift our framework for dealing with animal issues toward a recognition that at least some animals may be said to possess rights that are not subject to abrogation merely because humans will benefit from that abrogation. Moreover, I distinguish legal welfarism from other types of regulatory systems, such as those that might attempt to regulate animal treatment through the imposition of prohibitions. As I mentioned above, when the state prohibits altogether certain types of animal treatment, it may recognize animal interests that are not subject to abrogation simply on the basis of consequential considerations; legal welfarism treats virtually all animal interests as subject to sacrifice in favor of human interests, however trivial relative to the animal interest at stake.

The law requires that we "balance" the interests of humans and animals in order to decide what constitutes "humane" treatment and "unnecessary" suffering. The problem is that the framework of legal welfarism contains numerous normative considerations that render empty, for the most part, any attempt to "balance"—at least as far as animal interests are concerned. The result of legal welfarism is that in many instances a relatively trivial human interest is balanced against an animal's most fundamental interest in not experiencing pain or death, and the human interest nevertheless prevails. We all reject "unnecessary" cruelty, but we still allow bow hunting, pigeon shoots, rodeos, and all sorts of activities that are difficult to justify on any coherent moral ground. These practices result in unspeakable cruelty to animals, and none of these practices serves any purpose beyond mere entertainment. Nevertheless, such practices are protected under the law. A legal system that relies primarily on laws requiring "humane" treatment or prohibiting "unnecessary" suffering simply cannot protect beings that are, as a matter of law, regarded as the personal property of their owners. Three examples will illustrate the problem.[8]

First, in *New Jersey Society for the Prevention of Cruelty to Animals v. Board of Education,*[9] a local humane society sought to recover penalties against a school board when a high school student was permitted to induce cancer in live chickens. The state anticruelty law made it a misdemeanor to " '[i]nflict unnecessary cruelty upon a living animal or creature' " or to " 'needlessly mutilate or kill a living animal or creature.' "[10] The statute also provided that " '[p]roperly conducted scientific experiments' " were not covered.[11] There was no claim that the experiment was one for which there was any medical need. Indeed, the court noted that it was long known that the virus involved caused cancer in chickens and had "been the subject of many experiments over the years."[12] Nevertheless, the court deferred to scientific experts who, as "a result of Federal Government grants of some eight million dollars," concluded "that the use of living animals is essential at the high school level for biological studies in that it . . . helps students have sympathy for living things."[13]

Second, according to a 1992 article, scientists have determined that the same genetic mutation that causes quarter horses to have desirable physical appearance can also "cause the muscles to periodically seize up with spasms so uncontrollable that the afflicted animal may topple over and even die." The article continues:

> now that scientists have identified the guilty mutation and have developed a relatively simple test to detect it, a debate is roiling the fierce, high-stakes world of horse breeding on whether it is fair to continue propagating a potentially dangerous trait in a breed simply because the characteristic can reap so many rewards for the human owners.[14]

Presumably, those who would opt for breeding for the mutation would regard any resultant suffering or death of the horse as "necessary."

Third, it was reported in 1993 that a landmark tourist attraction located in the area of New York known as Chinatown had regrettably ceased to exist. The attraction consisted of a specially trained chicken who lived in a small coop that was fitted into a vending machine. When a customer dropped fifty cents into the machine, the chicken, called Willy by his owner, would play tic-tac-toe with the customer—and would almost always win. Willy had spent all of his life—two years—living in the machine. His predecessor spent eight years in the coop, and other performing chickens have been in the Chinatown games arcade since the 1960s. A glass front left the coop, which had a wire floor, exposed constantly to hordes of tourists who stared at these birds and challenged them to "play." The coop was located "next to the rows of noisy electronic zappers and death rays," not far from another chicken, whose name was not reported by the *Times,* and who amused patrons by dancing rather than playing tic-tac-toe. When a customer dropped seventy-five cents into the machine, the chicken "walk[ed] through a trap door to a round metal tray resembling a wobbly turntable. As the tray teeter[ed], the chicken flap[ped] its wings and shuffle[d] to balance itself in a manner that look[ed] like dancing."[15]

The tone of the report about Willy was a mixture of maudlin sentimentalism and attempted humor. The writer stated that although it is the "job" of chickens to die, "for those of us who have played the chicken, the sight of its empty box evokes feelings of sadness, if not quite tragedy." "It showed a great deal of heart almost to the end. Just two days before it died it was still pecking its way through games with whoever dropped 50 cents into the slot in front of its coop." Willy was "not like meat from Frank Perdue. It was our playmate, and since we have always been a particularly self-centered species, that elevated it." The dancing chicken "in the best show-business tradition . . . carries on despite the death of its comrade." The arcade owner is thinking about replacing Willy but complained that trained chickens cost more than $1,000 " 'which is a good deal of money when you consider that the last one only lived two years.' "[16]

There was not one word in the lengthy report about the propriety of this amusement from the standpoint of the humane treatment of animals. And despite New York's strongly worded anticruelty statute, the American Society for the Prevention of Cruelty to Animals, located in New York City, has not prohibited this senseless and wholly unnecessary exploitation of these birds.

## "Unnecessary" Cruelty: The "Balance" of Unprotected Animal Interests

It is difficult, if not impossible, to understand the use of "necessity" in any of the three preceding examples. In the first example, a high school student's infliction of pain and death on chickens is justified as necessary to the child's development of a "sympathy for living things." Most of the time, those who use animals in experiments justify that use by pointing to alleged benefits to human and animal health and the supposed necessity of using animals to obtain those benefits. In this case, however, there was no claim of such benefit, and it is certainly difficult to maintain that inducing cancer in an animal is "necessary" to achieve the stated goal of teaching young people "sympathy for living things." Similarly, those who use animals in teaching usually justify such use as "necessary" for the development of professional skills. In this case, however, the student was in secondary school and clearly did not need to learn such skills at that point in his educational career. Rather, the human interest, described as helping students to develop "sympathy" for animals, was held to outweigh the animals' fundamental interests in not being used for such purposes.

In the second example, the continued breeding for the mutation is "necessary" for horse owners to profit. There is no claim that the continued breeding will result in any benefit whatsoever—other than monetary profit for human beings. Monetary benefit, then, is sufficient to constitute the "necessity" required when we seek to justify animal exploitation—at least as far as some horse breeders are concerned. As the third example illustrates, human amusement is considered enough of a justification for animal exploitation that the *Times* writer did not consider it necessary even to address the issue of humane treatment in the article.[17] The third example is also reflective of the concerns raised in the context of the pigeon shoot I described in the Preface.

If animal use is "necessary" in these three cases—which are, by far, not the most egregious examples that could be used—then when is animal use "unnecessary" and what, exactly, does "necessity" mean? When we turn to legal doctrine to try to understand the notion of "necessity," we see that the notion that applies to human/animal conflicts stands in marked contrast to the notion employed when human/human conflicts are involved. Every first-year law student has read *Regina v. Dudley & Stephens,*[18] a case involving cannibalism. Dudley and Stephens, together with Brooks and Parker, were shipwrecked in a storm 1,600 miles from the Cape of Good Hope. The four young men were afloat in a small boat that had survived the storm, but the boat had no water and only two small cans of turnips, and the nearest land was over a thousand miles away. After having no food for nine days or water for seven days, Dudley and Stephens killed Parker without the latter's consent.[19] They then drank Parker's blood and ate his body. Four days after Parker was killed, a passing ship rescued the men, and Dudley and Stephens were tried for the murder of Parker.[20] At trial, the defendants argued that their killing of Parker should be excused under the doctrine of "necessity" because it was "necessary" for Dudley and Stephens to preserve their own lives.[21] The court rejected this argument, holding that there is no "absolute and unqualified necessity to preserve one's life." In rejecting this notion of necessity, the court asked, "Who is to be the judge of this sort of necessity? By what measure is the comparative value of lives to be measured?"[22]

In *Dudley & Stephens* the jury found specifically that at the time of the murder, Parker was in a much weaker physical condition than the other three men, that it was likely that Parker would have died before the other three men even if he had not been murdered, and that there had been no reasonable prospect that the men would be saved.[23] Nevertheless, the court found that the defendants' actions were not justifiable as "necessary."[24] Although Dudley and Stephens had interests in remaining alive, so did Parker, and Parker's right was upheld even though his "sacrifice" had beneficial consequences for a greater number of other people. This is the whole point of a right: as a general matter, it cannot be abrogated even if the violation produces beneficial consequences for others. To put it another way, when it comes to killing innocent human beings or inflicting injuries on them, we tend to reject utilitarian thinking in favor of treating persons as ends, rather than as means to ends. Moreover, the court correctly pointed out that any appeal to the "necessity" for homicide would invariably involve the courts in value judgments about the relative value of human rightholders and in formulating criteria for determining what constitutes "necessity."

Indeed, if a researcher needed fifty innocent unconsenting human beings in order to perform an experiment that would result in a cure for cancer, most people would not permit the use of humans in the experiment. Although the use of the humans might be "necessary" in a very direct and causal way, most people would regard the necessity argument as ignoring the rights claims of the potential victims. We simply use the concept of "necessity" in different ways when we talk about humans and nonhumans. In *Dudley & Stephens* the four men also killed and ate a turtle fairly early in their voyage. But the court never discussed any legal or moral issue connected with the death of the turtle. The level of human need that results in the "necessity" for animal suffering or death is clearly different from the level "needed" for human suffering or death.

The problem is that many animal exploiters assert that the notions of "necessity" are the same and equally protective of human and animal life.[25] This assertion is simply not true. When we balance human and animal interests in order to see whether suffering is "necessary" or "justified," our notion of "necessity" is shaped by the fact that we generally balance two very different entities. Human beings are regarded by the law as having interests that are supported by rights. In the case of *Dudley & Stephens,* the three men were all rightholders, and the court sought to balance competing claims of right. Nonhuman animals are regarded by the law as incapable of having rights—or, at least, the same type of rights possessed by humans—despite an increasing consensus that animals possess some moral rights that ought to be recognized by the legal system. Our entire legal approach to resolving human/animal conflicts, which, as I mentioned above, rests on the notion of animal welfare and not animal rights, virtually guarantees that animal interests will be regarded as of lesser import, even when the human interest is trivial relative to the animal interest. Moreover, there are other normative considerations involved that make it difficult, if not impossible, for animals to prevail. For example, we often assume without question that we can accord "humane" treatment to animals used in sometimes quite painful medical experiments. Thus, to the extent that humans have rights and animals do not, animal interests are, of necessity, accorded less weight.

A critic may reply that "necessity," when used to discuss moral necessity, as opposed to causal necessity, is inherently imprecise whether applied to animals or humans. This criticism requires that I first distinguish briefly two senses of the term "necessity." Necessity, as I am presently discussing that notion, refers to moral necessity; a judgment that treatment does not result in "unnecessary" suffering is a moral judgment and is quite different from the usual case of a judgment of causal necessity. There is, however, a sense in which judgments about "necessary" suffering all concern causal necessity. For example, those who use animals in biomedical experiments make moral judgments about necessity (i.e., they routinely deny that animal suffering is "unnecessary"), but they also make a general judgment about causal necessity: they maintain, for the most part, that animal use is necessary—in a causal way—if humans are to achieve progress in fighting disease, developing medicines and new products, and so forth. On this view, progress and animal exploitation are causally linked. Similarly, someone who supports the use of animals in rodeos (in which animals are brutally treated and killed routinely) may argue that animal use is necessary—in a causal way—given the nature of the activity. Although I am more concerned about moral judgments about necessity, the line is difficult to draw, and in a sense, the problem is precisely that from the point of view of the person seeking to exploit the animal, almost all judgments about necessity are of a causal type; the exploiter is asserting that the animal use is necessary given the nature of the practice, which will, by definition, involve animals. From an external point of view (i.e., the perspective of one not involved in the activity), these judgments say more about morality than they do about causation.

Although there is ambiguity surrounding the notion of moral necessity as applied to humans or animals, judgments of moral necessity are more problematic when animals are involved. For example, if one of my colleagues were to tell me that I was being "unnecessarily" harsh in my classroom behavior with my law students who gave wrong answers in recitation, that comment would most certainly represent a value judgment (or, perhaps, a series of such judgments) that probably could not be reduced to any noncontroversial or "precise" assertion. Although there is inherent imprecision in the notion of necessity, my point about its differential application to animals goes well beyond any such imprecision. To return to my colleague's criticism: if I responded in class to a student's wrong answer by shooting and killing the student, my colleague's criticism would not be particularly meaningful, since my reaction already transcended what could be called "necessary" by any standard. Indeed, although my shooting the student could be criticized coherently on numerous moral and legal grounds employing a wide range of moral discourse, I doubt that anyone would think it sensible (or even coherent) to discuss whether I inflicted "unnecessary" suffering or death on the student. The point is that when we are talking about human beings, not every action is open to discussion and ultimate characterization as "necessary" or "unnecessary," even taking into consideration the linguistic imprecision. The reason is, as illustrated by *Dudley & Stephens,* that humans have certain rights that protect their interests and those interests are simply excluded from the balancing process. In the case of animals, *every* animal interest that we acknowledge (and we do not recognize many, and some philosophers argue that animals have no interests at all) is subject to being compromised. Therefore, even though judgments of moral necessity are inherently imprecise even as they apply to humans, they are qualitatively more problematic when animals are involved, because there is, by virtue of the fact that animals are not rightholders, no animal interest that cannot be sacrificed if some human decides that the animal's death or suffering is "necessary."

## Animal Property and Legal Welfarism

The lopsided results generated by such an unbalanced balancing approach are exacerbated when the property rights of humans are involved, because animals are a form of property. Humans are entitled under the laws of property to convey or sell their animals, consume or kill them, use them as collateral, obtain their natural dividends, and exclude others from interfering with an owner's exercise of dominion and control over them. A property owner's treatment of an animal may ostensibly be limited by anticruelty laws, but property rights are paramount in determining the ambit of protection accorded to animals by law.

The property status of animals dominates the way in which the political and legal systems think about nonhumans. For example, President Clinton recently proclaimed the first week of May as "Be Kind to Animals and National Pet Week."[26] In the proclamation, President Clinton made the following observations concerning animals: (1) in colonial times, animals acted as beasts of burden and carried our belongings; (2) animals helped early settlers to earn a living and otherwise to sustain themselves; (3) animals serve the blind as guides; (4) animals assist in military, customs, and law enforcement efforts; (5) animals ease the loneliness of the ill and the elderly; and (6) animals entertain us and our children in our daily lives. It should be noted that in every instance of our interaction with animals mentioned by President Clinton, the emphasis is upon the instrumental value of animals and not on any inherent value that the animals may have. This is reflective of the notion that animals are property; they are, as a matter of law, *solely* means to human ends. As such, their value is measured in terms of their usefulness to humans, and not in terms of their own interests, the existence of which cannot be denied. Moreover, property rights have an explicit constitutional basis and are considered to be "natural rights," reflecting the moral ontology of English philosopher John Locke.[27]

The property aspect of animals is almost always a major component in the resolution of human/animal conflicts, because even if the property status is not explicit, in almost all circumstances in which human and animal interests conflict a human is seeking to act upon her property. As far as the law is concerned, it is as if we were resolving a conflict between a person and a lamp, or some other piece of personal property. The winner of the dispute is predetermined by the way in which the conflict is conceptualized in the first place. The human interest in regarding animals as property is so strong that even when people do not want to consider animals as mere "property" and instead view animals as members of their family (as in the case of dogs, cats, and other companion animals), the law generally refuses to recognize that relationship. For example, if one person negligently kills the dog of another, most courts refuse to recognize the status of the animal as family member and limit the owner to the same recovery that would be allowed if the property were inanimate.

There are rights other than the right of private property that serve to support the interests against which we balance the unprotected interests of animals, but these other rights usually depend on legal welfarism's fundamental assumption that animals are property. For example, as I show in Part III, defenders of the use of animals in biomedical experiments often argue that their use of animals is protected by their right of free inquiry, which, in turn, they connect with the guarantee of free speech contained in the First Amendment to the United States Constitution. I argue that the right of free inquiry cannot serve to justify animal experimentation and that, in any event, such a claim would depend ultimately on the property status of animals. So, even though there are other human rights that may be relevant in the balancing process, these rights often assume the property status of animals.

The status of animals as property, as well as the resulting inability to "balance" animal and human interests, is effectively obscured by our discussion of the relevant issues in "normative" terms. As a general matter, our discussion of issues concerning the nature of law, the nature of rights, the process of judicial decision making, and the character of legal reasoning is "cast in terms of conflicts among normative conceptions of justice, efficiency, rights, morality, order, self-determination, community, and so on."[28] We must be more skeptical about normative analysis because it may serve to legitimize the oppression of certain members of society. For example, Richard Delgado argues that in the literature debating surrogate motherhood, in vitro fertilization, and egg transfer, the primary moral issues concern the need to ensure informed consent and to protect the contractual freedom of the parties. Delgado argues that these concerns focus on the "micro" issues and hide the fact that the development of such technologies

> invariably sharpen the differences in resources and control between the "haves" and the "have-nots." Reproductive technologies are likely to do so even more than other types of technology, since they are developed and distributed by a group (the medical profession) that is already empowered and has high prestige, and then distributed mainly to patients (a vulnerable group) who are largely female and infertile.[29]

Precisely the same problem occurs when we discuss the regulation of animal exploitation. When we purport to regulate animal exploitation, we talk in normative terms of the "humane" treatment of animals (e.g., of the minimum size of cages in which animals used in experiments are housed) and the prevention of "unnecessary" pain (e.g., through the use of anesthetics and analgesics). Although these "micro" ethical issues make it appear as though we are taking animal interests most seriously, such concerns fail to take into account that any laws and regulations affecting animals are interpreted and applied by an empowered group (i.e., the owners of animals) to sentient beings who arguably constitute the most disempowered group in our society—nonhuman animals. The total disparity in the economic power between the two groups—humans and animals—is manifested in the legal approach to the resolution of human/animal conflicts.

The reliance on these normative concepts obscures the fundamental issue to be decided: Is our exploitation of nonhumans justified in the first place? These normative concepts assume, *sub silentio,* an affirmative answer to this question.

The normativity of the law as it concerns animals supports structures regulating animal use that focus our attention on notions like "humane" treatment and "unnecessary" suffering and away from the status of animals as property and the primary consequence of that status: that these terms have completely different legal meanings from the ones they have in ordinary language. That is, normativity obscures the realities of legal welfarism, which dictates that the level of animal protection be limited to that which most efficiently facilitates the exploitation of animals.

To the extent, then, that legal thought prescribes that our treatment of animals requires that we balance competing human and animal interests—and with the help of normative analysis—we delude ourselves in thinking that animals can ever prevail. Our myriad laws and regulations that purport to protect animals are unable to achieve even a minimally acceptable level of protection as long as humans are the only rightholders and animals are regarded as "property."

Despite the universally accepted moral maxim that we ought not to kill or inflict pain on animals unless it is "necessary," our legal system, which embodies legal welfarism, is structured so that virtually any animal exploitation can be regarded as "necessary." That is, the law has developed a distinct structure for dealing with animal claims, and that structure, by deflecting attention to normative concerns that serve only to highlight the "micro" issues, guarantees that animal claims never even get into court. Even if a claim does get into court, the animal interest is weighed as trivial relative to the human interest at stake.

Legal welfarism has four basic and interrelated components. First, legal welfarism characterizes animals as the property of human beings. The only difference between domestic animals, which, by definition, must be owned by someone, and wild animals is that in the latter case ownership in the animals is held by the state and may be transferred to nongovernmental owners.

Second, legal welfarism interprets the property status of animals to justify the treatment of animals exclusively as means to human ends.

Third, legal welfarism provides that animal use is "necessary" whenever that use is part of a generally accepted social institution.

Fourth, legal welfarism does not proscribe "cruelty" as that term is understood in ordinary discourse. Rather, legal welfarism interprets "cruelty" to refer to animal use that, for the most part, fails to facilitate, and may even frustrate, that animal exploitation. For example, we tolerate practices in animal agriculture, such as castration and branding without any pain relief, and we do not label these practices "cruel," because they facilitate our institutional use of animals for food. We do not, however, permit farmers to starve these castrated and branded animals to death merely because the farmer does not wish to be bothered to feed the animals. The difference in treatment is not attributable to any differences in the *quality* of treatment. Rather, castration and branding are regarded (by those who own animals used for food) as "necessary" and are, as a result, permitted by the legal system, whereas allowing animals to starve for no reason other than neglect does not facilitate the exploitation of the animals for food or any other purpose.

## Maximizing the Value of Animal Property

In the preceding section I argued that legal welfarism permits any animal exploitation that is not wholly gratuitous. To put the matter another way, legal welfarism, or the treatment accorded to animals under the law, is determined not by reference to any moral ideal but by the property status of the animal and by what conduct is perceived to maximize the value of animal property. According to traditional economic analysis, people are rational maximizers of their satisfactions, and resources tend to gravitate toward their most valuable uses if voluntary exchange is permitted.[30] The Coase Theorem states that the initial assignment of a property right does not determine the ultimate use of the property, precisely because, in the absence of transaction costs,[31] resources are ultimately used in a way that maximizes wealth irrespective of the initial distribution of rights.[32] How this wealth maximization occurs depends in large part on the transaction costs involved, but, according to the law-and-economics theorists, wealth maximization not only serves to explain most of the doctrines of the common law but also serves as a normative principle that guides judges in future decisions.[33] Interestingly, advocates of this approach often argue that the principle of economic efficiency is either "neutral" or consistent with a morally desirable form of utilitarian thought. Critics of the economic approach to law have argued that the flaw in the indifference toward the initial distribution of rights is revealed by the economist's willingness to have human slavery as an initial starting point.[34] Defenders of the approach reply that even if initial property rights were distributed so that "one person owned all the others, soon most of the others would have bought their freedom from that person because their output would be greater as free individuals than as slaves, enabling them to pay more for the right to their labor than that right was worth to the slave owner."[35] Nevertheless, "the theoretical possibility exists that efficiency might dictate slavery or some other monstrous rights assignment."[36] In such cases, the answer is found not in economic theory but elsewhere: "we do not permit degrading invasions of individual autonomy merely on a judgment that, on balance, the invasion would make a net addition to the social wealth. And whatever the philosophical grounding of this sentiment, it is too deeply entrenched in our society at present for wealth maximization to be given a free rein."[37]

Irrespective of the debate about the efficiency of human slavery, the implications of economic theory for animals are far less ambiguous. Property rights in animals have historically been allocated to people—and animals remain property—because that allocation of rights is thought to maximize the value of the animal to human beings. Indeed, our allocation to humans of rights in the bodies of animals reflects the notion that it is more efficient to relegate animals to property status (with all of the consequences that are entailed and *because of* all the consequences that are entailed) than it is to value animals for themselves and to accord them dignity and respect. Moral concern for animals is not a "cost-justified policy."[38] The fact that we allocate property rights in animals means that we do not value animals in themselves, or that we do not value animal protection (beyond what is necessary to ensure efficient exploitation of animals) in itself. The property status of animals clearly maximizes the wealth of animal resources in that the property status of animals makes possible a market in which there are offering and asking prices. Indeed, it would make no sense to talk about the productive value of animals if animals were not property; the only measure of their productivity involves their value to human beings. The productive value and the property status of animals are inextricably intertwined. The value of animals is dependent on their property status, and in the absence of a pervasive system of animal servitude, it is unlikely—to say the least—that animals would "voluntarily" offer themselves to be used as food sources or as laboratory "equipment." In a system in which animals are property, they are, unlike human slaves (assuming the validity of certain economic theories), going to remain property because although there may be uses for the animal that maximize wealth even more, all uses depend on the status of the animal as the property of humans. Animals are not capable of buying their freedom, and even if there are many affluent altruists who suffer great discomfort from their knowledge of animal exploitation, it is unlikely that they will be able to influence the treatment of animals in any significant way. Although the economic analysis of statutes differs somewhat from common-law rules, statutes also seek to provide only that level of protection of animals that is consistent with the most productive use of the animal in the particular context. Moreover, since animals are the property of owners and we assume that the owners of property seek to maximize the value of their own property, we rely to a great extent on self-governance to ensure that animals are given the level of welfare needed to ensure their most efficient exploitation. Indeed, the fundamental economic notions of Pareto superiority, an economic state where no one is worse off and at least one person is better off than in an alternative state, and Pareto optimality, an economic state in which no person can be made better off without harming another person, assume that people are the best judges of their relative well-being and of their valuation of their own property, which includes their animal property.[39]

Even when society regulates the uses of property, that regulation is, at least ideally, supposed to maximize social wealth, and in some cases the owner of the property may be entitled to compensation if the property is taken outright or is regulated to such a degree that there is a constructive "taking" of the property. Regulation of the use of animals represents the only instance of property regulation where the regulation is, at least ostensibly, for the benefit of the property and not for the purpose of maximizing social wealth—although, for those people who are concerned about the treatment of animals, the regulation of animal use may represent a benefit. We seek to achieve the optimal level of regulation given the value of the property and the overall social wealth that results from the regulation.

For the most part, however, the suffering of animals represents a truly "external" cost of animal use because there is no easy way to quantify and "internalize" that cost for purposes of determining what course of action best serves the goal of economic efficiency. Indeed, to the extent that the regulation of animal use produces a social benefit, we do not measure that benefit from the point of view of the animal, because the animal is only property that has no entitlements protected by right or otherwise. Rather, any social benefit must be understood in terms of the benefits that humans perceive to come from such regulation. As one government agency charged with regulating animal use has stated, "animal welfare is an anthropomorphic attribute" that requires the measurement of the "increase in the level of public perception in animal welfare as the level of stringency of the regulations also increases." Such measurements involve a "lengthy and cost prohibitive study of marginal increases in social welfare or utility."[40]

The tension that arises from the perceived need to maximize the value of property—in this case, animal property—and the costs of regulation of property use mean, in effect, that the standards of animal welfare—the legal standards for determining what constitutes "unnecessary" suffering or "cruel" treatment—are, for the most part, determined not by some moral ideal but by the perceived *legitimacy* of the use to which the animals are put. And without any notion of absolute prohibitions on the use of animals, virtually all uses of animals that generate social wealth are regarded as legitimate. To put it another way, "humane" treatment and "unnecessary" suffering are determined by what most productively facilitates particular forms of animal exploitation. If the use objected to results in the infliction of suffering but that suffering facilitates that use and generates social wealth, then the use, however "inhumane" it may be in terms of the ordinary use of the word, results in "necessary" suffering that is not proscribed. If there is no socially recognized economic benefit generated by the conduct and the conduct consists largely of the infliction of gratuitous suffering, then the law may proscribe the conduct because overall social wealth is diminished. Moreover, legal welfarism requires structures that exclude the imposition of costs on animal ownership without corresponding economic benefits for (animal) property owners. That is, if we assume (as we do) that property owners know best how to use property and that it is difficult to quantify the social benefit of increased animal welfare, then any changes to the regulatory scheme that depart from these assumptions will be regarded (probably correctly) as diminishing the efficient use of animal resources. For example, as I show in Chapter Four, courts have developed rules to bar claims that are perceived to represent inefficiency in the system of animal ownership.

Economic analysis of child protection offers an insight that helps to elucidate the preceding point. Generally speaking, given that society wishes "to maximize the aggregate welfare of all of its citizens," "children require a considerable investment of both parental time and market inputs (food, clothing, tuition, etc.)" in order "to realize their potential as adults—in economic terms, to achieve a high level of lifetime utility."[41] Society has laws to protect children, such as requirements of financial and educational support and restrictions on child labor, in order to ameliorate the underinvestment of resources in children's human capital.

Although, as a historical matter, the concern for child welfare and the concern for animal welfare were closely connected, the economic basis for the former is quite different from that for the latter. Although we want both children and animals to be "productive" and we want to maximize their "potential" to achieve a "high level of lifetime utility," these goals, in the context of children, necessarily recognize the value of human autonomy and the role of law in attempting to protect the "potential" of children. With animals, however, the situation is quite different in that the only investment of resources required to ensure that the "potential" of animals is recognized is that level that most efficiently facilitates the exploitation of animals as means to human ends.

For example, the level of investment required to ensure that an animal used for experiments achieves its "potential" is the level that ensures that the use of the animal will result in usable data. Given that animals are property, any additional protection is economically inefficient because wealth is not maximized—and, indeed, is diminished—by this additional protection. If the only "capital" represented by animals is their value as means to human ends, then the only investment required (the content of animal welfare) is that level of investment that facilitates the efficient exploitation of those animals. There are two relevant qualifications of this notion. First, society may wish to "purchase" more protection for animals because animal cruelty may have negative effects on people in precisely the same way that poverty imposes various costs on the middle class, such as increased incidence of crime. That is, animal cruelty may be equated to an overall diminution of moral sensibility that translates into undesirable treatment of people by other people. The problem is that it is difficult, if not impossible, to measure this effect, so it becomes similarly difficult, if not impossible, to know what level of additional protection for animals ought to be "purchased" so that people will treat other people better. Second, affluent altruists are, in theory, in a position to "purchase" more protection for animals through the political process, but the transaction costs associated with the purchase of greater protection, in the face of an economy that is very dependent on animal exploitation, are staggering and would reduce to *de minimis* the amount of additional protection purchased.

Before we conclude that the notion of "humane" treatment embodied in legal welfarism is just another concept whose meaning has been twisted out of recognition by lawyers and judges and that legal welfarism does not embody ordinary notions of "necessary" suffering, we should consider that the tenets of legal welfarism pervade much of our ordinary-language discourse about animals. Indeed, it is precisely because most of us are in certain respects legal welfarists that we fail to see the contradictory relationships that we have with animals, and that these contradictions are at the very foundation of legal welfarism. There is no doubt that most people in this country have had an experience with an animal, usually a dog or cat, who is regarded as a member of the family for all intents and purposes. Our ability to relate in this way to these companion animals obviously accounts for some of the strong reaction, including opposition, that many people have, for example, to the use of dogs or cats in biomedical experiments. In a recent essay legal scholars Alan

Freeman and Betty Mensch observe that although "our culture tolerates those who lavish affection and resources on pets," we have a "paradoxical and contradictory relationship with pets [that] is but a subset of our relationship with animals generally. Animal suffering makes us anxious and uncomfortable, yet most of us want to make 'rational' use of animals for our own well-being."[42] We resolve this contradiction through the doctrine of legal welfarism, which through the treatment of animals as property facilitates the keeping of "pets" by people and at the same time permits any economically efficient, or "rational," exploitation of animals that we wish to use for food, or entertainment, or clothing.

Most people accept the underlying tenets of legal welfarism at least with respect to some activities. That is, most people may express serious reservations about the treatment of laboratory animals (especially when dogs and cats are involved) or about animals trapped or raised for their fur. Such objections usually are aimed at the perceived disparity between the meaning of "humane" treatment used by researchers and furriers, which is embodied in the law that permits researchers and furriers to accord animals this (low) level of protection, and the notion of "humane" treatment as it is used (by the objectors) in ordinary, nonlegal moral discourse. Although these objectors may reject the exploitation of animals by others, they may themselves engage, usually indirectly, in animal exploitation as well.[43] Most people eat meat and do not for a second lament the deaths of the billions of farm animals slaughtered annually for food even though meat is no longer considered "necessary" for human health and may even be dangerous for people to consume and unsound for environmental as well as moral reasons.[44] Although we may experience sorrow for the death of a beloved companion animal, we feel no sorrow for animals killed for food. Indeed, the only time we lament the deaths of farm animals is when they die *unproductively;* then we care about their deaths but only to the extent that we care about the unproductive destruction of other nonanimal property. For example, a recent newspaper article reported that a grandson of an Amish bishop was charged "with setting fires that burned $1 million worth of barns and livestock last year on six Amish dairy farms."[45] The purpose of such a story is not to report that animals died and that their deaths are per se a reason for our concern; rather, the matter is reported to inform us that someone engaged in the unproductive destruction of animal and nonanimal property. The destruction of the animals for productive uses (i.e., for slaughter) occurs at a staggering rate of thousands *per minute,* yet we never read newspaper stories about the number of animals killed at the local abattoir. It would be bizarre to lament these deaths, because we regard them as productive—and therefore acceptable— uses of animals.

Similarly, the slaughtering guidelines developed by livestock expert Temple Grandin, promulgated by the American Meat Institute, and actually endorsed by some animal advocates state explicitly that although the standards will improve animal welfare, their primary goal is to achieve a slaughtering process that is "efficient and profitable." Indeed, Grandin emphasizes throughout her report that "proper" slaughtering procedures can "make the difference between profits and losses due to meat quality or worker safety."[46] "Humane" slaughter conforms to those standards that can, with few, if any, exceptions, be justified as ensuring that food animals are not "wasted" unnecessarily—that is, that food animals are not subjected to conduct that diminishes overall social wealth with no corresponding benefit for animal owners. The Grandin/Meat Institute standards suggest strongly that it is very difficult to get protection for animals that cannot be cost-justified, especially since concerns about animal protection do not figure into the "benefit" to be assessed.

We may lament the way in which animals are killed, but again, our concerns go to "unnecessary" suffering, which is unproductive; suffering that results in a more efficient production of animal products is tolerated. The proof of this proposition is that consumers do not, in sufficient numbers, value a reduction in animal suffering in the slaughter process enough to demand more "humanely" produced meat. Instead, most of us are quite content to express our concern for animals mistreated in modern agriculture but are unwilling to pay for alternatives.[47] If we start to tinker with "necessity" and "humane" treatment as it involves exploitation, we have to start tinkering with that concept as it affects the indirect exploitation in which many of us are most active participants. In a sense, then, the normativity of law helps us to deal with the dissonance between the level of exploitation permitted by legal welfarism and our own ordinary-language concepts of "humane" treatment and "unnecessary" suffering.

## Conclusion

In this chapter, I have argued that our legal treatment of animals is characterized by a balancing process that requires us to weigh interests protected by powerful rights against interests protected by no rights. I called this balancing process legal welfarism and described its central tenets. I argued that the prohibition of gratuitous animal use has to be understood in light of the general tendency of the common law to maximize the value of property.

In the next chapter, I explore in greater detail the notion of animals as property.

# CHAPTER TWO

## The Dominion of Humans over Animals, the "Defects" of Animals, and the Common Law

THE CONCEPT of property has generated a rich and considerably complex philosophical and jurisprudential literature.[1] There are at least two primary characteristics of the legal conception of property that account for this complexity. First, the fact that legal conceptions are often used very differently in legal and nonlegal contexts is confusing, and

> the word "property" furnishes a striking example. Both with lawyers and with laymen this term has no definite or stable connotation. Sometimes it is employed to indicate the physical object to which various legal rights, privileges, etc., relate; then again— with far greater discrimination and accuracy—the word is used to denote the legal interest (or aggregate of legal relations) appertaining to such physical object.[2]

Modern jurisprudence considers property not to be a "thing" but, as Professor Bruce Ackerman has observed, a "set of legal relations between persons governing the use of things."[3] The second reason for confusion, which is related to the first, is that to the extent that property is considered to be a set of relations, it is often not clear what the incidents of ownership are in any particular case and how these incidents of ownership are related to someone whom we might be inclined to label an "owner." Often the rights and obligations of ownership (or property considered as a set of relations) may be divided among several persons, none of whom (or all of whom) may be readily labeled the "owner."

These problems are thankfully not part of the present inquiry. Although there is certainly a sense in which these issues are relevant to all discussions of property, they are particularly germane to discussions of real property, or estates in land, rather than to personal property. Indeed, as one scholar has correctly argued, the confusion between "property" and "ownership" is particularly important "if property is in the earth. . . . It has been argued that 'the' modern idea of ownership emerged in England, at least, in the seventeenth century, and part of the evidence for that thesis concerns new powers given to persons holding various sorts of estates in land."[4] Although discussions of "property" and "ownership"

33

consume large sections of treatises on real property, discussions of these topics in books on personal property are usually quite succinct.[5] This is, of course, not to say that the jurisprudential issues that concern personal property, as opposed to estates in land, are insignificant or unimportant. It is only to say that these issues may be simplified when—as in the case of much, but certainly not all, personal property—the *object* of property is readily identifiable and the incidents of ownership, including the identification of an "owner," do not involve the complexities that arise when estates in land, including the innumerable legal distinctions that allow ownership to be divided among many different people sometimes living over many generations, are involved.

There is no question that animals are regarded as property under the law and have held the status of property for as long as anyone can recall. In a 1993 article, Professor Robert Ellickson states that the need to provide incentives to people to cultivate crops and domesticate animals resulted in the first property rights.[6] Biotechnology critic Jeremy Rifkin argues that the domestication and ownership of animals are very closely related to the development of the very idea of property or money. For example, "the very word 'cattle' comes from the same etymological root as the word 'capital.' In many European languages, the word 'cattle' was synonymous with the words 'chattel' and 'capital,'" The Spanish word for property, *ganaderia,* is virtually identical to the word for cattle, *ganado.* The Latin word for money, *pecunia,* is derived from *pecus,* which means cattle.[7]

Rifkin's observations support the contention that throughout the course of legal history, animals have assumed the status of personal property, subject to "absolute" dominion by humans and to the same use that humans could make of any inanimate property. "[A]nimals are owned in the same way as inanimate objects such as cars and furniture."[8] They "are by law treated as any other form of movable property and may be the subject of absolute, *i.e.,* complete ownership . . . [and] the owner has at his command all the protection that the law provides in respect of absolute ownership."[9] Because animals held the status of property, laws to protect them were slow to develop; and, as I show in subsequent chapters, such laws, when eventually enacted, did more to protect human ownership rights and economic interests than to protect the animal from abusive conduct.

When we say that animals are considered as "property" under the law, we mean both that animals are the object of property and that there are incidents of ownership that constitute the property relationship. Over the centuries, the common law has evolved rules, which are fairly simple when compared with those legal rules that concern real property or estates in land, that embody fairly settled incidents of ownership. These rules concern such matters as the means of obtaining ownership of animals, the "bailment," or leasing, of animals, and the warranties that accompany the sale of animals.[10] In short, no legal scholar has argued that there is much jurisprudential confusion surrounding the notion of animals as property. As a general matter, we know what animal "property" is, and we understand the incidents of ownership of animal property.

This is, of course, not to say that any normative—as opposed to descriptive—

analysis of animal property would not require a complex and complicated treatment. Such a normative analysis might involve questioning the very justification of private property as a social institution, as Marx and others have done. On the other hand, normative analysis might be less ambitious in accepting that private property is a legitimate institution but may propose that property concepts, and property distribution, ought to conform more to underlying moral notions. For example, scholars such as Professor Charles Reich maintain that "property performs the function of maintaining independence, dignity and pluralism in society by creating zones within which the majority has to yield to the owner";[11] other commentators, such as Professor Ellickson, argue that property theory should be grounded in the "anthropological record" and that property policy should reflect how people actually behave.[12]

In this chapter, I explore the origins of the property status of animals in the common law. In a sense, a full description of the property status of animals awaits the further chapters of the book. My analysis reveals, I hope, that the ownership of animal property is, for all intents and purposes, no different from the ownership of other sorts of personal property—and therein lies the problem I discussed in the Introduction and Chapter One. Animals are property, and our current system of animal protection, legal welfarism, requires that animal interests be balanced against human interests. The problem is that the law has not developed any doctrines that require that animal property be treated differently because an animal is different from inanimate property, such as a tool. Rather, the law only requires that animal property not be "wasted" or that animals not be killed or made to suffer when there is no legitimate economic purpose. Although property owners may "waste" their tools and thus the law may be said to recognize that animal property is different from other sorts of property, this level of protection is a far cry from that which most people think animals already receive under the law and that which most people think animals should receive under the law.

The reason for this state of affairs is found in our understanding of the very concept of property and in the distinction between persons and property. Most legal theorists argue that there cannot be any legal relations between persons and things and that things cannot have rights.[13] Property is understood as that which does not have any inherent interests that must be respected. That is, although I may have an interest in owning property, my property is itself not regarded as a carrier of interests. This distinction between various interest carriers does not, of course, correspond to the distinction between human beings as persons and everything else as things. After all, corporations are considered "persons," but they are not human beings. Rather, corporations are entities that have certain legally recognized interests, and so we consider them "persons." But whether an entity is a carrier of interests, and therefore a person, or is not considered a carrier of interests, and therefore a thing, is not a matter of empirical reality. We do not find carriers of interests in the natural world; rather, that an entity is or is not a carrier of interests is a conclusion we come to after we engage in moral reasoning about whether the entity may be said to have interests.[14] When we characterize animals as property, we assert, in effect, that an animal is an entity without interests and is not entitled to the benefits (i.e., interest recognition) of persons. We assert not only that animals are without interests but that entities with interests (i.e., persons) cannot have any reciprocal relationship with animals. So, the mere characterization of animals as property within the legal system tells us from the outset that the law does not regard animals as carriers of interests. The doctrines of legal welfarism are the logical consequence of this characterization.

As I discussed earlier, certain theorists—most notably Professor, now Judge, Richard Posner—claim that the common law is best understood as a system for promoting economic efficiency, a state of affairs in which resources are used to their maximum value.[15] Under this theory, rights are incentives for using property in an efficient way. The economic analysis of law has a descriptive component, which seeks to describe common-law doctrines in economic terms, and a normative component, which seeks to guide the development of the law in terms of economic efficiency.[16] I am not concerned with the latter, but I do maintain that the cornerstone of what I call legal welfarism is that—as a general and descriptive matter, and with certain exceptions—the common law affords only that level of protection to animals that is consistent with the exploitation of animals solely as means to human ends. This level of protection, which is explored in future chapters, generally goes no further than to prohibit the "wasting" of animal resources without any resulting quantifiable benefit.

In the present chapter it is my intention to discuss animal property in a general and descriptive way and to discuss the particular importance of property in the American constitutional system. In the next chapter I offer two examples where animals are treated as property in two very different contexts. I then discuss the doctrine of standing, which determines whether a court has the jurisdiction to hear a particular case. I argue that the doctrine of standing as it concerns animal issues has been shaped by the property status of animals. It is my hope that the examination in this and the following chapters will provide some texture for the general thesis about the balancing of animal and human interests in light of the property rights in animals held by humans.

## Dominion and Defects

In Western legal systems, there are two types of justifications that are usually given for the status of animals as property. The first is the theological justification found in Genesis (1:20–28), in which man is given "dominion over the fish of the sea, and over the birds of the air, and over the cattle, and over all the earth, and over every creeping thing that creeps upon the earth." The notion of "dominion" is, of course, ambiguous and is certainly consistent with a state of affairs in which humans regard animals as wards to be cared for in light of the interests of the animals.[17] That is, although the theological justification places human beings (specifically men) in a preferred position over animals in the hierarchy of God, human, animal, plant, and inanimate object, the theological justification does not, per se, imply that animals are "inferior" to humans or "defective" in a way that would justify particular forms of animal exploitation.

Developing alongside the first justification, the second seeks to justify human superiority over animals based not merely on a divine hierarchy but on the notion that animals ought to be exploited by humans because animals possess some "defect" that makes them qualitatively different from humans and thereby deserving of subjugation by humans. This is not to say that these views about animal "defects" were not related to theological concerns or that they did not play a role in theological theories. Rather, the distinction is between a humanocentric (or patriarchal) worldview, which sees humans (or men) in a position superior to everyone and everything else as a result of divine ordering but does not necessarily regard this hierarchy as saying anything else about the nature of those who occupy lower rungs on the ladder, and a worldview that sees the "other" (in this case, animals) as "inferior" to humans (or men) in some substantive way that justifies exploitation of animals by humans. These ideas are, nevertheless, related, and may be traced through different historical periods.

For example, Aristotle (384–322 B.C.) created a hierarchy in which nonhumans were considered lesser beings because although they possessed a nutritive and sensitive soul, they lacked a human soul that was rational in addition to nutritive and sensitive. Aristotle found "naturally with the male and female; the one is superior, the other inferior; . . . [men] who are as much inferior to others . . . are slaves by nature"; and "plants are created for the sake of animals, and animals for the sake of men; the tame for our use and provision; the wild, at least the greatest part, for our provision also, or for some other advantageous purpose, as furnishing us with clothes and the like."[18] Indeed, Professor Richard Sorabji has argued that a "crisis both for the philosophy of mind and for theories of morality" was "provoked when Aristotle denied reason to animals."[19] This is not to deny that the Greeks believed that at least some animals were powerful gods who appeared in nonhuman form and should be worshiped for fear of retaliation. At the same time, these attitudes did not discourage the use of animals even for trivial purposes such as cockfighting and dog- and catfighting.[20]

The Romans, who brought exotic animals from foreign lands and established private zoos, considered animals nothing more than objects of amusement. "Countless thousands of animals, maddened with red-hot irons and by darts tipped with burning pitch, were baited to death in Roman arenas. At the dedication of the Colosseum by Titus, five thousand died in a day; lions, tigers, elephants and even giraffes and hippos perished miserably."[21] The Romans were among the first to describe legal doctrines about the ownership of wild animals. Moreover, it was during this time that humans began using animals for medical experiments.[22]

Thomas Aquinas (1225–74), who adopted and espoused the views of Aristotle, claimed that because man was made in the image of God and possessed rationality and prudence, "man should be master over animals," and "the subjection of other animals to man is proved to be natural."[23] Kindness toward animals was desirable only because it encouraged humans to be kinder to each other or prevented the damage of human property (the animal). Similarly, René Descartes (1596–1650) argued that it was the error of "weak minds" to suppose "that the souls of the beasts are of the same nature as ours."[24] According to Descartes, the use of language by humans demonstrated that humans were conscious, and since animals did not exhibit linguistic behavior, they could not be regarded as conscious beings or beings that were sentient. Descartes and his colleagues performed experiments on living, unanesthetized animals, the screams of which Descartes compared to the noise of a malfunctioning machine. It is quite plausible that Descartes's views helped to expand the practice of vivisection.[25]

These two types of justifications have a synergistic effect on each other. Genesis placed humans in a "superior" position to animals but left vague what precise relationship would exist between humans and animals. Subsequent thinkers such as Aquinas, who interpreted Aristotle for a Europe that was not acquainted with the ancient Greek philosophers, and Descartes based their interpretations of "dominion" upon the perceived "inferiority" or "defects" of those lower on the ladder. Although I have chosen to comment on Aristotle, Aquinas, and Descartes, my selection is somewhat artificial because there were many other thinkers who identified the same or similar "defects"—lack of a soul, lack of rationality, inability to use language—in order to justify human oppression and absolute ownership of animals.[26]

## Animals and the Common Law

### The Common Law and Property

There can be little doubt about the importance of property in common law. Moreover, property rights in the Anglo-American context have generally been regarded not merely as "positive" rights created by law but as "natural" rights. The theorist most influential in shaping the ideas that eventually became part of the common law of property was English philosopher John Locke.[27] For Locke, "a right is a natural right if its binding force is nonconventional and it could be possessed in the state of nature." The right to property was not only a natural right in this sense but also in the sense that the right was nonconsensual. Locke needed a theory of natural right because "if property is a consensual, conventional, or legal notion, the rules of property can change as consent, conventions, and laws change, making our rights in effect subject to whatever constraints society deems proper."[28] Locke recognized that private property was a difficult concept in light of the biblical suggestion that God gave the world to all humankind in common.[29] Locke recognized further that property in animals was particularly problematic because "they are produced by the spontaneous hand of Nature." Nevertheless, Locke argued that in order for animals to be useful to humankind, to whom, Locke acknowledged, they had been provided by God in common, it was necessary "to *appropriate* them some way or other before they can be of any use, or at all beneficial to any particular Man."[30] That is, Locke recognized that in order for any particular person to take advantage of an animal, it was necessary for the person to have a right in that animal so as to be able to exclude others. A legitimate appropriation was precisely a justification for excluding others from the use of that which has been appropriated.

Locke resolved the ostensible inconsistency by arguing that the sole ground of original and exclusive property rights was the labor of the individual.[31] Locke assumed that although animals were owned in common, a person, who had property in his body and the labor of his body, could join his labor to the animal. An animal might not be a person's private possession, but when a person, for example, hunted and killed a hare, that person had "thereby removed her from the state of Nature, wherein she was common, and hath *begun a Property*."[32] "Thus this Law of reason makes the Deer, that *Indian's* who hath killed it; [it is] allowed to be his goods who hath bestowed his labour upon it, though before, it was the common right of every one."[33]

Locke's theory was as simple as it was powerful: although God gave everything to humankind in common, such an arrangement could only benefit humankind if individuals could use those resources to benefit themselves. This tension between collective resources and individual use is resolved by limiting appropriation to what the individual can convert from the state of nature through the mixing of the unowned resource with her own labor. Since animals could only be useful to humans by the mixing of labor with the animals, the concept of animal property fit comfortably in Locke's scheme, which, of course, necessarily assumed that animals were no different from any other sort of "resource" and had no property interests in their own labor, which they, like humans, mixed with objects in the state of nature.[34] Private property, being a "natural" right, existed before the creation of political authority, which was created and obliged in order to protect such natural rights. Labor represented humankind's creative acts upon the creations of God and was an essential part of individual liberty.

Locke's theory of property had an extraordinary influence on the common law. William Blackstone, one of the greatest commentators on the common law, or the system of judge-made law prevalent in the United States and inherited from Great Britain, stated that "[t]here is nothing which so generally strikes the imagination, and engages the affections of mankind, as the right of property; or that sole and despotic dominion which one man claims and exercises over the external things of the world, in total exclusion of the right of any other individual in the universe."[35] In discussing the philosophical foundation of the right of property, Blackstone rejected "whatever airy metaphysical notions may have been started by fanciful writers upon this subject," and, relying upon Genesis, considered that "by holy writ, the all-bountiful Creator gave to man 'dominion over all the earth; and over the fish of the sea, and over the fowl of the air, and over every living thing that moveth upon the earth.' "[36] Blackstone relied on Locke's theory and formulated a broad notion of property that would not tolerate the "least violation of it."[37]

## The Common Law and Animal Property

Although Genesis is ambiguous about whether this passage means that humans have power over everything or property rights in everything or both or neither, humans have consistently treated this grant as a property right over animals probably because of the use of animals as food. Originally, humans had to hunt for food, and this proved to be inadequate. Subsequently, humans gathered "together such animals as were of a more tame and sequacious nature [in order to] establish a permanent property in their flocks and herds."[38] It then became necessary to establish social institutions of animal property. The doctrine of dominion made property status for animals a feasible alternative in the first instance; the various notions of animal "defects" allowed the perpetuation of the institution through rationalization provided by philosophical and theological doctrine.

Locke, the primary architect of common-law property theory, did not even entertain the possibility that animals had a property interest in their bodies or that they could act on objects in the state of nature and thus conjoin their labor with those objects. Although Locke recognized that animals had a fairly complex psychology,[39] he explicitly condemned "any such *Subordination* among us that may Authorize us to destroy one another, as if we were made for one anothers uses, *as the inferior ranks of Creatures are for ours*."[40] To the extent that Locke regarded as important the "humane" treatment of animals, he did so because "the custom of tormenting and killing beasts will, by degrees, harden [the] minds [of children] even towards men; and they who delight in the suffering and destruction of inferior creatures, will not be apt to be very compassionate or benign to those of their own kind."[41] Locke observed that "the exclusion [as jurors] of butchers" from the trial of capital crimes proved that society regarded the killing of animals as leading to an undesirable attitude toward humans. Interestingly, Locke did not advise that butchering animals be prohibited so that butchers would no longer be excluded from jury duty. Rather, Locke criticized only the "mischief" of (primarily) children, which he defined as the "spoiling of any thing to no purpose," and he admonishes that children be taught to "be tender to all sensible creatures, and to spoil or waste nothing at all."[42] The child who acts with "mischief" toward the animal probably does nothing worse than what is done by the butcher in the abattoir; indeed, at the time Locke was writing, it would have been difficult to imagine a more heinous place than the local slaughterhouse. Nevertheless, the child is admonished not because the child inflicts pain on, or kills, an animal. The butcher engages in those acts as well. The particular "mischief" of the child lies in the fact that the child "spoils" property for "no purpose." Locke's views—articulated in the seventeenth century—resonate in modern legal thought, in which animal protection is limited to proscribing the infliction of pain or death on an animal "for no purpose." Accordingly, the level of protection accorded to animals is very low because any improvement in the treatment of animals is costly to the owners of animals, and unless the protection facilitates the use for which the animal property is sought, the regulation is economically inefficient.

At common law, humans were said to have had "absolute" possession of personal property, which meant that although there might be some restrictions imposed on the use of personal property (i.e., I could not use my club to injure an innocent person), the possessor had "solely and exclusively, the right, and also the occupation, of any movable chattels; so that they cannot be transferred from him, or cease to be his, without his own act or default." All inanimate objects, such as money, jewels, and plates, fell into this category of inanimate property that could be possessed "absolutely." However, animals "have in themselves a principle and power of motion, and (unless particularly confined) can convey themselves from one part of the world to another," and accordingly, property rights in animals were analyzed by Blackstone under a different framework.[43]

Blackstone distinguished between domestic animals, or *domitae naturae,* and wild, or feral, animals, or *ferae naturae.* Domestic animals, he wrote, "we generally see tame, and are therefore seldom, if ever, found wandering at large." Feral animals are those "usually found at liberty."[44] The ability of animals to move was a key concern. As a result of the distinction between *domitae naturae* and *ferae naturae,* the early common law tended to focus nearly exclusively on whether a particular animal fell into one category or another. This classification was crucial because the property rights in domestic animals differed from the property rights in wild animals. Domestic animals might be the absolute possession of a human because these "continue perpetually in his occupation, and will not stray from his house or person, unless by accident or fraudulent enticement, in either of which cases the owner does not lose his property." "Other animals, that are not of a tame and domestic nature, are either not the objects of property at all, or fall under our other division, namely, that of *qualified, limited,* or *special property;* which is such as is not in its nature permanent, but may sometimes subsist, and at other times not subsist."[45]

Qualified property in wild animals was obtained in three ways: *per industriam hominis,* or taming them "by art, industry, and education" or confining them within one's immediate power; *ratione impotentiae,* or the constructive possession of young wild animals that are too weak to leave the possessor's land; and *propter privilegium,* or the privilege to hunt, take, and kill animals to the exclusion of others.[46] This qualified property was defeasible when the wild animals escaped or passed from the control of the qualified owner, unless the animals had *animus revertendi,* which was determined by the usual habit of the animal, such as a tame hawk, to return to the original owner after the animal had left the owner's control.[47]

Needless to say, considerable litigation concerned the property status of various animals. For example, in *Manning v. Mitcherson,*[48] Mitcherson's canary escaped and was caught by Manning. The court held that the bird still belonged to Mitcherson: "To say that if one has a canary bird, mocking bird, parrot, or any other bird so kept and it should accidentally escape from its cage to the street, or to a neighboring house, that the first person who caught it would be its owner, is wholly at variance with our views of right and justice."[49] In *Pierson v. Post,*[50]

Pierson killed a fox that he knew was being pursued by Post and Post's hounds. The New York court held that Post had no qualified property in the fox: even "pursuit, accompanied with wounding, is equally ineffectual for [the purpose of obtaining qualified property], unless the animal be actually taken."[51] Some years later, the same court revisited the issue and had to decide how severe a wound had to be to allow for qualified property to vest in a party other than the one that actually killed the animal. In *Buster v. Newkirk,*[52] Newkirk wounded a deer but then abandoned the hunt until the next morning, when he discovered that Buster had killed the deer the night before. The court denied Newkirk any qualified property on the ground that although Newkirk had wounded the animal, the wound was not severe enough to bring the animal "within the power and control of" Newkirk.[53] Numerous other cases involved what type of confinement was necessary for qualified property *per industriam,* what constituted pursuit, what constituted *animus revertendi,* and what types of animals were subject to consideration as qualified property.

Two important qualifications inform the above admittedly abbreviated description. First, although all domestic and wild animals that were qualified property *were* the property of the possessor, it was not a crime to steal from the owner any animals that were "kept for pleasure, curiosity, or whim, as dogs, bears, cats, apes, parrots, and singing-birds,"[54] Because these animals were not fit to serve as food. The owner could maintain a civil suit for money damages against a person who took one of these nonfood animals, but, at common law, no crime was committed. The common-law rule has largely been changed by statute in both the United States and England so that both civil and criminal penalties apply to any person who takes any animal legitimately possessed by another.

Second, state and federal governments, subject to certain relatively insignificant limitations, have considerable power to allow the hunting and killing of animals.[55] Accordingly, qualified property in an animal does not necessarily vest in a person who reduces an animal to her control.

In sum, the common law developed against a theological and philosophical background that, for various reasons, considered animals to possess some "defect" that justified human oppression of animals. Despite changing philosophical views—such as the virtually unanimous rejection of the notion that animals do not feel pain, the rejection of various theological notions, and clear evidence of the ability of animals to think—the common-law concept of animals as the "absolute" property of humans continues to this day.

## Private Property and Ownership

As I mentioned at the outset, private property has been thought to be a difficult concept to define because there is some indeterminacy inherent in it. The concept of property denotes different legal relations between a person and other people concerning a thing. These legal relations, however, are reflective of the various ways in which persons may be said to have property rights. The *Restatement of*

*Property,* borrowing from the work of Professor Wesley Hohfeld, describes four such relations or aspects of the notion of property right. A "right" is "a legally enforceable claim of one person against another, that the other shall do an act or shall not do an act." A "privilege" is "a legal freedom on the part of one person as against another to do a given act or a legal freedom not to do a given act." A "power" is "an ability on the part of a person to produce a change in a given legal relation by doing or not doing a given act." An "immunity" is "a freedom on the part of one person against having a given legal relationship altered by a given act or omission on the part of another person."[56] For example, if we assume that my pen is my private property, I have a claim to be able to use my pen for writing purposes, and you have a duty to refrain from interfering in that use; I have a privilege not to use my pen, and no one has a right to make me use it; I have the power to alter legal relations with another by selling or lending the pen; and I have an immunity in that no action of another person can affect my ownership of the pen without my agreement. "Complete property" is the "totality of these [claims], privileges, powers and immunities which it is legally possible for a person to have with regard to" property.[57] Other relations may focus more on my duties with respect to the use of my pen. That is, although I may use my pen to write or, if I wish, to stir my coffee, presumably I cannot, without justification, use my pen to injure someone.

If a person has "complete property" in a piece of property, it would not be difficult for us simply to define private property as the complete collection of rights (and duties) described. The problem is that the person can have one relation with respect to a piece of property while not having another such relation. For example, I may lend my pen to you for a charge, on the agreement that you will return it to me in two weeks. For that two weeks, you have a claim to use of the pen and others are under a duty not to interfere with that use. In lending the pen, I have changed my legal relationship to you, but because I was free to lend and did not sell the pen, you are disabled from keeping the pen beyond the time of our agreement; and since you must return the pen to me, you may not use the pen as carelessly as I might choose to use it, given that if I wish, I am free to destroy the pen entirely. The indeterminacy arises because the various sticks that make up the bundle of "complete property" may not all be held by the same person at the same time.

Moreover, although we talk about "absolute" property or "absolute" ownership, no such thing really exists. All property is subject to restrictions on its use. For example, as mentioned above, just because a person owns something does not mean that she can use it to injure others. Also, there may be laws that prohibit certain items—for example, illicit drugs—from qualifying as property at all. And there are other sorts of restrictions on the use of property. A person who owns a building designated a historic landmark may be restricted from changing the building, or federal or state environmental laws may have an impact on what can and cannot be done with one's land. In the case of animals, there are ostensibly laws that limit their use by property owners. These laws include anticruelty statutes and federal laws regulating the slaughter of animals and the treatment of animals used in experiments. These restrictions are treated in subsequent chapters.

In an excellent analysis of the concept of property, philosopher Jeremy Waldron argues that private property is a concept of which there are many conceptions. Waldron argues that "[t]he concept of property is the concept of a system of rules governing access to and control of material resources."[58] "In a system of private property, the rules governing access to and control of material resources are organized around the idea that resources are on the whole separate objects each assigned and therefore belonging to some particular individual." In explaining the notion of belonging, Waldron states that a correlation between an object and a particular person expresses "the idea of *ownership* or *belonging*. 'Ownership,' then . . . is a term peculiar to systems of private property. The owner of a resource is simply the individual whose determination as to the use of the resource is taken as final in a system of this kind."[59]

A. M. Honoré has argued persuasively that the "liberal" conception of ownership involves a number of "standard incidents" that "are not individually necessary, though they may be together sufficient" conditions of ownership. These are (1) the right to possess (the right to have exclusive physical control of a thing); (2) the right to use; (3) the right to manage (powers to license and contract with respect to the thing); (4) the right to the income, such as rents, fruits, and profits; (5) the right to the capital (the power to alienate the thing and the liberty to consume, waste, or destroy the thing); (6) the right to security (the right to keep the item if the person so chooses and remains solvent); (7) the incident of transmissibility (the ability to bequeath the thing to successors); (8) the incident of absence of term (the ability to determine the length of time that someone else may have an interest in the property); (9) the prohibition of harmful use; and (10) liability to execution (the owner's interest may be taken away by execution of a judgment or insolvency).[60]

Animals fit this private property/ownership paradigm quite neatly. With the exception of wild animals (which can be reduced to ownership), we usually consider any particular animal as assigned and therefore belonging to a specific person, who may be identified. Such an individual is entitled to exclusive physical possession of the animal, the right to use the animal for economic or other gain, the right to manage the animal by making contracts with respect to the animal or to use the animal as collateral for a loan; and, perhaps most important, the individual to whom the animal is assigned can, with no exceptions, consume, waste, or destroy the animal. The greatest power that one being can have over another is the right to take the life of the other. It has never been seriously questioned that the owners of animals can kill their animals with complete impunity. The individual is also under a duty to ensure that the animal does not harm others, and may be restricted in other ways as well. Otherwise, the owner can bequeath the animal, keep the animal, and be liable to have the animal taken in execution of a legal judgment or insolvency. Although there is a requirement that animals not be treated "inhumanely," for the most part this requirement amounts to no more than an adoption of Locke's principle that animals not be "wasted" or "spoiled."

Honoré's notion of "liberal" ownership demonstrates the social view of ownership, reflected in ordinary language. In an important essay, philosopher Frank Snare analyzed property in terms of constitutive rules and argued that certain rules of social behavior must be observed in order for property to be said to exist in a particular community.[61] According to Snare, the proposition "John owns X" is true if John has a right to use X and if John has a right to exclude others from using X. Moreover, John must be able to transfer use and exclusion rights; any violator of John's right must be subject to punishment; anyone who damages X may be required to pay damages; and John may be held liable if X is used to injure the person or property of another. Although this "ordinary-language" analysis of property ownership does not apply in more complicated cases in which the standard incidents of ownership are distributed among different people, it captures almost perfectly the way in which animal property has been, and is currently, viewed by the common law. This notion of "liberal" ownership is closely related to the notion that the concept of property is very much connected to the freedom of individuals to use their property in the way that they see fit. To put the matter in terms of economic theory, the liberal theory of ownership respects the principle that the individual is the best person to decide how much she values the property.

The liberal theory, of course, begs the question against other theories that advocate state ownership of property or public ownership of property.[62] For example, rather than apply a "liberal" notion of ownership to animals, we could just as easily say that all sentient beings other than human beings are the property of the state, and although humans may use animals for human purposes, the state has a property interest in animals and must ensure that all animals are treated "humanely." Indeed, under modern law, the actual situation is ostensibly similar; although individuals own their animals, the state technically has an interest in the animal to ensure that the animal is treated "humanely." As I discuss in subsequent chapters, the problem is that this is interpreted to mean that the state is required only to ensure that the owner does not, in Locke's terminology, "waste" or "spoil" the animal—that is, that the owner does not use the animal in ways that are not efficient. This scheme *assumes* that the liberal theory of ownership ought to prevail and that state regulation (it does not even amount to state ownership) must accommodate that liberal conception of ownership.

Indeed, as seen above, there is at least one instance in which we depart from the liberal theory of ownership in favor of some other: in the case of wildlife, it has been stated by various courts that the state holds all wildlife in trust for the people of the state. Again, even that scheme, in which there is more of a property interest vested in the state through the trusteeship notion, the liberal theory predominates because individuals can reduce wildlife to private property through wildlife capture rules. The liberal theory of property, and the notion of property ownership, then, far from being self-justifying notions, are really normative concepts that focus on one value—the freedom of the property owner to use the property in ways that she thinks best, and the ability to exclude others from using the property—to the exclusion of other moral values.

Specifically, the liberal theory of property assumes that animals have no interests, or, at least, no interests that will ever prevail against human interests. That is the whole point of classifying animals as "property." Indeed, to classify something as property in a legal sense is to say that the thing is to be regarded solely as a means to the end determined by human property owners. The property concept should be contrasted with the notion of rights, which generally implies that the rightholder is *not* to be treated solely as a means to an end with respect to the substance of the right. If we say that an animal is property, we mean that the animal is to be treated under the law primarily (if not exclusively) as a means to human ends, and not as an end in herself. This is not to say that we do not give legal "protection" to property. For example, in some states and foreign countries, art work is protected from being defaced not only by vandalism laws but by laws that seek to protect the artistic integrity of the work. These laws, however, are not intended to recognize any inherent interest that must be protected; rather, the sole concern of the law is to protect the personal integrity of the artist. Similarly, laws that restrict our exploitation of endangered species do not recognize any rights in animals; rather, the concern is to ensure biological integrity for human purposes. As soon as a species is no longer "endangered" or "threatened," its members are routinely hunted or otherwise exploited.

## The Importance of Property and the Constitutional Scope of Regulation

In the present section, I briefly examine the importance of the concept of property in American constitutional jurisprudence. The purpose for this examination is to provide the reader with some understanding of the issues raised by the regulation of property in the United States.

Blackstone was studied carefully by lawyers in the American colonies, and for the colonists, for whom the cry "Liberty and Property" was the motto of the revolutionary movement, "property and liberty were inseparable, as evidenced by the colonists' willingness to break with England when the mother country seemingly threatened property ownership." However, there were restrictions on the use of property that were dictated by governmental regulation and by custom. For example, "the abundance of game in North America fostered public hunting rights. In sharp contrast with English law, the colonies recognized a general customary right to hunt on privately owned unenclosed land."[63]

According to many theorists, a strong Lockean theory of property rights characterized the prerevolutionary period, and most of the framers of the Constitution agreed that the right to own private property was an important value. Professor James Ely argues that as a result of the endorsement of a strong property rights philosophy, "many provisions of the Constitution pertain to property interests and were designed to rectify the abuses that characterized the revolutionary era," although "unlike many of the early state constitutions, the federal Constitution did not proclaim the natural right of property ownership or declare that a person could not be deprived of property except by due process of law." Ely claims that "the framers were content to rely primarily on institutional and political arrangements to safeguard property owners."[64] The scheme envisioned by the framers would establish various safeguards, such as a strong executive and an independent judiciary, to ensure that the majority could not, through the legislature, interfere with property rights.

Ely places the various constitutional protections of property interests into four categories. The first three categories involved provisions that "restricted the power of the new national government with respect to property and economic activity,"[65] provisions "intended to strengthen the hand of the national government over economic matters,"[66] and provisions that placed restrictions on state power.[67] The fourth category involved provisions concerned with the protection of slave property, and Ely notes that "no other type of property received such detailed attention from the framers." Although many delegates to the constitutional convention shared "a tepid antislavery sentiment that occasionally surfaced in the debates," the delegates never considered the abolition of slavery, since "such a move not only would have been impossible to implement but also would surely have caused the collapse of the convention." Federalists and Anti-Federalists, who held fiercely opposing views about the nature of government, nevertheless "shared the prevailing view that respect for property was an essential element of republicanism."[68] Indeed, the primary difference between these opponents focused on whether the national government, as the Federalists maintained, or the state governments, as the Anti-Federalists maintained, would better govern commerce and protect privacy.[69]

In drafting a proposed bill of rights, Federalist James Madison sought to increase property protection beyond the institutional and political arrangements that had been included in the Constitution. Although Congress rejected Madison's broad declaration that government was instituted, in part, to protect the right to acquire and to use property, Madison gained approval of the Fifth Amendment, which provides that there shall be no deprivation of property (or life or liberty) "without due process of law" and that no private property shall "be taken for public use, without just compensation."[70]

There are, of course, competing views of the role played by private property notions in the formation of the Constitution. For example, some scholars argue that the predominant political philosophy during the Revolutionary War was one of republicanism, which sanctioned the idea of the sacrifice of individual rights for the public good.[71] Neither Jefferson nor Franklin believed that property was an inalienable right, supporting the argument that the prevailing philosophy of property was anti-Lockean. But disillusionment with state legislatures that sanctioned uncompensated takings prompted a political shift away from republicanism toward liberalism, with its attendant concern for the sanctity of property rights as inextricably connected to notions of personal liberty.

Whatever the origins of constitutional concern for property rights in general, and of the Fifth Amendment takings clause in particular, it is clear that Locke's views (or the standard version of Locke's views) were, on any interpretation, a historical winner in terms of the extent of property protection ultimately contained in the Constitution and Bill of Rights. Since no one ever questioned the status that animals would have under the law, the important issue for present purposes is to what degree, if any, the law permits the regulation of the use of animal property. That issue provokes an antecedent question: does a "taking" mean the physical appropriation of property, or does it contemplate regulation as well?

Although Madison intended the Fifth Amendment takings clause to be limited to the physical taking of property, and although the Supreme Court has acknowledged this interpretation,[72] it is clear, as Professor Bruce Ackerman has noted, "there is no indication that any individual Framer (let alone the whole bunch) had worked out a particular theory of compensation law that would suggest a determinate way of separating out those contexts in which compensation was required from those in which losers should be left to tend their wounds without communal assistance."[73]

The Supreme Court has long rejected the notion that "all property within the State is held, and all contracts are entered into subject to the future exercise of the police power of the State,"[74] and has held that government regulation can constitute a "taking"; nevertheless, the Court has often failed to provide criteria that may be used to distinguish the uncompensable regulation of the use of property from its compensable taking. In a 1992 decision on the subject, *Lucas v. South Carolina Coastal Council,*[75] the Court invalidated a state regulation that prohibited the development of coastal wetlands and that had the effect of precluding Lucas from developing his beachfront property. The Court held that "[w]here the State seeks to sustain regulation that deprives land of all economically beneficial use, we think it may resist compensation only if the logically antecedent inquiry into the nature of the owner's estate shows that the proscribed use interests were not part of his title to begin with." In cases where the taking does not effect a deprivation of all economically beneficial use, it may be possible to receive compensation dependent upon " 'the economic impact of the regulation on the claimant and . . . the extent to which the regulation has interfered with distinct investment-backed expectations.' "[76]

Although *Lucas* dealt with real, as opposed to personal, property, the principles would apply to animal property, and especially uses of animals involving land, such as cattle grazing or the construction of a research laboratory. Although the state can regulate the use of property pursuant to police power to abate nuisances, it may not deny an owner all economic or beneficial use of property through regulation or frustrate investment-backed expectations. American law, echoing common-law principles, has historically permitted animal users virtually unlimited discretion to treat their animal property as they wish. Significant regulation of the ownership of animal property would at least be suspect.

## Conclusion

In this chapter I have provided, albeit in a rather abbreviated fashion, some general thoughts on the status of animals as property in the common-law system. In particular, I have emphasized that the "liberal" theory of property ownership is closely connected to the notion that property owners should have maximum freedom to use and value their property. The problem is that by classifying animals as property, the law has already decided that animal interests will not be protected whenever (or almost whenever) human property rights are at stake.

In the next chapter, I examine two examples of the animals-as-property paradigm. These examples illustrate how legal welfarism operates in standard legal doctrine.

# CHAPTER THREE

## *Two Examples of Legal Welfarism*

I NOW CONSIDER two examples of the status of animals as property in the context of concrete legal doctrines. The first example concerns a "bailment" contract involving animals. For purposes of such contracts, animals are treated exactly like inanimate property subject to the same type of bailment contract. The human actors who are parties to the contract rely on legal rules that relegate the animal to property status. The purpose of discussing bailment contracts is not to educate the reader on arcane topics in the law of personal property. Rather, I hope that the discussion demonstrates the extent to which the legal system has incorporated animals as property without any regard for their status as sentient beings different from inanimate objects.

The second example concerns the treatment of animals as property in the somewhat unusual context of veterinary malpractice in which some of the people involved not only do not regard animals as property but regard them as members of their families or as close companions who share no similarities with the inanimate objects that we think of as property. Nevertheless, the legal system regards these companion animals as property, thus demonstrating the strong institutional need of the legal system not to depart from the traditional characterization of animals, even though this characterization simply fails to reflect the reality of how we see at least some animals in our society.

The two examples used here—bailments and the law of liability for veterinary malpractice—illustrate the legal welfarism thesis in two very different ways. The first example—that involving the law of bailments—represents a classic case of legal welfarism: animals are treated as property no different from any other sort of property. To put the matter in the terminology of the last chapter, the attributes of ownership are not divided among the putative owners and "others," such as the state or private animal protection agencies, who have the responsibility to ensure that the animal is treated properly. Moreover, the use of property is not regulated in any other way, and humans with possession of animals are not restricted in their treatment of animals beyond that which facilitates the exploitation of the animal.

The rules surrounding liability for veterinary malpractice represent a curious, but distinct, manifestation of the doctrine of legal welfarism. Legal welfarism, which embraces the notion that animals are (and should be) regarded as property, allows individuals to own animals with very little, if any, supervision by the government or anyone else who may have concern for the welfare of the animals. Legal welfarism permits the development and perpetuation of an extensive system of private animal ownership. One consequence of this unlimited license to own animals is that some people, for various reasons, develop close bonds with the animals they own. It might be said, then, that the liberal ownership of animals permitted under legal welfarism, which normatively accepts the status quo of animal property, respects and reinforces social expectations that animals are property and can be the subject of exclusive ownership by people. This type of ownership, although not the only type of ownership, also facilitates the development of relationships in which people feel justified—even obligated—in expending a considerable amount of resources on their animals. For example, if, for moral reasons, the ownership of animals was, as the ownership of land is often, divided among several people, so that humans had use and possession of the animal but state agents could routinely inspect the owner's premises and circumstances to ensure that the animal was being treated properly, the "owner" might be more inclined to view the government (or the public) as a "part owner" for purposes of providing resources for the animal's welfare.

Legal welfarism militates against such expectations on the part of animal owners, who usually view their ownership as exclusive. When animals owned by such people are injured or killed through the tortious acts of others, the owners understandably expect that the legal system will require that their loss (pecuniary and nonpecuniary) be reimbursed by the culpable party. The usual response of the system—that damages are restricted to the fair market value of the animal, which is the typical measure of damage to property in general—respects and reinforces the defendant's expectation that animals will be treated as property no different from any other. Of course, the justification for such respect may be purely economic; for example, damages for the negligent injury to animals caused by a veterinarian may be restricted to fair market value because the veterinarian has, in a sense, not contracted to pay greater damages, this state of affairs being reflected in the veterinarian's professional fees, which would be higher but for the limitation of liability. Such a response, however, proves the very point that is part of the background for my entire argument: that by treating animals as property we delude ourselves into thinking that a moral issue can be resolved by economic analysis.

Again, I caution the reader that these examples are not intended as exhaustive statements of legal rules and principles. Rather, these are abbreviated descriptions designed to provide some idea about the place of animals in our legal system. Although some more technical material is included, it is generally placed in the endnotes.

## Animals as Property: Bailment Contracts

In bailment contracts, the owner of property uses the property as a commodity to be exchanged, lent, or hired to another party. Although the owner, the bailor, retains title to the property and may, accordingly, be considered the "owner," the other party, the bailee, has temporary dominion and control over the property. As one court has said, a bailment contract may be defined as "the holding of a chattel by one person under an obligation to return or deliver it to another after some special purpose is accomplished."[1] Animals and inanimate objects are both the subjects of bailment contracts. Examples of animal bailments include hiring horses for others to ride, hiring animals for farm work, allowing animals to graze on certain lands in return for the animals' milk or wool, and hiring animals out for stud purposes. Under the law, bailments involving animals are treated like any other type of bailment contract and are subject to the same rules and duties. No distinction is made between bailments involving living creatures and those involving inanimate objects.[2]

There are three basic types of bailments:[3] where the bailee performs a gratuitous service involving the property for the sole benefit of the bailor or owner (e.g., the bailee agrees to care for an animal while the owner is away);[4] where both the bailor and bailee receive a mutual benefit from the bailment (e.g., the bailor hires out a horse for the bailee to use and receives payment);[5] and where the bailor lends the property to the bailee for the bailee's sole benefit (e.g., the bailor lends a horse to the bailee but receives no compensation).[6] If the bailment is for the sole purpose of the bailor, then the bailee is responsible for gross negligence alone and need only exercise "slight care" in maintaining the well-being of the animal and in protecting the animal from harm. If the bailment is for the mutual benefit of the parties, then the bailee must exercise ordinary prudence in treatment of the animal.[7] If the bailment is for the exclusive benefit of the bailee, then the bailee is liable for slight neglect to the animal.[8]

The bailor may, if she chooses, specify that a lesser standard of care be provided in maintaining an animal and may even hold the bailee harmless from liability for injuring or destroying the animal.[9] The commercial value of an animal may be considered in determining the appropriate standard of care. This standard-of-care concept exists to ensure that the owner's interest in the chattel is protected, not to safeguard the animal from abuse or harm by the bailee. Courts have not expressed the view that the law demands a higher or different duty of care because the bailed property is a living, sentient creature, although at least one court rejected the argument that a bailee owed a lesser duty to the bailor in the case of animals than in that of inanimate objects. Although the bailee argued that "there are risks inherent in the care of animals" and that bailees cannot be held accountable for injuries that occur to the bailed animal, the court ultimately rejected the challenge.[10] The bailor may, however, specify that the bailee is to keep the bailor's animal on a "starvation diet," a notion that would have no meaning applied to inanimate objects.

The bailee's responsibility in fulfilling the bailment contract is twofold. First, the bailee must satisfy the applicable standard of care while the animal is in the bailee's possession, "preserving the animal's value unimpaired."[11] Second, the bailee must return the animal in the same condition in which the animal was delivered.[12] At a minimum, the bailee must provide the "necessaries of life" to the animal,[13] but absent a special agreement, the bailee is not considered an insurer of the animal[14] and is not bound to replace the animal if the animal dies through natural causes.[15] The bailee may be bound to provide ordinary veterinary care to an animal, but would not be expected to go beyond what is minimally necessary to preserve the animal's value.

The bailor's duties with respect to the bailment are more limited than the bailee's. As with inanimate objects, the bailor must deliver animals in a satisfactory condition, suitable for the purpose they are meant to serve.[16] If the bailor does not provide an animal that satisfies, this implied warranty that the animal is not sick or injured, the bailee may be absolved from the animal's later injury and death.[17]

In the event of a breach of a bailment contract involving animals, the remedies are the same as they would be for other property. A bailor who cannot regain possession of his animals from the bailee is entitled to the fair market value of the property lost.[18] Similarly, if the bailee breaches his duty of care and, as a result, the animal's value is lessened, the bailor may recover money damages. If the bailment is for the mutual benefit of the bailor and bailee or for the exclusive benefit of the bailor, and the bailor fails to provide any promised compensation to the bailee, the bailee may have an agistment lien against the animals, which are the bailor's property.[19] If an animal is abandoned in the care of the bailee, the bailee may exercise her right to keep and use the animal in return for the care provided.[20] In one case, the court reasoned that if the bailee incurred an expense in maintaining the animal, he was entitled to make reasonable use of the property as compensation.[21] Because animals have the status of property, they can also serve as security for a loan.[22]

Many opinions have been written on the topic of bailments involving animals, and they all relegate animals to the same status as inanimate objects from which the owner could derive some benefit or value. Animal bailments are viewed simply as transactions in which goods and services are provided in exchange for benefit to either or both parties. None of the bailment decisions discusses the peculiar status of animals as sentient beings or expresses any concern to protect animals from harm.[23] All of the cases recognize that the primary obligation of the bailee is to ensure that the economic value of the bailed animal is preserved. This point is underscored in *Deiro v. American Airlines*.[24] In *Deiro,* the plaintiff had checked his nine greyhounds for transport on a flight from Oregon to Boston. During the stopover in Dallas/Fort Worth, the airline left the cages containing the dogs exposed to the sun, in a temperature of approximately a hundred degrees. The airline did not provide the dogs with proper ventilation or water and refused the plaintiff's requests to let him attend to his dogs. By the time the plane landed in Boston, seven of the dogs had died from heat exposure, and the remaining two were seriously ill. The plaintiff sued for damages of approximately $900,000 for the seven deaths and for the treatment needed for the other two.[25] The appellate court held that the clause on the back of the plaintiff's ticket limiting the airline's liability for lost or damaged luggage to $750 also applied to its liability for the dogs.[26]

Similarly, in *Mitchell v. Union Pacific Railroad,*[27] the plaintiff sued the railroad company after his valuable show dog died during transit from Chicago to Los Angeles. The plaintiff had thoroughly questioned the baggage clerk about whether he would be allowed to feed and walk the animal during the journey, and the clerk had assured the plaintiff that he would be allowed to do so.[28] After the train left for Chicago, however, the plaintiff was denied all access to the dog and was told that the baggage car was locked and that the dog would not receive any care. The dog died from lack of water and lack of ventilation. The plaintiff was able to recover more than the $25 limit for baggage specified on his ticket only because the court found that he had no actual notice of the limitation of liability.[29] Although the jury awarded $12,000 in compensatory and punitive damages for the death of the dog, the district court, on remand, reduced the award to $5,000 in compensatory damages, representing the fair market value of a dog able to perform tricks.[30]

## Animals as Property: Liability for Veterinary Malpractice

Some writers on property maintain that "legal relations in our law exist only between persons. There cannot be a legal relation between a person and a thing or between two things."[31] In Chapter Five, I consider the possibility that the law may permit legal relations to exist between persons and things. For the time being, however, my concern is to focus on the indisputable fact that whether humans may have legal relations to property or not, they can certainly have strong emotional and personal relations with what we call pets, or companion animals. The point of the discussion is to demonstrate how far the law will go in acknowledging that people can have meaningful relationships with animals, though it nevertheless preserves intact the legal dogma of animals as property.

More people than ever before have dogs, cats, birds, and other animals with whom they live and whom they regard as members of the family. Over 125 million dogs, cats, horses, and birds lived in American homes in 1989. The veterinary profession has benefited enormously from an increase in animal ownership and from the fact that animal owners now seek a higher level of care, including preventive treatment, than they did in the past. Revenues in the veterinary care field have risen an average of 7 percent per year for the last decade and, as of 1989, reached $5 billion per year.[32] It is obvious that humans who have these relationships with animals do not regard them merely as personal property. I now focus on the problems that arise when a pet is killed or injured as the result of the negligence of a veterinarian or other caretaker, such as a kennel or animal hospital.

Veterinarians and other animal caretakers can commit malpractice in several different ways.[33] For example, veterinarians have been successfully sued for causing injuries to humans during the course of treatment of an animal.[34] This usually occurs when an owner is allowed to help "restrain" her animal during a veterinary examination or procedure; the animal becomes upset and bites or otherwise attacks the person restraining the animal.[35] Injuries to humans can also occur after a veterinarian's treatment if the sick or injured animal reacts violently to medication or if the owner or someone in the owner's household inadvertently ingests some of the medication intended for the animal.[36]

Claims of veterinary malpractice have also been made by nonclients alleging injury to their animals as a result of the alleged negligent misdiagnosis or failure to diagnose a contagious disease of a client's animal and that animal's subsequent exposure to the nonclient's animal, as in an adjacent pasture. Other nonclients who have asserted malpractice claims against veterinarians include a farmer who was sued by food producers for selling them milk contaminated with insecticide. The farmer claimed that the veterinarian who had treated the cattle for illness resulting from ingestion of the insecticide should have warned him to withhold the milk from the market.[37]

For our purposes, however, the most important—and common—form of veterinary or caretaker liability is the claim of malpractice by reason of injuries inflicted upon the animal of a client. It is this type of claim that is addressed for the remainder of this discussion, all under the common term "veterinary malpractice."

Even though a pet owner does not usually regard a companion animal merely as a piece of property, we know that domestic animals such as dogs or cats are still considered the personal property of their owners, and remedies for negligence must be understood against this background. Laws regarding veterinary malpractice vary greatly from state to state. The traditional notions of veterinary malpractice allowed aggrieved owners of animals injured by their veterinarians to recover nothing more than market value, that is, the difference between the monetary worth of the animal before the incident complained of and that after.[38] Such measure of damages does not include consideration of how valuable an animal may actually be to an owner who would never contemplate a sale; it relies instead on what amount the animal would be worth to a stranger acting as a willing buyer in an arm's length transaction for fungible goods. Certainly many, if not most, owners would find that type of measurement of their animals' worth unsatisfactory. Nonetheless, for many years the market value approach was used exclusively in evaluating damages for injuries to animals and indeed is still used today in many states.[39]

In a representative case from the Supreme Court of Alaska, a lower-court ruling was upheld limiting damages to fair market value for the destruction of a dog. In *Richardson v. Fairbanks North Star Borough,*[40] plaintiffs called the local animal shelter when they discovered their dog, Wizzard, was missing. They were told that the shelter had Wizzard in its custody and that they could reclaim him between 8:00 A.M. and 5:00 P.M. The Richardsons arrived at the shelter at 4:50 P.M. and saw

Wizzard chained in the back of the facility. Shelter employees told the Richardsons that the shelter was already closed and that they would have to return the next day to pick up the dog. When the Richardsons returned as instructed, they were advised that Wizzard had been killed. Since the killing violated an ordinance that required the shelter to keep animals at least three days before killing them, the Richardsons sued. The shelter admitted that adequate records were not kept on its animals.[41]

The trial court awarded the Richardsons only $300 for the senseless destruction of Wizzard, based on its assessment of the dog's fair market value. The Richardsons appealed, claiming that the trial court should have accepted evidence about Wizzard's value as a pet and their emotional pain and suffering upon his death. On appeal, the Supreme Court of Alaska in *Richardson* affirmed this ruling, holding that "since dogs have legal status as items of personal property, courts generally limit the damage award in cases in which a dog has been wrongfully killed to the animal's market value at the time of death." The court added that "in cases involving working dogs, especially those of mixed lineage without a marketable pedigree, courts have based the damage award on the dog's utility." The court refused to allow any recovery for mental or emotional distress, because the plaintiffs had failed to show that they had suffered the requisite amount of emotional distress from the intentional killing of a pet. The court made that finding despite the fact that the Richardsons had rejected an offer of $2,000 from the shelter, and then it awarded the defendant shelter $3,763 for costs of suit and attorney's fees, which the Richardsons had to pay.[42]

Another typical fair market value case involved an atypical "pet."[43] Archie Ubanoski of Houston, Texas, bought a steer for his son to enter in livestock shows. The steer cost $2,256. Ubanoski took the steer to the shared offices of three Houston veterinarians for cosmetic dehorning. To immobilize the steer for this extremely painful procedure, the doctors attached an electric clip on the steer's lip and inserted a probe into the steer's rectum. The current from the electric clip was supposed to paralyze the steer's muscles so the veterinarian could do the procedure without movement from the steer, which might cause further injury (and diminuition of value) to the steer. When the power was activated, the steer fell to the ground, the clip was dislodged, the current stopped, and the steer stood up. The same thing happened on the second attempt. On the third try, the clip remained on the steer's lip, and the steer stayed on the ground, so the dehorning finally took place. The steer, however, was unable to stand again and was euthanized one month later. A necropsy revealed a recent fracture of the hip bone. Ubanoski sued the veterinarian for negligence, alleging that their failure to use a restraining chute to keep the steer from falling and their use of the electrical immobilization device caused the steer to be crippled. The jury awarded Ubanoski $31,450 upon a finding that the veterinarians were negligent and that their negligence caused the harm to the steer.[44] The appellate court reversed the judgment, stating that the general rule for measuring damages to personal property is the difference in the market value immediately before and immediately after the injury, and reasoning that the amount of the award was not an accurate measure of the steer's fair market value given that the steer could still be sold for slaughter.[45] The court determined that the jury had relied on purely speculative evidence concerning the potential value of the steer, threw out the jury's verdict, and ordered a new trial.[46]

Many of today's most common household pets are mixed-breed dogs and cats, often obtained at minimal or no cost from shelters. As such, they have no discernible "market value." Thus, their owners frequently forgo legal remedies when the animals are negligently injured or killed, because they cannot recoup their true damages in the courts. An owner may suffer tremendous emotional distress when left without a beloved family pet, yet the loss of this unique being goes completely uncompensated under the market value approach.

The market value system of assessing damages for injury to personal property has gradually expanded to the point were some states now allow recovery for emotional distress of an owner resulting from harm to an animal caused by a veterinarian or other person, whether or not market value is also a factor.[47] Typically, claims for damages based on emotional distress are pursued through one of four avenues. It is important to recognize, however, that these cases do not remove animals from the category of personal property. Indeed, the "emotional-distress" cases focus exclusively on the reaction of a property owner to the loss of property. Moreover, the "emotional-distress" cases that involve animals are not unique breaks from past precedent; rather, these cases merely apply established principles of law concerning emotional distress over the loss of other personal property— specifically, family heirlooms—to the loss of another type of personal property.

First, in some courts, plaintiffs are allowed to recover the "actual value"[48] of their property. The sentimental value of the animal to the owner may be a component of such actual value and of any damage award based thereon, especially where there is no discernible market value. One of the first courts to consider the actual, or intrinsic, value of a pet was the New York City Civil Court, in *Brousseau v. Rosenthal*, a 1980 case.[49] Plaintiff left her healthy eight-year-old mixed-breed dog at a kennel for two weeks. When she returned to pick up her pet, she was told the dog had died. Plaintiff sued the kennel for loss of companionship and loss of protection. The court found the kennel liable for the death under the law of bailments and acknowledged the market value approach for damages to personal property but nevertheless held that Brousseau was not limited to a nominal award just because the dog had been given to her, was a mixed breed, and had no ascertainable value. The court held that an assessment of the dog's "actual value" to the owner was required in order to make her whole. Because her pet was Brousseau's sole and constant companion, and because loss of companionship had been long recognized as an element of damages in New York, the court said it must be considered in any award to plaintiff even though measuring such a loss in pecuniary terms is quite difficult.[50] Despite the judge's obvious sympathy for Brousseau's loss of her treasured pet, the judge awarded her only $550.[51]

In Illinois, a court held that actual value should be used to compute damages where the property in question has no market value.[52] Joseph and Anita Jankoski had taken their pet German shepherd to the Preiser Animal Hospital for some diagnostic tests. The hospital veterinarians administered anesthesia to the dog during the course of the exam, and the dog died. The Jankoskis sued the veterinarians for failing to administer the anesthesia properly and for failing to monitor the dog's condition. They sought to recover damages not for the dog's value but for their loss of companionship of the dog. The trial court stated that the Jankoskis could amend their complaint to ask for damages for loss of their property, but the Jankoskis refused because the dog had no value as property. The trial court then granted the veterinarians' motion and dismissed the suit. Upon the Jankoskis' appeal, the appellate court had to decide whether Illinois law recognized a legal claim for loss of companionship resulting from the negligently caused death of a dog. The appellate court agreed with the trial court that no action for loss of companionship of a dog could be brought in Illinois, because an animal is an item of personal property. The court said that while the usual measure of damages for personal property is its fair market value, where no such value exists the actual or intrinsic value of the property should be the basis of a monetary award. Although it refused to consider an independent claim for loss of companionship, the court did expressly state that "sentimental value" may be an element of the property's actual, or intrinsic, value. However, the court also stated, without reason, that damages for sentimental value would be severely circumscribed, thereby playing a game of semantics in which it could appear realistically to assess a human/animal relationship yet deny damages to the people who lost a cherished companion.[53]

Obviously, the actual, or intrinsic, value approach to assessing damages for the loss of a pet is better than the market value approach because it at least recognizes the reality of the relationship of a companion animal with the owner. It appears, however, that the damages awarded on the basis of actual, or intrinsic, value are not appreciably more than the meager amounts historically given on the basis of fair market value.

Second, some other courts take a different route to allowing sentimental value to play a part in damage awards for loss of property, through the tort of "negligent infliction of emotional distress."[54] Although this tort was once narrowly construed and applied only to incidents involving humans who were physically compromised by their emotional distress, at least one court has extended its applicability to incidents involving property damage alone.

The Hawaii Supreme Court, in a landmark 1981 case, upheld the right of plaintiffs to recover for emotional distress caused by the negligent killing of their family pet, even though none of the plaintiffs witnessed the event and even though they proved no physical manifestation (to them) of the alleged emotional harm.[55] The Campbell family was moving to Hawaii and was required by law to put their nine-year-old boxer dog, Princess, into a quarantine facility for 120 days. Upon her arrival at the quarantine station, Princess was examined and found to be in good health, except that she had a non-life-threatening growth on her gums. With the approval of the quarantine station personnel, Mr. Campbell arranged to have a veterinarian at the Kapalama Pet Hospital remove the growth. Three days later, Princess and six other animals were put into an unventilated van for transportation to the pet hospital. The animals were left in the van under direct exposure to the sun for over an hour. Princess died of prostration shortly after the van arrived at the pet hospital.[56]

The trial court found that Mr. and Mrs. Campbell and three of their four children (the fourth being too young) suffered severe mental distress over the death of Princess and were entitled to damages in the amount of $1,000. The court made new law by allowing the Campbells to recover damages against the quarantine station for simple negligence even though they had not witnessed the incident or suffered physically from it. Prior to this case, the killing of a pet had to be intentional or reckless, rather than just negligent, in order for the owner to recover for emotional distress only, with no concurrent physical symptoms.[57]

The Supreme Court of Hawaii affirmed the trial court's ruling by holding that as long as the serious mental distress was reasonably foreseeable by the negligent defendant, plaintiffs should be able to recover for the loss of their property, based on the symptoms and duration of the distress.[58] While this case certainly improved the lot of distraught owners of injured or killed pets, a $1,000 award for five people who were found to have suffered a prolonged period of severe mental distress seems sorely inadequate.

A third route for claiming loss of sentimental value may be through the tort of "intentional infliction of emotional distress." A court that only recognizes market value or actual value as the proper barometer of a pet's worth as an item of personal property may nonetheless allow damages for the emotional pain and suffering of an owner whose pet is intentionally or recklessly harmed or killed, or threatened with such action. This is so in several states, usually upon proof of outrageous or extreme conduct.[59] It is rare for a veterinarian or other animal caretaker to be charged with intentional (as opposed to negligent) injury to an animal; most such cases deal with neighbors or strangers committing or threatening acts of cruelty. However, cases involving veterinarians do occur.

For example, in 1983, Annette Powell and her children brought their dog to the Ashland Terrace Animal Hospital to be treated for injuries sustained when he was hit by a car.[60] Powell asked the veterinarian, Dr. J. L. Stanford, if she could make payment for the dog's treatment over a period of time because she did not have enough money to pay the bill of $155 in full when services were rendered. The veterinarian refused to make a financial agreement with her. Powell alleged that Dr. Stanford then threatened to "do away with" the dog unless she made payment in full. Based upon the veterinarian's demand, Powell brought suit to prevent Dr. Stanford from disposing of the dog and to seek damages for his intentional infliction of emotional distress upon her and her children.[61]

The veterinarian attempted to have the case dismissed before trial on the ground that he was simply complying with the provisions of a Tennessee statute that authorized him to dispose of the dog if his bill was not paid.[62] The doctor denied ever making any threat in the specific words alleged by Powell, that he "would do away with" the dog. The trial court granted the veterinarian's motion to dismiss the case against him, and Powell appealed. Powell alleged that the statute under which the veterinarian claimed he could dispose of the dog was unconstitutional. The appellate court refused to rule on the issue, because it had not been raised in the courts below, and the case was remanded back for full trial on the issues.[63] In remanding the case, the appellate court made an unnecessary but intriguing editorial comment: "In our view, a jury could reasonably conclude that such conduct of the defendant was extreme, outrageous and intolerable in present day society and that the mental and emotional injuries alleged by the plaintiffs to have resulted from the defendant's conduct are serious."[64]

While not ruling on Powell's case specifically, the court certainly opened the door for her to receive damages for intentional infliction of emotional distress if a jury believed that Stanford made the threat to "do way with" her dog. However, based on other cases of intentional infliction of emotional distress where the perpetrator was not a veterinarian or animal caretaker, the damages would probably be low and therefore insufficient to compensate a person who suffered substantially over the inhumane treatment of her pet.[65]

Finally, some courts allow damages for an owner's emotional distress only as part of a punitive damage award, regardless of the nature of the underlying tort. Punitive damages are designed to allow a jury to express its moral outrage in cases where the usual measure of damages, compensatory damages, would not be enough for that punitive purpose. The state of Florida is foremost in allowing damages in this context. Its courts have permitted punitive damage awards based on an owner's affection for a pet in incidents ranging from malicious destruction to reckless conduct to gross negligence.[66] In a 1967 case, *Levine v. Knowles,*[67] the plaintiff sought punitive damages for his mental pain and suffering against a veterinarian. Levine alleged that the veterinarian committed malpractice in the treatment and subsequent cremation of the body of plaintiff's pet Chihuahua, Tiki. Dr. Knowles treated Tiki for a routine skin ailment, and the dog died. Levine advised Knowles that he wanted an autopsy performed on the body, but instead the dog was cremated. Dr. Knowles claimed that the cremation was inadvertently done by an unknown employee, whereas Levine alleged that the cremation was done expressly to avoid an autopsy. The trial court granted a motion by the veterinarian to dismiss the case on the basis that punitive damages would not be allowed under the law for the loss of a pet.[68] The appellate court ruled that an owner of an animal has as much right to recover for a dead dog wrongfully destroyed as for any other item of personal property and that if the destruction was willful, wanton, reckless, or malicious, punitive damages would be recoverable. If they were not, the court reasoned, and if only nominal market value or actual value damages were available, such undesirable behavior would not be discouraged, since the defendant would be in the same position after committing the act as before.[69]

In 1978 a Florida court upheld a substantial award of damages against an animal hospital. In *Knowles Animal Hospital, Inc. v. Wills,*[70] a jury awarded $13,000 to the Wills family for the loss of their pet dog. The dog was at the hospital for an operation. After the procedure, the dog was placed on a heating pad and kept there for a day and a half, sustaining severe burns and disfigurement and dying shortly thereafter.[71] The Wills claimed the hospital was guilty of gross negligence and instituted suit for their mental pain and suffering and for punitive damages. The award consisted of $1,000 for compensatory damages and $12,000 for punitive damages, and the court stated that the hospital's conduct satisfied the necessary standard for malicious conduct.[72] This is the largest known award to date that has been upheld for punitive damages and mental-pain-and-suffering damages. Indeed, although other states have allowed punitive damages for the emotional distress of an aggrieved pet owner,[73] Florida appears to harbor the most liberal attitudes on the issue.[74]

In sum, the parameters of potential damage awards to animal owners for emotional distress caused by a veterinarian's malpractice vary from state to state. The existence and extent of an owner's emotional distress are often difficult to prove. Thus, at least so far, damages for emotional distress rarely rise above nominal levels.[75] There is a trend, based upon the different theories of law discussed above, toward compensating owners for mental pain and suffering when their pets have been wrongfully treated or killed. However, most awards still depend on the threshold issue of the market value of an animal, since that measure of damages has not been entirely abandoned in any state and is more capable of proof in many cases.

Although the tenor of the law is gradually changing such that an increasing number of states allow recovery for an owner's emotional distress caused by the negligent or intentional harming of the owner's animal, the law still falls short of protecting the animals themselves, because the animals are property. Since recovery is predicated upon an owner's reaction to the animal's injury, where there is no emotional distress there is no corresponding liability imposed on the veterinarian for the animal's treatment, even if the treatment was grossly negligent.

A system that looks to the owner's emotional state is capable of generating anomalous situations. For example, if an animal is unfortunate enough to live with a human who does not have a significant emotional attachment to the animal, the animal's plight is worsened by a legal system that refuses to hold a veterinarian liable for negligent acts performed on the animal. Conversely, if a stray animal brought to a veterinarian by a person who genuinely feels extraordinary affection for that animal is negligently treated, resulting in severe emotional distress to the good Samaritan, the veterinarian is not liable, because the person did not "own" the animal. Indeed, in a bizarre departure from the typical malpractice claim, a woman in Oregon was awarded $4,000 for mental anguish and $700 in punitive damages because a veterinarian *saved* her dog's life. In *Fredeen v. Stride,*[76] plaintiff had brought her injured dog, Prince, to the veterinarian to be destroyed, but his two assistants instead nursed the dog back to health and gave the dog to someone in the same neighborhood where the plaintiff lived. Fredeen claimed she suffered mental anguish when, about six months later, she discovered the dog was still alive, because she feared the possibility that her children would encounter the dog and attempt to reunite with him. The substantial damage award was based on the court's finding that the veterinarian had wrongfully converted the plaintiff's property.[77] Again, this judgment, awarded against a veterinarian who refused to kill a healthy animal, is a direct result of looking to the owner's reaction in order to determine the veterinarian's liability.

These emotional distress cases are interesting, however, from another viewpoint, as related directly to the notion of animals as property. That is, given that animals are legally regarded as property, the legal system can do no more than it would do if a thief stole a valuable family heirloom. Of course, pet owners undoubtedly take their animals to veterinarians in order to relieve their own distress, just as parents seek to relieve their own distress by taking a sick child to a doctor. It is clear, however, that the primary purpose behind most of these acts—whether taking a sick dog to a veterinarian or a sick child to a pediatrician—is altruistic; the dog owner or parent is motivated by the altruistic desire to alleviate the distress and pain of the animal or child. At most, the law looks at distress experienced by a person *after* the negligence or harm has occurred, and completely refuses to look at the animal's pain and distress. This is the expected result of treating animals strictly as chattels.

There are some rather weak indications that this attitude is changing. In 1979, in *Corso v. Crawford Dog and Cat Hospital,*[78] a New York court reversed earlier law and held that an action could be maintained against a veterinarian who had wrongfully failed to return the body of a dead animal to plaintiff for burial. The court stated that "a pet is not just a thing but occupies a special place somewhere in between a person and a piece of personal property." The court distinguished between a dog and an heirloom. The former is "not an inanimate thing that just receives affection; it also returns it . . . while [an heirloom is a] source of good feelings [but] is merely an inanimate object and is not capable of returning love and affection."[79] In another New York case, *Restrepo v. State,*[80] the court criticized a decision by a veterinarian who withheld proper treatment from a horse in order to ensure that the horse races started on time. The court criticized the decision as "unreasonable and inhumane" and reminded us "that the greatness of a nation can be judged by the way that its animals are treated."[81] Unfortunately, the higher courts of New York have not adopted these encouraging pronouncements. In a 1987 case, *Fowler v. Town of Ticonderoga,*[82] a dog owner whose dog was shot by the local dog-control officer claimed that the officer had acted negligently and maliciously and sought damages for the monetary value of the dog, damages for psychic trauma, and punitive damages. The court ignored *Corso* and held that "regarding plaintiff's claim for damages for psychic trauma, a dog is personal property and damages may not be recovered for mental distress caused by its malicious or negligent destruction."[83] In a 1994 case involving a dog killed in the baggage compartment of an airplane, the court explicitly characterized *Corso* and similar cases as "aberrations flying in the face of overwhelming authority to the contrary" by "viewing a pet as more than property."[84]

There are two final points to be mentioned in connection with the valuation of animals in terms of market value. First, a veterinary malpractice case is not the only instance when a pet owner is restricted to some valuation short of what the actual human/animal relationship reflects. For example, when one dog attacks another and the owner of the injured dog sues the owner of the aggressive dog, the fair market value measure is frequently employed. In *Julian v. DeVincent,*[85] DeVincent's large dog, which had previously attacked people, attacked and killed Julian's smaller dog (which was on Julian's porch at the time of the attack). The trial court awarded Julian $178.70 in damages: $49 for veterinary care, $29.70 for burial, and $100 for sentimental value and mental cruelty inflicted upon Julian's children by the event.[86] The Supreme Court of Appeals of West Virginia reversed the judgment in *Julian,* holding that damages "for sentimental value or mental suffering are not recoverable" and that recovery was limited to the assessed value of the dog. Because "there was no assessed value placed on [Julian's] dog for taxation purposes," and because Julian did not otherwise attempt to prove the value of the dog, the court denied recovery entirely.[87]

Second, in cases in which less valuable animals kill or injure more valuable animals, the law generally protects the interests of the owners of the more valuable animals even though the human interest in the relationships with the less valuable animals may be more valuable at least in an emotional sense. For example, some states have laws that provide that the owner of property containing livestock may seize or kill any trespassing dog, with immunity from civil or criminal actions. In *Katsaris v. Cook,*[88] the plaintiff's dogs trespassed on a neighbor's cattle ranch while the plaintiff was away on vacation. The defendant, an employee of the ranch, shot and killed the dogs and then dumped their bodies into a ditch. The plaintiff searched for the dogs for over a week, but the court held that the defendant had no duty even to tell the plaintiff what happened to the dogs. The court allowed damages only against the defendant ranch owner's wife based on her false statements to the plaintiff that she knew nothing about the location of the dogs.[89]

## Conclusion

In conclusion, the common law has long treated animals as property, based in part on the close connection between certain interpretations of Genesis and philosophical doctrines that attempt to provide justifications of property status for animals based on the supposed "defects" or "inherent inferiority" of animals. I have examined two very different examples of what I have characterized as legal welfarism, and both examples indicate that the law fails to provide a level of protection that goes beyond that accorded to inanimate property objects. In one of those contexts—liability for veterinary malpractice—the owners of animal property emphatically insist that their animal property be recognized as more than "just property." Although some courts have analogized animals to family heir-looms—another type of property with which we might form an emotional bond—there is absolutely no consideration for the animal as a sentient being with interests and inherent value.

In the next chapter, I consider another context in which the property status of animals is relevant as a general matter. That context involves the law of standing, or the rules that determine whether a court is empowered to adjudicate a particular case or type of case.

# CHAPTER FOUR

## *The Exclusion of Animal Interests from Legal Consideration—the Doctrine of Standing*

### The Concept of Standing: A General Overview

THERE IS CONTROVERSY about the precise relationship of moral standing to the notion of moral rights.[1] However, there can be little doubt about the relationship of legal standing to the notion of legal rights. Simply put, it makes no sense to say that someone has a legal right to something if that person does not possess standing to assert that right. For example, if Jane has a contractual right to receive payment from me but no court will grant her legal standing to pursue the enforcement of that right, then it is difficult to understand how we can sensibly say that Jane has that right. To be sure, sometimes the person who actually articulates the right and actually asserts the required standing is someone other than the rightholder. Children and the mentally incompetent have legal rights and legal standing, but their interests are often articulated by court-appointed guardians.

If animals have any legal rights, they will, of course, be incapable of articulating them on their own behalf. Rather, someone who, at least ideally, is acting in the best interests of the animals must articulate those interests. In this chapter I argue that despite the existence of laws that supposedly protect animals, animal interests are not taken seriously by the legal system, which through the doctrine of standing has done everything possible to ensure that matters involving animal interests are never brought into the courtroom.

My discussion focuses on the doctrine of standing as it has been developed in federal law and as it pertains to animal issues.[2] However, it is necessary to explore the concept of standing as a general matter to provide a sense of the direction in which the Supreme Court has gone in interpreting the constitutional provision that gives courts jurisdiction only over "cases and controversies." In so doing, I try conscientiously to respect the late Justice William O. Douglas's wise admonition that "generalizations about standing to sue are largely worthless as such."[3] In a very provocative treatment of the subject, Professor Cass Sunstein states quite accurately that "the law of standing has had many remarkable twists and turns."[4] Accordingly, I do not present a treatise or general discussion on the law of standing; rather, I discuss that notion as it applies to cases involving animals and, to a much lesser degree, cases involving environmental concerns, which are also applied in animal-related contexts.

Much of the interesting federal standing law relevant to animals has developed in two contexts. The first context involves cases that interpret various laws directed toward environmental protection. The second context involves cases concerning the use of animals in experiments. Resolution of standing issues in cases involving animals has tended to focus on ownership status and to reinforce property rights in animals even when it would clearly be in an animal's interests to do otherwise. The notion of property plays a most important role in determining the scope of standing doctrine and the extent to which we tolerate interference with the use of private property. Specifically, the controversy involving a group of macaque monkeys known as the "Silver Spring monkeys" has generated several decisions involving standing to protect animals. Those decisions establish that no one who has a mere interest in the welfare of these animals has standing to sue, because the animals are the private property of others. That is, the law of standing assumes that humans cannot have legally significant relationships with animals owned by others.

In addition, it is impossible for any animal advocacy group to take any legal action to protect animals used in experiments. Standing doctrine prohibits such groups from initiating suits in federal courts. Even when they instead seek to rely on state anticruelty laws in state courts, such groups may find that if the defendant receives federal funds—and in the context of animal experimentation, virtually all do—the defendant may be able to have the case transferred to federal court. Due to federal standing doctrine, the case will then be dismissed without a hearing on the merits.

Once again, the legal doctrine is structured around the notion of animals as property. To put the matter another way, courts have recognized that people may have standing to litigate issues involving nonowned, or "wild," animals, but do not have standing to litigate cases involving animals owned by others. This is perfectly consistent with what I have called legal welfarism. In the case of wildlife, the external costs, or the costs that do not get factored into the calculations of the costs of an act, dictate that society may underinvest in the protection of these animal resources and litigation by private litigants may be a desirable way to rectify this underinvestment.[5] For example, when a corporation seeks to develop an area in which there are animals, the business decision may not consider the impact of the development on the animals. In such a case, these external costs may be considered as a result of litigation initiated by a party who uses the area for, say, bird watching. In the case of animals that are owned, however, this underinvestment problem does not exist. We assume that property owners will use their animal and nonanimal property in ways that maximize the value of the property to the owner. We do not need any further private litigants to ensure that external costs are considered, because, as far as the traditional economist is concerned, there are no external costs involved if the animal is owned, and we do not need these private litigants to ensure that animal property is used efficiently. We rely on the self-interest of owners; and indeed, to allow private litigants to interfere with the relationship between the owner and the property would impose a cost on the owner that is unjustified in light of the assumption that the owner will act in her best interest.

Standing is a jurisdictional notion; that is, it concerns whether a court is empowered to act in a particular case. As the doctrine is applied in federal courts, it seeks to ensure that the constitutional requirement that there be a "case or controversy" has been satisfied.[6] The Constitution does not explicitly mention standing; the concept has developed as one way of ensuring that federal courts do not adjudicate matters that do not fall within the "case-or-controversy" limitation.[7] In addition to the constitutional dimensions of standing, there are what are called "prudential" considerations, which have been developed in the case law and contained in statutes. For example, the Administrative Procedure Act (APA) provides that judicial review is available to anyone "suffering legal wrong because of an agency action, or adversely affected or aggrieved by any agency action within the meaning of the relevant statute."[8] Courts interpreting the APA have held that review of an agency action requires that the plaintiff show that asserted injury be within the "zone of interests" of the relevant statute.[9] There are other "prudential" (i.e., not constitutional) considerations that often determine standing as an overall matter.[10]

The notion of standing and the notion of rights are clearly related. If there is no standing, or if standing is possessed by someone other than the rightholder, then the legal right means little. Standing is a prerequisite—perhaps the most important prerequisite—for the enforcement of rights.

In addition, it is clear that even if animals had rights, they could not assert those rights themselves. Rather, it would be necessary to have someone else assert those rights. Such a person might be a court-appointed guardian or an organization that advocates animal rights. I explore the notion of who should assert an animal's rights later, but for present purposes, it suffices to recognize the need for some party to act on behalf of the animals.

Recent decisions of the United States Supreme Court have established that the constitutional aspect of standing consists of three elements: (1) "plaintiff must have suffered an injury in fact, [or] an invasion of a legally-protected interest that is concrete and particularized, [and] actual or imminent"; (2) there must be a causal relationship between the injury and the defendant's conduct; and (3) it must be likely, not merely speculative, "that the injury will be redressed by a favorable decision."[11] For example, assume that I become convinced that your marriage is foundering and that I file a divorce proceeding on your behalf and without your permission or knowledge. The court would most certainly dismiss such a case because although I may be acting with what I perceive to be your best interests in mind, the law does not regard me as a party having the requisite interest in the matter. I have not suffered any "injury in fact" that would permit me to dissolve your marriage. If, however, your legal right to seek divorce is to have any meaning at all, then that right must be recognizable and enforceable by *some* party, and in that case, that "someone" would be you or your spouse.

The cases important for this inquiry commence with *Sierra Club v. Morton,*[12] a United States Supreme Court decision. The case concerned the Mineral King Valley, designated by Congress as a national game refuge, located in the Sierra Madre Mountains and adjacent to the Sequoia National Park. The United States Forest Service approved the construction of a $35 million ski resort in the Valley, and the Sierra Club, a well-known environmental organization, sought to stop approval by the Department of the Interior of a highway and power line required for the project. For standing, the plaintiffs relied on the APA. The Supreme Court held that persons had standing to challenge agency action if the challenged action caused them "injury in fact"[13] and if the alleged injury fell within the "zone of interests" that the agency was required to protect or regulate.[14] Although the Sierra Club alleged that its long-standing concern and expertise in environmental matters made it a "representative of the public," the Court rejected this, holding that the party seeking review must "be himself among the injured."[15] The Court pointed out that "the Sierra Club failed to allege that it or its members would be affected in any of their activities or pastimes by the Disney Development. Nowhere in the pleadings or affidavits did the Club state that its members use Mineral King for any purpose."[16] The message of the Court was clear: it was not denying standing in cases involving challenges to projects that would have a deleterious impact on environmental resources. Rather, the Court's holding was a "signal" to litigants like the Sierra Club to be sure to allege that individual members used the resource in question, because only then would there be the requisite "injury in fact."[17]

In a fascinating dissent, Justice Douglas questioned why it was necessary for the action to be brought on behalf of a person injured as a result of the action adverse to environmental resources. Why could the resources themselves not bring an action? Douglas argued for "the conferral of standing upon environmental objects to sue for their own preservation." He observed that the law permitted some inanimate objects to be parties in litigation: ships have legal personality, as do corporations.[18] Although environmental resources are under the control of federal or state agencies, this was not sufficient protection, because such agencies "are notoriously under the control of powerful interests who manipulate them through advisory committees, or friendly working relations, or who have that natural affinity . . . which in time develops between the regulator and the regulated."[19] Although Douglas would have as guardians for environmental interests those who frequented the area and knew its ecological values, he emphasized that the inanimate object or resource should itself have standing.[20]

Douglas's position was not without serious intellectual support. Shortly before *Sierra Club* was handed down, lawyer and philosopher Christopher Stone had written the now well-known essay "Should Trees Have Standing? Toward Legal Rights for Natural Objects."[21] Stone argued persuasively that "each time there is a movement to confer rights onto some new 'entity,' the proposal is bound to sound odd or frightening."[22] Like Douglas, he observed that the law already accepted as legitimate legal "entities" many inanimate objects, including "trusts, corporations, joint ventures, municipalities, Subchapter R partnerships, and nation-states."[23] Stone also noted that blacks and other minorities, women, and children had been deprived of significant rights as a result of some view of natural law and not merely as a legal convention that supported the status quo and that reflected a conceptualization of a person as an object that was necessary for some social purpose.[24] What is necessary, Stone argued, was that we recognize the rightless as having inherent value, and then we will be more inclined to extend rights.[25] He went on to argue that since nature has an inherent value independent of its status as a mere collection of objects to be exploited by people, the natural environment as a whole should have legal rights. These rights would be enforced by guardians just as are the rights of children or the mentally disabled.[26]

Although Stone's essay was clearly the most important, philosophically developed, and influential statement of environmental standing, similar ideas had resonated in the writings of earlier authors. For example, in a brief essay, law professor Clarence Morris argued that it was merely "homocentric conceit" that allowed the legal system to recognize legal relations as a form of human relations that can run only between people or aggregates of people.[27] Morris claimed that natural objects should possess legal rights that would be articulated by a guardian.

The important point about *Sierra Club* is that the Supreme Court did not bar environmental organizations from seeking redress for environmental damage; rather, the Court held that the Sierra Club's generalized interest in environmental matters was insufficient to grant it standing. In order for the organization to have standing, it was necessary for it to plead that its members would suffer the requisite injury in fact. That is, the organization had to allege, for example, that at least some of its members used the Mineral King Valley for recreational purposes. The difference between the majority opinion and Justice Douglas's dissent, as well as the academic writing by scholars such as Stone and Morris, was that Douglas, Stone, and Morris would grant standing directly to the natural objects and then allow the articulation of rights by a guardian or some other party, whereas under the majority's approach, standing would (and could) be possessed only by a human whose enjoyment of the resource in question was affected by some governmental act.[28]

This approach to standing continued in other Supreme Court cases involving animal-related issues. In *Animal Welfare Institute v. Kreps*,[29] the plaintiff animal welfare organizations challenged a decision by the federal government waiving a moratorium under the Marine Mammal Protection Act on the taking or importing of marine mammal products. The director of the National Marine Fisheries Service was empowered to waive the moratorium and issue permits authorizing marine mammal importation. When the director decided to issue permits for the killing of set numbers of Cape fur seals, plaintiffs sued, but the trial court dismissed the suit on the ground that plaintiffs lacked standing.[30] The United States Court of Appeals for the District of Columbia Circuit reversed, holding that plaintiffs had alleged, as required by *Sierra Club*, that the director's decision impaired the interests of the plaintiff organizations and their members: "Through sanctioning the seal harvesting method of the South African Government, the [director's] decision impairs the ability of members of the Plaintiff organizations to see, photograph, and enjoy Cape fur seals alive in their natural habitat under conditions in which the animals are not subject to excessive harvesting, inhumane treatment and slaughter of pups that are very young and still nursing."[31]

In *Japan Whaling Association v. American Cetacean Society*,[32] animal protection organizations and environmental groups sought standing to require the secretary of commerce to certify to the president that Japan was in violation of a whaling moratorium and was thus "diminishing the effectiveness" of the International Convention for the Regulation of Whaling. The president was required to impose economic sanctions on any nation so certified. Although the Court ultimately did not require the secretary of commerce to certify Japanese lack of compliance, it rejected the argument that the plaintiffs did not have standing, because, in accordance with *Sierra Club*, plaintiffs "alleged a sufficient 'injury in fact' in that the whale watching and studying of their members will be adversely affected by continued whale harvesting."[33]

Similarly, in *Alaska Fish & Wildlife Federation v. Dunkle*,[34] various wildlife conservation groups sued the United States Fish and Wildlife Service to challenge certain cooperative agreements that permitted the hunting of migratory birds in Alaska. In response to a standing challenge, the United States Court of Appeals for the Ninth Circuit, relying on *Sierra Club*, held that defendants' actions would injure "those who wish to hunt, photograph, observe, or carry out scientific studies on the migratory birds."[35] In *American Horse Protection Association, Inc. v. Frizzell,* a United States District Court in Nevada held that the plaintiff, an organization dedicated to the protection of wild horses, had standing under *Sierra Club* because its members " '*have in the past and have the right in the future to be users and enjoyers of the lands and wildlife which is the subject of this suit.*' "[36] Similarly, in *Wilkins v. Lujan*,[37] plaintiffs were granted standing to challenge the removal of wild horses where plaintiffs alleged that they would be deprived of the ability to view the horses.[38]

The issue of organizational standing in a context involving animals was more extensively discussed in *Humane Society of the United States v. Hodel*,[39] where the plaintiffs sought to challenge a decision by the Fish and Wildlife Service expanding hunting in wildlife refuges. Plaintiffs alleged that Humane Society members "suffered from the knowledge that animals in the reserves were being killed and maimed."[40] The United States Circuit Court held that this mental distress did not suffice to give standing to plaintiffs under the Supreme Court's decision in *Valley Forge Christian College v. Americans United for Separation of Church & State, Inc.*, in which the Supreme Court held that psychological suffering produced by some governmental action was generally insufficient grounds for standing.[41] In addition, the circuit court held that the Humane Society's generalized interest in the enforcement of laws that promote the humane treatment of wildlife was similarly insufficient. However, the court did hold that the allegation that Humane Society members who visited refuges would be subjected to animal corpses, environmental degradation, and a depleted number of animals and wildlife to view sufficed to grant standing under *Sierra Club*.[42] The circuit court then went on to examine whether the Humane Society could assert these legitimate interests on behalf of its members. Relying on a 1977 Supreme Court decision, the court held that an organization can bring an action on behalf of its members when the individual members would have a right to sue (i.e., they suffered or will suffer a cognizable injury under *Sierra Club*) and the interests defended by the organization are germane to its purposes, and that participation of the individual members is not necessary.[43] The court concluded that the Humane Society had met the requirements for organizational standing.[44]

Standing may also be predicated on an agreement between the parties that gives plaintiff an interest in the matter. For example, in *Animal Protection Institute of America v. Hodel*,[45] the plaintiff animal advocacy organization argued that it had standing to enjoin the transfer of title in wild horses and burros to those who planned to slaughter the animals for commercial purposes. The court rejected the claim that standing could be based on the enjoyment of the animals by members of the organization, because the animals had already been removed from the range and plantiff's suit concerned the disposition of those animals. The court did hold, however, that the organization had standing because it had an agreement with the secretary of the interior enabling it to inspect the animals in governmental holding pens to make sure that the animals were treated humanely.[46]

Standing doctrine seemed to take an interesting turn in *Animal Lovers Volunteer Association, Inc. v. Weinberger*.[47] In *Animal Lovers,* an animal protection organization sought to enjoin the navy from the aerial shooting of feral goats on San Clemente Island, a military enclave to which there is no public access. The circuit court held that the navy's goat control program had no direct sensory impact on the organization's own environment or any other environment to which organization members had access, and that a "general contention that because of their dedication to preventing inhumane treatment of animals, [Animal Lovers'] members will suffer distress if the goats are shot does not constitute an allegation of individual injury."[48] The court stressed that Animal Lovers could not interfere "with the the government's method of ridding its own property of goats" unless there was a "distinct and palapable" injury to Animal Lovers' members.[49]

What made *Animal Lovers* interesting was that although it seemed to be applying *Sierra Club* in a straightforward way, the case involved a twist. Animal Lovers argued that the court's application created an "actual-use" test, which made it impossible for anyone to challenge the navy's action, because the island was a military enclave. The court responded that Animal Lovers had "confused its alleged standing with its right of action. A right of action may exist where a particular party does not have standing." The court pointed out that another animal protection organization, the Fund for Animals, had brought two earlier actions to stop the navy from removing the goats from San Clemente Island. On both occasions, the navy agreed to permit the Fund to trap and remove the goats, but these rescue efforts were only partially successful. After each Fund rescue, the navy announced that it would begin to shoot the remaining goats, and after the second such instance, the Fund withdrew. Animal Lovers was lead by Harold Baerg, who was a plaintiff in these earlier actions with the Fund. Accordingly, Animal Lovers commenced its action knowing that the Fund had been permitted to bring two identical actions against the same defendant. The court distinguished the two plaintiffs by characterizing Animal Lovers as lacking "the longevity and indicia of commitment to preventing inhumane behavior which gave standing to Fund for Animals, and which might provide standing to other better known organizations."[50] Rather, Animal Lovers had the same general abhorrence to cruelty to animals as did the public.

*Animal Lovers* appeared to open the standing door to organizational plaintiffs that could satisfy the vague standard of "longevity and commitment to preventing inhumane behavior."[51] Nevertheless, just one year after the Ninth Circuit decided *Animal Lovers,* another federal circuit court held that *Animal Lovers* did, indeed, apply an actual-use test, and prohibited anyone else from having standing. This subsequent development occurred in the context of a widely publicized case involving the Silver Spring monkeys. Interestingly, the court made a distinction between standing when the animals in question are privately owned and standing when the animals are publicly accessible, and then placed the former effectively outside the range of any meaningful judicial remedies.

## Standing: Animals as Private Property

In order to understand how the law of standing became coupled with the notion of property, it is necessary to discuss briefly the factual background of the Silver Spring monkeys case.[52]

Edward Taub was the chief animal experimenter at the Institute for Behavioral Research (IBR),[53] whose work was funded by the National Institutes of Health (NIH). Taub was supposedly investigating the possibility of training human stroke victims to regain use of their limbs. Using macaque monkeys, Taub created an animal "model" of limb atrophy by a surgical procedure called somatosensory deafferentation, which involved servering the nerves so that all sensation to the limb was abolished. Taub would then perform experiments to see whether the monkey could be taught to use the deafferented limb by the application of electric shocks and other forms of painful stimuli.

In May 1981, Alex Pacheco, then a college student and chairperson of the newly formed People for the Ethical Treatment of Animals (PETA), sought a job at IBR. Pacheco wanted some experience in an animal laboratory, so that he could better defend his antivivisection views, and he looked in the government listing of registered research facilities and found the one closest to his home. Pacheco did not reveal to Taub his affiliation with PETA and instead told Taub that he wanted to pursue a career in medical research. Pacheco began to document the egregious conditions in which the monkeys were kept, and at night and on weekends he brought scientific experts through the laboratory to render their opinions on the condition of animal care at IBR. One expert, a primatologist, stated that he had "never seen a laboratory as poorly maintained."[54] He remarked on the filth of the premises, the inadequate food supply, and untreated wounds and injuries suffered by the monkeys. Wire protruded through the cages, making it difficult for the animals to move in their cages; lights were kept on twenty-four hours a day; and due to lack of care, the monkeys had severely mutilated themselves in various ways, including chewing their own fingers and mutilating their deafferented limbs. A veterinarian remarked that the monkeys were unable to seek relief from contaminated cage floors and that mouse urine and droppings pervaded the entire facility.[55] Taub had an amputated monkey hand on his desk that he used as a paper weight. Although the United States Department of Agriculture (USDA) was charged with making regular inspections of the facilities, it found no serious deficiencies.

Pacheco provided his information to the Montgomery County Police, who investigated the matter. In January 1982, Taub's lab was raided by the police, who seized the seventeen remaining primates. The police did not know where to place the mutilated monkeys. The National Zoo refused to help, and local animal shelters were not properly equipped. A local animal advocate volunteered to keep the monkeys in the basement of her home, and PETA paid for the costly modifications that were necessary. Meanwhile, Taub's attorneys moved to regain possession of his property, and the judge granted the motion. The monkeys then disappeared, taken by persons unknown, before Taub could get them.[56] However, it was clear that without the monkeys the State of Maryland could not prosecute Taub. The monkeys were returned to the police, and despite assurances from the police to the contrary, they were given back to Taub. After one of the seventeen monkeys died under suspicious circumstances, the court ordered the monkeys to be held at an NIH facility in Poolesville, Maryland. The NIH suspended Taub's grant, claiming that Taub was guilty of, among other things, providing inadequate veterinary care to the monkeys.

Taub was charged with seventeen counts of violating the Maryland anticruelty statute. At trial, Taub was found guilty on six counts of failing to provide adequate veterinary care to the monkeys. He appealed to the intermediate appellate court in Maryland, which found Taub guilty of one count of failing to provide necessary veterinary care. In *Taub v. State,* Taub appealed to the Maryland Court of Appeals, which reversed his conviction altogether on a ground that Taub's attorneys never raised in the briefs before the court.[57] According to the court, the state anticruelty statute under which Taub was prosecuted was not meant to apply to animals used in scientific experiments. Although that statute contained no explicit exemption for these animals, the court reasoned that the legislature sought to prohibit the infliction of "unnecessary" or "unjustifiable" pain. Surely the legislature must have been aware of the practice of vivisection and of the federal regulation of that activity; the court reasoned that the state legislature recognized that vivisection was an activity in which the infliction of pain on an animal was "purely incidental and unavoidable."[58] Shortly thereafter the Maryland legislature amended the state anticruelty statute to cover all animals, including animals used in experiments, irrespective of the source of funding for those experiments.[59]

Despite what seemed to be the conclusion of the Taub case, the criminal prosecution during 1981–83 was only the beginning of what would be one of the most enduring animal rights struggles. There were several more phases of the case, and all were important for what they had to say not only about the animal rights movement but about the judicial and institutional response to efforts by that movement to seek redress.

First, animal protection groups brought two actions focused on the USDA, which is responsible for enforcing the federal Animal Welfare Act (AWA), and on the NIH, which also oversees the use of animals in federally funded experiments. In one suit, *Humane Society of the United States v. Block,* the plaintiffs attempted to get the USDA to enforce against Taub the provisions of the AWA.[60] In a second suit, *Fund for Animals v. Malone,* the plaintiffs sought a declaration concerning USDA and NIH control of the treatment of animals used in research, and requested an injunction to prevent the return to Taub of the Silver Spring monkeys.[61] Both cases were dismissed on the grounds that the enforcement of the AWA was within the discretion of the USDA and NIH, and no duty was owed to members of the public on the issue of animal treatment.

Meanwhile, the focus of the Taub matter shifted over to the question of who owned the monkeys, which were, at the time, being held by the NIH. The animal advocates pointed out correctly that the animals were maintained by the NIH at taxpayers' expense, and they offered to provide a sanctuary for the monkeys, using private funds both for the physical facilities and for a qualified primatologist who could help to rehabilitate the monkeys. The NIH maintained, however, that the monkeys were owned by IBR and that only IBR could relinquish ownership. IBR, supported by numerous research organizations and encouraged to stand firm against animal advocates, refused to deal directly with the animal advocates. Although IBR tried to relinquish ownership to NIH so that NIH (rather than IBR) could then dispose of the monkeys to a humane group, NIH refused to accept ownership, even though NIH had custody of the monkeys and was (with taxpayers) supporting them.[62] Shortly after the conclusion of the criminal case, and in light of the unwillingness of IBR and NIH to allow the animals to be placed in an appropriate sanctuary, PETA, together with several other animal protection organizations, brought a civil suit in state court in Maryland, seeking designation as guardians of the monkeys. The suit was removed to federal court but was dismissed for lack of standing, and plaintiffs appealed to the United States Court of Appeals for the Fourth Circuit.[63]

Plaintiffs alleged that they had standing on three grounds. First, they argued that they had a financial interest in the monkeys because they had paid significant sums of money to house the animals after the Maryland police took custody of them and before the monkeys were transferred to NIH. The Fourth Circuit rejected this argument, holding that plaintiffs' expenditures were incurred voluntarily in an effort to help the Maryland authorities and that plaintiffs "did not acquire any interest in the monkeys, who remained the property of IBR and in the custody of" Maryland police.[64] Second, plaintiffs alleged that they had a personal interest in encouraging the "civilized and humane treatment of animals." The Fourth Circuit rejected this alleged ground of standing as the generalized interest that was rejected in *Sierra Club*.[65]

Third, and most interesting, plaintiffs attempted to meet *Sierra Club* on its own terms and alleged that their personal relationship with the monkeys would be disrupted if the monkeys were returned to IBR. The court rejected this argument as well, holding that "whereas the parties described in *Sierra Club v. Morton* could use the park if the defendants complied with the law, these plaintiffs could not see the monkeys in the IBR laboratory if the defendants satisfied all requirements of care."[66] In other words, because the monkeys were the private property of IBR, no private person or organization could claim standing to challenge the treatment of what the court essentially regarded as pieces of property. Not only did the court not look to see whether plaintiffs had the "longevity and indicia of commitment to preventing inhumane behavior," as articulated in *Animal Lovers*,[67] but the court used *Animal Lovers against* plaintiffs. The court held that plaintiffs' situation was like that described in *Animal Lovers* because the injury in that case was "abstract at best . . . and insufficient to remove [Animal Lovers] from the category of concerned bystander."[68] The court analogized the plaintiffs in *Animal Lovers,* who did not have access to the federal enclave on which the goats were located, to the plaintiffs in the IBR case, who would not otherwise have had access to the monkeys had Taub not been charged with violating the Maryland anticruelty statute.

The Fourth Circuit's analysis here is questionable, and its reliance on *Animal Lovers* less than honest. The Ninth Circuit, in *Animal Lovers,* made it clear that an organization did not have standing when it had no prior history and could not be differentiated from any other member of the public.[69] Not only were the plaintiffs in the IBR case more established than the plaintiff in *Animal Lovers,* but Alex Pacheco, chairperson of PETA, had actually worked in the laboratory and documented abuses of the monkeys. Surely Pacheco's interest in the disposition of the monkeys was distinguishable from that of members of the general public. Moreover, the Ninth Circuit, in *Animal Lovers,* explicitly held that under some circumstances a plaintiff could have standing to challenge illegal acts even if those acts occurred on the defendant's private property and that there was no "actual-use" requirement embedded in standing.[70] The Fourth Circuit embraced an actual-use requirement in holding that if animals were privately owned and plaintiff would not otherwise have access to the animals, plaintiff could not gain standing. The Fourth Circuit rejected as insufficient for standing not only plaintiffs' access to the monkeys while they were out of the IBR laboratory as the result of their confiscation by state authorities, but also Pacheco's access to the monkeys while working in the laboratory and the relationship he had developed with them.

The linkage of standing with private property was solidified further in another case—this one from the United States Court of Appeals for the Fifth Circuit—that also involved the Silver Spring monkeys.[71] In 1983 the court order that granted possession of the monkeys to NIH expired, but NIH "continued to act as keepers of the monkeys with the consent and cooperation of IBR, the monkeys' owners."[72] In 1986 NIH transferred some of the monkeys to the Delta Regional Primate Center of Tulane University. NIH had provided written assurances to members of Congress that the animals would be subject to no further experimentation and would live the remainder of their natural lives at Delta.[73]

Despite these assurances, NIH announced in 1988 that it planned to euthanize three of the monkeys and would perform an experiment on the monkeys before they were euthanized. PETA and others sued NIH, IBR, and Tulane in Louisiana state court, and defendants removed the case to federal court. After the federal district court granted an injunction against the euthanasia and experimentation, the defendants appealed to the Fifth Circuit.[74] Plaintiffs argued that they had standing on grounds of a long-standing and sincere commitment to the Silver Spring monkeys and because their role as advocates for the monkeys would be impaired, both of which were rejected by the Fifth Circuit as being impermissible grounds under *Sierra Club*.[75] Plaintiffs also argued that individual members of plaintiffs' organizations had relationships "with the monkeys . . . which were established prior to any previous litigation in related matters and which continued during such litigation."[76] Presumably, this referred to Pacheco's relationship with the monkeys while he worked in the laboratory, as well as to that relationship and others that occurred when the monkeys were removed from IBR.

The Fifth Circuit rejected this ground as well, holding that the Fourth Circuit had "previously rejected the virtually identical argument." Like the Fourth Circuit, the Fifth Circuit relied on *Animal Lovers*. The Fifth Circuit rejected those cases in which animal groups had been found to have standing, holding that "unlike the *privately-owned* laboratory animals involved in the present situation, the animals in the majority of those cases were feral ones which, were the challenged conduct of the defendants to be enjoined, the members of the plaintiff organizations could freely enjoy."[77] The court held that in only one case was an animal protection group allowed to "protest the treatment of *privately-owned* animals"; in that case a humane society with law enforcement powers challenged a regulation that required dairy farmers to brand certain cows on the face.[78]

The Fourth and Fifth Circuit holdings on standing are terribly troubling, since they go far beyond *Sierra Club*, although they purport to be literally faithful to that decision. Pacheco developed a relationship with the monkeys while he was working in the laboratory. Pacheco continued, and others also developed, a relationship with the monkeys when they were removed from the laboratory. Nothing in *Sierra Club* or any other decision requires that a plaintiff cannot get standing by virtue of another's wrongful act but for which plaintiff would not have standing. All that *Sierra Club* requires is that the plaintiff have more than a generalized interest in the problem.

In addition, nothing in *Sierra Club* requires a distinction between privately owned animals and wild animals so that a plaintiff who develops a relationship with a privately owned animal as a result of the illegal conduct of the owner or the legal conduct of the plaintiff cannot have standing. Surely Pacheco and the other plaintiffs were not in the same position as other members of the public; surely the interest of Pacheco and the others cannot be described as a "mere interest in a problem."[79] Moreover, the Fifth Circuit held that in other cases in which standing had been granted, the plaintiffs could have freely enjoyed the resource if the conduct of defendants were enjoined. Again, plaintiffs in the IBR litigation sought guardianship over the animals. The Department of Health and Human Services did not reinstate Taub's grant, and had plaintiffs been given an opportunity to present their evidence, a court could have found that Taub's conduct constituted a violation of the federal law and regulations and could have awarded guardianship to the plaintiffs.[80]

In any event, the purported distinction between the Silver Spring monkeys situation and the other cases represents a distinction without a difference; the criterion required for standing under *Sierra Club* is actual injury, and that requires that plaintiff have an interest that goes beyond a "mere interest," or an interest distinguishable from that of other members of society.[81] To say that plaintiffs in the IBR situation did not meet this criterion, because the animals were privately owned, is incorrect. However, the distinction conjured up by the Fourth and Fifth Circuits does serve an interest that I have maintained before: it insulates the owner of property from having others interfere with that ownership even when the object of ownership is a highly intelligent sentient being.

Moreover, whether Pacheco's care of the animals after they were removed from IBR was voluntary or not, he clearly had an agreement with the Maryland authorities to ensure that the animals would be treated humanely. From the time that the animals were transferred to the NIH facility in Poolesville, and until they were taken to Tulane, Pacheco was permitted to visit the animals regularly. On numerous occasions he made suggestions to NIH concerning the treatment of the animals, and many of these suggestions were adopted. In a sense, Pacheco was like the plaintiff organization in *Animal Protection Institute,* which was granted standing based on an agreement between the Animal Protection Institute and the Bureau of Land Management that allowed the former to monitor the treatment of animals seized by the government.[82] Pacheo had an explicit agreement with the Maryland authorities and an implicit agreement with NIH. In any event, to say that Pacheco was indistinguishable from other members of the public or that his harm was purely "abstract" or "ideological" is nonsense.

In many respects, the decisions of the Fourth and Fifth Circuits demonstrate that the injury-in-fact test is, as Professor Sunstein has argued, anything but factual.[83] That is, courts distinguish between injuries in fact and what might be called purely ideological harms. Sunstein observes that "in classifying some harms as injuries in fact and other harms as purely ideological, courts must inevitably rely on some standard that is normatively laden and independent of facts."[84] For example, a challenge by blacks to a grant of tax deductions to segregated schools is regarded as "abstract" and ideological;[85] a challenge by someone who uses a resource that will be adversely affected by governmental action satisfies the injury-in-fact test. Sunstein is correct that whether there is an injury in fact is determined on a case-by-case basis and on the basis of unstated political values. The test is susceptible to virtually any interpretation, depending upon the court deciding the case.

## Standing and the Federal Animal Welfare Act

In the Fourth Circuit IBR decision, the court discussed another alternative ground for standing. This ground concerns whether the AWA itself provides plaintiffs with a cause of action.[86] The law provides for standing if a federal statute explicitly so provides. "Congress may enact statutes creating legal rights, the invasion of which creates standing, even though no injury would exist without the statute."[87] For example, many federal environmental statutes contain a "citizen suit" provision that allows people to bring environmental suits without showing actual injury to themselves beyond violation of general rights (e.g., to clean water) provided for in the statutes. "The question whether a statute creates a cause of action, either expressly or by implication, is basically a matter of statutory construction."[88] Indeed, as Professor Sunstein argues, the original notion of standing is closely related to whether the legislature has granted the right to bring suit.[89]

The Fourth Circuit examined the AWA and found that Congress did not intend the goal of humane treatment of research animals "to come at the expense of progress in medical research."[90] The court noted that Congress had delegated enforcement of the statute to the USDA, requiring that the secretary of agriculture establish standards to ensure the humane handling, care, treatment, and transportation of animals, but that the secretary is explicitly prohibited from regulating in any way the " 'design, outlines, guidelines, or performance of actual research or experimentation by a research facility as determined by such research facility.' "[91] The secretary is empowered to inspect facilities and may remove an animal from a laboratory when that animal is suffering as the result of noncompliance with the act but only if the animal is no longer needed for the experiment or test for which the animal was being used. The secretary can levy fines of up to $1,000 per day, and the court noted that if private plaintiffs could sue to enforce the act, such might result in higher awards that would discourage scientists from pursuing careers in animal research.[92]

The court further stressed that in addition to limiting enforcement to administrative supervision, the act subordinated that supervision "to the continued independence of research scientists . . . '[who] still [hold] the key to the laboratory door.' "[93] The court unquestionably accepted the representations made in the amicus curiae brief of sixty-eight medical organizations, which emphasized the need for the use of animals in experiments. Finally, the court concluded that Congress intended the exclusive remedy to be the administrative remedy.

In *Animal Legal Defense Fund v. Yeutter,*[94] plaintiffs sued the USDA on the grounds that the USDA had failed to include birds, rats, and mice as "animals" within the meaning of the AWA. Rats and mice are the animals most commonly used in experiments, and because of the USDA's failure to include them within the definition of "animal," research facilities are neither obligated to provide the minimal protections of the AWA to these animals nor required to report the numbers of excluded animals on the USDA reporting forms. Plaintiffs sued under the APA in light of the Fourth Circuit's holding in the IBR case. Citing the *IBR* decision, the court in *Yeutter* stated that "plaintiffs' challenge to the regulations . . . must proceed under the APA because . . . [the Animal Welfare Act] does not create any private rights of action."[95] This required that plaintiffs show that they suffered an injury in fact, which is the constitutionally mandated part of standing doctrine, and that they show that the injury was within the zone of interests protected by the AWA, which is required under the APA. The court held that the plaintiffs satisfied the constitutional test, as well as the prudential test for standing.

In its analysis, the district court in *Yeutter* found that a primary function of the plaintiff organizations (the Animal Legal Defense Fund [ALDF] and the Humane Society of the United States [HSUS]) was the dissemination of information; and because research facilities were not required to report on the numbers and use of birds, rats, and mice, these humane organizations were unable to provide full information to their members on the use of animals in experiments. The court relied heavily on a Supreme Court case, *Havens Realty Corporation v. Coleman.*[96] In *Havens,* an African-American woman had asked at an apartment complex whether apartments were available and had been told falsely that none was available. The woman was what is known as a "tester": she had no intention of renting an apartment, and she believed that she would be lied to when she inquired about the availability of apartments because she was an African-American. When a suit was instituted under the Fair Housing Act, the defendants argued that the tester had no standing because she never had any intention of renting an apartment. They argued further that although the statute granted a cause of action to the tester, the statute was constitutionally defective because failing any intention to rent an apartment, the tester could not be injured. The Supreme Court rejected these arguments and held that Congress had seen fit to give the public a general right to information about racist practices in the allocation of housing.[97] The district court in *Yeutter* held that the plaintiffs satisfied the constitutional portion of standing doctrine based on their similar interest in information about animal use, their need to disseminate this information to their members, and their injury in being unable to do so as the result of the USDA failure to report the numbers of the most commonly used animals.

The court in *Yeutter* found also that because plaintiff organizations were seeking to provide information to their members, their interests were not tangential and, accordingly, fell within the "zone of interests" that the AWA sought to protect. The court noted that the goal of disseminating information was the same as the goal Congress sought to achieve by requiring annual reporting by research facilities: the humane treatment of animals.[98]

In another case, *Animal Legal Defense Fund v. Secretary of Agriculture,*[99] the plaintiffs challenged regulations, discussed in Part III of this book, concerning canine exercise and primate psychological well-being. Again, plaintiffs proceeded under the APA and were required to show both that they had suffered an injury in fact and that they were within the zone of interests protected by the AWA. The case was tried before the same court that had decided the standing issue (and ultimately the merits) in favor of the plaintiffs in *Yeutter.* The federal defendants did not challenge the standing of the plaintiffs, perhaps because of the earlier ruling on standing in *Yeutter.* In any event, the trial court in *Secretary* held that USDA had acted arbitrarily and capriciously in promulgating its regulations, which the court deemed to be not in compliance with congressional directives contained in the 1985 amendments to the Animal Welfare Act.

*Yeutter* and *Secretary* seemed to indicate that contrary to the Fourth Circuit's proscription against any private enforcement of the AWA, there may be standing under limited circumstances to challenge the administration of the AWA by USDA. Any such optimism in this regard, however, was eviscerated by the Supreme Court's 1992 decision in *Lujan v. Defenders of Wildlife.* In *Lujan,* a number of environmental groups sought to challenge a regulation of the secretary of the interior that required other federal agencies to confer with him under the Endangered Species Act[100] only with respect to domestic projects and projects on the high seas. The environmental groups argued that the consultation should also occur when federal agencies undertook in foreign lands action that might affect endangered species. The Supreme Court held that the groups lacked standing because they could not show that their members would suffer any concrete injury.[101] Specifically, although the plaintiffs had expressed an intention to return to these foreign lands in order to enjoy the endangered wildlife—so that the pleading rules of *Sierra Club* might apply to them—the Court made clear that any injury must be imminent, which the Court construed strictly to require *immediacy* of the harm. Because plaintiffs did not have "concrete plans"[102] to return to the foreign lands, the Court found that their injury was not imminent. Interpreting the imminence requirement in this way means that many plaintiffs who have been granted standing in the past no longer qualify.

In addition, the Court rejected another ground of standing alleged by plaintiffs. The Endangered Species Act contains a provision for "citizen suits," which allows "any person" to commence suit for a violation of the act. In a holding that has caused considerable concern, the Court held that Congress cannot confer standing to sue merely by authorizing citizens' suits in statutes; rather, a litigant must show the existence of a cognizable injury to her in order to have standing.[103] The decision in *Lujan* is in direct conflict with *Havens* and with the unanimous decisions of the lower courts that a legislative grant of standing to citizens without a showing of injury in fact was constitutional.[104] Indeed, in 1994, the federal appellate court for the District of Columbia Circuit vacated both *Yeutter*[105] and

*Secretary*[106] on grounds of standing, and *Lujan* played an important role in both cases. It is important to discuss these holdings in some detail because, in certain respects, they indicate that *Lujan* will probably further restrict the ability of animal advocates to have their claims heard in federal court.

In *Yeutter,* the appellate court held that plaintiffs lacked standing. As to the organizational plaintiffs—ALDF and HSUS—the court rejected entirely the "informational standing" theory relied upon by the trial court. The appellate court distinguished *Havens* as a case in which Congress had explicitly created a right to information about racist practices in housing. According to the appellate court, Congress did not create a similar right to information in enacting the AWA, and the plaintiffs could not suffer injury by being deprived of information to which they had no right in the first place. In addition, the court found that the organizational plaintiffs also did not fall within the zone of interests of the AWA because neither ALDF nor HSUS had asserted any interest expressly protected by the AWA.[107]

This portion of the appellate court's holding concerning the lack of standing of the organizations was not particularly noteworthy in that the appellate court did not need *Lujan* to vacate the lower court's decision. The appellate court simply adhered to the notion, articulated by the Fourth Circuit in the IBR case, that animal advocacy organizations had no standing to enforce provisions of the AWA. This interpretation of standing doctrine is completely consistent with the notion of legal welfarism. Animal advocacy groups are, in a sense, attempting to interfere in the relationship between property (the animals) and the property owner (the research institution). Assuming that the latter is using animal resources in an efficient manner (i.e., getting data that are regarded as valid), then the actions of advocacy groups can do nothing but add to the opportunity costs of animal ownership without producing any quantifiable benefit.

There are, however, aspects of the appellate court's reversal of *Yeutter* that require further discussion. Even if the appellate court correctly held that, unlike the Fair Housing Act, there was no right to information contained in the AWA, it would seem that the court's concern about whether Congress had granted such a right to information similar to that involved in *Havens* is, after *Lujan,* irrelevant. *Lujan* made clear that Congress cannot grant standing by creating rights unless a particular plaintiff has suffered an injury in fact and that such injury cannot merely be deprivation of the congressionally granted right. Indeed, the animal protection community has in recent years sought to get federal legislation that would overturn the Fourth Circuit *IBR* decision and amend the AWA to permit humane organizations to have standing to enforce the AWA under limited circumstances.[108] If Congress can create a general right to obtain truthful information about racism in housing, as the Court found in *Havens,* then Congress can also create a general right for humane organizations to obtain truthful information about what is occurring in federally funded laboratories. The problem is that after *Lujan,* it is not clear whether *Havens* is good law. That is, even if Congress did amend the AWA and create a right to information about animal use, *Lujan* might well portend that the deprivation of that right does not constitute the requisite injury in fact that is required for standing.

In addition, and relevant to the effect of *Lujan,* there was another plaintiff in *Yeutter* other than ALDF and HSUS, and the court also denied her standing even though she arguably satisfied the injury-in-fact test as it was understood pre-*Lujan*. The plaintiff, Dr. Patricia Knowles, was a psychobiologist who had worked in laboratories covered by the AWA from 1972 until 1988. Knowles argued that because rats and mice were not covered under the AWA, the inhumane treatment often accorded to these animals directly affected her ability to obtain reliable research results in the past and would do so in the future. From the standpoint of legal welfarism, Knowles made an entirely different claim because she was, in effect, stating that animal resources were not being used efficiently to ensure that the animals would serve their only useful purpose: the production of reliable research data. The appellate court recognized that this claim was different from the claimed standing of advocacy organizations like ALDF or HSUS. Nevertheless, the court declined to discuss whether there was an injury in fact present, and instead relied explicitly on *Lujan*'s notion that an injury in fact must be "imminent" and that the notion of imminence must be strictly construed. Since Knowles was not currently involved in activities covered under the AWA, any injury that she might suffer (loss of reliable research data) was too speculative.

Interestingly, one of the three judges on the appellate panel dissented from the court's holding on the issue of Knowles's lack of standing. The dissenting judge argued that the researcher did suffer an injury in fact precisely because she had lost data as the result of the fact that rats, mice, and birds were not covered under the AWA. As to the imminence requirement of *Lujan,* the dissenting judge argued that although the case was close, the plaintiff's allegations that she would be required to work with rats, mice, and birds in the future was different from the claims of the plaintiffs in *Lujan* that they might someday return to various foreign countries and observe the wildlife, and satisfied the imminence requirement.

In *Secretary,* the trial court had set aside certain USDA regulations concerning primate well-being and canine exercise as being not in accord with congressional directives. The appellate court also vacated the lower-court decision, holding that the animal advocacy organizations (ALDF and Society for Animal Protective Legislation) failed to satisfy both the constitutional and the prudential components of standing, based on established case law and the court's earlier analysis in *Yeutter*. In addition, the court rejected the notion that certain manufacturers of primate housing equipment had standing, since the AWA was not intended to protect such interests.

Again, the court in *Secretary* also denied standing to an individual plaintiff who would arguably have satisfied the standing requirements before *Lujan*. Dr. Roger Fouts is a highly respected primatologist and director of the Chimpanzee and Human Communication Institute at Central Washington University. Dr. Fouts argued that the vagueness of the USDA regulations (that had been rejected by the lower court) prevented him from establishing plans for the design of his research institute, including a chimpanzee housing facility that was presently under construction. Fouts claimed that he feared being out of compliance with these vague USDA regulations. The appellate court rejected Fouts's claim. The court held that if Fouts were out of compliance, it would be his university—and not Fouts—that would be liable, so that any injury in fact would be inflicted on the facility and not on Fouts. Moreover, the court, relying explicitly on *Lujan,* held that Fouts's injury (if any) was too speculative anyway because the USDA might ultimately determine Fouts's plan to have satisfied the regulations and that therefore no injury (to Fouts or his institution) would have occurred.

In a concurrence, Chief Judge Mikva stated that if the plaintiffs (both the organizations and the individuals) had alleged an interest in protecting specific laboratory animals under circumstances predating the litigation, they would have satisfied both constitutional and prudential standing requirements. This is fascinating, in part because it seems to conflict directly with the Fourth Circuit's *IBR* decision. It will be remembered that Pacheco had a relationship with the individual Silver Spring monkeys, which occurred as the direct result of his exposure to the animals before any litigation. Mikva's concurrence seems to indicate that had Fouts, for example, alleged an interest in a particular primate, he might have had standing, in light of the challenged USDA regulations, to challenge those regulations. If that were the case, however, it would seem difficult to distinguish Fouts's situation from Pacheco's. Although Judge Mikva was careful to limit such interest to one that predated the litigation, Pacheco's relationship with the Silver Spring monkeys, as I noted earlier, predated the litigation in that case, but the Fourth Circuit nevertheless found no standing.

An additional aspect of *Secretary* requires comment. When the district court decision was handed down (holding that the USDA had acted improperly in promulgating performance standards), the government filed a protective notice of appeal to preserve its right to appeal the decision, but did not indicate whether it would, in fact, appeal. A private trade-and-lobbying organization, the National Association for Biomedical Research (NABR), which represents and is supported by commercial animal users and suppliers (such as Merck Research Labs, Merrell Dow, and the Cosmetic, Toiletry, and Fragrance Association), universities, and individuals, sought to intervene as a defendant but was refused by the trial court. NABR argued that its interests would be adversely affected if the government did not appeal, and that it (NABR) should be permitted to intervene and to appeal. Without oral argument, the appellate court reversed the lower court's denial of intervention and allowed NABR to intervene as a defendant.

The fact that the appellate court permitted intervention in light of the uncertainty of the government's appeal is not terribly unusual. If the government had decided not to appeal and NABR had taken the appeal, the plaintiffs would presumably have challenged the constitutional standing of NABR to be sole defendant. What is unusual, however, is that the appellate court allowed NABR to remain a defendant-intervenor *after* the government decided to appeal; it is unusual because it is difficult to understand what interest NABR could have had that would not have been protected by the government. After all, the government was in the best position to know the importance to it of its own regulations. In any event, the appellate court's decision indicates how generous the courts can be to those who represent commercial exploiters of animals, while those very same courts interpret precedent in the most extreme way possible in order to ensure that animal advocacy groups never even get their claims heard on the merits.

Both *Yeutter* and *Secretary* indicate that *Lujan* will have a detrimental impact on standing in cases involving animals, even when standing would have been granted under the most restrictive reading of *Sierra Club* and its progeny. In *Yeutter,* the appellate court ignored the claims of a researcher who had worked in laboratories covered by the AWA for sixteen years and who had alleged that she had suffered, and would suffer, injuries as the result of USDA's failure to include rats, mice, and birds under the AWA. The court, relying on *Lujan,* held that because Dr. Knowles was not doing research at the time of the suit, she failed to satisfy the imminence requirement of *Lujan.* In effect, the appellate court required that a plaintiff in such a case must have a *present property interest* in order to have standing. Fouts, on the other hand, claimed that the vagueness of the USDA regulations made it *presently* impossible for him to plan his research facility and, in particular, the chimpanzee housing unit that he was constructing at the time. Fouts appeared to have had a present property interest. Nevertheless, the court ignored that interest on the ground that should Fouts's primate housing be deemed inadequate by USDA at some time in the future, it would be Fout's facility, and not Fouts, that would be responsible. The court completely ignored Fouts's own interest in his research and in the integrity of the facility that he was constructing.

The appellate court's rejection of standing on the part of animal advocacy groups reinforces legal welfarism, as I discussed above. Rejection of standing on the part of the researcher plaintiffs (Knowles and Fouts) does not, however, detract from that thesis. Even though Dr. Knowles phrased her injury to fit quite comfortably within the welfarism paradigm, she did not presently have any sort of property interest in research, and those who do have such an interest—researchers who are currently using rats, mice, and birds in research—disagreed with her view that the collection of reliable data requires that the USDA cover these animals under the AWA. The research community, including NABR, argued against inclusion of rats, mice, and birds; and the court interpreted the *Lujan* imminence requirement strictly. Similarly, in *Secretary,* the appellate court did not regard Dr. Fouts as representing the interests of the research community even though he clearly had a present interest; NABR was a defendant-intervenor in that case and made clear to the court that the research community favored the USDA standards that Fouts opposed. It should come as no surprise that despite what appeared to be Fouts's present interests, the court ignored those interests in favor of those of the party it regarded as having the more important property interests—the research community.

*Lujan,* then, will likely be problematic for those seeking to use the federal courts to protect animals (or the environment). It appears as though *Lujan*'s focus on injury in fact, and its rejection of the notion that Congress can create standing by conferring it in statutes, turns the notion of standing on its head. Sunstein argues persuasively that the original idea of "standing" was determined by whether there was a common-law action or an action statutorily created.[109] The concept of "injury in fact" played no role whatsoever and did not come into being until the Supreme Court "made it up" in 1970.[110] The Court has come full circle to the point of saying that it is the injury in fact that is the primary determinant of standing, and not whether Congress has created statutorily granted standing. Sunstein correctly points out that the distinction between an injury in fact and an ideological harm is inevitably dependent on normatively laden notions. That is, every litigant is convinced that she has suffered some injury in fact, and it is difficult, if not impossible, to create principles that determine which injuries in fact result in standing and which do not.

In any event, *Lujan* illustrates the difficulty that faces those who seek to use the judicial system to assist animals. In *Lujan,* Justice Scalia, echoing views in his earlier academic writings,[111] stated that when

> the plaintiff is himself an object of the action (or forgone action) at issue . . . there is ordinarily little question that the action or inaction has caused him injury, and that a judgement preventing or requiring the action will redress it. When, however, . . . a plaintiff's asserted injury arises from the government's allegedly unlawful regulation (or lack of regulation) of *someone else,* much more is needed.[112]

The Court in *Lujan* appeared to resurrect the distinction between *objects* of regulation and *beneficiaries* of regulation, a distinction that Sunstein correctly labels "a conceptual anachronism."[113] It is difficult to understand into which categories we should place animals used in experiments. An animal could be considered the object of regulation, although it is more likely that the object of such regulation is the research facility to which the regulations apply, because these regulations intrude on the legal interests of the facility—its right to use its property (nonhuman animals) as it deems fit. The animals may be considered the beneficiaries of the regulation, but since animals are considered property and not juridical entities that may use the court system, there is simply no conceptual facility for according them standing. Finally, it is unlikely that animal advocacy organizations could be considered beneficiaries of welfare regulations.

The problem is clear: regulations that concern animals cannot be challenged *whether animals are the objects or the beneficiaries of regulations*. Animals, like children and certain disabled persons, are unable to use courts without assistance, and although guardians are appointed to protect the legal interests of children and the disabled, they are not appointed to represent animal interests, because animals are property and ostensibly have no rights to protect. Accordingly, even when intelligent and sentient beings are considered to be the object of the government's action or inaction, they have no standing. When animal protection groups try to assert animal interests, they are told that they have no standing because the regulation does not concern them. This is all very neat and has one result: animals have no way of protecting their interests in court. The court in *Kreps,* which interpreted standing in the context of the Marine Mammal Protection Act, stated, "Where an act is expressly motivated by considerations of humaneness toward animals, who are uniquely incapable of defending their own interests in court, it strikes us as eminently logical to allow groups specifically concerned with animal welfare to invoke the aid of the courts in enforcing the statute."[114] In *Lujan,* the Supreme Court assumed that the executive would enforce the law and that lawsuits by citizens who did not have an injury in fact would violate the separation of powers even though Congress had conferred standing on all citizens. Where laboratory animals are concerned, it is folly to think that the law will ever be enforced properly by the executive when the primary guardians of those laws are the research facilities that own and use the animals in experiments.

Moreover, *Lujan* made clear that the requirement that any injury not be speculative was to be interpreted more strictly in light of the Court's holding on imminence. In *Lujan,* the plaintiffs alleged that they would return to the foreign areas in question as part of their professional work, and this was rejected by a majority of the Court as not satisfying the requirement that any injury in fact be imminent. Three members of the Supreme Court—Justices Blackmun, O'Connor, and Stevens—all expressed their concern that the Court in *Lujan* had interpreted the imminence requirement too strictly in light of past precedent. The problem with the Court's current position on imminence is similar to the problem identified by Professor Sunstein with respect to the Court's view on injury in fact: it is ad hoc and lends itself to completely elastic interpretation. Indeed, the appellate court in *Yeutter* and *Secretary* arguably applied an even more strict interpretation of imminence than required under the majority's view in *Lujan.* Both Dr. Knowles and Dr. Fouts would in all likelihood have been granted standing before *Lujan.* Although *Lujan* made the imminence standard more strict, both Knowles and Fouts had interests that were more immediate than those rejected in *Lujan.* Nevertheless, the ad hoc nature of the imminence requirement allows the increasingly conservative federal courts to close the courthouse door to unpopular causes.

In any event, the future of standing in animal-related cases brought in federal court is anything but hopeful.

## Federal Defendants and Standing in State Courts: The Ultimate Irony

The federal courts, led by an ever more reactionary Supreme Court, have developed a very restrictive standing doctrine. That doctrine basically closes the door of the federal court to cases involving animals unless the plaintiff can demonstrate an immediate injury in fact. This raises a question about the use of state courts to protect animal interests.[115] State courts also have standing requirements, but for the most part they are less rigorous than their federal counterparts because, in the latter case, constitutional considerations trigger concern about the assertion of jurisdiction by federal courts. Although state courts remain a somewhat untested ground of standing law as it concerns animals, some recent developments—again, involving the Silver Spring monkeys—do not augur well for the use of state courts and state law to challenge the propriety of the treatment of animals used in experiments.

I noted above that after the Silver Spring monkeys were transferred to the Delta Regional Primate Center, NIH decided to "sponsor" experiments on the animals that would end in their death. This announcement completely violated assurances, given by NIH in writing to Congress, that the animals would remain at Delta in comfort for the rest of their lives and without any further experimentation. In addition, the government had, again in writing, represented that it had "no research protocols, either ongoing or planned, for which these animals are appropriate,"[116] and IBR had tried earlier to transfer title to the monkeys to NIH because IBR had no plans for the monkeys and did not want to incur further expense for their care. NIH acknowledged these experiments were unprecedented because there was no peer review or protocol and the experiments were to be conducted using private funds supplied by a lobbying group, the Biomedical Research Defense Fund. The experiments were designed by a team of experimenters assembled by a neuropsychologist, Mortimer Mishkin, who was employed by the NIH but who held the relevant meetings at his home during weekends. Mishkin had served on the government panel that affirmed the termination of Taub's grant, and Mishkin was the lone dissenter on that panel. Moreover, Mishkin had spearheaded efforts to raise private funds to reimburse the government for its care of the Silver Spring monkeys so that IBR would continue to own the monkeys.

When PETA learned of the plan to experiment upon and kill the monkeys, it sought an injunction in state court, relying upon, inter alia, the Louisiana anticruelty statute. The state court issued an injunction against killing the animals. NIH—relying upon 28 U.S.C. § 1442(a)(1)(1988), which authorizes the removal from state to federal court by "any officer of the United States or any agency thereof, or any person acting under him, for any act under color of such office"— removed the action to federal court, although PETA opposed the removal on the ground that NIH had no real interest in the suit and had been misnamed as a defendant in the first place. PETA also argued that, in any event, only federal officers or persons acting under federal officers—and not federal agencies—could use the removal statute. The federal court permitted the removal and continued the injunction in effect. After twenty days, the temporary restraining order became a preliminary injunction, and defendants sought appellate review.[117] The federal appellate court held that federal agencies could remove under the statute and that, in any event, plaintiffs lacked standing in federal court under *Sierra Club* and its progeny.[118]

The Supreme Court granted discretionary review of the federal appellate decision and, in a unanimous decision, held that the removal statute applied only to federal officers or persons acting under them, and not federal agencies.[119] The Court remanded the case to the federal district court, which, in turn, remanded it to state court. Tulane University then re-removed the case back to federal district court, claiming that it was a person acting under a federal officer. The director of NIH and the secretary of health and human services sought to intervene or be joined as defendants. Plaintiffs opposed these motions and the removal on the ground that there was no legitimate federal interest in the case given that the care of the monkeys and the cost of the experiments had been borne by private sources precisely to ensure that IBR would retain ownership of the animals and that the experiments would not be subject to federal requirements or accountability. Plaintiffs argued further that Tulane had raised no federal defense and merely wanted to get into federal court long enough to have the case dismissed for lack of jurisdiction on standing grounds. The district court remanded the case to the state court to determine whether NIH and its officers were indispensable parties under state law. The federal appellate court vacated the remand and directed the district court to decide whether Tulane could properly remove the case to federal court.[120] The district court then decided that Tulane had properly removed the case and upheld federal jurisdiction. The district court went on to apply the appellate court's earlier decision that the plaintiffs lacked federal standing under *Lujan* and other cases, despite the fact that the Fifth Circuit's earlier dismissal on standing grounds was without jurisdiction in light of the Supreme Court's decision.

The decision—likely to be the final one in the sad history of the Silver Spring monkeys (unless the Supreme Court again intervenes)—is problematic in a number of respects. First, the Supreme Court has already determined that removal by itself does not establish federal jurisdiction; rather, it is necessary that a defendant who seeks to remove must present a colorable federal defense. Tulane did not assert any federal defense in its removal petition and only later asserted that plaintiffs lacked standing and that the experiments were protected from interference by the state because they constituted a federal project. The standing argument is not a relevant defense, because it could not have been raised in state court. For the reasons discussed above, the experimentation was not a federal project.

Second, there is substantial legal authority for the proposition that a corporation is not a "person" for purposes of the removal statute. For example, courts have approved corporate removal only when there was so close a relationship between the corporation and the government that the former could be said to be an "agent" or "fiscal intermediary" of the latter. In this case, Tulane clearly did not so qualify.

Third, a fair reading of the case law interpreting the requirement that a person "act under" a government official indicates that the official must exercise "direct and detailed official control" over the "person" seeking removal. In this case, it cannot credibly be argued that such a level of control existed. The Silver Spring monkeys were taken from IBR in 1981. NIH, which had funded the original experiments by Taub, conducted an investigation and terminated all federal grants for the experiments. On appeal, the Department of Health and Human Services affirmed the termination. NIH steadfastly maintained that IBR continued to own the monkeys throughout the criminal prosecution of Taub, the civil case seeking to have PETA declared guardian, and Taub's unsuccessful administrative appeals. NIH stated in writing that it had no research use for the animals. IBR continually asserted its rights of ownership and warned the NIH not to take any action concerning the monkeys without IBR permission, and both NIH and Tulane acknowledged IBR's rights. IBR subsequently paid for the care of the monkeys with private funds; the experiments that PETA sought to enjoin were also paid for with private funds. The experiments were approved by the Tulane animal care committee and *not* by the NIH.

Nevertheless, the district court found that Tulane was a "person" who "acted under" a government official. The court based this determination on NIH's alleged "financial and research" interests and on various affidavits and deposition testimony that contained self-serving assertions about NIH interest in the animals. Given the clear history of NIH's attempts to disavow any interest in the animals as a general matter and any interest in continued experimentation, it is difficult to know how the court could base a determination on such nonexistent "research" interests. Although NIH had stated that it had expended approximately $50,000 for care of the animals (presumably since 1981), there is no indication that this expenditure resulted in NIH getting any "control" over the monkeys or the experiments. Assuming that NIH had "financial and research interest" in the monkeys, such interest would be no different from the interest NIH would ordinarily have with respect to *any* research that it funded through competitive peer review. Indeed, those institutions that receive federal grants or contract funds have far more pervasive interests than those claimed by NIH in this case. Accordingly, *any* institution that receives such a grant or contract—virtually every university, college, drug company, and so forth—will be a "person" that "acts under" a federal officer.

Fourth, assuming *arguendo* that plaintiffs could not satisfy federal standing requirements, they certainly had standing in Louisiana state court, which has very liberal standing rules. Louisiana permits taxpayer suits challenging governmental action, as well as third-party suits that seek to vindicate ideological positions. In sum, it is now impossible for anyone to challenge the treatment of animals in federally funded laboratories. Under the decisions discussed above, animal organizations do not have standing to initiate a suit in federal court to protect laboratory animals, because there can be no injury in fact when the animals are owned and not feral. If, however, the animal protection group brings an action against a research facility in state court, then, even if the defendant has no colorable federal defense, the defendant can remove to federal court, where the restrictive standing doctrines can be used to dismiss the suit altogether. Even if state standing requirements are considerably more flexible than federal requirements, animal protection groups, and the animals whose interests they seek to protect, may not be able to benefit from those more liberal requirements.

## Conclusion

As a general matter, the law of standing is confused and confusing, and it is safe to say that the Supreme Court suffers from the confusion in the same way that the rest of us do. Standing decisions in which animals are involved never address the interests of animals. Rather, the sole question is whether the allegation of a plaintiff is sufficient to show that her enjoyment of the animals as "resources" is impaired by some action. Standing in these cases has little, if anything, to do with animals (or the integrity of natural resources); rather, the sole focus is the protection of completely humanocentric interests. Moreover, in the few cases in which plaintiffs sought to protect animals for their own sake, the courts, for the most part, drew a line between those animals that are "feral" and are "resources" available for enjoyment by all and those animals that are privately owned. In the latter case, it is virtually impossible, if not impossible, ever to satisfy the constitutional standing requirements. Although the rationale is never really stated explicitly, it is, nevertheless, quite clear: a plaintiff cannot suffer a legally cognizable injury as the result of an owner's treatment of her private property.

Federal standing, which, for purposes of cases involving animal interests, has always been limited, has become even more restricted. In *Lujan,* the Supreme Court articulated abstract (and ad hoc) notions about the injury-in-fact and imminence requirements of standing. The latter was relied upon in *Yeutter* and *Secretary* to deny standing to researcher plaintiffs who clearly would have had standing before *Lujan.* The *Tulane* case indicated that animal advocates may find themselves unable to seek redress in state courts if the defendant receives federal funds. In sum, there may be no courthouse available to those who seek to protect animal interests.

In the next chapter—the final chapter of Part I—I examine the general theoretical claim that the regulation of the use of animals may result in animals' having certain rights. This inquiry rounds out my general examination of the property paradigm as it concerns animals.

# CHAPTER FIVE

## Laws and Rights:
## *Claims, Benefits, Interests,*
## *and the Instrumental Status of Animals*

### The "Right" to Humane Treatment

THE CENTRAL THESIS of this book is that legal welfarism requires that we balance animal interests unprotected by claims of right against human interests protected by claims of right in general and, in particular, by claims of human property rights in those animals. In the past three chapters I have discussed the legal status of animals as property and have examined some of the consequences of that property status. I concluded that from the perspective of the law, and in the absence of any laws regulating the use of animal property by human owners, animals are treated exclusively as means to the ends determined by human property owners. I now examine the general claim that regulating the use of animal property does not thereby create rights in those animals as against their owners. If regulating animal property did create true animal rights, then I would need (at least) to reformulate my claim because my characterization of animal welfare as balancing animal interests unprotected by any claims of right would be a less-than-accurate description of that process.

As I indicated earlier, the use of "absolute" to modify ownership is not quite accurate to describe human ownership of animals or any other property. There are always some legal restrictions placed on the use of property. These restrictions may be viewed as background constraints on action or as specific rules of property use.[1] The most obvious restriction concerns prohibitions on the use of property in ways harmful to others. I may have "absolute" ownership of my baseball bat, but I cannot use it to injure people unjustifiably. There are, however, other restrictions as well. Although I may have "absolute" ownership of my very old townhouse, I may not change the outside of the structure if it is designated a historic landmark.

Once we recognize that property ownership is not absolute and is subject to restriction, the next question becomes whether these restrictions translate into some sort of "right" for the property. Although this question may be rather nonsensical as it applies to inanimate objects, it is a plausible question to ask when the property is a sentient being, such as a slave or a nonhuman animal. One commentator, Professor Reinold Noyes, answered that we could not have legal relations with property as a general matter because " 'legal relations in our law exist only between persons. There cannot be a legal relation between a person and a thing or between two things.' "[2] According to Professor Waldron, property "cannot have rights or duties or be bound by or recognize rules."[3]

Despite these generally accepted statements of property law, some writers have argued that regulatory laws—be they criminal laws or administrative regulations—really can create rights in animals. For example, a widely used reference book on laws concerning animals states that "America has the distinction of being the first country to acknowledge the rights of animals by enacting statutory legislation to protect them from cruel treatment."[4] The Animal Legal Defense Fund has launched a campaign to establish rights for animals to be free from "exploitation, cruelty, neglect, and abuse." These two comments assume that anticruelty laws— a most common form of the regulation of animal use—can create rights. That is, according to this view, a law that prohibits the "exploitation, cruelty, neglect, and abuse" of animals can be said to create a *right* to be free from "exploitation, cruelty, neglect, and abuse." Indeed, the notion that there is such a "right" suggests that a "wide range of animal protection positions can be couched in rights terminology."[5]

In this chapter, I argue that, as a theoretical matter, this view deceptively embodies and does not reject the notion that animals are entitled to no more than the balancing of interests that characterizes legal welfarism. In Parts II and III of this book, I examine the operation of anticruelty laws and the regulatory scheme created by the federal Animal Welfare Act (AWA) respectively, in order to show that theory and practice converge; regulation of animal use, whether by criminal statutes, in the case of anticruelty statutes, or administrative regulation, in the case of the AWA, does not give true rights to animals.

I emphasize from the outset that my primary concern is to examine the laws that currently characterize our legal treatment of animals. For the most part, these laws require a balancing to determine whether the conduct in question is "necessary," and permit *any* animal interest to be sacrificed as long as the consequences (for humans or other animal property) are deemed (by humans) to be sufficient. I am not considering alternative legal structures that seek to control animal use through the imposition of substantive prohibitions, such as a complete ban on particular types of experiments. Such laws might conceivably be thought to recognize animal interests and to embody a rights-type concept.

Whether the prohibition (as opposed to the regulation) of various types of animal exploitation can create rights for animals is not considered in any detail in this book. It suffices for present purposes to say that our legal system does not employ absolute prohibitions in most cases in which the property involved is animal property. Almost *any* use may be made of such property, subject to the regulation that I am discussing here—that the use is "humane" and does not result in "unnecessary" suffering. There are, however, some exceptions, such as bans on cockfighting or dogfighting. In many instances, these laws are neither enforced nor observed, but the laws do represent de jure prohibitions. And as I discussed earlier, these prohibitions are often more reflective of concerns other than animal protection.

Further work is needed to determine whether, and in what situations, prohibitions on the use of animal property may create protection similar to what is provided by human rights.

As a prelude to the central discussion, I review briefly some material concerning the criminal prosecution of animals.

## The Prosecution and Execution of Animals

In one sense these categorical assertions about the inability of animals to have legal relations with humans may be refuted simply by reference to the bizarre but nevertheless once extant prosecution of animals (as well as inanimate objects). From approximately the ninth century to the beginning of the twentieth century, there were hundreds of prosecutions and executions of animals for various crimes.[6] These trials occurred in Belgium, Canada, Denmark, England, France, Germany, Italy, Portugal, Russia, Scotland, Spain, Switzerland, Turkey, and New Haven, Connecticut.[7] The type of animals tried included "insects and rodents . . . asses, beetles, bloodsuckers, bulls, caterpillars, cockchafers, cocks, cows, dogs, dolphins, eels, field mice, flies, goats, grasshoppers, horses, locusts, mice, moles, rats, serpents, sheep, slugs, snails, swine, termites, turtledoves, weevils, wolves, worms and nondescript vermin."[8] The most commonly prosecuted animals were pigs, which were thought to be easily possessed by the devil. For example, in 1386 a sow was sentenced "to be mangled in the face and maimed in the forelegs" before being hanged, because it had torn the face and arms of a child.[9]

There are several explanations for the criminal prosecution of animals. The first is the simple principle of retaliation, based on the notion that "the moral equilibrium of the community had been disturbed by [the crime] and that somebody or something must be punished or else dire misfortune, in the form of plagues, [droughts], and reverses in men's fortunes would overtake the land."[10] This principle is thought to have been the basis for the trial of animals in ancient Greece.[11] The second principle concerned the animal as an agent. As noted in Chapter Two, Thomas Aquinas, a highly influential medieval theologian, viewed animals as irrational creatures. Aquinas argued that animals could be cursed or blessed only if they were acting as agents toward rational beings. If animals were acting as agents of God, then it would be blasphemy to punish them; if they were not acting as agents at all and merely behaved as irrational brutes, it would be wrong to punish them. The only appropriate ground for animal "responsibility" for crime, then, was that the animals were "instruments of Satan 'instigated by the powers of hell and therefore proper to be cursed.' On this ground alone the church had the right to excommunicate and punish them with death, for it is not the animals but the Devil through them that is aimed at." The theological explanation does not, however, implicate the culpability of animals. Rather, "the anathema of the church is not pronounced against the animals *per se,* but hurled at the devil through them, inasmuch as they are used by Satan to our detriment."[12]

A more interesting explanation—advanced by a Swiss jurist, Edouard Osenbrugen—is that since "only human beings can commit crimes and be responsible for them, since they alone are rational, animals, if so treated, must have undergone a kind of personification in men's minds." Osenbrugen supports this view by observing that in medieval times "domestic animals were regarded just as much a part of the household and entitled to the same legal protection as the human inmates" and that, under Germanic law, animals were permitted to give testimony in criminal cases. Osenbrugen concluded, then, "that beasts were vested, by an act of personification, with human rights and responsibilities."[13] Edward Westermarck argued similarly that animals were executed because "the beast or insect was retaliated upon for the simple reason that it was regarded as a rational being."[14]

The trial and execution of animals is a legal anomaly. Even if such trials and executions represented some notion of animal responsibility or rights, it would be difficult to jump to the conclusion that animals possessed rights or responsibilities under the law. For example, although some domestic animals may have been regarded as "part of the household," their owners were still able to exercise the incidents of property ownership, including the right to kill and consume these animals. Under such circumstances, it seems odd to say that such animals were vested with rights. In any event, these actions are unlikely to shed much light on the issue before us: whether property can have rights and responsibilities.

In a recent New Jersey case, a dog, Taro, was ordered to be killed because he allegedly bit a child and was found to be a "vicious" dog under state law.[15] Interestingly, the trial court refused to consider the proceeding as criminal in nature (and thus requiring certain procedural safeguards), even though the outcome of the proceeding was an order directing that the dog be killed, and instead treated the state law as merely regulating the use of animal property. After a great deal of international attention paid to Taro's plight, New Jersey governor Christine Whitman ordered that the dog's life be spared. Although the press reported that the governor "pardoned" Taro, the actual legal documents issued by the governor indicated that she "remitted the forfeiture" of Taro, pursuant to her constitutional power to "suspend fines and remit forfeitures."[16] The reason for this distinction is that only a person can be pardoned; where property is concerned, the correct gubernatorial remedy is to remit the forfeiture of the *property.* In any event, there was never any question of Taro having any rights or responsibilities. Rather, Taro was characterized by the system as a troublesome piece of property, no different from a dangerous tool or piece of machinery that is no longer of use, because its use presents a danger to people.[17]

We will never know the true justifications for the animal trials, and surely any justification that attributed rights to animals was manifestly in contradiction to social norms concerning the treatment and use of animals.

## When Do Laws Create Rights?

Putting aside the case of animal trials, it is clear that there are modern laws that regulate our use of animals, and many of these laws reflect our concern to ensure that animals are treated "humanely" and are spared any "unnecessary" suffering. For the most part, these laws become relevant when a human seeks to exercise some aspect of ownership of an animal and someone else objects. Do these balancing laws in some way establish "rights" on the part of the property? In order to answer this question, we must first determine what is meant by a "legal" right.

As a preliminary matter, it should be noted that any rights scheme requires some mechanism for the rightholder to demand the enforcement of or waive the right (as in choice theory) or to assert the interest of the rightholder (as in interest or benefit theory). The obvious problem is that animals are in a position similar to that of infants or the mentally disabled: they require someone to make the relevant assertions. In the case of disabled or incompetent human beings, we appoint a guardian *ad litem* to represent the interests of the rightholder. Although appointment of such a guardian for animals raises special problems, at least in theory, it is possible.[18]

For purposes of this discussion, I assume a "positivist" theory of law rather than a competing view, such as natural-law theory. The latter theory holds that the existence and validity of legal rules is dependent on the conformity of those rules to some moral standard. A positivist theory denies such a connection. Perhaps the best-known version of postivism is set forth in H.L.A. Hart's classic work of analytic jurisprudence, *The Concept of Law*.[19] Hart argues that a legal rule exists and is valid when that rule has met the requirement of validity of the system and when the system is, as a whole, efficacious. For example, a natural-law theorist might say that a law authorizing slavery is not valid because it violates fundamental moral conditions. The positivist would not focus on the moral issue and instead would look to see whether the rule was adopted in conformity with the accepted legal process (i.e., passed in an appropriate manner by the legislature or adopted in court ruling) and whether the system, as a whole, is efficacious. That does not mean, of course, that the positivist does not have moral views. The salient difference between positivists and natural-law theorists is most apparent in the criticism they mount against a particular law or legal system. The natural-law theorist denies the validity of an immoral rule; the positivist may accept that the rule is a valid rule of an efficacious legal system but argues that the law is immoral or unjust. I am assuming a positivist theory in that I accept that the legal system of the United States is an efficacious system and that the existence and validity of a law depend on whether it has been enacted in accordance with the appropriate criteria. Both of the rights theories that I discuss below provide criteria, independent of moral requirements, for identification of the existence of rights.

A legal right is a right that is recognized and enforced by the legal system. It is distinguished from a moral right, which does not have the force of law but which is often used as a reason for obtaining legal protection for the interest it represents.

Although we all have an intuitive sense of what a legal right is, the concept is complex and is used to describe several very different elements within the legal system. The theorist with perhaps the greatest influence in this regard is Professor Wesley Hohfeld, who, as we saw earlier, argued that "the term 'rights' tends to be used indiscriminately to cover what in a given case may be a privilege, a power, or an immunity, rather than a right in the strictest sense."[20] According to Hohfeld, a right, strictly speaking, is really a *claim* that has duty as its correlative: to say that Mary has a right against John that John stay away from Mary's land is equivalent to saying that John has a duty to Mary to stay off her land.[21] Claim rights may exist *in personam* in that the duty is identifiable with a particular person, or may be *in rem* in that the corresponding duty binds everyone. My ownership of my dog is a claim right in rem in that a correlative duty binds everyone not to interfere with my enjoyment of my dog unless I inflict gratuitous suffering on my dog, in which case the local authorities may no longer have a duty *not* to interfere with my ownership. However, if I enter into a contract to buy your cow, the corresponding duty—in this case the duty to transfer ownership of the cow—binds an identifiable person: you, the seller.

There are, however, senses of right other than claim right. For example, I may have a right to do something in the sense that I have a *privilege* to do it; having a privilege is the same as having no duty not to do X—privilege is the negation of duty.[22] Mary has a privilege to enter upon her own land in that she has no duty not to do so (assuming she has not rented it to someone else), and privilege is correlative with "no right" in that John has "no right" that Mary should not enter the land.[23] In addition, to say that Mary has a right may mean that Mary has a *power* to alter her legal relationships with respect to the property.[24] A power is the opposite of a disability and the correlative of legal liability.[25] That is, if I have a power over X, then I am not under a disability with respect to X, and everyone else is under a potential liability if I exercise my power. Finally, a right may be an *immunity,* which is the opposite of liability and the correlative of disability.[26] That is, if Mary owns X, John may be disabled from affecting her relationship with X; Mary is not liable to having her legal position altered.

A comparison of Hohfeld's analysis to Honoré's jurisprudential analysis of ownership and Snare's ordinary-language constitutive rules of property indicates that animal ownership fits comfortably within all three frameworks. Honoré, it will be recalled, proposed a "liberal" theory of ownership that reflected the concern for the freedom of owners. This resonated with Snare's notion that property required that the owner be able to decide how to use the property and that the owner be able to exclude everyone else from use of the thing. Similarly, Hohfeld's fundamental juridical conceptions accommodate Honoré's liberal theory and Snare's ordinary-language analysis. A property owner has a claim right in that others are under a duty not to interfere with her use of her animal property; the owner has a privilege to use the animal, and others have no right to interfere; the owner has a power to alter the relationship of herself and others to the animal; but the owner is otherwise immune from the exercise of others' rights as they affect her relationship to the animal.[27]

A simple application of Hohfeld's framework would lead to the view that animals have all sorts of rights. For example, in the production of goose liver pâté, geese are force-fed the equivalent (to humans) of twenty pounds of grain per day until their livers rupture. Presumably, workers on such farms have duties to force-feed the geese every day. This hardly suggests the existence of a right on the part of the goose to be force-fed. Part of the problem here is that Hohfeld never really clarified the idea of duty. As Professor Joel Feinberg has argued, when we talk about the violation of a duty, we usually mean that the rightholder has herself been wronged.[28] Surely no one (especially the goose) would argue that she had been wronged by not being force-fed. In this instance, Hohfeld's framework simply fails to capture the idea of duty that we ordinarily use when we talk about the violation of a duty incidental to the notion of claim rights. A more difficult example would involve regulations that require that researchers not inflict pain on animals unless the infliction is scientifically "necessary." Unlike the goose, a laboratory rat may be said to be "wronged" when the researcher fails to make the "necessity" determination in a particular case. However, this would be like saying that a woman was wronged—and her right violated—when her husband beat her with a rod that exceeded the width of his thumb. Although both the animal and the woman are wronged, it tugs at our intuitions to say that a woman has a "right" to be beaten with a smaller rod or that an animal has a "right" to have pain inflicted only when it is scientifically "necessary." Again, the problem has less to do with understanding "right" than with understanding "duty" and what it means to say that someone has been wronged by a breach of duty.

This is, of course, not to say that Hohfeld's framework does not have some utility with respect to the various relationships that people have with animals. When Hohfeld speaks of privilege, he contemplates the liberty to engage in an action that others may well be under a duty not to do.[29] For example, if I am curious about what occurs when I put a live cat in a functioning microwave oven and decide to satisfy my curiosity by performing such an experiment, I will probably be charged with violating the anticruelty statute because I have engaged in an "unproductive" use of the animal. However, if I happen to be a scientist at a major research institution, the exact same "experiment" will probably be immune from criminal prosecution because it is part of "science." In such an instance, Hohfeld's framework is useful to describe this situation: the scientist has a "right" that I do not have in the sense that a scientist has a privilege to do what I have a duty not to do. In this sense, the concept of "duty" is clearer, but overall, Hohfeld's framework is problematic because it allows claim rights to be found in contexts in which their existence is highly questionable at best.

There are, of course, many other theories of legal rights, but I focus further discussion on two theories that are popular in jurisprudential discourse and that address the relationship between claim and duty—a relationship that Hohfeld discussed but did not analyze satisfactorily in light of the ambiguous meaning of "duty." In addition, these two theories are thought by some to contain competing positions about whether animals have legal rights.

The first theory is called the will theory or choice theory of rights. The choice theory requires that a rightholder have moral control over the action of another person. For example, if I have a right that you fulfill some promise to me, that right assumes that I have autonomy and may either insist on your fulfilling the promise or may release you from the obligation. This theory may also be understood in terms of the components of the right of property referred to above. If John has a duty to do what Mary wants and John's obligation is contingent on Mary's choice to enforce or waive enforcement of that obligation, then Mary has a claim right. If Mary has a liberty or privilege to speak in the sense that she has no duty not to do so, then Mary has a liberty right. The liberty right differs from the claim right in that, with respect to the liberty right, Mary is not an active subject of the right but is rather a passive subject whose choice is protected by law. Nevertheless, she can choose not to exercise that right. With respect to the claim right, Mary is an active subject of the right and may demand or waive John's performance of the obligation owed.

If Mary has a power right, then she may affect a change in her legal position. Again, the "autonomy" portion of this right is reflected in the willingness of the system to respect Mary's exercise of her power. Finally, if Mary has an immunity right, others are disabled from changing Mary's legal position. A clear statement of the choice theory is offered by Professor L. W. Sumner: "Central to this conception [of protected choices] is the idea of the right-holder having the freedom to choose among a set of options, and of this freedom being protected by a set of duties imposed on others. The choice in question may be provided by a full liberty, in which case its protection will include claims of non-interference against others. But it may also take the simpler form of a claim, since . . . every claim necessarily involves the power either to demand performance by the duty-bearer or to waive it."[30]

It should be clear that under such a theory, animals are not likely to be said to possess rights. Professor Waldron states that the choice theory "has a number of controversial implications. It implies that it is a mistake to attribute rights to entities like foetuses or animals which are in principle incapable of exercising the choices which having rights essentially involves."[31] Indeed, perhaps the best-known attack on animal rights (moral or legal) is based on this notion that animals cannot exercise choice. Professor Carl Cohen defends the use of animals in research on the ground that they are not "capable of exercising or responding to moral claims."[32] For Cohen, the essence of having a right involves autonomy and the ability to act in an autonomous manner. This notion is very close to the choice theory of rights, and if will or choice is necessary for an animal to have a right, then it may be said safely that animals have no legal rights and, indeed, *cannot* be the subject of legal (or moral) rights. The obvious response to Cohen's argument is that there are human beings who are incapable of the autonomous behavior envisioned by the choice theory of rights. Cohen responds that the capacity for moral judgment

> is not a test to be administered to human beings one by one. . . . The issue is one of kind. Humans are of such a kind that they may be the subject of experiments only with their voluntary consent. . . . Animals are of such a kind that it is impossible for them, in principle, to give or withhold voluntary consent or to make a moral choice.[33]

Whatever one thinks of Cohen's argument, it is clear that animals (and, if Cohen is wrong, some humans) possess no rights under a choice theory.

The second theory of legal rights actually involves two closely related theories: "benefit" theory and "interest" theory.[34] The benefit theory, in its broadest formulation, holds that an individual can be said to have a right when she is the beneficiary of another's duty that is imposed for her benefit (the benefit theory) or when the legal system recognizes that she has interests that are worth protecting and that serve as a reason for imposing a duty on others (interest theory). If P stands to benefit from Q's duty to do (or to refrain from doing) X, then P has a right against Q—a right that many be characterized either as a right *that* Q should do X (or refrain from doing X) or as a right *to* the benefit that P stands to gain in the matter. Professors Lyons, MacCormick, Raz, and Waldron have been particularly prominent in the development of this theory. These theorists have tried to qualify the benefits theory in order to distinguish it from one that would accord rights to anyone who merely benefited from another's duty. For example, Waldron states that someone has a right "when the securing of a benefit to him is part of the point of holding another to be under the duty in question." The benefit that gives rise to the right must be so closely connected to the duty that "it becomes in a sense a test of the duty's performance."[35] Neil MacCormick states that a rule that confers rights must: (1) "concern 'goods' (or 'advantages,' or 'benefit,' or 'interests,' or however we may express the point)"; (2) "concern the enjoyment of goods by individuals separately"; and (3) provide normative protection to individuals in the enjoyment of the benefits so secured.[36] David Lyons argues that a qualified benefits theory identifies a person with a right as "one for whom a good is 'assured,' or an evil obstructed, by requirements or prohibitions upon others' behavior, in the sense that some other person or persons are required to act or forbear in ways designed or intended to serve, secure, promote, or protect his interests or an interest of his."[37]

Unlike the choice theory, there appears to be nothing inherent in interest theory that would preclude it, prima facie, from applying to animals. Indeed, as I mentioned above, Waldron regards its main competitor, choice theory, as controversial partly because the latter does not allow for the possibility of animal rights. Interest theory assumes, of course, that animals have interests. Although the denial of such interests appears to be an implausible philosophical move, the issue is not free from dispute. In his 1980 book, *Interests and Rights: The Case Against Animals,* Professor R. G. Frey argues that there are two senses of the word "interests." The first sense involves "having a good or well-being which can be harmed or benefited." In this first sense, animals do have interests; but then, Frey argues, so do man-made or manufactured objects. It is not good for a dog to be deprived of water, but it is also not good for prehistoric cave drawings to be exposed to excessive amounts of sunlight or for tractors to be deprived of oil. Although a dog needs water, so too does a tractor need oil.[38]

"Interest" in the second sense involves "having wants which can be satisfied or left unsatisfied."[39] Frey argues that "wants" cannot be equated with "needs," because manufactured objects, such as tractors, can have needs. Rather, "wants" must be equated with desires or preferences. The problem, according to Frey, is that desires presuppose beliefs in the truth or falsity of various sentences. For example, Frey claims that if I desire to own a Gutenberg Bible, my desire is linked with my belief that the sentence "My collection lacks a Gutenberg Bible" is true.[40] Put another way, if I have the desire to own a Gutenberg Bible, I must be able to distinguish between the two sentences "My collection contains a Gutenberg Bible" and "My collection lacks a Gutenberg Bible." This distinction requires that I have a grasp of the relationship between language and the actual state of affairs in the world, or, in this case, the state of the collection of my library books. In order to make such a distinction, Frey claims, I must have language capacities. Since animals do not possess language capacities, Frey reasons, they cannot have beliefs and, therefore, cannot have desires.[41] Frey also denies that animals can suffer; rather, he argues that " 'higher' animals can suffer unpleasant sensations."[42]

Obviously, if Frey is correct, any theory of animal rights linked to animal interests is in trouble. However, there are serious flaws in Frey's theory. First, because Frey denies that animals suffer—a notion linked closely to interests—it is difficult to understand his acknowledgment that animals can experience "unpleasant sensations." In a more recent article, Frey acknowledges that animals do suffer, and it is therefore difficult to understand how he can still (if he ever could) maintain that animals do not have interests.[43] Second, Frey's view that a belief is always a belief that a certain sentence is true has been effectively refuted by Professors Tom Regan and Bernard Rollin.[44]

Applying the qualified (i.e., not broad) interest theory, it appears at first glance as though animals may already have some rights within our legal system. For example, the regulations promulgated under the AWA require that "indoor housing facilities for rabbits shall be adequately ventilated to provide for the health and comfort of the animals at all times."[45] Under the interest theory, this arguably confers a legal right on a rabbit used in experimentation. The well-being, or interest of the rabbit in comfort and health, is a ground for holding the research facility under an obligation not only not to interfere with the rabbit's right but to take affirmative steps to ensure that the rabbit is comfortable. Moreover, the rabbit is the *intended* beneficiary of the obligation in that the research facility is required to perform these acts simply to promote or protect an interest of the rabbit. We may say in advance that if this benefit has not been conferred, the research facility has not performed the duty imposed. There are literally hundreds of such requirements under the AWA, and all may be analyzed in the same manner.

On closer inspection, however, there may be reasons that make it inappropriate to apply the interest theory to statutory schemes like the AWA or other laws that, under some interpretation of the interest theory, may be said to confer rights on animals by virtue of requiring that human and animal interests be balanced.

At least one interest theorist—Professor Joseph Raz—has explicitly ruled out the use of interest theory to establish rights for animals. According to Raz's view of interest theory, animals would be excluded for two reasons. Raz argues that under what he calls "the reciprocity thesis," "only members of 'the same moral community' can have rights."[46] Animals are "nonmembers" of the community, to whom we may owe duties but who do not possess rights. Moreover, Raz argues that animals may be "intrinsically valuable," or valuable apart from instrumental value, but nevertheless not be of ultimate value. For example, Raz argues that the relationship between a human and a companion animal may be intrinsically valuable but that the value of the animal is not intrinsic, because the animal's value ultimately derives from the animal's contribution to the happiness and well-being of the animal's human companion. On Raz's view, the capacity to have rights requires that the rightholder be of ultimate value.

Raz does recognize that some people may argue that the value of the human/animal relationship is related as well to the contribution of the relationship to the well-being of the animal, which may then be held to be ultimately valuable. If we took this view, then interest theory—or at least Raz's version of it—would be relevant to rights for animals. In the cases discussed above, however, interest theory could not be used. That is, any right that the rabbit used in experiments has to comfort is not given in recognition of the rabbit's ultimate value but, rather, concerns the *instrumental* value that the rabbits have for human purposes.

In addition, the notion of the animal as being of instrumental value goes to the core of concern about using interest theory in connection with rights for animals. In an essay about children's rights, MacCormick argues that "there is a significant difference between asserting that every child ought to be cared for, nurtured, and, if possible, loved, and asserting that every child has a right to care, nurture, and love." If the argument is that care, nurture, and love are important because "a healthy society requires well-nurtured children who will grow up into contented and well-adjusted adults who will contribute to the GNP and not be a charge on the welfare facilities or the prison service,"[47] then it would be absurd to say that children have a *right* to care, nurture, and love. Rather, the only claim being made is that by providing certain benefits to children, an ulterior end—keeping people from being charges on the taxpayer—is served. For MacCormick, the political aim of the law must be the well-being of the putative rightholder.

The problem with MacCormick's view is that at least on some accounts of political theory there is little legislation that counts as creating rights. For example, laws that ostensibly give workers rights to certain benefits, including but not limited to a safe workplace, may not be viewed as rights legislation, because even though the law protects the well-being of the worker, there is an ulterior end that is sought—greater productivity in the workplace.[48] It is clear that any theory like MacCormick's must analyze further what is an "ulterior end" and how such ends relate to the concept of "well-being."

For present purposes, however, we can say safely that irrespective of the theoretical relationship between the concepts of ulterior ends and well-being, animal rights cannot fit into the interest theory of legal rights, no matter how that theory is constituted. Because animals are regarded as property, they are regarded, *as a matter of law,* as means to human ends. The institution of property has no other function except to satisfy human interests irrespective of the theoretical basis of that institution. Whether one takes the view, as does Hegel, that the right to private property is a general right (held by all) that is justified because it facilitates the moral development of people or, as do Locke and Waldron, that the right is specific in that only those who, for various reasons, deserve to have property are beneficiaries of that right, the institution of property is still a means of serving human ends.

To say that a chattel can have rights requires that the instrumental status of the chattel be altered fundamentally. To say that an item (or animal) is a chattel is to say that it has no inherent value and that its value is exclusively instrumental. To change that status and to attribute some inherent value to the chattel is to deny its completely instrumental value. Regulations on the use of property do not deny the instrumental value of the property; on the contrary, such regulations are enacted to ensure that the instrumental use of property does not interfere with the activities of other people. These regulations in no way recognize the inherent value of the chattel. Interest theory requires that a rightholder be regarded as having at least some interests that cannot be sacrificed simply because of consequential considerations. Although certain legal prohibitions (such as an absolute ban on using animals in burn experiments) may recognize that at least some animal interests are not subject to being "balanced" away, the regulation of animal treatment under legal welfarism assumes that all animal interests are, at least in theory, subject to sacrifice.

Moreover, the law operates so that owners of property are given all the protection necessary to use their property in the ways that they wish. Although there are regulations imposed on some uses of property, such regulation is regarded as a serious matter and must be justified by the government. Moreover, if the regulation becomes too intrusive, the problem of a taking arises. In any event, the law regards property as something to be used by its owner without interference from the government, and as indicated by the cases concerning veterinary malpractice, the law refuses to depart from this conceptualization even when the owner no longer regards the property as mere property. Although someone may regard her dog or cat as having ultimate value in Raz's sense, the law refuses to recognize that value and sees animals only in consequential terms. That is, animals may be used and exploited if there is human benefit to be gained. Indeed, only the most egregious acts of pure sadism are punished by anticruelty laws. The reason for this is that in such cases there is no legitimate benefit to be gained from the activity and that any pleasure obtained by the person harming the animal is more than offset by myriad social values that we seek to protect. Because animals are regarded as property, they are regarded as means to human ends. "Humane" treatment and "unnecessary" suffering are interpreted in light of this status.

There may be restrictions on how humans use their animal property, but these restrictions are formulated within a context in which animals are *only* ulterior means to human ends, and these restrictions are often imposed to facilitate and not to moderate the use of animals as means to ends. Indeed, MacCormick recognizes this when he asks us to "consider the oddity of saying that turkeys have a right to be well fed in order to be fat for the Christmas table."[49] It would be inappropriate to respond to MacCormick that the turkey has a right but that the right of the turkey is simply overridden by the rights of humans to eat the turkey. As Waldron has correctly observed, "[i]n theories of rights which allow for the possibility of conflict [of rights], there is usually a requirement that a prima facie right cannot be overridden in favour of others without some moral compunction and without a feeling that something extra is owed in the future if at all possible to the person whose right has had to be sacrificed."[50]

Virtually all rights theories view rights as "barriers" to be used by the rightholder in order to prevent the rightholder's protected interest from being sacrificed. For example, Professor Ronald Dworkin, a leading rights theorist, argues that the background justification for political decisions in Western democracies is utilitarianism, or the principle that we ought to maximize the fulfillment of goals that people have for their own lives. According to Dworkin, rights are "trumps" over the background justification of utilitarianism when utilitarianism becomes corrupted by giving less weight to some preferences or persons than to others.[51] Dworkin argues that equal concern and respect for persons is a moral imperative, and to the extent that utilitarianism fails to provide for this concern and respect, rights become necessary.

There is simply no sense in which moral compunction is involved in overriding the supposed right of the turkey; there can be no feeling that something is owed to the turkey (who will be killed and consumed); and there is no sense in which the turkey's right acts as any sort of trump.[52] As I discussed earlier, in the context of Professor Tom Regan's theory of animal (and human) rights, those rights depend on the rightholder's being regarded as the subject of a life and an individual with inherent value. It is difficult to understand how the present status of animals as property subject only to the balancing laws of legal welfarism can be consistent with the status of animals as rightholders. If, as a matter of law, the system treats animals solely as means to ends and never as ends in themselves, possessing at least some interests that are not tradable, then it is difficult, if not impossible, to reconcile such treatment with the status of animals as individuals with inherent value, because the owner of the property may override that individuality and value whenever it is in the owner's interest to do so.

Finally, it should be noted that other rights theories are even less congenial to an animal rights perspective. For example, Dworkin views rights as "trumps" that act as a brake on the use of utilitarianism to justify important social, political, and legal decisions. Sometimes utilitarianism violates Dworkin's principle of equal concern and respect for individuals, and in such instances, rights are needed to "trump" the appeal to consequences. Dworkin does not consider the principle of equal concern to apply to nonhumans, however, and it is not even clear that Dworkin would require that animal interests be included in calculating the consequences. In any event, it is difficult to see how Dworkin would accommodate the interests of animals as long as they retain the status of property.

On the other hand, Hart attempts to formulate a theory of rights that identifies those human interests that are associated with the "essentials of human well-being." Although Hart's theory is different from Dworkin's in that the latter rejects a fixed notion of human well-being and the former decries using the inadequacies of utilitarianism upon which to build a rights theory, Hart's theory is still based upon human interests, and it is difficult to see how he could accommodate animal rights.

## The Nonbalancing "Balancing" Approach

The normative nature of the legal rules that concern animals requires that we balance human interests and animal interests. In this regard, it is instructive to consider the discussion on animals offered by libertarian philosopher Robert Nozick in his book *Anarchy, State, and Utopia*. Although Nozick is concerned more with moral notions than with legal ones, his discussion is nevertheless enlightening and will, I believe, illuminate the tension that exists when we try to apply the balancing approach of legal rules to resolve human/animal conflicts. Indeed, it appears as though Nozick has described precisely the system of animal welfare currently reflected in the legal system.

Nozick argues rights should not be understood as merely moral goals incorporated "into the end state to be achieved." Rather, he argues, rights should be understood as "side constraints upon the actions to be done."[53] He contrasts his view with that of a utilitarian, who seeks as a goal to minimize the violation of rights, which view, according to Nozick, would permit the violation of some rights if that violation were necessary to achieve the minimal overall violation of rights. The view of rights as "side constraints" is justified, according to Nozick, by the "underlying Kantian principle that individuals are ends and not merely means. . . . Individuals are inviolable."[54]

In an attempt to "illuminate the status and implications of moral side constraints," Nozick considers "living beings for whom such stringent side constraints (or any at all) usually are not considered appropriate: namely nonhuman animals."[55] He thinks that at least "higher" animals receive moral consideration but that this consideration is arguably utilitarian. That is, when addressing at least some instances of the treatment of nonhumans, we weigh whatever moral cost we attach to animal pain and death against whatever benefits are likely to be obtained as a result of that pain or death and determine whether the putative benefits outweigh the estimated costs. Although animals do not have any rights, human beings have duties toward animals only when the scales that weigh human and animal interests tip in favor of the animal. Nozick labels his position "utilitarianism for animals, Kantianism for people." According to this position, "human beings may not be used or sacrificed for the benefit of others; animals may be used or sacrificed for the benefit of other people or animals *only if* those benefits are greater than the loss inflicted."[56]

A consequence of this "Kantianism for people, utilitarianism for animals" principle is that "nothing may be inflicted upon persons for the sake of animals."[57] That is, it is never permissible to violate human rights for the sake of animals. At this point, Nozick, who accepts a very strong right of private property, asks (perhaps rhetorically) whether his principle would preclude inflicting "penalties [on humans] for violating laws against cruelty to animals?" He recognizes that his principle could lead to arguably absurd results. For example, it would ostensibly prohibit infliction of minor discomfort on one innocent person in order to save ten thousand animals from excruciating pain. Nozick concedes that if people derive great utility from animal exploitation, then the principle may require or allow "that almost always animals be sacrificed," which would make "animals too subordinate to persons."[58] He concludes his discussion by acknowledging that utilitarianism for animals "won't do as the whole story" but professes his inability to determine what other considerations are relevant, and he confesses that "the thicket of questions daunts us."[59]

Nozick's analysis prompts three observations. First, in an important sense he has accurately captured the way the legal system handles human/animal conflicts. He is correct to say that, for the most part, we apply consequentialist considerations to determine what to do with animals. We may exploit animals if the benefits of that exploitation outweigh the costs (presumably to the animals). Nozick recognizes, however, that utilitarianism comes in different shapes and flavors. Although a more enlightened utilitarian theory, such as that described by Singer, may require that animal interests be weighed equally against human interests in the utilitarian calculus, it is always possible that people may be "utility devourers with respect to animals, always getting counterbalancing utility from each sacrifice of an animal."[60] For these people, animals are merely means to ends and have no interests that are worth protecting as a matter of utilitarian theory.

Second, what Nozick does not acknowledge (although, as I mentioned, his is a normative, rather than a descriptive, theory) is that the status of animals as property ensures that animals are treated as means to ends and do not have their interests taken into account within the legal system. Our legal system does not embody the enlightened system of utility about which Singer writes. Rather, the law permits virtually any human benefit to justify the infliction of pain or death on an animal. Although utilitarian theory does not focus on rights and instead focuses on furthering interests to the maximum extent possible, animals do not possess interests for many of the same reasons that they fail to possess rights under either the choice or the interest theory. As long as animals have the status of property, as long as they may be bought, sold, and killed with relatively little interference by the state, then talk of animal interests is nonsense because these interests may *always* be sacrificed.

Third, even if animal interests were taken more seriously in the utilitarian calculus, Nozick's side constraints, or rights, would virtually always "trump" those animal interests. If rights are "side constraints" and these constraints prohibit certain activities, only people are beneficiaries of rights, or side constraints. One important right accorded to people in Nozick's theory is the right to own property. Interference in the exercise of this right is protected by a side constraint that dictates that others may not interfere with the exercise of the right. Since humans (not animals) are treated as ends only and not means, and since the humane treatment of animals is morally required only if such treatment promotes the general good but is actually prohibited if it treats humans as means to ends, then it is difficult to see how Nozick's principle can lead to the humane treatment of animals as long as animals are viewed as private property and property rights are viewed as central to our moral and legal structure.

In a system such as the one Nozick proposes, there is really no balancing to be done when human and animal interests conflict. Humans are to be treated *only* as ends, and animals are to be treated *only* as means to ends. The law, however, appears to embody a balancing approach. As Dworkin argues, utilitarian considerations are, if not the primary justification for political decisions, certainly an important component of those decisions. As mentioned above, utilitarian notions are explicitly built into statutory schemes like the AWA, which requires that we balance benefits and burdens before proceeding with animal experiments. In reality, however, the situation is identical with the scheme that Nozick proposes.

Utilitarianism holds that in order to determine what is morally right or wrong, one must look to the consequences of action and determine what will promote the greatest general balance of good (or happiness or pleasure) over evil (or unhappiness or pain). If one is a utilitarian, one has duty to maximize the collective "good," however that notion is understood. Some utilitarians, such as Jeremy Bentham and Peter Singer, have argued that animal suffering must be included in the consideration of the consequences of action, and only when human benefit outweighs animal suffering should animal suffering be permitted. Both Bentham and Singer would strictly construe the notion of human benefit so that many trivial interests would not justify animal exploitation.[61]

Although utilitarianism as a moral theory may look like an appealing way to avoid at least some animal suffering, the problem is that utilitarianism is generally regarded as incompatible with the notion of rights.[62] No theory that excludes rights can accurately capture the current state of the legal system that exists in the United States. That is, I do not deny that there are utilitarian elements contained in the law, and indeed, these elements are present in our legal consideration of animals. For example, current federal law directs that experimenters balance the expected benefit to be gained from animal research against the harm to animals. That requirement is utilitarian, although federal law by no means restricts the notion of benefit in the way proposed by Bentham or Singer. The problem is that what I would call "weak" utilitarian considerations may impose direct duties on humans toward animals, but legal rights are possessed *only* by humans. When the legal system mixes rights considerations with utilitarian considerations and only one of two affected parties has rights, then the outcome is almost certain to be determined in favor of the rightholder.

When the interest of an animal is juxtaposed against the interest of a human in exercising his or her right over property, the animal interest virtually never prevails, because humans have property rights and animals are usually the object of the exercise of that right. I call our legal (and moral) reasoning about animals a "hybrid" system because we juxtapose the interest of a rightholder with that of a nonrightholder who, in addition to being a nonrightholder, is also the object of the rightholder's exercise of right. Our myriad laws and regulations that purport to protect animals are *unable* to achieve even a minimally acceptable level of protection as long as humans are the only rightholders and animals are regarded as "property" *all* of whose interests may be traded away. In many instances, a relatively trivial human interest is balanced against an animal's most fundamental interest in not experiencing pain or death, and the human interest nevertheless prevails. Moreover, the fact that humans have property rights in animals explains why there are usually no effective sanctions attached to animal protection legislation: we are reluctant to impose sanctions—especially criminal sanctions—on a human whose only offense is against her own property and involves no injury to any other rightholder (person).

In most cases, legal rights are not subject to abrogation simply because others will benefit from that abrogation. That is the main purpose of a right: it stands as a barrier of sorts between the rightholder and everyone else. The right to own property reflects the view that even though the social consequences of nonownership may, in a utilitarian sense, be desirable, it is better if people are allowed to own things. It is generally thought that the right to own property is a right that should not be violated just because someone else will benefit from the violation of the right. As I discussed in Chapter Two, the right to own property is generally thought of as a natural, or respect-based, right in that it reflects "a certain mandatory way in which persons must be treated if their essential humanity is to be respected and preserved." This type of right is different from conventional, or policy-based, rights, which "give certain people certain powers or liberties against interference . . . [because such rights are deemed to be in] the general welfare or health of our political institutions."[63]

This is not to say that we do not sometimes violate property rights, but generally, there must be a sufficient justification for doing so. Violations of property rights are not taken lightly. For example, a state may decide to deprive someone of property, but the Constitution requires that various substantive and procedural safeguards be followed. In regulating the use of property, we are generally reluctant to tell people how they should use their property, as long as their use does not have adverse consequences for other rightholders, who are always humans.

A critic of this analysis may say that there are other instances in which the state limits people's property rights in order to accommodate some interest of their property. For example, in the United States, some buildings are given a "landmark" status that prevents the owner of the building from altering or destroying the building even when the market value of the building or the location is substantial. The critic may conclude that this type of regulation illustrates that there are instances in which the "interests" of property are effectively protected by the law and truncate human property rights.

The difficulty with this example is that the landmark designation really serves the collective interests of people, and it is rather peculiar to speak of the "interest" of the building. In most cases, the state regulates the exercise of property rights in order to achieve wealth maximization, but the designation of a building as a landmark clearly does not maximize material wealth (because the owner of the site is deprived of the full economic benefits from her property). Nevertheless, there are many instances apart from landmark designation in which the state regulates the exercise of a property right, such as when the government, acting under environmental laws, prevents a landowner from covering a wetland in order to develop property.

It is, however, difficult to view such regulation as undertaken on behalf of the environment, just as it is problematic to regard landmark designations as undertaken in the interest of historic sites. Rather, these instances of regulation serve human interests. In the case of landmark designations, the interest is in preserving cultural treasures so that future generations of humans can appreciate those treasures. In the case of environmental regulation, the interest is in preserving the environment so that future generations of humans can have a place in which to live and "resources" to exploit.

This point may be stated in the context of Professor Dworkin's distinction between goal-based, right-based, and duty-based theories of political and legal systems.[64] Dworkin argues that a goal-based theory takes some goal, such as "improving the general welfare," as fundamental, whereas a right-based theory takes a right, such as the right to liberty, as fundamental, and a duty-based theory takes a duty, such as the duty to obey God, as fundamental. There can be no doubt that our legal treatment of animals is goal-based on at least two levels. Legal welfarism states that the overall goal that governs animal use is to provide maximum benefits to people from animal exploitation. The goal of obtaining benefits from animal use is supposedly tempered by a second goal that seeks the "humane" treatment of animals and their protection from "unnecessary" suffering. The first goal arguably assumes that humans have the *right* to obtain benefits from the exploitation of animals. The second goal is balanced against whatever human rights are relevant in the situation and almost always includes the right of private property.

If a goal-based theory, such as utilitarianism, could provide for rights, then it might make no difference what theory was operative in protecting animals. The problem is that utilitarian theory cannot generate legal rights—or at least legal rights with moral force. If a legal right is morally defensible, then the moral defense of that right must exclude utilitarian justifications because, if it does not, the legal right will succumb to utilitarian considerations and lose its force as a prima facie reason to respect whatever interest is protected by the right.[65]

This is, of course, not to deny that some legal rights might be based upon assessments of the general welfare. For example, a right of a physician to perform surgery is a policy-based right in that it reflects the creation of a social role and the assignment of certain rights to those who occupy such roles. Such a right does not protect an interest that must be respected if we are to preserve and respect the essential humanity of people, and is to be distinguished from those rights that are respect-based.

Even if animals had rights, those rights would only be—and, given our legal system, could only be—policy-based rights that reflect considerations of utility. Animals possess no respect-based rights because we are permitted to kill animals, subject them to horrible pain, and use them for virtually any purpose imaginable. Human rights, or at least some of them, are respect-based and concern what we rightly or wrongly view as the essence of our humanity. For example, few would argue that the right to own and use property is a right that could be taken away simply if the government made a determination that social welfare would be better off if we eliminated the institution of private property. Indeed, many people argue—correctly, in my view—that overall social welfare would be drastically improved if the institution of private property were abolished or modified significantly to provide for redistribution of wealth. Nevertheless, there is no movement in the direction of abolishing or altering private property rights, because there is general consensus that the respect of private property rights is essential to respect for the individual and to the ability of the individual to keep and use the fruits of her labor.

The difference between respect-based rights and policy-based rights is one of utility: in the latter case, we employ consequentialist notions of utility in framing the right and use those very same notions in arguing for continuation or dissolution of the right; in the former case, utilitarian notions are generally insufficient as a ground for creation or dissolution of the right.[66] A fundamental right protected by law can generally be overridden only by a right that is even more compelling or under circumstances where the rights of many conflict with the rights of a few. Any rights that animals may be said to have are rights that are based on consequentialist considerations and may be disregarded as soon as the utilitarian calculus changes. That is, animal "rights" may be overridden by purely consequentialist considerations that do not even purport to vindicate rights considerations. When the human interest is further protected by a right, as is usually the case, and not just by utilitarian considerations, then the animal's interest is cast aside that much quicker. In our society, *any* human benefit, including entertainment and, in the case of biomedical research, curiosity, will suffice to eliminate any policy-based right that an animal has, because the human interest is usually protected by a panoply of human respect-based rights, including the right to own property.

## Persons and Rights

The problems discussed above are, of course, not restricted to laws concerning animals. There were laws that protected slaves and that ostensibly gave "rights" to those persons, but the laws were seldom, if ever, enforced or at all meaningful to the slave. Although slaves were obviously people, the law treated them as "chattels," or as the personal property of their owners, rather than as persons.[67] As I showed earlier, the law may regulate the use of property by persons, but that regulation does not mean that the property acquires any rights.

Only persons—natural or legal—can have rights. Although slaves were regarded de jure as persons *and* property, they were de facto treated as property under the law in that any de jure rights they had as persons were simply ignored whenever there was any conflict between the slave and the slave owner. As chattels, slaves could be sold, willed, insured, mortgaged, and seized in payments of the owner's debts. Those who intentionally or negligently injured another's slave were liable to the owner in an action for damage to property. As a general rule, slaves could not enter into contracts, own property, sue or be sued, or live as other free persons with basic rights and duties.[68] Thus, the civil, legal personality of slaves was essentially nonexistent. Slaves could neither own a horse nor contract to buy one; but the law had no difficulty in recognizing that a slave could steal one. Professor Alan Watson writes that "procedure for slaves' crimes was more summary, penalties were more severe when the offender was a slave, and there were crimes in effect that could only be committed by slaves."[69]

In *Creswell's Executor v. Walker,* the Alabama Supreme Court described the status of a slave as "a complete annihilation of [the] will" and declared that a slave "has no legal mind, no *will* which the law can recognize."[70] Many laws supposedly gave protection to slaves, but in reality there was no protection at all. For example, legislation enacted in 1798 in North Carolina provided that the punishment for maliciously killing a slave should be the same as for the murder of a free person. This law, however, "did not apply to an outlawed slave, nor to a slave 'in the act of resistance to his lawful owner,' nor to a slave 'dying under moderate correction.' "[71] Tennessee had a similar law. A law that proscribes the murder of slaves and then permits three general—and easy to satisfy—exceptions, combined with a general prohibition against the testimony of slaves against free persons, is certainly less than an effective deterrent to slave murder. Moreover, despite the fact that the North Carolina law superficially supported the idea that slave owners could not kill their own slaves with impunity, courts were unwilling to hold owners liable for batteries committed upon their own slaves. In *State v. Mann,*[72] the court held that a master is not liable for a battery upon his slave because the law cannot protect a slave from his own master. Mann had leased for one year a slave named Lydia. Lydia ran away from Mann while he was in the process of whipping her. When Mann ordered Lydia to stop running and she refused, Mann shot and wounded her. Mann was convicted at trial, but the appellate court reversed the conviction because even a "cruel unreasonable battery" on one's own slave is not indictable. The court held that it could not "allow the right of the master to be brought into discussion in courts of justice. The slave, to remain a slave, must be made sensible that there is no appeal from his master."[73] In a Virginia case, *Commonwealth v. Turner,* the court determined that it had no jurisdiction to try the defendant slave owner who beat his slave with "rods, whips and sticks," and held that even if the beating was administered "wilfully and maliciously, violently, cruelly, immoderately, and excessively," the court was not empowered to act as long as the slave did not die.[74] The court distinguished private beatings from public chastisement, which might subject the master to liability, "not because it was a slave who was beaten, nor because the act was unprovoked or cruel; but, because ipso facto it disturbed the harmony of society; was offensive to public decency, and directly tended to a breach of the peace. The same would be the law, if a horse had been so beaten."[75]

There are many reasons the law was reluctant to impose criminal liability on slave owners for brutal acts committed on their slaves. As mentioned above, the law was concerned that slaves not think that there was an appeal from the exercise of dominion by the master. Another reason, which is actually adopted in anticruelty cases involving animals, is that the master has a self-interest in his property that should militate against the infliction of "unnecessary" punishment. " 'Where the battery was committed by the master himself, there would be no redress whatever, for the reason given in Exodus 21:21, "for he is his money." The powerful protection of the master's private interest would of itself go far to remedy this evil' "[76] Indeed, Virginia had a law that a slave owner who killed a slave as part of disciplining the slave could not be said to have acted with malice, and could, therefore, not be convicted of murder, because of a presumption that the owner would never intentionally destroy his property.[77] As Professor Watson has noted, "At most places at most times a reasonably economic owner would be conscious of the chattel value of slaves and thus would ensure some care in their treatment."[78] This is related to the notion, expressed by Justinian, that " 'it is to the advantage of the state that no one use his property badly.' "[79]

Although free persons could be punished under the criminal law for battering another's slave (as well as be liable for damages in a civil action for damaging another's property), it was clear that the concern in such cases was for the property interest of the owner. In one case, *State v. Hale,* the court noted that there was a sharp parallel between laws prohibiting "public cruelty inflicted upon animals" and "wanton barbarity exercised even by masters upon their slaves."[80] The court held that slaves are protected from wanton abuse by strangers because "it is a more effectual guarantee of [the master's] right of property when the slave is protected from wanton abuse . . . for it cannot be disputed that a slave is rendered less capable of performing this master's service when he finds himself exposed by the law to the capricious violence of every turbulent man in the community."[81] Although by the middle of the nineteenth century most Southern states had slave "welfare" laws that were intended to protect the "welfare" of slaves by providing for substantial punishment for the cruel treatment of slaves, "few Southerners suffered the penalties of these laws, since juries were reluctant to convict, and slaves, who were often the only witnesses to such crimes, were barred from testifying against white men."[82]

Although there is certainly an analogy between slavery and the treatment of animals as chattels, there are also important dissimilarities as well. As I mentioned earlier, many economists argue that slavery will cease to exist where relevant markets are permitted to operate. According to this theory, persons work harder for their own account than they do for a "master," and if they are permitted to do so, they will borrow against their future earnings in order to escape servitude through their purchase of freedom. Therefore, even if a society begins with an allocation of rights in favor of slave owners, the inefficiency of slavery (persons are more productive as free people) will eventually result in a redistribution of rights as long as slaves are legally able to purchase their freedom. Even if this theory is correct and slavery is, indeed, inefficient, as well as obscenely immoral, an allocation of property rights in animals is unlikely to result in a similar redistribution of rights in favor of animals. The reason is clear: animals, unlike slaves, cannot purchase their own freedom. Moreover, in a society that is heavily dependent on the institutional exploitation of animals, it is difficult, if not impossible, for affluent altruists to make any significant dent in reducing animal exploitation.

When sentient beings are regarded as property, laws that regulate the treatment of the beings are generally not effective to protect the interests that the law may recognize the beings to possess. In slavery, the law placed restraints upon cruel masters, and these rules "may resemble those today hindering cruelty to animals."[83] The problem is that such rules fail to protect the supposed beneficiaries, who are without rights and legal personhood and whose interests are being balanced against those of a full person, who possesses legal rights and, as property, the very being whose interests are being balanced against her own.

## Rights and Legal Welfarism

Throughout this chapter, I have maintained that there is a very real distinction between the normative notion of rights and the regulation of animal property that is involved in legal welfarism. I want briefly to address two arguments that welfarist regulation and rights collapse. Although these arguments are closely related to some of the ideas I have already discussed, it is important to address them explicitly. At the outset of this chapter, I mentioned the argument advanced by some, that virtually any position on animal protection—including that level of protection currently provided to animals under the law—may be couched in rights terminology. For example, the Animal Legal Defense Fund maintains that a law that prohibits "exploitation, cruelty, neglect, and abuse" can be said to create a *right* of humane treatment.[84] In Part II of this book, I demonstrate that anticruelty laws have little, if anything, to do with rights. For now, I argue as a general matter that *any* type of "right" to humane treatment is not really a right at all, although the right may, on first glance, appear to be similar to a claim right. The putative holder is not really empowered to seek any particular type of treatment, and the supposed right does not, in any manner, serve to protect any animal interests that cannot be traded away for consequential reasons. All that this supposed "right" entitles animals to is to have animals interests balanced against the human interests. That is, the "right" to humane treatment does not prohibit any type of conduct or entitle animals to be regarded as ends in themselves. Rather, the "right" entitles animals to be treated merely as a means to human ends in determining whether particular animal use constitutes "exploitation, cruelty, neglect, and abuse." And this is just another way of saying that animals are "entitled" to the benefit of a balancing process that will invariably tip in favor of the human interests and against the animal interests.

The second argument that the rights/welfare distinction collapses requires that we further refine our notion of utilitarian moral thought. There are two basic forms of utilitarian theory.

> Act-utilitarianism is the view that the rightness or wrongness of an action is to be judged by the consequences, good or bad, of the action itself. Rule-utilitarianism is the view that the rightness or wrongness of an action is to be judged by the goodness and badness of the consequences of a rule that everyone should perform the action in like circumstances.[85]

For example, an act-utilitarian faced with the decision whether to tell a lie would look to the probable consequences of that particular act of lying; that is, she would appeal directly to the principle of utility. The rule-utilitarian might appeal to the rule, such as "Lying destroys the moral fiber of society," and not tell the lie even though it would maximize consequences in the particular case.[86]

L. W. Sumner, a philosopher who has examined the rights/welfare distinction in the context of animal protection, has argued that although the rights/welfare approaches are theoretically different, the conceptual gap may be closed if rights theorists recognize that rights may be defeasible if respecting the right may cause "substantial aggregate harm."[87] Such an approach, it is argued, would still retain the deontological (i.e., nonconsequential) notion that rights would act as a barrier against simple utilitarian cost/benefit analysis. Welfarists, on the other hand, should recognize that rights have the ability to help the utilitarian achieve the goal of maximizing aggregate consequences better than appealing directly to the principle of utility.

Sumner's argument is actually nothing more than a version of the distinction between act- and rule-utilitarianism. Sumner essentially argues that we ought to use rights notions instead of appealing to the principle of utility in individual cases, because respecting rights will result in maximizing utility over a number of individual cases, but that rights can always be overridden in a particular case if the failure to do so will result in "substantial aggregate harm." In a sense, Sumner's argument may be understood in terms of the distinction between right-based and policy-based rights. For Sumner, rights are policy based in that they are thought to maximize utility, although the negative consequences of respecting rights in an individual case may well justify their abrogation.

Although Sumner's suggestion is provocative, even he recognizes that engrafting onto a rights framework the notion of defeasibility in light of "substantial aggregate harm" would result in a "messier" rights theory.[88] Rule-utilitarian theory, however much it resembles rights theory, is not rights theory, just as policy-based rights, however much they resemble respect-based rights, are not respect-based rights. Ultimately, the rule-utilitarian will not allow rights to act as "trumps" if respecting rights does not maximize utility. Moreover, as David Lyons has argued convincingly, the rule-utilitarian will engraft exceptions onto a rule in precisely those situations in which an act-utilitarian will break a rule in order to maximize the desirable consequences.[89]

## Conclusion

To say that an animal (or human) is property is to say that, as a matter of law, the animal (or human) has no value, or holds no interests, apart from the value accorded, or the interests recognized, by the individual property owner. In other words, to classify something as property is to defend its treatment solely as a means to the ends chosen by the property owner. Although there are laws—criminal and civil—that attempt to regulate animal use, these laws do not create "rights" for animals in the way that we normally use that term to describe a type of protection that does not evaporate in the face of consequential considerations.

Instead, the "rights" supposedly created by these laws simply serve to facilitate our use of a "balancing" process to decide animal issues, but because these regulatory laws do not create rights, the entire balancing process is futile. As Nozick suggests, we have Kantianism for humans and utilitarianism for animals. Such a system provides only that level of protection that is consistent with facilitating the use of animals as means to human ends. Any utilitarian considerations in favor of animals are, in light of the property status of animals, likely to establish that level of animal protection consistent with maximizing the wealth represented by animal "resources."

# Part I Conclusion

IN THIS portion of the book, I introduced and described the doctrine of legal welfarism. According to legal welfarism, animals are the property of humans, and the regulation of our use of animal property is limited to that conduct that represents a "waste" of animal resources without any recognized social benefit. That is, although the law prohibits "inhumane treatment" or the infliction of "unnecessary" suffering on animals, the law limits its proscription to that conduct that can be said to represent purely gratuitous animal exploitation.

Legal welfarism is the only possible way to explain our almost universal embrace of principles of "kindness" to animals while we socially tolerate continuing and unequivocally barbarous conduct that almost no one would defend as "necessary." Indeed, although virtually every reader of this book will agree with the notion that animals ought not to be made to suffer "unnecessarily," many readers will be active consumers of animal products. The use of animal products as human food is certainly not necessary, and is probably harmful, especially when compared to the health benefits of a vegetarian diet. So, even though we are all "against" inflicting "unnecessary" pain on animals, most of us are unwilling to do what we can as individuals: give up eating animal products.

What we do tolerate as "humane" is so unquestionably *inhumane* that the conduct *could not* be justified morally in the absence of an explanation grounded in the assumptions that animals are property, that property valuation is best done by property owners, and that animal "welfare" should not go much (or any) further than what facilitates the production of "good" data from laboratory animals, of lean meat or cheap meat or whatever it is that consumers value in meat, or of enough animals so that hunters can kill "game."

Indeed, legal welfarism is so deeply ingrained that even when people regard animals as more than property and as members of human families, the law refuses to recognize this nonproperty status. The law excludes animals from the scope of legal concern and enforces this exclusion through the doctrine of judicial standing, according to which most animal interests are disqualified from the outset from even being considered in courts of law.

115

Finally, the regulation of the human use of animal property does not thereby create animal rights. On the contrary, as long as animals are regarded, as a matter of law, as means to human ends, legal standards that require "humane" treatment or prohibit "unnecessary" suffering will require nothing more than that animal interests be balanced against human interests—a balance that always weighs in favor of human property rights.

In the next section of the book, I apply this general view—that the regulation of the use of animal property does not create animal rights—to a common form of regulation represented by anticruelty statutes.

# PART II

---

## *A General Application of the Theory: Anticruelty Statutes*

These little animals, however worthless they may be, have a way of endearing themselves, especially to the women and children of the family.

*Miller v. State*

# CHAPTER SIX

## *The Purposes of Anticruelty Statutes*

IN PART I, I argued that laws that protect animal "interests" cannot be said to give rights to animals, because animals are regarded as a matter of law as means to human ends and *all* animal interests are tradable. Here I develop and test that hypothesis in a concrete context that involves the oldest and most salient form of regulation involving the use of animals by humans—anticruelty statutes.[1] I argue that contrary to what is commonly thought, these statutes do not have as a primary purpose the protection of animals and that they do not create rights for animals. To put the matter in terms of the thesis of legal welfarism, anticruelty statutes—like all regulations of animal use—focus our attention on considerations of "humane" treatment without revealing the normative assumptions that render that word meaningless in terms of the level of animal protection actually provided.

Some of the limitations inherent in anticruelty statutes are demonstrated clearly in a 1986 California case, *Jett v. Municipal Court.*[2] California has one of the nation's toughest anticruelty laws, and enforcement of the law appears to be more rigorous than in many other states. Jett owned Rocky, a fifty-year-old Aldabra tortoise, and exhibited him at a petting zoo located at a shopping center. In response to complaints of animal cruelty, local humane society officials investigated and found that Rocky had infected eyes, a cracked shell, diarrhea, dehydration, and toenails worn to the quick. The humane society confiscated Rocky and treated him for these various ailments, which, the court found, were "all indicative of lack of care and attention."[3] Jett was charged with inflicting needless suffering on an animal and permitting an animal to be on a street or lot without proper care or attention, both misdemeanor violations of the state anticruelty statute. He was convicted and was sentenced to pay a $500 fine and to relinquish ownership of Rocky.[4] Jett appealed his conviction and also sought the return of Rocky.

The court held that despite the fact that Jett's appeal of his criminal conviction was still pending, he was entitled to seek recovery of "his property."[5] The appellate court concluded that the trial court had no power to divest Jett of his ownership of Rocky. According to the court, California law did not provide for forfeiture of the animal in an animal cruelty case unless fighting animals were involved, and the court denied that "Rocky belongs in the ring."[6] The state argued that Rocky "should be equated with a child" and that "Jett's rights to Rocky should be terminated as parental rights must yield when necessary to protect the child's best interest." The court replied that although "a child preparing for homework or cleaning a bedroom may exhibit turtle-like qualities or creep toward school in turtle pace," the court refused to treat Rocky like a child for purposes of terminating Jett's ownership rights. The court concluded that "Jett is Rocky's owner and the [trial] court had no authority to divest him of ownership."[7] Rocky was ultimately returned to Jett, whose criminal convictions for violating the anticruelty statute were ultimately reversed.

*Jett* is illustrative of judicial attitudes toward enforcement of anticruelty statutes. First, courts often do not take violations of these statutes very seriously, as demonstrated by the supposedly "humorous" statements quoted above as well as by others in the opinion.[8] If *Jett* had involved child abuse, the court's attempts at humor would surely have been viewed as displaying bad taste, at the very least.

Second, the *Jett* court completely disregarded the spirit of the anticruelty law by holding that a court may *never* divest an owner of property rights in an animal, no matter how badly the owner treats the animal, unless the animal is used for fighting purposes. Such a ruling means that even if an owner is convicted of cruelty on multiple occasions or is convicted of heinously torturing an animal, a court has no authority to order the forfeiture of the animals. Under these circumstances, a conviction for cruelty is no victory whatsoever for the animal, whose owner may "retaliate" with even more cruel conduct. It is unlikely that the legislature intended such a result, and in any event, the failure of the law to provide explicitly for any meaningful protection for the animal demonstrates the general ineffectiveness of these statutes.

Third, the property status of animals precludes courts from fashioning sensible remedies that protect animals. In *Jett*, the state argued that Rocky should be treated like a child and that Jett's rights to Rocky should be extinguished in light of Rocky's interests. The court responded by observing that although parents have "custody" of their children, "Jett *owns* Rocky."[9] Jett's ownership interest in Rocky provided the basis for the court's refusal to consider whether it was in Rocky's interests to be taken from Jett. Even if the anticruelty statute provided Rocky with some "rights," it is difficult to understand what these rights were or how they were enforced for Rocky's benefit. Again, property considerations defeat the goal of animal protection that these statutes are supposedly designed to advance.

Fourth, the penalty for Jett's unquestionably cruel treatment of Rocky was $500. A fine so small would probably not have any deterrent impact on those who exploit or abuse animals, especially when that abuse is profitable, in which case such an insignificant amount might be considered nothing more than a cost of conducting business.[10]

Fifth, the conviction was ultimately reversed, which seems remarkable given the facts of the case.

## The Protection of People Through the Protection of Animals

Cruelty to animals was not an offense at common law.[11] Before the adoption of anticruelty statutes, domestic animals were accorded minimal protection through statutory prohibitions of malicious mischief and trespass. Malicious mischief statutes typically required that the offending act manifest malice toward the owner of an injured or killed animal.[12] Where the act manifested malice toward the animal but not toward the owner, the act did not generally constitute malicious mischief.[13] Courts generally allowed malice toward the owner to be presumed or inferred from the circumstances surrounding the incident.[14]

The shift from malicious mischief statutes to anticruelty statutes was supposed to represent a shift from pure property protection to a concern for animals whether they were owned or not. States began to introduce anticruelty statutes in the mid- to late nineteenth century. Two notable exceptions were the Massachusetts Bay Colony, whose 1641 legal code protected domestic animals from cruelty, and the state of New York, where as early as 1822 courts had held that wanton cruelty to an animal was a misdemeanor at common law.[15] For the most part, anticruelty statutes provide for minimal criminal penalties for those who engage in the prohibited conduct. Since cruelty to animals is a statutory offense, any determination whether the conduct complained of constitutes cruelty depends largely upon the language of the particular statute involved. The statutes designate the scope of protection, the type of animals protected, the conduct prohibited, the mental state of the actor, and the penalty. Most statutes apply to "any animal."[16] Many states prohibit depriving an animal of "necessary sustenance" and failing to provide food, water, or shelter.[17] Some states prohibit failing to provide animals with "necessary sustenance" without going further,[18] and some mention food or water but do not talk explicitly about "necessary sustenance."[19] Other provisions that are common include prohibitions against abandonment[20] and poisoning,[21] and requirements to provide sanitary living conditions[22] and humane transportation.[23]

A review of several statutes demonstrates that despite the variation among them, there are striking similarities. For example, Alabama prohibits the intentional or reckless subjecting of "any animal" to "cruel mistreatment" or "cruel neglect," and the killing or injuring "without good cause [of] any animal belonging to another."[24] The penalty for violation is imprisonment up to six months or a fine of up to $1,000, or both. California has a more complicated statute that prohibits the malicious or intentional maiming, torturing, mutilation, wounding, or killing of an animal, which includes "every dumb creature."[25] In another section of the statute, California imposes liability upon those who, without malice or intent (i.e., negligently or with no culpable state of mind), overdrive, overload, drive when overloaded, overwork, torture, cruelly beat or kill, or cause any of these acts to occur.[26] The former section carries a fine of up to $20,000 or imprisonment up to one year, or both. The statute defines "torture," "torment," and "cruelty" to include any act or omission "whereby unnecessary or unjustifiable physical pain or suffering is caused or permitted."[27] Delaware explicitly excludes "fish, crustacea or mollusca"[28] from the scope of its statute, which, like the Alabama statute, prohibits one from recklessly or intentionally subjecting an animal to "cruel mistreatment" or "cruel neglect," killing or injuring an animal belonging to another "without legal privilege or consent of the owner," and "cruelly or unnecessarily" killing or injuring an animal belonging to oneself or another.[29] "Cruelty" is defined to include "every act or omission to act whereby unnecessary or unjustifiable physical pain or suffering is caused or permitted."[30] "Cruelty to animals" includes "mistreatment of any animal or neglect of any animal under the care and control of the neglector, whereby unnecessary or unjustifiable physical pain or suffering is caused."[31] The statute gives "unjustifiable beating of an animal" as an example of "cruelty to animals." New York's law, which served as a model for those of many other states, states that one "who overdrives, overloads, tortures or cruelly beats or unjustifiably injures, maims, mutilates or kills any animal, whether wild or tame, and whether belonging to himself or to another, or deprives any animal of necessary sustenance, food or drink, or neglects or refuses to furnish it such sustenance or drink,"[32] or causes any of these acts, or abandons an animal,[33] or fails to provide food, drink, and shelter to a confined or impounded animal[34] is guilty of a cruelty offense. "Torture" and "cruelty" are defined to include every act or omission "whereby unjustifiable physical pain, suffering or death is caused or permitted."[35]

In order to understand the purpose of these statutes, it is important to differentiate between *direct* and *indirect* duties. A direct duty is one that is owned directly to the animal and does not merely concern the animal.[36] Even if the duty is owed directly to the animal, that relationship does not necessarily establish the further proposition that the animal has a right. For example, although John Chipman Gray maintained that the duties imposed by anticruelty statutes were owed directly to the animals, he refused to conclude that animals had any legal rights, because animals were not "moral agents." This notion is closely related to the idea that animals cannot claim their rights and, so, cannot be holders of any rights.

An *indirect* duty imposes an obligation that may concern animals but is not owed to the animal directly. For example, in the cases of veterinary malpractice referred to in Chapter Three, the duty of care is owed to the owner of the animal, not to the animal. Again, when I come to discuss animal experimentation, I advance the argument that most duties concerning animals are indirect duties designed to reassure the public and not to recognize animal interests. If the duty is owed only indirectly to animals and directly to human beings, then it makes no sense to speak of the indirect duty as giving rise to a legal right for the animals to whom the duty is owed.

Anticruelty laws purport to impose both direct and indirect duties. A stated purpose of these statutes is to protect animals through inculcating "a humane regard for the rights and feelings of the brute creation by reproving evil and indifferent tendencies in human nature in its intercourse with animals."[37] Anticruelty laws are said to "recognize and attempt to protect some abstract rights in all that animate creation, made subject to man by the creation, from the largest and noblest to the smallest and most insignificant."[38] As such, the duties imposed by these statutes are arguably owed directly to animals. As I mentioned above, however, the content of the duty owed would, for the most part, be nothing more than a duty to treat animals "humanely."[39] And as seen in the previous chapter, a right to humane treatment is really no right at all because the only benefit to animals is an entitlement to have their interests balanced against those of humans, whose interests (especially in property) are protected by claims of respect-based right.

Although some cases hold that anticruelty statutes are intended "for the protection of the animals themselves,"[40] other cases maintain that these statutes have a dual purpose "to protect these animals [and] to conserve public morals."[41] The former purpose is considered as secondary to the latter, and most courts agree that these statutes are intended to prevent humans from acting cruelly toward one another and regard cruel treatment of animals as leading to cruel treatment of humans. In the *Model Penal Code,* prepared by the American Law Institute, the drafters state that their review of state anticruelty legislation indicated that "the object of [anticruelty] statutes seems to have been to prevent outrage to the sensibilities of the community."[42] As such, the duty imposed is indirect because it concerns animals but is not owed directly to animals. Rather, under this view, the purpose of the statutes is to improve human character and not to protect animals. It is as if laws against murder had as their primary justification preservation of public morals; in such a case, the duty not to murder would be considered indirect, since it would be owed, not to the individual potential victim, but to society as a whole. Anticruelty laws have sought the improvement of human beings through the development of their sensibilities. For example, in *Stephens v. State,* the court condemned cruelty to animals because it "tends inevitably to cruelty to men. . . . [H]uman beings should be kind and just to dumb brutes; if for no other reason than to learn how to be kind and just to each other."[43] In *Bland v. People,* the court upheld the constitutionality of a law prohibiting the ownership of horses with docked tails, holding that "constantly seeing the disfigured and mutilated animals tends to corrupt public morals."[44] Similarly, in *Commonwealth v. Higgins,* the Massachusetts Supreme Court noted that a statute that prohibited trapping animals in a manner that caused suffering was "directed against acts which may be thought to have a tendency to dull humanitarian feelings and to corrupt the morals of those who observe or have knowledge of those acts."[45] A particularly interesting statement of the indirect-duty theory occurred in *Miller v. State,*[46] in which the defendant's conviction for shooting his neighbor's dog in front of his neighbor's wife and children was reversed. Although the appellate court did not think that the defendant violated the anticruelty statute, it remonstrated the defendant for committing "a serious breach of propriety and a lack of neighborly consideration in killing the dog in [the owner's] yard in the presence of the [owner's] family. They doubtless loved the little fice. These little animals, however worthless they may be, have a way of endearing themselves, especially to the women and children of the family."[47] The explicit rejection of any duty owed directly to the animal is apparent.

This notion of indirect duty continues to be articulated even in more modern cases. For example, in *Knox v. Massachusetts S.P.C.A.*,[48] the court quoted and endorsed the above language from *Higgins* in a case involving the use of animals as prizes at a fair. In holding that cockfighting violated the anticruelty statute, the Supreme Court of Utah, in *Peck v. Dunn*,[49] traced the evolution of society's view toward cockfighting, noting that

> over the centuries the disposition to look upon such brutalities with favor or approval has gradually lessened, and compassion and concern for man's fellow creatures of the earth has increased to the extent that is now quite generally thought that the witnessing of animals fighting, injuring and perhaps killing one another is a cruel and barbarous practice discordant to man's better instincts and so offensive to his finer sensibilities that it is demeaning to morals.

The court stated that "legislation against [cruelty] is justified for the purpose of regulating morals and promoting the good order and general welfare of society."[50] In *C. E. America, Inc. v. Antinori*,[51] the Florida Supreme Court held that the plaintiff could not lawfully hold a "Portuguese-style bloodless simulated bullfight" in which the bull would not be killed, because the event would violate the state anticruelty law as well as a separate statute that prohibited fights between a person and a bull. In explaining its holding, the court noted that such an exhibition would necessarily "[shock] the sensibilities of any person possessed of humane instincts."[52] Similarly, in *Brackett v. State,* Georgia's anticruelty statute was interpreted to protect "public sensibilities."[53]

Although the reported cases rely on both justifications—protection of animals (direct duty) and improvement of human character (indirect duty)—and the commentators seem to ignore the implications of these two justifications, I believe that questions of animal protection really have little, if anything, to do with animal protection and everything to do with issues of human character. A close examination of some features of these statutes indicates quite clearly that they have an exclusively humanocentric focus, and the duties that they impose give rise to no corresponding rights for animals.

## Anticruelty Statutes and the Protection of Property

The most interesting characteristic of anticruelty statutes for our purposes concerns the distinction between these statutes and statutes that provided relief for malicious mischief. In the case of malicious mischief statutes, the duty was owed to the property owner simply because that person owned the property, and the nature of the property was irrelevant to the obligation. Malicious mischief statutes

pertained to inanimate objects, such as rocks, as well as to animals. In the case of anticruelty statutes, the duty generally extends beyond those animals that are owned by people and, in many states, includes "any animal," defined as "all living creatures except human beings," although some states protect "the property interests of a person in the ownership of an animal."[54] Anticruelty statutes "must be considered wholly irrespective of property, or of the public peace, or of the inconveniences of nuisances. The misdemeanors attempted to be defined may be as well perpetrated upon a man's own property as another's."[55] Although there was supposedly a dramatic difference between the theory of the anticruelty statutes and that of the malicious mischief statutes, the distinction collapsed in at least four respects. That is, anticruelty statutes, like malicious mischief statutes, also focus primarily on property concerns.

First, as seen above, the primary rationale for the anticruelty statutes is essentially that cruelty to animals has a detrimental impact on the moral development of human beings. In both anticruelty reasoning and malicious mischief reasoning, the animal is viewed as instrumental to some goal of humans, and the duty to the animal is indirect. Whether that goal involves the refinement of moral sensibilities or the right of people to enjoy their property rights in animals and other chattels is, from this point of view, irrelevant. Moreover, the emphasis on animals as means to ends does nothing to change the status of animals in society; they still remain property or, in the case of wild animals, potential property.

Second, the anticruelty statutes are, and have always been, limited in ways that effectively protect property interests in animals and protect nonanimal property interests as against animal interests. The first limitation is that cruelty may be justified when it is necessary to "assist development or proper growth, fit the animal for ordinary use, or to fulfill the part for which by common consent it is designed."[56] So, for example, the branding and castration of animals, and the killing of animals for food, either in slaughterhouses or for sport, are generally exempt. As a general matter, experiments on "laboratory animals" are also exempt either explicitly in the statute or through judicial interpretation. The second limitation is that cruelty may be inflicted in order to discipline or govern the animal. The training of dogs and the discipline of horses, unless excessive, are not prohibited. In *State v. Avery*, the court upheld a cruelty conviction but made it clear that the beating of an animal, if "solely for the purpose of training, however severe it might be, . . . would not be malicious, within the meaning of the statute, and therefore it would be no offense."[57] In *People ex rel. Walker v. Court*, the court held that although a dog is not a "beast of burden," it is "not cruelty to train and subject him to any useful purpose. His use upon a 'treadmill' or 'inclined plane,' or in any mode by which his strength or docility may be made serviceable to men, is commendable and not criminal."[58] Finally, if the cruelty is inflicted pursuant to the protection of a person or, more commonly, the protection of property, it is permitted. For example, in *Miller v. State*,[59] the defendant was convicted of cruelty to animals when he shot and killed a dog while the dog was on the owner's premises. The defendant claimed that the owner gave him permission to kill the dog because the dog was worrying the defendant's sheep; the owner admitted to giving permission to kill the animal, but only if the dog was found actually in the act of bothering sheep. The court reversed the conviction, holding that the defendant did not need to catch the dog worrying the sheep, but might kill the dog as long as the "killing was a fair act of prudence on the part of the person doing the killing, reasonable regard being had as to the value of the dog, the value of the property menaced, and the probability of present or future depredations." As long as the dog showed "itself to be a menace to property more valuable than itself," the dog might be killed.[60] Indeed, although the law generally forbids the use of deadly physical force against persons who threaten property,[61] the use of deadly physical force against animals who threaten property is routinely, although not ubiquitously, permitted even when the property interests at stake are relatively trivial.

Many of the reported cases interpreting anticruelty statutes involve the killing of animals in order to protect property, and the law has always permitted deadly physical force to be used against animals in the defense of property. For example, in *State v. Jones,* the state had an exception to the anticruelty statute that permitted the killing of an animal who " 'is found injuring or posing a threat to any person, farm animal or property.' "[62] Jones shot a dog he found destroying Easter baskets that he had purchased for his children. The court held that the exception applied to property other than farm property and that the statute authorized the killing of the dog.[63] In *Hunt v. State,*[64] a shepherd, in the mistaken belief that a hunting dog was about to harm his sheep, shot the dog. The court held that the shooting did not constitute cruelty in that the statute was designed to "inculcate a humane regard for the rights and feelings of the brute creation" but was not meant to limit humankind's "proper dominion" over animals.[65] The court made clear that if the defendant sincerely and reasonably believed it was necessary to kill an animal in order to protect property, killing would not violate the anticruelty law even if the defendant's apprehension was unwarranted. In *People v. Jones,*[66] the court reversed the conviction of a defendant who castrated a bull who was bothering his cows. The court stated that if a reasonable person believed that the castration was necessary to the enjoyment of her property, then there could be no malice. The court also held that evidence that a cross-bred calf would have been worth much less than a full-blood calf was admissible to show that the defendant did not act with malice when he castrated the bull, but was acting only to protect his economic self-interest. In *Hodge v. State,*[67] the defendant placed a steel-jaw trap in a bucket of slop and placed the bucket in his garden in order to catch a dog who was making "nightly incursions" on the defendant's property. A "valuable" dog came along and attempted to eat the slop, thus triggering the trap. The dog's tongue was entirely ripped out. In reversing the defendant's conviction under the anticruelty statute, the court noted that the injured dog was clearly the animal responsible for trespassing on the defendant's property and that "if a night-prowling dog, in the habit of invading premises and breaking up hen's nests, and sucking the eggs, while so transgressing is caught in a steel-trap, though set by the owner for that purpose, and thus suffers pain or mutilation, we are not prepared to say that it would be *needless* torture or mutilation within the meaning of the statute." The court held that the statute was "not intended to deprive a man of the right to protect himself, his premises and property, against the intrusions of worthless, mischievous or vicious animals."[68] Absolutely nothing in the opinion indicated that the defendant considered or pursued alternatives to the action he took, and the court showed absolutely no interest in questioning whether the defendant had any other, less dangerous options available. Rather, the court held the statute was never intended to address the situation in which a person sought to protect her property against the actions of animals. Although the use of deadly physical force against animals in order to protect property is limited by some modern cases and differs by jurisdiction, the fact remains that property concerns are sufficient to justify killing an animal, because the animal is itself regarded at best as property, whereas deadly physical force is virtually never permitted to be used against human beings in the defense of property.[69]

The third way in which the distinction between anticruelty and malicious mischief statutes collapses involves the property status of animals as it affects the interpretation of anticruelty statutes through a presumption similar to the one mentioned above in connection with slavery—that people took care of their property.[70] This presumption finds its origins in early-nineteenth-century common law. For example, in *Callaghan v. Society for the Prevention of Cruelty to Animals,* an Irish court, in upholding the propriety of dehorning cattle—a frightfully painful procedure—stated that "self-interest would prevent any farmer from resorting to a practice of this nature, if the result were merely to cause useless pain or torture."[71] The notion is often articulated explicitly in American cases. For example, in *Commonwealth v. Barr,*[72] the defendant was convicted of cruelty to animals because he had ordered his employees to feed his chickens a diet of mangels, or German beets, sour milk, and refuse, and no grain; forty of the chickens died, and most of the rest were ill. This dietary decision was apparently made by the defendant after consultation with his farm manager, but there is nothing to indicate whether the decision was made based upon any reliable information, and indeed, the appellate court described the decision to change the diet from grain to beets as an "experiment." The court reversed the conviction, holding that if the defendant changed the diet with a sincere belief that mangels were proper food for chickens, then the defendant could not be said to have exhibited a reckless disregard for the animals. The court noted that "[d]ead chickens, however, were the defendant's loss, and as he was their owner, the natural inference would arise that he would not deliberately or with gross carelessness bring about a result which was disastrous to himself."[73] In another more recent case, *Commonwealth v. Vonderheid,*[74] the defendant was convicted of cruelty to animals in connection with his operation of a traveling circus and roadside zoo. Humane law enforcement officers found that the animals were kept in a crowded condition, had insufficient food and bedding, and that the building leaked water. The reviewing court held a de novo hearing and took the unusual step of visiting the premises personally and concluded that this personal visit "dispelled any feeling of sorrow for these animals except that which is naturally present within a human being on seeing any wild animal in a cage whether it be in a circus, on television, or in a roadside menagerie."[75] In reversing the conviction, the court stated:

> Defendant is endeavoring to make his livelihood from the use of these animals. He has expended large sums of money to secure them, and he most certainly is not about to impair his investment by improper food or shelter. Even though some of the Southern planters before the Civil War may have cruelly treated some slaves, on the other hand, the slave that produced was well fed and housed by reason of their livelihood to the planter.[76]

The court went on to note that "businessmen of the immediate communities are concerned for the retention of [the roadside zoo] because it has in the past attracted many persons to the vicinity, and it is their opinion that their business would suffer a considerable blow in the summertime if this attraction was not permitted to remain in their vicinity."[77] Similarly, in *State v. Smith*,[78] the court found that an indictment for malicious mischief was insufficient because it did not aver that the animal was owned by another. The court relied, in part, on the notion that people do not abuse their animal property out of self-interest: "Our slaves are protected from the cruelty of masters by law, because they are persons as well as property. All other property is wisely left to the sufficient protection of self-interest of the owner, and the prevalent moral sentiment on that subject."[79]

Fourth, anticruelty statutes have never been interpreted to interfere with the killing of one's own animal even when such killing was not "necessary" in that the owner could have sought different arrangements for the animal. For example, in *Miller v. State,* discussed above,[80] the court said that if the dog owner had given consent to the killing of the dog, then the defendant's killing could not violate the anticruelty laws. The court held that although there may be instances in which an owner may be indicted for cruelty to animals, the owner has a privilege "of killing in some swift and comparatively painless manner a dog that is worthless or that has evinced dangerous tendencies; and if he may lawfully kill it, he may also consent that another person may do the execution." The court reasoned that if an owner could not kill her own animal, she might incur "considerable burden[s]," especially in the case of "a worthless cur-bitch," because the owner would then be obligated under the anticruelty statutes to provide care for the animal and her progeny because "cruelty may consist in neglect as well as in some overt act."[81] In *Smith,* discussed above, the court held that an indictment was defective because it failed to aver that the animal was owned by another and that the law should not attempt to regulate the use of animal property by the owner of that property. Similarly, in *Cinadr v. State,* the court, which emphasized that despite anticruelty laws "the right of property in domestic animals is not open to question," reversed the defendant's conviction for "needlessly" killing a hog, because "the exercise of judgment by the owner to slaughter [her own] animals [is not] the proper subject" of the anticruelty law.[82] *Miller* and *Cinadr* represent a position that is by and large accepted unanimously: the law generally does not require that an owner exert even minimal effort to make alternative arrangements for the animal that may result in the preservation of the animal's life. *Miller* illustrates that the application of anticruelty statutes to particular acts, such as the killing of one's own animal when there is absolutely no need (apart from convenience) to do so, is inextricably intertwined with property considerations that relate directly to the value of the animal.

So, although the anticruelty statutes were supposed to differ from malicious mischief statutes in that the latter were concerned with property, whereas the former were not, the putative distinction is, at best, meaningful in only a relatively insignificant way and is misleading. To the extent that anticruelty statutes apply — and they apply to a relatively minuscule amount of cruel or painful behavior directed toward animals — the statutes generally do not distinguish between owned and unowned animals, although many statutes provide higher penalties for killing the animal of another, which, of course, is a property notion. The distinction is misleading for the most part because virtually all instances of cruel conduct escape proscription because the thrust of these property-driven limitations is effectively to exclude from the scope of coverage of these statutes every act of cruelty that occurs as part of institutionalized animal exploitation. Institutionalized exploitation is, of course, based on the notion that animals are property and are properly treated as means to human ends. To say that animal exploitation is "institutionalized" is to say that society recognizes that the activity of which the exploitation is a part has some legitimate value for human beings. To put it another way, institutionalized exploitation is that which society (or some part thereof) has recognized as economically efficient or whose costs (including the "external" costs of animal suffering) are outweighed by the economic benefits of allowing property owners to determine the most highly valued use of their animal property. Once an activity is regarded as legitimate, animal killing or suffering that occurs as part of the activity is acceptable, and the balancing supposedly required by anticruelty statutes has already been done implicitly, to the animal's loss. That is, by virtue of its location within the ambit of some socially acceptable conduct, the activity is automatically deemed "humane" or "necessary." The only activities that remain to be prohibited by such statutes are those where no socially recognized benefit can be traced to the animal killing or suffering. In a society whose norms permit "benefit" to include the pleasure that comes from shooting captive pigeons or, as I discussed in Chapter One, the development of "sympathy for living things" that comes from the painful killing of animals in a high school biology class, virtually nothing — apart from blatant acts of sadism — will constitute a violation of the anticruelty statutes.

A review of the operation of these statutes demonstrates that they do not prohibit any use of animals that forms a part of any traditionally accepted activity. I call this the "institutional" structure of animal exploitation. Anticruelty laws are for the most part useless against such activities as hunting, fishing, target practice with live animals, scientific experiments involving live animals, particularly painful and stressful methods of agricultural husbandry and slaughter, circuses, zoos, or the uses of animals for other forms of entertainment. These activities are either explicitly exempted from the scope of the anticruelty statutes or are implicitly exempted because they are accepted activities and because incidental animal suffering is regarded as necessary to them. In all of these institutional forms of animal exploitation, the human participants and exploiters are necessarily committed to the view that animals are property that may be exploited, and all institutional uses are thought to involve economic benefit that is generated directly by animal exploitation. That is, the division between those activities that are considered cruel and those that are not is determined not by the nature of the action involved but rather by property-oriented concerns. For example, the actions incidental to animal slaughter for food purposes are most certainly "cruel," according to any ordinary understanding of that notion. Nevertheless, we do not regard such actions as cruel, because the activity is socially acceptable: the use of animals for food by those who own the animals is thought to provide social benefit in that the meat industry generates social wealth. If there is no economic benefit generated by the activity, or if the economic benefit is considered insignificant or is accompanied by other opportunity costs that we deem to be undesirable, such as the moral approbation connected to gambling that occurs at animal fights, then the activity is considered to be "cruel" even if, from the point of view of the animal involved, it does not differ in any material way from conduct considered to be "humane" or not cruel. If the activity is considered "cruel," it generally does not involve any economic benefit and may be said to represent a socially undesirable use of property because overall social wealth is diminished. In many ways, anticruelty cases reflect the notion articulated by Justinian in the context of Roman slavery: "It is to the advantage of the state that no one use his property badly." To the extent that the use of animals generates economic and social benefit, there is usually no question that the conduct falls outside the scope of these laws; where, however, the conduct is without corresponding benefit, and where the only or the primary value comes from the satisfaction of sadistic impulses, then the conduct, which can only represent a minute fraction of the conduct that would be called "cruel" in everyday language, will be prohibited by the law.

An interesting example of this phenomenon is found in *State v. Wrobel*,[83] a Connecticut case decided in 1964. Wrobel, a dog warden, responded to a call concerning several stray dogs who were gathered around the home of a Mrs. Parker "because a female dog she owned was in heat." When Wrobel arrived on the scene, he observed two stray dogs, one of which he caught and placed in his truck without incident. He placed a noose around the neck of the other dog, but the dog slipped the noose, and when Wrobel attempted to replace the noose, the dog bit him on the hand and arm. Wrobel then lifted the dog by one hind leg and carried him to the truck, and when the dog "locked its teeth onto the defendant's knee," Wrobel "seized the dog by both hind legs and slammed [the dog] against the truck." The dog, an apparently remarkable animal, then "locked its jaws onto defendant's right foot." Wrobel, who was still holding the dog upside down by his hind legs, "stepped on the dog's head with his left foot and pinned the dog to the ground."[84] The trial judge had instructed the jury that " 'cruelty' " was defined as " 'unjustifiable physical pain or suffering' " and that the jury had to decide whether Wrobel's acts were justified " 'in the performance of his duties' " as dog warden.[85] The jury returned a verdict against Wrobel, indicating that they found that Wrobel's actions were unjustified. Wrobel's conviction was reversed by the appellate court for several reasons, but the one relevant for present purposes concerned the jury instruction on justification. The appellate court held that the trial court's instruction on justification was "too abrupt."[86] According to the appellate court, "it was not enough, for the guidance of the jury, to define cruelty in its general sense or abstract connotation. What is cruelty under one set of circumstances may not be cruelty in another."[87] Although Wrobel's actions may have appeared "to be cruel to bystanders . . . [Wrobel's actions] may [have been] the practicable and reasonable means to accomplish the capture and impounding of the offending dog, and therefore not within the statutory meaning of cruelty."[88] In short, the jury should have considered Wrobel's actions as occurring in the context of animal control, a socially desirable activity that permitted Wrobel to beat, injure, or kill a stray animal if necessary. The appellate court seemed to think that the jury may have judged Wrobel's actions without reference to his being a dog warden, that is, that they considered his actions cruel "in the abstract." But the jury clearly was aware that Wrobel was a dog warden, and was similarly aware that the dog warden was authorized and required to impound stray animals. Nevertheless, the jury decided that Wrobel's actions were cruel because they involved more force than was necessary.

What is ultimately interesting about *Wrobel* is not whether the jury was indeed instructed properly concerning Wrobel's duties and privileges as a dog warden. Rather, what is interesting is that the appellate court inadvertently articulated the dichotomy that ultimately renders anticruelty statutes ineffective. The court was concerned that cruelty not be understood as an "abstract" proposition, that it be considered as part of whatever context in which it occurred. The court noted that Connecticut law permitted a person to kill a dog if the dog bit the person when the person was not on the premises of the owner or keeper of the dog at the time of the bite. The law was silent about the reason for the attack; the person was authorized to kill the dog even if the dog was provoked into attacking by the person. The permission to use lethal force against a dog who initiates an attack or is provoked into attacking represents a judgment about the use of force against animals that is qualitatively different from the amount of force that the law permits human beings to use against one another in situations of self-defense.[89] Therefore, the law has already balanced human and animal interests before a jury ever determines whether particular conduct is cruel or unnecessary. If that context permits force to be used against animals, then "cruelty" must be understood as conduct that goes *beyond* whatever force is justified by the social context. This framework, then, masks an important normative premise—that the institution or context justifies a particular level of suffering (or even death). The balancing of animal and human interests involves consideration of human institutions that themselves legitimate suffering in the first place. The only determination for the jury to make is whether conduct goes beyond the level of suffering that is inherently permitted in the first place, and there will be, as the appellate court obviously found in *Wrobel,* a de facto presumption against finding the level of force or suffering inflicted on the animal to be excessive.

In effect, the appellate court in *Wrobel* rejected the jury's verdict because the court believed that the jury did not sufficiently understand that the statutory scheme already permitted the infliction of suffering or death in situations in which an ordinary-language interpretation would not consider the suffering or death as necessary or humane. Accordingly, the appellate court ordered a new trial to ensure that the jury would understand that the question was not whether the infliction of suffering was necessary or humane as the jury would ordinarily understand those terms, but rather whether the conduct was unlawful in light of a statutory scheme that already permitted conduct that would not be considered necessary or humane. Indeed, some states, such as Connecticut, explicitly allow for the killing of dogs who bite, and this privilege to kill legitimizes force that would be excessive if applied in the context of human conduct.[90]

Further, to the extent that courts focus on whether there is any benefit—hence, any legitimacy—that results from the conduct, it should come as no surprise that the most commonly accepted form of benefit is respect for the freedom of a property owner to use her property or to inflict suffering or death on an animal in order to protect her property or that of another. Although the court in *Wrobel* did not discuss property issues explicitly, the court's description recounts the fact that Wrobel was called because the stray dogs had been on the property of Mrs. Parker, whose dog was in heat. Wrobel was protecting two property interests: the interest of Mrs. Parker in her real property, and her interest in her personal property, her dog. Again, the treatment of animals for purposes of property defense reflects a striking departure from the way in which property issues involving only humans are decided, and thus provides yet another instance in which a normative premise about our view of animals is made apparent. People are not permitted to kill human trespassers; they are not permitted to kill trespassers who bother their domestic animals. People are, however, often permitted to kill animals on their property and to kill animals who disturb their animal property.[91]

## Conclusion

Although anticruelty statutes were supposedly intended to represent a shift from protecting the (animal) property of people to protecting the animals themselves, these laws imposed primarily indirect duties on people in order to conserve public morals. Indeed, even the recent *Model Penal Code* maintains that the purpose of anticruelty statutes is to improve human character and not to protect animals.

Moreover, anticruelty laws reinforce human property rights in animals in several respects. In addition to viewing animals instrumentally as aiding in the moral development of humans, these laws are always limited in their application to ensure the protection of human property rights. Also, anticruelty statutes are usually interpreted against the background of the further assumption that (animal) property owners can be counted on, out of their own self-interest, to take care of their property. Finally, anticruelty statutes have never prohibited the completely unnecessary killing of one's own animal as long as the killing is done in a humane fashion.

In the next chapter, I examine further the various ways in which anticruelty statutes protect the property-oriented institutionalized exploitation of animals.

# CHAPTER SEVEN

## *Anticruelty Statutes and the Protection of the Institutionalized Exploitation of Animals*

THE PROTECTION of institutionalized animal exploitation through anticruelty statutes, protection that reflects property concerns, is effected by four different statutory devices.

First, some of the statutes require that a defendant act with a particular mental state, or *mens rea,*[1] and it is difficult to prove that a defendant who engaged in cruel but "accepted" or "customary" behavior acted with the culpable mental state required under the statute.

Second, many anticruelty statutes contain broad exemptions for virtually all of the activities that traditionally involve animal suffering and death, such as hunting, fishing, animal husbandry, and biomedical research.

Third, and perhaps most important, these statutes explicitly proscribe only those activities in which "unnecessary" or "unjustified" cruelty is imposed. The defendant can easily raise a reasonable doubt that would preclude criminal liability by arguing that the cruelty was "necessary" to achieve some "accepted" end, so that the conduct is not within the scope of the anticruelty statute. When the conduct in question is part of an accepted institutional exploitation of animals, the notion of necessity is not interpreted in its ordinary sense, and instead, the jury is directed to consider whether the conduct is justifiable by reference to the legitimate or accepted activity of which animal exploitation is a part. It is only when the conduct in question is not part of any institutional exploitation that we allow the jury to apply the common, or ordinary, lay understanding of necessity.

Fourth, virtually all of these statutes impose relatively minor penalties for violation. A light sanction has the effect of indicating to society that the conduct, while proscribed, is not viewed as being particularly deviant. More important, perhaps, these offenses are not taken seriously by law enforcement officials, who, in my experience, are reluctant to enforce the law even against clear offenders. In this chapter, I discuss these four devices that are used to severely limit the protection accorded to animals under these statutes. At the end of the chapter, I briefly discuss a 1993 decision of the United Stated Supreme Court that dealt with a state anticruelty statute.

## The Requirement of a Particular Mental State

Anticruelty statutes, which are almost exclusively criminal statutes, may be divided broadly into two categories: those that require the prosecution to prove that the defendant had a particular state of mind when committing the allegedly cruel act, and those that do not require proof of a culpable mental state. About half of the state statutes require that the prohibited act be accompanied by a particular mind state. These statutes prohibit actions performed maliciously, willfully, intentionally, knowingly, recklessly, negligently, or voluntarily.[2] If the statute does not require one of these mind states, then it is generally thought that the statute imposes strict liability, or liability without fault.[3] In those jurisdictions where a mind state is required, courts generally permit the required state of mind to be inferred from the circumstances, but it is obviously difficult to obtain a conviction, because the trier of fact is required to decide what was occurring in the mind of the defendant.

Although several different mental states are used, among which there is considerable confusion,[4] all have a purpose that is often explicitly recognized in the cases: to ensure broad discretion in the treatment of animals by humans by prohibiting only those acts performed with a culpable mental state. Courts have long held that if an act is "unjustifiable" but not accompanied by the requisite mental state, then the defendant is not liable.[5] For example, in *Regalado v. United States*,[6] Regalado was convicted of violating the anticruelty statute of the District of Columbia for beating a puppy. Regalado argued that the evidence was insufficient to convict him, because the state had not proved that he had the specific intent to harm the puppy, and that he was merely disciplining the puppy.[7] The court noted that the statute did not designate any particular mental state necessary for conviction and that the trial judge had instructed the jury that it was required to find that Regalado "willfully" mistreated the puppy. The court held that this meant more than general intent but less than the specific intent to harm the puppy. The required addition to general intent, or the intent to engage in the actions, was malice or a "cruel disposition." The court rejected the specific-intent standard because it would offer the animal's owner "the greatest protection," but a "general intent with malice requirement reflects the growing concern in the law for the protection of animals, while at the same time acknowledging that humans have a great deal of discretion with respect to the treatment of their animals." The court recognized that anticruelty statutes were "not intended to place unreasonable restrictions on the infliction of such pain as may be necessary for the training or discipline of an animal,"[8] and explicitly rejected liability based on " " "good intentions coupled with bad judgment." " "[9] Finally, the court recognized that "proof of malice will usually be circumstantial and the line between discipline and cruelty will often be difficult to draw."[10]

In *Regalado*, the court recognized that requiring the state to prove that the defendant intended to harm the animal would impose a heavy burden on the state because it is difficult to prove beyond a reasonable doubt that a defendant had a specific intent when committing an act. The court also recognized that the anticruelty statutes were never intended to prohibit people from disciplining or training and that a violation of the anticruelty statute required that the objectionable act be coupled with a "cruel" or "malicious" mind state. The addition of the malice requirement was specifically intended to ensure that the humans would not be prohibited from or punished for exercising their property rights in their animals unless the state could show beyond a reasonable doubt that the defendant acted with a cruel disposition.[11]

In *State v. Fowler,*[12] Fowler was convicted of willfully beating and torturing his dog Ike. After Fowler beat Ike and tied him up, Fowler's wife filled a hole in the backyard with water. Fowler than submerged Ike's head under water. The state's witnesses claimed that Fowler submerged the dog for various periods of time over fifteen to twenty minutes. Following this, the Fowlers untied Ike, hit and kicked him, and then tied him to a pole near the water hole. Fowler argued that he and his wife were professional dog trainers and that Ike had been digging holes in the backyard. After trying less harsh methods to no avail, Fowler called Koehler, a famous dog trainer, and Koehler recommended alternative strategies, including the water submersion method that Fowler ultimately used successfully to stop Ike from digging the holes. The trial court refused to allow evidence about the Koehler method or about the local humane society's approval of the Koehler method.[13]

The appellate court reversed Fowler's conviction, holding that the violation must be "willful," which "means more than intentional. It means without just cause, excuse, or justification." A "willful" act excludes "punishment administered to an animal in an honest and good faith effort to train it." The jury should have been instructed to return a verdict of not guilty if it "believed the defendant inflicted the punishment on his animal in a good faith effort to train him." Since the trial court had excluded evidence that Fowler had sought to introduce concerning the Koehler method of dog training, and since this evidence may have influenced the jury to believe that Fowler had sought only to discipline Ike, the appellate court granted a new trial.[14]

Cases like *Regalado* and *Fowler* illustrate clearly that when the prosecution must prove that the defendant acted willfully or maliciously, the defendant may often prevail by showing that the conduct was part of some institutionalized animal exploitation that per se involves inflicting suffering or death on animals. Such institutionalized exploitation is ostensibly justified by the benefit that humans receive from it. In order for the prosecution to prevail, it is necessary to show that the defendant not only intended to perform the actions in question but also intended to act with a culpable mental state that transcends the mere intention to engage in an act. This is, of course, not to say that some actors engaged in activities such as dog training are not motivated by a malicious desire to inflict suffering and death on animals. To the extent that these statutes are designed to elevate human character through the prohibition of certain acts, those who are motivated by cruelty to perform acts that are part of accepted and institutionalized animal exploitation should still be punished. The problem, however, is one of proof. If the actor is inflicting suffering or death on an animal as part of an accepted activity, it is generally very difficult to prove that the person acted maliciously or cruelly.

If a statute requires that an act be committed recklessly, that state of mind may accommodate in a more subtle way institutionalized animal exploitation or conduct that would otherwise constitute cruelty were it not for the presence of benefit derived from the conduct. For example, in *State v. Schott,*[15] Schott was convicted of intentionally and recklessly subjecting his domestic animals to cruel mistreatment and cruel neglect. The court held that a person acted recklessly when she disregarded a substantial risk that her conduct would result in a violation of the law, and that the " 'risk must be of such a nature and degree that . . . its disregard involves a gross deviation from the standard of conduct that a law-abiding person would observe in the actor's situation.' "[16] The relevant language here concerns what a law-abiding person would do in the actor's situation. A law-abiding farmer may perform all sorts of acts that result in great pain and suffering on the part of the farmer's animals but that are part of "commonly accepted practices of animal husbandry." Again, the anticruelty statutes do not provide a perspective from which a trier of fact may assess conduct by reference to ordinary-language notions of humane treatment; rather, the anticruelty statutes require that the trier of fact find that the conduct goes beyond that which is "commonly accepted" and which may involve great pain and suffering, and find that the defendant has engaged in "uncommon" conduct that is not recognized as legitimate for the reason that it provides no possible human benefit.

*Schott* illustrates these principles clearly. Police found dozens of cows and pigs dead or dying from malnutrition and dehydration on Schott's farm. One hog was found eating the remains of another, and when veterinarians called by the police attempted to perform necropsies, they had to "drive off hogs trying to eat the organs eviscerated from the [dead] animals."[17] The necropsies indicated that some of the dead hogs had nothing whatsoever in their stomachs except for feces that they had eaten, and there were six inches of feces at the hog facilities. The cattle were emaciated and dehydrated; their stomachs were completely empty; their ribs protruded grotesquely; and they suffered from sternal recumbancy.[18] Schott's defense was that bad weather had prevented him from caring for his livestock.[19] The jury returned a verdict of guilty, and the appellate court affirmed, holding that there was enough evidence to permit the jury to find beyond a reasonable doubt that Schott had intentionally or recklessly subjected his animals to cruel mistreatment and neglect.[20]

Schott's conduct was certainly not normal husbandry practice, and his conduct did not provide benefit to anyone. It is precisely this type of conduct—and, by and large, *only* this type of conduct—that anticruelty statutes prohibit. Schott's conduct certainly constituted a "gross deviation from the standard of conduct that a law-abiding person would observe in the actor's situation." That does not mean, however, that if Schott had been acting as a law-abiding person, he would not have done anything that would constitute cruel treatment as that notion is normally understood. Although the Nebraska statute did not explicitly contain an exemption to the anticruelty statute for farming practices, there can be no doubt that any attempt to use that statute to prohibit "normal" farming practices would have failed. Indeed, in 1990 Nebraska amended its statute, which now contains numerous explicit exemptions, including one for "commonly accepted practices of animal husbandry with respect to farm animals."[21]

Liability for cruelty through negligence is more unusual, although some statutes provide for liability if the defendant acted with criminal negligence,[22] and some state courts have interpreted their statutes to impose liability for ordinary negligence alone.[23] A statute that prohibits acts done "negligently" requires that an actor perform as would a "reasonable person" under the circumstances. A "reasonable person" is not necessarily a person who never inflicts suffering on animals that is considered "unnecessary" by others. Plenty of "reasonable people" are farmers, experimenters, rodeo performers, or animal trainers. Cruel treatment is not necessarily unreasonable; given the activity, it may be necessary to act in a cruel manner, as in the *Fowler* case. Rather, it is simply unreasonable for such people to inflict more suffering than is necessary to accomplish those ends society has accepted as legitimate, or socially necessary or desirable, or as generating benefits for human beings.[24]

Some statutes require a showing that the defendant acted intentionally, or, put another way, that defendant intended to commit the act that constitutes cruelty but did not necessarily act with malice or the specific desire to act cruelly toward the animal. For example, in *State v. Mitts,*[25] the defendants were convicted of confining several horses and then failing to feed them. In upholding the conviction on appeal, the court held that a requirement of criminal intent was satisfied by "the acts of intentionally confining animals and failing to supply them with sufficient food." It was not necessary "that the defendants had a malevolent purpose to starve the animals in their care."[26] Similarly, in *Jones v. State,* the court held that the state had to prove that a person own, possess, keep, or train a dog "'with the intent that such dog shall be engaged in an exhibition of fighting with another dog.'"[27] The requirement that an act be intentional is, in many respects, less difficult to prove than the other mind states described above.[28] If a statute requires that a defendant act intentionally, that means simply that the act must be a conscious, voluntary act; it does not mean (for the most part) that the defendant must intend that the conduct be cruel or that it result in torture of an animal. The intention requirement is less burdensome for the prosecution because it is more difficult to prove that conduct was performed willfully or maliciously than it is to prove that the conduct was done intentionally. In addition, it is more difficult to prove that the conduct was not in conformity with what a reasonable person would do (as required in negligence) or that it represented a risk the creation of which indicates that the actor departed seriously from the conduct of a law-abiding citizen. The problem is that even if a statute requires mere intentionality, there are other doctrines that require the prosecution to demonstrate that the conduct, in addition to being intentional, also constitutes the very type of gratuitous cruelty that is required when the other mental states are involved.

Under the *Model Penal Code* drafted by the American Law Institute and adopted by various states, cruelty to animals is defined as "purposely" or "recklessly" subjecting any animal to cruel treatment or cruel neglect, or killing or injuring any animal belonging to another without the owner's consent.[29] In order for a defendant to act "purposely" under the *Model Penal Code,* she must have the cruel conduct or neglect as a conscious objective.[30] In order for a defendant to act "recklessly," she must "consciously [disregard] a substantial and unjustifiable risk that the material element exists or will result from [her] conduct."[31] The level of proof required under the *Model Penal Code,* especially for cruelty that is purposely committed, is high and requires a showing similar to that required under *Fowler.* That is, if people inflict unnecessary or unjustifiable suffering on animals but do not do so with the conscious objective of inflicting that pain or suffering or do not consciously disregard a substantial or unjustifiable risk that the cruelty will result, then there can be no criminal liability.[32]

## Specific Exemptions

In addition to requiring the state to prove that a defendant acted with a culpable mind state, anticruelty statutes more directly exclude various activities; they contain explicit exemptions for activities that constitute, for the most part, the institutionalized forms of animal exploitation that account for the largest numbers of animals killed in our society. These exemptions serve to protect defendants irrespective of the actor's mental state at the time she committed the act. For example, the *Model Penal Code* explicitly exempts "accepted veterinary practices and activities carried on for scientific research."[33] The commentaries to the *Model Penal Code* section state that "[i]n light . . . of the wide differences of view as to when pain or death may justifiably be imposed on animals, it is at least necessary to exempt the professionally accepted practices of veterinarians and scientific researchers."[34] An Alaska statute states that it is a defense to prosecution for violation of the anticruelty statute that the defendant's conduct conformed to "accepted" veterinary practices, was part of research governed by "accepted" scientific standards, or was "necessarily incident to lawful hunting or trapping activities."[35] A California statute, contained in a section of the criminal code concerned with "crimes against property," provides that its anticruelty laws are not applicable to activities permitted under the game laws or laws for the destruction of certain birds, the killing of any venomous reptile or any other dangerous animals, the killing of animals for food, or the use of animals in experiments conducted under the authority of the faculty of a regularly incorporated medical college or university.[36] A Delaware statute exempts "accepted" veterinary practices and scientific experiments, as well as the killing of animals for food, "provided that such killing is not cruel."[37] Kentucky prohibits the killing of any animal[38] — a prohibition that is on its face the most stringent in the United States —

but a subsequent section of the statute exempts any activities in connection with hunting, fishing, trapping, processing animals for food, killing for "humane purposes," dog training, and killing animals for any authorized purpose.[39] Maryland law specifically provides that "[c]ustomary and normal veterinary and agricultural husbandry practices including but not limited to dehorning, castration, docking tails, and limit feeding, are not covered" by the anticruelty law. The statute continues: although it is the intention of the law to protect from intentional cruelty all animals, whether "they be privately owned, strays, domesticated, feral, farm, corporately or institutionally owned, under private, local, State, or federally funded scientific or medical activities . . . no person shall be liable for criminal prosecution for normal human activities to which the infliction of pain to an animal is purely incidental and unavoidable."[40] Nebraska exempts veterinary practices, experiments conducted by research facilities that conform to requirements of the federal Animal Welfare Act (AWA), hunting, fishing, trapping, animal races, rodeos, pulling contests, and "[c]ommonly accepted practices of animal husbandry."[41] Indeed, Nebraska provides *by statute* that it "shall be unlawful to brand any live animal other than by the use of a hot iron."[42] Oregon exempts "[a]ny practice of good animal husbandry," which is defined in another section as including "the dehorning of cattle, the docking of horses, sheep or swine, and the castration or neutering of livestock, according to accepted practices of veterinary medicine or animal husbandry."[43] Pennsylvania exempts "normal agricultural operations" from its statute and defines these activities as "practices and procedures that farmers adopt, use or engage in year after year in the production and preparation for market of poultry, livestock and their products in the production and harvesting of agricultural, agronomic, horticultural, silvicultural and aquacultural crops and commodities."[44] Virginia specifically exempts the dehorning of cattle.[45] The most frequent exemptions involve scientific experiments, agricultural practices, and hunting. Sometimes it is not clear whether a statute exempts a particular activity.[46]

In two respects, these exemptions effectively prevent the jury from considering whether conduct in a particular case constitutes "cruelty" or results in "unnecessary" suffering or death. First, and most obvious, the statutes exempt particular types of behavior, such as conduct involved in scientific experiments or animal husbandry. The exempted activities all represent classes of conduct that are thought to be beneficial to human beings. In other words, by exempting certain classes of conduct, the legislature makes a determination that such conduct is "necessary" or "humane." This determination is based on an assessment of the utility of the conduct to human beings.

Second, the exemptions do not, for the most part, provide that conduct must be reasonable—from the point of view of the jury—to be considered as falling within the exemption. Rather, the exemptions almost always provide that the conduct in question must represent the "accepted" or "normal" practices within the particular class of activity. This qualification has a most important—and subtle—effect: it removes from consideration the question whether a particular instance of the exempted conduct *should* fall within the exemption and leaves that determination to the "standards" of the profession or activity. For example, when a statute exempts "accepted" scientific procedures, that means that a practice is considered within the ambit of the exception if others in the profession state that the practice is "customary." That is, by incorporating the norms of the particular industry or activity, the exemption precludes the trier of fact from assessing whether conduct in a particular case was really necessary, or reflected gratuitous cruelty. There is no consideration whether the "customary" or "accepted" practice is "necessary" or "humane." What is particularly relevant for our present inquiry is that these exemptions effectively preclude *any* inquiry once the activity is determined to fall within the scope of the exemption. Again, any "balancing" has already been done by the statute in that the decision about what constitutes acceptable behavior is left to those who engage in the activity in question. This approach stands in marked contrast to that used to solve similar problems in the law. For example, in determining whether conduct constitutes negligence, juries may consider conformity to custom as evidence of reasonable behavior, but it has long been recognized that the customary nature of conduct does not make the conduct reasonable, and that the jury must determine whether the defendant balanced the amount of risk generated by her conduct with an appropriate amount of caution.[47]

An explicit recognition that such exemptions permit even inhumane or cruel or unnecessary suffering and death is found in *New Jersey Society for the Prevention of Cruelty to Animals v. Board of Education*,[48] discussed in Chapter One. In that case, the court denied that painful experiments on chickens by high school students violated the state anticruelty prohibition against the "needless mutilation or killing or the infliction of unnecessary cruelty." As part of its decision, it interpreted the exemption for "properly conducted scientific experiments performed under the authority of the state department of health" to mean that those covered by the exemption could "inflict even unnecessary pain or even needlessly mutilate or kill a living animal in the course of their work without being liable to prosecution from the S.P.C.A."[49] The court found that since the board of education had not obtained authorization from the state department of health, the school board could not inflict "unnecessary cruelty" or "needless mutilation." When the court went on to determine whether the experiment violated the statute, it permitted its understanding of necessity to be determined solely by the views of scientific experts who routinely and slavishly defend virtually any use of animals. Indeed, the complete lack of critical analysis of the notion of necessity is remarkable.[50]

Moreover, those who benefit from these exemptions are not likely to build considerations for the humane treatment of animals into their practices, and the existence of an exemption only serves to encourage even more inhumane practices if they are economically desirable. For example, despite claims by agribusiness that intensive farming methods are humane, no one without a financial interest in the food industry would maintain that modern animal husbandry is humane at all. Indeed, even those who eat meat are horrified when they learn about the hideous treatment accorded to animals used for food, and many people become vegetarians after they learn about these practices.[51] Nevertheless, exemptions for "accepted" animal husbandry practices permit the castration of animals, the dehorning of cattle, the debeaking of chicks, the branding of animals with hot irons — all without anesthesia — and the confinement of animals in conditions so crowded that the animals must be fed a constant supply of antibiotics to keep them from getting ill from the stress.[52]

## Economic Benefit and "Custom" as Necessity

If an anticruelty statute does not require proof of a mental state, then, technically speaking, an offender can be liable just by virtue of performing the offending act — for example, inflicting unnecessary suffering on an animal — even though she does not intend to act cruelly or maliciously. The problem is that the act in question — inflicting unnecessary suffering on an animal — is defined so that the only way to identify conduct as an "act" culpable under the statute is to identify the conduct as "unnecessary."

For all practical purposes, that identification serves, in part, the same function that culpable mental states served in *Regalado* and *Fowler:* to ensure that "necessary" suffering or death remains outside the scope of the statute. Moreover, cases interpreting such "strict liability" provisions often, despite the lack of proof of a culpable mental state, look to the defendant's motivation in order to determine whether the infliction of suffering or death was "necessary." Finally, when the statute proscribes unnecessary suffering but does not require consideration of a mental state, defendants who are in fact motivated by cruelty or who actually enjoy inflicting suffering on animals may not be subject to liability as long as the conduct in question is regarded as necessary. As a result, one of the primary purposes of the anticruelty statutes — the "elevation" of humans — is entirely lost.

All anticruelty statutes use the language of necessity or justification; that is, they do not prohibit all suffering and death — they only prohibit *unnecessary* or *unjustifiable* suffering or death, and they rarely prohibit any particular practice outright.[53] The statutory language is inherently ambiguous because courts must determine what constitutes "unnecessary abuse," "unnecessary pain," "unjustifiable pain and suffering," and "unjustifiable killing."[54] Although the anticruelty context is not the only one in which words like "necessary" are used, the animal context is unique. For example, most states have laws that prohibit the infliction of "unnecessary" or "excessive" punishment on children. At first glance, what constitutes "necessary" punishment of a child and what constitutes the "necessary" infliction of suffering on an animal may ostensibly raise the same type of issue. This appearance is deceptive. In the case of child abuse, the law for the most part looks to the "common understanding" of the term. That is, what constitutes cruelty to children is, by and large, determined by jurors who simply interpret the statute in light of their own understanding of the meaning of the words, against the backdrop of their personal views on appropriate methods of parenting. Although there is certainly massive exploitation of children in our society, that exploitation is routinely and widely condemned by most people and does not form the basis for institutional exploitation that is widely accepted.

What constitutes unnecessary suffering inflicted on animals, however, does not involve the jury in applying its own notions of cruelty and unnecessary suffering. Rather, what is "necessary" or "humane" treatment as far as animals are concerned depends on a most technical legal interpretation of "cruelty" or "necessary suffering" and not an interpretation based on ordinary-language meaning. Indeed, a theme that appears consistently in the cases is that the cruelty prohibited by anticruelty statutes is not necessarily that which would be considered as cruelty as that word is used in nonlegal contexts. This notion is reflected by John Ingham, who, writing in 1900, stated that despite anticruelty statutes it is permissible to inflict pain on animals in order to save a human life, to cure human or animal diseases, or to "assist development or proper growth, fit the animal for ordinary use, or to fulfill the part for which by common consent it is designed."[55] It is this third reason for inflicting pain that is most pertinent to the current inquiry. The notion of inflicting pain in order to fulfill the role of the animal "for which by common consent it is designed" suggests that social norms about animal exploitation govern the interpretation of anticruelty statutes and that the anticruelty statutes do not serve to shape those social norms. "Necessity," as it is used in anticruelty statutes, purports to require an inquiry into the factual state of the world, while in actuality it requires a value-laden assessment of which human activities are worthwhile and which are not. An example of this occurs in the context of using animals for food. Health professionals no longer emphasize the importance of meat in the human diet, and even the conservative American Medical Association has urged the increase of fruits and vegetables in the diet and has warned of the dangers of meat consumption. Despite this lack of necessity of meat consumption and the consequent unnecessary killing and suffering that is attendant to a meat diet, we continue to kill over eight billion animals for food annually in the United States alone. Moreover, even if we accept that meat production is "necessary," the practices of modern agribusiness, as well as traditional agriculture, cause great suffering to animals and are justified only by economic factors. Nevertheless, any challenge under the anticruelty statutes to meat production as a general matter, or the various practices of intensive agriculture, would most certainly fail because agricultural uses of animals would be explicitly excluded from the statute or would be interpreted judicially to be excluded. In the latter case, the exclusion would be based upon a determination that the legislature never sought to include agricultural uses within the ambit of the statute and that the practice in question merely facilitates the service of animals to humans.

Courts have from the outset interpreted these statutes not to apply to common forms of cruelty—as long as they are "socially acceptable." For example, in *Grise v. State,* the Arkansas court cautioned against an interpretation of the Arkansas anticruelty statute that would lead to "absurdities": society "could not long toler-ate a system of laws, which might drag to the criminal bar, every lady who might impale a butterfly, or every man who might drown a litter of kittens."[56] In *State v. Bogardus,* the Missouri court held that the shooting of captive pigeons purely for amusement purposes was not prohibited, because it was a "manly" sport and "services which the citizen is called upon to render to the State, in exigencies, may largely depend on the qualities acquired in manly sports, and from some of the most attractive of these a certain amount of injury to dumb animals seems in-separable."[57] In a separate opinion in which the court overruled Missouri's mo-tion for rehearing, the court held that shooting pigeons must be considered one of many "popular diversions which, however indifferent to the value of brute life, have never been held 'needless' for man's lawful delectation, [and] could not have been within the legislative contemplation when this indefinite prohibition was made a law."[58]

In a nineteenth-century Massachusetts case, *Commonwealth v. Lufkin,*[59] Mar-tin, a baker, drove in his horse-drawn cart to Lufkin's house in order to deliver bread and to collect money on an earlier bill. Lufkin and his wife emerged from the house, and Lufkin, angry at what he understood to be an "intimate" relation-ship between Martin and Lufkin's wife, ordered Martin away. After the two men argued for a short time, Lufkin struck Martin's horse with a large stick several times. In Lufkin's subsequent trial for cruelty to Martin's horse, Lufkin requested that the court instruct the jury that he had to intend to cruelly beat and torture the horse in order to be found guilty. The trial court refused to give the instruction, and Lufkin appealed.[60] The appellate court agreed that Lufkin's requested in-struction on intention was improper. The court was concerned, however, that the jury not be confused by that part of the lower-court opinion that pertained to the lawful right of an owner to inflict force on an animal for purposes of discipline or government. The court stated that "[t]he cruel treatment which the statute con-templates is the same, whether inflicted by the owner of the animal or by another." Accordingly, "[i]f the defendant's object was a lawful one for any person, and his act was not an excessive and cruel use of force for that object, he should have been acquitted."[61]

*Lufkin* is typical. We do not look to the allegedly cruel act and then "balance" in order to determine its legality or the legality of the activity of which the cruelty is a part. Rather, we look to the activity to see whether it is legal. If the activity is legal, we then look to the allegedly cruel act to see whether it involved excessive force given the legitimacy of the enterprise. Such a framework classifies as "nec-essary" that suffering or death which is more or less needed to perform the legal activities. This explains why the anticruelty laws have been unable to touch ac-tivities such as hunting or intensive agriculture. Those are legal activities, and the law permits the amount of force that is necessary to perform those activities, and usually looks to the customary practices of those activities to determine the amount of force that is necessary. The notion of "necessity" comes to be inter-preted as meaning that anything that is *causally* necessary to a legally sanctioned activity (i.e., is part of that activity) becomes *morally* necessary under the anti-cruelty law.

Moreover, courts have made absolutely clear that "[s]uch statutes were not intended to interfere, and do not interfere, with the necessary discipline and government of such animals, or place any unreasonable restriction on their use or the enjoyment to be derived from their possession."[62] Anticruelty statutes, then, are concerned only with the prohibition of *unnecessary* or *unjustifiable* cruelty, and these statutes are routinely interpreted to exclude, or explicitly exclude, the use of animals to save human life, to cure human diseases, to provide food, to facilitate the service of the animal for human purposes, and to protect property. As a result, the activities that involve the largest numbers of animals—the use of animals for food, including hunting, and the use of animals in experiments—are, from the start, *excluded* from the scope of anticruelty statutes. Moreover, even when the statute does not speak explicitly in terms of necessity and justification, those terms must be read into the statute, or else the statute would prohibit all animal exploitation. Indeed, in cases involving challenges to anticruelty laws on the ground of the supposed vagueness of terms such as "unnecessary" or "unjustifiable," courts have expressed concern that various accepted practices might come within the ambit of the statute were those terms interpreted in their ordinary senses.[63]

The exclusion of all acts that provide any benefit to humans, including entertainment alone, from the scope of anticruelty statutes means that the balancing of human and animal interests supposedly required by these statutes has already been done before a court even begins to interpret a particular statute in the context of a specific case. That is, anticruelty statutes are explicitly designed not to interfere with many activities that most people would regard as "cruel." For purposes of the law, it is only those acts that cannot be justified by reference to *some* human benefit that are considered "cruel." As one court stated, "the most common case to which the statute would apply is undoubtedly that in which an animal is cruelly beaten or tortured for the gratification of a malignant or vindictive temper."[64] This is not to say that the statute is never applied in other contexts; rather, the point is only that anticruelty statutes are explicitly designed not to apply to what most people would regard as "cruel" treatment or the infliction of "unnecessary" distress. As long as a defendant can offer some credible reason (i.e., a reason other than malignant or vindictive temper) for the action or omission, then the anticruelty statute usually does not apply. With respect to those activities that are "cruel" but involve some other activities that are deemed to be socially desirable, the statute simply does not apply. If the "end," such as the use of animals for food, is acceptable, then, with very few exceptions, the "means" of exploitation is also regarded as acceptable. In any event, the allegedly cruel conduct can never be viewed apart from the activity of which it is a part, because the status of that activity, with very few exceptions, determines whether the challenged conduct is cruel, or is rightly performed to further the service of the animal to human beings.

An early statement of the purpose of anticruelty laws indicates quite clearly that these laws were never intended to stop institutionalized exploitation. In *People v. Brunell,* the court, in its interpretation of the New York anticruelty law, remarked that concern for animals has been "cultivated by the christian religion" and that

> [i]t is impossible for a right minded man . . . to say that unjustifiable cruelty is not a wrong, a moral wrong at all events, and why should not the law make it a legal wrong? Pain is an evil. Why should dumb creatures, domesticated to obey us, confiding in us, indebted to us for their food and subsistence, bound and taught to obey us, be unnecessarily and unjustifiably inflicted with pain?[65]

The court here recognizes clearly that the purpose of the statute is not to alleviate the pain and suffering incidental to our use of animals but, rather, to alleviate only that suffering that goes beyond what is necessary for "appropriate" exploitation. This is a consistent theme of cases going back to the nineteenth century. Not "every treatment of an animal which inflicts pain, even the great pain of mutilation, *and which is cruel in the ordinary sense of the word,* is . . . necessarily within the Act."[66] Cruelty "does not mean merely inflicting pain. . . . Much pain is often inflicted where the operation is necessary, as for instance in the case of cautery, which is practised on animals. . . . *That is torture,* . . . but in my opinion, in this statute [cruelty] must refer to something done for no legitimate purpose."[67] It is not the anticruelty statutes that help shape our treatment of animals. Our treatment of animals—as long as it is not a completely gratuitous destruction of animals that represents an overall diminution of social wealth—is not even covered by the anticruelty statutes.[68] The balancing has already been done, and the scales of justice have—once again—been tipped in favor of the property owner and the owner of the animal.

As a theoretical matter, this understanding of the anticruelty laws can be traced directly to their primary role as "directed against acts which may be thought to have a tendency to dull humanitarian feelings and to corrupt the morals of those who observe or have knowledge of those acts."[69] The anticruelty laws are intended not to eradicate all or even most acts of cruelty to animals; rather, the statutes are directed only at acts that are "deviant." It may be argued that statutes prohibiting the "excessive" punishment of children are not intended to eradicate all acts of corporal punishment of children but are directed only against acts of punishment that are deviant or that depart from the socially accepted norm concerning the corporal punishment of children. The problem is that the notion of "deviant" conduct in these two instances differs radically in terms of the social context in which the norms of social acceptance are developed. Simply put, although children are certainly exploited, most of us do not endorse this exploitation; and, in any event, we do not eat children, we do not use them in experiments (without parental consent), and we do not exhibit them in cages at the zoo or chase them around an arena and rope them for human amusement; and to engage in any of these acts—irrespective of the "humane" nature of the means employed—

would itself represent deviant behavior. In the case of animals, however, we do use and kill animals for food, science, entertainment, and clothing, and the "deviant" view is the one that rejects such animal use. We simply do not regard our massive exploitation of animals as creating "dull humanitarian feelings" or corrupting "the morals of those who observe or have knowledge of these acts."[70] Accordingly, we have no real interest in applying the anticruelty laws to these activities and are instead concerned primarily with those that represent gratuitous cruelty, or those that are done without "any *useful* motive."[71] Such acts cause a diminution in overall social wealth because animals are exploited but no social benefit is generated.

In addition to the cases, discussed above, concerning the killing of animals in order to protect private property, a series of decisions going back to English common law supports an interpretation of anticruelty statutes to prohibit only those activities that represent a gratuitous abuse of animals with no corresponding social benefit. For example, cases dealing with the treatment of animals used for food have, from the inception of anticruelty cases, held that pain and suffering inflicted on animals is necessary when that treatment makes the animal more serviceable to humans. "Whenever the purpose for which the act is done is to make the animal more serviceable for the use of man the statute ought not to be held to apply."[72] Indeed, courts have always been concerned that "mere" killing not be prohibited by the anticruelty statutes, because that would mean that "he who kills his pig, or ox for the market would fall within the letter of the law, and, no exception being made in the statute as to the purpose of the killing, we must eat no more meat."[73] In *Bowyer v. Morgan,*[74] the court held that branding lambs on the nose with a hot iron did not violate the anticruelty law, because it was an act that, although it was "cruel" in causing pain to the animal, was "reasonably necessary" for identification purposes, and that the practice had become customary in Wales. Once we accept the legitimacy of eating animals, that which is necessary to facilitate that exploitation—even if it causes excruciating pain, as the veterinary experts on both sides in *Bowyer* agreed—falls outside the scope of the anticruelty statute. A close examination of the case, together with the summary of the opposing expert testimony given at trial, shows that the trial court considered the branding necessary, in large part because it was customary, even though less painful alternatives existed.

In another English case, *Lewis v. Fermor,*[75] the court held that if a person had a good-faith belief that imposing severe pain on animals would benefit the owner of the animals by increasing their value, then there could be no conviction for violating the anticruelty statute. In *Fermor,* the defendant, a veterinarian, was charged with violating the anticruelty statute by spaying sows. Prosecution witnesses all testified that the operation was severely painful and that it was useless. The defendant practiced in an area of England "where it is customary to perform this operation . . . in order to increase [the sows'] weight and development."[76] The court held that because the operation was customary and the defendant performed it with ordinary care, and because the defendant was performing the procedure to benefit the owner economically, there could be no conviction for violating the anticruelty law even if the operation ultimately proved useless.

Although the Queen's Bench in *Ford v. Wiley* held that the dehorning of cattle—a practice widespread in the United States at present and often protected by explicit exemptions to the anticruelty statute—constituted cruelty to animals, the author of the opinion, Lord Chief Justice Coleridge, made it clear that any procedure "without which an animal cannot attain its full development or be fitted for its ordinary use may fairly come within the term 'necessary.' "[77] He gave an example: "Mutilation of horses and bulls is necessary, and, if properly performed, undoubtedly lawful; because without it, in this country at least, the animals could not be kept at all."[78] In a concurring opinion, Justice Hawkins stated that although a horse may be "designed for draught and riding purposes, [the horse] is not in its natural untutored state so fitted. To prevent it from being unruly and unsafe, it requires to be broken, sometimes with a degree of severity, occasioning pain, which without such necessity would be utterly unjustifiable."[79] The determination whether a particular practice falls within the ambit of the statute turns on empirical questions of efficacy and utility and not on the abstract question of pain and suffering. So, when the evidence showed that dehorning increased the marketability of the cattle, an Irish court in *Callaghan v. Society for the Prevention of Cruelty to Animals* held that dehorning made the cattle "more serviceable for the use of man."[80]

In an early American case, *State v. Crichton,*[81] the court held that dehorning cattle could not be justified merely by increased profit or convenience of the owner, but could be justified if it facilitated the ordinary use for which the animal was designed. The court added that if the procedure could be shown to "render the flesh nutricious [sic] and wholesome" or if it could be proved that animals with horns cause more injury to each other than is caused in the dehorning process, then the procedure would be justified as facilitating the service of the steer for human purposes. Echoing Coleridge in *Ford,* the court noted that the "mutilation of horses, bulls, and other male species is necessary and undoubtedly lawful, for without it, they could not be fully developed and fitted for their ordinary use to man."[82]

Other cases dealing with animals used for food support the thesis that in any inquiry into whether a particular method or part of a method of husbandry or slaughter is humane, we generally look to what is "customarily" done; if the action comports with the custom, it is not considered cruel. In *Davis v. Society for Prevention of Cruelty,*[83] the ASPCA objected to the practice of hoisting a hog by one hind leg, in preparation for the infliction of a stab wound in the neck, and then plunging the hog into boiling water before the animal has lost consciousness through exsanguination. The ASPCA argued that the abattoir should hoist the hog by both back legs and use a leather belt instead of a chain to avoid limb dislocation in the animal, and that no hog should be plunged into the boiling water until the animal had lost consciousness. Although the abattoir initially agreed to these changes, the ASPCA determined that the practices were continuing and arrested several people involved in the slaughtering operations. The slaughterhouse then sought to have the ASPCA enjoined from interfering in the operation of the plant.[84] The court found that an injunction was not appropriate, in part because dislocating the limbs of animals to be slaughtered and immersing living animals into cauldrons of boiling water, which was not customary, constituted cruelty. It should be noted here that although the court agreed that a certain part of the slaughtering process was inhumane, it did not hold that the slaughtering process itself, which involved the shackling, hoisting, and stabbing of a conscious and unanesthetized animal, was inhumane.[85] Indeed, the ASPCA itself stated that it did not object to the shackling, hoisting, and stabbing of the animal, but that it was concerned primarily about limb dislocation attendant to the use of a chain around one hind leg of an animal and about the plunging of the conscious, freshly stabbed hog into the cauldron of boiling water.

In another case, *People ex rel. Freel v. Downs,*[86] one of two defendants, Downs, a captain of a merchant marine vessel, was charged with cruelty for his treatment of sixty-five turtles he transported from Cuba to New York. He perforated the turtles' fins, passed a rope through the holes, tied the fins together, and then placed them on their backs on the deck of the ship until the vessel reached New York, where the other defendant, Smith, took delivery. Smith cut the ropes binding the turtles and then stacked them side by side, on the edges of their shells, and transported them to a warehouse.[87] The court held that although there was testimony that the method of transportation to the warehouse caused discomfort to the turtles, the pain and suffering were "temporary," "unavoidable," and "necessary to preserve the safety of the property involved."[88] The court stated that there was a "legal license permitting the infliction of unavoidable pain" given that "[m]an is superior to animals, and some of them he uses for food and is permitted to slaughter them." The court continued:

> It must have come to the attention of many that the treatment of "animals" to be used for food while in transit to a stockyard or to a market is sometimes not short of cruel and, in some instances, torturable. Hogs have the nose perforated and a ring placed in it; ears of calves are similarly treated; chickens are crowded into freight cars; codfish is taken out of the waters and thrown into barrels of ice and sold on the market as "live cod"; eels have been known to squirm in the frying pan; and snails, lobsters, and crabs are thrown into boiling water.[89]

The court held that, as a matter of law, Smith could not be convicted of cruelty for the manner in which he transported the animals, because it was necessary and justified and was consistent with the manner in which animals intended for slaughter are transported; and accordingly, the court quashed the indictment against Smith.[90] The court refused to quash the indictment against Downs and required that he stand trial for perforating and tying the fins when alternative and more humane means of transportation were available.[91]

Other cases involving animals used for food have yielded similar analyses. A particularly interesting case is *Commonwealth v. Anspach*,[92] a case in which the defendant, a manager of a Sears, Roebuck store, was charged with violating the anticruelty statute by placing a small chicken in a bottle for the purpose of advertising a special chicken feed that was given to the confined chick. The bottle was nineteen inches high and had wire netting upon which the chicken stood. The court held that so confining the chicken did not constitute a violation of the anticruelty statute, because the custom in the industry was, according to the court, even more inhumane. One expert witness, upon whom the court relied, stated that young chicks were routinely placed in drawers that were only eight or nine inches high and had much less space than the chick involved in the case, that wire floors were common in brooder houses, and that commercial practice was tending toward restrictive chicken cages in any event. Moreover, the court noted that other farm animals are kept under very confined circumstances.[93] Again, the court did not analyze whether the conduct was cruel as that notion is ordinarily understood. Rather, the court assumed that if the challenged conduct was not worse than what was customary in the industry, then it could not be violative of the anticruelty law.[94]

In a 1993 case, *Commonwealth v. Barnes*,[95] the defendants were charged with violating the state anticruelty law by neglecting their horses. Defendants claimed that they intended to sell the animals for slaughter to make dog food and that, as a "normal agricultural operation," the failure to care for the horses was exempted from the scope of the anticruelty law. The appellate court affirmed the defendants' convictions, but the court made clear that the defendants had failed to prove that the severe neglect of horses was, indeed, an accepted custom in that industry. According to the court, the defendants' experts gave testimony that was inconsistent regarding both the severity and the prevalence of the practice and that the defendants provided no evidence that they had formed the definite intention to send the horses to slaughter for dog food.[96] The implication of *Barnes* is clear: had the defendants produced consistent expert testimony that the severe neglect was customary, and had they themselves provided creditable testimony that they had intended to use these horses for dog food, the exemption under the anticruelty statute for "normal agricultural operations" would have applied.

Cases involving the exploitation of animals in contexts other than food production support the thesis that institutional uses of animals—however much they may result in pain and suffering—are generally outside the scope of anticruelty laws. The use of animals in research is usually exempted through an explicit provision of the law or is otherwise adjudged by courts to be "necessary." In *Taub v. State,* a case that I discussed in Chapter Four and discuss further in the third part of this book, the Maryland high court reversed Taub's conviction under the anticruelty law because "there are certain normal human activities to which the infliction of pain to an animal is purely incidental and unavoidable" and scientific research using animals is one such activity.[97] What is even more disturbing is that humane societies have traditionally led the fight to protect vivisection and other "traditional" forms of animal exploitation. For example, in

*Vivisection Investigation League v. American Society for the Prevention of Cruelty to Animals,*[98] the League and an individual plaintiff sought to enjoin the ASPCA from using its name, or any similar name, based on the fact that the ASPCA had favored the enactment of a law, since repealed, that provided for "pound seizure," or the taking of shelter animals by research facilities for use in vivisection experiments. The League argued that the ASPCA had been formed for the purpose of opposing cruelty in all forms and that the ASPCA's support for vivisection and pound seizure violated its corporate purposes. The court disagreed:

> In the divine plan of all creation, two orders . . . were ordained, the human and all others. . . . From the origin of mankind, the dumb beast has been used to serve man for his primary needs of food and clothing, in addition to other ancient services, such as dragging his plow, transporting his burdens, guarding his home and being his companion. Now there has been added the more recent use of animals in furthering medical research in the discovery of scientific knowledge for the control of disease, in alleviating pain and in prolonging life. In its limited co-operation in this field of activity, the defendant evinces its primary love of humankind, to which is subordinated its love of animals.
>
> For the plaintiff to assert that defendant practices cruelty to animals because of its viewpoint begs the question raised by the complaint. What is cruelty? The dictionaries generally define cruelty as an inhuman act. Both organizations profess human [*sic*] behavior toward animals. This activity of the defendant represents but a small area of its full concern and activity. *And, of course, is not considered cruelty by [the ASPCA].*[99]

In another case, *Fund for Animals, Inc. v. Mud Lake Farmers Rabbit Committee,*[100] an animal protection organization sought to enjoin a "rabbit drive" where men, women, and children used baseball bats, tire irons, and wooden sticks to club jack rabbits, who were perceived as a threat to crops. The trial court found that children were permitted to participate in the "drive," that many of the animals were not killed but were permitted to suffer, and that some of the participants tossed rabbits at others who struck them with baseball bats. The trial court also found that the purpose of the anticruelty statute was to prohibit unnecessary abuse of animals and that " '[w]hen animals threaten the physical or financial survival of man, he is lawfully entitled to strike back and to use such tactics as appear necessary and reasonable.' " The court refused to enjoin the rabbit drive; it found that " '[k]illing, maiming to some extent, mutilating to some extent, causing of pain and suffering to rabbits are necessary incidents to a rabbit drive operated for their destruction.' "[101] The court did order that children under the age of sixteen not be permitted to participate and that the use of rabbits for "Bunny baseball" or for other sport or game activities be forbidden. The appellate court affirmed. Interestingly, although the plaintiff in the case—Fund for Animals—appealed the decision, it conceded on appeal that it was satisfied merely to stop the use of the rabbits for sport or game purposes and not to stop the drive altogether.

Despite the particularly cruel means of killing used in hunting, there is a dearth of cases that deal with it. This paucity of case law is due to a legal doctrine that effectively insulates hunting from challenge. Most of the more serious cruelty involved in hunting occurs when an animal is wounded, but not killed, by a hunter. Although the hunter is the direct cause of the animal's suffering, the common law has always taken the position that a hunter has no obligation to ensure that the animal is killed. In an English case, *Hooker v. Gray*,[102] the defendant was charged with violating the anticruelty law when he shot, but did not kill, a neighbor's cat. The wounded cat returned to the owner's yard and was discovered by the owner to be in great pain. The defendant knew that he had not killed the cat, although he testified that he had intended to kill the cat; and although he knew the identity of the cat's owner, he had done nothing to make the owner aware of the cat's plight or to alleviate the cat's distress. The appellate court affirmed the dismissal of the complaint on the ground that the defendant did nothing unlawful in shooting the cat, who was on the defendant's premises, with the intent to kill the cat. If the defendant had merely intended to wound the cat, the result would have been different, the court held.[103] Most important was the court's concern that given that the defendant's conduct in shooting the cat was not unlawful, it would be anomalous to impose liability on the defendant for failing to ensure that the cat was dead, and the court could not "possibly say that that is cruelty under the statute," because such a rule "would oblige anybody who was shooting animals, such as rabbits, hares, or any such thing, and who wounded one, to follow it up and to kill it at once. If the Legislature meant to say that that is the way in which shooting is to be conducted, they must say so in much plainer terms than they have said at present."[104] If the original act is lawful because it is explicitly permitted by the statute, or because it is held by a court not to contravene the statute, or because it is justified, as in the case of protection of person or property, then the actor is usually not under an obligation to ensure that the animal is not suffering as a result of that act. In *Hooker,* Justice Phillimore expressed in dicta that "[i]f a ferocious dog flies at me and I shoot or strike at it with the view of defending myself and thereby inflict a mortal wound, there may be, I think, no duty to that dog, because I was only defending myself."[105] That is, if inflicting the wound is justified by self-defense, then the actor has no duty to ensure that the dog is actually dead or to kill the dog if the defendant sees that the animal is suffering. If the injury-producing act is unlawful or unjustified, then the defendant may have a duty to ensure that the animal is not consequently suffering pain. For example, in *Laner v. State,*[106] the defendant shot trained wolfhounds who were running across land owned by others and along a country road, chasing deer. The defendant did not bother to see whether the dogs had been killed outright, and the dogs were, in fact, injured. In affirming the defendant's conviction, the court rejected the defendant's argument that the dogs represented a nuisance because they offended the decency of others, and replied that "we fail to see how the ancient sport of running the hounds or wolf hunting in any way can offend public decency." The court held that the defendant had violated the cruelty statute because "[h]e knew that he had hit the dogs and he was willing to let them drag themselves off and suffer and die."[107]

Unless a person is hunting illegally for whatever reason, the shooting of an animal does not constitute cruelty. Because the injuring act is lawful, the hunter incurs no duty to ensure that the animal is actually dead. Accordingly, there is no liability under anticruelty laws when hunters allow injured animals to escape and die lingering deaths.

There are many, many cases that effectively insulate from challenge various uses of animals that result in unspeakable pain and suffering to animals. There are very few cases that have held that the exploitation of animals that is part of some accepted activity constitutes cruelty.[108] A notable exception is *Humane Society v. Lyng,*[109] which involved a challenge to a regulation promulgated by the Department of Agriculture requiring that certain cattle be branded on the face with a hot iron. The court found that there had been no consideration of the cruelty issue by the government and that more humane marking alternatives had been rejected "based more on inconvenience to farmers than on inconvenience to cows."[110] Although *Lyng* demonstrated that on rare occasions courts look more carefully at agricultural practices, the case is idiosyncratic because hot branding of the face is not an "accepted" agricultural practice in that it was adopted only for purposes of facilitating a government program.[111]

If the primary purpose of anticruelty statutes is to improve human character, then it makes sense to say that the acts that the laws prohibit should be limited to those that reflect a malignant and sadistic character or those in which animal suffering provides no human benefit (other than sadistic enjoyment). Society — at least at this time — is not prepared to regard the hunter, the factory farmer, the scientist, or the rodeo performer as displaying a malignant or sadistic personality in providing benefits to humans. Ironically, this reluctance exists even though participants in these activities may enjoy inflicting pain on animals. If we want to improve human character, we will inevitably focus on "deviant" behavior, but we will exclude all behavior that is part of socially accepted practices. For example, if a person eats meat, that person is unlikely to be particularly critical of farming practices, especially when their improvement will result in higher meat costs.

A review of cases in which defendants have been found liable under anticruelty cases indicates that the activity proscribed by these statutes may be classified as conduct that generates no socially recognized benefit for the individual or society. Put another way, the conduct is not part of an institutionalized use in which the infliction of pain on an animal is regarded as a *causally* necessary part of an accepted activity.[112] Accordingly, the killing or maiming of an animal under such circumstances represents a destruction of property and a *morally* unnecessary infliction of pain or death. For example, in *State v. Tweedie,*[113] the defendant was convicted of killing a cat by placing the animal in an activated microwave oven at the defendant's place of employment. The appellate court, which affirmed the conviction, upheld the trial court's finding that "defendant was indifferent to the pain and suffering he caused the cat"[114] and that the defendant's only concern was that he might lose his job. In another case, *In re William G.*,[115] the minor defendant sought to have his male dog mate with a neighbor's female dog. When the mating attempt proved unsuccessful, the defendant kicked the female dog and threatened to kill her. The defendant later poured turpentine on the female dog and lit the dog on fire. The appellate court refused to overturn the defendant's conviction based on the alleged vagueness of the state anticruelty statute. The court held that persons of ordinary intelligence could not but conclude that "the burning of a dog to the extent that he [*sic*] had to be destroyed constitutes torture, torment and cruelty as defined by the statute."[116] A number of cases in which cruelty convictions were affirmed involved sadistic conduct, such as beating or burning an animal, that no one would argue provides any social benefit.[117] For example, in *Tuck v. United States*,[118] the court upheld the defendant pet-store owner's conviction for violating the anticruelty law when the defendant had placed a puppy and a rabbit in an unventilated display window and had then refused to remove the rabbit, whose body temperature registered as high as the thermometer was calibrated—at 110 degrees Fahrenheit. Tuck had to be physically restrained while officers removed the rabbit, who was salivating and had suffered a heat stroke.[119]

If, however, conduct can be "justified" as an effort to discipline or train an animal, then the conduct is generally outside the scope of the anticruelty laws. As we saw above, the law permits the infliction of significant pain on an animal for purposes of training and disciplining, and a conviction for violating the anticruelty laws will be sustained only when "such a punishment and such infliction of violence is foreign to and not dictated by any feeling incident to humanity, save that of cruelty."[120] "Normal" punishment—and the attendant pain and suffering—can always be justified if the actions are reasonably calculated to facilitate the exploitation of the animal as part of an activity that is socially accepted; excessive beating serves no socially recognized purpose and results in the destruction of property, which, even though the property may belong to the defendant, represents a net loss to society.

The vast majority of cases in which defendants are found to have violated anticruelty laws involve the neglect of domestic animals, rather than the commission of affirmative acts, such as beating, burning, or torturing. Some of these decisions concern the neglect of animals such as dogs, cats, or other animals that are not ordinarily kept as food animals, and most of these cases involve what appear to be eccentric people who kept too many animals in their homes under circumstances unhealthy to both the animals and the defendants. For example, in *Reynolds v. State*, the court affirmed the conviction of a defendant who had confined "eleven dogs, one parrot, two tarantulas, two fox, and at least one snake" in filthy, cramped, and otherwise unhealthy conditions in her home, and had confined two rabbits and seven cats in a nearby shed that was filthy and hot.[121] In *State v. Linder*,[122] the court refused the defendant's motion to controvert a search warrant, given that the defendant had told officers that she had approximately twenty-nine dogs living inside her house, that the officers had observed through a window that the defendant's premises were infested with flies and saturated with urine and feces, and that the officers had observed dogs in various stages of neglect and mistreatment. In *LaRue v. State,* the court upheld LaRue's conviction for cruelty because the defendant had kept at his home a large number of stray dogs that suffered from mange, blindness, dehydration, parasites, infections, pneumonia, and distemper and had to be euthanized.[123] Cases like *Reynolds, Linder,* and *LaRue* involve mistreatment of animals that is outside of any accepted institutional exploitation of animals and is, therefore, regarded as a completely unproductive use of animal property.

Most neglect cases, however, involve farm animals. Although there is an established and accepted institutional framework that can—and does—accommodate pervasive cruelty to farm animals, this cruelty may be said to have economic benefit. Indeed, those involved in the industry argue that practices characterized as cruel, such as veal confinement, are justified by economic considerations. The neglect of farm animals, however, involves conduct that does not fit into this institutional use and that, like the other cases in this section, involve the socially undesirable destruction of property. For example, in *State v. Walker,*[124] the defendants failed to provide food, water, and shelter to their herd of 130 cattle, and many of the cows died. In *State v. Brookshire,*[125] in which the court affirmed the defendant's conviction for cruelty, the defendant, who claimed to be physically injured and unable to care for his herd, failed to supply food or water to his cows, and approximately fifty perished. There are many such cases.[126]

In all of these cases, whether they involve active cruelty or neglect, the notion of necessity is understood in its ordinary-language sense. This represents a significant departure from cases involving institutional animal exploitation, where necessity is understood by reference to what is considered acceptable within the context of the socially accepted activity. For example, in *Tweedie,* the defendant argued on appeal that the statute, which prohibited "cruelly kill[ing]" animals, was unconstitutionally vague. The appellate court treated Tweedie's argument with a brief but pointed response: "No idiosyncrasy of a trier of fact is required to conclude that the killing of the cat in this case was cruel. . . . It would be absurd for us to conclude that the killing of the cat in this manner was not a cruel killing prohibited by the language of [the statute]."[127] In a neglect case, *Cross v. State,*[128] the defendant, who was convicted of "unreasonably" failing to provide "necessary" food, care, and shelter for his horse, argued on appeal that the language of the statute was vague. The appellate court, which affirmed the conviction, held that although the qualifying adverb and adjective were "not defined by statute, . . . [they] are words in common use and, therefore, must be understood according to their common meanings in the context in which they are employed."[129] Juries and courts are permitted to apply the notion of necessity in a manner that reflects the ordinary understanding of the term precisely because the action or omissions in these cases occur outside the context of institutionalized animal exploitation. As I showed above, in cases involving institutional exploitation the jury or court is precluded from employing the ordinary notion of cruelty or necessity through those devices that are designed to ensure that such exploitation is effectively removed from the ambit of the anticruelty statutes.

## Penalties and Enforcement Difficulties

In addition to the various doctrines, described above, that have the effect of removing virtually all institutionalized exploitation of animals from the scope of anticruelty laws, other aspects of these laws exacerbate the inability of the laws to provide any meaningful protection to animals. Most important is that with very few exceptions anticruelty laws provide for the minimal level of criminal culpability. Most states treat violations of anticruelty laws as summary offenses or misdemeanors and provide for penalties that do not usually exceed a fine of $1,000 or a prison term of one year. Some states provide for more severe penalties. For example, California law provides that cruelty to animals may be treated as a felony, with a fine of up to $20,000 and a prison term of up to one year.[130] Wisconsin law provides that in certain cases the maximum penalty may be two years imprisonment and a fine of $10,000.[131] In any event, imprisonment is hardly ever imposed on violators, and the punishment is typically a fine that is far less than the maximum that is authorized. If the particular animal involved is the property of another, then the penalties are higher in some states, and the owner can always seek redress in a civil suit—an option not available when the animal is either unowned or is the property of the person who killed or injured the animal.

Another doctrine that serves to blunt the ability of these laws to protect animals involves standing to invoke the jurisdiction of the court. Standing requirements, discussed in Chapter Four, determine whether the party bringing the suit has the requisite interest in the matter in light of the relief requested. In Chapter Four, I discuss federal standing law. It is important to consider state standing briefly given that anticruelty laws are primarily state laws and that restrictive state standing rules can have a distinct impact on the enforcement of these laws. For example, in *People for the Ethical Treatment of Animals v. Institutional Animal Care & Use Committee,*[132] the Oregon Supreme Court held that an animal advocacy organization did not have standing to challenge the decision of a university animal care and use committee to allow certain experiments. The court held that the animal group was not an "aggrieved" party under state law, because the group asserted interests—the protection of animals and the inappropriate use of tax revenues—that were "concerns for political choices, interests that are not 'substantial' for the purposes of standing for judicial review."[133] In *Jones v. Beame,*[134] the plaintiff sought a declaration that the city of New York was operating certain of its zoos in violation of the anticruelty law, and an injunction against the selling of animals by the zoo. The court did not reach the case on the merits, since it held that the complaint should have been dismissed because the plaintiff and the courts were in no position to interject themselves into the discretionary management of public business by public officials. In *Walz v.*

after the injury, and reasoning that the amount of the award was not an accurate measure of the steer's fair market value given that the steer could still be sold for slaughter.[45] The court determined that the jury had relied on purely speculative evidence concerning the potential value of the steer, threw out the jury's verdict, and ordered a new trial.[46]

Many of today's most common household pets are mixed-breed dogs and cats, often obtained at minimal or no cost from shelters. As such, they have no discernible "market value." Thus, their owners frequently forgo legal remedies when the animals are negligently injured or killed, because they cannot recoup their true damages in the courts. An owner may suffer tremendous emotional distress when left without a beloved family pet, yet the loss of this unique being goes completely uncompensated under the market value approach.

The market value system of assessing damages for injury to personal property has gradually expanded to the point were some states now allow recovery for emotional distress of an owner resulting from harm to an animal caused by a veterinarian or other person, whether or not market value is also a factor.[47] Typically, claims for damages based on emotional distress are pursued through one of four avenues. It is important to recognize, however, that these cases do not remove animals from the category of personal property. Indeed, the "emotional-distress" cases focus exclusively on the reaction of a property owner to the loss of property. Moreover, the "emotional-distress" cases that involve animals are not unique breaks from past precedent; rather, these cases merely apply established principles of law concerning emotional distress over the loss of other personal property—specifically, family heirlooms—to the loss of another type of personal property.

First, in some courts, plaintiffs are allowed to recover the "actual value"[48] of their property. The sentimental value of the animal to the owner may be a component of such actual value and of any damage award based thereon, especially where there is no discernible market value. One of the first courts to consider the actual, or intrinsic, value of a pet was the New York City Civil Court, in *Brousseau v. Rosenthal*, a 1980 case.[49] Plaintiff left her healthy eight-year-old mixed-breed dog at a kennel for two weeks. When she returned to pick up her pet, she was told the dog had died. Plaintiff sued the kennel for loss of companionship and loss of protection. The court found the kennel liable for the death under the law of bailments and acknowledged the market value approach for damages to personal property but nevertheless held that Brousseau was not limited to a nominal award just because the dog had been given to her, was a mixed breed, and had no ascertainable value. The court held that an assessment of the dog's "actual value" to the owner was required in order to make her whole. Because her pet was Brousseau's sole and constant companion, and because loss of companionship had been long recognized as an element of damages in New York, the court said it must be considered in any award to plaintiff even though measuring such a loss in pecuniary terms is quite difficult.[50] Despite the judge's obvious sympathy for Brousseau's loss of her treasured pet, the judge awarded her only $550.[51]

In Illinois, a court held that actual value should be used to compute damages where the property in question has no market value.[52] Joseph and Anita Jankoski had taken their pet German shepherd to the Preiser Animal Hospital for some diagnostic tests. The hospital veterinarians administered anesthesia to the dog during the course of the exam, and the dog died. The Jankoskis sued the veterinarians for failing to administer the anesthesia properly and for failing to monitor the dog's condition. They sought to recover damages not for the dog's value but for their loss of companionship of the dog. The trial court stated that the Jankoskis could amend their complaint to ask for damages for loss of their property, but the Jankoskis refused because the dog had no value as property. The trial court then granted the veterinarians' motion and dismissed the suit. Upon the Jankoskis' appeal, the appellate court had to decide whether Illinois law recognized a legal claim for loss of companionship resulting from the negligently caused death of a dog. The appellate court agreed with the trial court that no action for loss of companionship of a dog could be brought in Illinois, because an animal is an item of personal property. The court said that while the usual measure of damages for personal property is its fair market value, where no such value exists the actual or intrinsic value of the property should be the basis of a monetary award. Although it refused to consider an independent claim for loss of companionship, the court did expressly state that "sentimental value" may be an element of the property's actual, or intrinsic, value. However, the court also stated, without reason, that damages for sentimental value would be severely circumscribed, thereby playing a game of semantics in which it could appear realistically to assess a human/animal relationship yet deny damages to the people who lost a cherished companion.[53]

Obviously, the actual, or intrinsic, value approach to assessing damages for the loss of a pet is better than the market value approach because it at least recognizes the reality of the relationship of a companion animal with the owner. It appears, however, that the damages awarded on the basis of actual, or intrinsic, value are not appreciably more than the meager amounts historically given on the basis of fair market value.

Second, some other courts take a different route to allowing sentimental value to play a part in damage awards for loss of property, through the tort of "negligent infliction of emotional distress."[54] Although this tort was once narrowly construed and applied only to incidents involving humans who were physically compromised by their emotional distress, at least one court has extended its applicability to incidents involving property damage alone.

The Hawaii Supreme Court, in a landmark 1981 case, upheld the right of plaintiffs to recover for emotional distress caused by the negligent killing of their family pet, even though none of the plaintiffs witnessed the event and even though they proved no physical manifestation (to them) of the alleged emotional harm.[55] The Campbell family was moving to Hawaii and was required by law to put their nine-year-old boxer dog, Princess, into a quarantine facility for 120 days. Upon her arrival at the quarantine station, Princess was examined and found to be in good health, except that she had a non-life-threatening growth on her gums. With

# Part II Conclusion

IN PART II of this book, I have sought to test the thesis of legal welfarism in a general context—the use of anticruelty laws to regulate animal treatment. I have argued that anticruelty laws do not give rise to animal rights but instead merely require that level of animal protection that is most consistent with maximizing the freedom of the property (animal) owner and that effectively prohibits only those animal uses that Locke would regard as "wasteful." This level of protection is facilitated by a group of doctrines that effectively permit any animal treatment that is part of an institutionally recognized use of animals.

In Part III of the book, I test the thesis of legal welfarism in a particular but more specific and complicated context: the use of animals in scientific experiments regulated under the federal Animal Welfare Act.

# PART III

---

*A Specific Application of the Theory:*
*The Regulation of Animal Experimentation*

> It is an affront to my own ethical sensibility to hear arguments that
> the suffering of animals is of greater moral weight than are the
> advancement of human understanding and the consequent
> alleviation of human suffering.
>
> > C. R. Gallistel, "Bell, Magendie, and the Proposals to Restrict
> > the Use of Animals in Neurobehavioral Research"

# CHAPTER EIGHT

## *Animal Experimentation:*
## *Animal Property and Human "Benefit"*

THE PURPOSE of Part III of this book is to test whether the thesis of legal welfarism works in a specific context involving a particular use of animals in a highly complex regulatory structure. That is, although everyone objects to animal "cruelty" in the abstract, "cruelty" often occurs in particular institutionalized contexts and is not merely the result of random acts that are often the subject of anticruelty cases. In most of these particular situations involving animals, the status of animals as property does not explicitly determine the outcome of our balancing of human and animal interests. Indeed, were that the case, the futility of the balancing approach would be obvious, and we would all spare ourselves the time and energy involved in trying to apply the balancing framework. Rather, the property status of animals is hidden in the background, and even those who are aware of that status and who accept its legitimacy rarely justify their exploitation explicitly or exclusively on the property status of animals. They rely instead on notions of human welfare, human rights, and, in some cases, theological notions about humankind's supposed dominion and control over animals. The property paradigm gets played out in the context of institutional structures that protect the preordained outcome of the balancing process while still maintaining that animal welfare is an important part of the calculus.

For example, much of the rhetoric in defense of fur focuses on the notion that people should have a "choice" in their clothing. Indeed, one person, a celebrity with a history of supporting progressive social causes, when criticized for wearing a fur, replied in a letter, "For me to choose to wear a fur coat or not is none of your business." This is "MY choice."[1] What is intriguing about this comment is that if the writer reflected for a moment, she would see that her argument in favor of personal liberty, or choice—a value highly prized in liberal society—begs a most elementary question: do we *morally* have the right to make the particular choice at issue? Surely, when we legislate against murder, we remove or reduce "choice." When we outlaw racial discrimination, we remove or reduce "choice." But those "choices"—to kill or to discriminate against others on the basis of race—are regarded as options that a civilized society cannot afford to offer its citizens

165

without threatening a breakdown of moral fiber. So we all agree that at least some "choices" may—and, indeed, *should*—be restricted. Why, then, do we think that the fur issue should be analyzed differently? Why do so many well-meaning and intelligent people think that the fur issue may be resolved by resorting to a most question-begging reliance on the notion of "choice?"

The reason is that the "choice" argument necessarily assumes that animals may be used for the relatively trivial purpose of providing clothing thought to be stylish, and that assumption necessarily itself assumes that the human/animal conflict balancing has already been performed and that the animal has lost. The only reason that could possibly explain our willingness to inflict hideous pain and suffering on millions of animals mutilated in leghold traps or electrocuted, gassed, or strangled on fur farms is that we have already made the decision that animal life and suffering matter so little that massive pain and suffering can be justified by fashion. An animal's fundamental interest in life and in avoiding pain and suffering is outweighed by our desire to appear sensual or desirable or stylish. The status of the animal is as a *thing*; "it" has virtually no interests that we respect unless its abuse does not increase—but, in fact, decreases—overall social wealth. Buried deep below the choice "argument" is a set of assumptions about animals, and these are all based on notions of animals as property, as *things*.

With this thought in mind, I focus on experiments using live animals, or vivisection, to show how the paradigm of property functions to facilitate and guarantee the exploitation of animals.

The use of animals in science is a broad topic that extends beyond what we might regard as experiments using live animals and arguably covers drug and product testing, the production of research products that rely on animals, and the use of animals in scientific education. My focus here is limited: I examine the legal structures that have arisen in connection with the federal Animal Welfare Act (AWA). To the degree required, I also mention other laws in order to explain the federal structure. I not only omit the other uses of animals that might be considered in a discussion of the use of animals in science, I also exclude, except in passing, statutes other than the AWA that directly concern experiments using animals. My goal is not to provide an exhaustive review of the uses of animals in science. Rather, I wish to focus on one mechanism for the regulation of animal experimentation—the AWA—in order to demonstrate how systematically flawed the act is and how these flaws reflect my thesis about legal welfarism.

In this chapter I explore the current controversy concerning vivisection. In the next chapter, I examine the development of the AWA from its inception to its most recent amendments. As part of this discussion, I explore the normative considerations that form the foundation of the act, including its implicit assumption that animals are, indeed, property. In the following chapters, I review administrative and judicial interpretation of the AWA in order to demonstrate how these normative considerations dictate the outcome of our supposed balancing of human and animal interests.

## Animal Experiments and Protected Benefits

Just as in the case of furs, the defense of animal experimentation almost always rests on unarticulated assumptions about the immorality or, to a lesser degree, the impracticality of challenging certain widely held—and morally justified—notions about private property, but these assumptions are usually not revealed in the first level of debate. Rather, the scientist points to the supposed benefits of animal experimentation. These benefits may consist of three types: (1) benefits that already exist and are currently available allegedly as the result of animal use; (2) benefits that portend some direct application to a problem in the immediate or reasonably foreseeable future ("applied" research); or (3) benefits that consist of knowledge without any immediate or beneficial application ("basic" research).[2] Moreover, scientists point to their right to use animals as a necessary step in the generation of these benefits and ideas, and they often claim that their use of animals is constitutionally protected because, as a general matter, scientific inquiry is protected under the First Amendment.

The view that experimentation is constitutionally protected enjoys some support among legal scholars. For example, the late Professor Thomas Emerson, one of the leading experts on the First Amendment, observed that experimentation "is a vital feature in the development of new information, ideas, and theories." He analogized experimentation to "marching in a demonstration, the publication of a newspaper, and the organization of a political party."[3] That is, experimentation is a necessary precondition for scientific speech; and, so the reasoning goes, if the latter is protected, the former must be as well. Professor Rebecca Dresser has defended this general view in the particular context of animal experimentation, arguing that "there are convincing legal reasons for postulating" a First Amendment right to engage in animal experimentation and that only "compelling" state interests suffice to justify the regulation of animal experimentation.[4] She argues that the "interest in protecting free inquiry and its resultant social benefits are potentially matters of constitutional concern."[5]

Related to this notion that science is somehow "special" is the view that the public has a right to this knowledge, especially insofar as it promises cures for diseases or other improvements in human life. Although American law does not (yet) formally recognize a property right in health care, there can be no doubt that large numbers of our own population, as well as those in many other parts of the world, view health care morally as the right of every citizen. In any event, everyone agrees that the "public" (however broadly or narrowly defined) deserves the best scientific information even if there is disagreement about how best to distribute that information. These mutually reflective views necessarily support each other. Scientists seek to protect their perceived right to gather knowledge by arguing that such protection can only serve the public right to the best health care. And to a lesser degree, but in an increasing number of instances, scientists point to the proprietary value of their ideas—that is, to the more directly pecuniary rewards they can obtain in the form of patents or other financially valuable property.

Although these various types of benefits, together with their alleged constitutional protection, appear to represent values other than property in animals, they reflect property values in two respects. First, they represent the view that scientists (or scientists in conjunction with the public) have property interests in knowledge. Second, and more important for present purposes, is that the benefits arguments, and the argument that science is constitutionally protected, serve to obscure the property status of animals by ignoring that the status of animals is even a moral issue. As in the case of the fur debate, those who argue in favor of vivisection fail to discern that they are begging the most important questions. If understood literally, the argument that scientists have a right to gather information would mean that the law could not, at least as a prima facie matter, impose *any* limits on the ability to gather information. But surely the law imposes many limitations on the right to gather information. For example, there are laws that prohibit even scientists from experimenting with hallucinogenic drugs in order better to understand brain biochemistry, or that prohibit scientists from kidnapping children for use in experiments. These activities would surely permit scientists to gather useful information, but for a variety of reasons, we have collectively decided that such knowledge would come at an unacceptably high price. Similarly, the public is not entitled to *any* knowledge, or knowledge gained by any means. The public would surely benefit if more knowledge about cancer could be obtained, and such knowledge could surely be obtained more easily and more reliably if we used humans rather than rats in laboratory experiments. But most people agree that irrespective of the unquestionable public benefit, such information would come at too high a moral price.

The problem with either version of the benefits argument (i.e., from the researcher's or the public's point of view) is that it *assumes* an answer to the question, Do animals have rights? and does not *provide* one. That is, we cannot even make a benefits argument unless we have already decided that it is appropriate to treat animals solely as means to human ends—as property—though such treatment is precisely what is sought to be justified in making such an argument. We can see this point clearly by considering a simple example. Imagine that a researcher has designed an experiment that will produce information that will lead directly and immediately to a cure for cancer. In order to do this experiment, the researcher needs ten human beings, who will be exposed to painful procedures without anesthesia. At the end of the experiment, the humans will be killed. The researcher has tried to find willing human subjects, but no one has volunteered, and if the experiment is to be done at all, it will be necessary to use unwilling human subjects.

In my experience using this hypothetical in hundreds of class lectures and public talks, no one has ever agreed that it would be permissible to use the ten unwilling human subjects for such an experiment. Even when reminded that cancer causes enormous suffering not only to victims of cancer but to their families, and even when the hypothetical is qualified to restrict the pool of eligible subjects to those without families or friends who might care about or miss them, the answer remains that it would not be morally permissible to use unwilling subjects for this purpose.

It is difficult, if not impossible, to understand how someone who subscribed to utilitarian moral theory could refuse to allow the use of the unwilling subjects for the experiment.[6] After all, millions of people worldwide die from cancer, and many of those people suffer considerably from the illness before they die. Their families also suffer before and after the patients die. Surely, if utilitarianism as a moral theory means anything, it means that we are obligated to relieve the hideous suffering and death from cancer if we can do so in a way that inflicts harm on only a handful of people. Nevertheless, people overwhelmingly reject such a scenario, and they do so on the grounds that consequences simply do not matter when certain interests are involved. That is, many of us would allow consequences to determine the extent of protection of only some interests. We might, for example, accept that our collective interests in having expensive stereos in our homes ought to be sacrificed if the consequence would be the elimination of hunger. But when it comes to fundamental interests, like the interest in life and liberty that is protected under our system of law, then we are unwilling to sacrifice such interests even if desirable consequences would result from the sacrifice. In other words, we believe that there are certain interests that cannot be abrogated even if desirable and substantial benefits would result.

Our moral intuitions are very strong in this respect and, indeed, are embodied in the legal standards governing human experimentation. Although recent reports indicate that American citizens have been used as experimental subjects without their consent, any experimentation involving human subjects that is conducted or supported by the federal government, or subject to governmental regulation, legally requires that the investigator obtain the informed consent of the subject.[7] An institution that performs research with human subjects must have an Institutional Review Board (IRB) that reviews all such research[8] and limits permissible experiments to those that minimize risk and that anticipate benefits that make any such risk reasonable.[9] The IRB is also required to ensure that all potential human subjects are fully informed of all risks, benefits, and alternatives, and that all subjects understand that their participation is voluntary and that they may withdraw at any time without penalty.[10] There are explicit precautions about the use of vulnerable populations, such as children, prisoners, pregnant women, the mentally disabled, and the economically disadvantaged, because such persons may be more open to coercion, which is explicitly prohibited.[11] If there is no informed consent, or if the detailed requirements for informed consent are not strictly satisfied, then the research is absolutely prohibited, except when the research risk is minimal, defined as risk no greater than that "ordinarily encountered in daily life," when the waiver or alteration of informed consent requirements is necessary and will not adversely affect the rights and welfare of the subject, and, where appropriate, when the subject is provided with pertinent information after participation.[12]

The reason for the IRB and the informed consent requirements is clear: human beings have the *right* not be used in experiments against their will and without their knowledge irrespective of any putative benefit to be gained from particular research. So the cancer experiment described above would be illegal for two reasons: first, the subjects would, by definition, be unconsenting, and the experiment would violate their rights; and second, even if the subjects consented, the risks presented by the experiment (the certainty of death) would make the experiment impermissible.[13]

The moral and legal concerns involved in experiments with human subjects make clear that the status of experiments as morally or legally permissible requires a *prior* determination of the research subject's status as rightholder and of the scope of rights possessed by the subject. The anticipated benefits from any experiment—however great those benefits might be—are irrelevant if the rights of the subject are to be violated by not obtaining voluntary and informed consent or by exposing even a willing subject to risk of death. The benefits argument advanced in support of vivisection is intended to establish the propriety of conduct *without* a similar determination of the status of the animal as rightholder; indeed, the benefits argument assumes that the animal is *not* a rightholder, because it is appropriate for the law institutionally to treat the animal solely as a means to human ends. In a sense, the benefits argument is not really different from the type of argument used in the context of anticruelty statutes. These statutes do not challenge the "dominion" that humans have over animals, but require that such dominion be exercised with care, unless there are human interests involved. Similarly, the benefits argument never confronts the issue of animal rights; indeed, the argument avoids this issue by assuming that animals are property without rights and that their exploitation may be justified by reference to various benefits.

The same circularity affects the argument about the constitutional protection of science. Even if experimentation as a general matter had a constitutionally protected status, that protected status would still not suffice to protect the use of animals in experiments without the very same question-begging assumption that comes into play in the context of the benefits argument: animals are property and do not have any respect-based rights in the first place. If animals were not property and had respect-based rights, then arguments about the constitutional status of science would be irrelevant, just as they are in the case of experiments involving humans.

Moreover, an appeal to the already extant benefits of vivisection is, as an empirical matter, problematic. For the better part of the past hundred years, scientists have routinely used animals in the development of virtually every procedure or drug. There is, therefore, no easy way to know which procedures or discoveries were causally related to the use of animals and which were not. Moreover, even if animals were crucial in the development of certain procedures or discoveries, there are many other human diseases and scientific questions that have resisted a solution even though millions of animals have been killed in the process. Indeed, only a small portion of the serious ills affecting human beings have been solved, and the rest have thus far resisted solution. In addition, there have been myriad instances in which animal use has frustrated scientific process. For example,

> prior to 1963, all 27 prospective and retrospective studies of human patients showed a strong association between cigarette smoking and lung cancer. However, almost all efforts to cause lung cancer in laboratory animals failed. . . . This lack of correlation between human and animal data delayed health warnings for years; subsequently, thousands of people died of cancer.[14]

An appeal to past benefits is intended to evoke the past successes of animal experimentation. But such successes are difficult to link causally to animal use; the number of medical successes (whether or not linked to animal experimentation) is dwarfed by the number of still unsolved mysteries; and there is strong evidence that animal experimentation has retarded medical progress, not facilitated it.

Although all appeals to the supposed benefits of animal experiments assume the property status of animals and assume that animals have no respect-based rights, the argument that the benefits of basic research, which may have no application whatsoever, can justify the suffering and death of animals demonstrates most clearly the futility of the supposed balancing of human and animal interests. That is, an argument from basic benefits maintains that human curiosity is a sufficient justification for using animals in experiments. For example, one defender of animal experimentation, who acknowledges that "most" animals who suffer in the course of neurobehavioral research suffer in vain, nevertheless maintains that scientific knowledge outweighs animal suffering and states that "it is an affront to [his] ethical sensibility to hear arguments that the suffering of animals is of greater moral weight than are the advancement of human understanding and the consequent alleviation of human suffering."[15] Another researcher admitted that "when evaluated by the standards of utilitarianism, my research is useless, as is all other basic research, because it does not have an immediate, known beneficial application." He adds that such "research must be judged by the links that it adds to the chain of knowledge, even if those links seem at the time to lack value."[16]

If the acquisition of knowledge can count as a "benefit" that entitles or morally justifies a researcher in inflicting pain or death on an animal, and if scientists ultimately determine what "benefit" means, then virtually any use of animals can be justified.

## Three Questions

A central thesis of this book is that legal welfarism embodies certain normative notions about animals that effectively obscure the important and fundamental moral concerns at stake. In Part II, I argued that anticruelty statutes conceal the normativity of legal welfarism by fostering the notion that anticruelty statutes prohibit cruelty as commonly understood—a reasonable notion in light of the wording of anticruelty statutes—when, in operation, these statutes are interpreted to provide only that level of protection that is consistent with the efficient exploitation of animals as property. The argument about the normativity of laws concerning laboratory animals is similar but more complicated. We can see this by considering the three levels of moral questions presented by the use of animals in experiments. The treatment (or nontreatment) of these issues under the AWA will become clearer in subsequent chapters.

The first question is whether it is morally acceptable to use animals in experiments *at all*. Although this is a highly charged moral issue, we will see that the AWA does not really address it. The AWA and its regulations assume that using animals in experiments is morally acceptable.

The second question is, given that animals can be used in experiments, are there limits placed on the use of animals? The AWA purports to "regulate" animal use by limiting the infliction of unnecessary pain or discomfort except when there is scientific "necessity" for the pain. Determinations of scientific necessity are almost always left to the discretion of the scientists doing the experiment. The primary criterion for determining necessity is benefit, and as I argued earlier, almost anything that justifies animal use in a particular situation—including satisfying the curiosity of the experimenter—can count as a "benefit." This explains why there are so many experiments that even those who are sympathetic to animal experimentation regard as atrocities.[17]

In sum, then, the first two questions concerning vivisection—whether to use animals at all, and what limits should be placed on the types of experiments that may be done—are, for all intents and purposes, not addressed by the law. This position becomes clearer when in subsequent chapters I describe the regulatory scheme created by the AWA.

The third question involved in animal experimentation—and the only one addressed in the law—is whether, once the morality of experimentation is accepted and scientific autonomy is granted to determine what uses of animals yield scientific benefit, the animal is treated "humanely," given the use. For example, some years ago, it was revealed that researchers were conducting burn experiments on pigs, who were given neither anesthesia nor analgesia. Animal advocates obtained a video of the experiment, which shows researchers blowtorching a conscious pig who has been tied down. The purpose of the experiment was allegedly to determine whether the presence of severe burns had any impact on the pig's eating habits. There is absolutely nothing in the federal (or state) law that would prohibit such an experiment. So the law does not address (except insofar as it allows) experiments in general and this experiment in particular. The law says only that once a scientist has decided to perform such an experiment, she must do so "humanely" and not inflict "unnecessary" pain on the animal. I hope that most readers find this characterization of the matter at least ironic and, more appropriately, profoundly disturbing. In showing this video to startled audiences over the years, I get an almost uniform reaction from lay audiences: "But wait.

That has got to be against the law. Isn't it?" This reaction indicates how the normativity of law obscures matters. People are aware that there are laws that require that animals be treated "humanely." What they do not recognize, however, is that many of the normative questions involved are not addressed explicitly by the regulatory structure and, instead, are assumed in light of the property status of animals. The regulatory structure answers questions that most people would find to be the least interesting moral questions presented. Once we decide to blowtorch an unanesthetized pig, a matter that the law does not explicitly address but leaves to scientific determinations of "necessity" and "benefit," the law requires that the researcher perform the act in a "humane" manner. The only possible meaning that "humane" can have in this context is that the researcher does not inflict "gratuitous" pain on the animal, given that the infliction of hideous pain has already been approved. A prohibition on the infliction of gratuitous pain in this context is perfectly compatible—and, indeed dictated by legal welfarism. Any infliction of "gratuitous" suffering would be, in Locke's terminology, a "spoiling" of property and would, at least in theory, jeopardize research data and result in an inefficient use of animal resources.

Indeed, researchers claim that they need to observe animal welfare standards in order to obtain valid research data.[18] This claim means no more than that animal property must be exploited efficiently but need not be given any additional protection. If the treatment of the animal impairs the integrity of the data, then the animal has been used in an unproductive manner. Accordingly, the only aspect of the inquiry addressed by present welfare laws is that of efficiency, and in that regard animal welfare means no more than a standard to ensure that an animal is used productively for the purpose for which the animal is intended—in this case, the collection of data, which might be jeopardized by treatment that fell below the "welfare" standard.

In sum, the laws that regulate vivisection are in this way identical with anticruelty laws.

## Animal Experimentation: The Current Controversy

Another reason to choose the area of animal experimentation to illustrate the property thesis is that there is currently a heated debate about vivisection in our society.[19] This debate is both confused and confusing, in part because the participants on all sides have neglected the normative notions of property that shape the very institutions that are criticized by a growing segment of the public. I explore some of the dimensions of this controversy in this section.

The use of nonhuman animals in biomedical experimentation has long evoked strong criticism on both moral and scientific grounds.[20] Nevertheless, the practice of vivisection continues today with vigor. A 1986 study conducted by the Office of Technology Assessment of the Congress of the United States (OTA Report) reported that estimates of the animals used in the United States each year range from ten million to one hundred million.[21] Nonhuman animals are used for a variety of purposes,[22] which frequently involve subjecting animals to severe pain,[23] psychological distress, and deprivation[24] and to confinement for prolonged periods of time.[25]

A recent study conducted at Tufts University claims that "it appears as though animal use (or at least the use of the six species primarily counted by the USDA) has declined by almost 50% since 1967." This assertion is based largely on figures reported by the Institute for Laboratory Animal Resources (ILAR), a quasi-governmental organization that is vehemently pro–animal use. The Tufts study acknowledges that in addition to general data collection problems as the result of reporting inadequacies and inconsistencies, there were inconsistencies between various ILAR reports (depending on whom ILAR was reporting the data for), and that there were discrepancies between ILAR figures and USDA reports. Moreover, the Tufts study apparently credits figures that report a decreased use of rats and mice, which are not even required to be reported under current federal law and about which accurate data collection is almost impossible. Nevertheless, the Tufts authors quite incredulously conclude that "despite these problems," they (the Tufts authors) accept the ILAR figures.[26] Whatever credibility is accorded to the Tufts study, it is clear, as I argue in Chapter Ten, that animal use has not decreased since the 1985 amendments to the AWA, which promised a reduction in the number of animals used, through the creation of an animal care committee and centralized data storage concerning animal experimentation.

Vivisection is the most heavily regulated area of animal use. A number of federal and state laws and regulations purport to regulate or restrict vivisection in some manner or other, and as such, a highly developed institutional structure operates on the legislative, regulatory, judicial, and institutional levels. Also, the very pervasiveness and complexity of this structure, together with the rhetoric of the research community, ostensibly support claims that animals are adequately protected under the law and that the law even provides some rights to animals. Indeed, many writers have commented upon the extent to which vivisection is more regulated than other animal uses, and have argued that such regulation discriminates against scientists and demonstrates an anti-intellectual attitude on the part of animal advocates. The irony is that despite this welter of laws and regulations, vivisection involves probably the *least* restricted use of animals. The reason for this is that the regulatory structure, which prohibits any interference with the conduct or design of an experiment, essentially permits self-regulation of vivisection by the biomedical community.

For most of the twentieth century, vivisection has been regarded as a necessity. That is, scientists and medical professionals have argued—and many continue to argue—that animals must be used if there is to be progress. That attitude is being challenged in four respects.

First, there is growing skepticism concerning the principle of Cartesian reductionism—a theory that requires us to reduce an object to its constituent parts in order to understand it. In many respects, reductionist thought was responsible for the widespread acceptance of vivisection as a "scientific" practice. To the extent that reductionism is rejected, one of the primary theoretical foundations of vivisection simply collapses.

Second, and related to the first point, there is an increasing recognition that science, as a body of knowledge, should not be viewed as presenting "truth" in some abstract sense, or as constituting an epistemologically superior form of knowledge. This recognition is slowly eroding the pedestal upon which science has presided for many years.

Third, profound changes have taken place in moral thought concerning non-human animals. The past fifteen years have seen an explosion of highly sophisticated philosophical thinking about the issues of animal welfare and animal rights. I touched on these notions briefly in the Introduction.

Fourth, animal advocates' exposure of scandals involving vivisection has generated considerable public skepticism about the use of animals in research.

## Cartesian Reductionism

René Descartes, a seventeenth-century rationalist philosopher, believed that in order to understand nature, it was necessary first to determine the parts that constituted the whole and then to determine how these parts related to the whole. Descartes viewed the world atomistically and in many ways was the chief proponent of what is referred to as reductionist scientific methodology. As biologists Richard Levins and Richard Lewontin write:

> In the Cartesian world . . . phenomena are the consequences of the coming together of individual atomistic bits, each with its own intrinsic properties, determining the behavior of the system as a whole. Lines of causality run from part to whole, from atom to molecule, from molecule to organism, from organism to collectivity. As in society, so in all of nature, the part is ontologically prior to the whole.[27]

In order to understand things, we must first take them apart, and then reconstruct them.

It is easy to see how this reductionist approach supported the practice of vivisection. In order to understand "nature," Descartes believed that it was necessary to resolve the object to be examined into its constituent parts. If the "object" happened to be a nonhuman, then the correct approach was to observe the structure and function of each of the parts inside the nonhuman.

This type of examination caused Descartes no moral difficulty, because, as was discussed in Chapter Two, Descartes also believed that nonhumans were "machines" that possessed neither consciousness nor mind. According to Descartes, "there is no prejudice to which we are all more accustomed from our earliest years than the belief that dumb animals think."[28] Although Descartes offered many reasons for this view of nonhumans, perhaps the most important was his belief that humans had souls and nonhumans did not.[29] Descartes also believed that nonhumans lacked consciousness, because they did not speak. Of course, Descartes was aware that certain humans also lacked the ability to use speech, but he responded that such humans would nevertheless use signifying behaviors instead of speech. Descartes did not recognize that nonhumans used signifying behaviors as well, and accordingly, he concluded that nonhumans lacked consciousness. For Descartes, the use of nonhumans for any human purpose—however trivial—simply raised no moral issue.

Although vivisection certainly existed before Descartes, it was the acceptance of Cartesian thought that facilitated the spread of the practice. We are, however, now moving away from the Cartesian model in our view of the nature of science. Philosophers and sociologists of science have argued convincingly that our scientific methodology and our view of "nature" are, like other aspects of our social life, not dictated by something "out there" that we merely describe more or less accurately. Rather, our understanding of nature is very much related to our prevailing social ideology. And as Levins and Lewontin argue, our prevailing social ideology—as was Descartes's—is that of a bourgeois society in which the individual is considered ontologically prior to the social. Our understanding of social phenomena requires that we first understand the autonomous individuals involved before we attempt to understand the collective. And so the prevailing paradigm in science, for Descartes and up until now, has been reductionist.

This reductionist paradigm is also being challenged more and more effectively and by an increasing number of scientists and health-care professionals. For example, holistic and homeopathic medicine are enjoying widespread popularity in both medical and lay communities. These alternative approaches explicitly reject reductionist methodology, with its accompanying theories of causation that run from part to whole. Holistic medicine does not focus on disease at the cellular level; rather, it seeks to preserve the homeostasis of the organism considered as a whole. Even those who adopt a more traditional approach are questioning the value of animal experimentation in light of traditional scientific method.[30] Similarly, many environmental scientists are arguing that our reductionist framework is leading to massive environmental damage because that framework prevents us from thinking about the environment in whole and complete terms—as a collection of biotic communities.

In addition, no one—except some of those who use animals in experiments—seriously believes any longer that nonhumans are not conscious or that they do not feel pain. Indeed, even many researchers acknowledge that nonhumans are more like us than Descartes ever imagined. There are, of course, differences between nonhumans and humans, and no one would doubt the existence or significance of those differences, but they cannot serve as a wedge between human and nonhuman. For example, there is increasingly widespread acceptance that many nonhumans are capable of autonomous action and personal relationships, and that some animals are able to use human language.[31]

## The Nature of Science

Until recently, science has, as a general matter, been regarded as "truth" and as different from, and epistemologically superior to, other forms of knowledge.[32] As Galileo stated, "in the natural sciences . . . conclusions are true and necessary and have nothing to do with human will."[33] There are three reasons science is viewed as "truth." First, science is seen as an enterprise that merely describes the physical world, based on empirical observations.[34] Second, scientific knowledge claims are seen as being testable.[35] Third, scientific knowledge claims are seen to be the product of certain institutional imperatives that effectively produce intellectual "neutrality" among scientists.[36] This view of science as generating "objective truth" has allowed scientists to protect various practices, such as vivisection, as necessary for scientific progress.

Despite the seductive simplicity of the view that science is "objective truth," the assumptions supporting the empiricist view are being received with increasing skepticism. More and more, science is viewed as a political enterprise that does not possess the imprimatur of "objectivity."[37] For example, induction in science assumes a certain uniformity in nature, but such uniformity must either be established empirically, which is circular, or established formally, which means that the principle of uniformity does not refer to anything in the world.[38] Observational terms in natural laws derive their meaning from the more abstract and speculative terms of scientific theories,[39] and alternative theories cannot be compared, because the meaning of terms changes from theory to theory.[40]

The close relationship between fact and theory suggests that facts cannot even be formulated in the absence of theory and that theory, then, cannot be refuted unequivocally by means of theory-based facts. No fact may qualify automatically as the falsification of a theory. Furthermore, observation itself is subject to interpretation. An investigator may "*not know what he is seeing* . . . until his observations cohere and are intelligible as against the general background of his already accepted and established knowledge. . . . This is part of Goethe's meaning when he says that we see only what we know."[41]

Perhaps the most profound change in the standard view of science was brought about by Thomas Kuhn in his seminal work, *The Structure of Scientific Revolutions.* Kuhn argues that the standard notion of scientific progress as a succession of theories more closely approaching truth is inaccurate because theories cannot be compared. Rather, science consists of a succession of research traditions, or paradigms, that are shared by practitioners of the particular science. The prevailing paradigm defines what problems are worth considering and prescribes the appropriate methodologies for investigating those problems. As puzzles that cannot be accommodated by the prevailing paradigm present themselves, practitioners are forced to choose a new paradigm. The choice of the new paradigm, however, cannot be governed by any "objective" criteria, because all paradigms are logically different and the ultimate choice of a paradigm must be based on nonrational factors.

Once we recognize that science is not a "neutral" or "objective" activity and that value-oriented considerations govern not only the choice of problems scientists choose to investigate but also the content of the information they generate, the criticism of scientific practices, including vivisection, is facilitated. Vivisection can no longer be regarded as necessary in any absolute sense, but must be seen instead as a contingent practice that, for a number of reasons having more to do with historical and economic considerations and less to do with "truth," is simply part of the now generally accepted paradigm of biomedical science.

Moreover, this emerging critique of the supposed objectivity of science is helping us to see the flaws of this prevailing paradigm. For example, toxicity testing generally involves exposing nonhumans to high dosages of a substance over a relatively short period of time and then extrapolating in order to determine how humans who are exposed to relatively low doses over a much longer period of time will respond. The problem is that there are no methods of extrapolation that are not, on some level, controversial. Indeed, a growing number of scientists are admitting that there are serious flaws with every method of extrapolation and, indeed, that the basic theory of toxicity testing using nonhumans may be mistaken.

### Emerging Moral Theories

Unfortunately, the recognition that Descartes was wrong in his views about animal consciousness, and the acceptance of the indisputable fact that animals feel pain, did not result in a rejection by science of the practice of vivisection. Rather, animal experimenters have simply substituted other moral theories to justify their exploitation of nonhuman animals. According to these theories, humans are justified in exploiting nonhumans as long as humans can identify some "benefit" that results from that exploitation.

Such views have been challenged by theorists such as Tom Regan, Carol Adams, Peter Singer, Stephen Clark, Barbara Noske, Bernard Rollin, Mary Midgley, and Richard Ryder, who, as I mentioned in the Introduction, have argued that there is no philosophical justification for most of what we do to nonhumans. Indeed, a cornerstone of Regan's theory is that animal rights follow from the rejection of mistaken Cartesian notions about animal consciousness. Researchers often accuse animal advocates of being "irrational" or "emotional." What is particularly interesting about this is that the widespread acceptance of vivisection rests on largely theological notions about supposed animal "defects" in general and on Cartesian theological notions about souls in particular. The scientist who supports animal experiments, then, finds herself in the peculiar position of defending an activity that has historically been justified almost exclusively on theological grounds, while the animal advocate argues that nontheological point that species bias is irrational given secular views about the relationship between speciesism and other forms of discrimination, and our recognition that nonhumans share certain characteristics with humans. In any event, the philosophical rejection of speciesism has deeply permeated general philosophical thought, and probably no more than a few college ethics courses taught these days do not include some consideration of animal rights.

### Exposés of Cruelty

Recent events have created public skepticism about the efficacy of the regulation of vivisection. Beginning in 1980, animal advocates obtained powerful proof of egregious abuses of laboratory animals and serious violations of federal law.[42] The first case involved the application of a state anticruelty statute to the activities of an animal experimenter, Edward Taub, a case that I discussed in detail in Chapter Four.[43]

In another, perhaps even more important case, a federally funded laboratory at the University of Pennsylvania was closed as the result of violations of federal law. The Head Injury Clinical Research Laboratory was established at Penn in 1975 and was directed by Dr. Thomas Langfitt and Dr. Thomas Gennarelli. The lab used primates and other animals to develop a model of head injury. In one series of experiments, the researchers tried to develop a reproducible head-injury model in baboons and to study the consequences of such injury. The specific type of injury to be studied was axonal injury, or injury to parts of nerves located in the brain. Axonal injury is contrasted with vascular damage, or damage to blood vessels, which would include contusion and subdural hematoma. The researchers sought to produce a controlled axonal injury through "accelerating" the baboon's head, rather than produce a contusion injury through striking the head. In order to study acceleration injuries, researchers encased the shaved heads of baboons in helmets made of dental stone, and then fitted the heads into metal helmets that were attached to a device that accelerated the baboon's head forward at a force equivalent to as much as two thousand times the force of gravity.

On May 28, 1984, a group called the Animal Liberation Front illegally entered the laboratory and removed approximately forty-five hours of videotapes that the researchers themselves had filmed. These videotapes, which disturbed everyone who saw them, showed, among other things, partially and fully conscious baboons writhing on the operating table immediately before the head trauma was inflicted, lab personnel mocking the brain-damaged animals and using them for supposedly humorous purposes, and lab personnel performing surgery under nonsterile conditions and smoking cigarettes and pipes during surgery and in the presence of explosive gases.

Copies of the videotapes were distributed by the the Animal Liberation Front to a number of recipients, including People for the Ethical Treatment of Animals (PETA), which then proceeded to make a twenty-four-minute video that contained excerpts from the original tapes together with narration. The excerpted video, labeled *Unnecessary Fuss,* after a comment made by Gennarelli in a newspaper interview, was distributed throughout the United States, Canada, and Europe. Parts of the video were shown on nationwide television, and the case drew attention from around the world.

Langfitt, Gennarelli, the university, the federal government, and many in the scientific community all defended the research at the head-injury clinic. Although the head-injury experiments raised many questions, three issues were most significant. The first issue was whether the baboons experienced pain during the experiments. Langfitt and Gennarelli, as well as university and NIH personnel, all stated publicly that the baboons were anesthetized during the experiments and experienced no pain. However, the research protocol itself indicated that the baboons were not anesthetized, and this was confirmed by one of the world's leading experts on the subject of pain, Dr. P. D. Wall, editor of the journal *Pain*, a professor at University College, London, and a supporter of animal experimentation. After review of Gennarelli's published work, Wall stated that "these animals were not anesthetized at the time of the head injury." He noted that the researchers used "1 mg/kg phencyclidine intraperitoneal. This is a low dose given by an unconventional route. This short acting drug has been discontinued in the UK because it frequently induced an agitated psychotic episode during recovery. This drug has an effect lasting about 10 minutes in monkeys." Wall noted that although the researchers used nitrous oxide in addition to the phencyclidine, the nitrous was stopped after the researchers finished inserting various tubes into the baboon's body. The baboon was then given an hour to recover before the injury was inflicted, and one hour "is certainly adequate for a full return of sensation and movement."[44]

Despite Gennarelli's and Langfitt's assertions that the animals were in deep anesthesia at the time of the injuries, it is clear from the videotape that the animals were conscious and struggling against their restraints immediately before their heads were accelerated. In addition, the videotapes contained a particularly gruesome scene in which a small baboon is tied to an operating table while two men perform surgery on the animal's exposed brain. As the baboon begins to move violently, and clearly in response to painful stimuli, one of the researchers states, "We better get some nitrous." The other researcher tells the baboon to "stop moving," and the first researcher states, "It hurts him, for Christ's sake." Neither man gives any nitrous to the animal, and they continue cutting into the brain of a clearly conscious and unanesthetized animal.

The second issue was whether the experiments had produced, or could produce, any results for human head injury. Despite the fact that the head-injury lab was established in 1975 and had been the recipient of millions of dollars of federal money, Gennarelli was unable to point to a single significant practical application to the problem of human head injury. Moreover, there was a serious question whether any of Gennarelli's data were valid given that he added an uncontrolled variable concerning the removal of the baboons from the head-injury apparatus. The videotape showed researchers removing the dental stone helmets from the injured animals with a hammer and chisel. The experiment was intended to study axonal injury from acceleration and explicitly sought to avoid any vascular damage that would be caused by a contact injury. The use of the hammer and chisel introduced a contact force as a new and completely uncontrolled variable into the experiment, and this method of dental-stone removal was never revealed by the experimenters in the protocol that had been submitted to the government or in any of the published papers that came out of this research. Experts in the field have stated that the removal of the helmets in this manner invalidated the data. One brain researcher who did animal experiments himself stated:

> Anyone who has ever worked with the brain, and is familiar with the delicate vasculature connecting the dura matter to the brain must shudder at the damage done to

the brain from these very forceful and repeated blows to the skull. . . . I cannot imagine that anyone could observe this sequence of events and still contend that these experiments could have any experimental validity.[45]

Another expert, a professor of veterinary medicine, stated that

after using carefully designed equipment to deliver a precise insult, the workers were shown using a hammer and screwdriver to remove the apparatus from the animals' heads. I saw numerous, sharp blows delivered to the heads of baboons who had just been traumatized. It seems to me that the impact of these blows would add a highly un-controlled variable to the experiment, particularly since there could be compounding of minor damage in those animals subjected to lesser trauma.[46]

The third issue raised by the videotapes concerned the attitude of the re-searchers toward the baboons. Gennarelli publicly defended the way in which he and his colleagues cared for the baboons: "These animals are cared for in exactly the same manner as our human head-injured patients," and the staff "is highly ded-icated to . . . the care of these animals and their humane treatment."[47] Langfitt echoed these views: "We treat the baboons the way we would treat human be-ings,"[48] and "researchers would never laugh at the apes."[49] The videotapes indi-cated otherwise. Throughout the tapes, lab staff are seen to be mocking the ani-mals and treating them cruelly. In one scene, a lab worker states that a baboon has a dislocated shoulder, but then lifts the animal by that shoulder. In another scene, the worker films an animal strapped to an operating table and then pans over to an-other part of the room where a partially incapacitated baboon named B-10, who had suffered massive brain damage, was strapped in a high chair. The worker states, "Cheerleading in the corner we have B-10. As you can see, B-10 is still alive. He's wishing his counterpart well and hoping for a good result." In one scene, a lab worker poses with an animal who has massive cranial hemispherical sutures, and the lab staff, including Gennarelli, laugh at the animal, whom they tease as having the "punk look."

By spring 1985 the protest against continued federal funding of the head-injury laboratory had reached a pitch. Animal groups in the United States and Great Britain, where some parts of the research were performed, had amassed a formidable coalition of supporters. Over fifty members of Congress demanded that NIH stop federal funding, pending a full and impartial investigation. Although the university purported to convene a "blue-ribbon" committee to investigate allegations of wrongdoing, it was revealed that the chair of the com-mittee was himself connected to the research in one of its earlier phases. Not sur-prisingly, the "blue-ribbon" committee absolved the lab of any wrongdoing. James Wyngaarden, then director of the NIH, was himself a former member of the University of Pennsylvania faculty and had declared that " 'this is [consid-ered] to be one of the best labs in the world.' "[50] In addition, a separate NIH site visit revealed no deficiencies, although a USDA inspection had found over sev-enty violations.

In the midst of public reaction, the intensity of which was not seen before or after this case, NIH decided to continue funding the laboratory. This precipitated direct action by animal advocates, and on July 15, 1985, over one hundred protesters from around the country occupied the NIH for three days.[51] During that time, intense negotiations were held between the protesters and the NIH, and on July 18, 1985, the NIH, at the direction of Secretary of Health and Human Services Margaret Heckler, closed the lab pending a full investigation. Secretary Heckler's action was supposedly based on a report issued by the NIH on July 17, 1985, which found that the experiments were not always conducted with proper supervision, that professional and technical personnel were not adequately trained, and that there was inadequate anesthesia and analgesia provided to the animals. The report concluded that the conduct of the experimenters constituted "material failure to comply with" federal policy on laboratory animals.[52] The NIH report states that scientists reviewing the experiments "criticized procedures involving twenty-two experimental animals in the anesthetic/analgesic review category."[53] In fall 1985 the university and NIH indefinitely suspended the research, and USDA imposed a fine on the university.

The Gennarelli case stands as probably the most important animal rights case of this century. Well-respected researchers at a well-respected university were depicted on videotape—that they had taken themselves—as engaged in what could only be described as brutal and barbaric behavior. Moreover, the researchers, the university, and the government all exerted extraordinary effort to deny what was clearly and unambiguously shown in the videotapes and contained in the researchers' own writings.

Contrary to the response to these incidents by the scientific community, which ranged from frenzied attempts to portray the criticized scientists as heroes to dire predictions of the end of science, both cases, Taub and Gennarelli, demonstrated that the law is resilient in its reluctance to interfere with the use of animals and that the scientific community is virtually unregulated in its use of animals. Although the federal government terminated the grants supporting the research and imposed fines in these cases, the biomedical community[54] and federal officials have continued to defend these experimenters. The government has recently recommenced funding to Gennarelli for head-injury experiments that will involve pigs but not primates. Taub's criminal conviction was reversed because the court held that scientific experiments involving animals—however cruel—were not covered under the anticruelty statute, and the Philadelphia district attorney, Ed Rendell, adamantly refused to prosecute Langfitt and Gennarelli.

The handling of these and other cases also served to highlight the inability of federal administrative agencies to control recipients of federal funds, and the incapacity of the biomedical community to exercise any significant self-regulation or internal discipline. Even moderates who defend some use of nonhuman animals in experimentation have remarked that funding agencies have "not properly addressed" animal protection concerns and that self-regulation by the biomedical establishment "has either been inadequate or it has not allayed public fears."[55] This skepticism has led some to argue that only significant government intervention and actual prohibition of at least certain types of experimentation will ameliorate the problem. Others argue that a reform of the current regulatory scheme will suffice. In both the Taub and Gennarelli cases, there was considerable evidence that the regulatory process had simply failed. I consider that evidence later.

Even those in the animal protection community who favor the regulation, and not the abolition, of animal experimentation have argued through the years that these regulatory standards are inadequate in practical effect and not enforced vigorously.[56] The problem with vivisection has nothing to do with how the statutes are interpreted or enforced; rather, the problem is that the laws themselves prescribe standards that are essentially unworkable. Although our legal norms purport to embody a substantial interest in preventing the unnecessary suffering and death of nonhuman animals, that protection is always limited by considerations of the utility of animal exploitation. Moreover, scientific notions of the "necessity" of animal experimentation would most likely be part of any assessment of the propriety of regulation. Although the law prohibits the infliction of "unnecessary" suffering on animals, the "necessity" of animal suffering in the research context is effectively determined by the research community alone, and the community seemingly tolerates the use of animals for any "scientific" purpose. There is simply no " 'common, shared, socially institutionalized, legally codified pool of intuitions' "[57] that serves to provide any generally accepted norm limiting the use of nonhuman animals in experimentation. To the extent that there is any norm at all, it is that animals can be used for any purpose. A 1985 study found examples of experiments in which animals were shocked, scalded, irradiated, and burned, as well as subjected to drug addiction, sleep deprivation, maternal deprivation, blinding, and forced fighting.[58] In many of these federally funded experiments, no serious argument could be made that improvements in human or animal health were anticipated.

Although there is a social critique of the use of animals in biomedical experiments, I do not mean to suggest that this critique has had any effect on the legislative, regulatory, or judicial levels. Indeed, in the next three chapters, I show that the legislative structure of the AWA has remained pretty much the same for almost thirty years and that Congress has steadfastly refused to interfere in any way in the content or conduct of experiments involving animals. The regulatory agency responsible for enforcement of the AWA, USDA, has demonstrated little interest in enforcement of the AWA, particularly as it concerns research facilities. And because of restrictive notions of standing, cases involving animals rarely get into the courts.

So, despite a growing opposition to the use of animals in experiments, the prevailing legal standards are as they have always been: property owners (in this case, research facilities) are able to use their animal property in whatever ways they wish, as long as they do not "waste" animal resources.

## Conclusion

In this chapter, I have discussed the current controversy involving the use of animals in biomedical research, and the shifting social consensus that is facilitating a critique of the use of animals in experiments. I also discussed the notion of "benefit" as used in this context: any appeal to the supposed benefits of animal experimentation, or to the protected status of science, assumes that animals are property without respect-based rights. Moreover, the supposed balancing of human and animal interests means that any benefit, however small, including satisfying the curiosity of the experimenter, is sufficient to permit the infliction of pain or death on an animal.

In the next chapter, I discuss the development of the federal Animal Welfare Act.

# CHAPTER NINE

## *The Federal Animal Welfare Act*

THE PURPOSE of this chapter is to introduce the reader to the primary regulatory structure that governs vivisection in this country—the federal Animal Welfare Act (AWA) and its implementing regulations, which represent the first and still primary legislation on the subject of animals used in biomedical experiments. The AWA was first passed in 1966 and was amended in 1970, 1975, 1985, and 1990. Nevertheless, the AWA is not as stringent as the British legislation concerning animals used in experiments, the Cruelty to Animals Act of 1876, which was made even more stringent in 1986.[1]

As a preliminary matter, I stress three points. First, the AWA is not the only source of regulation of the use of animals in experiments, although it is clearly the most important. There are other sources of regulation, the most significant of which involves the Public Health Service (PHS), of which the National Institutes of Health (NIH) is a part. PHS funds most experimentation involving animals, and most of the research facilities registered under the AWA receive funding from PHS. All PHS-funded research must comply with the PHS *Policy on Humane Care and Use of Laboratory Animals* (PHS Policy)[2] and with the NIH *Guide for the Care and Use of Laboratory Animals* (NIH Guide).[3] In addition, Congress provided statutory authority to certain PHS/NIH policies in 1985, at the same time that it enacted amendments to the AWA.[4] Most notably, the 1985 amendments require that the secretary of health and human services develop guidelines for the care and treatment of laboratory animals,[5] that each "entity" that receives funds from PHS have an Institutional Animal Care and Use Committee (IACUC),[6] and that each application or contract proposal contain an assurance that the entity is in compliance with the requirements of the law.[7] Moreover, in promulgating regulations pursuant to the 1985 amendments to the AWA, USDA consulted closely with PHS/NIH personnel and, according to USDA, achieved "a mutually satisfactory document" in the form of the final rules.[8] I do not discuss PHS/NIH policies in depth, but I mention them when necessary to provide a full explanation of the AWA.

Another influential source of federal regulation is the *Principles for the Utilization and Care of Vertebrate Animals Used in Testing, Research, and Education,* promulgated by the Interagency Research Animal Committee

(IRAC).[9] The IRAC principles, which were the result of collaboration among fourteen federal agencies, form the foundation of the PHS/NIH policies. A potentially important source of regulation is the NIH peer review process itself, which determines those grant or contract applications that will be funded, although there is absolutely no indication that the peer review process has in the past, or is currently, serving as an effective forum for ethical review. Indeed, all indications are that the federally imposed system of regulation is moving away from centralized control of these issues and toward local institutional control through the IACUCs.[10]

Second, as I discussed in the preceding chapter, at least three different questions determined the texture of any regulation concerning animal experiments. The first question is whether animals can be used at all. If the answer to the first question is negative, then the regulation will take the form of a prohibition on the use of animals or, at least, a prohibition on state funding of experiments using animals. If the answer to the first question is affirmative, the second question is, given that animals may be used for some reasons, what particular experiments are appropriate for animal use? The third question concerns what sort of treatment must be given to animals that are used for the approved reasons and in approved experiments. In this chapter, I argue that the regulation provided by the AWA concerns *only* the third question. That is, in passing the AWA and its amendments, Congress has always deferred—unquestioningly—to the position of the research community that experimentation using live animals is necessary for human health and for scientific knowledge. Moreover, Congress has always deferred to the position of the research community that Congress should not—and, perhaps, as a matter of constitutional law, cannot—regulate the "design, outlines, or guidelines of actual research or experimentation by a research facility as determined by such research facility" or "interrupt the conduct of actual research or experimentation" or "prescribe methods of research."[11] As a result, those uses of animals that are "appropriate" are those decided by the particular research facility, presumably in conjunction with any funding agency that may be involved. In any event, nothing in the AWA allows governmental regulation of the content or method of research. Consequently, the only issue regulated by the AWA is what constitutes "unnecessary" suffering, Congress having already decided that the use of animals in experiments is, as a general matter, "necessary" and that the use of animals for any particular experiment is also "necessary." I conclude that the AWA provides little significant regulation because it, like the anticruelty statutes, basically permits anything that is, in the judgment of the experimenter, necessary to facilitate the completion of the approved activity. Given that the research community is delegated almost exclusive control of interpreting the relevant regulatory norms, the only time that animal treatment runs afoul of the regulations is when an experimenter inflicts pain or suffering on an animal and has no valid reason for doing so. In other words, as in the case of anticruelty statutes, the only thing prohibited by the AWA and its regulations is the infliction of gratuitous pain and suffering. We do not judge the activity as "humane" or "inhumane" by reference to any standard external to the professional norms of the research community, and those norms permit the infliction of severe and prolonged pain on animals as long as there is some "scientific" justification. Rather, "inhumane" treatment is defined exclusively as treatment that results in the "waste" of animal resources in experiments that do not produce reliable scientific data. Although some economists view legislation to be efficiency reducing (as opposed to judge-made laws, which are considered efficiency promoting),[12] congressional allocation of resources in the various versions of the AWA has strongly protected the rights of property owners to use their animal property as they wish and has allowed into the process little, if any, sentiment that transcends the minimal requirements of legal welfarism. In a sense, the legislature has struck a bargain with the research community that the courts enforce through restrictive notions of standing.

Third, in discussing the development of the AWA through its various amendments, I caution the reader that it is not my intention to present an exhaustive history of the statute and the circumstances surrounding its passage and subsequent amendments. My limited purpose is only to explain the more important requirements of the AWA as they affect animal care, treatment, and handling. It is clear that despite excellent histories of some phases of the humane movement, no scholar has yet produced a complete historical treatment of the AWA. This is unfortunate because the history of the AWA and its amendments, in light of the character of the humane movement in the 1960s and beyond, the various legislative and administrative approaches to that movement, and the responses of the research community, is both fascinating and essential to a full understanding of the conflict over animal rights that now exists.

I briefly discuss pre-AWA attempts to regulate the use of animals in experiments in order to provide a context in which to understand and evaluate the AWA.

## Efforts Before 1966 to Regulate the Use of Animals in Experiments

The use of animals in experiments in the United States was a relatively rare phenomenon before the mid-1800s. By 1870, however, the practice had become widespread, and students began to perform vivisection as part of their study of physiology. One of the first to push for regulation of vivisection was Henry Bergh, a New York humanitarian who founded the American Society for the Prevention of Cruelty to Animals.[13] Although there were local attempts to combat vivisection, the next significant attempt to legislate against vivisection occurred in the District of Columbia, which was "a major center for experimental medicine."[14] The bill was a more limited version of British legislation but had a similar orientation toward restricting painful experiments on animals and establishing a licensing procedure.[15] Although discussion of the cruelty involved in vivisection was extensive, there was equal concern over the "sharp difference of opinion among medical men as to the value of vivisection." Some researchers stated that "the discoveries already made warrant the claim that human suffering is to be mitigated and human life greatly prolonged through the instrumentality of torture and experimentation upon the lower animals." Other medical experts denied "that any real advances have been made in medical knowledge in the laboratory of the biologist, while at the same time they deprecate[d] and denounce[d] the cruelties inflicted upon dumb animals by the vivisectionist."[16] The report cited a survey taken of physicians in New York and Massachusetts, in which 1,239 replies were received: 28 were "evasive," 243 were in favor of unlimited vivisection, and 968 were opposed to vivisection.[17]

The hearings indicate that support for legislation was strong not only among researchers who were opposed to the use of animals in experiments but also among leading jurists, politicians, scientists, and even military leaders.[18] The report states further that "it would be interesting to cite the thousands of names of leading physicians, clergymen, educators, and others who have unsparingly denounced some of the practices of vivisectionists. It warms the heart to know that men like Chief Justice Coleridge, Dr. Morgan Dix, Dr. Phillip S. Brooks, Alfred Tennyson, Robert Browning, [and] John G. Whittier" opposed at least some vivisection.[19]

The opponents of the bill recognized that the legislation threatened the traditional freedom accorded to researchers not to be regulated, and "the physiologists and their allies could afford to take no chances."[20] William Welch of Johns Hopkins and Henry Bowditch of Harvard formed a committee of leading scientific organizations and produced a statement, signed by researchers around the country, opposing the bill. Interestingly, many of those who opposed the bill claimed, in a somewhat contradictory way, both that the legislation was unnecessary, because its provisions were already observed by those doing vivisection in the District of Columbia, and that if passed, the bill would prohibit experimentation with animals altogether in the District of Columbia. The opponents argued for the most part that the most invasive procedure used involved innoculations, which were subsequently exempted from the anesthesia provisions. Further, researchers were strongly opposed to any visitation of their laboratories by inspectors. The National Academy of Sciences opposed the legislation on the ground that it would impede science, and argued that the use of animals for any human benefit was "a law of nature" and would continue "as long as man claims dominion over the brute creation."[21] Largely as the result of the impressive array of opponents marshaled by Welch and Bowditch, the bill was defeated. The bill was reintroduced in 1899, 1900, and 1902 and was defeated.

Throughout the first half of the twentieth century, various bills regulating vivisection were proposed concerning vivisection in the District of Columbia, and hearings were occasionally held.[22] In 1946, animal advocates in Congress once again sought to regulate animal experiments in the District of Columbia, this time seeking to prohibit experiments on living dogs. Hearings were held, and the research community, including NIH, vigorously opposed the bill, presenting witness after witness who claimed to have been cured of some malady or other as the result of procedures that were tested on dogs. The bill was defeated.[23]

Literature on the humane movement in the United States has generally ne-glected to discuss (or even acknowledge) the numerous bills introduced at the federal level that preceded the AWA. These bills, like the unsuccessful bill in-troduced for the District of Columbia, were, for the most part, modeled on British legislation, passed in 1876, which had as its primary focus a centralized licens-ing authority and a presumption against painful experiments on animals. For ex-ample, in 1960 a bill was introduced in the Senate that prohibited animal use ex-cept "when no other feasible and satisfactory methods can be used," and required a certificate of compliance issued by the secretary of health, education, and wel-fare as a precondition to the receipt of federal funds for experiments.[24] The bill required that animals be anesthetized, and provided for painless euthanasia im-mediately upon the conclusion of the pain-causing procedure unless inconsistent with the object of the experiment. Any painful experiments could be conducted only by the holders of special licenses the qualifications for which were to be de-termined by the secretary, and any animals used for surgery training were re-quired to be anesthetized during the procedures and euthanized before recover-ing consciousness.

A bill similar to the 1960 bill was introduced in the House of Representatives in 1961, along with another bill that would have established an Agency for Labo-ratory Animal Control, to be headed by a commissioner of laboratory animal con-trol appointed by the president and approved by the Senate for a five-year term, during which the commissioner could not be removed from office except under circumstances that would justify the impeachment or removal of a federal judge.[25] This second bill provided strict criteria for qualification of individuals to use ani-mals in experiments, and it also provided that although the commissioner could approve the withholding of pain relief if the experiment warranted it, any animal who would suffer prolonged pain or stress as the result of an experiment was re-quired to be euthanized painlessly after completion of the procedure, whether or not the objective of the experiment had been attained.

Hearings were held on these bills, and needless to say, the response of the research community was predictably negative to both. For example, the American Medical Association (AMA) stated that the bills were "likely to cause serious interference with, and irreparable harm to, the conduct of highly important research." The AMA added that this attempt to regulate the use of animals in experiments "implies a shocking and unjustified indictment of scientists and doc-tors which is unwarranted."[26] State and local university regulations, codes of ethics, and the requirements for "proper scientific research" were, according to the AMA, "adequate to secure and protect the objectives of the proposed legisla-tion."[27] The National Society for Medical Research stated that "if a Texas mil-lionaire wanted to give his pet hound the world's finest care, he would be hard put to equal the kid-gloves treatment which thousands of dogs receive today in mod-ern animal research laboratories throughout the Nation."[28] Many commenters stated that since good research required animals who were well treated, the very demands of science obviated any need whatsoever to regulate scientists.[29] From

1962 to 1965, at least four more federal bills were introduced on regulating the use of animals in experiments. All of these bills were variations on the theme of centralized governmental regulation through a certificate-and-license process, and for the most part, their provisions were very similar.[30] The research community opposed all legislation. In response to various bills introduced in the Eighty-seventh Congress, the American Veterinary Medical Association stated that it was opposed to the bills, which required licensing, reporting, record keeping, pain relief unless scientifically necessary to do otherwise, and the establishment of a federal agency on laboratory animals to be headed by a lawyer, " 'because it would place laymen in the position of dictating to medical scientists the nature and extent of their research with animals.' " Moreover, the legislation erroneously presumed "that pain and treatment of animals can be interpreted in terms of man's response to the same conditions," and these issues " 'are best left to the veterinarians and other biological scientists who specialize in the care of experimental animals.' "[31]

At least one state made an early effort to regulate the use of animals in experiments, apart from efforts to use anticruelty statutes to regulate animal use[32] and in addition to any statutes that concerned the acquisition of abandoned animals by research facilities.[33] In 1947 Michigan enacted a law that established an advisory committee in the state department of public health, composed primarily of the deans of schools that used animals, as well as two representatives of humane societies, and empowered to promulgate rules and regulations "controlling the humane use of animals."[34] Under the law, no person can keep or use animals for experiments unless registered to do so, and although the state is required to grant registration to anyone who complies with the applicable standards, the state can also revoke or suspend the necessary registration. The law continues in existence today in essentially the same terms.[35]

## The Development of the Federal Animal Welfare Act

### The Laboratory Animal Welfare Act of 1966

Perhaps the most interesting thing about the AWA is that this first piece of American legislation on the subject of laboratory animals had little, if anything, in common with the efforts in the late 1890s and early 1900s in the District of Columbia or with the efforts in the 1960s to regulate on the federal level. Those efforts, which were, for the most part, modeled on British legislation, provided for centralized licensing facilities, reporting, and tightly controlled use of animals in painful experiments. The AWA began as the Laboratory Animal Welfare Act of 1966, which was signed into law by President Johnson. The 1966 act came about not as an attempt to regulate the use of animals in laboratories but rather as the result of public outrage over the practice of stealing companion animals for sale to laboratories. Senator Dole characterized the 1966 act quite accurately as "the dognapping bill of 1966."[36] Although certain animal protection advocates had attempted to ameliorate the hideous conditions involved in "dealing" between suppliers and laboratories, the matter was brought more sharply into focus when, in 1965, Congressman Resnick of New York introduced H.R. 9743, a bill to license dog and cat dealers. Resnick had been personally involved in an attempt to help a family recover a stolen dog who was taken by a dealer to a laboratory. The dog was killed by researchers before she could be rescued, but the incident proved to Resnick the desirability of federal regulation of dog and cat dealers.

The stated purpose of H.R. 9743 was "to protect the owners of dogs and cats and other animals from theft of such pets and to prevent the sale or use of stolen dogs and cats and other animals for purposes of research and experimentation."[37] Congressman Poage stated, "There is overwhelming evidence that a substantial percentage of cats and dogs sold to hospitals and research laboratories are family pets which have been stolen."[38] It is clear that the purpose of the bill was to protect the *property* of people—their dogs and cats—from being stolen. Other representatives and senators introduced bills similar to the Resnick bill.

On September 2, 1965, hearings on H.R. 9743 (and similar House bills) were held before the Subcommittee on Livestock and Feed Grains of the House Committee on Agriculture. Although H.R. 9743 was a modest proposal to protect property and could not reasonably be construed as any "threat" to animal experimentation, researchers vigorously opposed the bill. For example, the New York State Society for Medical Research charged those who supported the bill with making "emotional appeals," since, in reality, the theft of companion animals was "rare."[39] The New York State Veterinary College at Cornell University actually claimed that H.R. 9743 represented an "unnecessary restriction on the betterment of the welfare of animals," in part because it would "increase the cost of veterinary education by making those animals obtained more expensive."[40] Researchers from the State University of New York objected to the bill, stating that "restrictive legislation relating to the supply of dogs and cats will only serve to hamstring medical research in this country. The high quality of medical knowledge and treatment in the United States is a product of free, unhampered efforts of dedicated investigators."[41] The Medical Society of North Carolina, together with the medical schools of the University of North Carolina at Chapel Hill, Duke University, and Wake Forest College, stated that H.R. 9743 "would be detrimental and restrictive to legitimate scientific research and to medical education, and would render the legal acquisition of such animals for these purposes much more difficult and much more expensive."[42]

More hearings were held in the House of Representatives in 1966 concerning H.R. 9743 and the approximately thirty other similar bills on the subject.[43] Again the research community objected vociferously to the legislation, claiming that the problem of stolen animals had been exaggerated and that federal regulation would only drive up the cost of acquiring animals and, as a result, decrease the total amount of research. What was particularly interesting, however, was the reaction to the proposed legislation on the part of the Department of Agriculture, to which enforcement of the legislation was to be given. Although USDA did not object to the legislation, Secretary Orville Freeman stated that the primary animal-related functions of USDA pertained to livestock and poultry and that "there is question as to whether it would not be more desirable that a program such as that in question be administered by a Federal agency more directly concerned."[44] From the outset, USDA did not regard the welfare of laboratory animals to be within its scope of administrative concern. Perhaps this accounts for what the Congress's Office of Technology Assessment has subsequently labeled "a lukewarm commitment to enforcement" of the AWA by USDA, and for its subsequent opposition to amendments of the AWA.[45] Similar hearings were held in the Senate on March 25, 28, and May 25, 1966, and produced the same flurry of objections from the research community and a plea from USDA to lodge enforcement of the legislation with some other federal agency.[46]

Although there was initial opposition to the bill, public support was galvanized by an article in the February 4, 1966, issue of *Life* magazine. The article displayed shocking photographs of the conditions in which dog dealers kept animals destined for laboratories. Concerned persons sent more letters to *Life* than the magazine had received on any other article, and sent more letters to Congress than were sent on issues such as civil rights and the war in Vietnam. The NIH attempted to stop the Resnick bill first by proposing self-regulation in the form of the American Association for Accreditation of Laboratory Animal Care (AAALAC) and then by attempting to secure various exemptions. Despite these efforts by the research community, the bill was passed and signed into the law in 1966, with the USDA given responsibility to enforce the law and to promulgate regulations, the first of which were proposed in 1967.

The Laboratory Animal Welfare Act was, in every respect, a very moderate piece of legislation. The preamble to the act stated that its purpose was "to protect the owners of dogs and cats from theft of such pets, to prevent the sale or use of dogs and cats which have been stolen, and to insure that certain animals intended for use in research facilities are provided humane care and treatment."[47] The act defined "animal" as "live dogs, cats, monkeys (nonhuman primate mammals), guinea pigs, hamsters, and rabbits."[48] The act may, for present purposes, be considered as having addressed four areas.

First, the secretary of agriculture was directed to "promulgate humane standards and recordkeeping requirements governing the purchase, handling, or sale of dogs or cats by dealers or research facilities at auction sales."[49] In addition, the secretary was directed to "promulgate standards to govern the humane handling, care, treatment, and transportation of animals by dealers and research facilities." The act provided that "such standards shall include minimum requirements with respect to the housing, feeding, watering, sanitation, ventilation, shelter from extremes of weather and temperature, separation by species, and adequate veterinary care." The statute carefully specified, however, that in promulgating these standards, the secretary was not empowered to "prescribe standards for the handling, care, or treatment of animals during actual research or experimentation by a research facility,"[50] and was not authorized to propose any "rules, regulations, or orders for the handling, care, treatment, or inspection of animals during actual research or experimentation by a research facility as determined by such research facility."[51] The 1966 act, then, exempted research facilities from complying with humane standards during actual experimentation.

Second, the act required that dealers be licensed[52] and that research facilities be registered, though not licensed.[53] Research facilities were prohibited from purchasing dogs or cats from anyone but a licensed dealer.[54] Dealers were required to keep a dog or a cat for at least five business days after acquiring the animal before selling the animals.[55]

Third, dealers were required to mark or identify all dogs or cats transported, delivered for transportation, purchased, or sold in commerce.[56] Research facilities were required to keep records concerning dogs and cats but not monkeys, guinea pigs, hamsters, or rabbits.[57]

Fourth, the act directed that the secretary "shall make such investigations or inspections as he deems necessary to determine whether any dealer or research facility has violated or is violating any provision of this Act or any regulation issued thereunder."[58]

The act provided for penalties as well. In the case of dealers, the secretary was permitted to suspend or revoke the dealer's license, and dealers were liable to imprisonment for up to one year and a fine of up to $1,000.[59] In the case of research facilities, civil fines of $500 per violation per day were authorized if the facility knowingly violated a USDA order to cease and desist violating the act.[60]

## The 1970 Amendment

In 1970 Congress amended the Laboratory Animal Welfare Act of 1966, which became the Animal Welfare Act of 1970.[61] The amendment represented "a continuing commitment by Congress to the ethic of kindness to dumb animals" and reaffirmed that "small helpless creatures deserve the care and protection of a strong and enlightened public."[62] There were four fundamental changes effected by the 1970 amendment.

The first change was an expanded definition of "animal" to include "any live or dead dog, cat, monkey (nonhuman primate mammal), guinea pig, hamster, rabbit, or such other warm-blooded animal, as the Secretary may determine is being used, or is intended for use, for research, testing, experimentation, or exhibition purposes, or as a pet."[63] The definition of "animal" excluded farm animals.

The second change expanded the scope of persons covered by the act. The amendment expanded the definition of "research facility" to cover "any school (except an elementary or secondary school), institution, organization, or person that uses or intends to use live animals in research, tests, or experiments." The original act had restricted covered facilities to those which used dogs and cats. The amendment also expanded the definition of "dealer" to include not only those involved in the buying, selling, or transportation of animals for research purposes but also those involved in the supply of animals for educational purposes or for exhibition purposes or as pets, excluding most retail pet shops.[64]

Moreover, the amendment added a new category of covered person—"exhibitors"—defined as "any person (public or private) exhibiting any animals, which were purchased in commerce or the intended distribution of which affects commerce, or will affect commerce, to the public for compensation."[65] This permitted coverage of auctions, circuses, zoos, and carnivals but excluded pet shops, livestock shows, rodeos, and other exploitative practices. Record-keeping and inspection provisions were extended to these newly covered entities.

The third major change initiated through the 1970 amendment was an expansion of the standards for the humane treatment of animals. The original 1966 act required the secretary to promulgate standards for the "adequate veterinary care" of covered animals. The 1970 amendment expanded upon the concept of "adequate veterinary care" to include "the appropriate use of anesthetic, analgesic or tranquilizing drugs, when such use would be proper in the opinion of the attending veterinarian of such research facilities." Again, the amendment was careful to establish that in promulgating standards for the humane treatment of animals, the secretary was not in any way to affect the "design, outlines, guidelines, or performance of actual research or experimentation by a research facility as determined by such research facility."[66] In discussion of the amendment in the House, sponsor Tom Foley made clear that

> the bill does mandate adequate veterinary care, including the use of analgesics and tranquilizing drugs, but it does preserve complete control of the research institutions with respect to the use of analgesics or tranquilizing drugs. In other words, Congress imposes an ethic of adequate veterinary care including appropriate use of pain-relieving drugs but the decisions are exclusively in the hands of the research institutions, and their judgments are final.[67]

These sentiments were echoed in the Senate discussion, where one of the cosponsors of the amendment stated that although the amendment "sets forth the basic creature comforts which must be afforded to these animals, including the necessity for the avoidance of pain through appropriate drugs and veterinary care," the amendment also "recognizes the prerogatives of the medical community and the contributions which these animals are making to the health and welfare of mankind, and in no way authorizes the Secretary to control or interfere with scientific research or experimentation."[68] In addition, Senator Dole, another cosponsor, included in the record of the Senate debate an article carefully pointing out that those who sought regulation were at odds with those who sought the abolition of all research, and that the former did not seek to regulate the content or conduct of research in any manner.[69]

Although the 1970 amendment made crystal clear that there could be no regulation of research decisions or regulatory criticism of institutional judgments concerning the propriety of the use of anesthetics or analgesics, the amendment did require that each research facility file an annual report demonstrating that the facility followed "professionally acceptable standards governing the care, treatment, and use of animals, including appropriate use of anesthetic, analgesic, and tranquilizing drugs."[70] The amendment also authorized the secretary to promulgate humane standards and record-keeping requirements concerning the purchase, handling, or sale of animals by research facilities, dealers, exhibitors at auction sales, and operators of auction sales.[71]

The fourth major change wrought by the 1970 amendment created penalties for those who assaulted or interfered with inspectors in the performance of their duties.[72] In addition, the amendment made the research facility, dealer, exhibitor, or operator of an auction liable for the acts of agents and employees.[73]

### The 1976 Amendment

In 1976 Congress again amended the AWA,[74] this time focusing on three changes. The first change expanded the range of persons covered by the AWA to include the "intermediate handler," defined as "any person . . . who is engaged in any business in which he receives custody of animals in connection with their transportation in commerce," and the "carrier," defined as "the operator of any airline, railroad, motor carrier, shipping line, or other enterprise, which is engaged in the business of transporting any animals for hire."[75] The legislative history reports that witnesses testified to "hundreds of examples in which live animals which were injured, diseased, or otherwise unfit to travel were nonetheless shipped, with cruel results. Some animals were shipped in containers or crates which were either flimsy or constructed in a fashion virtually guaranteed to result in injury to the animal."[76]

Second, the 1976 amendment made it "unlawful for any person to knowingly sponsor or exhibit an animal in any animal fighting venture to which any animal was moved in interstate or foreign commerce."[77]

The third change expanded the definition of "dog" to include "all dogs, including those used for hunting, security, or breeding purposes."[78]

What is interesting about the 1976 amendment is that Congress amended the preamble of the AWA to reflect different priorities. The original AWA stressed that the purpose of the AWA was to protect against the theft of pets from their owners. In 1976 Congress rewrote the preamble and listed as the purposes of the act (1) to ensure the humane treatment of animals used in research facilities, (2) to assure humane transportation of animals, and (3) to protect owners of pets from theft of their property.[79] Although the emphasis had, according to the preamble, shifted from pet theft to humane treatment, the substance of the 1976 amendment was really no different from the 1970 amendment or from the 1966 act itself. That is, the original act sought to ensure that animals would receive humane treatment in research facilities, but accorded unbridled discretion to the facilities themselves to determine what type of treatment was "humane" under the circumstances, and accorded complete deference to the research community to determine its own uses of animals in experiments.

### The 1985 Amendment

Between 1976 and 1985, the entire context of the regulation of animal experimentation changed dramatically. As the result of various cases in which federally funded research facilities were shown to be involved in the egregious abuse of animals, Congress held hearings in 1981 that captured public attention.[80] Following those hearings, a bill was proposed in 1982 that would, among other things, increase accreditation requirements for facilities, create animal care committees as a permanent fixture of (local) peer review for projects involving animals, require "merit review" of projects to determine whether the scientific knowledge anticipated outweighed animal suffering and distress, and require the development of alternatives to the use of live animals. As expected, the research community opposed the legislation. William Raub, representing the NIH, argued that "the authorities now in law and the administrative mechanisms already at hand are adequate if they are utilized fully."[81] He added that the NIH "believe[s] that the existing system based in the USDA is fundamentally sound in attempting to insure that the statute meets with appropriate compliance."[82] The USDA agreed.[83] Although the legislation was defeated, the push for amending the AWA only intensified.

The result was that in 1985 Congress undertook the only really substantial revision of the AWA since its enactment in 1966. Representative Brown, who sponsored the legislation in the House, stated that "there has been an increasing concern among the public that some laboratories are below currently set standards." He added that there was a question "whether current law adequately addresses the humane care of laboratory animals. At present, there is no law which requires researchers to use painkillers during an experiment causing pain to animals."[84] Brown's bill, sponsored by Robert Dole in the Senate and labeled the Dole-Brown amendment, was passed in 1985 as part of the Food Security Act of 1985.

The 1985 amendment once again provided Congress with an opportunity to explain the congressional purpose behind animal welfare legislation. In 1966 that purpose was primarily to protect owners of animals from the theft of their property. In 1970 and 1976 the focus shifted more toward the importance of the humane treatment of nonhumans used in biomedical experiments. By 1985 Congress began to focus primarily on humane standards, on alternatives to the use of animals, and on the growing public opposition to vivisection. Accordingly, in the preamble to the 1985 amendment, Congress made four findings: (1) that the use of animals is instrumental for advancing knowledge and cures; (2) that alternatives to live animals are being developed and that these alternatives are more efficient than animal use; (3) that preventing unnecessary duplication of experiments is desirable in light of federal budgetary concerns; and (4) that measures that promote animal welfare are necessary to the progress of research in light of public concern about animals.[85] The 1985 amendment to the AWA changed the act in nine significant respects.

First, the amendment required that the secretary shall promulgate minimum standards to govern the "humane handling, care, or treatment of animals," and "for exercise of dogs . . . and for a physical environment adequate to promote the psychological well-being of primates."[86]

Second, the amendment purported to establish a *requirement* that pain relief be provided to animals used in experiments. The amendment directed the secretary to develop standards "for animal care, treatment, and practices in experimental procedures to ensure that animal pain and distress are minimized, including adequate veterinary care with the appropriate use of anesthetic, analgesic, tranquilizing drugs, or euthanasia."[87] As part of this requirement, the secretary was also directed to develop standards that would ensure that the experimenter "considers alternatives to any procedure likely to produce pain to or distress in an experimental animal."[88] The standards must include requirements for consultation with a veterinarian for the planning of painful procedures and pre- and postsurgical care, and prohibition of the use of paralytic agents without anesthesia.[89] The standards must require that "the withholding of tranquilizers, anesthesia, analgesia, or euthanasia [occur only] when scientifically necessary" and "continue for only the necessary period of time."[90]

Third, survival surgery[91] was limited to one recovery except in cases of "scientific necessity" or under circumstances determined by the secretary.[92]

Fourth, and perhaps most important, the amendment required that each research facility,[93] including federal facilities, have at least one Institutional Animal Care and Use Committee (IACUC).[94] The IACUC is to be appointed by the chief executive officer of each research facility and is to consist of not fewer than three members; at least one member must be a veterinarian, and one member must (1) not be affiliated with the facility, (2) not be a member of the immediate family of anyone affiliated with the facility, and (3) represent "general community interests in the proper care and treatment of animals."[95] Members of the IACUC are supposed to "possess sufficient ability to assess animal care, treatment, and practices in experimental research as determined by the needs of the research facility."[96] A quorum is required for all actions of the IACUC.[97] The IACUC is required to conduct, at least semiannually, an inspection of "all animal study areas and animal facilities" in order to ensure that practices involving pain to animals and the condition of the animals are in compliance with the AWA.[98] The IACUC must file a report of these inspections, including any dissenting views, and the report must remain on file at the facility for at least three years for inspection by the USDA or any federal funding agency.[99]

Fifth, the amendment required the establishment of an information service at the National Agricultural Library that will, in cooperation with the National Library of Medicine, provide information concerning (1) employee training, (2) unintended duplication of experimentation, and (3) improved methods of experimentation that could reduce animal use and animal suffering.[100]

Sixth, research facilities must train all those involved with animals concerning (1) humane animal maintenance and experimentation, (2) research or testing methods that will reduce the number of animals used and the pain caused to animals, (3) use of the information service provided by the National Agricultural Library, and (4) procedures for reporting deficiencies.[101]

Seventh, the amendment provided that if the federal funding agency determines that a facility is not complying with the requirements of the act with respect to a particular experiment, the agency may suspend funding for that project after giving the facility notice and an opportunity for correction.[102]

Eighth, each research facility was required to show upon inspection and to report at least annually that "professionally acceptable standards governing the care, treatment, and use of animals are being followed by the research facility during actual research or experimentation."[103] Specifically, the facility must provide (1) information on procedures likely to cause pain or distress to animals, and assurances that the experimenter considered alternatives; (2) assurances that the facility is adhering to the standards prescribed by the act; and (3) an explanation for any deviation from the standards.[104]

Ninth, USDA is now required to inspect each research facility at least once a year.[105] In the event that there are "deficiencies or deviations from such standards," the USDA must conduct follow-up inspections until these problems are corrected.[106]

The amendment retained the deference accorded to researchers in the earlier versions of the act. For example, although the amendments required that each research facility have an IACUC, the IACUC must take the research program of the facility as a given and cannot engage in any ethical review.[107] Moreover, except for the requirements that pain and distress be minimized unless scientific "necessity" requires otherwise, and the requirement that facilities report that animals were being experimented upon in a "humane" fashion, "nothing in this chapter . . . shall be construed as authorizing the Secretary to promulgate rules, regulations, or orders with regard to the performance of actual research or experimentation by a research facility as determined by such research facility."[108]

Just as the original 1966 Laboratory Animal Welfare Act caused an uproar of protests from the biomedical community, so did the 1985 amendment to the act. The USDA opposed the legislation, arguing that judgments about pain and suffering in animals were subjective and best left to researchers and that the exercise requirements and certain other provisions were unworkable.[109] Most professional organizations opposed the amendments. For example, the American Association of Medical Colleges' representative, Glenn Geelhoed, testified that the amendment was premature because "at this time . . . we are not aware of any grave systematic deficiencies that exist within our laboratories regarding the treatment of animals." Further, Geelhoed stated that "by citing very infrequent and rather severe, extreme cases, several organizations have painted a rather unfair and unrepresentative, distorted picture of what occurs in our research institutions."[110] The American Physiological Society testified that there was already a reduction in the numbers of animals used, and had this to say about people who were concerned about the abuse of animals in laboratories:

> By and large, statements of malicious animal abuse by those who oppose animal research and scientific inquiry are anecdotal and are largely without verification. Such statements are designed . . . to sow seeds of mistrust about science and research in the minds of those unfamiliar with the standards and regulations that govern all research practices involving the use of laboratory animals.[111]

More important, however, was the research community's serious concern that the amendment would empower the secretary to promulgate "standards for research facilities, including requirements for methodologies in experimental procedures."[112]

It should be noted that the AWA does not apply to individual researchers, but only to research facilities. Indeed, as was discussed in Chapter Four, it was on this basis that the appellate court in *Animal Legal Defense Fund, Inc. v. Secretary of Agriculture* found that Dr. Roger Fouts did not have standing.

## A Full Circle Back to Property Concerns: The Pet Protection Act of 1990

In 1990 Congress once again amended the AWA,[113] this time providing for regulation of random-source (i.e., from a pound or shelter and not purpose bred) animals used in research. Although the original purpose of the amendment was, at least in part, to stop the purchase of animals from auctions, which are notorious for egregious animal abuse, the proposed amendment contained language that suggested that USDA-licensed animal dealers *should* look to animal shelters as a source of animals. This language caused alarm among more concerned members of the humane community, who did not want to make it appear as though Congress was encouraging dealers to look to shelters as a source of animals for vivisection. The version of the amendment that ultimately became law omitted this objectionable language but, unfortunately, omitted all reference to auctions as an inappropriate source of animals as well. In a sense, the amendment returned Congress to its original concern about the theft of people's *property*—their "pets."

The 1990 amendment requires that public or private shelters must hold and care for a dog or cat for at least five days before selling the dog or cat to a USDA-licensed dealer.[114] This requirement assumes, of course, that the pound or shelter is not prohibited by state law from selling animals for research purposes through a "pound seizure" law and that the shelter does not otherwise have a policy against giving shelter animals to animal experimenters. This five-day period allows dogs and cats to be recovered by their human companions or adopted before sale to a USDA-licensed dealer. If, however, the shelter has a policy to euthanize animals before five days are up, then the shelter can euthanize the animals to prevent them from being sold to dealers.

This five-day holding period should also be considered in conjunction with other recently amended regulations concerning the length of time that a dealer (as opposed to a public or private shelter) must hold and care for an animal before selling the animal to researchers. If the animal is from a public pound, then the dealer must keep the animal for at least five full days before selling the animal.[115] If the animal is from a private or contract shelter, then the dealer must hold and care for the animal for at least ten days.[116] This means that animals from public pounds must be kept for a total of at least ten days (five at the shelter, five at the dealer), and animals from private shelters must be kept for a total of at least fifteen days (five at the shelter, ten at the dealer), before being sold to researchers.

The 1990 amendment also requires that before selling or otherwise providing a random-source dog or cat, the dealer must provide the recipient with a valid certification that contains information about the dealer, the animal, the place from which the animal was obtained, the date of acquisition, and a statement by the pound or shelter that it complied with the waiting period. The research facility must keep the original certificate for one year, and the dealer must keep a copy of the certificate for one year.[117]

The certificate must contain an assurance that the provider of the animal was informed that the dog or cat may be used for research or educational purposes. If the provider is a pound or shelter (the usual arrangement contemplated by this section), that means that the dealer must tell the pound or shelter that the animal may be used for research. Of course, since the pound or shelter is providing the animal to a USDA-licensed dealer, it is probably a good guess that the pound or shelter *knows* that a USDA-licensed dealer is probably going to sell the animals to a USDA research facility. Unfortunately, the amendment does not require that the pound or shelter inform people who turn in their animals to shelters of the possibility that their former companions may be used in laboratories.

The amendment provides for fines for dealers who violate the law. A dealer who violates the law three or more times shall have her license revoked, and the USDA may request injunctions against dealers. USDA has promulgated regulations to implement the Pet Protection Act.[118] However, the problem of random-source animals continues.[119]

## Analysis

This brief overview of the AWA prompts four observations.

First, the regulation of animal experimentation is deeply rooted in property concerns.

Second, the research community has consistently opposed the AWA and all of its amendments. Nevertheless, the research community routinely claims that it accepts—indeed, embraces—the AWA. In addition, USDA has, from the outset, not wanted to administer the AWA and, as I show in the next chapter, has done a less-than-adequate job of enforcement.

Third, to place this statutory overview in the context of the theoretical structure developed in the previous chapter, the AWA plainly states that it is legitimate—and perhaps morally obligatory—to use animals in experiments. The AWA also states that there are *no* limits placed on the permissible use of animals on the basis of experiment content or conduct. Indeed, the research community has strenuously opposed every congressional effort to ensure that there is *any* ethical merit review of experiments. Instead, Congress has explicitly accorded complete deference to the research community. The *only* animal care or use issues that Congress regulates through the AWA are *husbandry* issues. The AWA and its regulations provide certain standards for transportation of animals and require that animals used in experiments receive wholesome food, water, and air. But the regulation stops there, and the AWA has absolutely *nothing* to say about the content or conduct of actual experiments. This situation reflects the basic principles of legal welfarism. Animals are treated as the property or "resources" of the facility, and the only concern of the AWA is to ensure that these resources are used efficiently, which, in this situation, means that they produce reliable scientific data.

Fourth, and related to the third point, is that the AWA does not provide "rights" for nonhumans as I discuss that notion in Chapter Five. To the extent that the AWA recognizes animal interests, those interests may be sacrificed as long as there is some benefit involved. In any event, the animal interests that the AWA recognizes are, for the most part, interests that facilitate animal exploitation (i.e., that animals used in experiments have "interests" in minimal conditions of subsistence so that their use will result in reliable data) and not those discussed in the context of the interest or benefit theory of legal rights.

Since 1966 the AWA has refused to regulate the design or conduct of research by a research facility *as determined by such research facility*. Indeed, the 1985 amendment uses that phrase on three occasions: to prohibit regulation of the design, outlines, and guidelines of experimentation; to prohibit regulation of actual research; and to require that IACUC members be able to assess animal care, given the facility's research decisions. In other words, if the facility decides to do burn experiments, then that decision is not subject to governmental regulation, apart from any decision that might be made not to fund the experiment for whatever reason. The facility has determined to do burn studies, and the only issue germane to AWA regulation is whether that burn experiment is performed humanely.

When Congress amended the AWA in 1985, many people saw the amendment as representing the first congressional venture "beyond the laboratory door." That is, the 1985 amendment was thought to go further than ever before in regulating the actual conduct of research. Indeed, Representative Brown, who cosponsored the bill with Senator Dole, stated, "At present, there is no law which requires researchers to use painkillers during an experiment causing pain to animals. My legislation would require this as well as other strengthening measures, unless they would specifically interfere with the research protocol."[120] Commenters agreed that the amendment represented regulation that was qualitatively different from the prior amendments.[121] One commenter stated that under the 1985 amendment "for the first time, standards are to be promulgated to govern an aspect of actual research. These standards are to ensure that pain and distress are minimized during experimental procedures by requiring the appropriate use of anesthetics, analgesics, tranquilizers, and euthanasia."[122]

Such views, however, proved unwarranted. When Congress failed to pass the 1982 act that required ethical merit review by the granting agency, it made clear that it would accede to the demand of the research community that there be no regulation of the content of research.[123] The 1985 AWA amendment did *nothing* beyond what prior amendments had done concerning the use of painkillers during experiments. When Congress passed the Laboratory Animal Welfare Act in 1966, it provided that the secretary of the USDA was to establish standards for the treatment of animals in laboratories and that these standards should provide for adequate veterinary care. Nevertheless, Congress stated that the secretary was not to prescribe standards for animal care, treatment, or handling during actual research or experimentation.[124]

In 1970, when the act became the AWA, Congress required that research facilities provide to animals used in experiments "adequate veterinary care, including the appropriate use of anesthetic, analgesic or tranquilizing drugs, when such use would be proper in the opinion of the attending veterinarian." The amendment prohibited the secretary from promulgating any rules or standards "with regard to design, outlines, guidelines, or performance of actual research or experimentation by a research facility as determined by such research facility." But the 1970 amendment contained an explicit exception to the complete deference to the scientific community contained in the 1966 act; under the 1970 amendment, each research facility was required to report annually and show that "professionally acceptable standards governing the care, treatment, and use of animals, including appropriate use of anesthetic, analgesic, and tranquilizing drugs, *during* experimentation are being followed by the research facility during actual research or experimentation."[125]

In a sense, then, the 1970 amendment represented an attempt by Congress to ensure that animals received painkillers during experimentation, but continued the congressional deference to the research community. As Representative Foley stated, research institutions had the final say about animal care and treatment and the use of pain-relieving drugs. Foley went on to say that "it is not the intent in any way to override the exclusive and sole discretion of the research facility in the conduct of experiments and the use of analgesics and tranquilizing drugs on animals in laboratories for experimentation purposes."[126]

In 1985 Congress really went no further than it had already done in 1970. That is, although the 1985 amendment directed the secretary for the first time to promulgate standards for the treatment of animals *during* experiments, Congress had already in 1970 required facilities to report annually and to show that they were using professionally acceptable standards of veterinary care *during* actual experimentation. Under the 1985 amendment, the secretary is still prohibited from regulating the design, outlines, or guidelines of actual experimentation,[127] and is prohibited from interfering with the performance of actual research or experimentation as determined by the research facility,[128] except that the secretary is authorized to promulgate guidelines to ensure that appropriate pain relief is provided during experimentation, that the researcher considers alternatives to animal use, and that the experiment does not involve duplication of earlier experiments. The primary enforcement mechanism for these requirements is the same as it was in 1970: the facilities are required to report annually and to demonstrate that they are using appropriate pain relief during actual experimentation.[129]

The AWA scheme reflects considerations similar to those present throughout federal policy on animal experimentation. For example, the NIH Guide states that "the intent of research is to provide data that will advance knowledge of immediate *or potential* benefit to humans and animals.[130] Publications produced by NIH to guide animal care committee members do not prescribe any type of "ethical merit" review,[131] and the NIH guidelines for federal investigators discuss the acquisition of knowledge—in addition to improved health care—as a sufficient justification for using animals in experiments.[132] The preamble to the IRAC *Principles for the Utilization and Care of Vertebrate Animals Used in Testing, Research, and Education* states that "the development of knowledge necessary for the improvement of the health and well-being of humans" and animals requires animal experimentation.[133] Again, the language suggests that the development of knowledge may, in and of itself, be sufficient to justify animal experimentation. Like the AWA scheme, the PHS/NIH principles reflect the judgment that knowledge is a (permissible) benefit for the justification of animal experimentation, and that benefit—even of knowledge—is related to human well-being. This conflation is understandable in that it resonates in the language of scientists themselves. For example, one researcher claims that even though basic research involving animals may not have any application, it is nevertheless justified because "it may provide direction in our continued battle against ignorance" and may ultimately lead to important applications later on.[134] Another researcher argues that determinations about what type of basic research will ultimately be fruitful will be made "under conditions of high uncertainty" and that to regulate research would necessarily impede the "advancement of human understanding and the consequent alleviation of human suffering."[135]

The only difference between the 1970 amendment and the 1985 amendment is that under the latter the individual researcher must, at least in theory, justify withholding pain relief to the IACUC.[136] In addition, the researcher must provide written assurances that she has considered alternatives to animal use and that her experiment is not merely an unnecessary duplication.[137] Despite these ostensible changes, however, the ultimate determination whether to provide pain relief to the animal still rests with the individual researcher, who is permitted to withhold pain relief "when scientifically necessary" and for "the necessary period of time." That is, once the investigator justifies the position that infliction of pain is required by the experiment, the IACUC must abide by the researcher's decision and has no authority to interfere with actual scientific decisions. Nevertheless, it is clear that most legal reformers have placed a great deal of emphasis on the importance of the IACUC.[138]

Congress explicitly considered whether the IACUC would have the power to interfere in the conduct of actual experiments and rejected this role for the IACUC, stating that the IACUC would have no authority to regulate or in any way interfere with the "design, outlines, or guidelines of actual research or experimentation by a research facility as determined by such research facility."[139] Similarly, the Public Health Service Law forbids the IACUC from "prescrib[ing] methods of research."[140] Congress thereby protected the individual researcher from any scrutiny of scientific design, details concerning experimental methodology, or the merits of research—all of which are supposedly reviewed and regulated by the funding agency. Moreover, the IACUC is precluded from interfering in the conduct of actual research.[141]

Federal regulations promulgated in 1989 by the USDA make clear that the purpose of the IACUC is not to discuss or regulate *anything* related to scientific methodology or design. The USDA solicited comments from interested persons concerning the functioning of IACUCs. The agency noted that some commenters from the scientific community claimed that IACUC authority over experiments "would deprive researchers of the scientific discretion necessary for the conduct of research." The USDA rejected this concern, stating that the IACUC was not intended to pass upon the merits of actual conduct of research. Rather, "it is the mandate of Congress that [IACUCs] assess animal care, treatment, and practices." The USDA emphasized that the authority of an IACUC is "limited to the animal care and use portion of a proposal to determine how the research will treat or affect an animal and its condition, and the circumstances under which the animal will be maintained. It does not extend to evaluating the design, outlines, guidelines, and scientific merit of proposed research."[142]

In addition, as mentioned earlier, the IACUC is to evaluate animal use not by some absolute standard but by reference to the "needs of the research facility."[143] If the facility engages in particularly objectionable research, such as psychological research that relies on "negative stimuli" (i.e., pain) in "training" or "conditioning" animals, then that is the "need" of the research facility that must be used to measure "humane" treatment and "necessary" pain. Finally, it must be understood that in virtually every instance the IACUC is composed of people who vivisect or who support vivisection. As a practical matter, these people are unlikely even to try to interfere with the judgment of a colleague concerning the scientific "necessity" of a particular painful procedure. Although the researcher has to justify withholding pain relief to the IACUC, as a practical matter there will be no greater oversight of individual investigator decisions in this regard than before. The bottom line remains the same: the AWA prohibits the infliction of "unnecessary" suffering upon nonhumans used in experiments but allows the decision of what constitutes "necessity" to be made by the researcher.

This is an important point: the research community wants the public to believe that its use of animals is regulated effectively by the federal government and that the government articulates strong standards that control what experimenters do during the course of actual experimentation. But that is not the case, and it has never been the case under the act. For all intents and purposes, the act prohibits "unnecessary" cruelty but leaves the determination of what is "necessary" to the research community itself.

Similarly, the 1985 amendment marked the first time that Congress regulated the practice of "survival surgery," which involves an animal's recovering consciousness after a major operative procedure. In many research facilities, especially veterinary schools and medical schools, animals were used repeatedly in experimental procedures or for "practice" surgery. In 1985 Congress provided that researchers may not use an animal for "more than one major operative experiment from which it is allowed to recover" except when "scientific necessity" demands it or the secretary says otherwise.[144] Again, Congress simultaneously created a rule and an exception that was broad enough to swallow the rule.

In addition, in the 1985 amendment, Congress explicitly permitted researchers to depart from any of the newly required standards if the departure was explained in a report to the IACUC.[145] Again, once the researcher justifies such a departure on scientific grounds, the IACUC is without authority to interfere in the design, outline, or guidelines of the experiment. Although researchers must justify withholding pain relief to the IACUC, the IACUC cannot, under both the AWA and the regulations, make any ethical judgment about the experiment and cannot evaluate the scientific merit or design of the experiment.

Moreover, the USDA, which has the responsibility to enforce the AWA, is already doing what it can to ensure the impotence of IACUCs. For example, USDA had originally proposed that a quorum of an IACUC would be required for any experiment that caused "more than short-term minor pain or distress."[146] In the final rule, however, the USDA permitted *one member* of an IACUC to review experiments as an agent of the entire IACUC. Although any member can request full-committee review, in the absence of such a request one member of the IACUC has authority to approve an experiment involving pain or distress.[147]

In an important sense, the IACUC serves as enforcer of the standards of legal welfarism contained in the AWA. The IACUC's power extends to two main areas. First, the IACUC is empowered to ensure that experimenters follow the husbandry rules established by the AWA and its regulations. Such rules, however, impose no ethical limits on experiments and are designed only to ensure that animals receive food and water and are maintained in a reasonably clean environment. Such standards are designed to ensure that animals used in experiments produce reliable data. Indeed, as I show in Chapter Ten, when the USDA tried to promulgate husbandry rules (in the form of engineering standards) that exceeded what the research community thought was cost-effective, the research community vocally objected and caused USDA to retract the rules in favor of more rules preferred by the research community (performance standards).

Second, the IACUC can suspend or disapprove an experiment should it determine that the infliction of pain on animals is "unnecessary." This IACUC power must be closely scrutinized. The IACUC is not empowered to make any ethical judgments about an experiment. Accordingly, if the researcher decides to do a pain experiment, or an experiment that will otherwise involve pain, the IACUC is explicitly disempowered from making any moral judgment about the necessity of pain in that circumstance. The IACUC is similarly not empowered to make any determinations about the design of the experiment and, therefore, cannot gainsay an experimenter on those grounds. The only time that the IACUC may act with respect to the conduct or content of an experiment is if the experimenter (who has complete ethical and scientific autonomy) cannot justify the infliction of pain and the IACUC determines that the infliction of pain is "unnecessary." And that judgment can *never* occur in the context of an *ethical* analysis. Rather, any IACUC action *necessarily* involves a determination that the experimenter is wasting animal resources and threatening the production of reliable data by inflicting "unnecessary" pain on an animal.

The IACUC system was intended only to ensure that experimenters did not use animals inefficiently, and despite optimism that the IACUC system would reduce the overall numbers of animals used and the numbers of animals used in painful experiments, the results thus far are less than promising and certainly do not indicate any significant decline.

It is certainly plausible that by shifting responsibility for animal care-and-treatment issues over to the IACUC, the AWA actually will encourage greater animal use over time. The reason for this is plain. By delegating authority to the IACUC, the funding and regulatory agencies are permitting IACUC members to make judgments about the work of their colleagues. It is at least possible that this places pressure on academics, most of whom will at some point be submitting *their* protocols to a future IACUC. Moreover, IACUC members have to face directly the displeasure of their colleagues whose projects they have not approved. By transferring authority to the IACUC, federal law actually encourages continuation of the "old-boy" system under which researchers protect one another from outside attacks. Again, more work is needed on this point, but the initial indications are that the IACUC is not fulfilling its promise of improved animal protection.

## Conclusion

In this chapter I examined the development of the federal Animal Welfare Act through the antecedents to its enactment in 1966, its provisions, and its subsequent amendments. The act, which originated to protect property interests in pets, established an elaborate system of legislation but, in effect, delegates decision making about animal interests to animal owners (individuals, institutions, or the government), who believe, as a matter of philosophical principle, that it is acceptable to use animals in experiments and that, as scientists, they should not interfere with the experiments of others. The only concern promoted and protected by the act is to ensure against the infliction of wholly gratuitous suffering and death, which could not be justified "scientifically." The AWA in no way recognizes animal interests in the way that rights recognize and protect human interests.

In the next chapter, I consider the administrative enforcement of the act.

# CHAPTER TEN

## Administrative Regulation
## of the Animal Welfare Act

### The AWA as Symbolic Legislation

THERE ARE TWO primary mechanisms for enforcement of the Animal Welfare Act (AWA). Under the AWA itself, the United States Department of Agriculture (USDA) is charged with the administrative enforcement of the AWA. In addition to the administrative enforcement of the AWA by USDA, the federal courts are specifically empowered "to enforce, and to prevent and restrain violations of" the AWA.[1] In this chapter, I discuss the administrative enforcement of the AWA by the USDA. In the next chapter, I discuss the rather limited litigation involving the AWA.

As a general matter, the AWA may be considered to be "symbolic," as opposed to "functional," legislation as those concepts are articulated by Professor John Dwyer in a 1990 article on environmental law.[2] Dwyer argues that certain functional statutes "instruct [administrative] agencies to balance competing concerns in setting standards," whereas other statutes are more symbolic than functional because "the legislature has failed to address the administrative and political constraints that will block implementation of the statute"[3] and agencies usually "resist implementation"[4] of the statute as they seek to reformulate the symbolic legislation into a more functional regulatory scheme. When Dwyer speaks of symbolic legislation, he has in mind those regulatory schemes, such as the restrictions on toxic pollutants contained in the Clean Water Act[5] or hazardous air pollutants contained in the Clean Air Act,[6] that "impose short deadlines and stringent standard-setting criteria that are designed to address a single, overriding [public] concern to the exclusion of other factors."[7] It is precisely in these instances that agencies are unable to formulate functional regulatory programs.

When administrative agencies are required to implement symbolic legislation, they become anxious about judicial review of their actions and move slowly in this reformulation process precisely to avoid such review.[8] As a part of what Dwyer calls "the pathology of symbolic legislation,"[9] courts may enter the vacuum and seek to impose a functional regulatory program, and Dwyer claims that this judicial intervention improperly interferes with the agencies' responsibilities and ultimately fails to satisfy legislative goals. Dwyer argues that administrative agencies must seek to reformulate symbolic regulation through close interaction with Congress and with environmental groups, and he counsels against active judicial implementation of these regulatory schemes.

The AWA clearly qualifies as a piece of symbolic legislation. Although the AWA does not concern the dreaded health threats sought to be regulated by particular environmental statutes, it clearly is intended, especially in its more recent versions, to address the overwhelming public concern about the treatment of animals. Moreover, as part of its 1985 amendment, the AWA required the USDA in a relatively short time frame to set regulatory standards objectionable to researchers. The result was predictable and fits Dwyer's paradigm quite nicely. The 1985 amendment to the AWA sought to provide a legislative solution that ignored the political and administrative constraints that would necessarily frustrate implementation.

In addition to the problem of symbolic legislation, administrative enforcement of the AWA is stymied by other aspects of the regulatory process that seek to achieve only that level of enforcement that is accepted by the scientific community. As mentioned, the USDA is charged with enforcement of the AWA. The actual administration of the AWA is done by an agency of USDA, the Animal and Plant Health Inspection Service (APHIS). In 1989 APHIS was reorganized to include a new unit, Regulatory Enforcement and Animal Care (REAC), which is responsible for administration of the AWA. APHIS directs enforcement of the AWA through regional offices. USDA, pursuant to a delegation of congressional power, has adopted regulations that, at least according to USDA, are designed to implement the AWA.[10] The AWA regulations are contained in title 9 of the *Code of Federal Regulations* (C.F.R.). The C.F.R. contains rules adopted by the many different federal administrative agencies pursuant to the equally myriad statutes enforced by those agencies.

Title 9, chapter 1, subchapter A, of the C.F.R. has three parts. Part 1 contains definitions that are used in parts 2 and 3. Part 2 concerns largely administrative responsibilities of those covered by the AWA. It contains rules that implement the licensing and record-keeping requirements of the act. For example, Part 2 contains reporting requirements that are important because they are—at least in theory—the primary means available under the AWA to get information about what is, in fact, occurring at facilities, about the numbers of animals used and about the types of procedures to which animals are subjected.

Each reporting facility[11] must submit a report to APHIS on or before December 1 of each year. The report must be signed and certified by the chief executive officer or institutional official and shall cover the previous federal fiscal year. The report must contain the following: (1) an assurance that the facility followed professionally acceptable standards of animal care, treatment, and handling, including an appropriate use of pain-relieving drugs before, during, and after any animal use; (2) an assurance that each principal investigator considered alternatives to painful procedures; (3) an assurance that the facility has adhered to the standards and regulations under the AWA and that any deviations therefrom have been explained by the principal investigator to the IACUC and approved by the IACUC; (4) the location of all facilities in which animals were housed or used; (5) a report of the common names and numbers of animals used in procedures in which no pain was involved; (6) a report of the common names and numbers of animals used in procedures that involved pain but where appropriate pain relief was provided; (7) a report of the common names and numbers of animals used in procedures in which the animal was subjected to pain and appropriate pain relief was not provided, and a statement why such pain relief was not provided; and (8) the common names and numbers of animals being held for research or other purposes but not yet used for such purpose.[12]

Part 3 of title 9, chapter 1, subchapter A, of the C.F.R. concerns the standards applicable to the transportation, handling, care, and treatment of animals covered by the AWA. It is further subdivided into subparts. Subpart A concerns dogs and cats; subpart B concerns guinea pigs and hamsters; subpart C concerns rabbits; subpart D concerns nonhuman primates; subpart E concerns marine mammals; and subpart F concerns other warm-blooded animals. These regulations are very detailed. For example, the regulations concerning space requirements for the primary enclosure for guinea pigs provide that the enclosure must be such that each guinea pig contained therein can make "normal postural adjustments with adequate freedom of movement."[13] The interior height of the primary enclosure must be at least seven inches.[14] If the guinea pig is less than 350 grams, then the animal must have at least 60 square inches, or 387.12 square centimeters, of floor space. If the guinea pig weighs more than 350 grams or is a nursing female with litter, the animal must have at least 101 square inches, or 651.65 square centimeters, of floor space.[15] Each subpart, although slightly different, addresses such subjects as the primary enclosure, outdoor facilities, ventilation, light, temperature, food, water, veterinary care, sanitation, separation of species, transportation, and the qualifications of attending employees. Many of the regulations are directed more at the condition of the property being used to hold animals than at the animals themselves. If a cage has exposed wires, animals may be "unproductively" injured.

Indeed, the USDA regulatory scheme is remarkably faithful to its statutory authority, the AWA, in that USDA addresses only animal *husbandry* issues and does not in any way purport to require any type of ethical consideration for animals. These husbandry issues reflect the concern that research facilities use their animals "efficiently." For example, the AWA and its regulations require that animals used in experiments be provided with sufficient wholesome food and water. This requirement applies even when the animal is being used in a particularly painful or distressing experiment over which the AWA and USDA have no control. The reason for these husbandry requirements is clear; an animal that is not fed properly is not likely to produce good research data. If the animal is involved in a starvation study (which still go on), then the feeding requirements do not apply, because the efficient production of data so requires.

The AWA and its regulations clearly reflect the foundational premises of legal welfarism.

## Administrative Enforcement of the AWA: A New Use of "Necessity"

The administration and enforcement of the AWA by the USDA stands as a text-book example of what might be referred to as a completely nonfunctional regulatory program. As mentioned in Chapter Nine, the USDA has, from the beginning, not wanted anything to do with the AWA. Before being assigned enforcement of the AWA, the USDA dealt primarily with the production, treatment, and slaughter of food animals. USDA has never enjoyed a reputation as an organization interested in the humane treatment of animals as a general matter. Indeed, in one case, a court struck down a USDA regulation, holding that the regulation "does not reflect the views of an agency which gave serious consideration to the prevention of cruelty to animals."[16] In another case, a court held that the USDA declined "to consider the benefit to animals as worthy of serious consideration as it decides how best to carry out its mandate."[17] Although there have been various criticisms of USDA enforcement that have been made by courts, government, and humane organizations alike, the best indication of USDA's philosophy of animal welfare can be obtained from the USDA itself in its promulgation of regulations to implement certain 1985 amendments to the AWA. Although I discuss that process below as it pertains to particular features of the 1985 amendment, here I examine the general theoretical approach that animated USDA throughout this uncommonly lengthy and still unresolved regulatory procedure. Interestingly, but not unexpectedly, that analysis reflects the property paradigm that is the foundation of legal welfarism.

The controversy surrounding the USDA regulations to implement the 1985 AWA amendments finds its source in the tension between "engineering" and "performance" standards. In 1985 Congress, in amending the AWA, required that the secretary of agriculture promulgate "standards to govern the humane handling, care, treatment, and transportation of animals" and stated that these standards "shall include minimum requirements for exercise of dogs" and for the psychological well-being of primates.[18] In order to fulfill its statutory mandate, USDA proposed rules in 1989 that contained primarily "engineering" standards, or standards that prescribed numerical goals that had to be met. For example, USDA originally proposed that any dog who was required to be exercised had to receive thirty minutes of exercise daily. In response to outcry from the research community, which objected to these various requirements, USDA substituted "performance" standards, which are intentionally imprecise and allow individual facilities to develop "plans" for satisfying the statutory requirements and leave discretion to the attending veterinarian and, in certain circumstances, to the combined decision of the attending veterinarian and the local IACUC. For example, in the revised rules, the requirement of thirty-minutes of exercise daily was replaced by a requirement of "regular" exercise, the duration of which was to be determined by the attending veterinarian.

According to USDA and its defenders, this change from engineering to performance standards was necessary to ensure that "dogs in regulated facilities receive sufficient opportunity for exercise."[19] This is, of course, a rather curious assertion, given that the engineering standards were only *minimal* standards and that nothing prevented a facility from providing *more* for a particular animal who, according to the attending veterinarian or the IACUC, needed different treatment.

Similarly, in the case of dogs and primates, USDA first established minimum requirements for housing and then, after protest by the research community, provided that "innovative housing," or housing that falls below the minimum requirement, could be acceptable if approved by the IACUC and the attending veterinarian.[20] The reason for this change was, according to USDA, that "it would be unrealistic to conclude that the design standards currently in general use [and which were being supplanted by the regulations] cannot be improved upon, based on continuing research in engineering and animal behavior."[21] To put it another way, USDA invited facilities to experiment with adapting their *present* facilities without making the changes required by the regulations. Obviously, any facility that does not or cannot expend the funds necessary to improve conditions will be tempted to try to adapt that facility.

These changes were clearly made by the USDA in response to commenters who objected to the expenditure that the original USDA-proposed rules would require. Indeed, in revising the rules, USDA stated that the revisions, and the replacement of engineering standards by performance standards, would "effectuate the intent of Congress without imposing an *unnecessary, unreasonable, or unjustified* financial burden."[22] Once again we encounter these magical words that played a crucial role in the interpretation and understanding of anticruelty laws, but this time the concern is that rules to protect animals not impose "unnecessary" or "unjustified burdens on research facilities."[23] So, not only do we balance animal welfare against the benefits to humans of cures, or to researchers of knowledge, but we must also consider the effect of animal welfare on the *property* and the *property rights* of facilities. This depresses animal welfare yet one more level and ensures that animal interests will not prevail.

Further examination of the USDA regulatory process reveals why this is so. In proposing a regulation, an administrative agency is supposed to perform a cost/benefit analysis as required by Executive Order 12,291.[24] In performing a cost/benefit analysis on its regulations, USDA claimed that there were two potential costs that had to be measured: cost to the regulated facility of compliance, and cost to society of forgone cures obtained by animal research. USDA concluded that its revised, performance-based regulations would not interfere with animal research or the use of animals in research and that the performance-based regulation would serve the least-cost criterion by allowing more flexibility; "thus regulated establishments can meet requirements through several means of compliance."[25] The potential benefits are found, not in any fulfillment of our moral obligation toward exploited nonhumans used in experiments or tests, but in the "public perception" that the regulations are decreasing the use, pain, discomfort, and suffering of animals. This benefit cannot be quantified, however, because, according to USDA, "animal welfare is an anthropomorphic attribute"; or put another way, public perception about animal welfare cannot be measured easily, so the primary benefit of the USDA regulations cannot be determined.[26]

The process used by USDA in promulgating the revised, performance-based regulations involved balancing interests. The interests balanced, however, did not include the animal interests directly. Rather, the primary concern of the USDA was not to impose an "unnecessary" financial burden on facilities in terms of compliance costs. These financial and property-related institutional concerns, which USDA purported to be able to calculate, together with concerns about the benefits to people of cures supposedly discovered through animal research and the benefits that supposedly accrue to scientists and to society from knowledge gathering, were measured against a benefit that could not be quantified—public perception of animal welfare. Such a process is, however, to be expected when the "necessity" of animal exploitation is measured primarily in terms of what facilities can afford in the way of animal protection. Again, necessity is determined not by reference to any standard that is animal-centered but by reference to that which is deemed "necessary" to sustain the legitimate social institution in which the animal use occurs. If an institution is regarded as legitimate, then virtually any activity that facilitates the institution's activity is "necessary" as long as it does not result in a diminution of overall social wealth. In this case, the "necessity" of animal suffering represented by less stringent, performance-based rules is occasioned by the "necessity" of keeping compliance costs as low as possible. This is legal welfarism: any cost that exceeds the minimum necessary to ensure the efficient exploitation of property—in this case to obtain reliable data from animal property used in experiments—is rejected as inefficient. Moreover, the fact that the main benefit of these regulations is to be found in public perceptions of animal welfare suggests that the reason for such laws has more to do with ensuring that people feel good about animal research than with ensuring that animals are treated better.

Against the backdrop of this general discussion about the USDA orientation toward the AWA, I want to consider first, what USDA has to say (or not say) about it own enforcement program; second, criticisms of USDA enforcement that have been made by other governmental agencies and by conservative animal welfare organizations; third, two examples where USDA has provided wholly inadequate regulations to implement the AWA; and fourth, the USDA role in the Taub and Gennarelli cases.

## USDA Enforcement Statistics

Inspectors from APHIS/REAC supposedly make unannounced inspections of licensees (animal dealers and exhibitors) and registrants (research facilities). I say "supposedly" because it is common knowledge in universities that such inspections are frequently anything but unannounced and because research facilities often know that an inspection is imminent even if they may not know the exact date and time of the inspection. USDA itself recommends that there be four visits per site per year.[27] Their own figures, however, indicate that the present level of inspection does not even begin to satisfy the USDA's own standard. For example, in 1992 APHIS reported a total of 17,764 compliance inspections, with 4,839 inspections of 3,205 research facilities for an average of 1.51 inspections per site. The overall average was 1.87 inspections per site, and the average inspections per site for animal dealers (2.16) and animal exhibitors (1.94) were significantly higher than for research facilities.[28] In 1991 APHIS reported that there were 15,148 compliance inspections conducted. Of this number 3,987 were inspections of the 3,495 sites at 1,474 research facilities for an average of 1.14 inspections per site. For the same year, dealer inspections averaged 1.57 inspections per site, and exhibitors averaged 1.77 inspections per site, and the overall average of inspections per site was 1.54.[29] In 1990 APHIS reported a total of 13,050 inspections, with 3,589 compliance inspections of research facilities. The overall average was 1.40 inspections per site, with the average site inspection for research facilities at 1.12.[30] In 1989 there were 3,544 inspections of 2,851 inspection sites for an average of 1.24 inspections per site.[31] In 1988 there were 3,767 inspections of 2,878 sites for an average of 1.31 inspections per site.[32] For each year the average of inspections per site was lower for research facilities than for animal dealers and exhibitors.

In addition to conducting compliance inspections, USDA, again through APHIS/REAC, investigates violations and prosecutes enforcement actions. APHIS field investigators conduct compliance inspections and investigate complaints. If the APHIS inspector finds a violation of the AWA or its regulations, the inspector has the discretion to settle the matter by issuing an official notice of warning, which means that no real sanction is imposed on the offender, or, as of 1992, through what is called a "stipulation procedure," which allows the offender to settle the case at an early stage by paying a fine or agreeing to the suspension of a license before legal proceedings commence. If, however, the APHIS inspector believes that the violations are serious or repeated, she may submit the case to the Regulatory Enforcement staff, who then attempt to settle the matter through official warning or stipulation but who may refer the case to the USDA office of the general counsel for possible administrative action resulting in a decision and order by an administrative law judge. That order may involve license suspensions or revocations, cease-and-desist orders,[33] or civil penalties. The aggrieved party can then appeal to the federal courts. Obviously, the APHIS inspector has a great deal of discretion in that she may, if she so decides, settle cases without any referral whatsoever to the Regulatory Enforcement staff. Interestingly, the APHIS description of the investigations and violations neglects to indicate that the A PHIS field inspectors have this considerable discretion or power. For example, the 1992 APHIS Report states that "when an investigation reveals apparent violations, a case report and documentation are forwarded to the Regulatory

Enforcement staff."[34] But this is not accurate. The APHIS field inspectors may decide that even though there is a violation of the AWA or its regulations, those violations can be settled with no warning, an official warning notice, or a stipulation.[35] In 1992 APHIS reported that there were 980 cases, 105 of which were submitted to the Regulatory Enforcement staff, and 107 of which were submitted to the general counsel during fiscal year 1991. Of these 980 cases, 616 were resolved by an official warning, 115 through stipulation.[36] The 1992 APHIS Report does not provide figures for how many of these official warnings or stipulations were done at the local level by the field inspector and how many at the level of the Regulatory Enforcement staff. The distinction is important, since determinations about the seriousness of a violation are more likely to be reliable when made by the Regulatory Enforcement staff, which, presumably, is more removed from the relationship that a field inspector invariably develops with licensees and registrants after years of inspecting the same facilities. In 1992, 63 cases were resolved through administrative decision and order. There were 14 license suspensions or revocations, 48 cease-and-desist orders, and fines totaling $286,450.[37] In 1991 APHIS reported 701 investigations, with 125 cases submitted to the Regulatory Enforcement staff and 92 submitted to the office of the general counsel. Of the 701 cases, 485 were settled by an official warning and 78 through decision and judgment. There were 62 cease-and-desist orders, 37 license suspensions or revocations, and fines totaling $213,350.[38]

The APHIS enforcement reports omit two crucial numbers: the number of research facilities and sites not inspected at all and the number of investigations and prosecutions involving research facilities rather than animal dealers, animal exhibitors, or transporters. In 1985 the General Accounting Office released a study (GAO Report) of the USDA animal welfare program. The GAO Report, discussed at length below, made an important point about per site inspections. The GAO Report stated that APHIS animal welfare personnel indicated that the desired inspection level was four inspections per site per year.[39] In 1983, in the state of New York, 48.4 percent of licensed dealers were not inspected at all, 50.0 percent of research facilities were not inspected at all, 33.3 percent of exhibitors were not inspected at all, and 64.3 percent of carriers were not inspected at all.[40] When Congress amended the AWA in 1985, it added a requirement that research facilities be inspected at least once a year, and although USDA claims to satisfy that requirement, it is not clear that each *site* is inspected at least once per year.[41]

With respect to the investigation and prosecution of research facilities, a review of other USDA documents, including APHIS news releases and compilations of prosecutions, indicates quite clearly that the overwhelming number of administrative prosecutions are directed toward parties other than research facilities.[42] That is, the USDA is far more likely to prosecute animal dealers, exhibitors, or carriers than research facilities. When the USDA does take action against a research facility, it is almost always for failing to file the required annual report. Upon my request, APHIS did supply me with the numbers of formal civil or administrative complaints issued per year for all covered parties, and the number for research facilities in particular. In 1993 a total of forty-three complaints were issued, but only one was issued against a research facility. In 1992, seventeen complaints were issued, and only one was issued against a research facility. In 1991, seventy-five complaints were issued, and two of those were against research facilities. In 1990, twenty-seven complaints were issued, with two of those against research facilities. It is clear that dealers, exhibitors, and transporters are regulated far more than research facilities, which are ostensibly left to enforce the AWA themselves. Dealers, exhibitors, and transporters are far more likely to be involved in conduct that USDA can clearly identify as causing nonproductive, gratuitous harm to animal property than are research facilities. Moreover, for what are probably reasons of politics and economics, the USDA obviously defers to research facilities more than, say, to zoos or circuses.

### Critiques of USDA Enforcement

USDA enforcement of the AWA is routinely attacked by animal rights advocates as ineffective. Such criticisms, however, are often discounted because they are made by people who have an acknowledged objection to the use of animals in experiments under any circumstances. Although the dismissal of a criticism based upon the identity of its source is not logical, I do not wish to have the issue of USDA enforcement become enmeshed in a critique of particular animal rights advocates. Therefore, I will confine the criticisms to be reviewed to those made by other governmental agencies and those made by conservative animal welfare organizations. The irony is that the most effective critics of USDA enforcement of the AWA are those who support animal experimentation. Unfortunately, these criticisms still have had little effect.

GOVERNMENTAL CRITIQUES. There are two primary governmental analyses of the efficacy of USDA enforcement of the AWA. The GAO Report, issued in 1985, stands as a powerful indictment of the USDA. The GAO Report found that training and written guidance for USDA inspectors was insufficient, that the frequency of inspections was inadequate, that APHIS did not follow up on deficiencies in a satisfactory manner, and that inspection quality and reporting was uneven and inconsistent.[43] The report pointed out that although USDA complained that it did not have enough funding to do the job properly, USDA had proposed in 1983, 1984, 1985, and 1986 that funding for APHIS inspections be eliminated or reduced and that state, local, and private agencies take over the job of monitoring animal welfare. Indeed, the situation is reflected in testimony before Congress in 1988 concerning the proposed amendment to the AWA to provide for citizen suits to enforce the AWA. In opposition to the proposed legislation, Aubrey Taylor of the American Physiological Society stated that the problem was not that the AWA was not being enforced but that USDA did not have enough congressional funding for its enforcement activities. Taylor stated, "They [USDA] need more money. I think the number we saw was $6 million for 8,000 facilities. This is not a lot of money." The chairman of the subcommittee holding the hearing, Barney Frank, interrupted Taylor's testimony and asked James Glasser, APHIS administrator, "What was the budget request for this coming fiscal year?" Glasser replied, "In the range of $6 million." Frank asked, "Did you get what you asked for?" Glasser replied, "Yes, sir." Frank then stated that "agriculture did not ask for more money. That is an indication. If they had asked for a significantly greater amount of money and had been denied it, the argument that they were underfunded would be a defense, but when they are getting what they asked for, that suggests a lack of zeal in enforcement."[44]

The GAO Report indicated that APHIS generally uses veterinarians to inspect research facilities and larger exhibitors, such as zoos, and animal health technicians to inspect dealers, carriers, and small exhibitors. The report stated that of the 73 APHIS inspectors, 57 had obtained some training in animal welfare courses, but that 43 of the 57 had not had any formal training in recent years, and that 9 of the 25 inspectors in California and 6 of the 17 inspectors in Texas had never received any formal training.[45] APHIS has no more-recent data to indicate whether the training problem identified by the GAO Report is improved or has worsened.

In its discussion of the frequency of inspections of research facilities, the GAO Report indicated that there was a wide range by state in the average number of inspections per site. For example, in 1983 the average number of inspections per site for research facilities was 1.49 in Kansas but only .66 in California and .68 in New York.[46] These figures indicate that some sites were not inspected at all in 1983 — a fact confirmed elsewhere in the GAO Report. As I mentioned above, Congress added a requirement in 1985 that each research facility be inspected at least once a year, but it is not clear whether each *site* is inspected at least once per year. Given that a research facility may have numerous sites where animal experimentation is conducted, a requirement that the facility be inspected does not guarantee greater efficacy of USDA inspections.

Despite the fact that not all institutions were being inspected at least once annually, APHIS opposed the 1985 amendments, arguing that APHIS inspected "nearly all State-owned and privately owned research facilities."[47] The APHIS administrator at that time, Bert W. Hawkins, stated that APHIS tried "to visit each one of these registered facilities at least twice annually. . . . If we have a facility that has a long history of being up front, treating their animals very humanely, and submitting good reports, we might only visit it one time in 1 year."[48] It is clear, however, that Hawkins's testimony to Congress was significantly inaccurate. APHIS now claims that it does inspect each site, but there are no data to show that this is the case, and APHIS does not report this information in its annual report.[49]

Another portion of the GAO Report focused on the failure of the USDA to follow up on deficiencies. If a deficiency is minor, then reinspection occurs only if funds are available. Major deficiencies are supposed to trigger reinspections, but, as the GAO Report indicated, these reinspections are not always performed. In 1985 Congress, in amending the AWA, provided that USDA "shall" conduct follow-up inspections to ensure that all deficiencies and deviations are remedied. Again, APHIS claims that this problem has been rectified, but does not have any data to show that this is the case and does not report on this issue in its annual report.[50]

In a 1986 study produced by the Office of Technology Assessment (OTA Report), the authors state that "many groups concerned about animal welfare want the [AWA] and its enforcement strengthened" and that APHIS "inspectors, whose primary concern is preventing interstate transport of disease-carrying livestock and plants, spend about 6 percent of their time enforcing the research provisions of the Animal Welfare Act."[51] The OTA Report also states that the USDA has exhibited "reluctance to accept broader responsibilities under the [AWA]" and "remains opposed to its further extension."[52]

CRITICISMS BY CONSERVATIVE HUMANE ORGANIZATIONS. Many animal advocacy organizations are highly critical of the USDA enforcement (or lack thereof) of the AWA. Although many of these criticisms are perfectly valid, they are discounted—or ignored—because those who criticize are often opposed to any use of animals for research purposes. What cannot be discounted as easily is that not only do more progressive organizations regard USDA enforcement as ineffective, but so do organizations that have, by and large, supported biomedical research using animals. I review critiques by two such organizations—the Humane Society of the United States (HSUS) and the Animal Welfare Institute (AWI). Both critiques focus on the reporting requirements under the AWA, so it is necessary first to review those requirements.

*USDA Reporting Requirements.* Under the procedures promulgated by USDA, each research facility is required to file an annual report to APHIS that, among other things, provides an assurance that there is an "appropriate use of anesthetic, analgesic, and tranquilizing drugs, prior to, during, and following actual research, teaching, testing, surgery, or experimentation."[53] The report must provide the common names and numbers of covered animals that were used in procedures that caused no pain or distress, procedures that involved pain but where "appropriate" pain relief was provided, and procedures that involved pain but where no relief was provided because such relief would have "adversely affected" the purpose of the animal use.[54] The facility is required to provide an explanation of the procedures producing pain or distress and the reasons relief was not provided.[55]

USDA annual enforcement reports contain information about these three categories, which, incidentally, indicate that the IACUC system enacted in the 1985 amendments to AWA is not having much effect on the total number of animals used or the numbers of animals used in painful experiments. For example, in 1992 APHIS reported that of the total number of covered animals used (2,134,182), which represented the largest total number of covered animals used since at least the mid-1980s, 58 percent (1,241,373) were used for purposes that involved no pain and distress, 36 percent (772, 601) for purposes that involved pain or distress but where appropriate pain relief was provided, and 6 percent

(120,208) in procedures that involved pain or distress and where no relief was provided.[56] In 1991 APHIS reported that of the total number of covered animals used (1,842,420), 61 percent (1,131,139) were used in procedures that involved no pain or distress, 33 percent (602,415) were used for purposes that involved pain or distress but where relief was provided, and 6 percent (108,866) were used in procedures that involved pain and distress but for which no relief was provided.[57] The total number of research facilities registered in 1992 was 1,527, with 3,205 total sites; in 1991 there were a total of 1,474 facilities registered, with 3,495 total sites. The average number of animals used per facility was 1,398 in 1992 and 1,250 in 1991; the average number per site in 1992 was 666; the average number per site in 1991 was 527.[58]

The most interesting thing about this exercise—requiring research facilities to determine which category is appropriate for which animal—is that not even the USDA regards this as representing any reality about animal pain or distress. As I mentioned above, USDA and APHIS opposed the 1985 amendments to the AWA. This opposition was based, in part, on USDA's skepticism regarding the measurement of pain. For example, Secretary of Agriculture John Block opposed the requirement that the IACUC review the institutional "direct use of conscious animals," defined as "any use or procedure that involves more than momentary minor pain and discomfort."[59] Block stated that "we do not feel that 'pain' can be measured objectively" and should

> be a required element of professional judgment made by the trained doctors of veterinary medicine in charge of the research and researchers trained in other biomedical sciences. Therefore, we object to the bill's definition of the term "direct use of conscious animals" which would require the Secretary of Agriculture to promulgate regulations establishing standards for momentary minor pain and discomfort for various animal species.[60]

This portion of the bill was omitted in the final amendments. In addition, Block objected to the proposal that the secretary be required to establish "proper," rather than minimum, standards of care. Block's reason for this objection was that " 'minimum' is more definitive, and therefore, more enforceable in a court of law." "Proper" was removed from the final amendments, and "minimum" was used instead. Block also objected to the requirement of an "adequate exercise" standard for animals "because it would be extremely difficult to determine what is 'adequate' for the various species and number of animals that would be involved."[61] In the final law, the exercise requirement was eliminated for all species except dogs, and USDA took seven years to promulgate the regulations. Bert W. Hawkins, administrator of APHIS, made similar comments before the House and Senate subcommittees that held hearings on the amendments, and recommended against passage of the amendments. Hawkins stressed that it was not advisable to try to formulate more specific rules for animal care, because "the factors that it takes to administer the act are judgment factors, and no two of us can use judgment in exactly the same manner."[62] He gave an interesting example that indicated that at least as far as he was concerned, it was rather difficult to identify stress resulting from confinement:

> If one of you gentlemen had a saddle horse and I had one, and you kept yours in a padded stall and I gave mine freedom to roam; I might think that yours was being confined under conditions that were less than humane, and contrary, you might think that the free-roaming aspects of mine allowed him to come into contact with elements that might be very detrimental to him.[63]

These comments by Block and Hawkins reflect a general scientific skepticism about the very *existence* of pain and distress in animals, let alone skepticism about the efficacy of various methods used to quantify pain. Philosopher Bernard Rollin's book *The Unheeded Cry* is an extended argument why scientists should realize that the prevailing paradigm for understanding animal consciousness—including, and especially, the notion that animals do not feel pain—flies in the face of common sense, evolutionary theory, and reasoned thought as a general matter. Rollins reviewed the scientific literature and found that recognition of the phenomenon of animal pain is something that has occurred widely only in the past decade.[64] Indeed, in a paper published in 1982, the authors, a professor of animal science and a professor of philosophy, felt the need to devote a great deal of their paper to arguing for the plausibility of the position that animals feel pain.[65] The National Research Council wrote as late as 1992 that "there is general agreement on the need to minimize pain and distress, but it has been difficult to bring the necessary melange of information together and to disseminate it throughout the scientific community."[66] Professor Andrew Rowan wrote in 1984 that "some researchers seem intent on dispelling the notion that animals feel pain as humans do and develop terms that appear to be little more than an attempt to disguise the fact that animals are in pain."[67] Put simply, it is part of conventional wisdom that animals feel pain; an assertion to that effect uttered in a group of nonscientists would not evoke much controversy. The use of animals in research, however, is historically predicted on the Cartesian notion that animals have no souls and are incapable of feeling pain. However much we have rejected other aspects of Cartesian philosophy, we—or at least modern science—are lagging on the animal consciousness question. Indeed, both major mainstream American news magazines have had cover stories about the recent—and grudging—recognition by scientists that animals have consciousness.[68]

In light of this general scientific skepticism about the existence and measurement of pain in animals, and the USDA/APHIS endorsement of this skepticism, it should not come as any surprise that the reporting system required under the AWA comes under attack by even conservative animal advocates.

*The HSUS Critique.* The Humane Society of the United States (HSUS) has long been the conservative bastion of animal welfare and has not hesitated in distancing itself from the animal rights movement.[69] Nevertheless, HSUS has launched two significant attacks on USDA in recent years, both of which focused on USDA reporting requirements. The first HSUS challenge to USDA reporting requirements occurred in 1982, when HSUS unsuccessfully petitioned USDA to change the reporting procedures for research facilities under the AWA. The HSUS petition claimed that the reporting system failed to provide sufficient guidelines for "appropriate" pain relief and presented three reasons in support. First, the petition claimed that the AWA and its regulations failed to provide any meaningful criteria for determining what constitutes "pain" and "distress." The petitioners pointed out that "research facilities appear to apply different and conflicting standards in assessing the responses of animals used in similar procedures."[70] For example, one facility that performed ocular and dermal irritancy tests reported that " '[d]uring exposure to these corrosive substances [applied to the eye or shaved skin of the animal], and during the subsequent evaluation period, the animal may experience pain and distress.' "[71] Another facility that performed the exact same type of tests listed all animals used in these irritancy tests as animals involved in procedures that caused no pain or distress. It should come as no surprise that different research facilities evaluate the pain component of the same conduct differently. After all, many experimenters doubt that animals feel pain, and USDA/APHIS has gone on record before the Congress expressing the view that pain determinations are inherently subjective and cannot be regulated.

Second, the petitioners observed that the regulations stated that "routine procedures (e.g., injections, tattooing, blood sampling) should be reported" in the category of procedures causing no pain or distress.[72] The HSUS petitioners argued that the term "routine procedures" was inconsistently applied.[73] In one instance, a facility listed hamsters used in vaccine testing as animals subjected to pain or distress with no relief; another research facility listed hamsters used in the exact same tests as animals subjected to pain with no relief, but the USDA/APHIS chief staff veterinarian altered the designation to "animals subjected to pain with appropriate relief." When challenged about the change of designation, the USDA/APHIS stated that since the test involved injections and since injections were considered to be "routine procedures" under the AWA, the designation of "pain or distress — no relief" was not appropriate, although the veterinarian admitted that pain subsequent to the injection of the virus or bacteria was a real possibility.[74]

Finally, the HSUS petitioners found that a number of facilities failed to provide the required explanation why certain animals were subjected to pain or distress without "appropriate" relief, and other facilities that had provided explanations had provided nothing more than a statement that pain relief would "adversely affect the test results" but had not explained *why* pain relief would have that effect.[75]

Ten years later, in 1992, HSUS again petitioned the USDA to change the reporting requirements under the AWA.[76] Again USDA rejected the petition. This time HSUS argued that new items, such as information about the nature of the facility involved, should be included in facility reports. At present, a "research facility" may be a university, college, professional school, pharmaceutical company, contract testing or other commercial institution, or a government or military institution. HSUS also argued that sources of animals, the scientific purposes for animal use, and the numbers of animals on yearly and multiyearly bases should be reported specifically on the annual report. HSUS argued that certain controversial procedures, such as ocular irritancy tests, should be reported specially. Most important of all the suggested reporting changes, however, was that concerning the adoption of a pain scale. The petitioners argued that greater discrimination was required, something more precise than classifying procedures using a gross parameter such as "pain." Petitioners pointed out that certain scientific groups had endorsed such pain scales and that some foreign countries had adopted them.[77] HSUS also requested that USDA/APHIS include more information in its annual enforcement reports, including the numbers of animals used for specific purposes and the numbers of animals exposed to the varying degrees of pain or invasiveness as measured by the pain scale whose adoption petitioners had requested.[78]

*The AWI Critique.* The other major attack on USDA came from an organization that has traditionally been quite close to USDA/APHIS. The Animal Welfare Institute (AWI) has long been an institutional supporter of animal research, and its president, Christine Stevens, is regarded by many as having played a major role in securing the original Laboratory Animal Welfare Act in 1966 and the subsequent amendments to the AWA. The Institute has also worked very closely over the years with APHIS to improve laboratory animal welfare. In 1985 the Institute issued a study that had a devastating impact on public perception of animal welfare and that played a significant role in the congressional hearings that resulted in the 1985 amendments to the AWA.[79]

AWI did a simple—but very effective—study. Using the Freedom of Information Act, AWI requested the annual reports of 214 research facilities and then categorized them according to the level and longevity of violations. The AWI report emphasized:

> Many of these institutions have been accredited by the American Association for Accreditation of Laboratory Animal Care (AAALAC). It is sometimes claimed that accreditation guarantees good animal care and treatment over the entire three-year period between AAALAC visits (all of which are announced), but, as illustrated by our data, this is clearly fallacious.[80]

Of the fifty-eight facilities classified by AWI as having serious and chronic deficiencies as measured by USDA inspection reports, thirty-eight reported that there were no animals that suffered unrelieved pain. Thirty-three facilities were fully or partially accredited by AAALAC. Forty-two of the fifty-eight facilities received increases in federal funds for animal experimentation during the time period of the AWI study. With precious few exceptions—primarily for cases that attracted public attention—no USDA/APHIS administrative action was taken against these facilities, and in many cases, the number of federal dollars given to these facilities for animal experimentation increased dramatically.

For example, inspection reports of Ohio State University (OSU), a registered research facility with AAALAC accreditation, indicated that animals were persis-

researchers to estimate that the AWA covers only 4 to 5 percent of the animals used in federally funded laboratories in the United States.[90] As mentioned in Chapter Four and discussed further in Chapter Eleven, several conservative animal welfare groups, including HSUS and ALDF, challenged the secretary's exclusion of rats, mice, and birds, and the appellate court found that the plaintiffs lacked standing to challenge the exclusion.

Another example of USDA failure to implement regulations under the act involves the 1985 amendments to the AWA. As I discussed earlier in this chapter, these amendments required that the secretary of agriculture promulgate minimum standards for the humane handling, care, treatment, and transportation of animals covered by the AWA, including standards for "handling, housing, feeding, watering, sanitation, ventilation, shelter from extremes of weather and temperatures, adequate veterinary care, and separation of species," the "exercise of dogs," the "psychological well-being of primates," and, with respect to laboratory animals, standards for animal care "in experimental procedures."[91] As a result of these amendments, USDA undertook, as it was required to do by Congress, a revision of its regulations in order to implement the various changes effected by the 1985 congressional amendment. USDA proposed amendments to part 1 (definition of terms) and part 2 (regulations) in 1987.[92] The comment period was extended twice. In 1989 USDA reproposed amendments of parts 1 and 2, together with proposed standards for the exercise of dogs and the psychological well-being of primates because, according to USDA, members of the research community overwhelmingly requested that USDA revise its proposals and publish them with proposed amendments to part 3 so that the public could comment on the "interrelationship of the definitions and regulations in Parts 1 and 2 with the standards we are proposing in Part 3."[93] The amendment of parts 1 and 2 was completed in 1989,[94] and, as discussed in Chapter Nine, the most notable feature of these regulations concerns USDA's capitulation to the research community in ensuring that any protection accorded to animals by the IACUC was eviscerated. Although the amendments to parts 1 and 2 took a considerable amount of time to complete, they represented speedy action on the part of USDA when compared to the glacial promulgation of the rules of part 3, especially provisions for the exercise of dogs and the psychological well-being of primates, which amendments the USDA opposed in hearings before Congress.

USDA completed its revision of subparts B (guinea pigs and hamsters) and C (rabbits) of part 3 in 1990.[95] In 1991 USDA revised its regulations in part 3 concerning dogs and cats (subpart A) and nonhuman primates (subpart D) in response to the congressional directive to provide for adequate exercise for dogs and a psychologically suitable environment for nonhuman primates. The USDA originally proposed revisions to subparts A and D on March 15, 1989.[96] USDA revised and reproposed the rules on subparts A and D on August 15, 1990.[97] The reason for this inordinate delay in the issuance of any final rule on part 3, subparts A and D, was that there was intense opposition from the scientific community to the *concept* of exercise for dogs or of a psychologically stimulating environment for primates.

Although the differences among various versions of the proposed regulations are complicated, it is instructive to note a few.

When USDA first proposed amendments to subpart A in 1989, it required that (1) dogs be maintained in compatible groups unless not in accordance with animal care procedures as approved by the IACUC or unless certain other conditions are met; (2) dogs be permitted to see and hear other dogs; (3) dogs kept individually in cages, or pens or runs that are smaller than four times the size of the floor space required for the primary enclosure, be permitted daily exercise for thirty minutes in an area that affords certain minimum space to the dogs; (4) dogs held in groups be exercised daily unless the dogs are held in pens or runs that provide the greater of eighty square feet or 1.5 times the floor space required for the primary enclosure for each dog in the exercise area; (5) a single dog kept by a facility be given at least sixty minutes of daily "positive physical contact"; and (6) methods of exercise be determined by the attending veterinarian, though they may be provided by walking on a leash or release into an open area or suitable pen.[98]

In reproposing the rules in 1990, the USDA noted that, as a general matter, "a very large number" of commenters found the proposed regulations to be too stringent, to exceed statutory authority, and to conflict with congressional intent. Curiously, in reporting these comments and in reproposing the regulations in 1990, the USDA did not bother to identify the sources of the comments. Although the USDA reports that 7,173 comments were provided by the "general public" and 2,890 were provided by the "research community," no source is provided for comments to any individual section. It is clear, however, that most of the criticisms that the USDA reviewed and incorporated in the reproposed rules came from research facilities. Many commenters "opposed exercise requirements for animals on the grounds that they would be so expensive they would be prohibitive," and a "large number of commenters opposed the inclusion in the regulations of any requirements regarding exercise."[99] Many commenters attacked other parts of the original regulations on the grounds that the regulations "were excessive and without scientific documentation."[100] According to USDA, many commenters opposed the provision that dogs be kept in compatible groups, because the requirement was arbitrary and lacking in scientific documentation, because group housing could spread diseases and threaten lab personnel, and because the AWA did not require socialization. A "small number of commenters either opposed the requirement for sensory contact among dogs, or recommended that the need for sensory contact be determined by the attending veterinarian," and "several commenters stated that socialization needs of dogs can be met only if two or more dogs have complete body contact." After reviewing these comments, USDA decided, "based on the evidence presented to us, . . . we do not believe that it is essential for the health and well-being of dogs that they have sensory contact with other dogs, and do not believe that it is appropriate to include such a provision in the regulations as a required minimum standard."[101]

It is not clear what "evidence" available to the USDA in 1990 caused it to revise its view, made only the year before and supposedly based on the expertise of the APHIS staff, that "because of the social nature of dogs, we are also proposing to require . . . that all dogs be able to see and hear other dogs."[102] "Many commenters" claimed that the requirement of a minimum time period for social contact with humans or for exercise was "arbitrary and lacking in scientific documentation."[103] Based on the "scientific evidence available to us," and "because of the wide variation in behavioral characteristics of different breeds, and of individual animals within breeds, we do not believe that our proposed 'across the board' standards are the most appropriate way of ensuring that dogs in regulated facilities receive sufficient opportunity for exercise."[104] The USDA then proceeded to eviscerate most of the minimum "engineering" standards, or numerically specific minimal standards, in favor of vague and intentionally imprecise "performance" standards, which reflected that "effective methods of ensuring that dogs receive exercise can most appropriately be developed on a facility-by-facility basis, based on the judgment of the attending veterinarian."[105]

The reproposed rules eliminated the requirement that dogs held individually in cages, or individually in pens or runs that provide less than four times the floor space required for the primary enclosure, be permitted daily exercise, and stated that there was no exercise requirement for any dog kept individually in a cage, pen, or run as long as the total floor space was twice that required for the size of the primary enclosure. The reproposed rules stated that dogs kept in groups need not be exercised if the cage, run, or pen provided the floor space for each dog that would be required for the primary enclosure. In the event that a dog was required to be exercised, that exercise was only required to be given "regularly," and not daily for thirty minutes, as required in the original rule promulgated in 1989. If a single dog was kept at a facility, then the dog must receive daily physical contact, but the sixty-minute requirement was removed. Moreover, the reproposed rules eliminated the requirement that dogs be kept in compatible groups, and accorded even broader discretion to the veterinarian to determine the method and period of exercise.[106]

When USDA promulgated the final rule on dog exercise and socialization in 1991—six years after Congress passed the amendments directing that the secretary develop the regulations—the rule was quite different from either the 1989 proposed rule or the 1990 reproposed rule. In its preface to the rules, USDA stated that it received a total of 11,932 comments on the revised proposals, with 509 from dealers and exhibitors, 1,372 from research facilities, and 10,051 from members of the general public. Again USDA failed to identify which groups made which comments, but did state that "very many commenters" indicated that they were strongly in favor of replacing "engineering" standards with "performance" standards. "Many commenters" expressed concern that more-specific standards would interfere with research because of their "rigidity and specificity." "Many commenters" stated that "rigid" standards "interfere with professional judgment" and "are not scientifically justified."[107] The research community wanted less stringent performance standards, and for the most part, that is precisely what they got.

In the final rule, the housing of dogs and cats in compatible groups remains completely optional. Research facilities are required only to develop a "plan" for exercise, and the plan, which must be approved by the attending veterinarian, must provide for "regular" exercise for dogs confined with less than twice the floor space required in the primary enclosure. Dogs kept in groups are not entitled to exercise if there is the equivalent of the floor space required in the primary enclosure for each dog. Finally, the frequency, method, and duration of exercise is to be determined exclusively by the attending veterinarian and the IACUC. Exemptions are permitted if the attending veterinarian or the IACUC approves. Interestingly, when USDA first proposed regulations on dog exercise in 1989, it stated that "the consensus of APHIS veterinarians with training and experience in the care of dogs is that 30 minutes of daily exercise is a reasonable minimum for maintenance of a dog's health and well-being."[108] In 1991, when it promulgated final rules that eviscerated the exercise requirement, the USDA stated that a rule about the duration of exercise "would not take into account variation among the types of dogs and the use for which they are being held, and would be too restrictive to be applied generally to diverse facilities." Perhaps the most disturbing addition in the final rules is the exemption that provides for "innovative housing" that departs from the requirements provided for primary enclosures as long as the IACUC determines that the "innovative housing" is appropriate.[109]

The development of the regulations for the psychological well-being of primates reveals a similar pattern. In 1989 USDA promulgated a regulation that required research facilities to enrich primary enclosures, and provided examples of such enrichment, including perches, swings, mirrors, and toys. The original rule required that nonhuman primates be housed in compatible groups. Those primates housed individually were required to be provided with a minimum of four hours of exercise and social interaction daily unless the primary enclosure provided at least twice the volume required for the particular species. With respect to juvenile and infant primates, adults used in research, and animals showing signs of psychological distress, the facility, in consultation with the attending veterinarian, must provide more stimulation and interaction.[110] Moreover, the USDA stated explicitly in proposing the original rules in 1989 that "nonhuman primates need greater space than that required under the current regulations," and it explicitly rejected as being inadequate with respect to certain primates the enclosure sizes used by the NIH in its *Guide for the Care and Use of Laboratory Animals.*[111]

After objections from "many commenters" who claimed that these rules were too burdensome for research facilities and were not scientifically valid, USDA reproposed rules that were ultimately made final and that left psychological well-being and social grouping to a "plan [that] must be in accordance with the currently accepted professional standards as cited in appropriate professional journals or reference guides, and as directed by the attending veterinarian." The social-grouping requirement was reduced to a requirement that the facility "address" primate social needs as part of the facility "plan."[112] The exercise requirements were removed entirely, and exemptions were added for "scientific reasons" in addition to those exemptions authorized by the attending veterinarian.[113] The USDA explicitly embraced the same NIH standards for the size of primary enclosures that it had earlier rejected.[114] The final regulations for increased primary enclosures permitted a phase-in period lasting until 1994—nine years after the amendment of the AWA.[115] Last, echoing changes made in the final regulations on the size of primary enclosures for dogs, the USDA permitted "innovative" primate housing that did not meet even the less rigorous requirements for enclosure size as long as the IACUC determined that the housing was appropriate for the species.[116]

The objection by the research community to the engineering standards clearly reflects legal welfarism. The engineering standards were perceived as increasing compliance costs, when at least those who objected believed that they could get reliable data from their animals with the less costly performance standards. The USDA performance standards were challenged, once again by two conservative organizations—ALDF and the Society for Animal Protective Legislation. Although the district court held that the regulations were invalid, the decision was, as I discussed in Chapter Four, reversed by the appellate court on the ground that the plaintiffs lacked standing, and accordingly, the appellate court never reached the merits of the issue. I discuss the merits of the lower-court decision in Chapter Eleven.

These two examples—the failure of the USDA to promulgate regulations covering rats, mice, and birds, and the failure of the USDA to promulgate regulations to implement the 1985 amendments to the AWA in a timely fashion—in combination with USDA opposition to any extension of the AWA, serve to demonstrate that USDA sees itself primarily as representing the interests of the research community.

## USDA Action Involving the University of Pennsylvania Head Injury Lab and the Institute for Behavioral Research

As a final matter, it is interesting to examine the efficacy of the USDA inspection process from the perspective of the two major cases that revealed pervasive animal abuse in federally funded labs.

In the case involving the trauma experiments at the University of Pennsylvania Head Injury Lab, USDA inspectors had performed an inspection of the medical school (in which the lab was housed) on May 31, 1984, which was immediately after the Animal Liberation Front removed the videotapes from the laboratory but before public controversy about the experiments became heated. On May 31 USDA inspectors found five minor violations of the AWA, including dirty lighting fixtures and peeling paint in baboon areas, peeling ceilings, opened food containers, minor excrement buildup, and a dirty air vent in the rabbit areas.[117]

On June 5 the USDA performed another inspection of the same facility in the wake of the ensuing controversy and the accompanying international publicity.

This time, USDA found over seventy violations. The inspector noted that the "facility in general was in very poor condition," that "primate cages do not meet space requirements," that there were "deplorable conditions" for the animals, and that "animal husbandry practices are so poor that we recommend more and better qualified animal caretakers." The inspector recommended that "all animals should be moved out of there immediately."[118]

The May 31 USDA inspection found no serious deficiencies; the June 5 inspection found over seventy violations. The only thing that had changed between the two inspections was the public clamor over allegations by animal protection groups that the experiments violated the AWA. Clearly, the May 31 inspection did not accurately represent the true state of the animal facilities at the medical school; if the controversy surrounding the head-injury laboratory had not triggered greater public scrutiny of an inspection process that is generally conducted in secret and without any public attention whatsoever, it is unlikely that any subsequent inspection would have differed from the inaccurate report of May 31, since both inspections were performed by the same APHIS inspector.

In the earlier case involving Taub's experiments at the Institute for Behavioral Research, the efficacy of the USDA inspection process in its ability to detect serious deficiencies was again placed in question. During the time that Pacheco documented the wholly inadequate conditions in Taub's laboratory, USDA inspectors had—on two occasions—found no major deficiencies.[119] USDA also conducted an inspection of the IBR facilities after the animals were removed and, despite photographic evidence obtained by the Maryland police that showed numerous serious deficiencies, found the facilities to be adequate.[120] At Taub's trial, the USDA inspector admitted that although his report indicated that the IBR facilities were adequate, the inspection had been quite cursory, for he had failed to inspect, or did not inspect adequately, many parts of the IBR premises.

## Explanations of USDA Behavior

It is easy—and consequently tempting—to dismiss USDA behavior as exclusively the result of what is called agency "capture." All too often, administrative agencies that are intended by Congress to regulate industries or practices are "captured" by those industries or practices and, as a result, are entirely too deferential to those they regulate. This "capture" is illustrated by the relationship between USDA and research facilities that use animals.

The biomedical establishment in this country is very powerful and exerts enormous political influence. The USDA, as an administrative agency, is a branch of the executive portion of government and is a politically vulnerable agency. Over the years, the USDA has come to see itself as aligned more with the research community than with the general public. Moreover, the USDA views the animal protection community as adversarial to the interests of the USDA. In a sense, these attitudes are to be expected.

The USDA has, from the outset, been reluctant to take an aggressive posture on the regulation of animal welfare. Indeed, as one commentator pointed out, "The Animal Welfare Act leaves the Secretary of the USDA wide discretion in promulgating AWA regulations. In doing so, however, the Secretary has shown more of an interest in not rocking the boat than in aggressively enforcing the Act."[121] As can be expected, the research community has welcomed this nonaggressive approach by USDA. On the other hand, even very conservative elements within the animal protection community have criticized the abuses of animals in federally funded laboratories and have emphasized the need for greater USDA involvement. Predictably, the USDA has not welcomed this criticism from the humane community. Accordingly, USDA has come to find friendlier quarter with those that it regulates.

There is, however, a more important and relevant explanation that must be considered as well. In the beginning of the chapter, I explained the process that USDA uses to guide one aspect of its enforcement of the AWA—the promulgation of regulations. That process requires that the agency "balance" animal interests against the interests of people, including the interest of the public in obtaining cures, the interest of scientists in obtaining knowledge, and the interest of the particular facility in being able to use its animal property in a way that does not impose "unnecessary" or "unjustifiable" costs. Just as anticruelty laws do not use the notion of "cruelty" as that term is commonly understood, so too does USDA not interpret "minimal" requirements to refer to those that are absolutely necessary for animal welfare. Rather, USDA interprets that term in conjunction with another norm that is found nowhere in the AWA: that a requirement for "minimal" standards must not result in the imposition of "unnecessary" costs to the research facility. It is difficult to understand how the concepts of "unnecessary suffering" and "unnecessary cost" are supposed to fit in any manner that would have a positive impact on animals. Indeed, the entire regulatory process concerning implementation of the 1985 AWA amendments indicates that "necessary" animal suffering is determined by what constitutes "unnecessary" cost to the facility. Once the USDA determines that the costs of compliance are too high, then the scope of protection afforded to animals is severely restricted, and the resulting level of protection becomes what is "necessary." The problem is that there is no non-normative way of determining when compliance costs are "too high," since neither the benefit to animals nor the public perception of improved animal welfare can be quantified. The USDA does not recognize that there is a level of protection to which animals are absolutely entitled and below which the cost of compliance cannot serve to decrease protection; rather, property concerns in the form of compliance costs of the facility determine the extent to which the government is willing to regulate the use of other (animal) property.

The implications of this approach in the area of implementing regulations will surely be felt in the area of inspections as well. If USDA inspectors view their roles as ensuring that level of animal protection that is consistent with some nebulous notion of what constitutes acceptable compliance costs, inspectors will not, by definition, regard the facilities as under any obligation to provide certain minimal care irrespective of cost. Rather, they will believe that the regulatory framework should not impose an "unjustified" or "unreasonable" cost on the research facility, and that is the criterion that determines the acceptable level of animal care.

In a sense, this approach reflects what Professor Howard Latin characterizes as "archetypal 'laws' of administrative behavior."[122] For example, Latin argues that agencies avoid making decisions when they are unable to make scientifically credible judgments.[123] It is obvious that in the area of animal protection the scientific community is deeply divided about what will best facilitate the efficient use of animal resources. Indeed, as the USDA itself reported throughout the regulatory process involving the 1985 AWA amendments, and as the scientific press indicated, many in the scientific community disagreed that canine exercise or the psychological well-being of primates was a legitimate subject of regulation. Many of these comments went directly to a lack of scientific consensus. In such a situation, it should not be surprising that USDA is reluctant to regulate, even though continued controversy about animal husbandry is likely to persist indefinitely, especially when such uncertainty facilitates efforts by the scientific community to resist regulation.[124]

Latin also argues that agencies will not make regulatory decisions that will cause severe social or economic dislocation.[125] He gives as an example efforts by the Environmental Protection Agency to exempt certain marginal plants from air pollution requirements because of the severe economic impact and social dislocation that would result. Although it ostensibly appears as though the USDA was simply adhering to this administrative behavioral "law" in proposing regulations under the AWA, there are important differences. First, USDA assumed that, as a general matter, complying with the original engineering standards would impose "unreasonable" or "unnecessary" financial burdens on research facilities. Second, the AWA, unlike the other laws that Latin discusses, provided explicitly for the development of "minimal" standards.

Latin also argues that bureaucrats are often conditioned by criticism or negative feedback.[126] There can be no doubt that although USDA receives its share of criticism from scientists, the most vocal critics of the USDA enforcement of the AWA are found in the humane community. Accordingly, USDA has, as I mentioned above, developed a rather adversarial relationship with the humane community and seeks defense from the research community.

Finally, there is one administrative "law" that, contrary to explaining USDA behavior through compliance with the administrative norm, explains USDA behavior better through using a model of deviation from the norm. Latin maintains that regulators are influenced by certain norms that are part of their professional discipline and may have difficulty in complying with statutory mandates that are perceived to conflict with those norms.[127] As an example, Latin discusses how the scientific study of acid rain failed to contribute meaningfully to the policy debate on the issue, which was driven by cost/benefit considerations rather than scientific considerations. In the case of USDA enforcement of the AWA, however, there is no real divergence of science and policy issues. That is, the research community sees the issue of animal use as presenting a question of cost/benefit analysis. The benefits to humans almost inevitably outweigh the costs to animals, and the care and treatment of animals is driven by these and other cost considerations, including the cost to the facility of animal welfare measures. Similarly, the USDA views these issues as requiring a cost/benefit analysis, and accordingly, the USDA limits animal welfare to those instances where the costs of compliance are "justified."

## Conclusion

In this chapter, I examined the enforcement of the AWA by USDA. I argued that the USDA regulation reflects the central tenet of legal welfarism: that any costs of complying with animal welfare regulation be justified using a balancing framework that accords virtually no regard to animal interests. This balancing process is conceptually similar to the concerns that animate the implementation of anti-cruelty statutes.

In the next chapter, I examine judicial decisions that have sought to interpret the AWA.

# CHAPTER ELEVEN

## *The Animal Welfare Act in the Courts*

### The Reasons for the Lack of Judicial Interpretation

IN A WAY, the AWA is more "pathological" than the environmental statutes that are the focus of John Dwyer's inquiry mentioned at the beginning of Chapter Ten. In Dwyer's examples of environmental statutes, courts were required to fill the void created by agency inaction with results that Dwyer quite correctly finds problematic. The problem with the Animal Welfare Act is exactly the opposite. The reason for this concerns the doctrine of standing to a great degree, and to a lesser degree the penalties prescribed and actually imposed by the USDA. Until the Supreme Court severely restricted statutory standing in *Lujan v. Defenders of Wildlife,*[1] there was an enormous amount of litigation under the citizen suit provisions of the various environmental statutes. This litigation has permitted courts to shape regulatory structures in ways that Dwyer believes create mischief because judicial intervention often, according to Dwyer, frustrates congressional objectives. In the case of the AWA, however, there has never been much litigation because the courts have always decided standing issues against those who sought to enforce AWA provisions. The courts do not interpret the AWA and try to impose a functional regulatory scheme that has not been created by the responsible administrative agency for all of the reasons that Dwyer discusses. To place the matter within the framework discussed in Chapter One, the courts do not enforce the AWA, because, as a general matter, it is economically inefficient to do so as it will increase the costs of animal property use without any quantifiable benefit.

There is, however, another reason the AWA has not been subjected to much judicial interpretation, let alone judicial enforcement. The AWA provides that federal courts are "vested with jurisdiction specifically to enforce, and to prevent and restrain violations of the" AWA.[2] As I discussed in the previous chapter, all AWA cases (given that the courts have already decided that private parties have no standing to bring AWA-based cases) originate at USDA. Only if the research facility, dealer, exhibitor, or transporter is dissatisfied with the USDA resolution does she seek court action. A review of typical USDA sanctions, however, indicates that it

234

would be very cost ineffective for any party to take the proceedings further than USDA. First of all, research facilities are hardly ever prosecuted for violating the AWA by the USDA, with rare exceptions and almost always in cases involving the failure to submit annual reports. Accordingly, those portions of the AWA that deal with the care and treatment of animals used in experiments are not usually headed toward judicial interpretation, because the USDA never starts those cases in the first place. When the USDA does act against a research facility for violating substantive provisions of the AWA, the facility has usually engaged in egregious behavior and settles the case early. In the rather unusual instance that the USDA does prosecute an administrative action against a research facility for violating the AWA, the penalties are ludicrous. For example, in 1992 USDA reported that Adelphi University agreed to a $2,500 fine and a cease-and-desist order for operating an unregistered research facility for rabbits; the facility was "poorly ventilated and not substantially impervious to moisture, the primary enclosures were not clean and sanitary, and there was no established program to remove and dispose of animal waste."[3] If Adelphi had received an adverse administrative decision rather than settle for the fine and order, it could have obtained review in federal court but would have had to pay at least $10,000 for legal costs associated with that review. Moreover, court proceedings would publicly highlight the AWA violations, and most research facilities go to great lengths to keep their animal experimentation skeletons locked away in impregnable closets. The virtue of the USDA proceedings from this standpoint is that the interested public rarely becomes aware of what APHIS is doing, but it would most certainly learn of a federal court proceeding in which the USDA was trying to obtain enforcement of an order or other sanction against an unwilling research facility.

Even when the USDA sanctions other, less "prestigious" parties subject to the AWA—dealers, exhibitors, and transporters—the sanctions are pitifully insignificant even when the violations are most serious. In 1991 the USDA took action against Orville Britt, an unlicensed animal dealer who sold "at least 449 dogs and 18 cats" to other animal dealers.[4] If a dealer is unlicensed, that increases the chances the animals sold by that dealer are companion animals who were illegally obtained. Although Britt had agreed to pay a $10,000 civil penalty without admitting or denying the charges, the administrative law judge reduced the penalty to $3,000 and ordered that for five years Britt not engage in activities that would require a license. Again, it would have cost Britt four or five times his civil penalty had he sought review in a federal court, which would probably have deferred to the agency anyway.

Accordingly, those with the interest in seeking interpretation and enforcement of the AWA in court do not have the standing to do so, because animals used in experiments are the property of another and the courts have already declared that there can be no cognizable "injury" for standing purposes if a person has a relationship terminated with an animal who is the property of another. Those with the authority to enforce the AWA do so with something far less than vigor or enthusiasm. Those who are charged with violating the AWA are usually sanctioned in relatively insignificant ways and do not seek federal court review, because it is simply not worth the cost, which almost always is a multiple of the penalty imposed by the USDA, or because the sanctioned party wants to avoid the publicity that would be attendant upon a court proceeding. Consequently, the AWA remains symbolic both at the level of administrative enforcement and at the level of judicial interpretation. Put another way, despite a complex regulatory structure that has existed for almost thirty years, there is very little case law that concerns the enforcement of the AWA provisions as they relate to the care and treatment of animals used in research facilities. In light of the thousands of statutes passed over the decades, it is impossible to make a blanket comparative statement, but I do feel comfortable in expressing the view that there is not a single similar regulatory framework whose key provisions have virtually never been interpreted, much less enforced, in federal courts.

## Private Property and Standing

### General Interpretation of the AWA

As I showed in Chapter Four, the courts have taken a most restrictive view of standing as it applies to the AWA. Those who "use" animal "resources," for example, by visiting wildlife refuges, have standing to object to actions that will deprive or modify those opportunities. However, those who seek to protect animals covered by the AWA have no standing to do so, even when they have a personal and sustained relationship with those animals. The line drawn by the court is one explicitly predicated on the property status of the animals. If the animal is owned, then even if a person who is not the owner has a relationship with the animal, the courts have no jurisdiction to hear the case, because the animals are privately owned and no one but the owner can enjoy those "resources" freely, so no one other than the owner can claim an interest in the animals for purposes of satisfying standing requirements. As a result of this severely restrictive approach to standing, few cases have interpreted the AWA, and none has enforced its provisions. To the extent that the AWA represents a nonfunctional regulatory scheme that contains hopelessly vague notions about "necessary" suffering or animal use, courts have done little to clarify the confusion.[5]

As I mentioned in Chapters Four and Ten, two attempts by animal welfare organizations to litigate regulations promulgated under the AWA were rebuffed by the courts on the ground that the plaintiffs lacked standing. In *Animal Legal Defense Fund v. Yeutter,* plaintiffs challenged the exclusion of rats, mice, and birds from the AWA. In the other case, *Animal Legal Defense Fund v. Secretary of Agriculture,* the plaintiffs challenged the USDA promulgation of performance standards rather than engineering standards. Although the plaintiffs prevailed on the merits in both cases, the appellate court reversed both decisions in 1994 solely on the grounds of standing, and never discussed the merits of either case. A brief review of the lower-court decisions in both cases, however, demonstrates quite clearly that the plaintiffs had strong cases on the merits.

The original *Yeutter* decision in the lower court involved standing, and, as I discussed in Chapter Four, plaintiffs prevailed on standing at that stage, and thus went on to trial on the merits. In *Animal Legal Defense Fund v. Madigan*,[6] the federal district court held that the USDA had acted improperly by excluding rats, mice, and birds from its administrative interpretation of the definitional section of the AWA, and that the agency had also acted improperly by denying the plaintiffs' petition for rule making to include the excluded species. The court rejected the USDA argument that the secretary of agriculture had discretion to designate which species were protected under the AWA. According to the USDA, the legislative history of the 1970 amendments to the AWA, which added the definitional section, provided that " 'it would be expected that the Secretary would designate additional species of animals not previously covered as permitted by available funds and manpower.' " The court responded that this sentence of the legislative history had to be read in conjunction with the preceding sentence, which provided that the AWA would " 'define the term "animal" to include any live or dead dog or cat, monkey (nonhuman primate mammal), guinea pig, hamster, rabbit, or such other warm-blooded animal as the Secretary may determine is being used, or intended for use, for research, testing, experimentation, or exhibition purposes, or as a pet.' "[7] The court found that the sentence relied upon by the USDA should be read " 'to refer to the Secretary's power to designate *additional* species for the expenditure of Department funds and manpower, not for coverage by the AWA, which is mandated by the language of the Act.' "[8] Also, the court rejected USDA's argument that because Congress had amended the AWA twice since rats, mice, and birds were excluded by USDA regulation in 1971, Congress must be taken to have ratified the administrative interpretation of the definitional section to exclude rats, mice, and birds. The court held that when Congress reenacts legislation, it is presumed to ratify previous administrative interpretations of the law, but that in this case there was a dispute whether Congress had "actual knowledge of the regulation." In any event, the court refused to apply the presumption, because the regulation was directly violative of the clear language of the AWA.[9]

Interestingly, the USDA in *Madigan* acknowledged that including rats, mice, and birds within the scope of the AWA would further the congressional purpose to ensure that animals used in experiments were treated humanely. Despite this acknowledgment, the court stated that the USDA declined "to consider the benefit to animals as worthy of serious consideration as it decides how best to carry out its mandate.[10] So, although the USDA is the only body that may properly "balance" human and animal interests in deciding issues of animal welfare under the AWA, that agency refused to consider animal benefit in deciding the appropriate scope of coverage under the act.

In the other case, *Animal Legal Defense Fund v. Secretary of Agriculture*,[11] the same court as in *Madigan* held that the USDA had acted improperly in not promulgating adequate and reasonable regulations concerning exercise for dogs and the psychological well-being of primates. The district court agreed that the regulation for canine exercise, which left frequency, duration, and method of exercise to the attending veterinarian and IACUC, was "contrary to the Act's clear mandate that the Secretary, and not the regulated entity, establish minimum requirements in this area."[12] The court also held that the USDA had failed to propose minimum standards for the psychological well-being of primates and, instead, had left such determination to the "generally accepted professional standards" and the attending veterinarian. The court remarked that in 1989 USDA and the commenters agreed that "social deprivation is psychologically debilitating to non-human primates and that group housing for non-human primates was the best way to avoid this problem."[13] Accordingly, the court observed, USDA had originally proposed that group housing was required unless contrary to the health of the nonhuman primate, but in the 1990 reproposed version and the 1991 final rule, group housing was no longer required. The court also held that USDA's use of the NIH requirements for the size of primary enclosures for nonhuman primates was arbitrary and capricious in light of USDA's rejection two years earlier of the same NIH standards. In addition, the court found USDA's phase-in period for primary enclosures for primates to be arbitrary and capricious. Finally, the court held that the USDA had acted arbitrarily and capriciously by allowing regulated entities to decrease cage size for dogs and primates through the provision of "innovative housing."

In a criticism of the lower court's decision in *Secretary,* and before that decision was reversed on standing grounds, Charles R. McCarthy, former director of the NIH Office of Protection from Research Risks, which oversees the extramural use of animals in NIH-funded projects, argued that "the animals are the losers" in the court's decision.[14] McCarthy made two different points. First, he claimed that the use of "engineering" standards, such as numerical criteria for cage size or established guidelines for the frequency, duration, and method of exercise, as opposed to the "performance" standards contained in the final rule, will hinder the development of optimal methods for animal housing, exercise, and psychological well-being and impermissibly intervenes "between the veterinarian and his or her patients."[15] Second, McCarthy argued that engineering standards are inconsistent with the AWA, which, according to McCarthy, required exactly what the USDA promulgated in its final rule—general standards that would be applied in each case by the attending veterinarian but without there being any set criteria that had to be followed in a particular case.[16]

McCarthy's arguments are without merit. His first argument—that minimum requirements will ultimately harm animals because they will inhibit optimal housing and treatment—is disposed of easily: absolutely nothing in the trial court's analysis would have precluded the attending veterinarian's doing *more* for a particular animal. For example, if the original USDA rule that required thirty minutes of daily exercise for dogs had been proposed as a final rule, nothing would have prevented the attending veterinarian from ordering more exercise for a particularly large or athletic dog that needed more exercise. This is the fallacy of McCarthy's argument, which, incidentally, was the same argument made by the government before the trial court. The "engineering" standards favored by the trial court were simply minimal standards; nothing prevents a particular research facility from doing *more;* the only thing prohibited is doing *less.* McCarthy's argument may be restated as saying that animal welfare will be retarded if the attending veterinarian cannot require less space or less exercise than the minimal standards permit. McCarthy's argument is even more transparent in light of the fact that even the originally proposed rules that USDA ultimately rejected explicitly permitted departures from the minimal guidelines *as long as such departure was in the animal's interests.* What the original rules did not permit, and what the final rules do permit (and what McCarthy sought to defend), is the ability to tailor exercise or cage space to suit the needs of the *research facility* and not to serve the welfare of the animal. In reproposing rules and announcing final regulations USDA stated that the purpose of performance standards was to allow for *future* scientific determinations that might revise notions about exercise, socialization, or psychological well-being in a downward direction. Since virtually any position may be supported with some "scientific" study, and since basic issues of animal husbandry have never lent themselves to broad professional consensus, the attending veterinarian is left unfettered in making decisions about "commonly accepted practice." Moreover, facility plans are not likely to include massive capital investments when future revisions of "commonly accepted practices" may render those expenditures unnecessary. In light of cost considerations, about which the research community had expressed concern during the multiple-year notice-and-comment period, it is likely that local IACUCs will feel pressure to agree to less expensive plans than would have been required under the engineering standards proposed in 1989 by USDA and retracted in 1990 and 1991, as each facility waits—for many more years—to see what the "consensus" of the scientific community is on these issues.

McCarthy's second argument, based on the language of the AWA, is similarly faulty. In amending the AWA, Congress directed the secretary of agriculture—and not each regulated entity—to develop "minimal requirements" for dog exercise and primate psychological well-being. In the case of dog exercise, the AWA states that the "minimal requirements" are to be determined by an "attending veterinarian in accordance with general standards promulgated by the Secretary." In the case of primate psychological well-being, the AWA states that the "minimal requirements" are to be promulgated by the secretary, and there is no mention of the attending veterinarian.[17]

Although the language of the 1985 amendments to the AWA is not as clear as it could be, the legislative history indicates clearly that Congress was very concerned about the level of discretion that research facilities had before the AWA was amended, since that discretion affected husbandry issues, such as exercise and housing. Congress wanted to remove some of that discretion but also wanted to ensure that it did not encroach in any manner on actual research activities. Minimal requirements help to ensure that animal care, treatment, and handling do not fall below a certain level, and Congress correctly determined the need for such standards. The history of animal use for experiments is not one that contains a long list of improvements in animal welfare voluntarily undertaken by research facilities. On the contrary, research facilities have traditionally improved animal welfare only when required to do so, and even then, the effort has not been remarkable. As the USDA itself observed, the research community objected to the original legislation in 1966 that eventually became the AWA, because of concerns about added expense that "were not borne out."[18] In any event, the statutory language is silent about the role of the veterinarian in the standards for psychological well-being. It is unlikely that Congress meant to exclude the attending veterinarian from having a role in developing standards for both dogs and nonhuman primates. It is also clear, however, that Congress did not mean to have the attending veterinarian formulate those requirements, since the veterinarian is not even mentioned in connection with standards for nonhuman primates. The only sensible role for the attending veterinarian is precisely the role that the court described: tailoring exercise, space, and psychological well-being to each individual animal in light of the veterinarian's expertise and judgment, but such that these provisions not fall *below* a certain level.

The controversy over engineering standards provides a valuable case study in the application of legal welfarism. Congress legislated that USDA develop standards for primate well-being and canine exercise. This congressional directive was not unlike other parts of the AWA that require standards concerning feeding and housing and address other husbandry issues. USDA developed engineering standards, and the research community reacted strongly, arguing that these standards were not cost-justified and would place "unnecessary" financial burdens on the research facility. Instead, researchers argued for performance standards that would, in all likelihood, allow each facility to determine what measures of animal welfare are cost-justified by reference to whether *that* facility's personnel regard their research data as reliable. When challenged in court, these performance standards were found not to comply with the congressional mandate, but this finding was overturned on appeal on standing grounds: private parties do not have the ability even to try to protect the animal property of the facility. Legal welfarism ensures that the animal *always* loses the supposed balancing that is part of our normative structure.

Another of the few cases involving the AWA is *State v. LeVasseur*.[19] Kenneth LeVasseur was an undergraduate student at the University of Hawaii. In January 1975 he began to work at the university's marine laboratory at Kewalo Basin, Honolulu, as a research assistant. His primary responsibilities involved repairing and cleaning the laboratory's dolphin tanks and feeding and swimming with the dolphins. In May 1977, after working with the dolphins for over two years, LeVasseur decided that the dolphins were in great danger as the result of their confinement in the laboratory tanks. He and several other people removed two dolphins from their tanks at the laboratory and released the animals into the ocean. LeVasseur was charged and convicted of first-degree theft, and he appealed.[20]

The primary issue in LeVasseur's appeal was whether the trial court had erred in ruling that LeVasseur could not use a "choice-of-evils" defense. This defense, which has different formulations depending upon the jurisdiction, provided under Hawaii law that certain conduct, otherwise criminal, could be justified if the actor believes such conduct "to be necessary to avoid an imminent harm or evil to himself or to *another*" and if "the harm or evil sought to be avoided by such conduct is greater than that sought to be prevented by the law defining the offense charged."[21]

LeVasseur argued that he was trying to prevent greater harm to *another* in two senses. First, he argued that the dolphins should be included within the term *another*. The appellate court rejected this argument because the statute defined "another" as a *person,* and although corporations and associations can be considered as "persons" under the law, the court ruled that dolphins could not be so considered. Second, LeVasseur argued that the term "person" was also defined under Hawaii law to include the United States. LeVasseur maintained that the policy of the AWA was to prevent cruelty to animals, and that by releasing the dolphins, he was protecting the humane treatment policy of the United States. Although the court accepted that the AWA "and its accompanying regulations manifest a national policy to protect the well-being of laboratory animals like the instant dolphins,"[22] the court held that LeVasseur had acted improperly because he should have contacted the federal government and reported the life-threatening condition of the dolphins and should not have deliberately chosen theft as his means of helping the animals. In the court's view, the crime of property theft was as great an evil as the evil that LeVasseur sought to prevent—the death of the dolphins.

The decision in *LeVasseur* is completely understandable given the fundamental premise of the AWA—that nonhumans are the property of humans and can be exploited for human benefit. Given a characterization of nonhumans as property, the researchers at the university were only exercising one of their rights, the right to use the facility's property. It, therefore, should not be surprising that even though the court recognized that the policy of the AWA was to treat animals humanely, the evil that LeVasseur had sought to avoid, the inhumane treatment of the animals, was no greater than the evil that he had actually caused, the violation of the university's property rights.

In two cases, *Kerr v. Kimmell* and *Winkler v. Colorado Department of Health,*[23] courts held that the AWA does not prohibit states from providing additional regulation of animal use. The Supremacy Clause of the United States Constitution establishes the supremacy of federal law over state law.[24] This is not to say that state laws about a particular topic are prohibited just because the federal government has chosen to enact some laws on that topic.

Rather, there are five conditions under which federal law may preempt state law: (1) where Congress explicitly indicates that by legislating on a topic, Congress intends to preclude the states from exercising authority; (2) where the scheme of federal regulation is so comprehensive that it leaves no room for additional state regulation; (3) where the particular area of legislation is one in which federal interests are inherently dominant; (4) where there is a conflict between federal and state law such that a person cannot comply with both; and (5) where state law stands as an obstacle to the accomplishment of federal objectives.[25] In these two cases, parties challenged state laws and regulations concerning animal use on the ground that the state rules were preempted by the AWA. Neither challenge involved state restrictions on biomedical research. Rather, these cases concerned state regulation of breeders and importers.

In *Kerr,* the plaintiff, who owned a breeding business, objected to application of the Kansas Animal Dealers Act to her business. One of Kerr's claims was that the AWA prohibited states from enacting their own legislation dealing with operations like Kerr's. The court rejected Kerr's claim, holding that the AWA specifically stated that the states may promulgate their own rules on animal welfare.[26] In *Winkler,* the plaintiff, a commercial pet supplier, imported animals from out of state. He challenged a Colorado law that had the effect of prohibiting importation of pets into Colorado from states whose licensing laws and regulations for commercial pet dealers were not as stringent as those of Colorado. Winkler argued that the Colorado law was preempted by the AWA, which imposes licensing requirements on persons who ship animals for sale in interstate commerce. The court rejected the challenge, holding that in the AWA Congress had specifically provided for supplemental state law and that there was no conflict between the Colorado law and the AWA.[27]

These cases are important for their recognition that state law may supplement the AWA, but they say nothing about the substantive provisions of the AWA. In the future, animal advocates may be well advised to seek greater protection for animals on the *state* level, not on the federal level. Decisions such as these support such efforts.

A 1993 case involving the regulation of animal dealers illustrates judicial reluctance to punish violators even when the violations are egregious. In *United States v. Linville,*[28] Linville pleaded guilty to conspiring to defraud the USDA. Linville fraudulently obtained dogs from owners by promising (in writing) to provide them with a good home when, in fact, she sold the dogs to a registered USDA dealer, who, in turn, sold the dogs into medical research. The USDA had notified Linville that she needed to obtain a license in order to sell dogs to USDA dealers, and warned her that use of fraud or deceit in obtaining random-source (i.e., not purpose-bred) animals violated federal regulations. Finally, the USDA issued an official notice and warning to Linville, advising her that she was in violation of the AWA.[29] When the trial judge sentenced Linville, he increased her punishment under the federal sentencing guidelines, which, in relevant part, provide for an increase in sentence when an offence of fraud or deceit involves the violation of any "administrative order, injunction, decree, or process."[30] The appellate court reversed, holding that the sentence enhancement was impermissible because, although the USDA had issued an official notification of violation and warning, there was no adversary proceeding or "formal" order and the warnings directed to Linville were merely "relatively informal missives."[31] Although the USDA warning to Linville did not result from an adversary proceeding, it simply stretches credulity to hold that Linville's conduct did not violate administrative "process." The Linville case illustrates the extent to which at least some courts will go to protect the use of animals in research even when the dealer obtains animals through fraud.

## Cases Involving Animal Care Committees

Other cases concerning the AWA involve access to the documents and the meetings of the Institutional Animal Care and Use Committees (IACUCs) required under the 1985 amendments to the AWA. In the past several years, animal protection advocates have sought to gain entrance to the meetings of these IACUCs and to gain access to the various documents submitted by experimenters to the IACUCs, including the project review forms submitted by animal users to the IACUC and the minutes of IACUC meetings. The primary means of obtaining this access is through state "sunshine" laws—laws that require that meetings of certain agencies be open to the public and that certain records of agencies be made available to the public.[32] There is an important reason—apart from general public interest in the workings of government—that accounts for this interest in access to IACUC meetings and documents.

Although grant applications can usually be obtained eventually through the federal Freedom of Information Act if the researcher seeks federal funds, an interested party often does not become aware of an experiment until *after* it is funded, and animal experimentation at universities is being funded increasingly by commercial enterprises not subject to the access law. Access to the meetings and documents of an IACUC under state law provides information about an experiment *before* the experiment commences, irrespective of the funding source. Such early access is important because it facilitates the scrutiny of an experiment on scientific and moral grounds and thereby increases the chances that an effective critique may prevent the experiment from being performed. Once an experiment is funded, federal agencies have a vested interest in defending the process of "peer review" that, according to those agencies, chooses only the "best" work to fund. In addition, the experimenter and sponsoring institution have a greater incentive to fight any criticism of the experiment.

Another reason for the importance of access is that certain uses of animals never involve any application for federal funding. For example, many animals are used for teaching purposes rather than for funded experiments. Disclosure through the IACUC may be the primary means of learning about, publicizing, and preventing such exploitation.

Several cases have concerned access to IACUC meetings and documents. Although some research institutions have voluntarily provided the requested access,[33] others have not, and litigation has occurred. In some cases, courts have ruled in favor of access,[34] and in some, they have ruled against access.[35] Good examples of IACUC access litigation are found in two cases that were filed against the State University of New York (SUNY) by the American Society for the Prevention of Cruelty to Animals (ASPCA). A review of these cases is useful, first, because they indicate just how far courts will stretch existing law in order to ensure that IACUCs are protected from public scrutiny and, second, because the arguments made by SUNY against access in both cases reflect the increasingly received—and uncritical—wisdom that science should be regarded as a proprietary enterprise and that scientists are entitled to preferential treatment.

In *American Society for the Prevention of Cruelty to Animals v. Board of Trustees*[36] (SUNY I), the ASPCA sought access to the meetings of the Stony Brook IACUC. Under New York access law, a meeting of a "public body" must be opened to the public unless certain very restricted exemptions apply. The law provided that a public body is one that has two or more members, requires a quorum to conduct public business, and performs a governmental function for the state or an agency of the state. The trial court held that the SUNY IACUC was a "public body" because, under the AWA, the IACUC must consist of more than two members and requires a quorum in order to conduct public business. The court held that the IACUC performed a "governmental function" because of its "statutorily mandated nature," "the authority that [IACUC] maintains over research, and the fiscal implications of the [IACUC] determination on the proposed research."[37] The court recognized that in order for SUNY—a state agency—"to receive federal funding [an IACUC] must be maintained when research, tests, or experimentation on live animals is involved."[38]

The trial court's decision was overturned by the intermediate appellate court on several grounds. First, the appellate court held that the IACUC acted only as an "advisory body for the chief executive officer of the appointing research facility and/or the funding agency."[39] This holding ignored completely the plain language of the AWA and its implementing regulations, which state that although the IACUC may not interfere with the content or conduct of experiments, or engage in any ethical review, the IACUC has the authority to disapprove of, or even to suspend, an experiment or other animal use and that officials of the institutions "may not override or circumvent the [IACUC's] decision on a proposed activity, including a decision on suspension."[40]

Moreover, there is no provision in the AWA or its regulations that permits a federal funding agency to ignore IACUC findings or to permit the proposed experiment or to resume the suspended activity despite the IACUC decision. So, although the ultimate decision to fund an experiment may rest with a federal agency, neither the institution (in this case, SUNY) nor the funding agency may override the decision of the IACUC should it disapprove a proposed project or suspend an ongoing project on the limited grounds discussed in Chapter Nine. The appellate court's holding that the IACUC was merely an "advisory body" that conducted no public business directly contradicted the clear and unambiguous language of the AWA and its implementing regulations.

As part of its misunderstanding about the function of the IACUC, the appellate court held that the IACUC was "not involved in deliberations and decisions that go into the making of public policy."[41] In holding that the IACUC decisions do not constitute "public policy," the court, regarding the IACUC as an "advisory" body, ignored the fact that Congress, recognizing "the importance of public concern for the care and treatment of laboratory animals,"[42] had delegated to the IACUC some power to decide whether particular experiments would be approved or suspended on the limited ground of animal care and use. To characterize the IACUC as not empowered to make any policy decisions is to misunderstand completely the legal power that the IACUC possesses. The IACUC has no power over the content, conduct, or ethical or scientific merit of an experiment, but may take action against an experimenter who "wastes" animal resources.

Second, the appellate court held that the supposedly "advisory" function of the IACUC was, in any event, performed for the benefit of the federal, not state, government because the IACUC was created by, and required by, federal law.[43] The court completely ignored the fact that in order for SUNY—an admittedly *state* agency—to take advantage of federal funds for scientific experiments involving animals, it was necessary for SUNY to comply with federal requirements contained in the AWA. Another division of the same appellate court had held in a 1979 case that "applications for federal funds and the priorities to be attached thereto are matters of public concern and are the public's business."[44] Moreover, in another case, the court held that the State Medical Advisory Committee, which "was created in compliance with the Federal directives which mandate its existence in order to enable a State to take advantage of Federal provisions and to obtain Federal Funding," was subject to the Open Meetings Law because the commissioner of social services was prohibited from acting without first receiving the advice of the Medical Advisory Committee.[45] Nevertheless, the appellate court held that because the IACUC was a creation of federal law, it could not be performing a state function. This holding represented a marked departure from preexisting law.[46]

The court of appeals, New York's highest court, granted discretionary review of the appellate decision's reversal but upheld the judgment.[47] The court of appeals carefully avoided endorsing the intermediate appellate court's reasoning or holdings on its interpretation of the Open Meetings Law. The court of appeals held simply that the IACUC was not subject to the access law, because "even if it could be characterized as a governmental entity, it is at most a *Federal* body that is not covered under the Open Meetings Law."[48] This holding directly contravened New York access law, which had never drawn a distinction based on the source of the state's obligation. Indeed, to the extent that there was law on the subject, the courts had specifically held to the contrary. The court of appeals, like the intermediate appellate court, never even bothered to address this argument.

In *American Society for the Prevention of Cruelty to Animals v. Board of Trustees*[49] (SUNY II), the ASPCA sought access to the unredacted project review forms provided by experimenters to the IACUC. The trial court held that the forms were "public records" under the state Freedom of Information Act. Again, the intermediate appellate court reversed, this time confining its decision to the court of appeals' view that the IACUC, being a creature of federal law, could not perform a governmental function for the state of New York.

*SUNY I* and *SUNY II* are interesting for two reasons. First, they indicate how far courts will go in accommodating the desire of research institutions to keep their activities shielded from the scrutiny of the very same public that pays for those research activities through its federal and state taxes. There is simply *no* way that one can reconcile the decisions in these cases with preexisting law on the subject of access, and these decisions present a formidable threat to public access to information about animal experiments.

Second, throughout both cases, the source of law that established the IACUC, which ultimately determined the decisions in both cases, was not the primary or even one of the primary arguments relied on by SUNY. On the contrary, the issues that SUNY pressed hardest were that information discussed by the IACUC was "confidential" and that researchers had a proprietary interest in the information contained in review forms and discussed at IACUC meetings. Both arguments are invalid, but both involve the assertions of property rights in research, which, as I mentioned earlier, are often used in the balance against animal interests.

In amending the AWA to require the IACUC, Congress explicitly articulated two interrelated concerns about the IACUC treatment of "confidential" matters. First, in section 2143 of the act, Congress made clear that a research facility is not required to disclose to the public *or to the IACUC* "trade secrets or commercial or financial information which is privileged or confidential."[50] Second, in section 2157 of the AWA, Congress prohibited the "release of trade secrets" and imposed criminal penalties on any IACUC member who released "any confidential information of the research facility including any information that concerns or relates to—(1) the trade secrets, processes, operations, style of work, or apparatus; or (2) the identity, confidential statistical data, amount or source of any income, profits, losses, or expenditures, of the research facility."[51]

SUNY argued that access to IACUC meetings and documents must be denied because federal law made confidential *any* discussion of experimentation, including information about the treatment, care, and handling of animals used in experiments. According to this argument, any discussion about experimentation would invariably reveal information about the "processes, operations, style of work, or apparatus," disclosure of which is explicitly prohibited by section 2157.

The unspoken assumption in the argument that section 2157 makes "confidential" any discussion of experimentation, including information about animal care, treatment, or handling, is that section 2157 is different *in scope* from section 2143. That is, SUNY's argument rejected any connection between the two sections and assumed that in section 2157 the act prohibits disclosure of information *beyond* the proprietary information described in section 2143. This argument is invalid.

The two statutory sections are presented together in the legislative history of the 1985 amendments to the act, and thus it appears that the two sections should be read together.[52] Section 2143 explicitly provides that the research facility is not required to disclose to the public *or to the IACUC* "trade secrets or commercial or financial information which is privileged or confidential." If, contrary to section 2143, the research facility does choose to disclose such information to the IACUC, then section 2157 prohibits public disclosure of that information. Under the statutory scheme, the IACUC is simply *not required* to discuss that information the Act regards as "confidential"—for example, trade secrets or commercial or financial information. Indeed, the institution is not under any obligation even to provide such information to the IACUC. The institution may, however, decide to provide such information to the IACUC, or conceivably, the IACUC may come into possession of such information inadvertently. In such instances, the act—through section 2157—prohibits the disclosure of such information.[53]

In addition, to the extent that access opponents argue that section 2157 makes confidential *any* discussion of research, including information on animal care, treatment, and handling, these opponents need to address how Congress could constitutionally achieve such a result. That is, the First Amendment guarantees free speech. Those who argue that the proscription of section 2157 extends beyond proprietary information and covers even nonproprietary information, such as whether an animal is provided with anesthesia or analgesia or how an animal is euthanized, are merely arguing that Congress can impose a criminal penalty on IACUC members for their *speech* about the care and treatment of nonhuman animals. Surely, absent a compelling interest, the government may not impose a criminal sanction on the exercise of rights guaranteed under the First Amendment.[54]

Moreover, the argument that section 2157 extends beyond proprietary information conflicts with other aspects of the federal regulation of animal experimentation. For example, section 2157 is explicitly designated as "Release of Trade Secrets."[55] Moreover, once a project is funded, information about the experiment, including information about the care, treatment, and handling of nonhuman animals, becomes available under the Freedom of Information Act.[56] That is, the very information that the experimenters claim is protected is that which is made available under another federal statute.

Finally, the 1985 amendments to the Public Health Service Law, which were enacted contemporaneously with the 1985 amendments to the AWA and which also require the establishment of IACUCs, protect a research facility from *public* disclosure of "trade secrets or commercial or financial information" as the result of establishing the IACUCs.[57] This language tracks precisely the language used in section 2143 of the AWA. Both statutes concern the establishment of the same committee; both statutes address confidentiality concerns. To suggest that the *exact same* language used in these two federal acts, which were passed at the same time and which both concern the creation of an institutional committee to monitor animal care and treatment, should be construed *differently* violates every norm of statutory construction—and common sense.

SUNY also argued that research is a competitive endeavor and that a researcher needs to protect her creative ideas from being usurped by other experimenters before the experiment is funded or before the results are published. According to this argument, any information about an experiment is "proprietary" because premature disclosure may threaten the entire project in which the researcher has a clearly "proprietary" interest. This argument, like the earlier argument, has serious flaws. Once an experiment is funded, access to protocols is available through the Freedom of Information Act. This access would come far in advance of the protection the researcher could obtain under copyright or patent laws, and far in advance of publication in a scholarly journal. If competitive incentive is germane, then that incentive supports access denial well beyond the stage of the IACUC.

There is a further problem with both the confidentiality argument and the argument that researchers have proprietary interests in research that go beyond copyright or patent protection. Congress has already determined, and the Supreme Court has held, that the First Amendment prohibits the granting of a proprietary interest in ideas or facts.[58] Similarly, the Supreme Court has held that no one may have a proprietary interest in "the laws of nature, physical phenomena, and abstract ideas."[59] To the extent that researchers or their institutions claim that all information about experimentation is "confidential" or otherwise seek to assert proprietary interests in all information about experimentation, they face serious constitutional impediments.

Finally, SUNY erroneously assumed that an IACUC discussion of a proposed experiment would of necessity go into such detail that premature disclosure thereof would jeopardize funding for the project. But the act does not require that the IACUC engage in such a free-roaming discussion. Indeed, the statutory scheme appears to *prohibit* such a broad discussion. As we saw earlier, Congress made clear that the IACUC had absolutely no power to interfere in the conduct of actual experiments or to interfere with experiment design or methodology.

## Conclusion

In Chapters Ten and Eleven, I showed that the AWA was an example of "symbolic legislation" not only because, like most such legislation, Congress failed to provide any guidance to the implementing agency but also because, unlike most such legislation, courts, hampered by the jurisdictional rules of standing, cannot enter the vacuum and devise the regulatory process. And the AWA and its regulations explicitly fail to recognize the legitimacy of animal interests. In a sense, then, the "pathology" of the AWA as symbolic legislation is exacerbated by the impossibility of judicial intervention, however desirable (or not) it may be.

In any event, the AWA clearly illustrates the theory of legal welfarism. Despite an elaborate statutory scheme and ostensibly endless regulations, animals, characterized as the property of research facilities or the government and part of experimentation over which researchers assert a proprietary interest, receive little protection. Just as in the case of anticruelty statutes, what concerns us is that we not "waste" animal property. As long as researchers get good data from their animals, then the requisite level of "welfare" has been achieved. Determinations of necessity in particular instances are left to the discretion of researchers, and, as an overall matter, "necessary" animal suffering is determined by what constitutes "unnecessary" cost to the facility.

# *Part III Conclusion*

IN THIS PART of the book, I have tested the thesis of legal welfarism in a particular context in which those who use animals defend that use by appealing to principles other than mere property ownership. The context I examined was animal experimentation as regulated under the federal Animal Welfare Act. I argued that although our discourse about animal experimentation generally focuses on interests other than human dominion over property, those other interests necessarily assume the legitimacy of the property status of animals.

The Animal Welfare Act purports to create public regulation of animal use in science but, in reality, allows researchers to regulate themselves and their colleagues. This invites the "balancing" of human and animal interests in the context of a belief system—modern science—that accepts the institutional premise that animals may be used as means to human ends and that scientists should never make value judgments about, or legislate concerning the research of, others. Again, animals virtually always lose because the principles of legal welfarism shape all aspects of the analysis.

The administrative agency charged with enforcing the AWA—the USDA—has done a less-than-adequate job. The primary criterion for regulatory acceptability is whether the legislation is cost-justified without reference to the interests of individual animals used. The act cannot be said to create animal "rights" any more than do the anticruelty statutes examined in Part II. And the judicial system, which, through its doctrine of standing, fails to recognize the interest of animals *at all,* has not improved the enforcement of the AWA.

# EPILOGUE

# An Alternative to Legal Welfarism?

IN THIS BOOK, I have been concerned primarily with a particular form of welfarist thinking as it is reflected in the law pertaining to the treatment of nonhuman animals. There is general agreement that the law ought to prohibit the infliction of "unnecessary" pain on animals and that animals ought to be treated "humanely." However, the law requires that what constitutes "necessary" suffering or "humane" conduct be determined by balancing the interests of animals, who are regarded as property without claims of legal right, against the interests of humans, who have many rights, one of the most important being the right to own and use property. Accordingly, the balancing process requires a putative weighing of completely dissimilar ethical entities. Moreover, this balancing, as it occurs in the context of law, reflects what I called legal welfarism, or the doctrine that the welfare of animals is determined by what conduct will maximize the efficient use of animal property.

Legal welfarism is, I have argued, a direct result of characterizing animals as property. To label something property, is, for all intents and purposes, to conclude that the entity so labeled possesses no interests that merit protection and that the entity is solely a means to the end determined by the property owner. To the extent that the regulation of the use of animals reflects interests other than the owner's, those interests are still humanocentric. For example, as Part II demonstrated, even anticruelty statutes are designed primarily to serve human interests. In any event, the regulation of the use of animal property—whether by anticruelty laws or complex regulatory structures—cannot be said to create animal *rights*. A right, which is a complex notion, protects an interest that is not subject to abrogation merely because someone else will receive a benefit from annulling the right.[1]

I indicated in the introduction that legal welfarism was not the only type of welfarist theory and that many in the modern animal protection community espouse a theory, not of animal rights, but of some modified form of animal welfarism. The temptation to avoid the rights position in favor of some variant of welfarism is clear: an animal rights position requires a complete rethinking of the legal status of animals and portends significant economic and social conse-

253

quences in light of the pervasive exploitation of animals for everything from sources of food, clothing, and entertainment to the primary "model" for biomedical research. Animal advocates who pursue some modified form of welfarism use the familiar discourse of "unnecessary" suffering and "humane" treatment, which, as we saw, is part of the language of legal welfarism, but they seek to give interpretations of these terms that are supposedly more generous toward animals.

In this conclusion, I examine three of these alternative welfarist theories that do not currently inform legal welfarism but are proposed by various parties as moral theories that if accepted in the law, would improve the legal protection we accord animals. My goal is not to provide an exhaustive analysis of each theory; rather, I argue in a preliminary fashion that any form of welfarism suffers from the same fundamental flaws of legal welfarism by requiring that we balance interests in a theoretical framework that almost always ensures that animals will lose.

## Singer's Enlightened Utilitarianism

The first alternative position is the one advocated by Peter Singer[2] and other utilitarians who accept the utilitarian balancing framework but who believe that the consequences to consider include animal suffering and that many or most forms of animal exploitation do cause suffering. For example, Singer is a utilitarian who argues that in calculating the consequences of actions such as using animals in experiments, we must include animal suffering as one of the consequences, but that this balancing of interests must never be affected by considerations of species. To do otherwise, Singer argues, is to engage in "speciesism" — a bias in favor of one's species that is no more morally defensible than, say, discrimination based on race or sex.

A serious problem with Singer's analysis — which is similar to the classical hedonism of Bentham, except that Singer thinks that the intrinsic value to be maximized is the furtherance of interests of those affected and not their pleasure alone — is that Singer's "enlightened" form of utilitarianism will probably not work as long as animals are regarded as property. Singer argues, in essence, that we ought to take animal interests seriously when we seek to use the utilitarian balancing apparatus, and that we ought to accord equal consideration to equal interests. The problem is that as long as animals are treated as a form of property, their interests are not likely to be accorded more weight than they are under the framework of legal welfarism. Our current political and legal discourse defines animal interests in terms of "legitimate" human use of animals, which, in turn, serves to limit those interests. In the current legal and social contexts as they concern animals, animals have no interests beyond those that humans determine will facilitate animal use.

Moreover, Singer, as a utilitarian, rejects the notion of rights for animals and humans. Singer proposes that we substitute instead a utilitarian calculus that would weigh equal interests — human and nonhuman alike — equally. Even if we could make the necessary conceptual shift away from the status of animals as property and toward a more expansive notion of animal "interests," and even if Singer's enlightened utilitarian position would thereby dramatically reduce (but not eliminate) animal exploitation, its implementation in a legal system centered on rights (at least for humans) would be impossible as a practical matter.

In addition, Singer's reliance on equality and his rejection of speciesism (as well as other forms of racism) is problematic, especially in light of the fact that Singer is an *act* utilitarian. Even if we give equal consideration to the equal interests of nonhumans, it does not mean that we might not ultimately choose to discriminate against an animal if such discrimination would maximize the intrinsic value identified by Singer. Similarly, it may maximize value to discriminate on the basis of race, sex, or species.

Finally, the only way in which Singer can make his utilitarian theory egalitarian for people and animals and avoid the charge of speciesism is to argue that under certain circumstances it is morally permissible to use humans as well as animals for the benefit of others. For example, Singer has argued that under at least some circumstances it would be permissible to use nonconsenting humans in experiments. This illustrates the difficulties of trying to combine a consequential theory, such as utilitarianism, with a rejection of species discrimination: if it is permissible to exploit a nonhuman in a particular situation because of the good consequences, it may also be acceptable to exploit humans if the interests at stake are equal. This conclusion is obviously troubling.

## Taking Some Animal Interests Seriously

The second alternative position is somewhere between Singer's view and the conventional legal welfarist view embodied in contemporary laws concerning animals. It is difficult to describe this position precisely, because it is itself very imprecise and reflects a wide range of very different views. There are many welfarists who would not go as far as Singer but who would accept some position that is more protective of animals than the legal welfarism currently reflected in the law.

For example, some welfarists support more stringent regulation of research when painful experiments are involved. This position takes seriously the notion that animals have some limited interests that should be protected, but denies that humans and nonhumans can have equivalent interests or that the equal interests of humans and animals ought to be treated equally (Singer's view) and that animal interests may virtually always be overridden by human interests (the position of legal welfarism). Moderate reformers such as F. Barbara Orlans[3] and Andrew Rowan[4]—who endorse "responsible" animal experimentation, but who support a reduction in the numbers of animals used, the refinement of experimental procedures, and the gradual replacement of animals through the development of alternatives, and who may reject the legitimacy of certain types of experiments fit in this category.

The obvious difference between legal welfarism, enlightened utilitarianism as

represented by Singer, and this third version, in which at least some animal interests are taken seriously, concerns the justification that suffices to permit the exploitation of an animal. That is, even if we, like Singer, accept that we should
weigh consequences to animals in assessing the merits of actions, there is, at least
in theory, a point at which the benefits to humans of exploiting animals may outweigh the detriment to animals. Adherents of legal welfarism would permit animal exploitation when any human benefit—however trivial—is involved. For example, some who defend the use of animals to test irritancy frequently claim that
the "benefit" of having yet another shade of lipstick or yet another brand of oven
cleaner justifies the suffering and killing of animals used in irritancy tests. Other
welfarists may claim that it is morally permissible to use animals in experiments
as long as those experiments are substantially certain to result in important advances in our knowledge about disease.

## Welfare as a Necessary Step Toward Rights

The third variation of welfarism involves a view, not of the merits of welfare itself, but of the perceived connection between animal welfare and animal rights,
or, at least, the abolition, rather than the regulation of, particular forms of animal
exploitation.

Many of those in the animal protection movement use "rights" and "welfare"
interchangeably. Sometimes this occurs simply as the result of failure to understand the very different philosophical views that are involved in the debate. It is,
however, not always simple confusion that is to blame; some advocates think
that the distinction is ultimately unimportant because animal welfare is a necessary step on the road to animal rights. Those who accept this position generally
disagree with the view that animals should be treated as property and used as
means to achieve human benefit. They accept that animals possess certain rights
that should, as a normative matter, be protected by law. Nevertheless, they maintain that it is morally permissible to seek interim and incremental improvements
in our treatment of animals. For example, some people argue that animal experimentation ought to be made more humane, but unlike those who espouse legal
welfarism or another version of pure welfarism (i.e., those who accept the moral
legitimacy of consequentalist analysis), they believe that the use of animals in
experiments is morally unjustifiable, and they advocate a change in regulation
only as an interim step on the way to recognizing that animals have a right not
to be so used. Some people who supported the 1985 amendments to the AWA—
an admittedly welfarist statute that was amended in an admittedly welfarist manner—ultimately seek and support the complete abolition of animal use by researchers.

This third position assumes that a casual relationship exists between these interim changes and the ultimate goal of abolishing the exploitation, and that incremental changes will themselves eventually lead to recognition of rights. For example, some animal advocates argue that increased restriction on the practice of

vivisection will lead to the abolition of vivisection as long as the restrictions become more and more restrictive.[5]

The view that animal welfare reforms are an acceptable way of getting to the ultimate goal of animal rights has some intuitive appeal but, upon closer examination, is problematic. Any version of animal welfare requires that we balance human and animal interests. We might, like Singer, be more generous toward animals when we perform the utilitarian calculation that is at the heart of animal welfare theory, but we still do this interest balancing. As I have argued throughout this book, this balancing process is at the root of the problem: it explains why animals are so ruthlessly exploited despite social norms that reject inhumane treatment, for as long as animals are regarded as property under the law, virtually any attempt to balance interests will entail an unavoidable devaluation of animal interests simply because they are property. It is incongruous (at the very least) to posit that treating an entity as a means to an end will eventually lead to treating the entity as an end in itself.

Moreover, there is simply no empirical evidence to suggest that if we make animal exploitation more "humane" now, we will be able to abolish such exploitation later through the recognition of rights. Indeed, the evidence that we do have seems to lead to the opposite conclusion, namely, that reforming exploitation through welfarist means will simply facilitate the indefinite perpetuation of such exploitation. Although there are many examples that may serve to illustrate this point, we need look no further than the AWA. Although the AWA has been in force since 1966, animal experimentation shows no signs of ending soon. Rather than hasten the demise of vivisection, the AWA and its various amendments have fortified it through explicit congressional recognition of the legitimacy of the practice and by giving researchers an ostensibly strong law to point to when questioned about the abuses of animals in laboratories. For example, as shown in Part III of this book, researchers often rely on laws such as the AWA in an effort to convince the public that stringent regulations govern the use of animals in experiments. What these researchers do not point out—and what the American public does not know—is that the AWA and its amendments prohibit "unnecessary" animal suffering but leave to the exclusive discretion of vivisectors the determination of what constitutes "necessity." As a result of the 1985 amendments, which required that each research facility have an animal care and use committee, researchers now argue that the committees provide animals protection equivalent to that provided by human experimentation review committees. What the researchers do not bother to mention, however, is that human experimentation requires the informed consent of the human subject—a crucial concept that cannot be applied in the context of animal experimentation. The American experience is not unique; in Britain, welfarist regulation of animal experimentation proved a powerful public relations device that researchers could use to assure those concerned that research was being performed "humanely."

Finally, if animals do possess moral rights, then it is no more acceptable to ignore those rights now in the hope that some future animals will be granted enforceable rights than it would be were we talking about human rights. That is, if I have a moral right to some benefit, then it is morally unacceptable to deny me this right now in the hope that my children or my grandchildren will enjoy the benefit. Similarly, if animals possess moral rights not to be treated merely as means to human ends, then it is not morally acceptable to continue to treat animals solely as means to human ends in the hope that they will one day not be regarded as means to human ends. Such a position is blatantly inconsistent with respecting the moral inviolability of those animals who are exploited today. Reformist measures—even when they ultimately seek the recognition of animal rights or the abolition of animal exploitation—necessarily authorize such exploitation.

## Shared Characteristics of Various Welfare Theories

All forms of welfarism—including the theory that welfare is a step on the road to rights—are linked by the notion that it is morally justifiable to support the institutionalized exploitation of animals under some circumstances. Legal welfarism, which represents the status quo position used to interpret animal cruelty statutes and regulatory statutes, explicitly supports animal exploitation as morally justifiable, and rejects animal rights. Singer's view and the intermediate welfarist position would support animal exploitation as long as the balancing process included animal suffering as a cost and placed a more realistic value (or lack thereof) on the consequences of animal exploitation.

This feature, shared by all versions of welfarism—including the view that welfarism is a step toward the ultimate goal of animal rights—creates enormous confusion because it allows animal advocates, researchers, food producers, furriers, and anyone else to purport to subscribe to theories of animal welfare. Indeed, it is difficult to find an animal exploiter who does not claim to be a supporter of animal welfare. These exploiters claim to weigh animal interests in determining whether to proceed with vivisection, but they assign a relatively low weight to animal interests. An enormous amount of confusion surrounding the current debate is attributable precisely to elastic qualities of the welfare notion.

All versions of welfarism, including but not limited to legal welfarism, inevitably involve the use of a balancing construct. Because animals are regarded as property, it is difficult to understand how this balancing process could be adjusted to ensure greater animal protection. Indeed, *any* consideration of the consequences of animal exploitation must, by definition, occur in a context in which animal interests are systematically devalued or completely ignored in favor of human interests.

In this regard, the notion of animal welfare is very different from the notion of human welfare as that term is used in general discourse. Under *any* theory of animal welfare, *any* animal interest—including the animal's fundamental interests in life and in not experiencing pain—may be "sacrificed" as long as the consequences for humans are sufficiently important. The notion of human welfare is far more protective and does not assume that all human interests may be sacrificed. We may discuss whether a person is entitled to some benefit or other, but this discussion takes place against a background of assumptions, one of which is that humans possess certain rights that cannot be compromised. We may sensibly discuss whether to increase (or decrease) a benefit given to people; we cannot sensibly discuss whether we may use unconsenting humans for experiments or as food sources. Humans are not to be treated solely as means to human ends; animals, as property, are intended to be treated as means to human ends.

It is, of course, possible to conceive of a situation in which animals were not regarded as property but were also not regarded as rightholders. Presumably, animal interests would be taken more seriously if animals were not viewed, as a matter of law, solely as means to human ends. The problem is that if humans (and corporations, etc.) were the only rightholders, then any balance of human and animal interests would still balance interests protected by right against interests unprotected by right.

Alternatively, as mentioned above, we might eliminate rights entirely from our normative landscape and rely solely on interest balancing in the absence of any rights considerations related to humans *or* animals. This is the sort of system advocated by Singer, who, as a utilitarian, rejects moral rights for both humans and animals. The problem is that it is highly unlikely that we are going to abandon rights concepts where humans are concerned, precisely because most of us do not want recognition of our most important and fundamental interests to hinge on purely consequential considerations. Singer, as a consistent utilitarian, accepts that there might be circumstances in which human and animal exploitation (including use as nonconsenting subjects in medical experiments) could be morally justified in light of consequences. Even those people who are more communally minded would, I think, reject that position precisely because we cling to a notion that at least some of our interests ought not to be subject to abrogation simply because of consequential considerations.

Finally, any balancing of human and animal interests, whether or not animals are regarded as property, is likely to be problematic as long as no rights considerations serve to limit the results of the balancing process. To put the matter differently, the utilitarian notion of "consequences" cannot be interpreted in a way that does not prejudice the issue of animal protection. Even if we do accept that animals have interests, it is simply difficult to make determinations about the nature of those animal interests from a humanocentric perspective; it is because we systematically devalue and underestimate the interests of disempowered populations that rights concepts are necessary in the first place. Although rights theory rests ultimately upon a consideration of animal interests, rights theory does not permit the sacrifice of animal interests simply because human interests would be served. Rather, rights theory assumes that at least some animal interests are entitled to prima facie protection and that the sacrifice of those interests requires a justification not dissimilar to that required when we seek to override human interests protected by rights.

## Rights and Prohibitions?

Must we await the abolition of the property status of animals before we can talk about restructuring the legal system to reflect the recognition of animal rights, or can rights changes occur—in the legal system—without there being a complete abdication of the status of animals as property? In other words, can there be laws that regulate the use of animal property and that, unlike the ones I have examined in this book, actually do create rights? This is a most difficult question, about which I have four very preliminary observations. First, as I have argued throughout this book, there can be no doubt that as long as animals are regarded under the law as merely means to the human ends of property owners, it will be very difficult to have any true, respect-based animal rights. Animal rights, strictly speaking, imply the recognition of the inherent worth and value of the right-holder—something precluded by characterizing animals as property.

Second, I have argued that as long as the content of any such "right" is restricted to freedom from "unnecessary" suffering or entitlement to "humane" treatment, then the animal's "right" is only to have the animal's interests balanced against human interests protected by right. It is precisely this type of interest balancing that I have criticized throughout this book because the existence of such a "right" does nothing to alter the fundamentally skewed balancing process that systematically devalues (or, better, fails completely to recognize) animal interests.

Third, despite the unlikelihood of achieving animal rights within the present legal system, it may be possible to have a pluralistic system that characterizes animals as property but recognizes rights-type concepts on some level. That is, though it may not be meaningful to talk about animal rights within our present legal system if what we mean by rights is what Regan means by rights, we may nevertheless be able to achieve some rights-like protection for animals, protection based on the recognition of animal interests that are not susceptible to sacrifice merely on account of consequential considerations. The key to such a pluralistic situation lies in the distinction between *prohibiting,* or *abolishing,* exploitation or abuse and merely *regulating* it. This focus on abolition in the context of rights is really quite natural; at the core of just about every normative entity that we call a right is some notion that others are prohibited from interfering with the exercise of the right. This is particularly true of what Hohfeld called "claim" rights. A right, then, is a notion closely connected to the prohibition of activities that are judged to be inimical to the right. Prohibiting particular forms of animal exploitation is very different from merely prohibiting that exploitation when it is "inhumane" to do otherwise.

Fourth, any theory about prohibitions must take into account that not all prohibitions are the same. For example, a prohibition that absolutely banned certain experiments on the ground that no member of any sentient species should be subjected to this treatment would represent a different sort of prohibition from the ones now found in statutes such as the AWA. A rule that prohibits the withholding of food (unless "scientifically necessary") is nothing more than an attempt to facilitate efficient exploitation; it in no way recognizes animal interests in the way that rights recognize human interests.

## Legal Welfarism and Moral Theory

Given that the treatment of animals raises moral questions, one would think that legal welfarism, our current legal framework for resolving human/animal conflicts, would reflect, however imperfectly, some *moral* theory. That, however, is precisely the problem. There is no moral theory that even attempts to justify the present level of animal abuse permitted under the law. Indeed, even those philosophers, such as Professors R. G. Frey, Peter Carruthers, and Carl Cohen, who are critical of animal rights and supportive of at least some forms of animal exploitation are critical of the level of animal abuse currently allowed under the law. Legal welfarism is problematic simply because it incorporates the normative position, which cannot be justified by any theory, that virtually *any* human interest, even if trivial, is sufficient to justify depriving an animal of life or imposing on an animal horrendous suffering. The gap between the animal treatment permissible under legal welfarism and that which would be permitted under a defensible moral theory most deferential to the wishes of animal property owners (let alone between welfarism and animal rights) is enormous.

Even if we take animal interests seriously, our treatment of animals is unlikely to improve as long as we regard animals as the property of human owners. We could, of course, opt for a pluralistic system under which animals are still regarded as property but under which certain forms of exploitation are prohibited even though these prohibitions may adversely affect the value of the animal property to the owner.

An alternative legal status for animals in which they would no longer be regarded as property would probably entail dramatic economic and social consequences, given that our economy is heavily dependent on the level of animal exploitation protected by legal welfarism. Therein lies the intractable nature of the present controversy.

*Explanation of Legal Citations, Notes,
Selected Bibliography, and Index*

# Explanation of Legal Citations

I HAVE tried throughout this book to explain concepts in nonlegal terms. However, there is a necessary residual of such terminology, and where it is used, I have tried to provide an explanation. For purposes of legal citation, there are three types of legal materials with which we are primarily concerned: statutes, regulations, and decided cases.

A statute is a legal rule that is enacted by a legislature, such as Congress or a state legislature. The federal Animal Welfare Act (AWA) is one statute that I discuss in this book. Statutes are usually compiled in multivolume sets and broken down by subject matter into "titles." For example, title 7 of the *United States Code,* which is the compilation of federal statutes, concerns the general topic of "agriculture." The AWA is contained in title 7 and begins at § 2131 and ends at § 2157. When you see a citation such as 7 U.S.C. § 2143, that translates to section 2143 of title 7 of the *United States Code.*

When legislatures enact statutes, they often leave enforcement of these statutes to administrative agencies, which are also entrusted with promulgating regulations that implement the statutory directive. For example, Congress passed the original AWA in 1966 and entrusted enforcement of the AWA to an administrative agency, the United States Department of Agriculture (USDA), which has now created the Animal and Plant Health Inspection Service (APHIS) of the USDA. The USDA has promulgated regulations that seek to implement the AWA. The AWA is the *statute;* the USDA rules are known as *regulations* that implement the statute. The AWA is contained as part of the *United States Code;* the implementing regulations are contained in the *Code of Federal Regulations.* The *Code of Federal Regulations* is also organized in titles and sections. For instance, when you see a reference such as 9 C.F.R. § 1, that is a reference to section 1 of title 9 of the *Code of Federal Regulations.*

When an agency such as the USDA makes rules, it usually goes through what is referred to commonly as a notice-and-comment process. First, the agency proposes a regulation. This proposal is usually printed in the *Federal Register.* The notice usually invites comments and informs the reader whom to contact with those comments. The agency sometimes holds hearings at which interested persons may give their comments orally. The agency then considers (to a greater or lesser degree) the comments submitted, and proposes a final rule. The final rule eventually appears in the *Code of Federal Regulations.*

Statutory law and regulations are distinguished from *case law* in that the latter involves a rule articulated by a judge in deciding a controversy between two (or more) parties. In deciding these controversies, courts may apply and interpret a statute or regulation, or they may simply apply rules made by other judges in earlier cases. Each state has its own court system, and the federal government has its own system as well. In the federal system, there are essentially three different types of tribunals: the United States district courts, in which trials are conducted; the United States courts of appeals, in which appeals are taken from the district courts; and the United States Supreme Court, which hears appeals from the courts of appeals (and under unusual circumstances from district courts) and hears other cases that it takes in its discretion.

Cases from the district courts are reported in the *Federal Supplement,* which is abbreviated as "F. Supp." If you see a citation such as 345 F. Supp. 102 (S.D.N.Y. 1954), that means that the district court case appears at page 102 of volume 345 of the *Federal Supplement* and that the case was decided in 1954 by the United States District Court for the Southern District of New York.

Cases from the United States courts of appeals are reported in the *Federal Reporter,* first (older), second (more recent), and third (most recent) series. If you see a citation such as 222 F.2d 333 (3d Cir. 1954), that means that the case appears at page 333 of volume 222 of the *Federal Reporter* (second series) and that the case was decided in 1954 by the United States Court of Appeals for the Third Circuit. The Third Circuit hears appeals from district courts located in New Jersey, Pennsylvania, Delaware, and the Virgin Islands.

Cases from the United States Supreme Court are reported in one official reporter and several unofficial ones. The official reporter is the *United States Reports,* and is abbreviated as U.S. If you see a citation such as 434 U.S. 1 (1989), that means that the case, which was decided by the Supreme Court in 1989, appears on page 1 of volume 434 of the *United States Reports.*

State legal systems, like the federal system, have a court that hears trials. Some states have an intermediate appellate court like the federal courts of appeals, but some states have only one appellate court. State court cases are reported in "official" reporters, and at least some cases (usually those from the state's highest court) are also reported in commercial "regional" reporters that collect cases from several states. Citations to state court cases are similar to those for federal cases. If you see a citation such as 107 P.2d 305 (Cal. 1985), that means that the case appears on page 305 of volume 107 of the *Pacific Reporter* (second series), which reports cases from several western states. The information in the parentheses indicates that the case is from the California Supreme Court, the highest court in the state of California, and was decided in 1985. If the level of the court is not specified and only the state is indicated, it may be assumed that the case is from the highest court in the state. If the case is from a lower state court, that information will be contained in the parentheses.

All states have administrative agencies that, like federal administrative agencies, are supposed to administer and implement legislative directives. Many states have reporters similar to the *Federal Register,* in which state administrative agencies communicate with the public about proposed administrative actions.

Much of the interest in the area of animal protection does not happen in courts but instead before federal or state administrative agencies. For example, when a person makes a request under the federal Freedom of Information Act for information concerning a particular federally funded experiment using nonhuman animals, that person generally makes the request to the National Institutes of Health (NIH). If NIH refuses the request, then the requester usually takes an appeal to the Department of Health and Human Services before filing a court action under the Freedom of Information Act. Both the NIH and the Department of Health and Human Services are administrative agencies.

# *Notes*

## Introduction

1. *See* Jeremy Waldron, *The Right to Private Property* (Oxford: Clarendon Press, 1988), 27.

2. *See generally* Richard A. Posner, *Economic Analysis of Law,* 3d ed. (Boston: Little, Brown, 1986).

3. The economic approach that I discussed above is similar but not identical to utilitarianism. *See* David Lyons, "Utility and Rights," in 24 *Nomos: Ethics, Economics, and the Law,* ed. J. Roland Pennock and John W. Chapman (New York: New York University Press, 1982), 107.

4. Jeremy Bentham, *An Introduction to the Principles of Morals and Legislation,* ed. Laurence J. Lafleur (New York: Hafner Press, 1948), 310–11 n. 1. Bentham argued that "the question is not, Can they *reason*? nor, Can they *talk*? but, Can they *suffer*?" Some utilitarians stress quality of character rather than rules or acts.

5. *See generally* Peter Singer, *Animal Liberation,* 2d ed. (New York: New York Review of Books, 1990).

6. *See, e.g.,* Peter Singer, "Ethics and Animals," 13 *Behavioral & Brain Sci.* 45, 46 (1990) (postcommentary to Marian S. Dawkins, "From an Animal's Point of View: Motivation, Fitness, and Animal Welfare," 13 *Behavioral & Brain Sci.* 1–9 [1990]).

7. Ronald M. McLaughlin, "Animal Rights vs. Animal Welfare: Can Animal Use Meet the Needs of Science and Society?" in *Animal Research, Animal Rights, Animal Legislation,* ed. Patrick W. Concannon (Champaign, Ill.: Society for the Study of Reproduction, 1990), 11–15.

8. *See, e.g.,* Mimi Brody, "Animal Research: A Call for Legislative Reform Requiring Ethical Merit Review," *13 Harv. Envtl. L. Rev.* 423 (1989) (arguing for "ethical balancing"); Rebecca Dresser, "Assessing Harm and Justification in Animal Research: Federal Policy Opens the Laboratory Door," 40 *Rutgers L. Rev.* 723 (1988) (arguing for ethical merit review and procedures to alleviate pain and distress); idem, "Research on Animals: Values, Politics, and Regulatory Reform," 58 *S. Cal. L. Rev.* 1147 (1985) (arguing for committee review of animal experiments).

9. *See, e.g.,* Josephine Donovan, "Animal Rights and Feminist Theory," in *Ecofeminism: Women, Animals, Nature,* ed. Greta Gaard (Philadelphia: Temple University Press, 1993), 167. *See also* Mary Ann Glendon, *Rights Talk* (New York: Free Press, 1991); Elizabeth Kingdom, *What's Wrong with Rights?* (Edinburgh: Edinburgh University Press, 1991).

10. *See, e.g.,* Barbara Noske, *Humans and Other Animals* (London: Pluto Press, 1989).

11. In addition to the work discussed here and in Chapter Five, there is a wealth of excellent philosophical writing on the subject. *See, e.g.,* Stephen R. L. Clark, *The Moral Status of Animals* (Oxford: Clarendon Press, 1977); Mary Midgley, *Animals and Why They Matter* (Athens: University of Georgia Press, 1984); Bernard E. Rollin, *Animal Rights and Human Morality,* rev. ed. (Buffalo, N.Y.: Prometheus Books, 1992); S. F. Sapontzis, *Morals, Reason, and Animals* (Philadelphia: Temple University Press, 1987). Not all of these philosophers endorse a rights approach. For example, Midgley argues that the notion of rights is very unclear, and she opts for the view that animal interests matter but that preference for our own species is acceptable within limits and is analogous to the "special interest which parents feel in their own children." Midgley, *Animals and Why They Matter,* at 102. Sapontzis regards ethics as a practical activity embedded in culture but capable of development. In light of our ethical tradition, which tolerates animal suffering but also has supposedly pro-animal tendencies, our moral development would seem to require that we focus on "developing moral virtues, reducing suffering, and being fair." Sapontzis, *Morals, Reason, and Animals,* at 109. He adopts a view similar to that of Midgley when he rejects Singer's view that we owe animals equal consideration for their equal interests.

For discussions critical of animal rights and animal protection, see Peter Carruthers, *The Animals Issue* (Cambridge: Cambridge University Press, 1992); R. G. Frey, *Rights, Killing, and Suffering* (Oxford: Basil Blackwell, 1983); idem, *Interests and Rights: The Case Against Animals* (Oxford: Clarendon Press, 1980); Michael P. T. Leahy, *Against Liberation* (London: Routledge, 1991).

12. Tom Regan, *The Case for Animal Rights* (Berkeley and Los Angeles: University of California Press, 1983).

13. Two scholars have argued recently that, contrary to most interpretations, Descartes may have recognized animal consciousness. *See* Daisie Radner and Michael Radner, *Animal Consciousness* (Buffalo, N.Y.: Prometheus Books, 1989).

14. Although Regan's theory has certain general affinities to the views of philosopher Immanuel Kant, who is generally characterized as presenting a deontological (i.e., nonconsequential) moral theory, Kant did not recognize the existence of direct duties owed to animals and, instead, believed that all duties owed to animals were indirect duties in that our obligation not to be cruel to animals was based on our obligation not to mistreat other people, and animal abuse encouraged the mistreatment of other people. Regan obviously rejects the indirect duty portion of Kant. Regan also rejects Kant's view that rationality is required for a being to be treated as an end, rather than as a means to an end. Regan does, however, substitute the notion of complex consciousness as a morally relevant criterion. Some writers have argued that complex consciousness and rationality are closely related. *See, e.g.,* Donovan, "Animal Rights and Feminist Theory," at 170. Moreover, Kant endorsed a contractarian theory that Regan rejects. Regan's views represent other substantial modifications of the Kantian position that are not relevant here.

It should be noted that the view that Kant's philosophy is not consequential is questionable. *See* Jeremy Waldron, introduction to *Theories of Rights,* ed. Jeremy Waldron (Oxford: Oxford University Press, 1984), 113. J.J.C. Smart has also characterized Kant's view as involving a form of rule-utilitarianism. *See* J.J.C. Smart, "An Outline of a System of Utilitarian Ethics," in J.J.C. Smart and Bernard Williams, *Utilitarianism: For and Against,* (Cambridge: Cambridge University Press, 1973), 9. *But see* William K. Frankena, *Ethics* (Englewood Cliffs, N.J.: Prentice-Hall, 1973), 31 (arguing that Kant does not maintain that of California Press, 1983), 1–82; Bernard E. Rollin, *The Unheeded Cry* (Oxford: d University Press, 1989), 23–106.

6. Eugene Linden, "Can Animals Think?" *Time,* March 22, 1993, at 54, 61.

7. *See, e.g.,* Andrew N. Rowan, "Cruelty to Animals," 6 *Anthrozoös* 218 (1993).

8. These are by no means the most extreme examples. *See generally* Mason and ᵣ, *Animal Factories;* Hans Reusch, *Slaughter of the Innocent* (New York: Civitas Pub- ᵢns, 1978).

9. *New Jersey Soc'y for the Prevention of Cruelty to Animals v. Board of Educ.,* 219 200 (N.J. Super. Ct. Law Div. 1966), *aff'd,* 277 A.2d 506 (N.J. 1967).

10. Ibid., at 203 (quoting N.J. Stat. Ann. 4:22–17, 26) (emphasis deleted).

11. Ibid., at 202 (quoting N.J. Stat. Ann. 4:22–16).

12. Ibid., at 207.

13. Ibid., at 208.

14. Natalie Angier, "Mutation Bestows Beauty and Death on Quarter Horses," *N.Y.* ₛ, October 6, 1992, at C1.

15. Michael T. Kaufman, "Cross Out a Landmark on the Chinatown Tour," *N.Y.* ₛ, August 14, 1993, at 23.

16. Ibid.

17. It is interesting to note that the article on horses did discuss issues concerning the ess to the horses, but the article on the dancing chicken did not discuss such issues. reflects the fact that the social tolerance for abuse to animals is much lower for horses for chickens. In some jurisdictions, chickens are not regarded as "animals." Indeed, ᵢederal Humane Slaughter Act does not cover chickens, thus reflecting a social attitude ᵢhickens are, for some reason, not worthy even of that level of minimal protection.

18. *Regina v. Dudley & Stephens,* 1881–85 All E.R. 61 (Q.B.D. 1884).

19. Brooks did not agree to the killing of Parker. Ibid., at 62. For two fascinating dis- ᵢons of this case, see A.W.B. Simpson, *Cannibalism and the Common Law* (Chicago: ᵣersity of Chicago Press, 1984); Allen Boyer, "Crime, Cannibalism and Joseph Con- The Influence of *Regina v. Dudley and Stephens* on Lord Jim," 20 *Loy. L.A.L. Rev.* 9 ᵢ6).

20. *Dudley & Stephens,* 1881–85 All E.R. at 62.

21. The doctrine of necessity, which is also referred to as the "choice of evils" or ᵢser evils" defense, "legitimizes technically wrongful conduct that common sense, fair- , or utilitarian concerns convince us is justified but which does not fall within any other ᵍnized justification defense. Without the defense a system of criminal laws is neither ᵢnal nor just." Joshua Dressler, *Understanding Criminal Law* (New York: Matthew der & Co., 1987), 249. Dressler points out that although the history of the doctrine is ewhat murky and the extent of its use somewhat unclear, the doctrine is contained in Model Penal Code and has been adopted by approximately one-half of the states. Ibid., ₅0.

22. *Dudley & Stephens,* 1881–85 All E.R. at 67 (Coleridge, C.J.). It is interesting ᵢote that the jury produced a special verdict setting forth in great detail its factual find- ₛ. The jury could not decide, however, whether the killing constituted a murder, and ᵣred the matter to the Queen's Bench, which then rendered the decision that a mur- had taken place, based upon the jury's findings. The court then sentenced Dudley Stephens to death; Queen Victoria, however, commuted the sentences to six months' ᵢrisonment.

23. Ibid., at 62.

the consequences of promise breaking would be intolerable, but th
in a contradiction of will).

15. Regan, *Case for Animal Rights,* at 187–94.

16. Ibid., at 286.

17. Regan is not the first person to talk about animal rights. T
the equality of "brutes" in his facetious criticism of feminism, *A V*
*of Brutes,* published in 1792, in which Taylor compared women's
animals. Henry Salt published *Animals' Rights,* a progressive argun
in 1892. Regan is, however, the first modern philosopher to presen
ticated theory of animal rights based on moral philosophy, epistemc
science of animal behavior.

18. *See, e.g.,* Herbert Pardes et al., "Physicians and the Anim
324 *New Eng. J. Med.* 1640, 1641 (1991).

19. James M. Jasper and Dorothy Nelkin, *The Animal Rights*
Free Press, 1992), 178.

20. The animal rights movement should not necessarily be con
ophy of animal rights articulated by Regan. That is, many who ident:
mal rights advocates do not necessarily adopt Regan's theory or his c
ity requires that we no longer treat animals solely as means to hun
abolish, rather than regulate, most types of animal exploitation.

21. Pardes et al., "Physicians and the Animal Rights Movement

22. *See, e.g.,* Stephen R. Munzer, *A Theory of Property* (Cambrid
versity Press, 1990); Waldron, *Right to Private Property.*

## Chapter One

1. *See* Robert M. Baird and Stuart E. Rosenbaum, eds., *Anima*
*The Moral Issues* (Buffalo, N.Y.: Prometheus Books, 1991); Gill Langl
*perimentation: The Consensus Changes* (New York: Chapman & Ha
Phillips and Jeri A. Sechzer, *Animal Research and Ethical Conflict* (Ne
Verlag, 1989); Andrew N. Rowan, *Of Mice, Models, and Men* (Albany:
New York Press, 1984); Richard D. Ryder, *Victims of Science,* rev. ed.
Anti-Vivisection Society, 1983); Robert Sharpe, *The Cruel Deception*
Northamptonshire: Thorsons Publishing Group, 1988).

2. *See* Mark Gold, *Assault and Battery* (London: Pluto Press, 198:
*Animal Machines* (London: Vincent Stuart, 1964); Jim Mason and Pet
*Factories,* rev. ed. (New York: Harmony Books, 1990); Jeremy Rifkin, *E*
York: Dutton Books, 1992); Orville Schell, *Modern Meat* (New York:
1984).

3. *See generally* Richard D. Ryder, *Animal Revolution* (Oxford:
1989), 235–37; "Furriers on the Defensive," *Animals' Agenda,* April 199(

4. *See* Peter Batten, *Living Trophies* (New York: Thomas Y. Cro
Virginia McKenna et al., eds., *Beyond the Bars* (Wellingborough, Northam
sons Publishing Group, 1987).

5. *See* Donald R. Griffin, *Animal Thinking* (Cambridge: Harvard U
1984); idem, *The Question of Animal Awareness,* rev. ed. (New York: Rocl
sity Press, 1981); Tom Regan, *The Case for Animal Rights* (Berkeley and Lo

24. There is some question whether *Dudley & Stephens* would preclude the use of the doctrine in all homicide contexts. That is, the case might not have involved true necessity. The Queen's Bench stated that although Dudley and Stephens were in a very weakened condition, they were not in imminent danger of death at the time of the killing of Parker. Parker, also in an extremely weak condition, was not consulted and did not consent to the killing; moreover, Parker died as a direct result of the actions of Dudley and Stephens. Dressler suggests that if a mountaineer tied to another mountaineer cut the rope of the latter when the latter slipped and threatened to pull down both climbers, the result might be different because, among other reasons, the mountaineer who falls was certain to die, unlike Parker, who was likely, but not certain, to die. *See* Dressler, *Understanding Criminal Law,* at 255–56. This explanation, however, does not address the hypothetical, also raised by Dressler, that involves a terrorist who threatens to kill a hundred children unless an unwilling person kills an innocent party. In such a case, the person to be killed is killed by the affirmative act of the other, and the situation cannot be characterized as one involving permitting "nature to take its course rather than *causing* [the victim's] death." Ibid., at 256.

25. For example, those who use animals in research often argue that laws that protect human beings used in experiments and those that supposedly protect laboratory animals, both of which embody notions of necessity, provide equivalent protection to their respective subjects. *See, e.g.,* Herbert Pardes et al., "Physicians and the Animal Rights Movement," 324 *New Eng. J. Med.* 1640 (1991).

26. Proclamation No. 6560, 58 Fed. Reg. 27,919 (1993).

27. *See, e.g.,* John Locke, "The Second Treatise of Government," in *Two Treatises of Government,* 2d ed., ed. Peter Laslett (Cambridge: Cambridge University Press, 1967), 303–20; A. John Simmons, *The Lockean Theory of Rights* (Princeton, N.J.: Princeton University Press, 1992), 222–306.

28. Richard Delgado, "Norms and Normal Science: Toward a Critique of Normativity in Legal Thought," 139 *U. Pa. L. Rev.* 933, 933 (1991) (footnote omitted). American legal thought regularly produces a new framework, or "paradigm," of analysis that legal academics claim will alter the way in which legal issues are conceptualized or resolved. For example, in the early part of the twentieth century, American legal scholars widely accepted the principles of legal realism. Legal realism rejected the notion that legal decisions could be constructed as a logical consequence of legal rules, and, instead, argued that judges possess a great amount of discretion and that legal decisions are more a function of the social class and temperament of judges than the "neutral" application of supposedly "objective" rules. *See, e.g.,* John C. Gray, *The Nature and Sources of the Law,* 2d ed., ed. Roland Gray (New York: Macmillan, 1921). The principles of realism have been extended by adherents of an approach called "critical legal studies" (CLS), which, in essence, has sought to link the indeterminacy of the law with a "leftist" political agenda. That is, CLS theoreticians accept the realist view that law cannot be considered as a canon of logical rules that generate results in a value-neutral fashion, and that legal rules invariably (and unacceptably) represent the values of the dominant social class because most judges are members of that class or at least tacitly accept those values. *See, e.g.,* Allan C. Hutchinson, ed., *Critical Legal Studies* (Totowa, N.J.: Rowman & Littlefield, 1989). The most recent of these jurisprudential analyses concerns the indisputable fact that legal academicians speak of the law in "normative" terms. That is, as they discuss issues concerning the basic legal issues, they speak in "normative" terms that often obscure completely the power relationships upon which legal relationships rest.

29. Delgado, "Norms and Normal Science," at 949 (footnote omitted).

30. *See* Richard A. Posner, *Economic Analysis of Law,* 3d ed. (Boston: Little, Brown, 1986), 5–9. *See generally* A. Mitchell Polinsky, *An Introduction to Law and Economics* (Boston: Little, Brown, 1983).

It should be remembered that the notion of economic efficiency "was originally introduced to help solve a serious objection to the widely held moral theory, utilitarianism," and economic criteria "were first introduced to obviate the problem of interpersonal comparability" of welfare. Jeffrie G. Murphy and Jules L. Coleman, *The Philosophy of Law* (Totowa, N.J.: Rowman & Littlefield, 1984), 212.

31. "In general, transaction costs include the costs of identifying the parties with whom one has to bargain, the costs of getting together with them, the costs of the bargaining process itself, and the costs of enforcing any bargain reached." Polinsky, *Introduction to Law and Economics,* at 12.

32. *See* R. H. Coase, "The Problem of Social Cost," 3 *J.L. & Econ.* 1 (1960).

33. For a brief but readable discussion of the descriptive and normative functions of economic theory in this context, see Richard A. Posner, *The Problems of Jurisprudence* (Cambridge: Harvard University Press, 1990), 353–92.

34. *See, e.g.,* Ronald Dworkin, "Is Wealth a Value?" 9 *J. Legal Stud.* 191 (1980); Anthony T. Kronman, *"Wealth Maximization as a Normative Principle,"* 9 J. Legal Stud. 227 (1980).

35. Richard A. Posner, "The Ethical and Political Basis of the Efficiency Norm in Common Law Adjudication," 8 *Hofstra L. Rev.* 487, 501 (1980).

36. Ibid., at 502.

37. Posner, *Problems of Jurisprudence,* at 379–80 (footnote omitted). Judge Posner also argues that "[w]hile reprobating slavery we condone similar (but more efficient) practices under different names—imprisonment as punishment for crime, preventive detention, the authority of parents and school authorities over children, conscription, the institutionalization of the insane and the retarded." Ibid., at 379. We could add the exploitation of animals to this list precisely because it is in most respects similar to human slavery, and although we reject human slavery, we accept animal slavery because it is economically efficient, while human slavery may not be (and, according to Posner, is not) efficient.

38. Posner, *Problems of Jurisprudence,* at 377–78. Judge Posner claims that religious freedom is a cost-justified policy because even though there are some religions that we might not care about, we do value individual freedom for its own value and not instrumentally. Ibid.

39. *See* Murphy and Coleman, *Philosophy of Law,* at 212–13. It is important to understand that the principle of wealth maximization is not coextensive with the concepts of Pareto efficiency or optimality. For example, almost any widespread distribution of resources may be said to permit no change that leaves no person worse off and at least one person better off. Dworkin, "Is Wealth a Value?" at 193.

40. 56 Fed. Reg. 6426, at 6486 (1991) (preamble to rules promulgated by the U.S. Department of Agriculture).

41. Posner, *Economic Analysis of Law,* at 137.

42. Alan Freeman and Betty Mensch, "Scratching the Belly of the Beast," in *Animal Experimentation,* ed. Robert M. Baird and Stuart E. Rosenbaum (Buffalo, N.Y.: Prometheus Books, 1991), 161, 163, 164.

43. I use the term "indirectly" quite intentionally. In most cases, if a person is in-

volved directly with animal exploitation, that person will not be sympathetic to claims that others are exploiters of animals. This explains why organizations like the National Association for Biomedical Research routinely report instances in which other animal exploiters, such as animal trainers and furriers, route the efforts of animal rights advocates. Such alliances (e.g., between furriers and researchers) are ostensibly peculiar because researchers usually seek to justify the use of animals in experiments by reference to the supposed benefits of animal use, which researchers point to as distinguishing their use from that of others.

44. *See generally* John Robbins, *Diet for a New America* (Walpole, N.H.: Stillpoint Publishing, 1987).

45. Michael deC. Hinds, "Among Amish, Suspect in Arson Is Well Known," *N.Y. Times,* November 26, 1993, at A16.

46. Temple Grandin, *Recommended Animal Handling Guidelines for Meat Packers* (American Meat Institute, 1991), 1.

47. Many economic theorists claim that in order for someone "to value" something, the person must be willing and able to pay for it; and, by extension, for someone to value something more than someone else, the former must be willing and able to pay more for the item than the latter. Whether this understanding of the notion of valuation is adequate, it is clear that consumers unable to pay for more animal protection could simply stop purchasing meat. Moreover, one might say that the present price of meat and animal products is effectively subsidized by a number of completely external costs, including a high degree of animal suffering and environmental damage not represented in the price of the product. Although some consumers are willing to pay more for animal products produced in a supposedly more humane manner, such as "free-range" eggs or "organic" beef, it is difficult to know the motivations of purchasers, since the advertisements for such products usually appeal to the health interests of consumers.

## Chapter Two

1. There have been literally hundreds of books devoted to the philosophical analysis of the concept of property. For some excellent treatments, see Bruce A. Ackerman, *Private Property and the Constitution* (New Haven: Yale University Press, 1977); Lawrence C. Becker, *Property Rights* (London: Routledge & Kegan Paul, 1977); Alan Carter, *The Philosophical Foundations of Property Rights* (New York: Harvester Wheatsheaf, 1989); Paschal Larkin, *Property in the Eighteenth Century* (New York: Howard Fertig, 1969); C. B. Macpherson, ed., *Property* (Toronto: University of Toronto Press, 1978); Stephen R. Munzer, *A Theory of Property* (Cambridge: Cambridge University Press, 1990); Andrew Reeve, *Property* (Atlantic Highlands, N.J.: Humanities Press International, 1986); James Tully, *A Discourse on Property* (Cambridge: Cambridge University Press, 1980); Jeremy Waldron, *The Right to Private Property* (Oxford: Clarendon Press, 1988).

2. Wesley N. Hohfeld, *Fundamental Legal Conceptions,* ed. Walter W. Cook (New Haven: Yale University Press, 1923), 28.

3. Ackerman, *Private Property,* at 27.

4. Reeve, *Property,* at 13–14.

5. *See, e.g.,* Ray A. Brown, *The Law of Personal Property,* 2d ed. (Chicago: Callaghan & Co., 1955), 1–7; Noah Rotwein, *Personal Property,* revised by Charles S. Phillips (New York: Harmon Publications, 1949), 1–6; Horace E. Smith, *A Treatise on the*

*Law of Personal Property,* 2d ed., ed. by George Lawyer (Chicago: T. H. Flood & Co., 1908), 1–8.

6. Robert C. Ellickson, "Property in Land," 102 *Yale L.J.* 1315, 1365 (1993).

7. Jeremy Rifkin, *Beyond Beef* (New York: Dutton Books, 1992), 28.

8. Godfrey Sandys-Winsch, *Animal Law* (London: Shaw & Sons, 1978), 1.

9. T. G. Field-Fisher, *Animals and the Law* (London: Universities Federation for Animal Welfare, 1964), 19.

10. For a modern treatment of legal issues concerning animals as property, see David S. Favre and Murray Loring, *Animal Law* (Westport, Conn.: Quorum Books, 1983).

11. Charles A. Reich, "The New Property," 73 *Yale L.J.* 733, 771 (1964). A similar position—that property rules can and should be interpreted by reference to conceptions of human dignity that we wish to protect—is put forth by Professor Margaret Radin. *See* Margaret Radin, "The Liberal Conception of Property: Cross Currents in the Jurisprudence of Takings," 88 *Colum. L. Rev.* 1667, 1693 (1988). Professor Nicolaus Tideman argues that the development of moral knowledge will periodically require an adjustment in what constitutes a property right. *See* T. Nicolaus Tideman, "Takings, Moral Evaluation, and Justice," 88 *Colum. L. Rev.* 1714 (1988).

12. Ellickson, "Property in Land," at 1398. Professor Lawrence Berger also argues that community expectations are important in determining the extent to which the state may properly regulate property use. *See* Lawrence Berger, "A Policy Analysis of the Taking Problem," 49 *N.Y.U. L. Rev.* 165 (1974).

13. *See e.g.,* Waldron, *Right to Private Property,* at 27. There is more discussion on this point in Chapter Five.

14. *See e.g.,* Leonard Nelson, *System of Ethics,* trans. Norbert Guterman (New Haven: Yale University Press, 1956), 137–41.

15. *See generally* Richard A. Posner, *Economic Analysis of Law,* 3d ed. (Boston: Little, Brown, 1986)

16. For a discussion of the normative content of efficiency, see C. Edwin Baker, "The Ideology of the Economic Analysis of Law," 5 *Phil. & Pub. Aff.* 3 (1975).

17. *See* Andrew Linzey, *Christianity and the Rights of Animals* (London: S.P.C.K., 1987).

18. Aristotle, *Politics,* trans. William Ellis (London: J. M. Dent & Sons, 1935), 8, 14.

19. Richard Sorabji, *Animal Minds and Human Morals* (Ithaca, N.Y.: Cornell University Press, 1993), 7.

20. Gerald Carson, *Men, Beasts, and Gods* (New York: Charles Scribner's Sons, 1972), 10 (citing Jacques Boudet, *Man and Beast: A Visual History,* trans. Anne Carter [London, 1964], 48–49).

21. Richard D. Ryder, *Animal Revolution* (Oxford: Basil Blackwell, 1989), 22.

22. H. R. Hays, *Birds, Beasts, and Men* (New York: G. P. Putnam's Sons, 1972).

23. Thomas Aquinas, *Summa Theologica* (Question 96), trans. Fathers of the English Dominican Province (New York: Benziger Brothers, 1947), 486.

24. René Descartes, "Discourse on the Method," in *The Philosophical Writings of Descartes,* trans. John Cottingham et al. (Cambridge: Cambridge University Press, 1985), 141.

25. *See* John Vyvyan, *In Pity and in Anger* (London: Michael Joseph, 1969), 22–24.

26. The views of Aristotle, Aquinas, and Descartes have been refuted quite effectively by modern philosophers. *See, e.g.,* Tom Regan, *The Case for Animal Rights* (Berkeley and Los Angeles: University of California Press, 1983). It should also be noted, how-

ever, that contemporaries of all three men adopted views that favored moral consideration for animals. For an excellent historical survey, see Ryder, *Animal Revolution,* at 19–177.

27. *See* John Locke, *Two Treatises of Government,* 2d ed., ed. Peter Laslett (Cambridge: Cambridge University Press, 1967). For an excellent discussion of Locke's theory of rights, including property rights, see A. John Simmons, *The Lockean Theory of Rights* (Princeton, N.J.: Princeton University Press, 1992).

28. Simmons, *Lockean Theory of Rights,* at 224.

29. Locke, *Two Treatises of Government,* 25, at 303–4.

30. Ibid., 26, at 304–5.

31. Simmons, *Lockean Theory of Rights,* at 224–25.

32. Locke, *Two Treatises of Government,* 30, at 308. It is important to understand that although Locke is usually viewed as the chief theoretical architect of the property notions that animate modern capitalism, he placed considerable restrictions on the ownership of too much property by any one person.

33. Ibid., at 307.

34. Since Locke was concerned about natural rights, and not the positive rights created within a particular legal system, he could just have easily recognized that animals had a similar interest in their own conversion of the natural world through their efforts. Instead, Locke understandably avoided the entire issue, in favor of basing his ultimate starting point on the language of Genesis. Locke accordingly ignored any concern about whether animals had property interests in their own bodies.

35. 2 William Blackstone, *Commentaries on the Laws of England* (Chicago: Callaghan & Co., 1872), *2.

36. Ibid., *2–3.

37. 1 Ibid., *139.

38. 2 Ibid., *5.

39. *See* John Locke, *An Essay Concerning Human Understanding,* ed. John W. Yolton (London: J. M. Dent & Sons, 1961), 115–17.

40. Locke, *Two Treatises of Government,* 6, at 288–89 (emphasis added).

41. John Locke, "Some Thoughts Concerning Education," in 9 *The Works of John Locke in Ten Volumes,* 10th ed., ed. Thomas Tegg et al. (Germany: Scientia Verlag Aalen, 1963), 112.

42. Ibid., at 113.

43. 2 Blackstone, *Commentaries,* *388, 389.

44. Ibid., *391.

45. Ibid., *390, 391.

46. Ibid., *391, 394, 394–95.

47. The notion of qualified property in wild animals and the doctrine of *animus revertendi* were also accepted in the civil-law system derived from Roman law and applied throughout much of continental Europe. *See* A. M. Prichard, *Leage's Roman Private Law,* 3d ed. (London: Macmillan, 1961), 176–77.

48. *Manning v. Mitcherson,* 69 Ga. 447 (1882).

49. Ibid., at 450–51.

50. *Pierson v. Post,* 3 Cai. R. 175 (N.Y. Sup. Ct. 1805).

51. Ibid., at 177.

52. *Buster v. Newkirk,* 20 Johns. Cas. 74, 75 (N.Y. Sup. Ct. 1822).

53. Ibid.

54. 2 Blackstone, *Commentaries,* \*394.

55. *See* Michael J. Bean, *The Evolution of National Wildlife Law* (New York: Praeger, 1983); George C. Coggins, "Wildlife and the Constitution: The Walls Come Tumbling Down," 55 *Wash. L. Rev.* 295 (1980).

56. *Restatement of the Law of Property* §§ 1, 2, 3, 4 (St. Paul, Minn.: American Law Institute, 1936).

57. Ibid., 5 cmt. e.

58. Waldron, *Right to Private Property,* at 31. It should be noted that Waldron views restrictions on the use of property as involving "side constraints" on the use, and not as part of the definition of "property" or "ownership."

59. Ibid., at 38, 39.

60. A. M. Honoré, "Ownership," in *Oxford Essays in Jurisprudence,* ed. A. G. Guest (London: Oxford University Press, 1961), 107, 112–24. Honoré defines ownership as "the greatest possible interest in a thing which a mature system of law recognizes," a notion that he describes as a "liberal" notion of ownership. Ibid., at 108, 109. By "liberal," Honoré means to focus on doctrines of ownership that respect the right of individual owners to use their property as they see fit. In "mature" legal systems, be they capitalist or socialist, Honoré maintains that there will be some "liberal" (i.e., owner-centered) ownership of some property. By "greatest possible interest," Honoré means that there may be ownership even when there is regulation of use of the property or some of the incidents of ownership have been transferred.

61. Frank Snare, "The Concept of Property," 9 *Am. Phil. Q.* 200 (1972). For a discussion of Snare's theory, see Bruce A. Ackerman, *Private Property and the Constitution* (New Haven: Yale University Press, 1977), 231 n. 11.

62. "State ownership" and "public ownership," although often used interchangeably, are different terms. *See* Reeve, *Property,* at 29–37.

63. James W. Ely Jr., *The Guardian of Every Other Right* (New York: Oxford University Press, 1992), 17, 18.

64. Ibid., at 43, 46, 47.

65. Ibid., at 43. For example, Congress was prohibited from enacting bills of attainder, giving preference to ports, or declaring a forfeiture of property for treason except during the life of the offender.

66. Ibid., at 44. These provisions included the taxing power, the power to regulate commerce, the power to grant copyrights and patents, and the power to establish national bankruptcy laws, which the framers thought would "operate largely for the benefit of merchants and traders, as was the practice in England, and would protect creditors from fraudulent debtors."

67. Ibid., at 44–45. These provisions included the prohibition against state interference with freedom of contract.

68. Ibid., at 45, 46, 51.

69. *See* ibid., at 52.

70. U.S. Const. amend. V. Private property was subject to eminent domain under English law, but according to Ely, "this power was . . . gradually qualified by the practice of paying compensation to the owner." Ely, *Guardian of Every Other Right,* at 23.

71. *See, e.g.,* Bernard Bailyn, *The Ideological Origins of the American Revolution* (Cambridge: Belknap Press, 1992).

72. *See Lucas v. South Carolina Coastal Council,* 112 S. Ct. 2886, 2900 n. 15 (1992)

("early constitutional theorists did not believe the Takings Clause embraced regulations of property at all.").

73. Ackerman, *Private Property and the Constitution,* at 7.

74. *Pennsylvania Coal Co. v. Mahon,* 260 U.S. 393, 409 (1922).

75. *Lucas,* 112 S. Ct. 2886 (1992).

76. Ibid., at 2899 (footnote omitted), 2895 n. 8 (alteration and omission in original) (quoting *Penn Cent. Transp. Co. v. New York City,* 438 U.S. 104, 124 [1978]).

## Chapter Three

1. *Gilson v. Pennsylvania R. Co.,* 92 A. 59 (N.J. 1914). Other courts have defined the term similarly. *See, e.g., Gebert v. Yank,* 218 Cal. Rptr. 585, 588 (Ct. App. 1985) ("a bailment is the delivery of a thing to another for some special object or purpose, on a contract, express or implied, to conform to the objects or purposes of the delivery which may be as various as the transactions of men"); *Fulcher v. State,* 25 S.W. 625, 625 (Tex. Crim. App. 1864) (a "bailment may be defined as a delivery of personal property to another for some purpose, upon a contract, express or implied, that such purpose shall be carried out"). *See also* Ray A. Brown, *The Law of Personal Property,* 2d ed. (Chicago: Callaghan & Co., 1955), § 73; 8 C.J.S. *Bailments* § 2 (1988).

A specific type of bailment contract, involving the feeding and raising of animals, usually horses or cattle, is known as an agistment contract. Typically, an agistment contract provides a mutual benefit to the parties involved. *See* David S. Favre and Murray Loring, *Animal Law* (Westport, Conn.: Quorum Books, 1983), 5.1. *See also Heckman & Shell v. Wilson,* 487 P.2d 1141, 1146 (Mont. 1971); *Bramlette v. Titus,* 267 P.2d 620, 622 (Nev. 1954) (agistment contract involves an agreement in which "a man, for a consideration, takes in cattle to graze and pasture on his land") (internal quotation omitted); *Baker v. Hansen,* 666 P.2d 315, 320 (Utah 1983) (a contract to care for animals for a specified period of time is an agistment, which is a "species of bailment").

2. *See, e.g., Gebert,* 218 Cal. Rptr. at 590.

3. *See* Brown, *Personal Property,* 73.

4. *See, e.g., Elephant, Inc. v. Hartford Accident & Indem. Co.,* 239 So.2d 692 (La. Ct. App. 1970).

5. *See, e.g., Bramlette,* 267 P.2d at 621; *Buchanan v. Byrd,* 519 S.W.2d 841 (Tex. 1975). However, payment for services is not dispositive of a mutual bailment, which can exist even if the bailee performs the services for free, as long as the services are performed "incident [to the] business in which the bailee makes a profit." *Andrews v. Allen,* 724 S.W.2d 893, 895 (Tex. Ct. App. 1987) (bailment for mutual benefit existed where bailee transported plaintiff's horse for free because the parties typically performed "favors" for each other because it was good for their businesses).

6. *See, e.g., Raines v. Rice,* 15 S.E.2d 246 (Ga. Ct. App. 1941); *New York Fire Ins. Co. v. Kansas Milling Co.,* 81 So.2d 15 (La. 1955).

7. Brown, *Personal Property,* 81. Ordinary care is that degree of care which persons of ordinary prudence take of their own property of a similar kind under like circumstances. *See Hanes v. Shapiro,* 84 S.E. 33, 36 (N.C. 1915). *See, e.g., Griffin v. Ruping,* 220 N.Y.S.2d 399, 401 (Cty. Ct. 1961) (agreement to board and train a pointer dog for $35 per month constituted a bailment, and ordinary care was required).

8. *See Hanes*, 84 S.E. at 36 ("in bailments for the exclusive benefit of the bailee, [the bailee] will be liable even for slight negligence").

9. *See, e.g., Chasteen v. Childers*, 546 P.2d 935 (Kan. 1976) (valuable brood mares were kept on a "starvation diet" because bailor contracted only for such services); *Elephant, Inc. v. Hartford Accident & Indem. Co.*, 239 So.2d 692 (La. Ct. App. 1970) (court upholds signed agreement freeing bailee from any liability should animal die while in bailee's care).

10. *Gebert v. Yank*, 218 Cal. Rptr. 585, 590 (Ct. App. 1985). The defendants argued that there is an inherent risk in caring for some animals, such as high-spirited horses, because they are more prone to injury simply because of their nature. Ibid.

11. *Nutt v. Davison*, 131 P. 390, 392 (Colo. 1913). In *Ward v. Newell*, 315 S.E.2d 721 (N.C. Ct. App. 1984), the court held that the bailee breached the standard of ordinary care by allowing a mare left in his care to be impregnated by another horse, thereby making her unsuitable for her intended purpose. *Ward*, 315 S.E.2d at 723. *See Moers v. Pell*, 167 N.Y.S. 774 (App. Div. 1917) (plaintiff delivered healthy dog to defendant for breeding, and defendant breached duty of care by returning dog with distemper).

12. *See, e.g., David v. Lose*, 218 N.E. 2d 442 (Ohio 1966). Failure to return the animal in good condition will result in a breach of the bailment contract unless the bailee can demonstrate that the injury to the animal was not the result of negligence or that the animal was not delivered in good condition at the start of the contract.

13. *See, e.g., People v. Johnson*, 277 P.2d 45, 52 (Cal. Ct. App. 1954).

14. *See, e.g., Torix v. Allred*, 606 P.2d 1334, 1339 (Idaho 1980); *Butterfly v. Marcell*, 365 A.2d 252, 253 (Vt. 1976).

15. *See, e.g., Edgar v. Parsell*, 151 N.W. 714, 715 (Mich. 1915). Some bailment contracts may include a special agreement to treat the animals as fungible goods, which a bailee can simply replace with like animals when the original ones are injured or destroyed. *See* Favre and Loring, *Animal Law*, § 5.3.

16. *See, e.g., Lepel v. Hitch*, 468 F.2d 149 (10th Cir. 1972) (bailor had responsibility to deliver healthy cattle to bailee, with whom he contracted for feeding program); *Evans v. Upmier*, 16 N.W.2d 6 (Iowa 1944) (owner of livery stable had duty to deliver horse suitable for riding to bailee). The bailor also has the responsibility to inform the bailee whether the animal has any vicious traits. *Buffington v. Nicholson*, 177 P.2d 51 (Cal. Dist. Ct. App. 1947).

17. *See, e.g., Lepel v. Hitch*, 468 F.2d at 149; *Bramlette v. Titus*, 267 P.2d 620 (Nev. 1954).

18. *See, e.g., McPherson v. Schlemmer*, 749 P.2d 51 (Mont. 1988) (as in the case of personal property, an owner may recover for loss or injury to an animal the amount that will compensate the loss and return the owner to the position she was in before the loss occurred).

19. For example, the agister's lien statute in Kansas provides that "the keepers of livery stables, and all others engaged in feeding horses, cattle, hogs, or other livestock, shall have a lien upon such property for the feed and care bestowed by them upon the same, and if reasonable or stipulated charges for such feed and care be not paid within sixty (60) days after the same becomes due, the property, or so much thereof as may be necessary to pay such charges and the expenses of publication and sale, may be sold as provided in this act." Kan. Stat. Ann. 58–207 (1983). At common law this remedy was not available, but many states now provide for agistment liens by statute. *See, e.g., Hannahs v. Noah*, 158 N.W.2d 678 (S.D. 1968) (no entitlement to agister's lien as a matter of law); *Hatley v. West*, 445 P.2d 208 (Wash. 1968) (plaintiff entitled to agister's lien). *See also Griffin v. Ruping*, 220

N.Y.S.2d 399 (Cty. Ct. 1961) (bailee had lien on dog left in his care for training, after dog received emergency medical treatment).

20. *See, e.g., Kennet v. Robinson,* 25 Ky. 84 (1829).

21. *Alvord v. Davenport,* 43 Vt. 30 (1870).

22. *See, e.g., Hennen v. Streeter,* 31 P.2d 160 (Nev. 1934) (1,590 head of sheep served as security for a mortgage).

23. *See, e.g., Bramlette v. Titus,* 267 P.2d 620 (Nev. 1954) (grazing rights in exchange for payment); *Gebert v. Yank,* 218 Cal. Rptr. 585 (Ct. App. 1985); *Edgar v. Parsell,* 151 N.W. 714 (Mich. 1915). *Cf. Brousseau v. Rosenthal,* 443 N.Y.S.2d 285 (Civ. Ct. 1980). In *Brousseau,* the plaintiff boarded her eight-year-old mixed breed dog at the defendant's kennel. When she tried to recover the dog two weeks later, the defendant told her that the dog had died. The court characterized the arrangement as a bailment for mutual benefit and held defendant to a standard of ordinary care. *Brousseau,* 443 N.Y.S.2d at 285. However, the defendant's failure to return the dog shifted the burden of proving due care to the defendant, and the court held that the bailee had failed to rebut the presumption (under the circumstances) of negligence. The court also recognized that the plaintiff had suffered a "grievous loss" and that the actual market value of the dog, which was nominal, would not adequately compensate her. The court awarded damages of $550. *Brousseau,* 443 N.Y.S.2d at 286–87.

24. *Deiro v. American Airlines,* 816 F.2d 1360 (9th Cir. 1987).

25. Ibid., at 1361–62.

26. Ibid., at 1366.

27. *Mitchell v. Union Pac. R.R.,* 242 F.2d 598 (9th Cir. 1957).

28. Ibid., at 599.

29. Ibid., at 601.

30. *Mitchell v. Union Pac. R.R.,* 188 F. Supp. 869, 875–76 (S.D. Cal. 1960). *See also Gluckman v. American Airlines, Inc.,* 884 F. Supp. 151 (S.D.N.Y. 1994).

31. C. Reinold Noyes, *The Institution of Property* (New York: Longmans, Green & Co., 1936), 290 n. 13 (quoting *Restatement of the Law of Property* [St. Paul, Minn.: American Law Institute, 1936]).

32. American Veterinary Medical Association Study, in 15 *Pet Health News,* March 1989.

33. Some writers on the subject distinguish between veterinary malpractice and veterinary negligence. "Malpractice" is deemed to be the type of liability that involves a matter of medical science and requires special skills not ordinarily possessed by lay people and that results in alleged injury, loss, or death of a client's animal. "Negligence" refers to veterinary liability for alleged injuries suffered by the client personally or another human.

34. Joseph H. King Jr., "The Standard of Care for Veterinarians in Medical Malpractice Claims," 58 *Tenn. L. Rev.* 1, 33–35 (1990).

35. An owner present during her animal's examination can be hurt in other ways. In one case, a veterinarian's assistant who was taking blood from a dog's front leg accidentally punctured the owner's eye upon removing the needle from the dog. *See* "The Outcome of Six Claims," *Liability: The Am. Veterinary Med. Ass'n Tr. Rep.,* March 1988, at 3–4. In another case, an owner's hand was lacerated by suture scissors the veterinarian was using when the animal suddenly jumped from the table during the procedure. *See* "New Claims Reveal It's Easy for Helpers to Get Injured," *Liability: The Am. Veterinary Med. Ass'n Tr. Rep.,* March 1989, at 1–2.

36. The veterinarian may be charged with negligently failing to warn the client of

the dangerousness of the drug or failing to advise the client to use a muzzle and/or sedation on the animal to avoid injury. *See* King, "Standard of Care for Veterinarians," at 31–33.

37. Ibid., at 29.

38. *See Smith v. Palace Transp. Co.,* 253 N.Y.S. 87 (Mun. Ct. 1931) (price paid for property was important in appraising its value, while sentimental value of dog was not an element), *overruled by Corso v. Crawford Dog & Cat Hosp., Inc.,* 415 N.Y.S.2d 182 (City Civ. Ct. 1979).

39. *See, e.g., Fowler v. Town of Ticonderoga,* 516 N.Y.S. 2d 368, 370 (App. Div. 1987) (a dog is personal property; thus, damages for mental distress are not allowed); *Stettner v. Graubard,* 368 N.Y.S.2d 683, 684 (Town Ct. 1975) (market value, including usefulness and desirable character traits, is the correct measure of damages for the destruction of a dog).

40. *Richardson v. Fairbanks N. Star Borough,* 705 P.2d 454 (Alaska 1985).

41. Ibid., at 455.

42. Ibid., at 455–56.

43. *Collins v. Ubanoski,* No. B14–88-00461-CV, 1989 WL 131120 (Tex. Ct. App. Nov. 2, 1989) (unpublished opinion).

44. Ibid., at *1.

45. Ibid., at *2.

46. Ibid., at *3.

47. In 1949, the Supreme Judicial Court of Massachusetts allowed recovery for "actual value" where the property in question, an irreplaceable roll of film, had no market value. *Sarkesian v. Cedric Chase Photographic Laboratories, Inc.,* 87 N.E.2d 745 (Mass. 1949). Other cases discussed in the text built upon the *Sarkesian* holding.

48. *See* ibid., at 746.

49. 443 N.Y.S.2d 285 (Civ. Ct. 1980).

50. Ibid., at 285–87.

51. Ibid., at 287. *See also Zager v. Dimilia,* 524 N.Y.S.2d 968, 969–70 (Village Ct. 1988) (the Village of Pleasantville court held that the appropriate measure of damages for the death of a dog in the absence of known market value would be the actual, or "intrinsic," value, which the court interpreted as the cost of veterinary treatment).

52. *Jankoski v. Preiser Animal Hosp., Ltd.,* 510 N.E.2d 1084 (Ill. App. Ct. 1987).

53. Ibid., at 1085–87.

54. *See, e.g., Gill v. Brown,* 695 P.2d 1276 (Idaho Ct. App. 1985) (claim of negligent infliction of emotional distress could be sustained for loss arising from shooting of animal even though recovery could not be based on mental anguish suffered as a result of property loss); *City of Garland v. White,* 368 S.W.2d 12 (Tex. Civ. App. 1963) (facts showing that police shot dog in presence of owner support claim of negligent infliction of emotional distress). *But cf. Roman v. Carroll,* 621 P.2d 307 (Ariz. Ct. App. 1980) (the court denied recovery for negligent infliction of emotional distress where defendants' Saint Bernard dismembered plaintiff's poodle while plaintiff was walking the dog; the court held that the dog was property, and the plaintiff could not recover damages for distress).

55. *Campbell v. Animal Quarantine Station,* 632 P.2d 1066 (Haw. 1981).

56. Ibid., at 1067.

57. Ibid., at 1068.

58. Ibid., at 1069–71.

59. *See, e.g., Richardson v. Fairbanks N. Star Borough,* 705 P.2d 454 (Alaska 1985)

(damages for loss of animal limited to fair market value unless intentional infliction of harm caused severe emotional distress to owner), discussed *supra* in text accompanying notes 40–42. For a noncaretaker example, see *Gill v. Brown*, 695 P.2d 1276 (Idaho Ct. App. 1985) (damages for mental anguish upon reckless killing of pet donkey are unrecoverable for loss of property but could be sustained in separate action for intentional infliction of emotional distress if defendant's conduct was reckless and caused the owner mental pain and suffering).

60. *Lawrence v. Stanford*, 655 S.W.2d 927 (Tenn. 1983).

61. Ibid., at 928.

62. Tenn. Code Ann. § 63-1234 (recodified as Tenn. Code Ann. § 63-12-134).

63. *Lawrence*, 655 S.W.2d at 929.

64. Ibid., at 930–31.

65. A typical case is *City of Garland v. White*, 368 S.W.2d 12 (Tex. Civ. App. 1963). The police were responding to a call from a neighbor of White complaining that White's boxer dog had lunged at her. The dog growled at the police but did not otherwise threaten them. The police shot at the dog, who ran to his home. The police followed the dog into his owner's garage and killed him with a shotgun, without even attempting first to trap the dog by closing the garage door or contact the owner, who was home at the time. Ibid., at 14–15. White was found by the trial court and the court of appeals to have suffered mental anguish and physical pain to a degree that he was unable to work for a period of time, yet the award for his serious distress was only $200. Ibid., at 13.

66. *See also La Porte v. Associated Indeps. Inc.*, 163 So.2d 267 (Fla. 1964) (allowing recovery of damages beyond market value for the malicious destruction of a pet when a garbage collector purposely threw a trash can at a small dog and killed the dog).

67. *Levine v. Knowles*, 197 So.2d 329 (Fla. Dist. Ct. App. 1967).

68. Ibid., at 330.

69. Ibid., at 331–32. On remand, the defendant in *Levine* prevailed on a motion for summary judgment on the question of damages. The appellate court held that the plaintiff should have been allowed to present new evidence on damages, but the court went on to say that any punitive damages should bear a reasonable relationship to compensatory damages. *Levine v. Knowles*, 228 So.2d 308, 309 (Fla. Dist. Ct. App. 1969). There was some confusion in applying the "reasonable-relationship" test. In 1976 the Florida Supreme Court held that an award of nominal actual damages would support a claim for punitive damages, and there was no requirement of a "reasonable relationship" between actual and punitive damages. *Lassitter v. International Union of Operating Engineers*, 349 So.2d 622 (Fla. 1976). Florida courts still seem to disagree about whether a claim for intentional infliction of emotional distress alone (without being coupled with another tort) can support a claim for damages. *See, e.g., Gellert v. Eastern Airlines*, 370 So.2d 802, 805 (Fla. Dist. Ct. App. 1979).

70. *Knowles Animal Hosp., Inc. v. Wills*, 360 So.2d 37 (Fla. Dist. Ct. App. 1978).

71. Ibid., at 38.

72. The court applied the standard established in *La Porte v. Associated Indeps. Inc.*, 163 So.2d 267 (Fla. 1964).

73. For example, the Minnesota Supreme Court upheld an award for punitive damages against a police department responsible for killing a plaintiff's cat before a mandatory five-day impound period had elapsed. *Wilson v. City of Eagan*, 297 N.W.2d 146 (Minn. 1980).

74. *See also Johnson v. Wander*, 592 So.2d 1225 (Fla. Dist. Ct. App. 1992) (revers-

ing the trial court's summary judgment striking plaintiff's claims for punitive damages and mental distress under a set of facts that the court found "indistinguishable" from *Knowles Animal Hosp.*).

75. One noteworthy exception to the general rule is the *Knowles Animal Hosp.* case, discussed *supra*. However, it is not known whether the award was based on the suffering of the owner, the suffering of the animal, or the financial status of the defendant.

76. *Fredeen v. Stride,* 525 P.2d 166 (Or. 1974).

77. Ibid., at 168–69.

78. *Corso v. Crawford Dog and Cat Hospital,* 415 N.Y.S.2d 182 (City Civ. Ct. 1979).

79. Ibid., at 183 (Plaintiff was awarded $700 as reasonable compensation for her shock, mental anguish, and despondency, against the veterinary hospital for wrongful disposal of her dog's body, discovered when plaintiff opened the casket she had ordered for the dog and found the body of a dead cat instead).

80. *Restrepo v. State,* 550 N.Y.S.2d 536 (Ct. Cl. 1989).

81. Ibid., at 541–42.

82. *Fowler v. Town of Ticonderoga,* 516 N.Y.S.2d 368 (App. Div. 1987).

83. Ibid., at 370.

84. *Gluckman v. American Airlines, Inc.,* 884 F. Supp. 151 (S.D.N.Y. 1994). The court also held that there was no cause of action for negligent and intentional infliction of emotional distress, because the dog was property, and that there was no cause for action for the dog's suffering.

85. *Julian v. DeVincent,* 184 S.E.2d 535 (W. Va. 1971).

86. Ibid., at 535.

87. Ibid., at 536.

88. *Katsaris v. Cook,* 225 Cal. Rptr. 531 (Ct. App. 1986).

89. Ibid., at 536–38.

## Chapter Four

1. *See generally,* L. W. Sumner, *The Moral Foundation of Rights* (Oxford: Clarendon Press, 1987).

2. I do not discuss in any detail the doctrine of standing as it is applied in state law. In Part II of the book, however, there is a brief discussion of that topic in the context of the enforcement of state anticruelty laws.

3. *Association of Data Processing Serv. Orgs., Inc. v. Camp,* 397 U.S. 150, 151 (1970).

4. Cass R. Sunstein, "What's Standing After *Lujan*? Of Citizen Suits, 'Injuries,' and Article III," 91 *Mich. L. Rev.* 163, 168 (1992). There are hundreds of essays on the subject of standing. Excellent pieces include Sunstein's as well as Louis L. Jaffe, "Standing to Secure Judicial Review: Public Actions," 74 *Harv. L. Rev.* 1265 (1961); Steven L. Winter, "The Metaphor of Standing and the Problem of Self-Governance," 40 *Stan. L. Rev.* 1371 (1988).

5. It should be noted that many economists do not believe that litigation is a desirable way of considering or calculating external costs.

6. U.S. Const. art. 3, § 2.

7. Other doctrines that also seek to ensure that the "case-or-controversy" requirement is followed include the doctrines of ripeness and mootness. *See generally* Laurence

H. Tribe, *American Constitutional Law,* 2d ed. (Mineola, N.Y.: Foundation Press, 1988), §§ 3–10, 3–11.

    8. 5 U.S.C. § 702 (1988).

    9. *See Association of Data Processing Serv. Orgs., Inc. v. Camp,* 397 U.S. 150, 153 (1970); *Barlow v. Collins,* 397 U.S. 159, 164 (1970). The "zone-of-interest" test is called a "prudential" consideration, while the "injury-in-fact" requirement is constitutionally mandated. The prudential consideration seeks to determine whether a particular plaintiff should be heard to complain of a particular agency decision. *See Clarke v. Securities Indus. Ass'n,* 479 U.S. 388, 399 (1987). In this chapter, I focus primarily on the constitutionally required "injury-in-fact" test, which is the more important of the two, and the one most discussed in judicial decisions.

    In his discussion of standing, Professor Sunstein states that "the zone-of-interest test was intended to be exceptionally lenient." Sunstein, "What's Standing After *Lujan?*" at 185 (citing *Data Processing,* 397 U.S. at 154–55). Sunstein points out that "the first Supreme Court case denying standing on zone-of-interest grounds came in 1991." Sunstein, "What's Standing After *Lujan?*" at 185 n. 107 (citing *Air Courier Conference of Am. v. American Postal Workers' Union,* 498 U.S. 517 [1991]).

    10. The Supreme Court discussed "a set of prudential principles that bear on the question of standing" in *Valley Forge Christian College v. Americans United for Separation of Church & State, Inc.,* 454 U.S. 464, 474 (1982). First, the plaintiff must assert its own legal rights and interests rather than those of a third party. Second, "the Court has refrained from adjudicating abstract questions of wide public significance which amount to generalized grievances" better addressed by the representative branches. Ibid., at 474–75 (internal quotations omitted). Third, and as mentioned above, the Court has required that the complaint "fall within the zone of interests to be protected or regulated by the statute or constitutional guarantee in question." Ibid., at 475 (internal quotations omitted).

    11. *Lujan v. Defenders of Wildlife,* 112 S. Ct. 2130, 2136 (1992) (internal quotations omitted) [hereinafter *Lujan*]. These three elements are "the irreducible constitutional minimum" for standing. Ibid.

    12. *Sierra Club v. Morton,* 405 U.S. 727 (1972).

    13. Ibid., at 733. Just as the Constitution does not mention standing explicitly, it also makes no reference to the injury-in-fact test. Sunstein puts the matter this way: "One might well ask: What was the source of the injury-in-fact test? Did the Supreme Court just make it up? The answer is basically yes." Sunstein, "What's Standing After *Lujan?*" at 185 (footnote omitted).

    14. *Sierra Club,* 405 U.S. at 733.

    15. Ibid., at 734–35.

    16. Ibid., at 735.

    17. The Supreme Court in 1990 interpreted *Sierra Club* to hold that a plaintiff must show specific injury before a court will deny summary judgment to a defendant challenging standing. *Lujan v. National Wildlife Fed'n,* 497 U.S. 871, 888–89 (1990) [hereinafter *National Wildlife Fed'n*]. The Court in *National Wildlife Federation* required a sworn statement of specific facts setting forth the actual injury. The Court found insufficient an allegation that plaintiffs used land "in the vicinity" of land covered under challenged agency action. In a dissent in *Lujan,* 112 S. Ct. at 2151–60, Justices Blackmun and O'Connor argued that physical proximity was required in *National Wildlife Federation* because in that case the type of harm alleged to have been done to plaintiff's visual enjoyment of nature

was the result of mining activities. *Lujan,* 112 S. Ct. at 2154 (Blackmun, J., and O'Connor, J., dissenting). The dissent continued: "Many environmental injuries, however, cause harm distant from the area immediately affected by the challenged action." *Lujan,* 112 S. Ct. at 2154. *National Wildlife Federation* is having an impact on lower-court standing decisions. *See People for the Ethical Treatment of Animals v. Department of Health & Human Servs.,* 917 F.2d 15 (9th Cir. 1990).

18. *Sierra Club,* 405 U.S. at 742 (Douglas, J., dissenting).

19. Ibid., at 745–46 (footnote omitted).

20. Ibid., at 749–52.

21. Christopher Stone, "Should Trees Have Standing? Toward Legal Rights for Natural Objects," 45 *S. Cal. L. Rev.* 450 (1972).

22. Ibid., at 455.

23. Ibid., at 452 (footnote omitted).

24. Ibid., at 453–56 and n. 24.

25. Ibid., at 456.

26. Ibid., at 464–67.

27. Clarence Morris, "The Rights and Duties of Beasts and Trees: A Law Teacher's Essay for Landscape Architects," 17 *J. Legal Educ.* 185, 189 (1964).

28. The question of what must be pleaded has been revisited by the Supreme Court in two recent cases. *See Lujan,* 112 S. Ct. 2130 (1992); *National Wildlife Fed'n,* 497 U.S. 871 (1990). In *Lujan,* the Supreme Court held that standing could not be established by allegations that members of an environmental organization had observed endangered species in the locations covered by the action to be funded by the United States government and that they planned to return to those locations at some unspecified later time. *Lujan,* 112 S. Ct. at 2138. The Court also rejected the notion that any person who used part of a contiguous ecosystem had standing to challenge an action even if it occurred far away from the place that the person used and enjoyed. *Lujan,* 112 S. Ct. at 2139. The Court based its rejection of this notion on its earlier holding in *National Wildlife Federation,* in which the Court rejected the notion that plaintiffs could have standing by alleging that they recreated on land "in the vicinity" of land covered by agency action. *Lujan,* 112 S. Ct. at 2139 (citing *National Wildlife Fed'n,* 497 U.S. at 887–89).

29. *Animal Welfare Inst. v. Kreps,* 561 F.2d 1002 (D.C. Cir. 1977), *cert. denied,* 434 U.S. 1013 (1978).

30. Ibid., 561 F.2d at 1004–5.

31. Ibid., at 1007 (quoting Plaintiffs' Complaint). It should be noted that the *Kreps* court discussed two other possible bases of standing. First, the court held that under the statute in question, the Marine Mammal Protection Act, Congress somewhat ambiguously provided for citizen suits. *See* ibid., at 1005–6. This holding would now probably be invalid under the Supreme Court's decision in *Lujan,* 112 S. Ct. 2130 (1992), in which the Court held that even under citizen suit provisions enacted by Congress, plaintiffs must still show injury in fact. *Lujan,* 112 S. Ct. at 2136. Second, the court in *Kreps* held that the statute was enacted to protect animals and that it was thus "eminently logical to allow groups specifically concerned with animal welfare to invoke the aid of the courts in enforcing the statute." *Kreps,* 561 F.2d at 1007. This alternative ground would probably be impermissible even under *Sierra Club* on the ground that the interests of organizations cannot be generalized but must relate to concrete interests possessed by members of the organization and injured by the challenged action.

32. *Japan Whaling Ass'n v. American Cetacean Soc'y,* 478 U.S. 221 (1986).

33. Ibid., at 230 n. 4.

34. *Alaska Fish & Wildlife Fed'n v. Dunkle,* 829 F.2d 933 (9th Cir. 1987), *cert. denied,* 485 U.S. 988 (1988).

35. Ibid., 829 F.2d at 937.

36. *American Horse Protection Ass'n, Inc. v. Frizzell,* 403 F. Supp. 1206, 1214 (D. Nev. 1975) (quoting complaint, emphasis added by court).

37. *Wilkins v. Lujan,* 798 F. Supp. 557 (E.D. Mo. 1992), *rev'd on other grounds sub nom. Wilkins v. Secretary of the Interior,* 995 F.2d 850 (8th Cir. 1993), *cert. denied,* 114 S. Ct. 921 (1994).

38. Ibid., at 560–61.

39. *Humane Soc'y of the United States v. Hodel,* 840 F.2d 45 (D.C. Cir. 1988).

40. Ibid., at 49.

41. Ibid., at 51–52 (citing *Valley Forge Christian College v. Americans United for Separation of Church & State, Inc.,* 454 U.S. 464, 486 [1982]).

42. *Humane Soc'y,* 840 F.2d at 52.

43. Ibid., at 52–58 (citing *Hunt v. Washington State Apple Advertising Comm'n,* 432 U.S. 333 [1977]).

44. *Humane Soc'y,* 840 F.2d at 60.

45. *Animal Protection Inst. of Am. v. Hodel,* 860 F.2d 920 (9th Cir. 1988).

46. Ibid., at 923–24.

47. *Animal Lovers Volunteer Ass'n, Inc. v. Weinberger,* 765 F.2d 937 (9th Cir. 1985).

48. Ibid., at 938.

49. Ibid., at 939.

50. Ibid.

51. The "longevity-and-commitment" test has been used by other courts. *See, e.g., Fund for Animals, Inc. v. Lujan,* 794 F. Supp. 1015 (D. Mont. 1991), *aff'd,* 962 F.2d 1391 (9th Cir. 1992). In *Fund for Animals,* the same organization referred to in *Animal Lovers* sought to enjoin the shooting of bison. Although the court rejected standing based on psychological harm to Fund members, the court, citing *Animal Lovers,* held that the Fund had a long-standing interest in the matter and had litigated the issue in an earlier case in 1985 in which the Park Service failed to raise standing as an issue. *Fund for Animals,* 794 F. Supp. at 1022.

52. *See* Alex Pacheco and Anna Francione, "The Silver Spring Monkeys," in *In Defense of Animals,* ed. Peter Singer (New York: Basil Blackwell, 1985), 135–47. *See generally* Kathy S. Guillermo, *Monkey Business* (Washington, D.C.: National Press, 1993).

53. IBR subsequently changed its name to Institute for Behavioral Resources.

54. Affidavit of Dr. Geza Teleki, Joint Appendix at 78, *International Primate Protection League v. Institute for Behavioral Research, Inc.,* 799 F.2d 934 (4th Cir. 1986), *cert. denied,* 481 U.S. 1004 (1987) [hereinafter *IBR*].

55. Affidavit of Dr. Michael W. Fox, Joint Appendix at 82, ibid.

56. *See* Caroline Fraser, "The Raid at Silver Spring," *New Yorker,* April 19, 1993, at 66, 74 (speculating that members of the Animal Liberation Front, an underground organization dedicated to the liberation of animals used in laboratory research, may have been responsible for the monkeys' disappearance).

57. *Taub v. State,* 463 A.2d 819 (Md. 1983). The court noted that the issue had been raised in oral argument before the court for the first time. *See* ibid., at 820. It is, however, unusual for a court to entertain an argument for the first time at oral argument when that argument was not raised in writing for review by the court and was raised only in rebuttal by the opposing party.

58. Ibid., at 821.

59. 1983 Md. Laws 82 (codified at Md. Ann. Code art. 27, § 59 [1992]) ("It is the intention of the General Assembly that all animals, whether they be privately owned, strays, domesticated, feral, farm, corporately or institutionally owned, under private, local, state, or federally funded scientific or medical activities . . . shall be protected from intentional cruelty").

60. Civil Action No. 81–2691, filed in the United States District Court for the District of Columbia. There are no reported decisions in this case.

61. Civil Action No. 81–2977, filed in the United States District Court for the District of Columbia. There are no reported decisions in this case.

62. *See* Guillermo, *Monkey Business,* at 143. I represented PETA in efforts to negotiate relinquishment of the monkeys by IBR.

63. *IBR,* 799 F.2d 934 (4th Cir. 1986), *cert. denied,* 481 U.S. 1004 (1987).

64. *IBR,* 799 F.2d at 938. The Supreme Court also rejected plaintiffs' argument that they were entitled to ensure that NIH as a federal agency, and IBR as a recipient of federal funds, respected federal law. Ibid., at 937–38 (citing *United States v. Richardson,* 418 U.S. 166, 174–75 [1974]).

65. *IBR,* 799 F.2d at 938.

66. Ibid.

67. *Animal Lovers Volunteer Ass'n, Inc. v. Weinberger,* 765 F.2d 937, 939 (9th Cir. 1985).

68. *IBR,* 799 F.2d at 938.

69. *See Animal Lovers,* 765 F.2d at 939. ("To have standing, a party must demonstrate an interest that is distinct from the public at large. ALVA lacks the longevity and indicia of commitment to preventing inhumane behavior . . . which might provide standing to other better known organizations" [citation omitted].)

70. *See Animal Lovers,* 765 F.2d at 939 ("The fact that Fund for Animals was allowed to proceed with two earlier lawsuits demonstrates that a right of action may exist to prevent the Navy from engaging in certain practices, if illegal, even on its own property").

71. *See International Primate Protection League v. Administrators of the Tulane Educ. Fund,* 895 F.2d 1056 (5th Cir. 1990), *rev'd,* 500 U.S. 72 (1991) [hereinafter *Tulane*].

72. *Tulane,* 895 F.2d at 1058.

73. *See* Guillermo, *Monkey Business,* at 165–66.

74. *Tulane,* 895 F.2d at 1058.

75. Ibid., at 1060–61.

76. Ibid., at 1059.

77. Ibid., (emphasis added).

78. Ibid., at 1059–60. *See Humane Soc'y v. Lyng,* 633 F. Supp. 480 (W.D.N.Y. 1986). For further reading concerning the standing issue in the Fourth Circuit and Fifth Circuit cases, see Ruth R. Hamilton, Casenote, "Of Monkeys and Men—Article III Standing Requirements in Animal Biomedical Research Cases," 24 *Creighton L. Rev.* 1515 (1991); A. Camile Holton, Note, "*International Primate Protection League v. Institute for Behavioral Research:* The Standing of Animal Protection Organizations Under the Animal Welfare Act," 4 *J. Contemp. Health L. & Pol'y* 469 (1988); Bridget Klauber, Casenote, "See No Evil, Hear No Evil: The Federal Courts and the Silver Spring Monkeys," 63 *U. Colo. L. Rev.* 501 (1992); Marci Messett, Note, "They Asked for Protection and They Got Policy: *International Primate's* Mutilated Monkeys," 21 *Akron L. Rev.* 97 (1987). *See also* Larry

Falkin, Comment, "*Taub v. State:* Are State Anti-Cruelty Statutes Sleeping Giants?" 2 *Pace Envtl. L. Rev.* 255 (1985).

79. *See Sierra Club,* 405 U.S. at 739 (1972).

80. Accordingly, the redressability issue was satisfied. It could be argued that Pacheco was not an object of the regulatory scheme involved in the Animal Welfare Act but was, at most, merely a beneficiary. *See* Sunstein, "What's Standing After *Lujan?*" at 183–86. If, however, that distinction is applied to other cases, many plaintiffs who were granted standing in the past would no longer have standing.

81. *See Sierra Club,* 405 U.S. at 733, 739.

82. *See supra* notes 45–46 and accompanying text.

83. *See* Sunstein, "What's Standing After *Lujan?*" at 188–89.

84. Ibid.

85. *See* ibid., at 189 (citing *Allen v. Wright,* 468 U.S. 737, 755–56 (1984).

86. *IBR,* 799 F.2d at 939–40.

87. *Linda R. S. v. Richard D.,* 410 U.S. 614, 617 n. 3 (1973). *See also Warth v. Seldin,* 422 U.S. 490, 500 (1975); *Trafficante v. Metropolitan Life Ins. Co.,* 409 U.S. 205, 206–12 (1972).

88. *Transamerica Mortgage Advisors, Inc. v. Lewis,* 444 U.S. 11, 15 (1979) (citations omitted).

89. *See* Sunstein, "What's Standing After *Lujan?*" at 180–81.

90. *IBR,* 799 F.2d at 939.

91. Ibid. (quoting the federal Animal Welfare Act, 7 U.S.C. § 2143).

92. *IBR,* 799 F.2d at 939.

93. Ibid. (quoting H.R. Rep. No. 91–1651, 91st Cong., 2d Sess. [1970], *reprinted in* 1970 U.S.C.C.A.N. 5103, 5104).

94. *Animal Legal Defense Fund v. Yeutter,* 760 F. Supp. 923 (D.D.C. 1991), *vacated sub nom. Animal Legal Defense Fund, Inc. v. Espy,* 23 F.3d 496 (D.C. Cir. 1994) [hereinafter *Yeutter*].

95. Ibid., at 925 n. 4.

96. Ibid., at 926–27 (citing *Havens Realty Corp. v. Coleman,* 455 U.S. 363 [1982]). *See also Trafficante v. Metropolitan Life Ins. Co.,* 409 U.S. 205 (1972). In *Trafficante,* plaintiffs argued that their landlord's racially discriminatory renting practices deprived them of the benefits of interracial association. The Court allowed standing. *Trafficante,* 409 U.S. at 212.

97. *Havens,* 455 U.S. at 373.

98. *Yeutter,* 760 F. Supp. at 928. The "zone-of-interests" test is not a constitutionally mandated test; rather, it refers to "prudential" standing considerations. *See supra* notes 9 and 10.

99. *Animal Legal Defense Fund v. Secretary of Agric.,* 813 F. Supp. 882 (D.D.C. 1993), *vacated sub nom. Animal Legal Defense Fund, Inc. v. Espy,* 29 F.3d 720 (D.C. Cir. 1994) [hereinafter *Secretary*].

100. Endangered Species Act of 1973, Pub. L. No. 93–205, 87 Stat. 884 (1973) (codified as amended at 16 U.S.C. 1531–1544 [1988 & Supp. IV 1992]).

101. *Lujan,* 112 S. Ct. at 2137–40. A plurality of the Court also held that any injury would not necessarily be redressed by enforcement of the consultation provision. Ibid., at 2140–42.

102. Ibid., at 2138.

103. The Court was concerned about separation of powers. According to Justice Scalia, who wrote for the majority, Congress and the chief executive are to vindicate the public interest. "To permit Congress to convert the undifferentiated public interest in executive officers' compliance with the law into an 'individual right' vindicable in the courts is to permit Congress to transfer from the President to the courts the Chief Executive's most important constitutional duty, to 'take Care that the Laws be faithfully executed,' Art. II, § 3." Ibid., at 2145.

104. *See, e.g., Evans v. Lynn,* 537 F.2d 571, 578–79 (2d Cir. 1976), *cert. denied,* 429 U.S. 1066 (1977); *Friends of the Earth v. Carey,* 535 F.2d 165, 172–74 (2d Cir. 1976); *Natural Resources Defense Council, Inc. v. Train,* 510 F.2d 692 (D.C. Cir. 1975).

105. In *Yeutter* the trial court held that plaintiffs had standing to sue. In addition, the lower court had decided in favor of plaintiffs on the merits (i.e., that the USDA had wrongly failed to include rats, mice, and birds) in *Animal Legal Defense Fund v. Madigan,* 781 F. Supp. 797 (D.D.C. 1992). The appellate decision vacating the lower court on standing and on the merits is reported at *Animal Legal Defense Fund, Inc. v. Espy,* 23 F.3d 496 (D.C. Cir. 1994).

106. *Secretary* was similarly recaptioned as *Animal Legal Defense Fund, Inc. v. Espy.* The appellate decision, which vacated the lower court, is reported at 29 F.3d 720 (D.C. Cir. 1994).

107. In both *Yeutter* and *Secretary,* there was another plaintiff—a member of ALDF who sat on an animal care committee at an institution that used animals in experiments. In both cases, the court rejected any claim of standing by this individual, who, according to the court, was simply trying to enforce the AWA in the absence of any injury.

108. In 1988 I testified before Congress on the constitutionality of the proposed standing legislation. My analysis, which concluded that the proposed legislation was not in conflict with any constitutional standing requirements, was based on *Havens. See Animal Welfare Act, Hearings on H.R. 1770 Before the Subcomm. on Admin. Law & Governmental Relations of the Comm. on the Judiciary,* 100th Cong., 2d Sess. (1988), 24–25 (Statement of Gary L. Francione).

109. Professor Sunstein maintains that the use of the word "standing" in this context did not appear until fairly recently. Sunstein, "What's Standing After *Lujan*?" at 169.

110. Ibid., at 185, 186. The case to which Sunstein is referring is *Association of Data Processing Serv. Orgs., Inc. v. Camp,* 397 U.S. 150 (1970).

111. *See generally* Antonin Scalia, "The Doctrine of Standing as an Essential Element of the Separation of Powers," 17 *Suffolk U. L. Rev.* 881 (1983).

112. *Lujan,* 112 S. Ct. at 2137 (emphasis added).

113. Sunstein, "What's Standing After *Lujan*?" at 188.

114. *Animal Welfare Inst. v. Kreps,* 561 F.2d 1002, 1007 (D.C. Cir. 1977), *cert. denied,* 434 U.S. 1013 (1978).

115. *See generally* Falkin, "Are State Anti-Cruelty Statutes Sleeping Giants?"

116. Guillermo, *Monkey Business,* at 143 (quoting a letter from William Raub of the NIH to Joseph Vasapoli, chief executive officer of IBR).

117. *Tulane,* 895 F.2d at 1058.

118. Ibid., at 1058–62.

119. *International Primate Protection League v. Administrators of the Tulane Educ. Fund,* 500 U.S. 72 (1991).

120. *In re Administrators of the Tulane Educ. Fund,* 954 F.2d 266, 269 (5th Cir. 1992).

## Chapter Five

1. Waldron prefers to consider such restrictions as "background constraints." *See* Jeremy Waldron, *The Right to Private Property* (Oxford: Clarendon Press, 1988), 49.

2. C. Reinold Noyes, *The Institution of Property* (New York: Longmans, Green & Co., 1936), 290 n. 13 (quoting *Restatement of the Law of Property* [St. Paul, Minn.: American Law Institute, 1936]).

3. Waldron, *Right to Private Property,* at 27 (footnote omitted). It should be noted that although these statements by Noyes and Waldron are generally correct, "persons" can include nonnatural persons, such as corporations. Moreover, as Professor Raz notes, persons (whether natural or non-natural) can have relations with objects, such as corporate shares. *See* Joseph Raz, *The Concept of a Legal System,* 2d ed. (Oxford: Clarendon Press, 1980), 176.

4. Emily S. Leavitt and Diane Halverson, "The Evolution of Anticruelty Laws in the United States," in *Animals and Their Legal Rights,* 4th ed. (Washington, D.C.: Animal Welfare Institute, 1990), 1.

5. *See* Tufts University School of Veterinary Medicine, Center for Animals and Public Policy, "Animal Rights Versus Animal Welfare: A False Dichotomy?" *Animal Policy Report,* April 1993, at 1, 2.

6. E. P. Evans, *The Criminal Prosecution and Capital Punishment of Animals* (New York: E. P. Dutton, 1906), 313–34.

7. Ibid. It should be noted that there is evidence of animal trials in ancient Greece, although little is known of these trials. *See* Walter W. Hyde, "The Prosecution and Punishment of Animals and Lifeless Things in the Middle Ages and Modern Times," 64 *U. Pa. L. Rev.* 696, 696–700 (1916).

8. Hyde, "Prosecution of Animals and Lifeless Things," at 708.

9. Ibid., at 710.

10. Ibid., at 698.

11. Hyde states that before animal trials were instituted, an animal that did serious damage had to be given up to the injured party "only for the sake of retaliation." Ibid., at 701.

12. Ibid., at 717.

13. Ibid., at 719. It should be noted that the other primary legal scholar in this area, E. P. Evans, takes issue with this personification theory. He argues that although such personification notions may explain attributing personality to ships, it cannot account for the animal trials and excommunications. Evans, *Criminal Prosecution of Animals,* at 10–12.

14. Hyde, "Prosecution of Animals and Lifeless Things," at 723.

15. *See* N.J. Stat. Ann. § 4:19–17 et seq. (West Supp. 1993). *See also* Malcolm Gladwell, "Death Row Dog Gets New Leash on Life," *Wash. Post,* January 29, 1994, at G1.

16. *See* N.J. Const. art. 5, § 2, ¶ 1.

17. The Rutgers Animal Rights Law Center represented Taro's human companions in negotiations with Governor Whitman.

18. *See* Gary L. Francione, "Personhood, Property, and Legal Competence," in *The Great Ape Project,* ed. Paola Cavalieri and Peter Singer (New York: St. Martin's Press, 1993), 248, 254–56.

19. H.L.A. Hart, *The Concept of Law* (Oxford: Clarendon Press, 1961).

20. Wesley N. Hohfeld, *Fundamental Legal Conceptions,* ed. Walter W. Cook (New Haven: Yale University Press, 1923), 36.

21. Ibid., at 38.

22. Ibid., at 39; *see generally* 38–50.

23. Ibid., at 39.

24. Ibid., at 50–51.

25. *See* ibid., at 50–60.

26. Ibid., at 60; *see generally* 60–64.

27. For an excellent discussion of Hohfeld's framework, see Joel Feinberg, *Social Philosophy* (Englewood Cliffs, N.J.: Prentice-Hall, 1973). *See also* L. W. Sumner, *The Moral Foundation of Rights* (Oxford: Clarendon Press, 1987), 14–53.

28. *See* Joel Feinberg, *Rights, Justice, and the Bounds of Liberty* (Princeton, N.J.: Princeton University Press, 1980). *See also* Vinit Haksar, "The Nature of Rights," 64 *Archiv für Rechts- und Sozialphilosophie* 183 (1978).

29. *See* Hohfeld, *Fundamental Legal Conceptions,* at 39.

30. Sumner, *Moral Foundation of Rights,* at 46.

31. Waldron, *Right to Private Property,* at 96–97.

32. Carl Cohen, "The Case for the Use of Animals in Biomedical Research," 315 *New Eng. J. Med.* 865, 866 (1986).

33. Ibid., at 866.

34. *See* H.L.A. Hart, "Bentham on Legal Rights," in *Oxford Essays in Jurisprudence,* 2d ser. ed. A.W.B. Simpson (Oxford: Clarendon Press, 1973), 171, 183–201; Neil Mac-Cormick, "Rights in Legislation," in *Law, Morality, and Society,* ed. P.M.S. Hacker and Joseph Raz (Oxford: Clarendon Press, 1977), 189; Joseph Raz, "Right-Based Moralities," in *Theories of Rights,* ed. Jeremy Waldron (Oxford: Oxford University Press, 1984), 182.

35. Waldron, *Right to Private Property,* at 81.

36. MacCormick, "Rights in Legislation," at 204–5.

37. David Lyons, "Rights, Claimants, and Beneficiaries," 6 *Am. Phil. Q.* 173, 176 (1969).

38. R. G. Frey, *Interests and Rights: The Case Against Animals* (Oxford: Clarendon Press, 1980), 79.

39. Ibid., at 82.

40. Frey explicity adopts Quine's method for eliminating propositions in belief contexts in favor of sentences. *See* Willard V. Quine, *Word and Object* (Cambridge: Technology Press of MIT, 1960). Frey states that in the sentence "John believes that the window is open," "believes" does not relate the name "John" to the proposition named by "that the window is open." Rather, "believes" is part of the operator "believes that," which, when applied to a sentence, " 'produces a composite absolute general term whereof the sentence is counted an immediate constituent.' " Frey, *Interests and Rights,* at 87–88 (quoting Quine, *Word and Object,* at 216). That is, "the window is open" is a sentence and not a name and, therefore, not the name of a proposition. Moreover, Frey argues that it is not necessary "to entertain the concept of a sentence in order to have beliefs." Frey, *Interests and Rights,* at 88.

41. Frey discusses the literature surrounding the supposed ability of animals to learn language and, relying on Chomsky's theory of linguistics, rejects the notion that animals have language capabilities. In sum, Chomsky argues that a normal human being, if provided with a finite set of lexical elements and a finite set of sentence-producing rules, can generate an indefinite number of sentences. Frey maintains that the most promising evidence to

date indicates that animals can only use the signs that they are taught, and have a limited ability to devise new variants of the signs that they have been taught. Frey, *Interests and Rights,* at 91–100.

42. Ibid., at 170.

43. R. G. Frey, "The Significance of Agency and Marginal Cases," 39 *Philosophica* 39 (1987).

44. *See* Tom Regan, *The Case for Animal Rights* (Berkeley and Los Angeles: University of California Press, 1983), 37–49; Bernard E. Rollin, *The Unheeded Cry* (Oxford: Oxford University Press, 1989), 136–40.

45. 9 C.F.R. 3.51(b) (1992).

46. Joseph Raz, "On the Nature of Rights," 93 *Mind* 194, 204 (1984).

47. Neil MacCormick, "Children's Rights: A Test Case," in *Legal Right and Social Democracy* (Oxford: Clarendon Press, 1982), 154, 159.

48. The Marxist would not be inclined to find that there were rights created as the result of this arrangement. But then, Marxists would not be inclined toward rights in the first place, given that Marx did not believe in human rights in light of their focus on the social status of individuals considered apart from the community.

49. MacCormick, "Children's Rights," at 159.

50. Waldron, *Right to Private Property,* at 79.

51. *See* Ronald Dworkin, "Rights as Trumps," in *Theories of Rights,* ed. Jeremy Waldron (Oxford: Oxford University Press, 1984), 153. *See generally* idem, *Taking Rights Seriously* (London: Duckworth, 1977).

52. It is precisely these sorts of considerations that may be used to flesh out MacCormick's theory of "ulterior ends." That is, occupational legislation may, in some sense (e.g., in Marxist theory), treat the worker as an "ulterior end" because the worker's "well-being" is sought only as aid to further exploitation by the employer. Nevertheless, the types of considerations discussed by Waldron and Dworkin do distinguish the example of the worker from the one involving animals. I do not, of course, expect that any Marxists will be convinced or satisfied by this observation.

53. Robert Nozick, *Anarchy, State, and Utopia* (New York: Basic Books, 1974), 29.

54. Ibid., at 30–31. It must be noted that Nozick has a theory of rights that is rejected by many other philosophers. For example, Waldron rejects Nozick's theory, in part because the latter excludes rights "that cannot be stated in negative terms (negative in the sense that they are nothing but rights that certain actions should not be performed)." Waldron, *Right to Private Property,* at 74–75.

55. Nozick, *Anarchy, State, and Utopia,* at 35.

56. Ibid., at 39.

57. Ibid., at 40–41.

58. Ibid., at 41.

59. Ibid., at 42.

60. Ibid., at 41.

61. There are, of course, many types of utilitarian theories. *See generally* Amartya Sen and Bernard Williams, eds., *Utilitarianism and Beyond* (Cambridge: Cambridge University Press, 1982).

62. *See* Tom Regan, "The Case for Animal Rights," in *In Defense of Animals,* ed. Peter Singer (New York: Basil Blackwell, 1985), 13, 18–21.

63. Jeffrie G. Murphy and Jules L. Coleman, *The Philosophy of Law* (Totowa, N.J.: Rowman & Littlefield, 1984), 91.

64. Ronald Dworkin, *Taking Rights Seriously,* at 171–83.

65. *See* David Lyons, "Utility and Rights," in 24 *Nomos: Ethics, Economics, and the Law,* ed. J. Roland Pennock and John W. Chapman (New York: New York University Press, 1982), 107. For a response to Lyon's views, see Kent Greenawalt, *Utilitarian Justifications for Observance of Rights,*" in ibid., at 139; R. M. Hare, "Utility and Rights: Comment on David Lyon's Essay," in ibid., at 148.

66. Even Locke would have to concede that the right of private property could not be unconditional in that, for example, the state should be able to requisition food in a famine. *See* Gregory Vlastos, "Justice and Equality," in *Theories of Rights,* ed. Waldron, at 41, 46–47.

67. *See generally* Andrew Fede, *People Without Rights* (New York: Garland Publishing, 1992); A. Leon Higginbotham, Jr., *In the Matter of Color* (New York: Oxford University Press, 1978); Robert B. Shaw, *A Legal History of Slavery in the United States* (Potsdam, N.Y.: Northern Press, 1991); Alan Watson, *Slave Law in the Americas* (Athens: University of Georgia Press, 1989).

68. Daniel J. Flanigan, "Criminal Procedure in Slave Trials in the Antebellum South," in *The Law of American Slavery,* ed. Kermit L. Hall (New York: Garland Publishing, 1987), 191, at 191.

69. Watson, *Slave Law in the Americas,* at 72.

70. *Creswell's Executor v. Walker,* 37 Ala. 229, 236 (1861).

71. Stanley Elkins and Eric McKitrick, "Institutions and the Law of Slavery: Slavery in Capitalist and Non-Capitalist Cultures," in *Law of American Slavery,* ed. Hall, 111, at 155 (quoting William Goodell, *The American Slave Code in Theory and Practice* [New York, 1853], 180).

72. *State v. Mann,* 13 N.C. (2 Dev.) 263 (1829).

73. Ibid., at 267.

74. *Commonwealth v. Turner,* 26 Va. (5 Rand.) 678, 678 (1827).

75. Ibid., at 680.

76. Elkins and McKitrick, "Institutions and the Law of Slavery," at 115 (quoting Thomas R. R. Cobb, *An Inquiry into the Law of Slavery in the United States of America* [Philadelphia, 1858], 98).

77. Higginbotham, *In the Matter of Color,* at 36 (quoting 2 William W. Hening, *Statutes at Large of Virginia* [Richmond, Va.: Franklin Press, 1819–20], 279). *See generally* Fede, *People Without Rights.*

78. Watson, *Slave Law in the Americas,* at xiv.

79. Ibid., at 31 (quoting Justinian's *Institutes,* J.I.8.I.).

80. *State v. Hale,* 9 N.C. (2 Hawks.) 582, 585 (1823).

81. Ibid., at 585–86.

82. David B. Davis, *The Problem of Slavery in Western Culture* (New York: Oxford University Press, 1966), 58.

83. Watson, *Slave Law in the Americas,* at 32.

84. This position is also adopted in "Animal Rights Versus Animal Welfare: A False Dichotomy?" *Animal Policy Report,* April 1993, at 2, published by the Tufts University School of Veterinary Medicine Center for Animals and Public Policy.

85. J.J.C. Smart, "An Outline of a System of Utilitarian Ethics," in J.J.C. Smart and Bernard Williams, *Utilitarianism: For and Against,* (Cambridge: Cambridge University Press, 1973), 3, at 9. Some utilitarians focus on quality of character rather than particular acts or general rules.

86. For a general discussion of act- and rule-utilitarianism, see William K. Frankena, *Ethics,* 2d ed. (Englewood Cliffs, N.J.: Prentice-Hall, 1973), 34–60. *See also* Sen and Williams, eds., *Utilitarianism and Beyond.* Some theorists argue that the distinction between act- and rule-utilitarianism collapses. *See* David Lyons, *Forms and Limits of Utilitarianism* (Oxford: Clarendon Press, 1965); R. M. Hare, *Freedom and Reason* (Oxford: Oxford University Press, 1963).

87. L. W. Sumner, "Animal Welfare and Animal Rights," 13 *J. Med. & Phil.* 159, 168 (1988).

88. Ibid.

89. *See* Lyons, *Forms and Limits of Utilitarianism,* at 57–62.

## Chapter Six

1. I stress at the outset of this discussion that I do not intend to provide any sort of comprehensive discussion or analysis of the over one thousand cases I reviewed involving the interpretation of anticruelty statutes. Rather, the purpose of the discussion is to provide a theory based on cases that are representative. Moreover, in discussing any particular case or statute, I do not intend to represent that the current law of the jurisdiction is as reflected in that case or statute. In addition, I do not examine what might be called "federal anticruelty laws," such as the federal laws concerning humane slaughter or the transportation of animals in interstate commerce. For a description of these laws, see generally *Animals and Their Legal Rights,* 4th ed. (Washington, D.C.: Animal Welfare Institute, 1990). Finally, the reader should be aware that the cases discussed in this chapter are, by and large, appellate opinions that review convictions or acquittals that occurred in lower courts. There is little reliable empirical evidence available about the numbers of cases that are not investigated by law enforcement personnel, that are not prosecuted by officials, or that are not appealed in the case of a pretrial, trial, or post-trial decision in favor of the defendant. Also, many anticruelty cases are tried in courts of very limited jurisdiction, such as justice-of-the-peace courts. These decisions are usually not reported unless the cases proceed to higher levels of appellate review.

2. *Jett v. Municipal Court,* 223 Cal. Rptr. 111 (Ct. App. 1986).

3. Ibid., at 112.

4. Jett was acquitted of a third count charging violation of a local ordinance prohibiting animal cruelty. Ibid.

5. Ibid., at 113. Jett could not appeal that portion of the court's order that denied return of Rocky, so he pursued a mandamus action or civil action seeking return of Rocky. Ibid.

6. Ibid., at 115. The court held that if the animal is a fighting animal, an officer may—or, in the case of fighting dogs, shall—take possession of the animal, and a court may subsequently order forfeiture. Ibid., at 114. The court also held that in other provisions of the anticruelty law, animals seized were subject to a lien, but that the law contemplated a return of the animals upon satisfaction of the lien. Ibid., at 113–14.

The California anticruelty statute was amended in 1986 to provide that upon a conviction of a person charged with violating section 597, one of the statutes that Jett was charged with violating, all animals lawfully seized and impounded shall be "awarded to the impounding officer for proper disposition."

7. Ibid., at 115.

8. In an apparent attempt to display its erudition and to amuse itself, the court quoted

the play *Romeo and Juliet* to show that Shakespeare thought that tortoises were fishes. Unfortunately, the court misinterpreted Shakespeare. *See* ibid.

9. Ibid. (emphasis added).

10. California has recently increased penalties for violations of its anticruelty laws. There is no indication, however, that courts are imposing the more severe penalties.

11. According to one court, "if cruelty to animals was a criminal offense at common law, which some writers deny, it was superseded so entirely in England by statutes as to pass out of view." *State v. Prater,* 109 S.W. 1047, 1049 (Mo. Ct. App. 1908).

12. *See* John H. Ingham, *The Law of Animals* (Philadelphia: T. & J. W. Johnson, 1900), 545–56. *See also State v. Pierce,* 7 Ala. 728, 731 (1845); *Chappell v. State,* 35 Ark. 345, 346 (1880); *Brown v. State,* 26 Ohio 176, 182–83 (1875); *Wallace v. State,* 30 Tex. 758, 759 (1868).

13. *See, e.g., Chappel v. State,* 35 Ark. 345, 346 (1880).

14. *See, e.g., Wallace v. State,* 30 Tex. 758, 759 (1868) (holding that if the act is willfully done, the law presumes that it was done with intent as to the consequences of the act, which would necessarily result in an injury to the owner). *See also Hill v. State,* 43 Ala. 335, 338 (1869); *Chappel v. State,* 35 Ark. 345, 347 (1880); *Brown v. State,* 26 Ohio 176, 184 (1875).

15. *Stage Horse Cases,* 15 Abb. Pr. (n.s.) 51, 63 (N.Y. Comm. Pl. 1873).

16. A number of cases hold that various animals are not "animals" under the statute. *See, e.g., State v. Stockton,* 333 P.2d 735, 736 (Ariz. 1958) (gamecocks are not "animals" under anticruelty statutes); *State v. Claiborne,* 505 P.2d 732, 735 (Kan. 1973) (same); *Commonwealth v. Massini,* 188 A.2d 816, 818–19 (Pa. Super. Ct. 1963) (a cat is not a "domestic animal" for the purposes of the statute prohibiting poisoning of domestic animals); *Commonwealth v. Mainero,* 21 Pa. D. & C.2d 239, 240–41 (Luzerne Co. Ct. 1960) (a dog is not a "domestic animal" within the meaning of statute).

17. For example, New York provides that animal cruelty includes depriving "any animal of necessary sustenance, food or drink, or neglect[ing] to furnish it such sustenance or drink." N.Y. Agric. & Mkts. Law § 353 (McKinney 1991). The statute also provides that anyone having impounded or confined an animal must provide it with a supply of "wholesome air, food, shelter, and water." Ibid., § 356.

18. *See, e.g.,* N.C. Gen. Stat. § 14–360 (1993).

19. *See, e.g.,* Del. Code Ann. tit. 11, § 1325 (1987).

20. *See, e.g.,* Mont. Code Ann. § 45-8-211(1) (d) (1993).

21. *See, e.g.,* Haw. Rev. Stat. § 711-1109(1) (b) (1988).

22. *See, e.g.,* S.D. Codified Laws Ann. § 40-1-2.3 (1991).

23. *See, e.g.,* 13 Vt. Stat. Ann. tit. 13, § 352(a) (4), (10) (Supp. 1992).

24. *See* Ala. Code § 13A-11-14 (1975).

25. Cal. Penal Code § 597(a) (West Supp. 1993). The definition of animal as "every dumb creature" is found in ibid., § 599b (West 1988).

26. Cal. Penal Code § 597(b) (West Supp. 1993).

27. Ibid., § 599b (West 1988).

28. Del. Code Ann. tit. 11, § 1325(a) (11) (1987).

29. Ibid., § 1325(b) (Supp. 1992).

30. Ibid., § 1325(a) (1) (1987).

31. Ibid., § 1325(a) (4).

32. N.Y. Agric. & Mkts. Law § 353 (McKinney 1991).

33. Ibid., § 355.

34. Ibid., § 356.

35. Ibid., § 350(2).

36. It should be understood, however, that even if a law imposes a direct duty owed to an animal, the direct duty does not necessarily have anything to do with the animal's welfare and may pertain primarily to facilitating exploitation of the animal. For example, if I work at MacCormick's turkey farm, I may be said to have an indirect duty (imposed by an anticruelty statute) to the turkeys to feed them. Just as it would be bizarre to label this a situation in which the turkey has rights, it is similarly bizarre to view this direct duty as serving the welfare of the turkey or doing anything other than facilitating its exploitation. In addition, the content of the duty, whether direct or indirect, imposed by an anticruelty statute, is to treat animals "humanely."

37. *Hunt v. State*, 29 N.E. 933, 933 (Ind. Ct. App. 1892).

38. *Grise v. State*, 37 Ark. 456, 458 (1881). The court also stated that the anticruelty laws "may be found useful in elevating humanity, by enlargement of its sympathy with all God's creatures, and thus society may be improved." Ibid., at 459.

39. Similarly, if this direct duty results in the animal having a "right," this means only that the animal has a right to humane treatment.

40. *E.g., Oglesby v. State*, 37 S.E.2d 837, 838 (Ga. App. 1946). Most cases that talk in terms of animal protection as a goal of these statutes recognize this interest in the context of distinguishing anticruelty statutes from malicious mischief statutes, which focused more on the status of the animal as property. *See, e.g., State v. Prater*, 109 S.W. 1047, 1049 (Mo. Ct. App. 1908). (Malicious mischief statutes were "intended to protect the beasts as property instead of as creatures susceptible of suffering." Anticruelty statutes are "designed for the protection of animals.")

41. *See, e.g., Waters v. People*, 46 P. 112, 113 (Colo. 1896).

42. *Model Penal Code* (Philadelphia: American Law Institute, 1980), § 250.11 cmt. 1.

43. *Stephens v. State*, 3 So. 458, 459 (Miss. 1887). In *Stephens*, the court also stated that the statute was intended "for the benefit of animals, as creatures capable of feeling and suffering, and it was intended to protect them from cruelty, without reference to their being property." Ibid., at 458.

44. *Bland v. People*, 76 P. 359, 361 (Colo. 1904). The law was subsequently declared unconstitutional in *Stubbs v. People*, 90 P. 1114 (Colo. 1907), because of an amendment that allowed some uses of horses with docked tails. The *Stubbs* court held that irrespective of the validity of *Bland* when that case was decided, the exceptions to the prohibition that the amendment permitted were as likely to corrupt public morals as were those uses that remained prohibited, and the law could no longer be viewed as rationally related to the state's police power.

45. *Commonwealth v. Higgins*, 178 N.E. 536, 538 (Mass. 1931).

46. *Miller v. State*, 63 S.E. 571 (Ga. Ct. App. 1909).

47. Ibid., at 573.

48. *Knox v. Massachusetts S.P.C.A.*, 425 N.E.2d 393 (Mass. App. Ct. 1981).

49. *Peck v. Dunn*, 574 P.2d 367 (Utah), *cert. denied*, 436 U.S. 927 (1978).

50. Ibid., at 369.

51. *C. E. America, Inc. v. Antinori*, 210 So.2d 443 (Fla. 1968).

52. Ibid., at 446.

53. *Brackett v. State*, 236 S.E.2d 689, 690 (Ga. Ct. App. 1977).

54. *See People v. Iehl*, 299 N.W.2d 46, 48 (Mich. Ct. App. 1980).

55. *Grise v. State*, 37 Ark. 456, 459 (1881).

56. Ingham, *Law of Animals,* at 529.

57. *State v. Avery,* 44 N.H. 392, 397 (1862).

58. *People ex rel. Walker v. Court,* 4 N.Y. Sup. Ct. 441, 445 (App. Div. 1875). *Tinsley v. State,* 22 S.W. 39 (Tex. Crim. App. 1893), indicates how extreme discipline must be before a person runs afoul of the anticruelty statute. Tinsley was riding a horse who " 'shied' a little" when "some negroes undertook to place a hog on [the horse] at defendant's [insistence]." Tinsley then beat the horse "using all the power he possessed in dealing the blows," and the horse, in an effort to escape, jumped through a barbed-wire fence. Ibid., at 40. The court held that the beating went beyond what is allowed for discipline purposes, and constituted cruelty.

59. *Miller,* 63 S.E. at 571.

60. Ibid., at 573.

61. The primary exception to the use of deadly physical force to protect property concerns the use of force to protect the home. Although the common-law formulation of this privilege permitted deadly physical force to be used whenever a person reasonably believed that another intended to enter the former's dwelling imminently and unlawfully and that such force was necessary to prevent the intrusion, the scope of the privilege has been narrowed in most American jurisdictions. *See* Joshua Dressler, *Understanding Criminal Law* (New York: Matthew Bender & Co., 1987), 224–29.

62. *State v. Jones,* 625 P.2d 503, 503 (Kan. 1981) (quoting Kan. Stat. Ann. 21–4310 [Supp. 1979]).

63. *Jones,* 625 P.2d at 505. In addition to being charged for violating the anticruelty statute, Jones was charged with injuring a domestic animal belonging to another without the owner's consent. The court held that the statutory exception for protecting property did not apply to this second violation, although the state was required to prove that Jones acted maliciously, and "by way of defense, the accused may contend that the killing was justified under the circumstances, and that it was necessary to protect his livestock, his property, or someone's life." Ibid., at 504–5.

64. *Hunt v. State,* 29 N.E. 933 (Ind. Ct. App. 1892).

65. Ibid., at 933.

66. *People v. Jones,* 89 N.E. 752 (Ill. 1909).

67. *Hodge v. State,* 79 Tenn. 528 (1883).

68. Ibid., at 531–32.

69. *See* Dressler, *Understanding Criminal Law,* at 224–29. Many cases deal with the killing of animals to protect property, and these cases reflect four different approaches. Some courts hold that in order for the killing of an animal to be justified as a defense of person or property, the attack must be imminent. *See, e.g., Readd v. State,* 296 S.E.2d 402, 403 (Ga. Ct. App. 1982); *State v. Simmons,* 244 S.E.2d 168, 169–70 (N.C. Ct. App. 1978). Other courts hold that the defendant must have reasonably believed that the animal was going to commit an act harmful to persons or property. *See, e.g., Hunt v. State,* 29 N.E. 933, 933 (Ind. Ct. App. 1892). In some cases, courts have held that where there is a sincere belief (even if unreasonable or mistaken) that the use of force is necessary to protect person or property, there can be no liability under the anticruelty statute; these are generally cases in which the state must prove that a defendant intended to act in a cruel manner and in which an intent to protect property, however unreasonable or mistaken, would not constitute the requisite cruel intent. *See, e.g., Stephens v. State,* 3 So. 458, 458 (Miss. 1887). Some courts have held that in protecting person or property, one may only use the amount of force that is necessary and may not use deadly physical force unless killing is necessary to protect the prop-

erty or person, and that the primary remedy available to the property owner is to drive off or impound the offending animals and sue for damages. *See, e.g., People v. Dunn,* 114 Cal. Rptr. 164, 165 (Ct. App. 1974). Courts that have adopted this fourth standard, which is ostensibly more protective of animals, have sometimes determined that deadly physical force is necessary under circumstances that strain credulity. *See, e.g., Hodge v. State,* 79 Tenn. 528 (1883).

In many cases, the property threatened by animals consists of other animals. Although it may seem that a standard that allows the killing of animals to protect other animals really expresses a moral preference for the "attacked" animal, the standard applies even if the property is inanimate. *See, e.g., State v. Jones,* 625 P.2d 503 (Kan. 1981).

70. In the case of slavery, the presumption, explicit and formally legal, had to be rebutted by the prosecution. In the case of animals, the "presumption" is not formal or legal but serves more informally as an aid to interpretation of the defendant's actions with respect to the mental element required for the crime. That is, if the anticruelty law requires that a defendant act with willful neglect or cruel wantonness, the defendant's ownership of the animals may suggest that defendant did not act with the required mental state, in part because defendant would not act with willful neglect or cruel wantonness toward her own property.

71. *Callaghan v. Society for the Prevention of Cruelty to Animals,* 16 L.R. Ir. 325, 355 (C.P.D. 1885) (Murphy, J.).

72. *Commonwealth v. Barr,* 44 Pa. C. 284 (Lancaster County Ct. 1916).

73. Ibid., at 288.

74. *Commonwealth v. Vonderheid,* 28 Pa. D. & C.2d 101 (Columbia County Ct. 1962).

75. Ibid., at 106. The court stated that "because of the importance of this case, and the wide divergence of the respective contentions, the court made a personal visit to these winter quarters without any previous notice . . . and upon personal inspection" found the premises to be acceptable. Ibid., at 104. By "wide divergence of opinion," the court was apparently referring to the contrasting opinions of the defendant and the cruelty officers. It is, however, slightly disingenuous (to say the least) for the court to discredit, based upon the court's own visit after the fact, the testimony of the humane officers as to the condition of the animals at the time they inspected, when it is common for defendants in cases like this to be more careful just in case the cruelty officers (or someone else, such as the court) comes to reinspect the premises.

76. Ibid., at 106. The mention of slavery by the court in this context is quite interesting for reasons that will be apparent to the reader. An additional point to be made about the court's analogy is that, for the most part, *all* slaves were expensive and, if the court's analysis were correct, the planter would value them all.

77. Ibid., at 107.

78. *State v. Smith,* 21 Tex. 748 (1858), *overruled in part by State v. Brocker,* 32 Tex. 611, 614 (1870). *Brocker* held that it was not necessary to designate the name of the owner for purposes of an indictment under a statute prohibiting willful and wanton killing. *Brocker,* 32 Tex. at 613.

79. *Smith,* 21 Tex. at 751. It should be noted that although the statute in the *Smith* case was a malicious mischief law, the statute proscribed cruelty to animals.

80. *See supra* notes 59–61 and accompanying text.

81. *Miller,* 63 S.E. at 573.

82. *Cinadr v. State,* 300 S.W. 64, 64–65 (Tex. Crim. App. 1927).

83. *State v. Wrobel,* 207 A.2d 280 (Conn. Cir. Ct. 1964).

84. Ibid., at 282.

85. Ibid., at 283 (quoting trial court's jury instruction).

86. Ibid., at 284.

87. Ibid., (citation omitted).

88. Ibid., at 284–85.

89. *See* Dressler, *Understanding Criminal Law,* at 191–201.

90. The law generally permits the use of deadly physical force in self-defense only if a person believes that such force is necessary to protect against death, serious bodily injury, forcible rape, or kidnapping. *See* Dressler, *Understanding Criminal Law,* at 210. In *State v. Spencer,* the court reversed a conviction for violating the anticruelty statute; the defendant, who had set steel traps to catch skunks, found a cat in a trap and killed the cat when the cat bit the defendant. The court held that "there was apparently no way to release the hold except by killing the cat." *State v. Spencer,* 29 A.2d 398, 401 (N.J. Spec. Stat. Trib. 1942). This conclusion about the necessity of killing the cat is dubious at best and reflects the notion that killing an animal may be justified even when the animal presents a relatively insignificant threat to a person.

91. *See supra* notes 64–69 and accompanying text.

## Chapter Seven

1. Literally, "guilty mind." In Anglo-American criminal law, it is thought that a crime generally requires two components: an *actus reus,* or "guilty act," and the *mens rea.*

2. For an excellent overview of the degree of intent required, *see* Sonja A. Soehnel, Annotation, "What Constitutes Offense of Cruelty to Animals—Modern Cases," 6 A.L.R. 5th 733 (1992).

3. This general assumption about strict liability is not quite accurate. As this chapter and the next show, even if there is no mental state specified in the statute, almost all statutes incorporate the notion that only "unnecessary" suffering is prohibited. This notion is frequently construed to require an inquiry into the actor's motivation. In many cases, courts have held that the "unnecessary" suffering must have been caused by something more than the actor's negligence.

4. For example, if a statute requires that a defendant act "willfully," that may mean that the defendant must act intentionally, or that she intend to do that which results in cruelty and not necessarily intend to injure the animal; or it may be interpreted to require that she act with an intent to do the culpable act, that is, that she intend to overdrive the horse and not that she intend to do that which constitutes overdriving.

5. *See, e.g., State v. Prater,* 109 S.W. 1047, 1050 (Mo. Ct. App. 1908) (defendant must act maliciously and cannot be guilty of violating the anticruelty statute even if an act that injured or killed an animal is unjustifiable).

6. *Regalado v. United States,* 572 A.2d 416 (D.C. 1990).

7. The "general intent" of a criminal offense "is the mental state provided in the definition of the offense that pertains to the conduct that constitutes the [act requirement] of the offense." Joshua Dressler, *Understanding Criminal Law* (New York: Matthew Bender & Co., 1987), 109. A specific-intent offense requires proof of an additional mental state besides the "general intent." Ibid. One example of a specific-intent offense is larceny, which is "the trespassory taking and carrying away of the personal property of another with the in-

tent to deprive the other of the property permanently." The act of taking away the victim's property "must be performed with a specific purpose—with the intent to deprive [the victim] of the property permanently. [The defendant] is not guilty of larceny if he has some other motive at the time he commits [the act]—even a bad motive such as the intent to keep the property temporarily." Ibid., at 110.

8. *Regalado,* 572 A.2d at 420.

9. Ibid., at 419 (quoting *Carson v. United States,* 556 A.2d 1076, 1078 [D.C. 1989] [quoting *Mullen v. United States,* 263 F.2d 275, 276 (D.C. Cir. 1958)]).

10. *Regalado,* 572 A.2d at 421. In a Michigan case, a court held that a "jury could properly infer wilful and malicious intent to kill, even when the defendant disclaims such intent, from evidence that he intentionally set in motion a force likely to cause death or grievous bodily harm—here kicking the dog." *People v. McKnight,* 302 N.W.2d 241, 243–44 (Mich. Ct. App. 1980).

11. For other cases involving maliciousness as the required state of mind, *see People v. Dunn,* 114 Cal. Rptr. 164 (Ct. App. 1974); *State v. Joy,* 819 P.2d 108 (Idaho Ct. App. 1991); *State v. Jones,* 625 P.2d 503 (Kan. 1981); *People v. Iehl,* 299 N.W.2d 46 (Mich. Ct. App. 1980).

12. *State v. Fowler,* 205 S.E.2d 749 (N.C. Ct. App. 1974).

13. Ibid., at 750–51.

14. Ibid., at 751. Other cases involving willful intent include *State v. Voelkel,* 202 A.2d 250 (Conn. Cir. Ct. 1964); *State v. Flynn,* 687 P.2d 596 (Idaho Ct. App. 1984); *State v. Price,* 772 S.W.2d 9 (Mo. Ct. App. 1989); *State v. Prater,* 109 S.W. 1047 (Mo. Ct. App. 1908). It is interesting to note that in *Voelkel* the court interpreted willfulness to mean "intent, that is, design, to cause harm, either actual or constructive." *Voelkel,* 202 A.2d at 254. That is, the court seemed to require that the state prove specific intent (intent to cause harm to the animal). If specific intent is required, then according to the court's analysis in *Regalado,* willfulness should impose a heavier burden on the prosecution than does showing that the defendant acted with malice. But at least one commenter on the subject of anticruelty statutes has argued that the malice standard is more onerous than the willfulness standard. *See* Soehnel, "What Constitutes Cruelty to Animals," 6 A.L.R.5th at 755–56. This disagreement is more indicative of the general confusion in the law concerning mental states than it is attributable to the correctness of one view or another.

For another case involving dog training, see *State v. Stanfield,* 314 N.W.2d 339 (Wis. 1982), *overruled on other grounds by State v. Poellinger,* 451 N.W.2d 752 (Wis. 1990). In *Stanfield,* where the defendant used sticks, chains, and cattle prods to train dogs, and where the dogs were returned to their owners in disabled or seriously deteriorated physical condition, the defendant's conviction for cruelty to animals was reinstated. The Wisconsin Supreme Court held that the jury was entitled to find that "the methods and devices advocated and used by Stanfield can easily cross over the line and become the means of animal abuse." *Stanfield,* 314 N.W.2d at 344. There is no doubt that the physical condition of the dogs determined the outcome of the case, and no suggestion that Stanfield's training was inherently improper.

15. *State v. Schott,* 384 N.W.2d 620 (Neb. 1986).

16. Ibid., at 624 (quoting Neb. Rev. Stat. § 28-109[19] [Reissue 1979]).

17. *Schott,* 384 N.W.2d at 623.

18. Sternal recumbancy occurs when the animal is so weakened as to be unable to bring the legs underneath the body, so that the knees of the animal are behind her. *See* ibid.

19. Ibid., at 624.

20. Ibid., at 624–26.

21. In 1990, Nebraska amended its anticruelty statute to include numerous exemptions—*see* Neb. Rev. Stat. § 28-1013 (Supp. 1992)—and to require that culpable actions be done intentionally or knowingly rather than intentionally and recklessly; *see* Neb. Rev. Stat. § 28-1008 (Supp. 1992).

22. *See, e.g.,* Utah Code Ann. § 76-9-301 (1) (Supp. 1993).

23. In *People v. Untiedt,* 116 Cal. Rptr. 899 (Ct. App. 1974), and in *People v. Farley,* 109 Cal. Rptr. 59 (App. Dep't Super. Ct. 1973), courts have held that mere negligence is enough, whereas in *People v. Brian,* 168 Cal. Rptr. 105 (App. Dep't Super. Ct. 1980), the court held that criminal negligence, amounting to reckless or gross departure from the ordinary standard of care, was required. The mental state of criminal negligence is similar to that of recklessness.

24. There is an additional mental state that requires that the activity be done "knowingly." This state of mind is most often relevant in cases involving attendance at animal fights. *See, e.g., People v. Superior Court,* 247 Cal. Rptr. 647 (Ct. App. 1988), *cert. denied,* 488 U.S. 1030 (1989).

25. *State v. Mitts,* 608 S.W.2d 131 (Mo. Ct. App. 1980).

26. Ibid., at 134.

27. *Jones v. State,* 473 So.2d 1197, 1199 (Ala. Crim. App. 1985) (quoting Ala. Code § 3-1-29 [1975]). *See also Moody v. State,* 320 S.E.2d 545 (Ga. 1984).

28. It should be noted, however, that "intent" is used ambiguously in the criminal law and may be more like willfulness or malice.

29. *Model Penal Code* (Philadelphia: American Law Institute, 1980), § 250.11.

30. *Model Penal Code* (Philadelphia: American Law Institute, 1985), § 2.02(2) (a) (i).

31. Ibid., § 2.02(2) (c). Under the *Model Penal Code* formulation of the "reckless" standard, it must be shown that the defendant consciously disregarded the risk. This imports a subjective standard (i.e., did the particular defendant, empirically, know about and disregard the risk) into the state's burden of proof beyond a reasonable doubt. Although proof of conscious disregard may be inferred from the circumstances, the proof requirement is rigorous.

32. For an example of the confusion engendered by the requirement of a mental element, see *People v. Wilhelm,* 676 P.2d 702 (Colo. 1984), in which the Colorado Supreme Court held that one section of the anticruelty statute required proof of a mental element, while another section imposed strict liability on defendants.

33. *Model Penal Code,* § 250.11.

34. Ibid., § 250.11 cmt. 2.

35. Alaska Stat. § 11.61.140(b) (1–3) (1989).

36. Cal. Penal Code § 599c (West 1988).

37. Del. Code Ann. tit. 11, § 1325(b) (4) (Supp. 1992).

38. Ky. Rev. Stat. Ann. § 525.130(l) (c) (Michie Supp. 1992).

39. Ibid., § 525.130(2) (a–d) & (3).

40. Md. Ann. Code art. 27, § 59 (1992).

41. Neb. Rev. Stat. § 28-1013 (Supp. 1992).

42. Ibid., § 54-101.01 (1988). The statute provides that freeze brands, which are generally considered to be less painful to animals, may be used for limited purposes.

43. Or. Rev. Stat. § 167.320(2) (1990); ibid., § 167.310(l) (b).

44. 18 Pa. Cons. Stat. Ann. § 5511(q) (Supp. 1993).

45. Va. Code. Ann. § 3.1-796.122(C) (Michie Supp. 1993).

46. For example, although Pennsylvania does not exempt scientific experiments per se, it provides that search warrants shall not issue in cases involving scientific research. This prohibition on the issuance of search warrants effectively exempts scientific activities even though there is no specific exemption for these activities and even though the Pennsylvania statute provides explicit exemptions for other activities. *See* 18 Pa. Cons. Stat. Ann. § 5511(1) (Supp. 1993).

47. In *United States v. Carroll Towing Co.,* 159 F.2d 169 (2d Cir. 1947), Judge Learned Hand first framed the "economic interpretation" of negligence: "if the probability be called P; the injury, L; and the burden, B; liability depends upon whether B is less than L multiplied by P: i.e., whether B [is less than] PL." Ibid., at 173. Custom may be evidence of reasonableness, but it is not dispositive. *See, e.g., The T.J. Hooper,* 60 F.2d 737 (2d Cir. 1932).

48. *New Jersey Soc'y for the Prevention of Cruelty to Animals v. Board of Educ.,* 219 A.2d 200 (N.J. Super. Ct. Law Div. 1966), *aff'd,* 277 A.2d 506 (N.J. 1967).

49. Ibid., at 205.

50. *See supra* Chapter One, notes 9–13 and accompanying text.

51. *See generally* Jim Mason and Peter Singer, *Animal Factories,* rev. ed. (New York: Harmony Books, 1990).

52. *See* ibid., at 36.

53. A notable exception is cockfighting, which is prohibited in most states. Also, many states prohibit the dyeing or coloring of animals. *See, e.g.,* Wis. Stat. § 951.11 (Supp. 1992).

54. For the most part, challenges concerning the vagueness of language used in anti-cruelty cases have occurred in the context of neglect cases, where courts have rejected such challenges, holding that the language requiring that "sufficient" food or water be provided requires a commonsense, ordinary-language interpretation. The one area in which vagueness challenges have succeeded has involved statutes prohibiting animal fights and specifically prohibiting "presence" at such events. Courts have often held such statutes to be unconstitutional. *See, e.g., People v. Superior Court,* 247 Cal. Rptr. 647 (Ct. App. 1988), *cert. denied,* 488 U.S. 1030 (1989); *State v. Abellano,* 441 P.2d 333 (Haw. 1968); *State v. Wear,* 472 N.E.2d 778 (Ohio Ct. App. 1984). *But see State v. Tabor,* 678 S.W.2d 45 (Tenn. 1984) (statute prohibiting presence at cockfight not vague).

55. John H. Ingham, *The Law of Animals* (Philadelphia: T. & J. W. Johnson, 1900), 529.

56. *Grise v. State,* 37 Ark. 456, 459 (1881).

57. *State v. Bogardus,* 4 Mo. App. 215, 217 (1877).

58. Ibid., at 220. It should be noted that Judge Lewis, who wrote the denial of rehearing, had only concurred in the judgment and did not agree with the court's reasoning. In the denial of rehearing, Judge Lewis made it clear that he had a personal distaste for hunting, but he acknowledged that there was a universal love for such "sports." He went on to say that he rejected the notion that pigeon shooting was required as preparation for serving the state: "All possible superiority in marksmanship could be quite as easily attained without the sacrifice of any life. . . . In all the 'manhood' that may be devoted to bloody conquests over defenceless creatures, already captive, we cannot feel sure of finding the material that would best serve to defend the State." Judge Lewis doubted that the motivation of the pigeon shooter reflected a no-more-elevated "tendency than was that of the ancient tyrant who plucked out the eyes of a slave in order to show the deftness of his fingers." Ibid.

For another case holding that live-bird shoots do not violate the anticruelty statute, see *Commonwealth v. Lewis,* 21 A. 396 (Pa. 1891). Some states have held that such shoots violate the anticruelty law. *See, e.g., Waters v. People,* 46 P. 112 (Colo. 1896); *State v. Davis,* 61 A. 2 (N.J. 1905), *aff'd* 64 A. 1134 (N.J. 1906).

59. *Commonwealth v. Lufkin,* 89 Mass. (7 Allen) 579 (1863).

60. Ibid., at 579–80.

61. Ibid., at 582, 583.

62. *Stephens v. State,* 65 Miss. 329, 331 (1887).

63. *See, e.g., Wilkerson v. State,* 401 So.2d 1110, 1112 (Fla. 1981) (in connection with a challenge to the vagueness of the statutory term "unnecessary," the court stated that defendant had raised "difficult questions concerning the applicability of this statute to hunters, fishermen, and pest exterminators"). *See also State v. Kaneakua,* 597 P.2d 590, 593–94 (Haw. 1979) (defendant charged with violating law against cockfighting raised issues concerning whether "various local customs" inflicted "unjustifiable" pain and suffering on animals).

64. *Lufkin,* 89 Mass. (7 Allen) at 581.

65. *People v. Brunell,* 48 How. Pr. 435, 437 (N.Y. City Ct. 1874).

66. *Murphy v. Manning,* 2 Ex. D. 307, 313–14 (1877) (Cleasby, B.) (emphasis added).

67. *Lewis v. Fermor,* 18 Q.B.D. 532, 534 (1887) (Day, J.).

68. It may, of course, be argued that even if cruelty is gratuitous, it still does not fall within the scope of the anticruelty statute. For example, it is difficult to find the redeeming social value of rodeos in light of the enormous amount of animal suffering that occurs at such events. Nevertheless, many people still regard rodeos as legitimate entertainment. Perhaps my thesis should be revised so that the only type of activity that falls within the anticruelty statutes is activity that results in gratuitous suffering and death but has no symbolic importance or value to anyone other than the actor.

69. *Commonwealth v. Higgins,* 178 N.E. 536, 538 (Mass. 1931).

70. *See supra* Chapter Six, note 45 and accompanying text.

71. *Grise v. State,* 37 Ark. 456, 460 (1881) (emphasis added).

72. *Murphy,* 2 Ex. D. at 314 (Cleasby, B.). *See also Brady v. M'Argle,* 14 L.R. Ir. 174, 183 (Ex. D. 1884) (Dowse, B.).

73. *Horton v. State,* 27 So. 468, 468 (Ala. 1900).

74. *Bowyer v. Morgan,* 95 L.T.R. 27 (K.B. 1906).

75. *Lewis v. Fermor,* 18 Q.B.D. 532 (1887).

76. Ibid., at 534 (Day, J.).

77. *Ford v. Wiley,* 23 Q.B.D. 203, 209 (1889) (Coleridge, C.J.).

78. Ibid., at 215.

79. Ibid., at 219 (Hawkins, J., concurring).

80. *Callaghan v. Society for the Prevention of Cruelty to Animals,* 16 L.R. Ir. 325, 333 (C.P.D. 1885) (Harrison, J.). Interestingly, Justice Murphy in *Callaghan* noted that philosopher and jurist Jeremy Bentham was not opposed to all pain and suffering inflicted on animals, but only to pain that was gratuitous and that did not have the purpose of making the animal more serviceable to humans. *See* ibid., at 335. Bentham is closely identified with animal *welfare* and not animal *rights.*

81. *State v. Crichton,* 4 Ohio Dec. 481 (Police Ct. 1892).

82. Ibid., at 482.

83. *Davis v. Society for Prevention of Cruelty,* 16 Abb. Pr. (n.s.) 73 (N.Y.C.P. 1874).

84. Ibid., at 74–76.

85. *See* ibid., at 78–79.

86. *People ex rel. Freel v. Downs,* 136 N.Y.S. 440 (City Magis. Ct. 1911).

87. Ibid., at 442.

88. Ibid., at 444.

89. Ibid., at 445.

90. Ibid., at 446.

91. Ibid., at 451–52.

92. *Commonwealth v. Anspach,* 188 A. 98 (Pa. Super. Ct. 1936).

93. Ibid., at 99.

94. In *Commonwealth v. Sanshuck,* 41 Pa. D. & C. 587 (D. Ct. 1941), the court held that locking the wings of a duck while weighing the animal was acceptable even though the prosecution produced evidence that the procedure caused injury and suffering to the animals. The defendants testified—and the court appeared to accept—that wing locking was acceptable, in part because the alternative, tying the duck's feet, caused more harm to the ducks. The court noted that wing locking is the "simplest, safest, and most expeditious method" of weighing a duck, and "[t]here is no remote suggestion of a sadistic or inherently cruel attitude on the part of either of the defendants." Ibid., at 589.

95. *Commonwealth v. Barnes,* 629 A.2d 123 (Pa. Super. Ct. 1993).

96. Ibid., at 132.

97. *Taub v. State,* 463 A.2d 819, 821 (Md. 1983). The Maryland anticruelty statute (at the time) explicitly provided that "no person shall be liable for criminal prosecution for normal human activities to which the infliction of pain to an animal is purely incidental and unavoidable." *See* ibid., at 821.

98. *Vivisection Investigation League v. American Soc'y for the Prevention of Cruelty to Animals,* 203 N.Y.S.2d 313 (Sup. Ct.), *aff'd,* 207 N.Y.S.2d 425 (App. Div. 1960).

99. *Vivisection Investigation League,* 203 N.Y.S.2d at 315 (emphasis added).

100. *Fund for Animals, Inc. v. Mud Lake Farmers Rabbit Comm.,* 673 P.2d 408 (Idaho 1983).

101. Ibid., at 410 (quoting findings of trial court).

102. *Hooker v. Gray,* 96 L.T.R. 706 (K.B. 1907).

103. Ibid., at 707 (Alverstone, C. J.).

104. Ibid., (Darling, J., concurring). There is some language in *Hooker* that suggests at least some of the justices did not believe the evidence supported the finding that the defendant was aware the cat was suffering. This language is at odds with the court's statement of the case, which indicated that the defendant was aware that he had severely wounded, but not killed, the cat.

105. Ibid., at 708 (Phillimore, J., concurring).

106. *Laner v. State,* 381 P.2d 905 (Okla. Crim. App. 1963).

107. Ibid., at 908, 909.

108. In addition to cases that have held the shooting of live birds to violate the anticruelty statute, at least one case has found that fox hunting violated the law. *See Commonwealth v. Turner,* 14 N.E. 130 (Mass. 1887). It is clear, however, that in *Turner* the court did not hold that all fox hunting violated the statute; rather, the court held only that taking a captive fox and throwing the animal to the dogs, to be mangled and killed, constituted a violation of the statute.

109. *Humane Soc'y v. Lyng,* 633 F. Supp. 480 (W.D.N.Y. 1986).

110. Ibid., at 486.

111. There are some indirect attacks on the use of animals for food, experiments, and hunting; and whether these activities are protected by an explicit exemption or not, the attacks are usually unsuccessful. For example, in *Animal Legal Defense Fund Boston, Inc. v. Provimi Veal Corp.,* 626 F. Supp. 278 (D. Mass.), *aff'd,* 802 F.2d 440 (1st Cir. 1986), the plaintiff argued that a state consumer protection statute required the defendant to inform consumers about the cruel conditions involved in raising veal calves. The court rejected this argument, holding that the anticruelty statutes are enforced by public officials and not private organizations, and that if the defendant were required to inform consumers of this conduct, it would be tantamount to enforcing "by means of an injunction obtained in a private lawsuit, a criminal statute enforceable only by public prosecutors and, in legislatively-sanctioned circumstances, private groups, among which the [plaintiff] is not numbered." Ibid., 626 F. Supp. at 281.

112. Obviously, the legislature may—and on very rare occasions does—determine that a particular activity constitutes cruelty, and courts will generally uphold that determination. For example, in *State v. Longhorn World Championship Rodeo, Inc.,* 483 N.E.2d 196 (Ohio Ct. App. 1985), the court held that a statute prohibiting the use of bucking straps on rodeo animals was not an unconstitutional exercise of police power. In the cases discussed in this chapter, I am dealing with the application of general anticruelty statutes and not with specific prohibitions, which are, in any event, rare. For obvious reasons, the latter constitute a far more effective way to address the issue of animal cruelty.

113. *State v. Tweedie,* 444 A.2d 855 (R.I. 1982).

114. Ibid., at 857.

115. *In re* William G., 447 A.2d 493 (Md. Ct. Spec. App. 1982).

116. Ibid., at 496.

117. *See, e.g., Willis v. State,* 410 S.E.2d 377 (Ga. Ct. App. 1991) (conviction upheld where the defendant shot a dog with a pellet gun for no reason); *Motes v. State,* 375 S.E.2d 893 (Ga. Ct. App. 1988) (conviction upheld where the defendant set a dog on fire because the dog was barking); *State v. Bruner,* 12 N.E. 103 (Ind. 1887) (court reversed dismissal of cruelty charges where defendant tortured a goose by burning the animal); *Commonwealth v. Gentile,* 150 N.E. 830 (Mass. 1926) (court affirmed defendant's conviction for burning a dog without any reason); *State v. Neal,* 27 S.E. 81 (N.C. 1897) (court affirmed defendant's conviction where the defendant impaled and beat the owner's chickens in order to protect the defendant's pea plants, and held that killing the animals in order to protect the peas was not permitted); *City v. Macasek,* No. 85-CRB-16326, 1987 WL 5446 (Ohio Ct. App. Jan. 15, 1987) (conviction upheld where the defendant gratuitously and severely kicked a cat).

118. *Tuck v. United States,* 477 A.2d 1115 (D.C. 1984).

119. Ibid., at 1117. *See also Smith v. State,* 285 S.E.2d 749 (Ga. Ct. App. 1981) (court upheld a conviction for cruelty to animals where the defendant illegally operated a pet shop and then abandoned the animals).

120. *Tinsley v. State,* 22 S.W. 39, 40 (Tex. Crim. App. 1893).

121. *Reynolds v. State,* 569 N.E.2d 680, 681 (Ind. Ct. App. 1991).

122. *State v. Linder,* 593 N.Y.S.2d 422 (Crim. Ct. 1992).

123. *LaRue v. State,* 478 So.2d 13 (Ala. Crim. App. 1985). *Cf. Biggerstaff v. State,* 435 N.E.2d 621 (Ind. App. 1982) (defendant's conviction for violating anticruelty statute was upheld where five Great Danes owned by defendant but kept at another location had been neglected and were emaciated, dehydrated, and infected with hookworms).

124. *State v. Walker,* 236 N.W.2d 292 (Iowa 1975).

125. *State v. Brookshire,* 355 S.W.2d 333 (Kan. Ct. App. 1962).

126. *See also, Moore v. State,* 107 N.E. 1 (Ind. 1914) (defendant convicted of depriving horse of light, bedding, food, water, and exercise); *State v. Jordan,* 136 A. 483 (Me. 1927) (defendant convicted of failing to provide cows with proper food where such failure was not caused by any necessity); *State v. Klammer,* 41 N.W.2d 451 (Minn. 1950) (defendant convicted of failing to provide necessary food and shelter to horses, which were to be slaughtered and used as food for ranch mink); *People v. Arcidicono,* 347 N.Y.S.2d 850 (D. Ct. 1973) (defendant convicted of failing to provide adequate food and shelter to a horse even though the horse's owner instructed the defendant not to change the diet and did not provide adequate funds for the defendant to feed grain to the horse), *aff'd,* 360 N.Y.S.2d 156 (Sup. Ct. 1974); *State v. Bauer,* 379 N.W.2d 895 (Wis. Ct. App. 1985) (defendants convicted of failing to provide adequate food, water, and shelter to horses); *Wildman v. State,* 230 N.W.2d 809 (Wis. 1975) (defendant convicted of failing to provide adequate care to cattle).

Another category of cases involves the use of lame or injured animals for work purposes. As a general matter, courts will uphold convictions where the defendant uses or hires out an animal that the defendant knows to be lame, and has no reason for doing so. Again, under such circumstances, there is no social benefit generated, and in the case of bailments, the bailee may be harmed financially by hiring a lame animal. *See People v. O'Rourke,* 369 N.Y.S.2d 335 (Crim. Ct. 1975); *People v. Koogan,* 11 N.Y.S.2d 49 (App. Div. 1939); *State v. Goodall,* 175 P. 857 (Or. 1918).

127. *State v. Tweedie,* 444 A.2d at 857.

128. *Cross v. State,* 646 S.W.2d 514 (Tex. Ct. App. 1982).

129. Ibid., at 515. *See also People v. Allen,* 657 P.2d 447, 451 (Colo. 1983) ("necessary" and "proper" care to be understood in the ordinary sense); *Tuck v. United States,* 467 A.2d 727, 732 (D.C. 1983) (notions such as "unnecessarily" failing to provide an animal with "proper" care " 'are to be understood in their ordinary sense' " [quoting *State v. Persons,* 46 A.2d 854, 855 (Vt. 1946)]); *State v. Vance,* 125 A.2d 800, 803 (Vt. 1956) (words "unnecessarily'" and "proper" in connection with neglect case are to be understood in the ordinary sense that the defendant could have provided food and drink but failed to do so).

In some neglect cases, courts employ a "reasonable-person" standard and require that the jury determine the degree of care that would be used under the same or similar circumstances. *See, e.g., State v. Groseclose,* 171 P.2d 863, 864–65 (Idaho 1946). Although that standard and the "ordinary-language" standard are likely to produce the same result in neglect cases where there is no benefit generated by the ostensibly cruel conduct, the "reasonable-person" standard, when used in a context of institutionalized cruelty, may lead to a counterintuitive result.

130. Cal. Penal Code § 597 (West Supp. 1993).

131. Wis. Stat. Ann. § 951.18 (West Supp. 1992).

132. *People for the Ethical Treatment of Animals v. Institutional Animal Care & Use Comm.,* 817 P.2d 1299 (Or. 1991).

133. Ibid., at 1303–4. For more on animal care committees, see Part III, *infra.*

134. *Jones v. Beame,* 392 N.Y.S.2d 444 (App. Div. 1977), *aff'd,* 380 N.E.2d 277 (N.Y. 1978).

135. *Walz v. Baum,* 345 N.Y.S.2d 159 (App. Div. 1973).

136. Ibid., at 160 (emphasis added).

137. *Pennsylvania Soc'y for the Prevention of Cruelty to Animals v. Bravo Enters., Inc.,* 237 A.2d 342 (Pa. 1968).

138. Ibid., at 349. Although the Pennsylvania anticruelty statute now provides that hu-

mane agents and police officers have standing to seek injunctive relief—*see* Pa. Cons. Stat. Ann. § 5511(i) (1983 & Supp. 1994)—the courts in Pennsylvania have apparently chosen to ignore this standing. *See, e.g., Mohler v. Labor Day Committee,* No. S-1081-1994 (Pa. Ct. Common Pleas, August 16, 1994) (court dismissed action filed by three state humane agents seeking declaratory and injunctive relief to enjoin the pigeon shoot described in the Preface to this book).

139. *State v. Roche,* 37 Mo. App. 480 (1889).

140. Ibid., at 482. This case is a good example of the confusion that arises in the use of terms that describe mental states. According to the court, the crime of cruelty to animals did not require any particular intent, but only required that the act itself not be "accidental." Surely Roche did not "accidentally" overdrive the horse; rather, at best, he intended to perform the acts that constituted overdriving but did not intend to overdrive the horse. If intent were really immaterial, the court would have had no difficulty in upholding the conviction, because Roche did not act accidentally at all.

141. *Church of the Lukumi Babalu Aye, Inc. v. City of Hialeah,* 113 S. Ct. 2217 (1993). Freedom of religion is protected by the First Amendment.

142. There were several ordinances at issue that the Court found were aimed directly at the Santeria religion. The ordinance that I discuss incorporated the Florida state anticruelty law that was facially neutral.

As a general matter, the protection of religious freedom "embraces two concepts, freedom to believe and freedom to act. The first is absolute but, in the nature of things, the second cannot be. Conduct remains subject to regulation for the protection of society." *Cantwell v. Connecticut,* 310 U.S. 296, 303–4 (1940). Among members of the Court there has recently been considerable confusion about what standard is to be used in evaluating the incidental regulation of religious conduct through neutral laws of general applicability. This confusion was addressed by the Religious Freedom Restoration Act, 42 U.S.C. 2000bb (1994), which provides that the government bears the burden to prove that it has a compelling state interest in any law—even a neutral law that applies generally—if the law incidentally and substantially burdens religion.

In the Hialeah case, the Court found that the ordinances were either directly aimed at religion or, in the case of the ordinance that incorporated the state anticruelty statute, interpreted in a non-neutral manner and in a way that was not generally applicable to all killings.

The Court left open the question whether a truly neutral anticruelty statute could be applied to these types of killings, considered apart from their religious context.

143. *Church of the Lukumi Babalu Aye,* 113 S. Ct. at 2223 (quoting Fla. Op. Att'y Gen. 87-56 [1988]).

144. Richard A. Posner, *The Problems of Jurisprudence* (Cambridge: Harvard University Press, 1990), 378, 379.

145. Laurie Asseo, "Court Upholds Harsher Terms for Hate Crimes," *L.A. Times,* June 13, 1993, at Al.


## Chapter Eight

1. Letter from Whoopi Goldberg to Doug Stoll, July 1983 (on file with the author).

2. I am aware that there has been a great deal written about the distinction between basic and applied science, and the distinction is not always an easy one to make. *See, e.g.,*

Jürgen Habermas, *Toward a Rational Society,* trans. Jeremy Shapiro (Boston: Beacon Press, 1970); George F. Kneller, *Science as a Human Endeavor* (New York: Columbia University Press, 1978); Herbert Marcuse, *One-Dimensional Man* (Boston: Beacon Press, 1964); Jerome R. Ravetz, *Scientific Knowledge and Its Social Problems* (Oxford: Clarendon Press, 1971); Liebe F. Cavalieri, "Science as Technology," 51 *S. Cal. L. Rev.* 1153 (1978); Barry Furrow, "Governing Science: Public Risks and Private Remedies," 131 *U. Pa. L. Rev.* 1403 (1983); Hans Jonas, "Freedom of Scientific Inquiry and the Public Interest," *Hastings Center Rep.,* August 1976, at 15. For purposes of this book, these problems are largely irrelevant.

3. *See, e.g., Science Policy Implications of DNA Recombinant Molecule Research: Hearings Before the Subcomm. on Science, Research, and Technology of the House Comm. on Science and Technology,* 95th Cong., 1st Sess. (1977) (testimony of Thomas Emerson). For other general defenses of the view that scientific inquiry possesses constitutional status, see Ira Carmen, *Cloning and the Constitution* (Madison: University of Wisconsin Press, 1985); Richard Delgado and David R. Millen, "God, Galileo, and Government: Toward Constitutional Protection for Scientific Inquiry," 53 *Wash. L. Rev.* 349 (1978); Steven Goldberg, "The Reluctant Embrace: Law and Science in America," 75 *Geo. L.J.* 1341 (1987); idem, "The Constitutional Status of American Science," 1979 *U. Ill. L.F.* 1; John A. Robertson, "The Scientist's Right to Research: A Constitutional Analysis," 51 *S. Cal. L. Rev.* 1203 (1978).

For an analysis that shows scientific experimentation is not constitutionally protected conduct as a general matter, see Gary L. Francione, "Experimentation and the Marketplace Theory of the First Amendment," 136 *U. Pa. L. Rev.* 417 (1987).

4. Rebecca Dresser, "Research on Animals: Values, Politics, and Regulatory Reform," 58 *S. Cal. L. Rev.* 1147, 1191 (1985).

5. Rebecca Dresser, "Assessing Harm and Justification in Animal Research: Federal Policy Opens the Laboratory Door," 40 *Rutgers L. Rev.* 723, 767 (1988).

For an analysis that contends animal experimentation should not receive constitutional protection, see Gary L. Francione, "The Constitutional Status of Restrictions on Experiments Involving Nonhuman Animals: A Comment on Professor Dresser's Analysis," 40 *Rutgers L. Rev.* 797 (1988).

6. It is possible that someone who subscribed to rule-utilitarianism, as opposed to act-utilitarianism, might argue that consequentialist theory could justify not using the ten human subjects. Under rule-utilitarianism, we ask whether a particular rule, such as "One should always tell the truth," serves the principle of utility if followed as a general matter even if the relative consequences of not observing the rule in a particular case do not serve the principle of utility. Act-utilitarianism requires that we examine the consequences of particular acts. *See* Chapter Five. A rule-utilitarian may argue, for example, that the consequences of applying the rule that humans can be used in experiments against their will would be disastrous and that the experiments, however valuable, would be morally wrong. There is, however, a great deal of criticism of rule-utilitarianism as not representing "true" (i.e., truly consequentialist) utilitarianism.

7. *See generally* 42 U.S.C. § 289 (1988); 42 U.S.C. § 300v-1(b) (1988); 45 C.F.R. §§ 46.101–46.409 (1993). For general information on human experimentation, see Robertson, "The Scientist's Right to Research."

8. 45 C.F.R. §§ 46.103, 46.107.

9. The regulations provide that risk is minimized "by using procedures which are consistent with sound research design and which do not unnecessarily expose subjects to

risk" and "by using procedures already being performed on the subjects for diagnostic or treatment purposes." 45 C.F.R. § 46.111(a) (1).

10. 45 C.F.R. § 46.116(a) (2), (3), (4), (8). Other requirements pertaining to informed consent include informing the subject of the nature of the research, confidentiality protections, compensation or medical treatment if the subject is injured, and an explanation of who may be contacted with respect to subject rights.

11. *See, e.g.,* 45 C.F.R. § 46.111(a) (3), (b). Also, special regulations govern the use of prisoners as research subjects (*see* 45 C.F.R. §§ 46.301–46.306) and children as research subjects (see 45 C.F.R. §§ 46.401–46.409).

12. 45 C.F.R. § 46.116(d) (1–4). The informed consent provisions do not apply to state and local government research designed to evaluate public benefits programs as long as any waiver or alteration of informed consent requirements is necessary, because the research could not otherwise be carried out.

13. Additional safeguards under state law would prohibit a person from killing herself as part of an experiment.

14. *A Critical Look at Animal Research* (New York: Medical Research Modernization Committee, 1990), 1 (footnote omitted).

15. C. R. Gallistel, "Bell, Magendie, and the Proposals to Restrict the Use of Animals in Neurobehavioral Research," 36 *Am. Psychologist* 357, 360 (1981).

16. John M. Orem, "Demands That Research Be Useful Threaten to Undermine Basic Science in This Country," *Chron. Higher Educ.,* March 14, 1990, at B1, B3.

17. *See Beyond the Laboratory Door* (Washington, D.C.: Animal Welfare Institute, 1985).

18. *See* American Medical Association, *Use of Animals in Biomedical Research: The Challenge and the Response* (AMA white paper, 1989), 17; National Academy of Sciences, Institute of Medicine, *Science, Medicine, and Animals* (Washington, D.C.: National Academy Press, 1991), 96.

19. In the past decade, the amount of literature concerning animal experimentation has exceeded that which was produced in the first eighty years of the twentieth century. For books and collections of essays, see, e.g., Gill Langley, ed., *Animal Experimentation: The Consensus Changes* (New York: Chapman & Hall, 1989); William Paton, *Man and Mouse,* 2d ed. (New York: Oxford University Press, 1993); Mary T. Phillips and Jeri A. Sechzer, *Animal Research and Ethical Conflict: An Analysis of the Scientific Literature, 1966–1986* (New York: Springer-Verlag, 1989); Bernard E. Rollin, *The Unheeded Cry* (Oxford: Oxford University Press, 1989); Andrew N. Rowan, *Of Mice, Models, and Men* (Albany: State University of New York Press, 1984); Richard D. Ryder, *Victims of Science,* rev. ed. (London: National Anti-Vivisection Society, 1983); Susan Sperling, *Animal Liberators* (Berkeley and Los Angeles: University of California Press, 1988); David Sperlinger, ed., *Animals in Research: New Perspectives in Animal Experimentation* (Chichester: John Wiley & Sons, 1981). For articles, see, e.g., Carl Cohen, "The Case for the Use of Animals in Biomedical Research," 315 *New Eng. J. Med.* 865 (1986); Gallistel, "Bell, Magendie, and the Proposals to Restrict the Use of Animals," at 357; Thomas D. Overcast and Bruce D. Sales, "Regulation of Animal Experimentation," 254 *JAMA* 1944 (1985). For two influential pro-experimentation statements, see American Medical Association, *Use of Animals in Biomedical Research;* National Academy of Sciences, Institute of Medicine, *Science, Medicine, and Animals.*

20. *See* Richard D. French, *Antivivisection and Medical Science in Victorian Society*

(Princeton, N.J.: Princeton University Press, 1975); Coral Lansbury, *The Old Brown Dog* (Madison: University of Wisconsin Press, 1985); James Turner, *Reckoning with the Beast* (Baltimore: Johns Hopkins University Press, 1980). *See also* Rowan, *Of Mice, Models, and Men,* at 42–63; Richard Barlow-Kennett, "Address to the Working Classes," in *Vivisection in America,* 4th ed., ed. Francis P. Cobbe and Benjamin Bryan (London: Swan, Sonnenschein & Co., 1890), 1; Franklin Lowe, "Using Animals in Research: What's Going on Here?" *Chron. of Higher Educ.,* September 18, 1985, at 80 ("The use of animals in research [and teaching] has been criticized since its beginning"); Andrew N. Rowan and Bernard E. Rollin, "Animal Research—For and Against: A Philosophical, Social, and Historical Perspective," 27 *Persp. Biology & Med.* 2–8 (1985). *See generally* Tom Regan, *The Case for Animal Rights* (Berkeley and Los Angeles: University of California Press, 1983); Bernard E. Rollin, *Animal Rights and Human Morality,* rev. ed. (Buffalo, N.Y.: Prometheus Books, 1992); Peter Singer, *Animal Liberation, 2d ed.* (New York: New York Review of Books, 1990).

21. U.S. Congress, Office of Technology Assessment, Rep. No. OTA-BA-274, *Alternatives to Animal Use in Research, Testing, and Education* (Washington, D.C.: U.S. Government Printing Office, 1986), 10 [hereinafter OTA Report]. The OTA Report indicated that all data on the numbers of animals used are "unreliable" for a number of reasons, the most important of which is that although federal law requires that certain institutions report their annual use of certain animals, there are no data enumerating how many institutions do not report animal use, and many animals commonly used in laboratories are not presently required to be included in the reports. The OTA Report estimates that between 17 million and 22 million animals are used annually in the United States and that available data did not justify predictions of future trends of usage. Ibid., at 64–66. OTA estimated that a minimum of 1.6 million animals are used by the federal government each year. Ibid., at 49. Philosopher Sidney Gendin criticized the OTA Report on the ground that "OTA ignores the fact that more than one-half of all research goes unreported because unfunded. Secondly, funded researchers consistently understate the number of animals used for several reasons I will not enumerate. My personal guess is that 120–150 million animals is the right ballpark figure." Ibid., at 41.

22. Rowan, *Of Mice, Models, and Men,* at 10–15.

23. *See, e.g., Beyond the Laboratory Door;* Jeff Diner, *Physical and Mental Suffering of Experimental Animals* (Washington, D.C.: Animal Welfare Institute, 1979); Dallas Pratt, *Alternatives to Pain in Experiments on Animals* (New York: Argus Achives, 1980).

24. *See, e.g.,* Diner, *Physical and Mental Suffering of Experimental Animals;* Brandon Reines, *Psychology Experiments on Animals: A Critique of Animal Models of Human Psychopathology* (Jenkintown, Pa.: American Anti-Vivisection Society, 1982). *See also* Martin L. Stephens, *Maternal Deprivation Experiments in Psychology: A Critique of Animal Models* (Boston: New England Anti-Vivisection Society, 1986).

25. Rowan, *Of Mice, Models, and Men,* at 67.

26. Andrew N. Rowan et al., *The Animal Research Controversy* (Grafton, Mass.: Tufts University School of Veterinary Medicine, 1994), 15. The Tufts authors also credit figures on animal use reported by pharmaceutical companies, which, in my view, represents dubious methodology. Curiously, the Rowan study was funded by the Pew Charitable Trusts, the president of which was Dr. Thomas Langfitt, who was the principal investigator with Dr. Gennarelli of the primate head-injury experiments at the University of Pennsylvania.

27. Richard Levins and Richard Lewontin, *The Dialectical Biologist* (Cambridge: Harvard University Press, 1985), 1–2.

28. René Descartes, *Philosophical Letters,* ed. and trans. Anthony Kenny (Oxford: Clarendon Press, 1970), 243 (letter from Descartes to Henry More, February 5, 1649).

29. *See* ibid., "Discourse on the Method," in *The Philosophical Writings of Descartes,* vol. 1, trans. John Cottingham et al. (Cambridge: Cambridge University Press, 1985), 111, 112.

30. *See, e.g.,* Stephen R. Kaufman and Betsy Todd, eds., *Perspectives on Animal Research,* vol. 1 (New York: Medical Research Modernization Committee, 1989); Stephen R. Kaufman et al., eds., *Perspectives on Medical Research,* vol. 2 (New York: Medical Research Modernization Committee, 1990). Both volumes contain essays critical of animal experimentation, written by physicians, psychologists, veterinarians, and "pure" scientists.

31. *See, e.g.,* Daisie Radner and Michael Radner, *Animal Consciousness* (Buffalo, N.Y.: Prometheus Books, 1989).

32. The myth of the superior status of science has misled even those who have otherwise launched powerful attacks on the knowledge claims of every discipline except science. For example, Durkheim, Marx, and Mannheim all recognized that cultural variations affect the content of knowledge and that the development of science is linked to social conditions. *See* Emile Durkheim, *The Rules of Sociological Method,* 8th ed., ed. George E. G. Gatlin, trans. Sarah A. Solovay and John H. Mueller (New York: Free Press, 1966), 35; Karl Marx, "Economic and Philosophic Manuscripts of 1844," in *The Marx-Engels Reader,* 2d ed., ed. Robert C. Tucker (New York: W. W. Norton, 1978), 66, 90–91. Nevertheless, all three accepted that the actual content of true scientific knowledge was not so linked. For Durkheim, scientific investigation involved defined phenomena; and "to be objective, the definition must obviously deal with phenomena not as ideas but in terms of their inherent properties. It must characterize them by elements essential to their nature, not by their conformity to an intellectual idea." For Marx, "only when science proceeds from nature—is it *true* science." *See also* Howard L. Parsons, ed., *Marx and Engels on Ecology* (Westport, Conn.: Greenwood Press, 1977).

33. Galileo, *Dialogue Concerning the Two Chief World Systems—Ptolemaic and Copernican,* trans. Stillman Drake (Berkeley and Los Angeles: University of California Press, 1953), 53.

34. *See, e.g.,* Israel Scheffler, *Science and Subjectivity* (Indianapolis, Ind.: Bobbs-Merrill Co., 1967), 8–9.

35. *See, e.g.,* Karl R. Popper, *Conjectures and Refutations* (New York: Basic Books, 1962), 36–37.

36. *See* Robert K. Merton, *The Sociology of Science* (Chicago: University of Chicago Press, 1973), 268–69.

37. *See, e.g.,* Stanley Aronowitz, *Science as Power* (Minneapolis: University of Minnesota Press, 1988).

38. Norwood R. Hanson, *Perception and Discovery,* ed. Willard C. Humphreys (San Francisco: Freeman, Cooper & Co., 1969), 408.

39. *See generally* Mary B. Hesse, *The Structure of Scientific Inference* (Berkeley and Los Angeles: University of California Press, 1974), 1–44, 283–302.

40. *See, e.g.,* Paul K. Feyerabend, *Problems of Empiricism: Philosophical Papers,* vol. 2 (Cambridge: Cambridge University Press, 1981), 52–61.

41. Hanson, *Perception and Discovery,* at 108–9.

42. *See, e.g.,* Carol Grunewald and Jim Mason, "The Head Injury Lab Break-in," *Animals' Agenda,* May 1985, at 1; Michael D. Ware, "The ALF Strikes," *Animals' Agenda,* July/August 1984, at 1. *See also* Kathy S. Guillermo, *Monkey Business* (Washington, D.C.: National Press, 1993).

43. *See supra* Chapter Four, notes 52–59 and accompanying text.

44. Wall's comments are contained in a letter from Wall to Clive Hollands, December 17, 1984 (on file with the author).

45. Statement of Dr. Jay Glass concerning the Head Injury Clinical Research Center (on file with the author).

46. Statement of Dr. Nedim Buyukmihci, professor of veterinary medicine, University of California at Davis (on file with the author).

47. Thomas Gennarelli, "From the Experimental Head Injury Laboratory," *University of Pennsylvania Almanac,* October 9, 1984, at 6, 7.

48. Dick Pothier, "Penn Researcher Says Lab Is Humane," *Philadelphia Inquirer,* May 31, 1984 at 1-B, 4-B (statement of Thomas Langfitt, principal investigator, Head Injury Laboratory, University of Pennsylvania).

49. *Philadelphia Daily News,* May 31, 1984 (statement of Thomas Langfitt, principal investigator, Head Injury Laboratory, University of Pennsylvania).

50. Jeffrey L. Fox, "Lab Break-In Stirs Animal Welfare Debate," 224 *Science* 1319, 1320 (1984) (quoting James B. Wyngaarden, NIH director).

51. The author and Roger Galvin were co-counsels to the protesters.

52. U.S. Public Health Service/National Institutes of Health, *Evaluation of Experimental Procedures Conducted at the University of Pennsylvania Experimental Head Injury Laboratory 1981–1984 in Light of the Public Health Service Animal Welfare Policy* (Bethesda, Md.: National Institutes of Health, July 17, 1985), at 5.

53. Ibid., at 30.

54. *See, e.g.,* Jeri A. Sechzer, ed., "The Role of Animals in Biomedical Research," 406 *Annals N. Y. Acad. Sci.* 150–54 (1983) (comments of Neil Miller of Rockefeller University defending Taub). Dr. Rowan, who does not oppose all animal experimentation but is a strong supporter of animal welfare, has commented that "Taub garners much sympathy by presenting himself as a modern-day Galileo, victimized by anti-intellectual forces, despite the fact that the action against him centered solely on his treatment and care of his monkeys rather than on the merits of his research." Rowan, *Of Mice, Models, and Men,* at 274.

55. Rowan, *Of Mice, Models, and Men,* at 279, 275.

56. *See, e.g.,* Lauren S. Rikleen, "The Animal Welfare Act: Still a Cruelty to Animals," 7 *B.C. Envtl. Aff. L. Rev.* 129 (1978); Mark Solomon and Peter C. Lovenheim, "Reporting Requirements Under the Animal Welfare Act: Their Inadequacies and the Public's Right to Know," 3 *Int'l J. Stud. Animal Prob.* 210 (1982). Even the OTA Report acknowledged that the current federal reporting system on the various uses of animals, and the numbers used, lack "clear definition and uniform reporting." OTA Report, at 66.

57. Rebecca Dresser, "Research on Animals: Values, Politics, and Regulatory Reform," 58 *S. Cal. L. Rev.* 1147, 1194 (1985) (quoting Bernard E. Rollin, "The Teaching of Responsibility" [Hume Memorial Lecture, November 10, 1983], at 13).

58. *See generally* Animal Legal Defense Fund, "Submission to the USDA on Pain and Anesthesia with Reference to the Improved Standards for Laboratory Animals Act of 1985."

## Chapter Nine

1. For a comparative discussion of British and American legislation on the use of animals in experiments, see Judith Hampson, "Legislation and the Changing Consensus," in *Animal Experimentation: The Consensus Changes,* ed. Gill Langley (New York: Chapman & Hall, 1989), 219.

2. U.S. Public Health Service/National Institutes of Health, *Public Health Service Policy on Humane Use of Laboratory Animals* (Bethesda, Md.: National Institutes of Health, 1986) [hereinafter PHS Policy].

3. U.S. Public Health Service/National Institutes of Health *Guide for the Care and Use of Laboratory Animals* (Bethesda, Md.: National Institutes of Health, 1985) [hereinafter NIH Guide]. The NIH Guide was prepared under contract by the Institute of Laboratory Animal Resources of the National Academy of Sciences.

4. 42 U.S.C. § 289d (1988).

5. 42 U.S.C. § 289d(a). These guidelines were already formulated and contained in the NIH Guide. The 1985 statute provided greater authority for those already extant guidelines.

6. 42 U.S.C. § 289d(b).

7. 42 U.S.C. § 289d(c).

8. 56 Fed. Reg. 6426, at 6428 (1991).

9. The IRAC principles are contained as part of the PHS Policy and the NIH Guide.

10. Other federal sources of regulation include the Good Laboratory Practices Rules of the Food and Drug Administration and the Environmental Protection Agency, the Endangered Species Act, and the various policies of federal agencies and departments that perform intramural or fund extramural animal research. For a discussion of these sources of regulation, see OTA Report. In addition, the states remain free to use anticruelty laws in the context of animal experimentation, but, as we have seen, this source of regulation has not been promising.

11. The quoted language is taken from various sections of the federal Animal Welfare Act, which is discussed *infra*.

12. *See* Richard A. Posner, *Economic Analysis of Law,* 3d ed. (Boston: Little, Brown, 1986), 495.

13. *See* James Turner, *Reckoning with the Beast* (Baltimore: Johns Hopkins University Press, 1980), 85. Turner states that "Bergh tried in 1867 to smuggle a ban on vivisection into an anticruelty bill then before the legislature. [John Call] Dalton [a prominent animal experimenter] and the state medical society foiled this maneuver, but battle was joined several more times in the seventies."

14. Andrew N. Rowan, *Of Mice, Models, and Men* (Albany: State University of New York Press, 1984), 49. Efforts in the District of Columbia were triggered by the British legislation. Senator McMillan introduced the bill, which was patterned very closely on the British act and severely limited causing unrelieved pain in animals used for vivisection. The bill provided that the experiment must be intended to advance physiological knowledge, advance knowledge necessary for saving or prolonging lives, or alleviate suffering. In addition, the experimenter needed to have a license, the cornerstone of the British law, granted by the commissioners of the District of Columbia, to do experiments that had the potential to cause pain. The commissioners could, at their discretion, append to any license conditions that would facilitate the goals of the legislation. Most important, the bill provided that an animal must be anesthetized throughout the entire experiment, and killed before recov-

ering if the pain was likely to persist. The bill prohibited the use of animals for education purposes in public schools, but provided an exception for qualified instructors in medical schools, hospitals, and colleges as long as the animal use was "absolutely necessary" for instruction, the anesthesia provisions of the bill were observed, and the instructor held a certificate required under the bill. The salient difference between a license and certificate was that the latter was limited in duration or applied to specific experiments. The bill prohibited any experiments using dogs, cats, horses, asses, and mules, unless the experimenter could demonstrate the need for such species. Further, the bill prohibited any painful experiments from being performed before the general public.

The bill provided that the commission could require registration of all facilities in which vivisection was practiced, and that all places in which animals were used in experiments for instructional purposes had to be registered and approved by the commission. Further, the bill provided that the commissioners could direct any licensee to report on her experiments, that the Washington Humane Society (and other commission appointees) had the power to make inspections without notice of the facilities, and that the application for a license or certificate be signed by three licensed and practicing physicians and by a professor of physiology, anatomy, medicine, medical jurisprudence, or surgery. The commissioners could disallow or suspend a certificate at any time and could revoke a license "on their being satisfied that a license ought to be revoked." The bill empowered judges sitting in criminal cases to permit an experiment if necessary for the purposes of a case. Finally, the bill imposed a sanction of a fine not exceeding $150 for a first offense and, for a subsequent offense, a fine not exceeding $300 or a term of imprisonment not exceeding six months.

The bill was referred to the Committee on the District of Columbia, which in turn referred it to the commissioners of the District of Columbia. The commissioners held a public hearing on the bill and then appointed a committee consisting of Dr. George M. Sternberg, surgeon general of the United States, Dr. William C. Woodward, health officer of the District of Columbia, and Henry B. MacFarland, of the Washington Humane Society, to study the bill and make recommendations. The report states that Sternberg and Woodward claimed that no legislation was needed and that MacFarland supported a modified version.

An amended form of the bill was recommended for passage. The amended bill contained exemptions to the prohibitions on the infliction of pain contained in the earlier bill. The amended bill provided that in innoculation experiments, or tests of drugs or medicines, the animal need not be anesthetized or killed afterward. Moreover, the amended bill provided that anesthesia was not required during the process of recovery from surgical procedures. The amended bill sought to weaken the role of the commissioners of the District of Columbia by permitting an authorized officer of the federal government or of the District of Columbia to issue licenses, and by transferring power over laboratory inspections from the commission to the president, who was to appoint four inspectors who would serve without compensation. The role of the Washington Humane Society was eliminated entirely. The power of the commission to revoke a license was not mentioned in the amended bill, although the ability of the commission to disallow or suspend certificates remained. There were other minor changes in the amended bill. *See* S. Rep. No. 1049, 54th Cong., 1st Sess. (1896).

15. For additional discussion of the legislation proposed for the District of Columbia, see Patricia P. Gossel, "William Henry Welch and the Antivivisection Legislation in the District of Columbia, 1896–1900," 40 *J. Hist. Med.* 397 (1985); *see also* Turner, *Reckoning with the Beast,* at 114–15.

16. S. Rep. No. 1049, at III.

17. Ibid., at VII.

18. The legislation was endorsed by Justices John M. Harlan, H. B. Brown, David J. Brewer, E. D. White, R. W. Peckham, and George Shiras Jr. of the United States Supreme Court; Justices Walter S. Cox, A. B. Hagner, and C. C. Cole of the Supreme Court of the District of Columbia; Chief Justice W. A. Richardson and Justices C. C. Nott and Lawrence Weldon of the United States Court of Claims; Bishop John J. Keane, rector of the Catholic University; General and Mrs. Nelson A. Miles; Mrs. U. S. Grant; Major R. H. Montgomery; and Major Frank Smith (U.S. Army). Ibid., at VI.

19. Ibid., at VII.

20. Turner, *Reckoning with the Beast,* at 114.

21. S. Rep. No. 1049, at 127 (statement of Wolcott Gibbs, president of the National Academy of Sciences).

22. For example, hearings were held in 1940 concerning the regulation of vivisection in the District of Columbia.

23. *Prohibit Vivisection in the District of Columbia: Hearings on H.R. 5572 Before the House Comm. on the District of Columbia,* 79th Cong., 2d Sess. (1946).

24. *See* S. 3570, 86th Cong., 2d Sess. (1960).

25. *See* H.R. 1937, 87th Cong., 1st Sess. (1961); H.R. 3556, 87th Cong., 1st Sess. (1961).

26. *Humane Treatment of Animals Used in Research: Hearings on H.R. 1937 and H.R. 3556 Before a Subcomm. of the House Comm. on Interstate and Foreign Commerce,* 87th Cong., 2d Sess. (1962), 364 (statement of F.J.L. Blasingame).

27. Ibid., at 365.

28. Ibid., at 317 (statement of R. A. Rohweder).

29. *See, e.g.,* ibid., at 321 (statement of J. Swearingen, American Public Health Association).

30. The bills were H.R. 4856, 88th Cong., 1st Sess. (1963); H.R. 8957, 88th Cong., 1st Sess. (1963); H.R. 12408, 88th Cong., 2d Sess. (1964); S. 1071, 89th Cong., 1st Sess. (1965). Of these bills, the only one that took a radically different approach from what had been before Congress since at least 1960 was H.R. 8957, which, in essence, provided for federal financial and other assistance to improve facilities and provide for better employee training.

31. L. Meyer Jones, "Why AVMA Says No to Proposed Federal Legislation on Humane Care of Laboratory Animals," 142 *J. Am. Veterinary Med. Ass'n* 293, 295 (1963) (quoting AVMA letter).

32. In 1913–14, those opposed to vivisection brought charges against faculty members of the University of Pennsylvania, claiming that their use of animals in experiments violated the anticruelty law. Although five indictments were issued, the jury did not return verdicts of conviction. National societies opposed to vivisection then planned to initiate cruelty charges against all prominent surgeons who used animals in experiments. The plan never materialized. See William J. Shultz, *The Humane Movement in the United States 1910–1922* (New York: Columbia University, 1924), 157.

33. *See, e.g.,* Wis. Stat. Ann. § 174.13 (West 1989) (providing for the release of unclaimed dogs to research institutions). This law was passed originally in 1949.

34. *See* Act of June 19, 1947, No. 241, 1947 Mich. Pub. Acts 369.

35. *See* Mich. Stat. Ann. § 14.15 (2672)-(2676) (Callaghan 1988 & Supp. 1993). There have been some recent efforts to exercise more state and local authority over animal

experimentation. For example, legislators in New York have sought to fortify regulatory procedures to include an IACUC. In Cambridge, Massachusetts, animal welfare advocates succeeded in getting an ordinance that permits some local regulation of animal experimentation.

36. 116 Cong. Rec. 40,461 (1970) (statement of Sen. Dole).

37. *Regulate the Transportation, Sale, and Handling of Dogs and Cats Used for Research and Experimentation: Hearings on H.R. 9743 et al. Before the Subcomm. on Livestock and Feed Grains of the House Comm. on Agric.,* 89th Cong., 1st Sess. (1965), 2 (statement of Rep. Poage).

38. Ibid., at 4.

39. Ibid., at 19 (statement of L. Greenbaum).

40. Ibid., at 57 (statement of L. Nangeroni).

41. Ibid., at 88 (statement of W. Kinter, A. Farah, and S. Martin).

42. Ibid., at 89 (statement of E. Beddingfield Jr.).

43. *Regulate the Transportation, Sale, and Handling of Dogs and Cats Used for Research and Experimentation: Hearings on H.R. 9743 et al. Before the Subcomm. on Livestock and Feed Grains of the House Comm. on Agric.,* 89th Cong., 2d Sess. (1966).

44. Ibid., at 12 (statement of Orville Freeman).

45. OTA Report, at 298.

46. *Animal Dealer Regulation: Hearings on S. 2322, S. 3059, and S. 3138 Before the Senate Comm. on Commerce,* 89th Cong., 2d Sess. (1966). For the history of the 1966 legislation, see 1966 U.S.C.C.A.N. 2635. For the text of the law, see 1966 U.S.C.C.A.N. 400.

47. Laboratory Animal Welfare Act, Pub. L. No. 89-544, 80 Stat. 350 (1966).

48. Ibid., § 2(h).

49. Ibid., § 12.

50. Ibid., § 13.

51. Ibid., § 18.

52. Ibid., §§ 3, 4.

53. Ibid., § 6.

54. Ibid., § 7.

55. Ibid., § 5.

56. Ibid., § 11.

57. Ibid., § 10.

58. Ibid., § 16.

59. Ibid., §§ 19(a), (c).

60. Ibid., § 20.

61. Animal Welfare Act of 1970, Pub. L. No. 91-579, 84 Stat. 1560.

62. House Committee on Agriculture, *Report on Animal Welfare Act of 1970,* H.R. Rep. No. 1651, 91st Cong., 2d Sess. (1970), 1, *reprinted in* 1970 U.S.C.C.A.N. 5103, at 5104.

63. Animal Welfare Act of 1970, § 3.

64. Ibid.

65. Ibid.

66. Ibid., § 14.

67. 116 Cong. Rec. 40,155 (1970) (statement of Rep. Foley).

68. Ibid., at 40,460 (statement of Sen. Cotton).

69. Ibid., at 40,461 (article by Ann Cottrell Free). This article was also presented during deliberations in the House. *See* ibid., at 40,157.

70. Animal Welfare Act of 1970, § 14,

71. Ibid., § 13.

72. Ibid., § 17.

73. Ibid., § 10.

74. Animal Welfare Act Amendments of 1976, Pub. L. No. 94-279, 90 Stat. 417.

75. Ibid., § 4.

76. House Committee on Agriculture, *Report on the Animal Welfare Act Amendments of 1976,* H.R. Rep. 801, 94th Cong., 2d Sess. (1976), 8.

77. AWA Amendments of 1976, § 17.

78. Ibid., § 3.

79. Ibid., § 2.

80. *See The Use of Animals in Medical Research and Testing: Hearings Before the Subcomm. on Science, Research, and Technology of the House Comm. on Science and Technology,* 97th Cong., 1st Sess. (1981).

81. *Humane Care and Development of Substitutes for Animals in Research Act: Hearing on H.R. 6245 Before the Subcomm. on Science, Research, and Technology of the House Comm. on Science and Technology,* 97th Cong., 2d Sess. (1982), 10 (statement of William Raub).

82. Ibid., at 18.

83. *See* ibid., at 33 (statement of Dale Schwindaman of APHIS testifying on behalf of the USDA).

84. *Improved Standards for Lab. Animals Act; and Enforcement of the Animal Welfare Act by the Animal and Plant Health Inspection Serv.: Hearing on H.R. 5725 Before the Subcomm. on Dep't Operations, Research, and Foreign Agric. of the House Comm. on Agric.,* 98th Cong., 2d Sess. (1984), 2 (statement of Rep. Brown).

85. Food Security Act of 1985, Pub. L. No. 99-198, § 1751, 99 Stat. 1354, 1645.

86. 7 U.S.C. § 2143(a) (2) (1988), For purposes of the 1985 amendment, I am citing the United States Code provisions because the amendment is part of the current law.

87. 7 U.S.C. § 2143(a) (3) (A).

88. 7 U.S.C. § 2143(a) (3) (B).

89. 7 U.S.C. § 2143(a) (3) (C) (i–iv).

90. 7 U.S.C. § 2143(a) (3) (C) (v).

91. "Survival surgery" is a term used to describe surgery from which an animal is permitted to recover, usually to be used in further experimental procedures. For example, veterinary schools routinely used animals for multiple "practice" surgeries. I became aware of one case in which an animal at the University of Pennsylvania School of Veterinary Medicine was subjected to more than a dozen major "practice" surgeries.

92. 7 U.S.C. 2143(a) (3) (D) (i–ii).

93. The act defines "research facility" to include "any school (except an elementary or secondary school), institution, organization, or person that uses or intends to use live animals in research, tests, or experiments, and that (1) purchases or transports live animals in commerce, or (2) receives funds under a grant, award, loan, or contract from a department, agency, or instrumentality of the United States for the purpose of carrying out research, tests, or experiments." 7 U.S.C. § 2132(e).

94. 7 U.S.C. § 2143(b) (1). Federal facilities are governed by § 2143(c). The AWA specifies the IACUC as a "committee." The USDA and Public Health Service use the ex-

pression "Institutional Animal Care and Use Committee" as a "generic term for a committee whose function is to ensure appropriate and humane animal care and use." 54 Fed. Reg. 36,112, at 36,115 (1989). Similarly, under 42 U.S.C. § 289d (1988), which concerns the Public Health Service, "each entity which conducts biomedical research under this Act" shall have an "animal care committee." This committee, "which shall be appointed by the chief executive officer of the institution," shall review the animal care and use at the facility on at least a semiannual basis, keep records of such reviews, and file certain assurances and reports with the director of the National Institutes of Health. Institutions covered by the NIH Guide had been required under certain circumstances to have a committee before 1985.

95. 7 U.S.C. § 2143(b) (1) (A), (B) (i–iii).

96. 7 U.S.C. § 2143(b) (1).

97. 7 U.S.C. § 2143(b) (2).

98. 7 U.S.C. § 2143(b) (3).

99. 7 U.S.C. § 2143(b) (4) (A), (B).

100. 7 U.S.C. § 2143(e).

101. 7 U.S.C. § 2143(d).

102. 7 U.S.C. § 2143(f).

103. 7 U.S.C. § 2143(a) (7) (A).

104. 7 U.S.C. § 2143(a) (7) (B) (i–iii).

105. 7 U.S.C. § 2146(a).

106. Ibid.

107. *See* 7 U.S.C. § 2143(b) (1).

108. 7 U.S.C. § 2143(a) (6) (A) (ii).

109. *Improved Standards for Lab. Animals: Hearing on S. 657 Before the Senate Comm. on Agric., Nutrition, and Forestry,* 98th Cong., 1st Sess. (1983), 5–6 (statement of Bert Hawkins). The position taken by the USDA concerning the 1985 amendments is most relevant as it concerns the subsequent history of the USDA's inability and, perhaps, unwillingness to promulgate regulations to implement the amendments. I discuss this at greater length in the next chapter.

110. *Hearing on H.R. 5725,* at 47 (statement of Glenn Geelhoed on behalf of the American Association of Medical Colleges).

111. *Hearing on S. 657,* at 48 (statement of Walter Randall on behalf of the American Physiological Society).

112. Ibid., at 49.

113. Food, Agriculture, Conservation, and Trade Act of 1990, § 2503, Pub. L. No. 101–624, 104 Stat. 3359, 4066–68. This is codified at 7 U.S.C. § 2158 (Supp. 1991).

114. 7 U.S.C. § 2158(a) (1).

115. 9 C.F.R. § 2.101(a) (1993).

116. 9 C.F.R. § 2.101(a) (1).

117. 7 U.S.C. § 2158(b) (3).

118. *See* 58 Fed. Reg. 39,124–30 (1993).

119. *See* Julio Moran, "Three Sentenced to Prison for Stealing Pets for Research," *L.A. Times,* September 12, 1991, at B1.

120. *Hearing on H.R. 5725,* at 2 (statement of Rep. Brown).

121. *See, e.g.,* Rebecca Dresser, "Assessing Harm and Justification in Animal Research: Federal Policy Opens the Laboratory Door," 40 *Rutgers L. Rev.* 723 (1988). *See also* Gary L. Francione, "The Constitutional Status of Restrictions on Experiments Involving

Nonhuman Animals: A Comment on Professor Dresser's Analysis," 40 *Rutgers L. Rev.* 797 (1988).

122. Esther F. Dukes, "The Improved Standards for Laboratory Animals Act: Will It Ensure that the Policy of the Animal Welfare Act Becomes a Reality?" 31 *St. Louis U.L.J.* 519, 523 (1987). Dukes does acknowledge, however, that in 1970 Congress provided that professionally acceptable veterinary procedures should be followed during actual experimentation. Ibid., at 522.

123. See H.R. 6245, 97th Cong., 2d Sess. (1982).

124. Lab. Animal Welfare Act, § 13.

125. Animal Welfare Act of 1970, § 14 (emphasis added).

126. 116 Cong. Rec. 40,155 (1970) (statement of Rep. Foley).

127. 7 U.S.C. § 2143(a) (6) (A) (i) (1988).

128. 7 U.S.C. § 2143(a) (6) (A) (ii).

129. 9 C.F.R. § 2.31(d) (1).

130. NIH Guide, at 1.

131. *See* U.S. Public Health Service/National Institutes of Health, *Institutional Animal Care and Use Committee Guidebook* (Bethesda, Md.: National Institutes of Health, 1992).

132. *See* U.S. Public Health Service/National Institutes of Health, *Using Animals in Intramural Research: Guidelines for Investigators* (Bethesda, Md.: National Institutes of Health, 1992), § 2.3.

133. NIH Guide, at 82.

134. John M. Orem, "Demands That Research Be Useful Threaten to Undermine Basic Science in This Country," *Chron. Higher Educ.,* March 14, 1990, at B1.

135. C. R. Gallistel, "Bell, Magendie, and the Proposals to Restrict the Use of Animals in Neurobehavioral Research," 36 *Am. Psychologist* 357, 360 (1981).

136. 9 C.F.R. § 2.31(d) (1). Under earlier proposals, such justification was required to be provided to the funding agency. *See, e.g.,* H.R. 6245, 97th Cong., 2d Sess. (1982).

137. 9 C.F.R. § 2.31(d) (2), (3).

138. *See, e.g.,* Rebecca Dresser, "Research on Animals: Values, Politics, and Regulatory Reform," 58 *S. Cal. L. Rev.* 1147 (1985). Professor Dresser was one of the authors and editors of the NIH *Institutional Animal Care and Use Committee Guidebook.*

139. 7 U.S.C. § 2143(a) (6) (A) (i).

140. 42 U.S.C. § 289d(a).

141. 7 U.S.C. § 2143(a) (6) (A) (ii)–(iii).

142. 54 Fed. Reg. 36,142 (1989).

143. 7 U.S.C. § 2143(b) (1).

144. 7 U.S.C. § 2143(a) (3) (D) (i).

145. 7 U.S.C. § 2143(a) (3) (E).

146. 54 Fed. Reg. 36,132 (1989).

147. 9 C.F.R. § 2.31(d) (2) (1993).

## Chapter Ten

1. 7 U.S.C. § 2146(c) (Supp. IV 1992).

2. John P. Dwyer, "The Pathology of Symbolic Legislation," 17 *Ecology L.Q.* 233, 233 (1990).

3. Ibid.

4. Ibid., at 234.

5. *See* 33 U.S.C. § 1317 (1988).

6. 42 U.S.C. § 7412 (1988 & Supp. III 1992).

7. Dwyer, "Pathology of Symbolic Legislation," at 233.

8. *See* ibid., at 234.

9. *See* ibid., at 233.

10. These regulations are *not* statutes. Only Congress can enact a federal statute. Rather, these regulations are rules that look and read a great deal like statutes but are adopted by the administrative agency to which Congress entrusts implementation of the statute. For example, when, in the wake of the depression, Congress enacted legislation to protect those who invested in the securities markets, Congress created an administrative agency—the Securities and Exchange Commission (SEC)—to implement the congressional legislation. The SEC has, pursuant to the various statutes that it administers, promulgated rules and standards intended to effect the goal of investor protection and market stability.

Similarly, in the case of the AWA, Congress could not legislate for every possible circumstance. Such all-encompassing legislation would make statutes even more unreadable than they are at present. Accordingly, Congress delegated authority to enforce the AWA to an already existing federal administrative agency—USDA.

11. "Reporting facility" is defined as "that segment of the research facility, or that department, agency, or instrumentality of the United States, that uses or intends to use live animals in research, tests, experiments, or for teaching." 9 C.F.R. § 2.36(a) (1993).

12. 9 C.F.R. § 2.36(b) (1–8) (1993). One may obtain these reports for a particular institution by making a request under the federal Freedom of Information Act (FOIA). FOIA, which is contained in title 5 of the United States Code at section 552, permits the public to get a wide range of documents from the federal government. To obtain these reports, write to the FOIA officer at USDA: USDA/APHIS, Coordinator, Freedom of Information Act, Room 771A, 6506 Belcrest Road, Hyattsville, Maryland 20782. To obtain the grant applications that were filed for experiments funded by the federal government, write to NIH FOIA Officer, Office of Communications, National Institutes of Health, Building 31, Room 2B43, Bethesda, Maryland 20205. Make sure that your requests are specific.

13. 9 C.F.R. § 3.28(b) (1). The regulation provides that guinea pigs acquired on or after August 15, 1990, must be provided more space, except for breeding females, who are provided with less space under the new regulations. 9 C.F.R. § 3.28(c) (1).

14. 9 C.F.R. § 3.28(c) (1) (ii). If the guinea pig was acquired before August 15, 1990, the interior height need be only 6.5 inches. 9 C.F.R. § 3.28(b) (2) (i).

15. 9 C.F.R. § 3.28(c) (1) (iii). For guinea pigs acquired before August 15, 1990, the regulations provide for 90 square inches for animals weighing 350 grams or more, and 180 square inches for "breeders." 9 C.F.R. § 3.28(b) (2) (ii).

16. *Humane Soc'y v. Lyng,* 633 F. Supp. 480, 486 (W.D.N.Y. 1986). The plaintiff humane society and two dairy farmers sued Lyng, who was then secretary of USDA, because USDA had required farmers involved in a milk production program to hot brand the face of cattle to be slaughtered under the program. The USDA had considered and explicitly rejected a less painful, but slower, alternative to the hot facial brand. In striking down the regulation as an arbitrary and capricious exercise of administrative authority and as unnecessarily cruel, the court stated that "had defendants truly been concerned with unnecessary

cruelty to animals, they would have at least allowed the farmers the option of either method" of branding. Ibid., at 487.

17. *Animal Legal Defense Fund v. Madigan,* 781 F. Supp. 797, 805 (D.D.C. 1992), *vacated sub. nom. Animal Legal Defense Fund, Inc. v. Espy,* 23 F.3d 496 (D.C. Cir. 1994).

18. 7 U.S.C. § 2143(a) (2) (B) (1988). Required minimal standards also included those "for handling, housing, feeding, watering, sanitation, ventilation, shelter from extremes of weather and temperatures, adequate veterinary care, and separation by species where the Secretary finds necessary for humane handling, care, or treatment of animals." 7 U.S.C. § 2153(a) (2) (A).

19. 55 Fed. Reg. 33,448, at 33,467 (1990). For a defense of the switch from engineering standards to performance standards based on achieving the optimal welfare of the animal, see Charles McCarthy, "Improved Standards for Laboratory Animals?" 3 *Kennedy Inst. Ethics J.* 293 (1993). I discuss McCarthy's analysis in Chapter Eleven.

20. 9 C.F.R. § 3.6(d) (1993) (dog enclosures); § 3.80(c) (primate enclosures).

21. 56 Fed. Reg. 6446 (1991).

22. 55 Fed. Reg. 33,448, at 33,451 (1990) (emphasis added).

23. Recall that the AWA also covers exhibitors, dealers, and transporters as well. I have limited my examination to those provisions of the AWA that concern animals used in experiments.

24. *See* Exec. Order No. 12,291, 3 C.F.R. 127 (1982).

25. 56 Fed. Reg. 6426, at 6485 (1991).

26. Ibid., at 6486 (1991).

27. U.S. General Accounting Office, *Report to the Chairman, Subcomm. on Agric., Rural Dev. and Related Agencies, Senate Comm. on Appropriations: The Dep't of Agriculture's Animal Welfare Program* (1985), 21 [hereinafter GAO Report].

28. U.S. Department of Agriculture Animal and Plant Health Inspection Service, *Report of the Secretary of Agric. to the President of the Senate and the Speaker of the House of Representatives: Animal Welfare Enforcement Fiscal Year 1992* (1993), 2–3 [hereinafter (year) APHIS Report]. Also, please note that all years referred to in the context of USDA enforcement reports are to the fiscal year, which begins on October 1 and ends on September 30.

29. 1991 APHIS Report, 2, 5.

30. 1990 APHIS Report, at 2. In 1990 and before, USDA appeared to estimate that each research facility had 2.2 sites per facility. After 1990, USDA has claimed to use the actual site figures.

31. 1989 APHIS Report, at 7, 15.

32. 1988 APHIS Report, at 14. It is not clear whether the 3,767 inspections include prelicensing inspections, which are announced inspections. If the number includes such inspections, then the overall average for compliance inspections would be less than 1.31 inspections per site.

33. Cease-and-desist orders differ from warnings in that if the party bound by the order does not comply, sanctions may be imposed.

34. 1992 APHIS Report, at 12.

35. Telephone interview with APHIS Public Information Office, Wednesday, November 3, 1993. The figures reported by APHIS indicate that not all official warnings or stipulations involve the Regulatory Enforcement staff. For example, in 1992, there were 980 cases, but only 105 were submitted to the Regulatory Enforcement staff. Nevertheless,

731 cases were settled with an official notice of warning or a stipulation. If the Regulatory Enforcement staff received only 105 cases, they could not have disposed of 731 cases.

36. 1992 APHIS Report, at 12.

37. Ibid.

38. 1991 APHIS Report, at 10.

39. GAO Report, at 21.

40. Ibid., at 22.

41. According to Dr. Jerry DePoyster, Veterinary Medical Officer, USDA/APHIS/REAC, "all sites are inspected at least once per year." Letter from DePoyster to Francione, November 29, 1993 (on file with the author) [hereinafter DePoyster letter].

42. *See, e.g.,* U.S. Department of Agriculture, Animal and Plant Health Inspection Service, *Prosecutions for Animal Welfare Violations, 1968–1980* (1980); APHIS News, 1983–93.

43. GAO Report, at i–vi.

44. *Animal Welfare Act: Hearing on H.R. 1770 Before the Subcomm. on Admin. Law and Gov'tal Relations of the House Comm. on the Judiciary,* 100th Cong., 2d Sess. (1988), 61.

45. GAO Report, at 8.

46. Ibid., at 20.

47. *Improved Standards for Lab. Animals Act; and Enforcement of the Animal Welfare Act by the Animal and Plant Health Inspection Serv.: Hearing on H.R. 5725 Before the Subcomm. on Dep't Operations, Research, and Foreign Agric. of the House Comm. on Agric.,* 98th Cong, 2d Sess. (1984), 24 (statement of Bert Hawkins, APHIS administrator). *See also Improved Standards for Lab. Animals: Hearings on S. 657 Before the Senate Comm. on Agric., Nutrition, and Forestry,* 98th Cong., 1st Sess. (1983), 54 (statement of Bert Hawkins).

48. *Hearing on H.R. 5725,* at 24.

49. DePoyster letter ("All sites are inspected at least once per year").

50. Ibid.

51. OTA Report, at 14.

52. Ibid., at 297.

53. 9 C.F.R. § 2.36(b) (1) (1993).

54. 9 C.F.R. § 2.36(b) (5)–(7).

55. 9 C.F.R. § 2.36(b) (7).

56. 1992 APHIS Report, 16–19.

57. 1992 APHIS Report; 1991 APHIS Report. In 1990 APHIS reported a total of 1,578,099 covered animals used, with 58 percent (920,330) not subjected to pain or distress, 36 percent (568,145) subjected to pain or distress but provided with adequate relief, and 6 percent (89,624) subjected to pain or distress without relief. There were 1,470 registered facilities in 1990 for an average of 1,073 animals per facility, and 488 per site. 1990 APHIS Report, at 7, 15–18. In 1989 APHIS reported a total of 1,754,456 covered animals used, with 58 percent (1,019,350) not subjected to pain or distress, 35 percent (619,219) provided adequate relief from pain or distress, and 7 percent (116,587) not provided relief from pain or distress. There were 1,296 registered facilities, for an average of 1,354 animals per facility and 615 per site. 1989 APHIS Report, at 7, 10, appendix. In 1988 APHIS reported that 1,635,288 covered animals were used, with 35.7 percent (583,617) not subjected to pain or distress, 58.7 percent (961,271) provided with adequate relief from pain

or distress, and 5.5 percent (90,400) not provided with relief from pain or distress. There were 1,308 registered facilities for an average of 1,250 animals per facility and 568 per site. 1988 APHIS Report, at 5–7, 19–21. In 1987 APHIS reported a total of 1,969,123 covered animals used, with 58 percent (1,146,503) not subjected to pain or distress, 35 percent (692,247) provided with adequate relief from pain or distress, and 7 percent (130,373) not provided with relief from pain or distress. There were 1,260 registered facilities for an average of 1,563 animals per facility and 710 animals per site. 1987 APHIS Report, at 9–12.

As I mentioned earlier, before 1991 APHIS estimated that each registered facility had an average of 2.2 sites; according to the 1991 report, APHIS now uses the actual number of sites per facility. Also, in 1992 APHIS created a separate category for research facilities that were "inactive" or were not presently conducting covered activities. The actual numbers of animals, which are in parentheses, come directly from the APHIS reports and often do not match the reported percentage, which has been adjusted.

58. *See* 1992 APHIS Report, at 6–7, 16; 1991 APHIS Report, at 5, 15. A recent study has concluded that there has been a substantial reduction in the number of animals used in experiments. *See* Andrew N. Rowan et al., *The Animal Research Controversy* (Grafton, Mass.: Tufts University School of Veterinary Medicine, 1994). As I explain in Chapter Eight, the Tufts conclusion is questionable.

59. *Hearing on S. 657,* at 178 (statement of John Block).

60. Ibid., at 178, 179.

61. Ibid., at 179. The House bill had a requirement for the exercise of dogs, which the USDA also opposed.

62. *Hearing on H.R. 5725,* at 24 (statement of Bert Hawkins). In trying to make the case against amending the AWA, Hawkins made a better case for why the AWA was virtually useless in the protection of animals: the "judgments" about animal care and treatment are invariably relegated to those who do the experimentation; and surely, their "judgments" about appropriate animal care and treatment should not determine the criteria to be used in assessing the adequacy of that care and treatment.

63. Ibid., at 24.

64. Bernard E. Rollin, *The Unheeded Cry* (Oxford: Oxford University Press, 1989).

65. Frank Hurnik and Hugh Lehman, "Unnecessary Suffering: Definition and Evidence," 3 *Int'l J. Stud. Animal Prob.* 131 (1982).

66. National Research Council, Commission on Life Sciences, Committee on Pain and Distress in Laboratory Animals, *Recognition and Alleviation of Pain and Distress in Laboratory Animals* (Washington, D.C.: National Academy Press, 1992), ix.

67. Andrew N. Rowan, *Of Mice, Models, and Men* (Albany: State University of New York Press, 1984), 75.

68. *See* Jerry Adler, "The (Secret) World of Dogs," *Newsweek,* November 1, 1993, at 58; Eugene Linder, "Can Animals Think?" *Time,* March 22, 1993, at 54.

69. *See* Gary L. Francione, "A Common Bond," *Animals' Voice,* April/May 1991, at 54–55.

70. Mark Solomon and Peter C. Lovenheim, "Reporting Requirements Under the Animal Welfare Act: Their Inadequacies and the Public's Right to Know," 3 *Int'l J. Stud. Animal Prob.* 210, 212 (1982) (article adapted from a petition for rule making filed by HSUS with the USDA on February 22, 1982).

71. Ibid, (quoting annual report of Unilab Research, Berkeley, Calif.).

72. 9 C.F.R. § 2.36(b) (5) (1993).

73. Solomon and Lovenheim, "Reporting Requirements," at 213.

74. Ibid., at 213–14.

75. Ibid., at 214–15.

76. *See* Humane Society of the United States, *Petition for Changes in Reporting Procedures Under the Animal Welfare Act Before the Animal and Plant Health Inspection Service of the United States Department of Agriculture* (October 1992).

77. Ibid., 5–11. HSUS also requested that USDA implement standardized reporting procedures for facilities that do not use any animals during the reporting period. *See* ibid., at 12.

78. Ibid., at 13–14.

79. *See Beyond the Laboratory Door* (Washington, D.C.: Animal Welfare Institute, 1985). ("We are publishing this report to document massive noncompliance with the Animal Welfare Act.")

80. Ibid., at 2 (footnote omitted).

81. Ibid., at 60–62.

82. Ibid., at 3.

83. *See* ibid., at 54–56.

84. *See* ibid., at 33–37.

85. 7 U.S.C. § 2132(g) (1988).

86. Rowan, *Of Mice, Models, and Men,* at 67.

87. OTA Report, at 278.

88. 54 Fed. Reg. 36,112, at 36,113 (1989).

89. 7 U.S.C. § 2132(g) (1988). The USDA has indicated that it will regulate, under the AWA, the use of horses and other farm animals used for biomedical or nonagricultural research. *See* 55 Fed. Reg. 12,630 (1990).

90. *See* Anne Griffin and Jeri A. Sechzer, "Mandatory Versus Voluntary Regulation of Biomedical Research," 406 *Annals N.Y. Acad. Sci.* 187, 188 (1983). *See also* Henry Cohen, "The Legality of the Agriculture Department's Exclusion of Rats and Mice from Coverage Under the Animal Welfare Act," 31 *St. Louis U.L.J.* 543 (1987).

91. 7 U.S.C. § 2143(a) (1988).

92. For the proposed amendments to part 1, see 52 Fed. Reg. 10,292 (1987); for the proposed amendments to part 2, see 52 Fed. Reg. 10,298 (1987).

93. 54 Fed. Reg. 10,822, at 10,823 (1989). For the USDA reproposal of the amendments to part 1, see 54 Fed. Reg. 10,822 (1989); for the USDA reproposal of the amendments to part 2, see 54 Fed. Reg. 10,835 (1989).

94. For the final amendment of part 1, see 54 Fed. Reg. 36,112 (1989); for the final amendment of part 2, see 54 Fed. Reg. 36,123 (1989).

95. For the revisions of part 3, subparts B and C, see 55 Fed. Reg. 28,879 (1990).

96. *See* 54 Fed. Reg. 10,897–10,954 (1989).

97. *See* 55 Fed. Reg. 33,448 (1990).

98. *See* 54 Fed. Reg. 10,897, at 10,934–10,935 (1989).

99. 55 Fed. Reg. 33,448, at 33,450, 33,469 (1990).

100. Ibid., at 33,469 (1990).

101. Ibid., at 33,468 (1990).

102. 54 Fed. Reg. 10,897, at 10,904 (1989). *See also* 55 Fed. Reg. 33,448, at 33, 467 (1990).

103. *See* 55 Fed. Reg. 33,468, at 33,469 (1990).

104. 55 Fed. Reg. 33,467 (1990). In *Secretary,* the trial court cited this passage as appearing in the preamble to the final rules, in 56 Fed. Reg. 6426, at 6447 (1991). *See Secretary,* 813 F. Supp. at 887 n. 9. This is incorrect. The passage was part of the preamble to the reproposed rules in 1990.

105. 55 Fed. Reg 33,448, at 33,469 (1990).

106. *See* ibid., at 33,516, 33,517 (1990).

107. *See* 56 Fed. Reg. 6426, at 6427 (1991).

108. 54 Fed. Reg. 10,897, at 10,905 (1989).

109. 56 Fed. Reg. 6426, at 6447, 6446 (1991). The USDA stated that "we encourage the design and development of primary enclosures that promote the well-being of dogs and cats by providing them with sufficient space and the opportunity for movement and exercise. Accordingly, we provided . . . that innovative primary enclosures *not precisely meeting the floor area and height requirements provided for dogs and cats* . . . could be used at research facilities when approved by the" IACUC. Ibid., at 6446 (emphasis added).

110. 54 Fed. Reg, 10,897, at 10,944–10,949 (1989).

111. Ibid., at 10,919 (1989).

112. 56 Fed. Reg. 6426, at 6499–6500 (1991); 55 Fed. Reg. 33,448, at 33,525 (1990).

113. 56 Fed. Reg, 6426, at 6500 (1991); 55 Fed. Reg. 33, 525, at 33,526 (1990).

114. 56 Fed. Reg. 6426, at 6471 (199 1

115. Ibid., at 6499 (1991).

116. Ibid., at 6471 (1991). The USDA stated that "we encourage the design and development of primary enclosures that promote the psychological well-being of nonhuman primates by providing them with sufficient space and unrestricted opportunity for movement and exercise, and by allowing them to interact physically and socially with other nonhuman primates. Accordingly we propose to allow the use of primary enclosures that *do not provide the minimum space otherwise required.*" Ibid. (emphasis added).

117. *See* USDA Inspection Report, University of Pennsylvania, School of Medicine, May 31, 1984 (on file with the author).

118. *See* USDA Inspection Report, University of Pennsylvania, School of Medicine, June 5, 1984 (on file with the author).

119. *See* USDA Inspection Report, Institute for Behavioral Research, April 24, 1981, and July 17, 1981 (on file with the author).

120. *See* USDA Inspection Report, Institute for Behavioral Research, September 15, 1981, and September 17, 1981 (on file with the author).

121. Esther F. Dukes, "The Improved Standards for Laboratory Animals Act: Will It Ensure that the Policy of the Animal Welfare Act Becomes a Reality?" 31 *St. Louis U.L.J.* 519, 527–28 (1987).

122. Howard Latin, "Regulatory Failure, Administrative Incentives, and the New Clean Air Act," 21 *Envtl L.* 1647 (1991).

123. Ibid., at 1659–66.

124. Similarly, Latin argues that agencies will not meet deadlines if appropriations, personnel, information, or other resources are not adequate. *See* ibid., at 1666–70. Apart from whether USDA lacks resources, it is clear that any uncertainty about scientific judgments will be relevant to this behavioral "law" as well.

125. Ibid., at 1657–69.

126. Ibid., at 1673–76.

127. Ibid., at 1670–73.

## *Chapter Eleven*

1. *Lujan,* 112 S. Ct. 2130.

2. 7 U.S.C. § 2146(c) (Supp. IV 1992).

3. USDA, *NEWS,* February 6, 1991, at 1.

4. Ibid.

5. I should again emphasize that I am only discussing those cases that concern the AWA as it relates to animals used in experiments, The AWA also covers animals used in other contexts, such as animal exhibits. For example, in *Haviland v. Butz,* 543 F.2d 169 (D.C. Cir.), *cert. denied,* 429 U.S. 832 (1976), Haviland owned and operated an animal show that included dogs and ponies. After USDA notified Haviland that he was an "exhibitor" under the AWA and needed to obtain a USDA license, Haviland sued. According to Haviland, the AWA did not cover his dog and pony show.

The court disagreed with Haviland, holding that the AWA had been amended in 1970 to cover animals used for exhibition purposes and that Haviland's dog and pony show certainly constituted such an exhibition. The court also rejected other arguments that Haviland made concerning the constitutionality of the AWA. A contrary decision would be difficult to imagine. In amending the AWA in 1970, Congress clearly meant to cover these types of animal acts.

6. *Animal Legal Defense Fund v. Madigan,* 781 F. Supp. 797 (D.D.C. 1992), *vacated sub. nom. Animal Legal Defense Fund, Inc. v. Espy,* 23 F.3d 496 (D.C. Cir. 1994).

7. *Madigan,* 781 F. Supp. at 802 (quoting H.R. Rep. No. 1651, 91st Cong., 2d Sess. 1970], 6, *reprinted in* 1970 U.S.C.C.A.N. 5103, 5108).

8. *Madigan,* 781 F. Supp. at 802 (quoting Henry Cohen, "The Legality of the Agriculture Department's Exclusion of Rats and Mice from Coverage Under the Animal Welfare Act," 31 *St. Louis U.L.J.* 543, 545 n. 19 [1987]),

9. *Madigan,* 781 F. Supp. at 802–3.

10. Ibid. at 805.

11. 813 F. Supp. 882 (D.D.C. 1993), *vacated sub nom. Animal Legal Defense Fund, Inc. v. Espy,* 29 F.3d 720 (D.C. Cir. 1994).

12. Ibid. at 886.

13. Ibid. at 889.

14. Charles McCarthy, "Improved Standards for Laboratory Animals?" 3 *Kennedy Inst. Ethics J.* 293, 301 (1993).

15. Ibid. at 300.

16. Ibid. at 296–99.

17. 7 U.S.C. § 2143(a) (2) (B) (1988).

18. 55 Fed. Reg. 33,448, at 33,451 (1990).

19. *State v. LeVasseur,* 613 P.2d 1328 (Haw. Ct. App.), *cert. denied,* 449 U.S. 1018 (1980).

20. Ibid., at 1330–31.

21. Ibid., at 1332 (emphasis added).

22. Ibid., at 1333.

23. *Kerr v. Kimmell,* 740 F. Supp. 1525 (D. Kan. 1990); *Winkler v. Colorado Dep't of Health,* 564 P.2d 107 (Colo. 1977) (en banc).

24. U.S. Const. art. VI, § 2.

25. *See Hillsborough County v. Automated Medical Lab., Inc.,* 471 U.S. 707, 713 (1985).

26. *Kerr,* 740 F. Supp. at 1530. The court cited 7 U.S.C. §§ 2143(a) (8), 2145(b).

27. *Winkler,* 564 P.2d at 110–11.

28. *United States v. Linville,* 10 F.3d 630 (9th Cir. 1993).

29. Ibid., at 631.

30. Ibid., at 630 (quoting United States Sentencing Guidelines, § 2F1.1 [b] [3] [B] [1992]).

31. Ibid., at 633.

32. In most instances, state "sunshine" laws apply to public agencies. Most litigation has focused on IACUCs at public institutions, such as *state,* as opposed to *private,* universities. It remains an open question, however, whether these state access laws apply to IACUCs at private institutions as well. It is at least arguable that the IACUCs at all institutions should be regarded as carrying out the governmental function of ensuring the humane treatment of nonhuman animals.

33. For example, the University of Florida at Gainesville has voluntarily opened IACUC meetings to interested members of the public since the mid-1980s.

34. *See, e.g., Students for the Ethical Treatment of Animals v. Huffines,* 399 S.E.2d 340 (N.C. Ct. App. 1991) (IACUC records subject to disclosure law) (I was counsel of record in that case); *Animal Legal Defense Fund, Inc. v. Institutional Animal Care & Use Comm.,* 616 A.2d 224 (Vt. 1992) (University of Vermont IACUC subject to both the public records law and the public access law).

35. *See, e.g., Medlock v. Board of Trustees,* 580 N.E.2d 387 (Mass. App. Ct.), *cert. denied,* 586 N.E.2d 10 (Mass. 1991) (open meeting law did not apply to IACUC meetings). In *People for the Ethical Treatment of Animals v. Institutional Animal Care & Use Comm.,* 817 P.2d 1299 (Or. 1991), an animal advocacy group sought to challenge the decision of the University of Oregon IACUC to permit an experiment on barn owls. The Oregon Supreme Court held that the group had no standing to challenge IACUC decisions. Unreported decisions in California and Virginia also denied access.

36. *American Soc'y for the Prevention of Cruelty to Animals v. Board of Trustees,* 541 N.Y.S.2d 183 (Sup. Ct. 1989), *rev'd,* 568 N.Y.S.2d 631 (App. Div. 1991), *aff'd,* 591 N.E.2d 1169 (N.Y. 1992) [hereinafter *SUNY I* ]. I was counsel of record in this case.

37. *SUNY I,* 541 N.Y.S.2d at 185.

38. Ibid., at 183–84.

39. *SUNY I,* 568 N.Y.S.2d at 634.

40. 54 Fed. Reg. 36,123, at 36,133 (1989). *See also* 9 C.F.R. § 2.31(d) (8) (1993) (institutional "officials may not approve an activity involving the care and use of [laboratory] animals if it has not been approved by the IACUC").

41. *SUNY I,* 568 N.Y.S.2d at 634 (quoting N.Y. Pub. Off. Law § 100).

42. 54 Fed. Reg. 36,123, at 36,128 (1989).

43. *SUNY I,* 568 N.Y.S.2d at 634.

44. *Oneonta Star Div. of Ottaway Newspapers, Inc. v. Board of Trustees,* 412 N.Y.S.2d 927, 930 (App. Div. 1979).

45. *MFY Legal Servs., Inc. v. Toia,* 402 N.Y.S.2d 510, 512 (Sup. Ct. 1977).

46. The court appeared also to hold that because the IACUC requirements applied to private and public institutions alike and because IACUC meetings at private institutions would not be open to the public, the IACUC could not perform a governmental function. *See SUNY I,* 568 N.Y.S.2d at 633–34. This portion of the court's decision is mystifying for a number of reasons. First, the issue of whether the access requirements would apply to a private institution was never raised before the trial court and was mentioned for the first

time by the appellate court, which simply assumed away a legal issue that had never been raised or briefed. Second, it is not unusual for access requirements to apply to a state actor, but not to a private actor engaged in the very same conduct. For example, SUNY conceded that its board of trustees meetings must be open to the public. It is generally thought that the board of trustees meeting of a private New York university would not be open, but public and private boards do the exact same thing at their respective institutions. The SUNY board meeting is open precisely because it is a state university, and its state status carries with it additional obligations. Third, the appellate court's view that the differential application of IACUC requirements to public and private institutions was meaningful suggests that the court accepted SUNY's argument that only governmental—and not proprietary— actions of a state actor can be considered a "governmental function." But the governmental proprietary distinction, which was used in the context of determining the tort liability of municipalities, has been regarded as an anachronism by both federal courts (*see e.g., Garcia v. San Antonio Metro. Transit Auth.*, 469 U.S. 528, 531 [1985]) and by the courts of New York (*see, e.g., In re County of Monroe*, 530 N.E.2d 202 [N.Y. 1988]).

47. *SUNY I*, 591 N.E.2d at 1169.

48. Ibid., at 1170.

49. *American Soc'y for the Prevention of Cruelty to Animals v. Board of Trustees*, 556 N.Y.S.2d 447 (Sup. Ct. 1990), *rev'd*, 584 N.Y.S.2d 198 (App. Div. 1992). I was counsel of record in this case.

50. 7 U.S.C. § 2143(a) (6) (B) (1988).

51. 7 U.S.C. § 2157 (1988).

52. *See Improved Standards for Lab. Animals Act; and Enforcement of the Animal Welfare Act by the Animal and Plant Health Inspection Serv.: Hearing on H.R. 5725 Before the Subcomm. on Dep't Operations, Research, and Foreign Agric. of the House Comm. on Agric.*, 98th Cong., 2d Sess. (1984), 13–14, 17–18.

53. This interpretation of the statutory scheme finds support in the regulations of the USDA, which has indicated that the federal confidentiality concerns are limited to proprietary information in the form of trade secrets, patent rights, and other commercial or financial information. *See* 54 Fed. Reg. 36,123, at 36,141 (1989). The USDA also made it clear that the IACUC may not, in any manner, regulate scientific design and methodology. *See* ibid., at 36,142. Also, the NIH will not release any "confidential commercial or financial information" pursuant to a request under the federal Freedom of Information Act. Upon a request for copies of a research grant application, NIH first consults with grantees to "advise [NIH] if the release of the material . . . requested would adversely affect any patent rights or reveal any other confidential commercial or financial information" (NIH form letter on file with the author).

54. U.S. Const. amend. 1.

55. There is not one shred of legislative history to suggest that Congress intended to prohibit the release of information other than what Congress explicitly designated in section 2143 as "trade secrets or commercial or financial information."

56. See 5 U.S.C. § 552 (1988).

57. 42 U.S.C. § 289d(e) (1988).

58. See 17 U.S.C. § 102(b) (1988); *Harper & Row, Publishers, Inc. v. Nation Enters.*, 471 U.S. 539 (1985). *See also* Gary L. Francione, "Facing *The Nation:* The Standards for Copyright, Infringement, and Fair Use of Factual Works," 134 *U. Pa. L. Rev.* 519, 537–40 (1986).

59. *Diamond v. Chakrabarty*, 447 U.S. 303, 309 (1980).

## *Epilogue*

1. As I have stated earlier, the mere protection of an interest, even when that protection is not contingent on consequential considerations, does not necessarily mean that a right exists.

2. *See generally* Peter Singer, *Animal Liberation,* 2d ed. (New York: New York Review of Books, 1990).

3. F. Barbara Orlans, *In the Name of Science: Issues in Responsible Animal Experimentation* (New York: Oxford University Press, 1993).

4. Andrew N. Rowan, *Of Mice, Models, and Men* (Albany: State University of New York Press, 1984).

5. There are, of course, variants of this third welfarist alternative. For example, someone who subscribes to this third alternative may maintain that although welfarist changes may not themselves lead to abolition, the incremental changes, with the attendant educational and legislative campaigns, will effect a gradual change in social consciousness about the status of animals, which will then lead to abolition of vivisection or the recognition of rights. Although this variant does not require a causal relationship between the changes and the final goal, it accepts that there is a causal relationship between the efforts to achieve the change and the goal of abolition. A person might also maintain that there is no causal relationship between incremental change and raised consciousness, or between these changes and the ultimate goal of animal rights, but that incremental change is simply preferable to no change at all while other—and causally unrelated—efforts to raise consciousness continue.

# Selected Bibliography

*Animals: Philosophy, History,*
*Animal Rights, and Animal Welfare*

Achor, Amy Blount. *Animal Rights.* Yellow Springs, Ohio: WriteWare, 1992.

American Medical Association. *Use of Animals in Biomedical Research: The Challenge and the Response.* AMA white paper, 1989.

Animal Welfare Institute, ed. *Beyond the Laboratory Door.* Washington, D.C.: Animal Welfare Institute, 1985.

Baird, Robert M., and Stuart E. Rosenbaum, eds. *Animal Experimentation: The Moral Issues.* Buffalo, N.Y.: Prometheus Books, 1991.

Baker, Ron. *The American Hunting Myth.* New York: Vantage Press, 1985.

Barlow-Kennett, Richard. "Address to the Working Classes." In *Vivisection in America,* 4th ed., edited by Francis P. Cobbe and Benjamin Bryan. London: Swan, Sonnenschein & Co., 1980.

Batten, Peter. *Living Trophies.* New York: Thomas Y. Crowell Co., 1976.

Bekoff, Marc, and Dale Jamieson, eds. *Interpretation and Explanation in the Study of Animal Behavior.* Vol. 1. Boulder, Colo.: Westview Press, 1990.

————, eds. *Interpretation and Explanation in the Study of Animal Behavior.* Vol. 2. Boulder, Colo.: Westview Press, 1990.

Boudet, Jacques. *Man and Beast: A Visual History,* translated by Anne Carter. New York: Golden Press, 1964.

Carruthers, Peter. *The Animals Issue.* Cambridge: Cambridge University Press, 1992.

Carson, Gerald. *Men, Beasts, and Gods.* New York: Charles Scribner's Sons, 1972.

Cavalieri, Paola, and Peter Singer, eds. *The Great Ape Project.* New York: St. Martin's Press, 1993.

Clark, Stephen R. L. *The Moral Status of Animals.* Oxford: Clarendon Press, 1977.

————. "The Rights of Wild Things." 22 *Inquiry* 171 (1979).

Clarke, A. B., and Andrew Linzey, eds. *Political Theory and Animal Rights.* London: Pluto Press, 1990.

Cobbe, Francis P., and Benjamin Bryan, eds. *Vivisection in America.* London: Swan, Sonnenschein & Co., 1890.

Cohen, Carl. "The Case for the Use of Animals in Biomedical Research." 315 *New Eng. J. Med.* 865 (1986).

Cohn, Priscilla N. "Pro and Con: Should Animals Be Used for Research?" *Philadelphia Inquirer,* May 25, 1986, at P-1.

Diner, Jeff. *Physical and Mental Suffering of Experimental Animals.* Washington, D.C.: Animal Welfare Institute, 1979.

———. "A Review of the Scientific Literature, 1978–1984." In *Beyond the Laboratory Door,* edited by the Animal Welfare Institute. Washington, D.C.: Animal Welfare Institute, 1985.

Donovan, Josephine. "Animal Rights and Feminist Theory." In *Ecofeminism: Women, Animals, Nature,* edited by Greta Gaard. Philadelphia: Temple University Press, 1993.

Feinberg, Joel. "The Rights of Animals and Unborn Generations." In *Philosophy and Environmental Crisis,* edited by William T. Blackstone. Athens: University of Georgia Press, 1974.

Fox, Michael A. *The Case for Animal Experimentation.* Berkeley and Los Angeles: University of California Press, 1986.

Francione, Gary L. "A Common Bond." *Animal's Voice,* April/May 1991, at 54.

Fraser, Caroline. "The Raid at Silver Spring." *New Yorker,* April 19, 1993, at 66.

Freeman, Alan, and Betty Mensch. "Scratching the Belly of the Beast." In *Animal Experimentation,* edited by Robert M. Baird and Stuart E. Rosenbaum. Buffalo, N.Y.: Prometheus Books, 1991.

French, Richard D. *Antivivisection and Medical Science in Victorian Society.* Princeton, N.J.: Princeton University Press, 1975.

Frey, R. G. *Interests and Rights: The Case Against Animals.* Oxford: Clarendon Press, 1980.

———. *Rights, Killing, and Suffering.* Oxford: Basil Blackwell, 1983.

———. "The Significance of Agency and Marginal Cases." 39 *Philosophica* 39 (1987).

Gaard, Greta, ed. *Ecofeminism: Women, Animals, Nature.* Philadelphia: Temple University Press, 1993.

Gallistel, C. R. "Bell, Magendie, and the Proposals to Restrict the Use of Animals in Neurobehavioral Research." 36 *Am. Psychologist* 357 (1981).

Garattini, Silvio, and D. W. van Bekkum. *The Importance of Animal Experimentation for Safety and Biomedical Research.* Dordrecht: Kluwer Academic Publishers, 1990.

Garner, Robert. *Animals, Politics and Morality.* New York: St. Martin's Press, 1993.

Gold, Mark. *Assault and Battery.* London: Pluto Press, 1983.

Gossel, Patricia P. "William Henry Welch and the Antivivisectionist Legislation in the District of Columbia, 1896–1900." 40 *J. Hist. Med.* 397 (1985).

Grandin, Temple. *Recommended Animal Handling Guidelines for Meat Packers.* American Meat Institute, 1991.

Griffin, Anne, and Jeri A. Sechzer. "Mandatory Versus Voluntary Regulation of Biomedical Research." 406 *Annals N.Y. Acad. Sci.* 187 (1983).

Griffin, Donald R. *Animal Thinking.* Cambridge: Harvard University Press, 1984.

———. *The Question of Animal Awareness.* Rev. ed. New York: Rockefeller University Press, 1981.

Grunewald, Carol, and Jim Mason. "The Head Injury Lab Break-In." *Animals' Agenda,* May 1985, at 1.

Guillermo, Kathy S. *Monkey Business.* Washington, D.C.: National Press, 1993.

Hampson, Judith. "Legislation and the Changing Consensus." In *Animal Experimentation:*

*The Consensus Changes,* edited by Gill Langley. New York: Chapman & Hall, 1989.

Harrison, Ruth. *Animal Machines.* London: Vincent Stuart, 1964.

Hays, H. R. *Birds, Beasts, and Men.* New York: G. P. Putnam's Sons, 1972.

Hendriksen, C.F.M., and H.B.W.M. Koeter, eds. *Animals in Biomedical Research.* Amsterdam: Elsevier, 1991.

Humane Society of the United States. "Petition for Changes in Reporting Procedures Under the Animal Welfare Act Before the Animal and Plant Health Inspection Service of the United States Department of Agriculture." 1985.

Hurnik, Frank, and Hugh Lehman. "Unnecessary Suffering: Definition and Evidence." 3 *Int'l J. Stud. Animal Prob.* 131 (1982).

Jasper, James M., and Dorothy Nelkin. *The Animal Rights Crusade.* New York: Macmillan, 1992.

Kaufman, Stephen R., Kathryn Hahner, and Joan Dunayer, eds. *Perspectives on Animal Research.* Vol. 2. New York: Medical Research Modernization Committee, 1990.

Kaufman, Stephen R., and Betsy Todd, eds. *Perspectives on Animal Research.* Vol. 1. New York: Medical Research Modernization Committee, 1989.

Keen, William Williams. *Animal Experimentation and Medical Progress.* Boston: Houghton Mifflin Co., 1914.

Langley, Gill, ed. *Animal Experimentation: The Consensus Changes.* New York: Chapman & Hall, 1989.

Lansbury, Coral. *The Old Brown Dog.* Madison: University of Wisconsin Press, 1985.

Leahy, Michael P. T. *Against Liberation.* London: Routledge, 1991.

Leffingwell, Albert. *An Ethical Problem.* London: G. Bell & Sons, 1914.

Linzey, Andrew. *Christianity and the Rights of Animals.* London: S.P.C.K., 1987.

Linzey, Andrew, and Tom Regan, eds. *Animals and Christianity.* New York: Crossword, 1988.

Lowe, Franklin. "Using Animals in Research: What's Going on Here?" *Chron. of Higher Educ.,* September 18, 1985.

Mason, Jim, and Peter Singer. *Animal Factories.* Rev. ed. New York: Harmony Books, 1990.

McCarthy, Charles. "Improved Standards for Laboratory Animals?" 3 *Kennedy Inst. Ethics J.* 293 (1993).

McCloskey, H. J. "Moral Rights and Animals." 22 *Inquiry* 23 (1979).

McGinn, Colin. "Evolution, Animals, and the Basis of Morality." 22 *Inquiry* 81 (1979).

McKenna, Virginia, Will Travers, and Jonathan Wray, eds. *Beyond the Bars.* Wellingborough, Northamptonshire: Thorsons Publishing Group, 1987.

McLaughlin, Ronald M. "Animal Rights vs. Animal Welfare: Can Animal Use Meet the Needs of Science and Society?" In *Animal Research, Animal Rights, Animal Legislation,* edited by Patrick W. Concannon. Champaign, Ill.: Society for the Study of Reproduction, 1990.

Medical Research Modernization Committee. *A Critical Look at Animal Research.* New York: Medical Research Modernization Committee, 1990.

Midgley, Mary. *Animals and Why They Matter.* Athens: University of Georgia Press, 1984.

Morton, Eugene S., and Jake Page. *Animal Talk.* New York: Random House, 1992.

National Academy of Sciences, Institute of Medicine. *Science, Medicine, and Animals.* Washington, D.C.: National Academy Press, 1991.

National Research Council, Commission of Life Sciences, Committee on Pain and Distress in Laboratory Animals. *Recognition and Alleviation of Pain and Distress in Laboratory Animals*. Washington, D.C.: National Academy Press, 1992.

Newkirk, Ingrid. "Total Victory, Like Checkmate, Cannot Be Achieved in One Move." *Animal's Agenda,* January/February 1992, at 43.

Noske, Barbara. *Humans and Other Animals*. London: Pluto Press, 1989.

Office of Technology Assessment. *Alternatives to Animal Use in Research, Testing, and Education*. Washington, D.C.: Office of Technology Assessment, 1986.

Orem, John M. "Demands That Research Be Useful Threaten to Undermine Basic Science in This Country." *Chron. Higher Educ.,* March 14, 1990, at B1.

Orlans, F. Barbara. *In the Name of Science: Issues in Responsible Animal Experimentation*. New York: Oxford University Press, 1993.

Overcast, Thomas D., and Bruce D. Sales. "Regulation of Animal Experimentation." 254 *JAMA* 1944 (1985).

Pacheco, Alex, and Anna Francione. "The Silver Spring Monkeys." In *In Defense of Animals,* edited by Peter Singer. New York: Basil Blackwell, 1985.

Pardes, Herbert, Anne West, and Harold A. Pincus. "Physicians and the Animal Rights Movement." 324 *New Eng. J. Med.* 1640 (1991).

Parsons, Howard L., ed. *Marx and Engels on Ecology*. Westport, Conn.: Greenwood Press, 1977.

Paton, William. *Man and Mouse*. 2d ed. New York: Oxford University Press, 1993.

Phillips, Mary T., and Jeri A. Sechzer. *Animal Research and Ethical Conflict: An Analysis of the Scientific Literature, 1966–1986*. New York: Springer-Verlag, 1989.

Pratt, Dallas. *Alternatives to Pain in Experiments on Animals*. New York: Argus Archives, 1980.

Rachels, James. *Created From Animals*. New York: Oxford University Press, 1990.

Radner, Daisie, and Michael Radner. *Animal Consciousness*. Buffalo, N.Y.: Prometheus Books, 1989.

Regan, Tom. *The Case for Animal Rights*. Berkeley and Los Angeles: University of California Press, 1983.

———. "The Case for Animal Rights." In *In Defense of Animals,* ed. Peter Singer. New York: Basil Blackwell, 1985.

———. "An Examination of One Argument Concerning Animal Rights." 22 *Inquiry* 189 (1979).

———, ed. *Matters of Life and Death*. 2d. ed. New York: Random House, 1986.

Regan, Tom, and Gary L. Francione. "A Movement's Means Create Its Ends." *Animals' Agenda,* January/February 1992, at 40.

Regan, Tom, and Peter Singer, eds. *Animal Rights and Human Obligations*. 2d ed. Englewood Cliffs, N.J.: Prentice-Hall, 1989.

Reines, Brandon. *Psychology Experiments on Animals: A Critique of Animal Models of Human Psychopathology*. Jenkintown, Pa.: American Anti-Vivisection Society, 1982.

Rifkin, Jeremy. *Beyond Beef*. New York: Dutton Books, 1992.

Robbins, John. *Diet for a New America*. Walpole, N.H.: Stillpoint Publishing, 1987.

Rodd, Rosemary. *Biology, Ethics, and Animals*. Oxford: Clarendon Press, 1990.

Rollin, Bernard E. *Animal Rights and Human Morality*. Rev. ed. Buffalo, N.Y.: Prometheus Books, 1992.

———. "Definition of the Concept of 'Humane Treatment' in Relation to Food and Laboratory Animals." 1 *Int'l. J. Stud. Animal Prob.* 234 (1980).

————. *The Unheeded Cry.* Oxford: Oxford University Press, 1989.

Rollin, Bernard E., and M. Lynne Kesel, eds. *The Experimental Animal in Biomedical Research.* Vol. 1. Boca Raton, Fla.: CRC Press, 1990.

Rowan, Andrew N., "Cruelty to Animals." 6 *Anthrozoos* 218 (1993).

————. *Of Mice, Models, and Men.* Albany: State University of New York Press, 1984.

Rowan, Andrew N., Franklin M. Loew, et al. *The Animal Research Controversy.* Grafton, Mass.: Tufts University School of Veterinary Medicine, 1994.

Rowan, Andrew N., and Bernard E. Rollin. "Animal Research—For and Against: A Philosophical, Social, and Historical Perspective." 27 *Persp. Biology & Med.* 1985.

Royal Commission on Vivisection. *Evidence by the Honble. Stephen Coleridge.* London: NAVS, 1907.

Ruesch, Hans. *Slaughter of the Innocent.* New York: Civitas, 1978. Reprint, 1983.

Rupke, Nicolaas A. *Vivisection in Historical Perspective.* London: Crook Helm, 1987.

Ryder, Richard D. *Animal Revolution: Changing Attitudes Towards Animals.* Oxford: Basil Blackwell, 1989.

————. *Victims of Science.* Rev. ed. London: National Anti-Vivisection Society, 1983.

Salt, Henry S. *Animals' Rights Considered in Relation to Social Progress.* Clarks Summit, Pa.: International Society for Animal Rights, 1980.

Sapontzis, S. F. *Morals, Reason, and Animals.* Philadelphia: Temple University Press, 1987.

Schell, Orville. *Modern Meat.* New York: Random House, 1984.

Sechzer, Jeri A., ed. "The Role of Animals in Biomedical Research." 406 *Annals N.Y. Acad. Sci.* (1983).

Serpell, James. *In the Company of Animals.* Oxford: Basil Blackwell, 1986.

Sharpe, Robert. *The Cruel Deception.* Wellingborough, Northamptonshire: Thorsons Publishing Group, 1988.

Shultz, William J. *The Humane Movement in the United States 1910–1922.* New York: Columbia University, 1924.

Singer, Peter. *Animal Liberation.* 2d. ed. New York: New York Review of Books, 1990.

————. "Ethics and Animals." 13 *Behavioral & Brain Sci.* 45 (1990).

————, ed. *In Defense of Animals.* New York: Basil Blackwell, 1985.

Smith, Jane E., and Kenneth M. Boyd, eds. *Lives in the Balance.* Oxford: Oxford University Press, 1991.

Sorabji, Richard. *Animal Minds and Human Morals.* Ithaca, N.Y.: Cornell University Press, 1993.

Sperling, Susan. *Animal Liberators.* Berkeley and Los Angeles: University of California Press, 1988.

Sperlinger, David, ed. *Animals in Research: New Perspectives in Animal Experimentation.* Chichester: John Wiley & Sons, 1981.

Stephens, Martin L. *Maternal Deprivation Experiments in Psychology: A Critique of Animal Models.* Boston: New England Anti-Vivisection Society, 1986.

Sumner, L. W. "Animal Welfare and Animal Rights." 13 *J. Med. & Phil.* 159 (1988).

Taylor, Thomas. *A Vindication of the Rights of Brutes.* London: Edward Jeffery, 1792.

Tufts University School of Veterinary Medicine, Center for Animals and Public Policy. "Animal Rights Versus Animal Welfare: A False Dichotomy?" *Animal Policy Report,* April 1993.

Turner, James. *Reckoning With the Beast.* Baltimore: Johns Hopkins University Press, 1980.

U.S. Congress. Office of Technology Assessment. *Alternatives to Animal Use in Research,*

*Testing, and Education*. Washington, D.C.: U.S. Government Printing Office, 1986.

U.S. General Accounting Office. *Report to the Chairman, Subcommittee on Agriculture, Rural Development and Related Agencies Committee on Appropriations United States Senate: The Dep't of Agriculture's Animal Welfare Program*. Washington, D.C.: General Accounting Office, 1985.

U.S. Public Health Service/National Institutes of Health. *Evaluation of Experimental Procedures Conducted at the University of Pennsylvania Experimental Head Injury Laboratory 1981–1984 in Light of the Public Health Service Animal Welfare Policy*. Bethesda, Md.: National Institutes of Health, July 17, 1985.

———. *Guide for the Care and Use of Laboratory Animals*. Bethesda, Md.: National Institutes of Health, 1985.

———. *Institutional Animal Care and Use Committee Guidebook*. Bethesda, Md.: National Institutes of Health, 1992.

———. *Public Health Service Policy on the Humane Use of Laboratory Animals*. Bethesda, Md.: National Institutes of Health, 1986.

———. *Using Animals in Intramural Research: Guidelines for Investigators*. Bethesda, Md.: National Institutes of Health, 1992.

Vance, Richard P. "An Introduction to the Philosophical Presuppositions of the Animal Liberation/Rights Movement." 268 *J. Am. Med. Ass'n.* 1715 (1992).

Vyvyan, John. *In Pity and in Anger*. London: Michael Joseph, 1969.

Ware, Michael D. "The ALF Strikes." *Animals' Agenda,* July/August 1984, at 1.

Westcott, E. *A Century of Vivisection and Anti-Vivisection*. London: C. W. Daniel Co., 1949.

## Animals and the Law

Animal Welfare Institute, ed. *Animals and Their Legal Rights*. 4th ed. Washington, D.C.: Animal Welfare Institute, 1990.

Bean, Michael J. *The Evolution of National Wildlife Law*. New York: Praeger, 1983.

Blackman, D. E., P. N. Humphreys, and P. Todd, eds. *Animal Welfare and the Law*. Cambridge: Cambridge University Press, 1989.

Brody, Mimi. "Animal Research: A Call for Legislative Reform Requiring Ethical Merit Review." 13 *Harv. Envtl. L. Rev.* 423 (1989).

Coggins, George C. "Wildlife and the Constitution: The Walls Come Tumbling Down." 55 *Wash. L. Rev.* 295 (1980).

Cohen, Henry. "The Legality of the Agriculture Department's Exclusion of Rats and Mice from Coverage Under the Animal Welfare Act." 31 *St. Louis U.L.J.* 543 (1987).

Cohn, Priscilla N. "Animals as Property and the Law." In *Law and Semiotics,* vol. 1, edited by Roberta Kevelson. New York: Plenum Press, 1987.

Dresser, Rebecca. "Assessing Harm and Justification in Animal Research: Federal Policy Opens the Laboratory Door." 40 *Rutgers L. Rev.* 723 (1988).

———. "Research on Animals: Values, Politics, and Regulatory Reform." 58 *S. Cal. L. Rev.* 1147 (1985).

Dukes, Esther F. "The Improved Standards for Laboratory Animals Act: Will It Ensure that the Policy of the Animal Welfare Act Becomes a Reality?" 31 *St. Louis U.L.J.* 519 (1987).

Evans, E. P. *The Criminal Prosecution and Capital Punishment of Animals.* New York: E. P. Dutton, 1906.

Falkin, Larry. Comment, *"Taub v. State:* Are State Anti-Cruelty Statutes Sleeping Giants?" 2 *Pace Envtl. L. Rev.* 255 (1985).

Favre, David S., and Murray Loring. *Animal Law.* Westport, Conn.: Quorum Books, 1983.

Field-Fisher, T. G. *Animals and the Law.* London: Universities Federation for Animal Welfare, 1964.

Francione, Gary L. "The Constitutional Status of Restrictions on Experiments Involving Nonhuman Animals: A Comment on Professor Dresser's Analysis." 40 *Rutgers L. Rev.* 797 (1988).

———. "Future Research Without Nonhuman Animals: An Introduction." In *Proceedings of the First International Medical Conference: Future Medical Research Without the Use of Animals: Facing the Challenge,* edited by Nina Natelson and Murry Cohen. Tel Aviv: CHAI, 1990.

———. "Personhood, Property, and Legal Competence." In *The Great Ape Project,* edited by Paola Cavalieri and Peter Singer. New York: St. Martin's Press, 1993.

Francione, Gary L., and Anna E. Charlton. *Vivisection and Dissection in the Classroom.* Jenkintown, Pa.: American Anti-Vivisection Society, 1990.

Hamilton, Ruth R. Casenote, "Of Monkeys and Men—Article III Standing Requirements in Animal Biomedical Research Cases." 24 *Creighton L. Rev.* 1515 (1991).

Holton, A. Camille. Note, *"International Primate Protection League v. Institute for Behavioral Research:* The Standing of Animal Protection Organizations Under the Animal Welfare Act." 4 *J. Contemp. Health L. & Pol'y* 469 (1988).

Hyde, Walter W. "The Prosecution and Punishment of Animals and Lifeless Things in the Middle Ages and Modern Times." 64 *U. Pa. L. Rev.* 696 (1916).

Ingham, John H. *The Law of Animals.* Philadelphia: T. & J. W. Johnson, 1900.

Jones, L. Meyer. "AVMA Statement on Proposed Laboratory Animal Legislation." 142 *J. Am. Veterinary Med. Ass'n* 293 (1963).

———. "Why AVMA Says No to Proposed Legislation on Humane Care of Laboratory Animals." 147 *J. Am. Veterinary Med. Ass'n* 1131 (1965).

King, Joseph H., Jr. "The Standard of Care for Veterinarians in Medical Malpractice Claims." 58 *Tenn. L. Rev.* 1 (1990).

Klauber, Bridget. Casenote, "See No Evil, Hear No Evil: The Federal Courts and the Silver Spring Monkeys." 63 *U. Colo. L. Rev.* 501 (1992).

Leavitt, Emily S., and Diane Halverson, "The Evolution of Anticruelty Laws in the United States." In *Animals and Their Legal Rights,* 4th ed., edited by the Animal Welfare Institute. Washington, D.C.: Animal Welfare Institute, 1990.

Lesser, William H., ed. *Animal Patents.* New York: Stockton Press, 1989.

Messett, Marci. Note, "They Asked for Protection and They Got Policy: *International Primate*'s Mutilated Monkeys." 21 *Akron L. Rev.* 97 (1987).

Morris, Clarence. "The Rights and Duties of Beasts and Trees: A Law Teacher's Essay for Landscape Architects." 17 *J. Legal Educ.* 185 (1964).

Rikleen, Lauren S. "The Animal Welfare Act: Still a Cruelty to Animals." 7 *B. C. Envtl. Aff. L. Rev.* 129 (1978).

Sandys-Winsch, Godfrey. *Animal Law.* London: Shaw & Sons, 1978.

Solomon, Mark, and Peter C. Lovenheim. "Reporting Requirements Under the Animal Welfare Act: Their Inadequacies and the Public's Right to Know." 3 *Int'l J. Stud. Animal Prob.* 210 (1982).

Stone, Christopher. "Should Trees Have Standing? Toward Legal Rights for Natural Objects." 45 *S. Cal. L. Rev.* 450 (1972).


## General Philosophy, Social and Political Philosophy, Jurisprudence, and Law (Excluding Property Law and Slave Law, Which Are Listed Separately Below)

Altman, Andrew. *Critical Legal Studies.* Princeton, N.J.: Princeton University Press, 1990.
American Law Institute. *Model Penal Code.* Philadelphia: American Law Institute, 1980, 1985.
Aquinas, Thomas. *Summa Theologica.* Translated by Fathers of the English Dominican Province. New York: Benziger Brothers, 1947.
Aristotle. *Politics.* Translated by William Ellis. London: J. M. Dent & Sons, 1935.
Aronowitz, Stanley. *Science as Power.* Minneapolis: University of Minnesota Press, 1988.
Bailyn, Bernard. *The Ideological Origins of the American Revolution.* Enlarged ed. Cambridge: Belknap Press, 1992.
Baker, C. Edwin. "The Ideology of the Economic Analysis of Law." 5 *Phil. & Pub. Aff.* 3 (1975).
Bentham, Jeremy. *An Introduction to the Principles of Morals and Legislation.* Edited by Laurence J. Lafleur. New York: Hafner Press, 1948.
Blackstone, William. *Commentaries on the Laws of England.* Chicago: Callaghan & Co., 1872.
Boyer, Allen. "Crime, Cannibalism, and Joseph Conrad: The Influence of *Regina v. Dudley and Stephens* on Lord Jim." 20 *Loy. L.A. L. Rev.* 9 (1986).
Carmen, Ira. *Cloning and the Constitution.* Madison: University of Wisconsin Press, 1985.
Cavalieri, Liebe F. "Science as Technology." 51 *S. Cal. L. Rev.* 1153 (1978).
Coase, R. H. "The Problem of Social Cost." 3 *J. L. & Econ.* 1 (1960).
Daniels, Norman, ed. *Reading Rawls.* Stanford, Calif.: Stanford University Press, 1989.
Delgado, Richard. "Norms and Normal Science: Toward a Critique of Normativity in Legal Thought." 139 *U. Pa. L. Rev.* 933 (1991).
Delgado, Richard, and David R. Millen. "God, Galileo, and Government: Toward Constitutional Protection for Scientific Inquiry." 53 *Wash. L. Rev.* 349 (1978).
Descartes, René. "Discourse on the Method." In *The Philosophical Writings of Descartes,* translated by John Cottingham et al. Cambridge: Cambridge University Press, 1985.
———. *Philosophical Letters.* Edited and translated by Anthony Kenny. Oxford: Clarendon Press, 1970.
Dias, R.W.M. *Jurisprudence.* 3d ed. London: Butterworths, 1970.
Dressler, Joshua. *Understanding Criminal Law.* New York: Matthew Bender & Co., 1987.
Durkheim, Emile. *The Rules of Sociological Method.* 8th ed. Edited by George E. G. Gatlin, translated by Sarah A. Solovay and John H. Mueller. New York: Free Press, 1966.
Dworkin, Ronald. "Is Wealth a Value?" 9 *J. Legal Stud.* 191 (1980).
———. *Life's Dominion.* New York: Knopf, 1993.
———. "Rights as Trumps." In *Theories of Rights,* edited by Jeremy Waldron. Oxford: Oxford University Press, 1984.
———. *Taking Rights Seriously.* London: Duckworth, 1977.
Dwyer, John P. "The Pathology of Symbolic Legislation." 17 *Ecology L.Q.* 233 (1990).

Feinberg, Joel. *Reason and Responsibility.* 2d ed. Encino, Calif.: Dickenson, 1971.

———. *Rights, Justice, and the Bounds of Liberty.* Princeton, N.J. : Princeton University Press, 1980.

———. *Social Philosophy.* Englewood Cliffs, N.J.: Prentice-Hall, 1973.

Feyerabend, Paul K. *Against Method.* London: Verso, 1975.

———. *Problems of Empiricism: Philosophical Papers.* Vol. 2. Cambridge: Cambridge University Press, 1981.

Francione, Gary L. " Experimentation and the Marketplace Theory of the First Amendment." 136 *U. Pa. L. Rev.* 417 (1987).

———."Facing *The Nation:* The Standards for Copyright, Infringement, and Fair Use of Factual Works." 134 *U. Pa. L. Rev.* 519 (1986).

Frankena, William K. *Ethics.* 2d ed. Englewood Cliffs, N.J.: Prentice-Hall, 1973.

Furrow, Barry. "Governing Science: Public Risks and Private Remedies." 131 *U. Pa. L. Rev.* 1403 (1983).

Galileo. *Dialogue Concerning the Two Chief World Systems—Ptolemaic and Copernican.* Translated by Stillman Drake. Berkeley and Los Angeles: University of California Press, 1953.

Gewirth, Alan. *Human Rights.* Chicago: University of Chicago Press, 1982.

———. *Reason and Morality.* Chicago: University of Chicago Press, 1978.

Glendon, Mary Ann. *Rights Talk.* New York: Free Press, 1991.

Goldberg, Steven. "The Constitutional Status of American Science." 1979 *U. Ill. L.F.* 1.

———. "The Reluctant Embrace: Law and Science in America." 75 *Geo. L.J.* 1341 (1987).

Gray, John C. *The Nature and Sources of the Law.* 2d ed. Edited by Roland Gray. New York: Macmillan, 1921.

Greenawalt, Kent. *Conflicts of Law and Morality.* New York: Oxford University Press, 1987.

———. "Utilitarian Justifications for Observances of Rights." In 24 *Nomos: Ethics, Economics, and the Law,* edited by J. Roland Pennock and John W. Chapman. New York: New York University Press, 1982.

Guest, A. G., ed. *Oxford Essays in Jurisprudence.* London: Oxford University Press, 1961.

Habermas, Jürgen. *Toward a Rational Society.* Translated by Jeremy Shapiro. Boston: Beacon Press, 1970.

Hacker, P.M.S., and Joseph Raz, eds. *Law, Morality, and Society.* Oxford: Clarendon Press, 1977.

Haksar, Vinit. "The Nature of Rights." 64 *Archiv für Rechts- und Sozialphilosophie* 183 (1978).

Hanson, Norwood R. *Perception and Discovery.* Edited by Willard C. Humphreys. San Francisco: Freeman, Cooper & Co., 1969.

Hare, R. M. *Freedom and Reason.* Oxford: Oxford University Press, 1963.

———. *Moral Thinking.* Oxford: Clarendon Press, 1981.

———. "Utility and Rights: Comment on David Lyons's Essay." In 24 *Nomos: Ethics, Economics, and the Law,* edited by J. Roland Pennock and John W. Chapman. New York: New York University Press, 1982.

Hart, H.L.A. "Bentham on Legal Rights." In *Oxford Essays in Jurisprudence,* 2d ser., edited by A.W.B. Simpson. Oxford: Clarendon Press, 1973.

———. *The Concept of Law.* Oxford: Clarendon Press, 1961.

———. *Essays on Bentham.* Oxford: Clarendon Press, 1982.

Hesse, Mary B. *The Structure of Scientific Inference*. Berkeley and Los Angeles: University of California Press, 1974.

Hohfeld, Wesley N. *Fundamental Legal Conceptions*. Edited by Walter W. Cook. New Haven: Yale University Press, 1923.

Holmes, Oliver W. *The Common Law*. Edited by Mark DeWolfe Howe. Boston: Little, Brown, 1963.

Honoré, A. M. "Ownership." In *Oxford Essays in Jurisprudence,* edited by A. G. Guest. London: Oxford University Press, 1961.

Hutchinson, Allan C., ed. *Critical Legal Studies*. Totowa, N.J.: Rowman & Littlefield, 1989.

Jaffe, Louis L. "Standing to Secure Judicial Review: Public Actions." 74 *Harv. L. Rev.* 1265 (1961).

Jonas, Hans. "Freedom of Scientific Inquiry and the Public Interest." *Hastings Center Rep.,* August 1976, at 15.

Kant, Immanuel. *Groundwork of the Metaphysic of Morals*. Edited and translated by H. J. Paton. New York: Barnes & Noble, 1950.

Kingdom, Elizabeth. *What's Wrong with Rights?* Edinburgh: Edinburgh University Press, 1991.

Kneller, George F. *Science as a Human Endeavor*. New York: Columbia University Press, 1978.

Kronman, Anthony T. "Wealth Maximization as a Normative Principle." 9 *J. Legal Stud.* 227 (1980).

Kuhn, Thomas S. *The Structure of Scientific Revolutions*. 2d ed. Chicago: University of Chicago Press, 1970.

Latin, Howard. "Regulatory Failure, Administrative Incentives, and the New Clean Air Act." 21 *Envtl L.* 1647 (1991).

Levins, Richard, and Richard Lewontin. *The Dialectical Biologist*. Cambridge: Harvard University Press, 1985.

Locke, John. *An Essay Concerning Human Understanding*. Edited by John W. Yolton. London: J. M. Dent & Sons, 1961.

———. "Some Thoughts Concerning Education." In *The Works of John Locke in Ten Volumes,* vol. 9, 10th ed., edited by Thomas Tegg et al. Germany: Scientia Verlag Aalen, 1963.

———. *Two Treatises of Government*. 2d ed. Edited by Peter Laslett. Cambridge: Cambridge University Press, 1967.

Lyons, David. *Forms and Limits of Utilitarianism*. Oxford: Clarendon Press, 1965.

———. "Rights, Claimants, and Beneficiaries." 6 *Am. Phil. Q.* 173 (1969).

———. "Utility and Rights." In 24 *Nomos: Ethics, Economics, and the Law,* edited by J. Roland Pennock and John W. Chapman. New York: New York University Press, 1982.

MacCormick, Neil. *Legal Right and Social Democracy*. Oxford: Clarendon Press, 1982.

———. "Rights in Legislation." In *Law, Morality, and Society,* edited by P.M.S. Hacker and Joseph Raz. Oxford: Clarendon Press, 1977.

Machan, Tibor R. *Individuals and Their Rights*. LaSalle, Ill.: Open Court Press, 1989.

Marcuse, Herbert. *An Essay on Liberation*. Boston: Beacon Press, 1969.

———. *One-Dimensional Man*. Boston: Beacon Press, 1964.

———. *Studies in Critical Philosophy*. Boston: Beacon Press, 1973.

Martin, Rex. *Rawls and Rights*. Lawrence: University of Kansas Press, 1985.

Melden, A. I. *Rights and Persons*. Berkeley and Los Angeles: University of California Press, 1977.

Merton, Robert K. *The Sociology of Science*. Chicago: University of Chicago Press, 1973.

Minow, Martha. *Making All the Difference*. Ithaca, N.Y.: Cornell University Press, 1990.

Murphy, Jeffrie G., and Jules L. Coleman. *The Philosophy of Law*. Totowa, N.J.: Rowman & Littlefield, 1984.

Nelson, Leonard. *System of Ethics*. Translated by Norbert Guterman. New Haven: Yale University Press, 1956.

Nozick, Robert. *Anarchy, State, and Utopia*. New York: Basic Books, 1974.

Paton, George W. *A Textbook of Jurisprudence*. 3d ed. London: Oxford University Press, 1964.

Pennock, Roland J., and John W. Chapman, eds. *Ethics, Economics, and the Law*. Vol. 24 of *Nomos*. New York: New York University Press, 1982.

————, eds. *Human Rights*. Vol. 23 of *Nomos*. New York: New York University Press, 1981.

Perry, Michael J. *Morality, Politics, and Law*. New York: Oxford University Press, 1988.

Polinsky, A. Mitchell. *An Introduction to Law and Economics*. Boston: Little, Brown, 1983.

Popper, Karl R. *Conjectures and Refutations*. New York: Basic Books, 1962.

Posner, Richard A. *Economic Analysis of Law*. 3d ed. Boston: Little, Brown, 1986.

————. "The Ethical and Political Basis of the Efficiency Norm in Common Law Adjudication." 8 *Hofstra L. Rev.* 487 (1980).

————. *The Problems of Jurisprudence*. Cambridge: Harvard University Press, 1990.

————. "Utilitarianism, Economics, and Legal Theory." 8 *J. Legal Stud.* 103 (1979).

————. "The Value of Wealth: A Comment on Dworkin and Kronman." 9 *J. Legal Stud.* 243 (1980).

Prichard, A. M. *Leage's Roman Private Law*. 3d ed. London: Macmillan, 1961.

Quine, Willard V. *Word and Object*. Cambridge: Technology Press of MIT, 1960.

Ravetz, Jerome R. *Scientific Knowledge and Its Social Problems*. Oxford: Clarendon Press, 1971.

Rawls, John. *A Theory of Justice*. Cambridge: Belknap Press, 1971.

Raz, Joseph. *The Concept of a Legal System*. 2d ed. Oxford: Clarendon Press, 1980.

————. "On the Nature of Rights." 93 *Mind* 194 (1984).

————. "Right-Based Moralities." In *Theories of Rights,* edited by Jeremy Waldron. Oxford: Oxford University Press, 1984.

Robertson, John A. "The Law of Institutional Review Boards." 26 *UCLA L. Rev.* 484 (1977).

————. "The Scientist's Right to Research: A Constitutional Analysis." 51 *S. Cal. L. Rev.* 1203 (1978).

Scalia, Antonin. "The Doctrine of Standing as an Essential Element of the Separation of Powers." 17 *Suffolk U. L. Rev.* 881 (1983).

Scheffler, Israel. *Science and Subjectivity*. Indianapolis, Ind.: Bobbs-Merrill Co., 1967.

Sen, Amartya, and Bernard Williams, eds. *Utilitarianism and Beyond*. Cambridge: Cambridge University Press, 1982.

Simmons, A. John. *The Lockean Theory of Rights*. Princeton, N.J.: Princeton University Press, 1992.

Simpson, A. W. B. *Cannibalism and the Common Law*. Chicago: University of Chicago Press, 1984.

————, ed. *Oxford Essays in Jurisprudence*. 2d ser. Oxford: Clarendon Press, 1973.

Smart, J.J.C. "An Outline of a System of Utilitarian Ethics." In J.C.C. Smart and Bernard Williams, *Utilitarianism: For and Against*. Cambridge: Cambridge University Press, 1973.

Smart, J.J.C., and Bernard Williams. *Utilitarianism: For and Against*. Cambridge: Cambridge University Press, 1973.

Sumner, L. W. *The Moral Foundation of Rights*. Oxford: Clarendon Press, 1987.

Sunstein, Cass R. "What's Standing After *Lujan?* Of Citizen Suits, 'Injuries,' and Article III." 91 *Mich. L. Rev.* 163 (1992).

Thomson, Judith Jarvis. *The Realm of Rights*. Cambridge: Harvard University Press, 1990.

Tribe, Laurence H. *Abortion*. New York: W. W. Norton & Co., 1990.

————. *American Constitutional Law*. 2d ed. Mineola, N.Y.: Foundation Press, 1988.

Tucker, Robert C., ed. *The Marx-Engels Reader*. 2d ed. New York: W. W. Norton, 1978.

Vlastos, Gregory. "Justice and Equality." In *Theories of Rights,* edited by Jeremy Waldron. Oxford: Oxford University Press, 1984.

Waldron, Jeremy. Introduction to *Theories of Rights,* edited by Jeremy Waldron. Oxford: Oxford University Press, 1984.

————, ed. *"Nonsense upon Stilts."* London: Methuen, 1987.

————, ed. *Theories of Rights*. Oxford: Oxford University Press, 1984.

Wellman, Carl. *A Theory of Rights*. Totowa, N.J.: Rowman & Allanheld, 1985.

Winter, Steven L. "The Metaphor of Standing and the Problem of Self-Governance." 40 *Stan. L. Rev.* 1371 (1988).

## Property Materials

Ackerman, Bruce A. *Private Property and the Constitution*. New Haven: Yale University Press, 1977.

American Law Institute. *Restatement of the Law of Property*. St. Paul, Minn.: American Law Institute, 1936.

Barzel, Yoram. *Economic Analysis of Property Rights*. Cambridge: Cambridge University Press, 1989.

Becker, Lawrence C. *Property Rights*. London: Routledge & Kegan Paul, 1977.

Berger, Lawrence. "A Policy Analysis of the Taking Problem." 49 *N.Y.U. L. Rev.* 165 (1974).

Brown, Ray A. *The Law of Personal Property*. 2d ed. Chicago: Callaghan & Co., 1955.

Carter, Alan. *The Philosophical Foundations of Property Rights*. New York: Harvester Wheatsheaf, 1989.

Casner, A. James, and W. Barton Leach, eds. *Cases and Text on Property*. 3d ed. Boston: Little, Brown, 1984.

Dukeminier, Jesse, and James E. Krier. *Property*. 2d ed. Boston: Little, Brown, 1988.

Ellickson, Robert C. "Property in Land." 102 *Yale L.J.* 1315 (1993).

Ely, James W., Jr. *The Guardian of Every Other Right*. New York: Oxford University Press, 1992.

Keyes, Wade. *An Essay on the Learning of Partial, and of Future Interests in Chattels Personal*. Montgomery, Ala.: H. & T. F. Martin, 1853.

Larkin, Paschal. *Property in the Eighteenth Century*. New York: Howard Fertig, 1969.

Macpherson, C. B., ed. *Property*. Toronto: University of Toronto Press, 1978.

Munzer, Stephen R. *A Theory of Property*. Cambridge: Cambridge University Press, 1990.

Nedelsky, Jennifer. *Private Property and the Limits of American Constitutionalism.* Chicago: University of Chicago Press, 1990.

Noyes, C. Reinold. *The Institution of Property.* New York: Longmans, Green & Co., 1936.

Radin, Margaret. "The Liberal Conception of Property: Cross Currents in the Jurisprudence of Takings." 88 *Colum. L. Rev.* 1667 (1988).

Reeve, Andrew. *Property.* Atlantic Highlands, N.J.: Humanities Press International, 1986.

Reich, Charles A. "The New Property." 73 *Yale L.J.* 733 (1964).

Rotwein, Noah. *Personal Property.* Revised by Charles S. Phillips. New York: Harmon Publications, 1949.

Schouler, James. *A Treatise on the Law of Personal Property.* 5th ed. Albany, N.Y.: Matthew Bender & Co., 1918.

Smith, Horace E. *A Treatise on the Law of Personal Property.* 2d ed. Edited by George Lawyer. Chicago: T. H. Flood & Co., 1908.

Snare, Frank. "The Concept of Property." 9 *Am. Phil. Q.* 200 (1972).

Tideman, T. Nicolaus. "Takings, Moral Evolution, and Justice." 88 *Colum. L. Rev.* 1714 (1988).

Tully, James. *A Discourse on Property.* Cambridge: Cambridge University Press, 1980.

Waldron, Jeremy. *The Right to Private Property.* Oxford: Clarendon Press, 1988.

Williams, Joshua. *Principles of the Law of Personal Property.* Philadelphia: T. & J. W. Johnson & Co., 1872.

## Slavery Materials

Catterall, Helen T. *Judicial Cases Concerning American Slavery and the Negro.* Vols. 1–5. New York: Octagon, 1968.

Davis, David B. *The Problem of Slavery in the Age of Revolution, 1770–1823.* Ithaca, N.Y.: Cornell University Press, 1975.

———. *The Problem of Slavery in Western Culture.* New York: Oxford University Press, 1966.

Elkins, Stanley, ed. *Slavery.* New York: Grosset & Dunlap, 1963.

Elkins, Stanley, and Eric McKitrick. "Institutions and the Law of Slavery: Slavery in Capitalist and Non-Capitalist Cultures." In *The Law of American Slavery,* edited by Kermit L. Hall. New York: Garland Publishing, 1987.

Fede, Andrew. *People Without Rights.* New York: Garland Publishing, 1992.

Flanigan, Daniel J. "Criminal Procedure in Slave Trials in the Antebellum South." In *The Law of American Slavery,* edited by Kermit L. Hall. New York: Garland Publishing, 1987.

Fogel, Robert W. *Without Consent or Contract.* New York: W. W. Norton, 1989.

Fogel, Robert W., and Stanley Engerman. *Time on the Cross.* Vol. 1. Boston: Little, Brown, 1974.

Genovese, Eugene. *The Political Economy of Slavery.* New York: Pantheon Books, 1966.

———. *Roll, Jordan, Roll.* New York: Pantheon Books, 1974.

———. *The World the Slaveholders Made.* New York: Pantheon Books, 1969.

Goodell, William. *Slavery and Anti-Slavery.* New York: Negro Universities Press, 1968.

Hall, Kermit L., ed. *The Law of American Slavery.* New York: Garland Publishing, 1987.

Higginbotham, A. Leon, Jr. *In the Matter of Color.* New York: Oxford University Press, 1978.

Ruchames, Louis, ed. *The Abolitionists*. New York: G. P. Putnam's Sons. 1963.

Shaw, Robert B. *A Legal History of Slavery in the United States*. Potsdam, N.Y.: Northern Press, 1991.

Sherman, Henry. *Slavery in the United States of America*. New York: Negro Universities Press, 1969.

Watson, Alan. *Slave Law in the Americas*. Athens: University of Georgia Press, 1989.

Tushnet, Mark V. *The American Law of Slavery, 1810–1860*. Princeton, N.J.: Princeton University Press, 1981.

# Index

Names of individuals and organizations are indexed only when they are discussed in the text apart from their involvement as parties in cases or as sponsors of legislation. Selected cases and statutes in the text are indexed. The endnotes, which are extensive, are not internally indexed; the material therein can be accessed through the numbered references in the indexed text.

345

# *Culture and Customs of Thailand*

# Culture and Customs
# of Thailand

∽o∾

## ARNE KISLENKO

Culture and Customs of Asia
*Hanchao Lu, Series Editor*

**GREENWOOD PRESS**
**Westport, Connecticut • London**

**Library of Congress Cataloging-in-Publication Data**

Kislenko, Arne.
   Culture and customs of Thailand / Arne Kislenko.
     p. cm. — (Culture and customs of Asia, ISSN 1097–0738)
   Includes bibliographical references and index.
   ISBN 0–313–32128–0
   1. Thailand—Civilization. 2. Thailand—Social and customs. I.
Title. II. Series.

   DS568.K5 2004
   959.3—dc22      2004002116

British Library Cataloguing in Publication Data is available.

Library of Congress Catalog Card Number: 2004002116
ISBN: 0–313–32128–0
ISSN: 1097–0738

First published in 2004

Greenwood Press, 88 Post Road West, Westport, CT 06881
An imprint of Greenwood Publishing Group, Inc.
www.greenwood.com

Printed in the United States of America

**Copyright Acknowledgments**

The author and publisher gratefully acknowledge permission to excerpt passages from the following sources:

The passage for the epic Thai poem *Ramakian* as it appears edited and translated into English in Theodora Bofman, *The Poetics of the Ramakian* is reprinted with permission by the Center for Southeast Asian Studies, Northern Illinois University, © 1984.

The passage from *Facets of Thai Cultural Life*, published by the Foreign News Division, is reprinted with permission by the Government Public Relations Department, © 1984.

The poem *Fate of the Urbanites*, found cited in Apinan Poshyananda, *Modern Art in Thailand: 19th and 20th Centuries* (Singapore: Oxford University Press, 1992) is reprinted with permission by Vasan Sitthiket.

For Mc B—the queen of Tom Yum Goong and banana roti

# Contents

# Illustrations

# Series Foreword

Geographically, Asia encompasses the vast area from Suez, the Bosporus, and the Ural Mountains eastward to the Bering Sea and from this line southward to the Indonesian archipelago, an expanse that covers about 30 percent of our earth. Conventionally, and especially insofar as culture and customs are concerned, Asia refers primarily to the region east of Iran and south of Russia. This area can be divided in turn into subregions commonly known as South, Southeast, and East Asia, which are the main focus of this series.

The United States has vast interests in this region. In the twentieth century the United States fought three major wars in Asia (namely the Pacific War of 1941–45, the Korean War of 1950–53, and the Vietnam War of 1965–75), and each had profound impact on life and politics in America. Today, America's major trading partners are in Asia, and in the foreseeable future the weight of Asia in American life will inevitably increase, for in Asia lie our great allies as well as our toughest competitors in virtually all arenas of global interest. Domestically, the role of Asian immigrants is more visible than at any other time in our history. In spite of these connections with Asia, however, our knowledge about this crucial region is far from adequate. For various reasons, Asia remains for most of us a relatively unfamiliar, if not stereotypical or even mysterious, "Oriental" land.

There are compelling reasons for Americans to obtain some level of concrete knowledge about Asia. It is one of the world's richest reservoirs of culture and an ever-evolving museum of human heritage. Rhoads Murphey, a prominent Asianist, once pointed out that in the part of Asia east of

Afghanistan and south of Russia alone lies half the world, "half of its people and far more that half of its historical experience, for these are the oldest living civilized traditions." Prior to the modern era, with limited interaction and mutual influence between the East and the West, Asian civilizations developed largely independent from the West. In modern times, however, Asia and the West have come not only into close contact but also into frequent conflict: The result has been one of the most solemn and stirring dramas in world history. Today, integration and compromise are the trend in coping with cultural differences. The West—with some notable exceptions—has started to see Asian traditions not as something to fear but as something to be understood, appreciated, and even cherished. After all, Asian traditions are an indispensable part of the human legacy, a matter of global "common wealth" that few of us can afford to ignore.

As a result of Asia's enormous economic development since World War II, we can no longer neglect the study of this vibrant region. Japan's "economic miracle" of postwar development is no longer unique, but in various degrees has been matched by the booming economy of many other Asian countries and regions. The rise of the four "mini dragons" (South Korea, Taiwan, Hong Kong, and Singapore) suggests that there may be a common Asian pattern of development. At the same time, each economy in Asia has followed its own particular trajectory. Clearly, China is the next giant on the scene. Sweeping changes in China in the last two decades have already dramatically altered the world's economic map. Furthermore, growth has also been dramatic in much of Southeast Asia. Today, war-devastated Vietnam shows great enthusiasm for joining the "club" of nations engaged in the world economy. And in South Asia, India, the world's largest democracy, is rediscovering its role as a champion of market capitalism. The economic development of Asia presents a challenge to Americans but also provides them with unprecedented opportunities. It is largely against this background that more and more people in the United States, in particular among the younger generation, have started to pursue careers dealing with Asia.

This series is designed to meet the need for knowledge of Asia among students and the general public. Each book is written in an accessible and lively style by an expert (or experts) in the field of Asian studies. Each book focuses on the culture and customs of a country or region. However, readers should be aware that culture is fluid, not always respecting national boundaries. While every nation seeks its own path to success and struggles to maintain its own identity, in the cultural domain mutual influence and integration among Asian nations are ubiquitous.

Each volume starts with an introduction to the land and the people of a nation or region and includes a brief history and an overview of the economy.

This is followed by chapters dealing with a variety of topics that piece together a cultural panorama, such as thought, religion, ethics, literature and art, architecture and housing, cuisine, traditional dress, gender, courtship and marriage, festivals and leisure activities, music and dance, and social customs and lifestyle. In this series, we have chosen not to elaborate on elite life, ideology, or detailed questions of political structure and struggle, but instead to explore the world of common people, their sorrow and joy, their pattern of thinking, and their way of life. It is the culture and the customs of the majority of the people (rather than just the rich and powerful elite) that we seek to understand. Without such understanding, it will be difficult for all of us to live peacefully and fruitfully with each other in this increasingly interdependent world.

As the world shrinks, modern technologies have made all nations on earth "virtual" neighbors. The expression "global village" not only reveals the nature and the scope of the world in which we live but also, more importantly, highlights the serious need for mutual understanding of all peoples on our planet. If this series serves to help the reader obtain a better understanding of the "half of the world" that is Asia, the authors and I will be well rewarded.

*Hanchao Lu*
Georgia Institute of Technology

# Preface

Like many countries in the world today Thailand is undergoing tremendous change. Just thirty or so years ago it was a poor, developing country, dominated by an autocratic government. Today, Thailand is rapidly industrializing, dramatically improving the living standards of its people, and gradually developing a more democratic society. Yet despite such profound changes, traditional Thai culture has not only survived, but in many respects prospered. Based on the twin pillars of the Buddhist faith and a deep reverence for its monarchy, Thai culture has unified the people and helped to protect the country against the many challenges and threats it has faced in its recent past. Moreover, Thai culture has proved to be flexible and dynamic, adapting to many pressures and incorporating many changes. In this way Thais have retained many of their customs and cultural values, while at the same time confronting the twenty-first century with confidence.

This book is designed to introduce Thailand, and to present its traditional culture and customs against the backdrop of modern times. Although famous for its food, and despite its increasing popularity as a tourist destination, Thailand remains relatively unknown to most Westerners. In part this is because the country and its population are much smaller than those of other Asian nations like Japan or China. In part it is also because, compared with other Asian peoples, the Thais do not emigrate in large numbers, and therefore have not had the same impact on Western culture. There are, for example, few cities in the West that can boast a "Thai-town," whereas most large centers in North America and Europe have a "Chinatown" and other ethnic

areas. As well, Thailand is not a major international political, military, or economic power, and thus seldom makes the news in the West.

However, this is by no means to suggest that the country is unimportant. Both historically and from a contemporary perspective Thailand has great importance. It is the only country in Southeast Asia to have avoided colonization by Western powers. It was the first country in Asia to establish diplomatic relations with the United States, and over the course of the 170 years since doing so it has remained a remarkably consistent friend and ally. Thailand avoided the bloody revolutions and wars that have characterized Southeast Asia in the last half century, and has emerged today as a considerable economic and political power in the region. It is the world's largest producer of rice and natural rubber; a major international tourist destination; and it has the world's longest-reigning monarch. Alongside the beautiful ancient temples and palaces, Thailand is also a country of progress and potential. Alongside the mystery and exoticness of its culture, Thailand is also remarkably open, familiar, and friendly. There's little wonder that it's often called "the Land of Smiles."

Some will caution that such serene images of the country are misleading. On many fronts Thailand is struggling with the pressures of modernization and reform. Globalization threatens many aspects of traditional Thai culture. Democratic freedoms as they are known in the West have not entirely taken root. Corruption in government and business remains a serious problem. Prostitution and the drug trade continue, and nearly one million Thais suffer with AIDS. There is no question that these and other problems deeply affect Thailand. In fact they represent fundamental challenges to the social, economic, and political development of the country. However, as wrong as it would be to ignore these problems, so too is it wrong to think that they define Thailand. Hollywood movies and Western television tend to present a Thailand full of nothing but seedy bars, drug warlords, and brutal justice. Such images are equally misleading stereotypes.

Of course to truly experience Thailand and its culture, you have to make the trip. I made my first journey to Thailand in 1990 as part of a backpacking adventure throughout Southeast Asia. After nearly 24 hours on planes, I walked into the humidity of a Bangkok summer night, and life was never the same again. The indescribable sights and smells of that city intrigued me, and my travels through the rest of the country were just as captivating. Like so many other travelers in Thailand, I was struck not only by the beauty of the country and the richness of its history, but also by the friendliness and sense of fun among its people; indeed, I was so taken by Thailand that I very nearly stayed for good. Although I did go home, Thailand continued to change my life. It struck me that in a world of such incredible and encompassing change,

Thailand represents an important center. How do a people balance old ways against the new? How can a society adapt to a new age of technology and globalization and still retain a sense of its traditional culture and customs? In the trips I've made back to Thailand since, I still ask these questions, and the Thais seem to have at least some of the answers.

# Acknowledgments

There are a number of people and institutions to which I am indebted in helping me research and write this book. I would like to thank Twekiat Janprajak, First Secretary of the Royal Thai Embassy in Ottawa, for his tremendous assistance on a number of fronts. Special thanks are owed to my friend Kaveechok Lertvachara for his advice, assistance, and guided tours of Bangkok. I am also very grateful for the help of Kayla Shubert and the use of materials from the Tourism Authority of Thailand in Toronto. Photographs in this book have also been drawn from some very gifted artists who deserve special thanks: my good friend Brent Wardrop, Jonathan Wong, and Carine Lindauer. I am equally grateful to the General Library at the University of Texas, Austin, which provided map illustrations. Sincere thanks are owed to the librarians at the University of Toronto libraries and the Royal Ontario Museum for their help as well.

Financial and moral support for this project came chiefly from the Department of History at Ryerson University, and in particular I would like to acknowledge the great encouragement of its recent past, and present, chairs, Al Wargo and Ron Stagg. Special thanks to my friends and colleagues Dr. Thomas Barcsay and Dr. John Cook, Chair of the Department of English at Ryerson, for their advice and assistance with some of the chapters, and to Mima Cvetkovic Petrovic for help with photo selection. My other friends both at Ryerson and the University of Toronto also deserve my gratitude. For her patience and support in seeing this book through I would like to thank Wendi Schnaufer, Acquisitions Editor at Greenwood Publishing. I am also indebted to the staff at Impressions Book and Journal Services and to copy editor Jonathan Dore for their excellent work. Lastly, I must of course thank my family and friends for just about everything in life.

# Note on Transliteration and Thai Names

There are several methods employed in transliterating Thai, which can make for considerable confusion. This book tries to follow as closely as possible the "sound-based" system commonly used in English-language works, which is based on the Royal Thai General System. Alternative phonetic spellings are in many instances given in brackets. Given their complexity to those unfamiliar with tonal languages, accents on Thai words have not been placed. The reader should keep in mind some helpful points about this language reference system. "Ph" is pronounced "P" as in "Peter," not as an "f" sound. The "h" in "Th" is silent, as in "Thomas" rather than "that." Thais refer to themselves by their first names, and that is reflected in this book. Surnames and honorary titles are given where applicable.

Before 1939 and from 1945 to 1949, Thailand was officially named "Siam." Historians and anthropologists use the word *Tai* in referring to the people—and signifying a common linguistic and cultural identity—in the period before the creation of a unified political entity. In this book I refer to the Tai people prior to the establishment of Siam; Siam and the Siamese prior to 1939; and to Thailand and the Thais thereafter. However, direct quotations from sources may use the terms "Siam" and "Siamese" regardless of chronology. Proper names and most place names have not been translated, but alternative names and rough English-language meanings have been given where appropriate. Many Thai words and phrases and their translations are included in the glossary. Some translations have been provided by the various sources used in researching this work. Additional translations have been provided by Thai-English Translation (www.thai-english-translation.com) and by the author.

# Chronology

| | |
|---|---|
| ca. 40,000 B.C.E | Relatively permanent hunter-gatherer sites in Southeast Asia |
| ca. 20,000–10,000 B.C.E | Emergence of agricultural settlements in Southeast Asia |
| ca. 10,000 B.C.E | Linguistic and cultural differentiation in Southeast Asia begins |
| ca. 5000 B.C.E | Evidence of copper and bronze working in northeastern Thailand |
| ca. 3000 B.C.E | Evidence of iron working and pottery making in northeastern Thailand |
| Early centuries C.E. | Chinese references to "Tai" people living in southern China and Southeast Asia |
| ca. 6th–8th centuries | Division of Tai-speaking peoples with emergence of Chinese and Vietnamese empires |
| ca. 6th–9th centuries | Rise of *Dvaravati* civilization in central Southeast Asia |
| ca. 8th–9th centuries | Nan-Chao kingdom in southern China and northern Southeast Asia centralizes region and links Indian and Chinese cultures |
| ca. 8th–13th centuries | Expansion of southern Tai-speaking peoples in present-day Thailand, Laos, Burma, and northeastern India |

| ca. 9th–13th centuries | Rise of *Khmer* civilization in Southeast Asia, based at Angkor (in present-day Cambodia) |
| --- | --- |
| ca. 11th–13th centuries | Rise of Pagan empire in Burma |
| ca. 11th–13th centuries | Rise of small Tai-speaking states on the frontiers of Pagan and Khmer empires |
| 1253–1300 | Mongol armies invade Southeast Asia, undermining Pagan and Khmer empires |
| 1279–1298 | Establishment of *Sukhothai* Tai kingdom under King Ramkhamhaeng |
| 1281–1292 | Establishment of *Lan Na* Tai kingdom based at Chiang Mai under King Mangrai |
| 14th–16th centuries | Expansion of *Ayutthaya* Tai kingdom |
| 1558–1569 | Burmese armies sack major Tai kingdoms |
| 1583–1590 | Tai rebellions against the Burmese led by Naresuan |
| 1590 | Naresuan crowned King of Ayutthaya |
| 1590–1593 | Annual Burmese campaigns against Ayutthaya fail at the Battle of Nong Sarai (1593) |
| 1593–1605 | Expansion of Ayutthaya through attacks on Burmese lands and development of trade and diplomatic relations with China |
| 1610–1688 | Height of Ayutthaya's expansion marked by development of trade and diplomatic relations with European states and internal rivalries |
| 1688 | Anti-Western and anti-Christian revolution in Ayutthaya |
| 1688–1733 | Further expansion of Ayutthaya's influence in Cambodia and Laos, but frequent rebellions in frontier provinces |
| 1733–1758 | "Golden age" of Ayutthaya under King Borommakot with bureaucratic and political reform, continued expansion, and the spread of Buddhism |
| ca. 1740–1760 | Resurgence of Burmese empire |
| 1760–1767 | Burmese armies invade and occupy Tai kingdoms, culminating in the siege and destruction of Ayutthaya (1767) |
| 1767–1768 | *Thonburi* Tai kingdom founded by Taksin |
| 1768–1782 | Thonburi campaigns against the Burmese and their allies in northern Tai kingdoms, culminating in the capture of |

|  | Chiang Mai (1776) and the expansion of influence in Cambodia and Laos |
|---|---|
| 1782 | Ramathibodi (King Rama I) moves the capital from Thonburi to Bangkok |
| 1782–1809 | Rama I presides over substantial legal, political, and bureaucratic reform; the resurgence of Buddhist clergy; the development of the arts; and the expansion of foreign relations |
| 1785–1793 | Continuing wars with the Burmese, gradually ending with Tai victories and consolidation of Tai kingdoms as Siam |
| 1809–1824 | Rama II confronts growing European power in Southeast Asia and competes with the Vietnamese empire in Cambodia |
| 1824–1826 | British war with Burma leads to the Burney Treaty with Britain (1826) and alleviation of European threats to Siam |
| 1827–1848 | Siamese military campaigns extend the Bangkok empire's control into Laos, Cambodia, and the Malay states |
| 1851–1868 | The reign of Mongkut (King Rama IV)—best known for its artful diplomacy with European powers and for educational, legal, and political reforms aimed at the modernization of Siam |
| 1868–1873 | Chaophraya Suriyawong rules as Regent for young Prince Chulalongkorn, continuing the development of Siam |
| 1873–1910 | The reign of Chulalongkorn (Rama V)—best known for reforms ending slavery, limiting powers of the royal court, employing Western advisers, and introducing Western ideas about government and economics |
| 1885–1893 | British victories in Burma and the French conquest of Vietnam pressure Siam, eventually leading to the Franco-Siamese conflict (1893) and the loss of Laos |
| 1904–1909 | Improving relations between Britain and France force Siam to cede more territory in the Malay peninsula and Cambodia, as well as to sign unequal trade treaties |
| 1910–1925 | The reign of Vajiravudh (Rama VI)—marked by economic decline and tension within the armed forces and bureaucracy over continued reforms: also noted for the development of ideas about modern Thai nationalism |

| ca. 1920–1930 | Siamese intellectuals studying abroad begin to question the absolute rule of monarchs and become increasingly influenced by Western ideas |
| --- | --- |
| 1930–1932 | Dramatic effects of the global Great Depression on Siam's economy |
| 1932 | (June) a small group of Western-educated government officials seize government in a coup; King Prajadhipok (Rama VII) agrees to adopt a constitution ending the absolute rule of the monarchy |
| 1932–1938 | Officials behind the coup lead the People's Party government, but are divided by numerous factions and disagreements over the direction of Siam: Thai nationalism becomes more extreme, influenced by the rise of totalitarian regimes in Europe and Japan |
| 1935 | King Rama VII abdicates: ten year-old Prince Ananda Mahidol is asked to take the throne with regents |
| 1938–1940 | Controversial era with Luang Phibunsongkhram (Phibun) as Prime Minister: Thai nationalism dominated by anti-Western ideas, especially with the outbreak of World War II in Europe: Phibun renames country "Thailand" |
| 1940–1941 | France falls to Germany in World War II—French Indochina ruled by weak, German-controlled Vichy government, which is forced to give transit and other rights to Japanese forces: Thailand takes the opportunity to reclaim territory in Laos and Cambodia, leading to Franco–Thai War |
| 1941 | (December) Japanese request transit through Thailand on the way to attack British colonies in Burma and Malaya: amid confusion, the Japanese invade |
| 1942–1944 | Under pressure from Japanese forces, Thailand signs treaty with Japan (Dec. 1941) and then declares war on Britain and the United States (Jan. 1942)—although considerable "Free-Thai" movement inside Thailand and abroad opposes Phibun's government and works with the Allies |
| 1944 | With mounting Japanese defeats, Phibun's government is overthrown and new civilian administration tries to mend relations with Western powers |
| 1944–1948 | Coalition governments deal with British and French demands for territory and compensation given Thailand's role in the war |

| 1946 | (April) Thai Supreme Court rules that war-crimes charges against Phibun are unconstitutional, allowing him to return to political life, and (June) King Ananda mysteriously killed, both events stimulating demands for strong government |
|---|---|
| 1948 | Military leaders force the resignation of a civilian government and re-install Phibun as Prime Minister |
| 1948–1957 | Phibun's second government dominated by intense factionalism; tremendous corruption; rising anti-Chinese sentiment; and the development of close relations with the United States based on mutual concerns about communist expansion in Southeast Asia |
| 1951 | (November) Bhumipol Adulyadej returns to Thailand, from exile in Switzerland, to resume duties as King Rama IX |
| 1957 | (September) army coup led by General Sarit Thanarat forces Phibun from office and from the country |
| 1957–1973 | Sarit and his successor Thanom Kittachakorn continue firm military government in Thailand and develop very close economic, military, and covert relations with the United States as it fights communism in Indochina |
| 1973 | Growing opposition to military government and Thai support for the U.S. war in Vietnam leads to massive demonstrations and (in October) riots: Thanom flees the country and a civilian government takes power |
| 1973–1976 | Civilian governments attempt to implement democratic reforms and to improve Thailand's relations with its neighbors after the withdrawal of American forces from Vietnam (1975) |
| 1976 | Increasing division of Thai politics characterized by the resurgence of extreme conservatism amid fears that civilian rule has encouraged communism and undermined Thai culture and society: (October) bloody riots in Bangkok traumatize Thailand |
| 1976–1980 | Thailand deals with political turmoil at home while facing Vietnamese expansion through the invasion of Cambodia (1978): flood of Cambodian refugees poses serious economic and political problems for Bangkok |
| 1980–1988 | General Prem Tinsulanonda takes over as Prime Minister and oversees era of political reform and economic growth |

1991–1992          After many allegations of corruption against his govern-
                   ment, the Thai military forces Chatichai Choonavan
                   from power (February 1991): elections (March 1992)
                   allow a military-dominated party to form the govern-
                   ment

1992               (May) large demonstrations against the military's return
                   to power erupt in violence in Bangkok: the intervention
                   of King Bhumipol prevents any escalation and pressures
                   the military to stand down

1992–2004          Continuing democratization is gradually changing Thai
                   politics: dramatic economic growth halted by Asian
                   financial crisis of 1997, but Thailand continues with
                   substantial modernization and reform

# 1

# Introduction

## GEOGRAPHY AND ENVIRONMENT

Thailand lies in the heart of mainland Southeast Asia, extending like an elephant's trunk south between the Andaman Sea and the Gulf of Thailand. Here it borders Malaysia, while to the west and north lies Myanmar, or Burma. Laos makes up Thailand's northern and eastern borders, and in the southeast is Cambodia. With a total area of 198,115 square miles (513,115 square kilometers), it is slightly smaller than the state of Texas; and about the same size as France. From north to south, Thailand measures almost 1,550 miles (2,500 kilometers), and east to west it covers 775 miles (1,250 kilometers). Its coastline on the Gulf extends 1,140 miles (1,840 kilometers), while on the Andaman Sea the distance is almost 540 miles (870 kilometers).[1]

There are four primary natural regions in the country; the North, the Central Plains or Chao Phraya River basin, the Northeast or Korat Plateau, and the South or Peninsular Thailand. The North is predominantly mountainous, and is covered by forests, ridges, and valleys. The Central Plains essentially form one large, very fertile valley, which serves as the main agricultural region of the country. The Northeast is a mostly hilly area with a hot and dry climate prone to droughts, cyclically mixed in with often torrential rains and flooding. The South also has hills and mountains, amid rainforests and long coastlines.

Thailand has a tropical climate, dominated by warm temperatures and high humidity. The most important climatic factor is the monsoons, which generally run from May through September. In the North, Northeast, and Central Plains, the monsoons provide three fairly distinct seasons: the "rainy

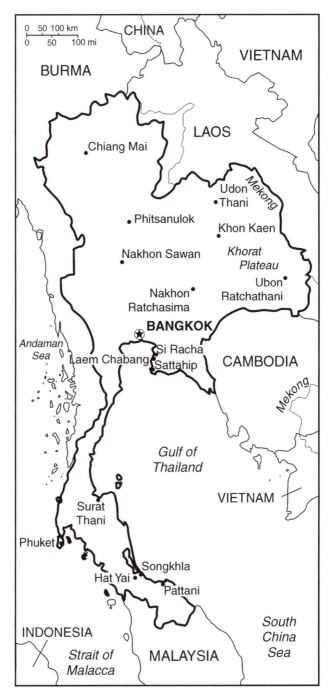

Map of Thailand.

season" from roughly July to November; the "cool season" from November through March; and the "hot season" from March through July. Not surprisingly, temperatures reach their highest in March and April—the "hot season" just before the monsoons. In the North and Northeast temperatures can easily reach 104 degrees Fahrenheit (40 Celsius); an additional factor is the humidity, which often exceeds 80 percent. Conversely, these regions also have Thailand's lowest temperatures during the "cool season," when at night in the mountains it often dips as low as 50 degrees Fahrenheit (10 Celsius). On average the country's temperature range is between 75 and 100 degrees Fahrenheit (24–38 Celsius), with the most consistent weather in the South.[2]

## THAI PEOPLE

With a population of approximately 62 million people and an annual population growth rate of 1.5 percent (in 2000), Thailand is the fourth most populous nation in Southeast Asia (behind Indonesia, Vietnam, and the Philippines). About 75 percent of the people are ethnic Thais. Within this population there are numerous subdivisions based on dialect, which follows a regional order. The majority are the Siamese, who live primarily in the Central Plains and the capital city, Bangkok, which with nearly 7 million residents represents more than 10 percent of Thailand's population alone. The North, Northeast, and South have their own distinct dialects, the latter two of which are often referred to respectively as Thai-Lao and Thai Pak-Thai. Beyond these divisions are a number of smaller groups scattered primarily in the North and Northeast who speak other Thai dialects.

### Chinese

Approximately 10 percent of the population is ethnic Chinese, most of whom are now descendants of nineteenth- and early-twentieth-century immigrants. Although best represented in Bangkok, ethnic Chinese populations can be found throughout the country. Many people of Chinese descent have intermarried with Thais over the years, and have therefore tended to blend in with the mainstream population. Historically, ethnic Chinese populations have faced considerable—sometimes extreme—persecution throughout Southeast Asia. In Thailand there have been periods of intense anti-Chinese feeling, usually driven by nationalistic governments. However, in comparison to other countries in the region, Thailand's treatment of the Chinese is markedly better. Today the Chinese-Thai are free to speak their own languages and promote their own cultures.

## Malay and Other Groups

A further 5 percent of Thailand's population is ethnic Malay, most of whom live in the South adjacent to Malaysia. The majority of these people are Muslims. Given their religious and linguistic differences, in the past the Malay population has hosted a fairly serious separatist threat, and even an armed rebellion. Although the problem has subsided since the 1980s, regionalism in Southern Thailand remains a political problem in Thailand.[3] The remaining 10 percent of Thailand's population is made up of smaller, non-Thai ethnic groups like the Vietnamese, Khmer (Cambodians), and Burmese, many of whom fled war and revolution in their own countries during the twentieth century.

## Hill Tribes

These smaller ethnic groups also include the so-called hill tribes—a collection of diverse peoples who, over the past 500 years or so, have migrated from Tibet, China, Vietnam, Burma, and Laos into the upland areas of Northern Thailand. There are seven major such tribes in Thailand; the Karen (or Kariang, or Yang), the Hmong (or Meo), the Yao (or Mien), Lahu (or Mussur), the Lisu (or Lisaw), the Akha (or Ekaw), and the Lawa. There is also an assortment of smaller tribes including the Palong, Khamu, Htins, and Mlabri. In total there are about 20 different hill tribes in Thailand, with a population of roughly 750,000. Many do not speak Thai, but have distinct tribal languages. Most of the tribes speak Tibeto-Burman languages, although some, like the Yao and Hmong, speak a dialect related more to the Mongolian and Chinese linguistic families. Only a few, like the Yao, have a written language. All of the minorities have different social and political organizations, unique customs, and their own religious beliefs. Most are animists, believing that all things—even inanimate objects—have souls or spirits; however, some members of groups such as the Karen and Lahu have over time converted to Christianity. Similarly, many of the Lawa and Yao have adopted Buddhist practices. Some tribes, such as the Karen and Lawa, have become more assimilated into mainstream Thai society, while others, such as the Akha, have resisted the process. Many hill-tribe communities remain quite isolated from the rest of the country, and are committed to maintaining their unique cultures.

Given that many hill-tribe communities cross over national borders, and that some of them, as mentioned above, are not actually native to Thailand, a number of them have been caught up in regional politics with sometimes violent consequences. The Karen, most of whose numbers live in Burma,

have been involved for more than fifty years in rebellions against the Burmese government. Groups like the Hmong were caught up in the horrors of war in Laos and Vietnam. They all consider Thailand to be a refuge, but their presence has often complicated relations between countries. The largest of the minorities is the Karen, with about 300,000 people in Thailand. The Karen in Thailand are actually a family of tribal subdivisions; the Sgaw, Pwo, Pao, Kayah, and Padaung. Most live along the Thai border with Burma, where the majority of Karen (some five million) live. The Hmong number about 60,000, with another 50,000 who fled war and poverty in Laos concentrated in refugee camps in the Northeast. There are roughly 50,000 Yao with an additional 10,000 also in refugee camps along the Lao frontier. Thailand has about 25,000 Lahu, while both the Lisu and Akha number approximately 20,000. The Lawa are the smallest of the major groups, with about 15,000.

For the most part the hill tribes live on the fringes of Thai society. Most of them are considerably poorer than the average Thai. Some are not recognized as Thai citizens and are instead considered refugees or illegal migrants in the country. Consequently these minorities struggle to maintain a largely subsistence lifestyle. Living in predominantly rural and isolated communities, the hill tribes often survive on slash-and-burn farming, which produces only a basic subsistence.[4] Increasingly the Thai government is assisting them in moving toward a more systematic and permanent agriculture, as well as other economic activities. The Thais are especially interested in encouraging the minorities away from opium cultivation, which for some, like the Hmong, Lisu, Yao, and others, has been a longstanding practice. In this way they have become implicated with the infamous "Golden Triangle" narcotics trade—controlled chiefly by Thais and foreigners—in the border area shared by Thailand, Burma, and Laos. Ideal for the cultivation of opium poppies, the region has become a major world exporter of heroin, which has become a sad economic and political fact of life for some members of hill tribes—and a dangerous alternative to poverty.[5]

In their search for other means of making a living, and to supplement their incomes from farming, some of the tribes have embraced Western tourism for their economic livelihood. In their colorful traditional dress, hill tribes have become a regular sight, selling handicrafts, jewelry, and textiles on the streets of large Thai cities like Chiang Mai. In addition, hikers exploring the mountains of Northern Thailand often stay in hill-tribe villages, bringing much-needed revenue. Exposure to modernity has, however, seriously affected hill-tribe communities. Many young people now want to leave their villages for life in Thai cities, which usually comes as an enormous culture shock, with many dangers. Traditional ways are being eroded by the impact of new technologies and new ideas. For some of the hill tribes the choice for the

future is not very pleasant: war and persecution in neighboring countries, or modernity and assimilation in Thailand.

## THAI LANGUAGE

The official national language of Thailand is Thai. It is spoken by the vast majority of people regardless of their ethnic background. It is a tonal language that is uninflected and mostly monosyllabic. There are five tones in Thai; the low tone, the high tone, the mid tone, the rising tone, and the falling tone. Getting the proper tone is essential, as they can totally change the meaning of words. This can be very difficult for Westerners, who speak mainly nontonal languages—such as English—and who use emotional expression of words and phrases for emphasis. A classic example is with the Thai word *mai,* which can mean wood, new, burn, and no—all depending on the tone used in pronunciation. Written Thai uses tone markers to indicate the appropriate sound.

The spoken language uses both male and female forms. This is chiefly expressed by the syllable *khrap* for men, and *kha* for women, which are used at the end of sentences or phrases in polite speaking. These syllables also stand as the Thai word for yes. The language employs rules based primarily on to whom one is speaking. There is an informal Thai, used with friends and colleagues of the same age and social rank; a formal Thai, used with elders and people who warrant special respect; and a "Royal" Thai, used only for addressing members of the Royal family.

Thai grammar is relatively simple because there is no conjugation of verbs as in English or French. They have no tense and do not change spelling or pronunciation based on any time references. The time is indicated by adding words like *wan-nii* (today), and also by the use of syntactic markers—short words added to the verb in the same way English shows past tense by using "-ed" on the end. The basic word order in Thai grammar is subject-verb-object, although it is quite common to put the object first. Nouns do not change when indicating the plural and do not require definite or indefinite articles. Adjectives always follow the noun, and, as in English, superlatives (such as "most" or "best") are frequently used.[6] There are 15 basic vowel structures and 44 consonants in Thai, some with approximate English equivalents. However, being a tonal language, Thai has different vowel and consonant sounds: 48 for vowels and 21 for consonants. The "extra" consonants indicate the tonal value of the word, while vowel symbols are written in combination to indicate the appropriate sound. Unlike Japanese or Chinese, the Thai writing system is not ideogram based (in which characters represent whole words); rather, each character represents a sound, like Western lan-

guages. Consonants are placed horizontally from left to right, without spaces, to form syllables, words, and sentences. Vowels are written above, below, before, or after the consonant they modify. However, the consonant sound is always heard first when the syllable or word is spoken. The official written script, based on an ancient script from South India, was invented during the reign of King Ramkhamhaeng in 1283, but it went through several changes over the following few centuries. The national script used today was devised during the reign of King Narai in 1680.[7] Over the centuries Thai has been influenced by and even adopted the vocabulary of other languages, mainly Khmer (Cambodian), Pali (a sacred language used by Buddhists throughout Asia, originally from India), Sanskrit (an old language from India and the ancestor of modern Indian languages), and, increasingly, English.

Other languages are also used in Thailand. Chinese, Malay, and the indigenous languages of the hill tribes are most common. With a sizeable population of foreigners living in Bangkok, other languages can be heard there as well. English has rapidly become the second language of the country. It is mandatory in public schools and is now widely spoken and understood, particularly in major cities. In fact, Bangkok has recently introduced English-language road signs in many locations throughout the city.

## HISTORY

### The Beginnings of the Tai People

Scholars still debate the origins of the Tai people and the beginning of their civilization. Archaeological evidence indicates that permanent settlements existed in what is today Thailand as long as 10,000 years ago. From this some experts believe that the Tai are indigenous, and emerged from earlier settlers in the region. Other experts contend that the Tai people are originally of Mongolian stock from north and northwestern China. Noting similarities in mythologies and other cultural traits, still other experts argue that the Tai came from civilizations in the Western Pacific Ocean. However, based on both archaeological evidence and linguistic theories, most anthropologists believe that Tai people migrated originally from southwestern China.

The debate began to be more pronounced in the 1960s, when excavations near Ban Chiang in Northeast Thailand revealed evidence of rice cultivation dating back to at least 4000 B.C.E. Moreover, the discovery of ornaments and weaponry point to bronze-age metallurgy around 3000 B.C.E.—before ancient cultures in the Middle East and China had reached this stage—making Southeast Asia one of the original cradles of human civilization. Complicating the argument is the relatively vast dispersion of Tai-speaking peoples,

who range throughout the region into eastern India and southern China. It is clear that there were several major migrations back and forth in this area. The first written records regarding the existence of the Tai people date back to China around 2000 B.C.E. It is from this evidence and linguistic mapping that most experts conclude the Tai came originally from what is today Szechuan province in China, and that they may have moved in and out of Southeast Asia beginning as early as 5000 years ago. It is also clear from later records of Indian missionaries that by the second and third century C.E. the Tai people lived in a "land of gold" *(Souvannaphoum)* stretching across much of Southeast Asia.[8] This is likely a reference to alluvial gold deposits known at the time in rivers and streams of Southeast Asia.

We know that during the first millennium C.E. the Tai population increased, but were politically subsumed within the powerful empires of the Chinese, Vietnamese, Khmer, Pagan, Mon, and Burmese. By the eighth century Tai peoples were divided into five language and regional subgroups: the northern Tai (Chuang) in southern China; the upland Tai in present-day Vietnam; the Lao; the western Tai (such as the Shan and Lahu); and the central Tai or Siamese, who settled in the middle of what is modern-day Thailand. Despite their division, most Tai kept their identity, language, and religion, and over time developed a unique culture.

### Ancient Empires

By the third and fourth centuries C.E. one of the largest and earliest-known Tai populations lived in southern China, in today's Yunnan province. By the eighth and ninth centuries they were incorporated into the kingdom of Nan-Chao, whose rulers were likely of Tibeto-Burman stock. During this time the kingdom ruled important trade routes between Southeast Asia and India and China, and therefore became a kind of cultural crossroads.[9] Nan-Chao also blocked the region from direct contact with China, which was largely controlled by the expansionist Tang Dynasty. Most importantly, Nan-Chao expanded its reach into much of northern Southeast Asia, which helped to bring the Tai peoples together.

Between the sixth and ninth centuries C.E. much of what is today Northeastern Thailand was dominated by the Dvaravati civilization. There is considerable controversy over whether the Dvaravati was an "empire" or "kingdom" in the traditional sense, as very little is known about its history. However, most scholars agree that the Dvaravati was dominated by the Mon, whose people likely originated in eastern India before migrating, centuries before, over much of present-day Burma. The Dvaravati may have also embraced Tai peoples indigenous to the area. Regardless of exactly who made

up the Dvaravati, there is little question that it had an extremely important role in the evolution of the Tai states.

The Dvaravati period brought to the region a culture, dominated by mythological and religious influences originating in India, particularly Hinduism and Buddhism. Hinduism had developed as a polytheistic religion in India by between roughly 1000 and 500 B.C.E., and Buddhism began in the sixth century B.C.E. as an offshoot of the Hindu religion. It made its way into Southeast Asia during the second and third century B.C.E., but did not take full root for almost 1000 years. Still, it is clear that by the seventh century the Dvaravati was a predominantly Buddhist civilization, but one that also retained a great deal of Hindu characteristics.[10] By adopting and incorporating Hinduism and local animistic beliefs, Buddhism gradually became the dominant religion in the region. The Dvaravati helped it spread to the Tai people.

By the eleventh and twelfth centuries C.E., the Dvaravati civilization was rapidly declining. One challenge came from another Mon people with their capital at the ancient city of Pagan, in today's northern Burma. Pagan expanded into an empire, consolidating many Mon and Burmese kingdoms. Another threat came from the Khmer empire, centered at the magnificent city of Angkor in present-day Cambodia. While little is known of how the rise of Pagan affected the Tai, historians agree that many of their peoples were brought under Khmer rule. The Khmer controlled much of Southeast Asia through a complex series of provinces, and introduced to the Tai people new cultural elements, many of which were also derived from India.[11] However, the balance of power in Southeast Asia changed even more dramatically during the thirteenth century. Mongol conquests of southern China pushed many Tai south. By 1253 Mongol armies had sacked much of Nan-Chao. As the Mongols pressed further southward they weakened regional empires, allowing the Tai people some independence from the Mon, Pagan, and Khmer. The most important consequence of this was the emergence of the kingdom of Sukhothai (the "rise of happiness"), which is widely regarded as the first truly Tai kingdom.

### Sukhothai

Sukhothai was originally an outpost of the Khmer empire. While the Mongol invasions distracted the Khmer, local Tai chieftains rebelled and set up their own government in 1238. The first king, Sri Indraditya, and his son, Ramkhamhaeng, expanded their power through a complex series of marriages, diplomatic alliances, and war. Sukhothai's influence increased into what is today Laos and Burma. Ramkhamhaeng also helped encouraged the

establishment of other independent Tai kingdoms, the most important of which was Lan Na (or Lanna) based at the city of Chiang Mai under the rule of King Mangrai. He had been successful in a similar revolt against the Mon, but still faced war with the Mongols. With Ramkhamhaeng's help, Lan Na survived, forming the first real unity alliance of Tai states.

After a series of failed attempts to invade the kingdom, the Mongols pursued diplomacy with Sukhothai. The great warrior king Kublai Khan sent a mission to the kingdom in 1282 in the hopes of securing Sukhothai's neutrality in a Mongol war with the Pagan. Within a few years Sukhothai had peace with the Mongols, and established various diplomatic and trade missions throughout Asia. Through such connections, the kingdom prospered, and maintained its independence in the face of more powerful empires.

Sukhothai also prospered by encouraging the spread of Buddhism, which was gradually adopted as the official religion, while retaining some Hindu and animistic aspects in practice. The development of a common religion, especially one so tolerant of local traditions and practices, helped to further the Tai. In this regard many people regard the Sukhothai era as a golden age in Tai history, renowned for its unity and its artistic and cultural achievements.[12] The magnificent ruins and art from the period certainly point to a highly developed and prosperous kingdom. Stone inscriptions dating from 1292 also serve as the first written record of the Tai people. In fact, during the reign of Ramkhamhaeng a formal writing system, derived from the Mon and Khmer, was introduced, which subsequently became the basis for the modern Thai language.

### Ayutthaya

Despite such achievements, Sukhothai was not without its rivals. After decades of warfare between Tai rulers, Sukhothai was defeated by the kingdom of Ayutthaya (or Ayudhya) in 1378. Ayutthaya was also originally an outpost of the Khmer empire, situated on an island at the confluence of the Chao Phraya, Lopburi, and Pasak rivers. This location was extremely important in a variety of ways. First, during the rainy seasons, much of the area would flood, providing ideal conditions for rice cultivation, which in turn allowed the city to maintain a larger population. Secondly, with easy access to the countryside and, more importantly, the Gulf of Thailand and the sea, Ayutthaya developed important trade routes. With its abundant rice harvests, the city in fact exported rice throughout much of Asia. Third, the cyclical floods provided Ayutthaya with a natural fortress for much of the year, thus protecting it from invading armies. With these advantages Ayutthaya became one of the largest and wealthiest cities in Asia, if not the world, establishing

nearly 400 years of continuous monarchical rule. By the seventeenth century it was at least as big as Paris or London, complete with roads, canals, dykes, and a multicultural population. Sitting behind high walls and well fortified, Ayutthaya must have seemed invulnerable.

The Ayutthaya period witnessed great artistic and architectural achievements, as well as the expansion of trade ties throughout Asia and the Middle East. Many of its kings also went to war, especially against the Khmer, to expand their territories. In doing so they developed a complicated bureaucratic system and set fairly rigid social and political hierarchies, which influenced Thailand right through the twentieth century. This order was based on the Khmer concept of *devaraja* (or *thammaraat* in Thai)—the Hindu idea that kings were divine beings. Beneath them were the princes *(chao)*, the nobles *(khunnang)*, and the commoners *(phrai)*. The only classless division was the Buddhist priesthood *(sangha)*, which was at the center of society and drew from all classes.

Ayutthaya, however, had rivals of its own. Almost a century of continuing war with the Burmese and Cambodians eventually led to Ayutthaya's collapse in 1569. Ayutthaya did recover, and in 1583 King Naresuan (ruled 1590–1605) led a revolt against the Burmese. He managed to increase Ayutthaya's influence in the region through the expansion of trade and diplomatic relations, both with China and several European powers new to Southeast Asia. Still, the threat from the Burmese continued as new challenges with the Europeans emerged.

### European Contact

The first Europeans to deal with the Tai were the Portuguese in the early sixteenth century, but it was not until the early seventeenth century that the Dutch, and then the British and French, made significant contact. Both Europeans and Tai rulers were motivated by trade interests. Tai lands provided exotic and valuable goods, like silk, hardwoods, spices, and rice for European markets. In return the Tais received metals, new technologies, and textiles. However, the Tais faced the problem of balancing their independence with the economic and political benefits of Western contact. European powers had imperial designs on Southeast Asia and, over the next 200 years, would carve out colonies in the region—posing a serious threat to the Tais.

One of the early examples of foreign pressure came with Constantine Phaulkon, a Greek adventurer who served as an adviser at the court of King Narai between 1675 and 1688. Working secretly for the French, Phaulkon convinced Ayutthaya to refuse the English and Dutch trading rights, thereby giving France a virtual monopoly. He also encouraged the king to allow

French soldiers to help guard the kingdom against reprisals. However, powerful members of the royal court distrusted the French—indeed all foreigners—and took advantage of Narai's illness with dropsy to usurp power. Phaulkon was arrested and executed, while the French soldiers were expelled. The modern Thai word for foreigners, *farang,* evolved from the incident, and comes from the Ayutthaya reference to *farangset,* or French (presumably from the local pronunciation of *français*). More importantly, the episode—and King Narai's death soon after—prompted an internal power struggle in the kingdom that led to a revolution of sorts in 1688. Fearful of foreign influences and being caught between the competing interests of European states, Ayutthaya began to withdraw from contact with the Western world.

In the meantime, the Tais still confronted their regional enemies. In 1760 another war with the Burmese erupted. The Burmese brutally sacked and destroyed Ayutthaya in 1767, and took over most Tai lands. Still, Tai independence survived—within a year a new Tai kingdom emerged, based at Thonburi, near the present-day capital of Bangkok. Led by a General-King named Taksin (ruled 1767–1782), Thonburi's armies gradually recaptured most of Ayutthaya's lands and extended Tai control into Laos. Despite his tremendous military and political accomplishments in rejuvenating and reuniting the Tai peoples, Taksin came to an unfortunate end. Believed to have gone mad, Taksin was forced to resign as king, and then was killed according to an old custom for royalty, by being wrapped in a velvet sack and beaten to death with clubs of sandalwood. His successor was Thong Duang, the commander-in-chief *(Chaophraya Chakri)* of the Tai armies. He was crowned King Ramathibodi, or Rama I (ruled 1782–1809), and moved the capital to Bangkok, which quickly grew into a major cosmopolitan city—and still today has the longest official place name in the world.[13] Rama I also introduced reforms in Tai law, politics, and trade. In the process he oversaw the establishment of a unified central Tai empire, later known as Siam. He also began the Chakri dynasty, which still rules Thailand today.

### Siam and the Era of Imperialism

By the eighteenth century most foreigners referred to both historical and contemporary Tai kingdoms as "Siam." There is great debate about the origins of the term, but most scholars believe it is derived from *Sayam* in the Sanskrit language of India, meaning "swarthy" (in reference to the appearance of the Tai people). Other experts argue that the word is best translated as "golden," in reference to the Indian missionaries' depiction of *Souvannaphoum*—the "golden lands" where the Tai people lived. Still others have argued that the term is Khmer in origin, meaning "dark," and that it may

have been their name for Sukhothai. Regardless of the precise meaning of the word, Siam is clearly an imported reference. Not surprisingly, the Tai called themselves "Tai," which basically translates as "free." The use of the word likely emerged to describe the difference between the lowest class of people living in Ayutthaya and of Sukhothai. Whereas the former adopted slavery as a practice, the latter did not. Therefore even the poorest in Sukhothai could call themselves "Free Tai." Their kingdom was referred to as *Muang Tai*, or "Land of the Free." Based on early contact with the Chinese and Indians, there are European references to the kingdom of "Sian" from the early fourteenth century. The first recorded Portuguese to actually visit the region arrived at Ayutthaya in 1511. They called the land a variety of names, eventually settling on "Siao." An English explorer first used the name "Siam" during a voyage there in 1592. The Tai continued to refer to their home as *Muang Tai* through the mid-nineteenth century, but in 1856, with the signing of a trade treaty between Great Britain and the kingdom, the term Siam became official.[14]

Throughout the nineteenth century Siam's power grew, but serious threats to Tai independence still remained. The British colonized Siam's mortal enemy, Burma, while the French pushed into the Mekong River through Cambodia and Laos. The Europeans demanded preferential trading privileges from Siam, and challenged Bangkok's authority in remote provinces. Through skillful diplomacy the Siamese avoided war, and managed to hang on to the largest empire in Southeast Asia. This was based on playing off European interests and rivalries against one another, and on forming only temporary alliances.

Two of Siam's most revered kings, Mongkut, or Rama IV (ruled 1851–1868), and his son Chulalongkorn, or Rama V (ruled 1868–1910), were particularly instrumental in maintaining independence against European imperialism. Mongkut introduced political, bureaucratic, and cultural reforms designed to modernize Siam. He also courted the United States in order to balance the influence of European powers, and broaden Siam's international position. Chulalongkorn continued this process, but conflict with the British and French late in the nineteenth century led to an enormous territorial readjustment for Siam. By 1910 Siam surrendered its possessions in Malaya and Burma to the British, and gave up Cambodia to the French, losing nearly half of the empire's territory. This was essentially the price of Siam's independence.

### Revolution and Military Government

When World War I broke out in 1914, Siam declared neutrality, but after the United States intervened in 1917, Siam quickly followed suit. By joining

the Allies the Siamese earned a place at the Paris Peace Conference, where, with American help, they negotiated an end to special privileges that the British and French had had in the kingdom. After the war, Siam endured a serious financial crisis, which was worsened by the worldwide Great Depression beginning in 1929. During the reign of King Prajadhipok, or Rama VII (ruled 1925–1935), Western-educated Siamese intellectuals demanded reforms to modernize the kingdom. A small group of them even staged a daring coup in 1932, forcing Prajadhipok to renounce the absolute rule of the monarchy. Then, in 1935, he abdicated the throne. The new king, Ananda Mahidol (ruled 1935–1946), was just ten years old, leaving Siam effectively without a monarch.

Throughout the 1930s Siamese politics were marked by tremendous infighting. This gave the military an opportunity to dominate the government. The key figure during this time was Prime Minister Plaek Khittasangkha (Luang Phibunsongkhram, or Phibun; ruled 1938–1944 and 1948–1957). He wanted to create a "new nation" *(sang chat)*, renaming the country *Prathet Thai* or Thailand (meaning "Country of the Free") in 1939. Phibun considered Siam to be a foreign term, and hoped that turning to a nationalistic name would help modernize the country. He also pursued more nationalistic policies and a series of cultural "reforms," such as banning languages other than Tai, and enforcing traditional dress codes.

Phibun also pursued a dangerous foreign policy. He admired Japanese militarists and European dictators, even referring to himself as the "Thai Führer." Encouraged by the outbreak of World War II in 1939, Phibun launched a brief war with the French in 1940, and reclaimed former territory in Laos and Cambodia with support from the Japanese. However, most Thais did not like the anti-Western nationalism that Japan and Phibun represented. In December 1941, after being denied access through the country to attack the British in Malaya, the Japanese invaded Thailand. Phibun quickly gave in to the Japanese, in the hope of protecting Thai independence. Following Pearl Harbor and other Japanese victories against the Western powers, Phibun joined an alliance with Japan. One month later, in January 1942, Thailand declared war on Britain and the United States.

### War and an Uneasy Peace

Many Thais opposed their government's decision and joined resistance groups. Others saw cooperation with Japan as the only way to protect their country from an otherwise harsh Japanese occupation. Still others welcomed the Japanese as being preferable to Western domination. They saw the war as an opportunity to regain territory that had been lost over the centuries to

European invaders. Officially, Thailand was the only independent ally of Japan. However, Thai resistance movements worked closely with western forces operating throughout Southeast Asia, and during the war Thai opposition to the Japanese grew. In 1944, Phibun was deposed as Prime Minister. A civilian government returned to power, facing the difficult task of explaining Thailand's war-time role to the Allies.[15]

The new leaders successfully convinced the United States that Thailand's declaration of war was not the will of the Thai people. As after World War I, they even managed to lobby the United States for help negotiating with the British and French, who wanted their territory back and payment as a result of the war. Thailand did have to pay, surrendering money and goods as well as the territory it took during the war in Burma, Malaya, and Laos. This ushered in a period of unstable government between 1944 and 1947, characterized by a proliferation of political parties and ideologies. One of the most important leaders during this time was Pridi Phanomyong, who along with Phibun had been one of the coup plotters in 1932. Pridi was a champion of the left in Thai politics. In March 1946 he became Prime Minister, but rumors about his ties to communists weakened him. In June 1946, King Ananda was mysteriously killed, and Thai conservatives linked Pridi to the incident, forcing him to resign. This eventually led the Thai military to retake control of the country. Facing little organized opposition within the country, and little response from the international community, the military then restored Phibun to power in April 1948.

### Thailand and the Cold War

Phibun's history was a concern to countries such as the United States, but his strong leadership was considered an asset during the late 1940s, when revolutions began throughout much of Asia. The United States was particularly anxious to prevent the spread of communism, and therefore saw Phibun as an ally. Throughout the 1950s American economic, technical, and military assistance poured into Thailand. This helped to develop a stronger economy in Thailand, but it also supported military rule.[16] Many Thais worried about such close relations with a foreign power, and became concerned about American influence on their culture.

An ancient Siamese proverb likens foreign policy to "the bamboo in the wind"—always solidly rooted, but flexible enough to bend whichever way the wind blows in order to survive. This reflects a philosophical approach to international relations, the precepts of which are very much enshrined in Thai culture and religion. Throughout their long history the Thais had consistently crafted a cautious, calculated foreign policy—jealously guarding

their independence and desperately trying to avoid permanent alliances. In this respect, Phibun was worried about drawing too close to the United States. On the one hand, he was very pleased to have American aid and support. On the other hand, he worried that by allying so closely with the United States, Thailand would alienate and anger the new People's Republic of China (PRC), established as a communist state in October 1949 after the long and bloody Chinese Revolution.

The PRC was no superpower at that time, but to the United States and other Western powers it represented a serious threat. Few decision makers in Washington distinguished between Chinese communism and the communism of the Soviet Union, with which the United States had a steadily worsening relationship after World War II. Americans had always viewed communism with great suspicion and fear. However, as the war came to a close the United States and Soviet Union found themselves confronting each other as the only two great powers left—and each was determined to extend their influence and ideas. In this respect, most Americans considered the Chinese Revolution to be just another form of Soviet expansion, particularly when the PRC intervened against American-led United Nations forces during the Korean War (1950–1953).

Between 1955 and 1957 Phibun cautiously applied this traditional "bamboo" pragmatism to Thailand's foreign relations, believing that it was needed to ensure the country's survival in the emerging Cold War in Asia. This was, however, a dangerous foreign policy—wooing the Americans while at the same time secretly pursuing relations with the Chinese. Worried that communism would eventually engulf Thailand, military officials plotted against their leader, overthrowing Phibun in a coup in September 1957. Another Army General, Sarit Thanarat (ruled 1957–1963), took over. Sarit considered himself the defender of traditional institutions, and introduced harsh reforms to preserve Thai culture. The king, Bhumipol Adulyadej (pronounced *Phumiphon Adunyadet,* who has ruled since 1946), was at the center of Sarit's nationalism, and symbolized Thai unity. Sarit was, however, also notoriously corrupt, amassing a huge fortune while in office. Still, the country's economic progress made Sarit popular with the people.

In foreign policy, Sarit cooperated closely with the United States in fighting the Cold War. Thailand was the focus of the American-led Southeast Asian Treaty Organization (SEATO), which was aimed at containing the spread of communism through a regional, multinational mutual defense pact. Despite military rule, Thailand was also promoted by Washington as a stable, progressive country—the "model" for economic and political development in Asia, and an alternative to the chaotic nationalism and revolution that characterized its neighbors. In 1967 Thailand joined the Association of

Southeast Asian Nations (ASEAN), another regional forum designed to strengthen this development still further. American aid began to transform the country dramatically, unquestionably helping Thailand's economic progress—but the price was potentially very high. Sarit had doubts about American commitment to the region. He feared that the United States was not fully prepared to combat communism, or that it would fight and lose—either way leaving his country vulnerable. His concerns were accentuated by a growing communist insurgency within Thailand. Focused on the Northeast and along the border with Malaysia, the presence of communist rebels—many trained or supported by North Vietnam and the PRC—seemed to confirm that Thailand was next on a timetable for revolution. In actuality, the Thai insurgency was never a serious threat to the country's stability, but at the time, with conflicts in Laos, Cambodia, and Vietnam rapidly developing, both the Thais and the Americans feared the worst.

### The War in Vietnam

Throughout the 1960s, as the United States became more deeply involved in containing the spread of communism in Southeast Asia, Thailand's importance in this process grew. Next to South Vietnam, it was the most important Asian ally the Americans had. Thai assistance was invaluable for American efforts to negotiate a settlement to the intricate conflict in neighboring Laos. Simultaneously, a considerable number of U.S. covert operations in Indochina were orchestrated from Thailand, making it essential to America's "secret wars" in the region. Sarit's successor, Thanom Kittikachorn (ruled 1963–1973), built an even closer relationship with the United States. Thailand played a pivotal role during the American war in Vietnam. It hosted thousands of American soldiers and huge amounts of military equipment. Over 11,000 Thai soldiers went to fight in Vietnam, one of the largest contingents from an American ally. Approximately 80 percent of the bombs dropped on Vietnam came from planes flying from bases in Thailand. Thai support also gave some credibility to U.S. claims that it was defending Asian allies from communism. For their efforts the Thais were well compensated by the United States. Military and economic aid continued to pour into the country. However, the Thais did have legitimate security concerns too. Communist forces in Laos, and later Cambodia, posed a serious threat to Thailand. Most Thais therefore supported American efforts to combat communism elsewhere in Southeast Asia, rather than wait for it to overrun their country.

Still, some Thais warned that their culture was threatened by such a large American presence. By 1968 there were nearly 45,000 U.S. servicemen sta-

tioned in Thailand, and thousands more based in Vietnam came in on leave. Cities like Bangkok were dramatically transformed with neon lights, massage parlors, and wild bars. Prostitution, crime, and the drug trade increased. American money flooded in, seriously affecting the nature of the Thai economy. By the late 1960s nearly $22 million per year was spent by U.S. soldiers based in Thailand or on leave there from Vietnam alone. Annual official aid reached a high of $130 million. Development was rapid, but not always even—in many ways dividing Thai society even more. Corruption, especially among government officials, was a significant problem. Many Thais thought that Americans were crude, and that they did not show respect for Thai culture. Stories about American soldiers and their offensive behavior were often exaggerated in the Thai media, and more openly anti-U.S. attacks appeared regularly in some of Bangkok's respected newspapers. But more than anything, most Thais feared that the United States was not winning the war in Vietnam, and that one day Thailand would be surrounded by communist countries that remembered, and resented, its role in their wars.[17]

### Reaction and Revolution

When the United States did begin to withdraw from Vietnam in the early 1970s, Thailand underwent dramatic changes. Many Thais wanted a change in the direction of the country's foreign policy, favoring accommodation with the communist governments that eventually came to power in Vietnam, Laos, and Cambodia. There was also pressure from a new generation of younger Thais who wanted more democracy and an end to military rule. Throughout 1973 there were continuing protests. Then in October of that year, a large demonstration by students at Thammasat University in Bangkok exploded into violence and revolution. The military and police used brutal force in an attempt to break up the demonstration. Only intervention by the revered king prevented more violence. Thanom and other top government officials fled the country, temporarily ending military rule in Thailand.

The civilian governments that followed allowed for greater political and social freedoms. They also moved to establish better relations with communist China and Vietnam, especially as the United States disengaged from Southeast Asia. By 1976, however, many Thais worried that the country was now too radical, and favored a return to military rule. Again demonstrations filled the streets of Bangkok. Clashes in October between students and conservative extremists killed thousands. Once again the Thai military took the opportunity to intervene, this time controlling a new civilian government behind the scenes. Governments into the 1980s were officially civilian, but run in effect by the military. Nonetheless, some democratic reforms did take

hold. Regular elections were held without the military's intervention, allowing for a relatively peaceful transition of power. In addition, fairly diverse political parties began to emerge, slowly changing the landscape of Thai politics and paving the way for more reform.

## Boom and Bust

Thailand survived the revolutions that engulfed its neighbors, and emerged in the 1980s as a fairly stable developing state. However, external relations remained problematic. In 1978, Vietnam invaded Cambodia, driving thousands of refugees into Thailand and placing the Vietnamese military on the Thai border. Bangkok developed an important, although superficial, alliance with China, and supported Cambodian resistance against the Vietnamese. Economically, Thailand pursued close relations with Japan and Southeast Asian nations, stimulating growth for much of the decade.

In the 1990s political reform resurfaced as the major issue in Thailand. The military openly seized power in February 1991, with the promise of fair elections. Voting in March 1992 was marred by fraud, which provoked protest and eventually violence when another general became prime minister. The King again intervened, criticizing the military and calling for peace. Since then coalition governments have struggled with reforming Thailand's political structure and economy. For much of the decade, the Thai economy boomed, making the country one of the financial "Tigers" of Asia. In 1997, however, a disastrous economic collapse reversed Thailand's fortunes, and doubts about its long-term stability resurfaced.

## Thailand Today and Tomorrow

Thailand is now recovering from the economic crash of 1997. It is also still going through the process of political restructuring. There is a new constitution, and there have been considerable changes to business, finance, and electoral practices. However, corruption remains a major issue affecting both the economy and government.[18] There are serious questions about the new government's connections to big business, and about its commitment to genuine reform. Issues like corruption have in fact taken center stage in Thailand. The drive to democratize the country, beginning in the 1970s, has now gained considerable momentum, and will likely grow in the years to come. Illustrative of this is the fact that in the early 1960s, only about 15,000 Thais attended university in the country, with another 2,000 training abroad. By the early 1990s there were more than 600,000 university students in the country, and more than 8,000 overseas.[19] As in many other societies, edu-

cation and economic prosperity are the engines of reform in Thailand. The more Thais open up to the world, the more they will demand changes at home.

There are also serious concerns about the effects of globalization on Thailand. With American economic aid throughout much of the Cold War, Thailand entered the twenty-first century far more developed than some of its neighbors. In many ways, parts of Bangkok are almost indistinguishable from any Western city—complete with skyscrapers, traffic jams, fancy hotels, and McDonald's restaurants. But "progress" has not been without consequences. Many people point out that economic growth has not ended poverty or any number of other problems that Thailand faces. Moreover, many people lament the erosion of traditional Thai society and cultural values, and fear that the country has become too Westernized in its pursuit of development.

Notwithstanding these problems, Thailand remains a relatively stable and progressive nation. Thais enjoy a well-defined sense of nationhood, and fairly good foreign relations both regionally and internationally. More importantly, profound reverence for the Buddhist faith and the Thai monarchy continues to be a pillar of Thai society. It is clear that these institutions and ideas have served Thailand well through some tumultuous history, and it is very likely that they will continue to be called on as the country faces the future.

## NOTES

1. National Identity Board, *Thailand into the 2000s* (Bangkok: Office of the Prime Minister, 2000), p. 1.

2. Ibid., p. 2. See also Joe Cummings and Steve Martin, *Lonely Planet Thailand,* 9th edition (Melbourne: Lonely Planet Publications, 2001), pp. 27–29.

3. Peter Chalk, "Separatism and Southeast Asia: The Islamic Factor in Southern Thailand, Mindanao, and Aceh", *Studies in Conflict and Terrorism* 24 (summer 2001): pp. 241–69.

4. Jane Richardson Hanks and Lucien Mason Hanks, *Tribes of the North Thailand Frontier* (New Haven, CT: Southeast Asia Studies, Yale University, 2001), pp. 211–213.

5. See Alfred McCoy, *The Politics of Heroin: CIA Complicity in the Global Drug Trade,* revised edition (Chicago: Lawrence Hill, 1992). On the Golden Triangle see also Bertil Lintner, *Burma in Revolt: Opium and Insurgency Since 1948* (Chiang Mai: Silkworm Books, 1999) and Ronald D. Renard, *Opium Reduction in Thailand 1970–2000: A Thirty Year Journey* (Chiang Mai: Silkworm Books, 2001).

6. Richard G. Robertson, ed., *Robertson's Practical English-Thai Dictionary,* 20th edition (Rutland, VT: Charles E. Tuttle, 1990), vii–xi. See also Joe Cummings, *Thai Phrasebook* (Melbourne: Lonely Planet Publications, 1984), pp. 7–16.

7. University of British Columbia language library at *www.library.ubc.ca/edlib/worldlang/thai/index.htm.*

8. Rong Syamananda, *A History of Thailand,* 5th edition (Bangkok: Thai Watana Panich, 1986), pp. 6–9.

9. David K. Wyatt, *Thailand: A Short History* (New Haven, CT: Yale University Press, 1982), pp. 12–15.

10. Robert L. Brown, *The Dvaravati Wheels of the Law and the Indianization of Southeast Asia* (Leiden: E.J. Brill, 1996), pp. 10–12.

11. Charles F. Keyes, *The Golden Peninsula: Culture and Adaptation in Mainland Southeast Asia* (Honolulu: University of Hawaii, 1995), pp. 74–78.

12. Wyatt, *Thailand: A Short History,* chapter 3, passim.

13. Tanapol Chadchaidee, *Essays on Thailand,* 10th edition (Bangkok: Thanapol Vittayakarn, 1994), p. 116. Bangkok is officially called *Krungthep, Maha Nakorn, Amorn Ratanakosindra, Mahindrayudhya, Mahadilokpop Noparatana Rajdhani, Burirom, Udom Rajnivet Mahastan, Amorn Pimarn Avatarn Satit, Sakkatuttiya Vishnukarm Prasit,* which means "the city of angels, the great city, the residence of the Emerald Buddha, the impregnable city (of Ayutthaya) of God Indra, the grand capital of the world endowed with the nine precious gems, the happy city, abounding in enormous royal palaces which resemble the heavenly abode where reigns the reincarnated God, a city given by Indra and built by Vishnukarm."

14. Rong, *A History of Thailand,* pp. 4–5, 82–92.

15. E. Bruce Reynolds, *Thailand and Japan's Southern Advance 1940–1945* (New York: St. Martin's Press, 1994), chapters 6 and 7 passim. On the Thai resistance movement see, John B. Haseman, *The Thai Resistance Movement During World War II* (Chiang Mai: Silkworm Books, 2002).

16. See Daniel Fineman, *A Special Relationship: The United States and Military Government in Thailand, 1947–1958* (Honolulu: University of Hawaii Press, 1997).

17. Arne Kislenko, "The Vietnam War, Thailand, and the United States," in Richard Jensen, Jon Davidann, and Yoneyuki Sugita, eds, *Trans-Pacific Relations: America, Europe, and Asia in the Twentieth Century* (Westport, CT: Praeger Publishers, 2003), pp. 217–245.

18. See Duncan McCargo, ed., *Reforming Thai Politics* (Copenhagen: Nordic Institute of Asian Studies, 2002).

19. Niels Mulder, *Inside Thai Society: Religion, Everyday Life, Change* (Chiang Mai: Silkworm Books, 2000), pp. 10–16. See also, Niels Mulder, *Thai Images: The Culture of the Public World* (Chiang Mai: Silkworm Books, 1997), chapter 5.

# 2

# Thought and Religion

## BUDDHISM

### History and Basic Beliefs

Buddhism is the state religion of Thailand. It has played a critically important role in the historical development of the country, and remains today one of the pillars of Thai society. Nearly 95 percent of all Thais are Buddhists, and for many their religion is an essential part of everyday life. Largely because of the country's location at the crossroads of Southeast Asia, Thai Buddhism has taken on the influences of many different cultures, and in many ways reflects the flexibility and openness of the Thai people. Buddhism in Thailand is intricately interwoven with Hinduism, ancient local folklore, and an assortment of gods, demons, and monsters, making it a complex but fascinating religion.

With more than 300 million followers, Buddhism is the fourth largest religion in the world today after Christianity, Hinduism, and Islam. It originated in Northern India in the sixth century B.C.E., and was founded by a prince named Siddhartha Gautama. Renouncing his royal rights, he began a reform movement against what he saw as the Hindu religion's formalities and indifference to inequality. Siddhartha became a wandering philosopher, traveling around India in a search of meaning and enlightenment. After enduring considerable hardship, he eventually achieved "enlightenment" and became Buddha ("one who has awaken"). By the time of his death in 483 B.C.E., Buddha had a large following. His disciples continued to develop his ideas, and over the following 250 years the journeys, experiences, and teachings of Siddhartha Gautama became the basis of Buddhism. The written form of these

teachings is called the *Tipitaka. Tipitaka* literally means "three baskets," in reference to the three different kinds of teachings it offers. The "discipline basket" *(Vinaya Pitaka)* gives rules for the practice of Buddhism at its ultimate, highest level. The "teaching basket" *(Sutta Pitaka)* contains the lessons, lectures, and sayings of Buddha. The "metaphysical basket" *(Abidhamma Pitaka)* deals with Buddhist theology and cosmology. Together, the writings in the *Tipitaka* are voluminous—many times larger than the Christian Bible. There are also writings about the traditions of Buddhism called *sutras.*

The basic teachings of Buddhism are called the truth *(dhamma).* Buddha taught that there were three dimensions to the existence of all life: suffering or unhappiness *(dukkha)*; impermanence *(annica)*; and the state of being without ego, or insubstantiality *(anatta).* Buddhists believe that *annica* is the truth that nothing physical or mental lasts forever. The desire to keep objects, ideas, and personal experiences despite this fact produces *dukkha. Anatta* is the realization that nothing we have and nothing we think is permanent or substantial. Buddha defined the development of these dimensions through what are called the *skanhda,* literally meaning "bundles" or "heaps." There are five *skandhas,* which shape the human mind and give rise to ego: form, perception, concept, consciousness, and feeling.[1] According to Buddhist doctrine, in the beginning of existence there was no ego. Humans, however, lost confidence in the world around them and felt panicked and threatened, leading to the first *skandha* of form. How we deal with ideas and experiences leads us to perception: we either like something, dislike it, or feel ambivalent. Then comes concept; an attempt to label or identify the experience in order to deal with it. That is followed by the realization and acceptance of our egos—our consciousness. Finally, with the *skandha* of feeling, emotions are generated and used to explain or act upon our egos. It is said that Buddha told his disciples: "Through our senses the world appears. Through our reactions we create delusions. Without reactions the world becomes clear."[2]

*Skandhas* lead in turn to the "Six Realms," which are essentially states of mind that all humans go through. Buddhists believe that all humans go through these realms in their search for truth. In the realms we have certain perceptions of ourselves and everything around us. For example, we seek to satisfy ego by acting or possessing something. However, once we do that we usually want more and therefore become dependent—even addicted—to want. This is referred to as the "Hungry Ghost" realm, because we are haunted by our wants and desires—we do not ever really get rid of them. The second realm is the "Animal" realm, in which we act based on instinct to protect and secure ourselves, mostly out of fear or ignorance. This leads to the third realm, "Hell," in which our anger and frustration with the world is vented out, leading to confusion and unhappiness. The fourth realm is called

the "Jealous God" realm, which is characterized by mistrust, envy, paranoia, and pride. We are lustful and jealous of others and consider ourselves to be better than we are—in a sense, gods of our own making. In this realm we define ourselves through competition, material rewards, and the opinions of others. The fifth realm, or "God" realm, is where we achieve some sense of spirituality and believe ourselves to have overcome all the others. The problem is that this realm is an illusion; a reminder that just because we create ideas and beliefs about ourselves doesn't mean they actually exist. The God realm is therefore a trick—and once we realize it, we fall back through the other realms of existence and start again. Buddha taught that only in the last realm, the "Human" realm, can people liberate themselves. Although the human realm is full of doubt and want, it is the only place in which people can work to attain a better understanding of life.[3]

From these principles come the "four noble truths" of Buddhism: first, that all forms of existence have *dukkha;* second, that *dukkha* is caused by want, or more literally "grasping" *(tanha)*; third, that by eliminating the cause of *dukkha* it will stop; and fourth, that there is an eightfold path (the *Atthangika-Magga* or *Magga)* to end *dukkha.* This path includes having right view or understanding, right intention, right speech, right discipline, right livelihood, right effort, right mindfulness or attentiveness, and right concentration. These eight ways to live have also been called the "Middle Way" because they are designed to avoid all excesses and extremes. Each of these eight ways belong to particular pillars of Buddhist practice: wisdom *(panna)*, morality *(sila)*, and concentration *(samadhi).* The ultimate goal of Buddhists is to transform their character and transcend the material view of the world and life. In doing so, they will achieve a state of liberation or absolute truth—literally, "cessation" *(nirvana* or *nibbana* in Thai)—and the end of all suffering.[4]

Somewhat similar to the Ten Commandments in Judaism and Christianity, Buddhism has the five precepts of morality *(sila)*; do not kill, do not steal, do not lie, do not be unchaste, and do not consume alcohol or drugs. Basically, these precepts encourage people to lead a moral life, to appreciate that their actions and thoughts have consequences, and to develop wisdom and understanding. Like Hinduism, Buddhism accepts the principle of *karma* and reincarnation. *Karma* is the belief that actions today affect not only this life, but the next, and that there is no real beginning or end to life. In this regard, Buddhists may not achieve *nibbana* in one lifetime, but rather spend several lifetimes in the circle of birth, living, and death before fully letting go of all their desires, wants, and egos. In order to achieve a better life, Buddhists must therefore make merit (in Thai, *bun)* through good works and good behavior.

Unlike the monotheistic religions of the Middle East, however, in the traditional sense Buddhism does not have a god or gods. There is no ultimate

judge or judgment day. Buddha never claimed to be a god, and did not become one once he achieved *nibbana.* He was simply a man who taught the path to enlightenment. There is also no absolute "heaven" or "hell" equivalent to the Christian or Islamic concept. *Nibbana* is a state of being, not a place for souls.[5] There is also no such thing as a "good Buddhist" or a "bad Buddhist." Buddhism stresses that the individual is the only one who can determine his or her own behavior. Similarly, whereas Christianity is based in part on "blind faith," Buddhism encourages people to question everything—even their religion. Also unlike other religions, Buddhism does not seek to convert people. It acknowledges and accepts all other religions—and especially their moral teachings. In this way, Buddhism is a very tolerant religion that discourages the use of labels and judgments.

Central to these concepts is the Buddhist belief in soul and character traits. Rather than assuming that each person has a singular soul, Buddhism deals with different, complicated, "layers of being." *Khwan* (loosely translated as "soul stuff") is the physical and psychological integrity of being. It is shaped by things such as birth, life, and loss, but it does not transcend the individual after death. *Winyan* (consciousness) does extend beyond death and is in fact the only element or layer that does, but it lacks personal attributes. In some respects it can be seen as the so-called spirit of a person, but not in the same way that other religions consider the spirit as an exact model or form of the individual. Rather, it is an impersonal plane of existence for one's essence. Interwoven with this is the Buddhist belief in character traits that shape all people. *Sandan* (subliminal consciousness) is in effect one's nature: intrinsic qualities that make up the person but that are detrimental to his or her progression toward achieving *nibbanna.* They are essentially flaws that require many lifetimes to overcome. *Nisai* ("that on which anything depends") is basically the set of accomplishments—both good and bad—that an individual can achieve. This affects a person's success in this life and also their progression in the next. The last and most important character trait is *chai* (heart or mind). It is best defined as one's disposition or attitude: a term like *chai di* means "good-natured," while *chai dam* refers to someone's "black-heart."[6] These character traits are generally used to describe or judge a person in life, with the *khwan* considered the integrating element: a kind of guardian that brings all elements together. *Winyan* is much like the product that results, and it shapes the *karma* one has for other lives.

## Theravada Buddhism

Buddhism is in fact not a single religion, but has several major divisions. Most of these are the result of local traditions, beliefs, and customs that have

become part of Buddhist practices in particular regions and countries. There are three major Buddhist systems in the world: the Southern *(Theravada)* school, the Northern *(Mahayana)* school, and the Tantric *(Vajrayana)* school. Thai Buddhism is almost exclusively Theravada. There are more than 100 million Theravada Buddhists in the world, most in Thailand, Sri Lanka, Burma, Laos, Cambodia, and parts of Vietnam. The Theravada school started in Sri Lanka shortly after monks from India introduced Buddhism there. It first came to Thailand in the third century B.C.E. but did not become fully entrenched until the Sukhothai era, between the thirteenth and fifteenth centuries.

The main difference between Theravada and other Buddhist schools revolves around how Buddha is seen. Theravada recognizes only one Buddha: the historic *(sakyamuni)* Buddha, Siddhartha Gautama. Theravada emphasizes Buddha's humanity and does not consider him a deity. Temples and statues devoted to Buddha are, of course, the design of those who followed his teachings. Although people pray and worship before the idols, in a formal sense Theravada Buddhists are simply thanking Buddha for his teachings. The principle focus in this is on meditation and concentration.

In contrast, those in the Mahayana school deemphasize the humanity of Buddha, instead considering him to be one of the beings of wisdom *(bodhisattvas)*. The *bodhisattvas* are essentially a series of lives that Buddha led before becoming Buddha. His life as Siddhartha Gautama was his final life, but before that he had many lives working toward being Buddha. Thus Mahayana considers him to be more of a spiritual being than a man.[7] From this belief comes the doctrine of a future Buddha *(maitreya)*, which holds that another Buddha will come to purify the world. In this way Mahayana recognizes several Buddhas, regarding them as more godlike than men, and hence has more elaborate forms of rituals and worship. There is also a theology, the *trikaya,* and a cosmological belief in other "world systems" *(sukhavati)* beyond the earth.

Scholars believe that Mahayana Buddhism emerged during the first century C.E. as a reaction to the orthodoxy of the Theravada school. By deemphasizing Buddha's divinity, and by placing so much stress on a strict, moral existence, the Theravada school did not appeal to everyone. Literally translated, Mahayana means "the greater ox-cart," in reference to the belief that it is an open, less demanding, and more realistic interpretation of Buddhist teachings. Originally followers of the Mahayana sect derisively called the Theravada the "lesser ox-cart" *(Hinayana)*.

Different still, the Tantric *(Vajrayana)* school emphasizes earthly, human behavior. It embraces existence and all the emotions Theravada Buddhism seeks to control. Although it accepts the belief that existence is illusory, Tantric Bud-

dhism holds that it can only be transcended through indulging in life. As well, the Tantric sect believes in magic and multiple deities, and it involves a high degree of ceremony and symbolism.[8] As a result, it is considered to be more "radical" by both the Theravada and Mahayana schools. Tantric Buddhism developed in India in the fifth and sixth centuries based on texts that described meditation techniques and rituals, called *tantras*. Followers believe that Buddha intended to teach a select group of disciples special meditation exercises that would accelerate their enlightenment. The movements of the body and sensual pleasure are emphasized as keys to metaphysical insight, which in turn leads to greater realization. The sect's main symbol, a thunderbolt, reflects this belief in a faster, more powerful achievement of *nirvana*.

In addition to these divisions, the schools have some different practices and emphasize different scriptures. The language of the scriptures also differs. Theravada Buddhist scriptures were written in ancient Pali, which originated in India, whereas Mahayana scriptures were originally in Sanskrit (also from India) but were then translated into local languages. Of the two schools, the Mahayana is the larger, and includes people in China, Japan, most of Vietnam, Nepal, and Tibet. Other schools, like the Vajrayana, have a wide geographical dispersion and are particularly popular in the West. Within Theravada Buddhism there are further divisions to consider. During the Sukhothai period, two main streams developed, differentiated by their emphasis on training and practice. One was called the "city-dwellers" *(gamavasi)*, which stressed the study of books and scriptures *(gantha dhura)*. The other was called the "forest-dwellers" *(arannavasi)*, which focused on meditation practices *(vipassana dhura)*. The names derived from where monks of both camps went to pursue their focus: *gamavasi* to urban centers with access to libraries and other collections, and *arannavasi* to seclusion in rural areas where they could meditate without distraction. However, these divisions were also political, and both factions competed for influence within the royal court. During the reign of King Mongkut (Rama IV, 1851–1868), the rivalry intensified. He had been a monk for 27 years prior to coming to the throne, during which time he became deeply dissatisfied with what he believed was the corruption of Buddha's teachings. As king, Mongkut implemented a host of reforms designed to "purify" the practice of Buddhism in Siam, most of which favored the *gamavasi* tradition. Complicating matters, Mongkut sponsored the creation of a new, separate order *(nikai)* of monks, called the *Thammayut* ("those who are yoked to the teaching"), which quickly came to be seen as having a more disciplined, orthodox approach to religion. Because of its connection to Mongkut, the *Thammayut* also became closely associated with the monarchy. Those from the *arannavasi* tradition eventually developed into another order, the *Mahanikai*

("Great Society"), which along with subsequent subdivisions, helped to perpetuate the schism within Theravada Buddhism.[9]

Today the two orders are still divided, and their rivalry is still political. In fact, their division is one of the major problems currently confronting the Buddhist religion in Thailand, as is discussed below. Despite its royal backing, the *Thammayut* remain the minority in Thailand, although it does count among its adherents the current king and prince, both of whom were ordained in the order. Both orders have considerable influence in government and, particularly, in Thai education, each with control over some of the country's major state universities. Beyond their historical and political distinctions, the two orders can also be distinguished by the color of their robes: *Thammayut* monks have red or brown robes, while *Mahanikai* monks wear orange ones.

## Buddhism in Thailand

Theravada Buddhism in Thailand claims the longest unbroken tradition in the world. In all other countries where the Theravada school is dominant, there have been periods when the religion was persecuted or disbanded. In fact, after years of oppression by the Dutch, Buddhism in Sri Lanka collapsed in the eighteenth century. It took Thai Buddhists to restore the religion and rebuild the order of monks there. Not surprisingly, Theravada Buddhists—and especially Thais—consider theirs the more traditional or "older" school of the religion. However, despite this claim, Theravada Buddhism has in fact changed significantly across the centuries and from country to country. In Thailand, Buddhism has absorbed a great deal of local beliefs, superstitions, and folklore. In this way, Buddhism in Thailand is in many ways unique.

Buddhism in Thailand is governed by the Triple Gems *(Tiratana)*. These are the Buddha, his teachings (the *dhamma*), and the Buddhist community *(sangha)*. Images of the Buddha are everywhere in Thailand. They are of course found in palaces, temples *(wat)*, and museums. However, they can also be found in nearly every home, hotel, restaurant, office building, and corner store. The *dhamma* is recited in temples and during prayers but can also be seen throughout Thai folktales, in popular movies, and in Thai schools, where it is regularly taught.[10] The *sangha* is probably best seen through the large number of monks *(phra)*, highly visible with their shaved heads and bright orange or red robes, found throughout the country. In fact, ancient Indian accounts of Thailand refer to it as "The Land of Yellow Robes" because of all the monks.

All men are expected to join the *sangha* at some point, usually between the ages of 12 and 20. Only those 20 years of age or older are ordained, but younger boys serve as apprentices *(nen)*. The period of service varies, but usually lasts a

few months. This is considered an important passage in any man's life, and a good way to make merit, especially in honoring one's parents. Even kings and other royals become monks at some point in their lives. The ordination ceremony, or *buat phra,* is marked over a period of a week. Six days before he becomes a monk, a man goes to the *wat* and takes part in regular daily events. The day before he is ordained there is a large celebration with much food, usually attended by the entire community in addition to his family. On the day of his ordination the man's head and eyebrows are shaved as a symbol of his renouncing earthly beauty. Family members help in the process as part of the ritual. A special white robe is then given to the man by his mother; this is regarded as one of the most important life moments for both. He is then led by a procession of family and friends to the *wat,* where he symbolically rejects material goods by tossing coins to the crowd. In the temple he is asked ceremonial questions by the head abbot, such as "are you a snake?" This stems from Buddhist mythology, in which a snake tried to become a monk by tricking Buddha. Based on this the man is often called a snake *(nak)* in the service before he is ordained. The *nak* is then blessed and formally admitted to the order, after which he is given his colored robes and taught how to wear them properly.

All monks take 227 vows as part of their ordination, as prescribed by the scripts on monastic service *(Vinaya Pitaka).* These include vows of piety and celibacy, in addition to many other promises that require considerable discipline. For example, monks are allowed only a few, very basic possessions; their robes, a small bowl for eating, and a cup for drinking. Those who enter the monkhood permanently, or for an extended period of time, undergo a formal training called the *nakthan,* which requires in-depth study of Buddhist scriptures, teachings, and philosophy. They also take nine different levels of Pali language training, collectively called the *parian.* On the whole, a monk's education is very rigorous, requiring serious concentration and self-deprivation. As a result of this lifestyle, monks are highly regarded in Thai society for their restraint and commitment to their way of life. At any given time there are approximately one-half million monks in Thailand scattered throughout the country's 32,000 monasteries.

There is also a monastic order for women called the *mae chii.* Similar to the men, these Buddhist nuns take vows and devote their service to the religion. However, the number of vows taken is considerably fewer—eight—which earns them less merit, and therefore less prestige. The *mae chii* are also generally less involved with important ceremonies and do not have the same influence within the religious hierarchy. However, there is a movement within Theravada Buddhism to restore an ancient order of female monks called the *bhikkhuni,* which was in every way equal to the male order. Currently, there are about 12,000 *mae chii* in Thailand.[11]

Monks are very active in Thailand and perform a variety of services beyond their religious duties. Many *wat* double as community centers, schools, playgrounds, healthcare facilities, shelters, and even guesthouses for weary travelers. Accordingly, monks often have many different functions. Moreover, because every male is expected to become a monk at some time during his life, the monastic orders reinforce important cultural and family values. Tolerance, respect, and self-sacrifice are constantly emphasized, and as a result a strong sense of community and belonging is fostered. And because service in the *sangha* is so common, the hierarchy of the religion is less apparent, and monks are considered very much a part of regular Thai society.

The Buddhist *sangha* does have a spiritual leader, the Supreme Patriarch of the Buddhist Order, who is appointed from a group of *thera,* or elders, by the king. By Thai law, the king has to be Buddhist and is officially recognized as the "Upholder of All Religions."[12] He is therefore the ultimate head of Buddhism in Thailand. For practical reasons, the supreme patriarch deals with all the ecclesiastical affairs of the *sangha.* However, the government of Thailand is also involved with the organization and function of the Order. Through a series of four complex national laws passed between 1903 and 1992, the government has come to officially defend, regulate, and serve the *sangha.* For example, the director general of the Department of Religious Affairs serves as a member of the Sangha Supreme Council *(Mahathera Samakhom)*, which is the consultative body advising the supreme patriarch. In this way the division between religion and state, although official, is much less marked than in most Western societies.

Today, the *sangha* confronts some serious challenges. In the past few years, it has been rocked by scandals: monks caught gambling, having sexual trysts, and generally being corrupt. It has also been threatened by the emergence of two relatively new Buddhist sects—the *Dhammakaya* (roughly translating as "the refined inner body, eternal and free"), and the *Santi Asoke* ("peace and no sorrow"). The *Dhammakaya* sect emerged out of the teachings of a venerable monk named *Luang Poh Sod* in the early 1900s. He developed unique meditation techniques that followers claim gave him supernatural powers, such as the ability to contact the dead and to predict the future. By the 1970s the *Dhammakaya* tradition had distanced itself from such claims and gained considerable popularity in its advocacy of meditation as the key to self-realization and spiritual enlightenment. However, it differed from the mainstream *Mahanikai* on the degree to which meditation could transform the individual and create manifestations, with some adherents convinced that they had literally developed small statues of Buddha in their bodies.[13] The *Dhammakaya* order requires its monks to join for life and to avoid any association with folk-religion practices, such as exorcisms and blessing animist objects. More

important, the *Dhammakaya* has emerged for some Thais as an alternative to the mainstream *sangha,* which they see as being corrupted by its power.

Some Thai and Buddhist scholars have characterized the *Dhammakaya* as "religious fast-food"—a kind of quick-fix for the growing, middle-class, urban Thai population, who still seek spiritual guidance but reject the more austere, traditional practices. In this respect, the sect reflects profound generational and socioeconomic changes taking place in Thailand. Critics of the *Dhammakaya* also note that it has built up considerable wealth with donations of land and money from its followers and that it is run with the same high efficiency, and objectives, of a major business.

In contrast to this, the *Santi-Asoke* sect has adopted a more puritanical Buddhist lifestyle. It entirely rejects mainstream Buddhism as too commercial and too political. *Santi-Asoke* followers renounce their material possessions, join communes in the countryside, adhere to a strict vegan diet, and in effect withdraw entirely from modern society. The movement was started by a man named Mongkol Rakpong, who after a career as a TV entertainer, became a fully ordained monk in the *Thammayut* order and took the name Bodhiraska. After a few years, he left the order and joined the *Mahanikai*, but he quickly became disenchanted with that order, too. Consequently, Bodhiraska formed his own order, breaking openly from the *sangha* and challenging its authority by ordaining his own monks and nuns. He and his followers have frequently been arrested and jailed for their disregard of the *sangha* and Thai laws governing it. This, however, has in some respects increased support for *Santi-Asoke*, which is seen by some Thais as the voice of a more rural, traditional, even Utopian Thailand.[14]

## OTHER RELIGIONS

### Islam

Despite the close association between Buddhism and the Thai government, Thailand does recognize other religions. Freedom of worship in the country has been enshrined since 1932. The largest religious minority in Thailand are Muslims, most of whom live in the South. Islam came to Southeast Asia during the thirteenth century from Arab traders and explorers. Most Thai Muslims are ethnically Malay, reflecting the old territorial divisions of the Siamese Empire. Nearly 99 percent of them are Sunni Muslims, and only 1 percent Shiite. The Thai government has given Muslims considerable freedom and support, including a separate education system, special holidays, financial assistance, and the right to separate courts based on the laws of the Koran *(sharia)* for some cases. The king of Thailand also appoints a special state counselor for Islamic affairs (the *chularajamontri*) to the government

from among the most respected Muslim clerics in the country. There are approximately 3,100 mosques in Thailand, with 164 in Bangkok alone. There are also nearly 200 Muslim schools with both state and private religious institutions.[15] During the 1960s and 1970s, there was a sporadic armed rebellion in Southern Thailand by Muslim insurgents seeking separation from the country. Although this movement has died out, there are still some concerns about the potential for religious conflict in the area.

These concerns have been heightened since the terrorist attacks of September 11, 2001. In the past two years, Thai authorities, in close cooperation with American intelligence agencies, have arrested suspected operatives of Al-Qaeda and other terrorist groups working in the country. Most are connected to Jemaah Islamiah, a militant organization working throughout Southeast Asia, believed to be behind the October 2002 bombing of a Bali, Indonesia, nightclub that killed 202 people. Counterterrorism experts believe that Jemaah Islamiah operates cells within Thailand and that it is likely linked to Muslim separatist groups in the South. Since 9/11 there have been a number of attacks on Thai police and soldiers stationed in the South, with several dozen killed. The Thai government has responded with additional forces to the area and expanded connections to the U.S.-led "war on terror." It should be noted, of course, that the vast majority of Thai Muslims do not support such radical groups and that, with very few exceptions, relations between the Muslim and non-Muslim communities of Thailand remain good.

### Christianity

Christianity first came to Thailand through European missionaries in the sixteenth and seventeenth centuries. Most of the early missions were Catholic, but they were later joined by Protestant and other sects. Most converts to Christianity came from the Chinese or hill-tribe populations, but despite their resistance to conversion Thais have been very tolerant toward the religion and acknowledge that it has generally had a beneficial impact on the country. For example, Christians introduced Thailand's first printing press, made significant improvements to the country's health and education systems, and were very influential in effecting the reforms of nineteenth-century Siamese kings such as Chulalongkorn.

### Hinduism and Sikhism

Hinduism and Sikhism are also found in Thailand, predominantly among the Indian population of the country. It must be noted that although they are quite different religions, Buddhism and Hinduism share many customs and

traditions in Thailand. High priests of Hinduism, called *Brahmins,* take part in important religious ceremonies and festivals in Thailand. There are four main Hindu temples in Bangkok, as well as a number of other shrines, most in the capital. The most famous is the Erawan shrine, named after the elephant that the Hindu supreme god Indra rode. Here the god of creation, Brahma, is depicted with four faces. The image is supposed to be good luck, and many Thais—regardless of their faith—come to bring gifts and make requests. Bangkok also boasts an enormous Brahman swing, known as the Great Swing *(Sao Ching-Cha).* It was originally designed to honor the god of destruction, Shiva, in a yearly ceremony that involved people swinging as high as they could. Unfortunately this led to accidents, and the event was permanently cancelled long ago. Hindus have their own education system too, which promotes the religion and the study of the Hindi language.

### Chinese Religion

There are also a small number of other religions represented in Thailand. This includes a collection of indigenous animistic beliefs, found chiefly among the hill tribes of the North. However, the most conspicuous are what Thais call "Chinese religion," which includes Mahayana Buddhism, Confucianism, and Taoism. Most Chinese Buddhists in Thailand practice their religion in a very similar way to Thais. In part this is because many Chinese immigrants who came in the nineteenth and twentieth centuries were absorbed into the larger Thai culture through marriage or by harsh nationality laws. There are, however, some noticeable differences in the style of worship among those who continue a more uniquely "Chinese religion." There are separate Chinese temples throughout Thailand, although many people go to both regardless of the distinction. In Chinese temples images of the Buddha have a very different appearance, usually laughing and with a very fat belly. This symbolizes prosperity and good fortune. This style of Buddha is more in keeping with the Mahayana school, but also reflects the influence of cultural traits unique to China. There are also other deities represented as part of a complex mixture of Buddhism with Chinese folktales and superstitions. Some practices, such as the offering of food to the gods rather than to monks, also distinguish the Chinese religions.

### BUDDHIST RELIGION IN EVERYDAY LIFE

Thais consider their religious beliefs to be a deeply personal affair. Most do not necessarily believe in every aspect of Buddha's teachings, or follow every dimension of the religion literally. Instead, they consider Buddhism as a prac-

tical guideline for living their lives. For example, most Thais do believe in reincarnation, but also accept the importance of leading a better life whether or not this is their only one. Thus many Thais worship regularly, and do good works in order to gain merit in this life, with the hope of substantially improving their next. Many Thais also accept and follow other religious practices, particularly those associated with Hinduism and local folk beliefs, which they believe complement Buddhism.[16] In this respect it is very common to see Thais worship at a Buddhist temple, and then do the same at a Hindu shrine, all the while wearing an animist talisman.

### Prayers and Offerings

For Thai Buddhists, religion is very much part of everyday life, but to Western eyes it can be remarkably informal and unhierarchical. There is no official day of worship, and no formal, collective ritual. Rather, people go to pray whenever they want, but do not regularly receive preaching or other religious ministration from a monk or priest. Thais tend to go to *wat* depending on the phases of the moon, and sometimes according to astrological or numerological predictions, which are very popular in Thailand. A usual visit to the *wat* includes private or group meditation, making traditional offerings of lotus buds, and burning candles or incense sticks at altars. Lotus buds symbolize enlightenment because they grow on stagnant, dirty water, and thus represent the passage from darkness to light.[17] Some Thais will purchase and release caged birds as a way of accumulating merit, or buy thin goldleaf gilding squares to place on the Buddha. The so-called money tree (sprigs and branches of a smallish tree with money notes wrapped as leaves) is another popular offering, often carried to the *wat* in a procession with singers and dancers accompanying, in order to ward off evil spirits and entice donations. Many Thais also bring food for the monks, who regularly seek alms from the people. On occasion they may listen to monks recite or chant Buddhist teachings, or seek special advice and counsel for problems. However, for the most part Thais go to the *wat* as part of their regular day, thus reinforcing Buddhism's impact as a philosophy even more than a religion.

### Spirits

Even beyond the *wat* most Thais live by a blend of strong religious principles and animist beliefs. One of the most interesting and widespread practices involves so-called spirit houses *(haw phii wat* or *san phra phuum)*, which stem from the ancient belief that all things have souls and spirits. Almost every home in the country has a spirit house, which is usually no bigger than a

Buddhist monks receiving alms (courtesy of Tourism Authority of Thailand).

bread box, mounted on a pedestal or placed on a shelf. Spirits in the area are supposed to live there. Without one, they would live in the rest of the house, and possibly bring bad luck. There are serious considerations about the size, composition, color, and especially the location of the spirit house, all of which are factors in the overall aim of appeasing the spirits. There are also daily offerings, usually of food, candles, incense, or even small figures and toys, which are designed to maintain good relations with the spirits. Spirit houses are so important that they can in fact be found in nearly every building in the country—even office towers, Western hotels, and airports.

Similarly, many Thais will wrap special cloths around certain trees to honor the "ghosts of the tree" *(phii ton mai)*. Certain trees have certain spirits, and the cloth marks this fact. There are often small shrines, spirit houses, and offerings kept nearby too. Cutting down the tree is, of course, prohibited, but should it become absolutely necessary then a ceremony is required to warn the spirit and give it a chance to move. To help manage all the spirits, many Thais turn to the "spirit doctors" *(mo phii)*, who claim to have special powers over the ghosts. Ordinary people make up the majority of *mo phii*, but it is not unusual to have a monk act as one. Other spirits are also an element of everyday life in Thailand.[18] A very common one is *nang kwak*, a female spirit who is supposed to bring good fortune into the household. Usually portrayed sitting on her knees, dressed in traditional Thai clothes, she has one

Spirit house (*haw phii wat*) (courtesy of Tourism Authority of Thailand).

hand up in the gesture of drawing money toward her. Some Thais, especially those of Chinese descent, also worship their ancestors. Although none of these spirits or traditions were originally part of Buddhism, the examples all demonstrate how local, indigenous beliefs have become fully part of Buddhist practices.

### Ceremonies and Special Events

Religion affects nearly every major event in a Thai's life. As in other religious societies, birthdays, weddings, and deaths are very much shaped by the religious background in Thailand. Engagements traditionally require the blessing of a monk. They also require blessings from the parents and ancestors. Ancestors are usually offered food, candles, or incense in exchange for bestowing happiness on the couple. For a successful marriage, Thais usually have nine monks (a lucky number) perform at a wedding. Wedding ceremonies and practices are discussed further in chapter 8.

### Birth

When a baby is born there is a ceremony known as the *tham khwan sam wan,* or "making a soul after three days." This has nothing to do with Bud-

dhism but rather is based on the old animist belief that babies are placed in the mother's womb by a spirit. The baby is ritually "bought" with a coin by another woman, usually an elder not directly related to the mother. This is thought to trick the spirit who brought the baby into going to the wrong person in case it should ever want to claim the child back. It is also customary for the parents and family members of the baby to avoid praising the child's looks. In fact, it is more likely that they will say the baby is ugly, believing that this will ward off spirits who steal the souls of beautiful children. After one month another ceremony is performed to protect the baby from evil spirits. This involves cutting the child's hair, which is believed to be where evil spirits congregate. A celebration follows to welcome the baby into the community, and to thank the good spirits for allowing it to survive. When a child reaches puberty a similar practice involves shaving its head except for a long braid or topknot. This is then cut by an elder to mark the child's entry into adulthood. Although monks are not usually involved in these ceremonies, they are often consulted, especially in helping to choose an auspicious name for the child, or to give their blessings. Many Thais are given both formal, legal names and important nicknames. This is based on the belief that evil spirits focus more on a person during the first month of his or her life if only the baby's real name is used. These nicknames—whose purpose is therefore to "confuse" the spirits—are usually used by Thais right through their lives. As well, children are often ceremonially adopted by close family friends, much in the same way Christians have godparents. Some *tham khwan* ceremonies are also held during periods of illness, and at other important life moments. Animist traditions also apply to other circumstances. For example, in many communities it is taboo for pregnant mothers to eat chilies, go fishing, visit the sick, or attend funerals. All are believed to be bad for the unborn child.[19]

### Death

Thai religious beliefs are essential in death too. Monks preside over most rituals for the dead, such as the placing of a coin by family members in the mouth of the deceased—which allows him or her to buy their way into purgatory—and the tying of their hands with white thread in the traditional *wai* greeting. Candles, incense, and money may also be placed in the coffin to help the spirit in its journey. Monks then lead the procession to the *wat* with the coffin tied to them by thread, symbolizing their guidance into the next life. At the funeral itself, monks will assist in the cremation of the body—as Buddhism dictates—and then chant *mantras* (or incantations) for several days to help the spirit pass into its next life. A celebration of the person's life then follows, complete with food, drink, and merriment. This is considered

more respectful than mourning in the sense more familiar to most Westerners because the belief in *karma* and reincarnation means that the dead are
considered to be reborn into a new life.

### Water

Water is especially important to most Buddhist rituals. It can signify a rite
of passage, the eternal flow of life, fertility, and purification. For example, at
weddings it is used to bless the new couple. After death the corpse is bathed
by family members and dressed. Water is then ceremonially poured over the
right hand by mourners to wish the person well in rebirth. A jar of drinking
water commonly found outside many Thai homes is turned upside down, to
discourage the ghost from returning home. At funerals the body is also ritually sprinkled in water blessed by monks. For the coronation of kings, water
is taken from different sources throughout the country and used to anoint the
monarch.[20]

### Everyday Events

In Thailand Buddhism also influences other, less spectacular events such as
moving to a new home, buying a car, or going on a journey, all of which
require the blessing of a monk. Buddhist beliefs also affect ways in which people lead their lives—through, for instance, healthcare, which among traditional Thais involves a very holistic approach. Traditional Buddhists even
follow their own calendar, which takes the birth of Siddhartha Gautama as its
starting point. Although Thais of course recognize that, for instance, the year
of this book's publication is 2004, on the Buddhist calendar the year is 2547.
Almost all Thais carry with them an amulet or image of the Buddha (*phra
khruang*). These remind them of his teachings and are considered to be powerful against evil spirits. Other amulets bear the image of Buddhist scrolls or
mythological symbols. Talismans of animal bone or claw, conch shells, various medallions, and semiprecious stones are also very commonly worn for
good luck.

In addition to these beliefs, Buddhists are supposed to refrain from any
excesses and unnecessary acts. Nature is regarded as sacred, and the destruction of animals or other living things is to be avoided. Strict Buddhists are
therefore vegetarians, although this is not compulsory for all followers. Thai
monks, however, must not eat meat and even use a small filter when drinking
to make sure they do not accidentally eat any insects. Buddhism also prohibits war for any reason. No war is "justifiable" or "holy" in Buddhism, and
no reason is legitimate for killing someone. Thailand has certainly seen its

share of violence and conflict, but this does not mean that such beliefs are useless. Most Thais embrace these notions in their everyday life, and a careful observer can see this in the average Thai's behavior. Generally, Thais are very easygoing. They dislike any form of confrontation, especially with foreigners, and consider aggressiveness to be extremely rude. Similarly, traditional Thais are rather modest and avoid public demonstrations of affection. As well, most Thais are helpful and friendly, in part because this earns them merit, again demonstrating how Buddhist concepts influence their everyday lives. Social customs and attitudes such as these are covered further in chapter 10.

## NOTES

1. Peter Harvey, ed., *Buddhism* (London: Continuum, 2001), pp. 72–80.

2. Jack Kornfield, *Buddha's Little Instruction Book* (New York: Bantam Books, 1994), p. 34.

3. Buddhist Studies Dharma Education Association at *www.buddhanet.net/ e-learning/basic-guide.htm.*

4. Thanapol Chadchaidee, *Essays on Thailand,* pp. 42–43. See also Tom Lowenstein, *The Vision of the Buddha: Buddhism: The Path to Spiritual Enlightenment* (London: Duncan Baird, 2000), pp. 2–32.

5. Noble Ross Reat, *Buddhism: A History* (Berkeley, California: Asia Humanities Press, 1994), p. 33.

6. Northeast Illinois University, Center for Southeast Asian Studies, Thai Studies Web site at *www.thaibuddhism.net/maha_tham.htm.*

7. Smitthi Siribhadra, *Palaces of the Gods: Khmer Art and Architecture in Thailand* (London: Thames and Hudson, 1997), pp. 13–14.

8. Kanai Lai Hazra, *Thailand: Political History and Buddhist Cultural Influences,* volume 2: *Buddhism and Its Influence on Thai Culture* (New Delhi: Decent Nooks, 2000), pp. 337–40.

9. Northeast Illinois University, Center for Southeast Asian Studies, Thai Studies Web site at *www.seasite.niu.edu/Thai/* and *www.thaibuddhism.net/maha_tham.htm.*

10. Yoneo Ishii, *Sanga, State and Society: Thai Buddhism in History* (Honolulu: University of Hawaii Press, 1986), pp. 24–30.

11. Chitra Ghosh, *The World of Thai Women* (Calcutta: Best Books, 1990), pp. 45–59.

12. Hazra, *Thailand: Political History and Buddhist Cultural Influences,* p. 339.

13. Marja-Leena Heikkila-Horn, "Two Paths to Revivalism in Thai Buddhism: The Dhammayaka and Santi Asoke Movements," *Temenos* 32/1 (1996): 93–111, online at *www.abo.fi/comprel/temenos/temeno32/horn.htm.*

14. Ibid.

15. National Identity Board, *Thailand into the 2000s,* pp. 107–113. See also Ishii, *Sangha, State and Society,* pp. 110–119.

16. William Klausner, *Reflections on Thai Culture* (Bangkok: Siam Society, 1981), pp. 205–207.

17. Together with the *Bodhi* tree, the *Wheel of Law,* and the *chedi* or bell monument, the lotus is one of the four fundamental emblems of Thai Buddhism. See Brown, *The Dvaravati Wheels of Law and the Indianization of Southeast Asia.*

18. For more information on spirits in the Thai world and older customs, see Phraya Anuman Rajadhon, *Some Traditions of the Thai* (Bangkok: Thai Inter-Religious Commission for Development and Sathirakoses Nagapradipa Foundation, 1987).

19. Klausner, *Reflections on Thai Culture,* pp. 346–52. See also Robert and Nanthapa Cooper, *Culture Shock!* (Singapore: Times Books International, 1982), pp. 136–55.

20. Steve Van Beek, *The Chao Phya: River in Transition* (Kuala Lumpur: Oxford University Press, 1995), chapter 5 passim.

# 3

# Literature

## TRADITIONAL LITERATURE

The National Museum of Thailand in Bangkok houses the earliest-known written records of the Thai language, which are stone inscriptions dating back to 1292 commemorating the invention of the modern Thai alphabet by King Ramkhamhaeng some nine years earlier. The stone chronicles the life of the king, but also discusses Tai history, society, and the politics of the time. Stone inscriptions from the same period at Bangkok's Wat Po detail the proverbs of the king, and contain the very earliest record of Tai poetry.

### Sukhothai

Although the Sukhothai period in Thai history is perhaps best known for its sculpture, it was also the period in which Thai literature began. The best-known writings of the day come from Nang Nopamas, also known as Sri Chulalak, the daughter of a high official in Ramkhamhaeng's court, and later the king's consort. Another important writer of the Sukhothai period was King Lithai, who in 1345 authored a long poetic dissertation on the three worlds of Buddhist cosmology called the *Tribhumikatha* (or *Traibhumi Phra Ruang*). This became a model for many subsequent literary forms, as well as for other arts and even architecture.[1]

### Tribhumikatha

The *Tribhumikatha* divided the universe into three worlds: the World of Desires *(kamadhatu)*, the World of Form *(rupadhatu)*, and the World of

Absence of Form *(arupadhatu).* The World of Desires is where people live. At its center is Mount Meru—the home of Hindu gods and the axis of the cosmos—surrounded by seven mountains and oceans. At the base of the mountain is a land of demons (the *yakkhas*) who are enemies of the gods. In a land halfway up the mountain the sun and the moon revolve, and there live the Four Great Kings of the East, as well as wise beings and other divinities. At the summit of Mount Meru is one heaven, *Tavatsima,* where 33 Hindu gods and Indra, the most important god, live. This land is also where a tower of precious stones protects the hair and tooth of Buddha, which the gods come to praise. Above this level are other cosmic realms, far removed from earthly desires. They are the domain of Mara, who is a vengeful god, and the rough equivalent of Satan in Christian or Islamic theology. In Buddhist doctrine Mara tries to prevent Buddha from reaching enlightenment. In a more philosophical sense, Mara represents earthly suffering and want—*dukkha.* Beneath all these levels are the infernal regions, or hells. The World of Form is the home of other deities, led by Brahma, while the World of Absence of Form is where gods of supreme perfection exist: another kind of heaven.

### Jatakas

The *Tribhumikatha* was complemented by tales about the various lives of Buddha called the *jataka* (in Thai, *chaa-dok*). The *jataka* were already popular during the Sukhothai period, and remain an essential feature of Thai literature and art today. They were originally based on Hindu *jataka* stories imported from India. In total there are 547 such *jataka* tales in the central Buddhist canon, the *Tipitaka,* but over the course of the sixteenth, seventeenth, and eighteenth centuries extra stories based on local folklore were added to the tales to make them more familiar to Tai people. The most important ten "great *jatakas*" are called the *Tosachat* in Thai, and illustrate the virtues of existence as laid out by Buddha. These include abnegation, perseverance, benevolence, resolution, wisdom, moral thought, patience, equanimity, truth, and giving. Some, like the virtue of giving *(wessandon jataka)* are especially well represented in Thai literature as a recurring theme.[2] Tourists to Thailand today are also more likely to see this *jataka* portrayed in temple murals, paintings, and even street souvenirs than any other. Together the *Tribhumikatha* and the *Tosachat* dominated the subject matter of Tai literature and arts up until the modern age.

### Folktales

Folklore has had a major role in the shaping of Thai culture. It has influenced interpretations of the *jataka* stories, given rise to ghost stories, and

served as the basis for both songs and jokes still popular in Thailand today. One of the most important genres of folklore is the *chakchak wongwong*. These are tales of adventures in which the hero, usually a prince or king, seeks out the love of a beautiful woman. Along the way he often meets and loves several women, which leads to heartbreak, jealousy, family rivalries, and battles between enemies. Thai television soap operas and even modern movies still follow the outline of the *chakchak wongwong*. To some scholars, the popularity and endurance of these tales is based on the structure of the traditional Thai family, as well as the traditional roles of the sexes.[3] Others believe that the stories originated and continue to serve as a kind of socially acceptable outlet for the anger, frustration, and anxiety that family relationships can cause.[4]

Creation myths are also an important component of folklore in Thailand. Because Buddhism does not deal directly with the creation of the world, creation myths based on nature and spirits emerged. Many are connected with agriculture, and particularly the cultivation of rice—the mainstay of Thai diets both in ancient times and today. Spirits of the rice fields are very common in Thai myths, as are spirits of the sky, water, and earth. There are also village and ancestor spirits. Although specific creation myths differ between groups of Tai people in Southeast Asia, all share this emphasis on natural elements. Most involve the action of spirits who made the earth and then gave life to humans. For example, a Northern Thai version centers on two sky spirits who came to the world after a great fire. They loved the fragrance of the soil so much that they gave up being gods to become mortal, and then started the human race.[5] Other myths liken the earth to a giant gourd, which was grown in the sky by spirits. Still others deal with sky spirits who help create the world, animals, and people out of clay.

Thai folklore is also full of ghost stories, some of which remain the premise of children's games, popular comic books, television shows, and movies. The most famous is *Nang Naak*, about a young woman of that name who dies and comes back to haunt her village. For generations Thais have been drawn to this simple tale, so much so that it has become ingrained in their culture and spawned a number of different variations. No one is sure if Nang Naak was a real person, but many believe that in fact she lived in Bangkok during the mid-nineteenth century and died in childbirth. Some believe she lived during the eighteenth century, while others argue that the story is even older. In some versions she is an ordinary farm girl, in others she is a princess, or the daughter of a village chief. The common thread is that she is young, beautiful, and married to her childhood sweetheart, who leaves her—pregnant with their first child—to go and fight in the army. Before he returns, she dies—often in childbirth, or of a broken heart mistakenly fearing that her husband has been killed. Because of the power of love, her spirit lives and returns to

her house. There she and her baby take the form of humans, without the husband knowing that they are in fact dead. In most versions, the truth is revealed only by accident: when she reaches through the floor to pick up a lime, for example. Often the story has a more sinister side, in which the husband remarries or flees in fear of the ghost. Nang Naak becomes angry, and either torments her husband and his new wife or follows him. In some versions the ghost even kills people who try to stop her.

In many places in Thailand Nang Naak is so famous and important that she is revered, almost as a deity. The popularity of the legend may be derived simply from its universal appeal as a scary story. It could also be because the idea of spirits is tolerated within the Buddhist faith. Other interpretations stress *Nang Naak*'s representation of the paradox of women as portrayed in traditional Thai culture: feminine and nurturing, but at the same time jealous and dangerous.[6] The fairy tale *Champa Thong* also illustrates the duality of women in Thai folklore. Champa Thong is a princess, named after a beautiful flower because the tears she cries are like golden petals. She is so loved that one of her handmaidens gives her as a gift a rare crocodile egg, which the princess keeps in her palace. Once hatched, the crocodile becomes a killer and soon eats many people. Champa Thong quickly earns the wrath of the kingdom, including that of her father and mother, the king and queen. The king orders the crocodile killed, but when that fails, with the hunters being eaten too, he banishes his daughter. Accompanied by her handmaiden, Champa Thong tries to drown herself in the river, where she meets her pet crocodile. As it tries to eat her, the gods take pity on the princess and put her on a lotus leaf made of thorns. The crocodile is killed by the thorns, and Champa Thong returns to the kingdom—once again loved by the people.

Another popular character in Thai folktales is the trickster, usually a heroic figure who teaches or learns moral lessons and is known for his charm, wit, and verbal dexterity. The best-known is probably Sri Thanonchai, a character who emerged in folklore during the Ayutthaya period (see below) and remains popular throughout the country today. According to most interpretations, he was a young, novice monk who once served as an advisor to a king—although exactly who is often disputed. As a reward for his services, the king decided to give Sri Thanonchai land and asked him how much he wanted. Sri Thanonchai suggested that he would take "just enough for a cat to die in." He then tied a string to a cat and followed it around until it died, which was not before it covered a great deal of territory, thus tricking the king.

The story then details the many different ways the king and Sri Thanonchai played tricks on one another, most of which are tales of practical jokes designed to make people laugh. For example, the king serves Sri Thanonchai

a hot curry made of vulture meat—considered inedible—and makes him sick. In retaliation, Sri Thanonchai gives the king a special piece of chalk, which he claims will only write once the tip is licked. When the king does this, Sri Thanonchai reveals that it is in fact a piece of vulture excrement. In another version of the tale, Sri Thanonchai gives the king a special pot, supposedly containing the most beautiful fragrance in the world. The king opens it, breathing deeply, and is disgusted to find out that Sri Thanonchai had passed wind into the pot instead.[7] Although the story may seem to contradict the Thais' deep reverence for the monarchy by portraying the king as a sort of dupe, it is more about humor than politics. In fact, the king is much loved in the story for his equally good sense of fun and for his occasional tricking of the trickster. Bangkok's *Wat Pathum Wanaram*—constructed in 1857 on the orders of King Mongkut, who spent 27 years as a Buddhist monk—is even adorned with murals of the *Sri Thanonchai* tale.

### Ayutthaya

During the Ayutthaya period (1350–1767), Thai literature flourished. For much of this era Ayutthaya was as big as London or Paris, and just as advanced in its infrastructure. The artistic community prospered, and received much support from successive rulers. Poetry was especially well represented in Ayutthaya, and developed into the primary form of literature, complete with rules for measure and rhyme. Poems were not, however, just artistic creations. They were used to glorify the rule of kings, reinforce laws and moral values, and above all, help in the spread of Buddhism—which by the fifteenth and sixteenth centuries was the dominant religion among the Tai people. Most known poets during the Ayutthaya period were Buddhist monks, which would explain why so much of the work from this era was found in temples. In the early years of the Kingdom, between 1350 and 1448, monk poets wrote some of the most important literature in Thai history. *Lilit Oong Gaan Chaeng Naam* (Oath to the King) established in poetic form the duties of people to their rulers, and eventually became the oldest work in continuous use until the end of the absolute monarchy in 1932. *Lilit Yuan Paai* (Defeat of Chiang Mai) detailed Ayutthaya's military victories over Sukhothai and other kingdoms in conquering and reorganizing the Tai lands. It therefore became, and remains, an important historical record. The famed *Maha Jataka* (Great Life) told about Buddha and recounted some of his past lives, thus aiding in the development of Buddhist thinking.

Not all the poems of the day were for political or religious purposes. One of the most famous from the early period of Ayutthaya was a love story, much like Shakespeare's *Romeo and Juliet*. *Lilit Phra Law* tells of a prince who falls

in love with two daughters of his enemy and therefore tries to make peace with his rivals, only to be killed—along with the girls—by evil grandmothers who want to continue the war.[8] Another story emerging from the Ayutthaya period cleverly combined Buddhist teachings with ancient folktales. *Ruang Koong Naai Prasop* (The Story of Nai Prasop) involves the son of a wealthy family who joins the priesthood to earn merit for his parents. Shortly after his ordination he consults a local soothsayer for his fortune, only to discover that he is destined to marry the bride of a slave, lower than he. Brooding on his fate, Nai Prasop discovers an infant resting in a cradle under his bunk, placed there by her mother—a slave of his family—and realizes that this must be his future wife. He decides to drop a knife through the floorboards to kill the child but succeeds only in wounding her, leaving a scar on her groin. Fearing for their lives, the mother runs away with her baby. Nai Prasop and his family are then cursed with bad luck and lose all their wealth and possessions. Forced to wander and beg for his food, he is taken in by kindly old townsfolk, eventually falling in love with their daughter. After they wed, Nai Prasop discovers his bride has a scar on her groin, and realizes his fate has come true.[9] Tales like this were clearly designed to entertain, and to convey moral messages that people could easily understand.

Poetry was so important in Ayutthaya that it became one of the most important artistic and historical legacies of the kingdom. By the seventeenth century, poetry was very common, and moved beyond the realm of monks. Most people in the royal court were expected to write poems, so much so that the period between 1656 and 1688 is known as the "Flower Period" from this blossoming of poetry. The best-known writer from this time was the king himself, Narai, whose work remains among the most important in Thai history. Many of his poems reflected the changing times of the kingdom, which during his reign saw not only nearly continual war with the Burmese, but also expanding—and often dangerous—ties with European powers. His most famous work is perhaps the *Samutakot,* a long narrative poem that he began writing to mark his twenty-fifth birthday. The story is about a prince who falls asleep while hunting and is taken to heaven through magic by a beautiful princess. Although she returns him, the princess wants him back, and seeks him out. After finding him, she arranges a contest for all men to show off their strength in the hopes of winning her heart, which, of course, the prince wins. The story is about the importance of pride, dignity, and honor, which some scholars interpret to be a message to the Tai people during the tumultuous times they faced.[10] The poem was so long and detailed that Narai did not live to see it finished, and it was eventually completed after his death by members of his inner circle. Narai also wrote a number of shorter poems, many of which have been turned into children's lullabies over the centuries.

Most are about elephants, several thousand of which he kept as treasured members of the royal court.

The Flower Period also produced Sri Pat, who was an important member of Narai's court. He wrote poems about the politics of the time and his own relationship with the king, leaving a valuable record for the era. Another famous poet, the monk Horathibodi, compiled the first language primer for children, the *Chindamani,* and the first official history of the kingdom—both in poetic form. Famously, this era also produced a poetic prophecy about sixteen evils that would befall Ayutthaya. Its authorship remains unclear, but it foretold the destruction of the kingdom.[11]

The late period of Ayutthaya between 1688 and its collapse in 1767 also produced important poetic works. Again much of the poetry from this era reflected the turmoil that the kingdom experienced. However, this era also witnessed other key developments. For the first time, theatrical plays and songs on literary themes began to be produced. In 1740 the Crown Prince Senapitak wrote "Phleng Rua" (The Boat Song), which is still one of Thailand's best-known songs:

Looking at fish swimming together in pairs,
I think of you and feel sad.
Even fish know how to love,
So it serves me right for having left her behind.
Looking at the bright and beautiful moonlight fish
Only reminds me how much more beautiful you are.[12]

### Ramakian

During the seventeenth and eighteenth centuries Ayutthaya also saw development of the *Ramakian* (Glory of Rama), the most important and influential piece in the history of Thai literature, and the country's national epic. The *Ramakian* was derived from the Hindu *Ramayana*—one of the two great poetic dramas of Hinduism, relayed through an elaborate story, which came from India centuries before. It is clear from archaeological evidence that the *Ramayana* made its way into Thailand sometime in the twelfth century. Fragments of art and text left after the destruction of Ayutthaya prove that it was well established in the kingdom long before 1767.

The *Ramayana* centers on the ten-headed demon-king, Ravana (Tosakanth in Thai), who tries to steal King Rama's wife, Sita. Rama—a reincarnation of the Hindu god of preservation Vishnu—then builds an army of monkeys to get her back. The army is led by the monkey-god Hanuman, who ultimately succeeds after an epic journey and battle. Translated from Sanskrit into Thai,

Painting from the *Ramakian* (courtesy of Brent Wardrop).

the *Ramakian,* like the original, is full of gods, demons, and heroes. Uniquely Thai, however, are the addition of elements from local folk tales, and the removal of most Hindu religious references. Rama's life therefore became a past life of Buddha rather than a reincarnation of Vishnu. The story also contains a distinctly Thai sense of morality and even humor. Central characters from the *Ramayana,* like the monkey-god hero Hanuman or the villain Tosakanth, are often portrayed quite differently in the *Ramakian.* In the Indian version, for example, Hanuman is always very serious and "pure." In the Thai version, he is far more emotional and sensual.[13] A famous mural of the *Ramakian* in Bangkok's Wat Po temple even pictures him grabbing a woman's breast like an apple. Also in the Indian version, Ravana is purely evil, whereas in the Thai version Tosakanth is portrayed more sympathetically. His wrong-doings are motivated by love, not hate, as suggested in this exchange with Queen Sita:

> Her voice only increased his desire.
> Her voice was beautiful beyond comparison.
> The more he listened the more absorbed he became
> In her body and in the beauty of her words.
> He bowed down and said eloquently,
> "Beautiful lady, whom I love
> Throughout the Three Worlds,

There is no one whose features compare with yours.
Even if you curse me
I don't take your words seriously
I have mercy for you through my love.
Do not destroy my love and affection.
You are like a heavenly gem.
Throughout the sixteen levels of heaven there is no one who can compare
    with you?
I love you like my own heart.
I will cherish you against evil.
Woman, don't reject my love.
Queen, have mercy.
Be my well-being forever."[14]

The popularity and importance of the *Ramakian* were furthered by Tai rulers who favored the concept of *devaraja,* or god-kings. The story also gained famed because it was easily adapted to theater, which served to entertain as much as educate all Tai.[15] Scholars point out that the *Ramakian* embodies a multitude of Thai customs and cultural values still held dear today. Reverence for the king is the obvious centerpiece of the tale, but throughout the story a number of other Thai qualities are portrayed, such as respect for elders, the importance of welcoming people into the home, honoring the dead, and the practice of consulting astrologers. Justice, gratitude, integrity, and fidelity are major themes in the *Ramakian*, much more so than in the Indian *Ramayana*.[16] In this way, the story has made an indelible imprint on Thai cultural identity.

## Bangkok Period

Literature survived the collapse of Ayutthaya and continued to prosper during the more modern Bangkok period. King Rama I wrote a famous version of the *Ramakian* in 1798, in which elements of Buddhist philosophy were added and the institutions and accomplishments of Ayutthaya ingrained. His version of the *Ramakian* provided the source for the beautiful murals adorning Thailand's holiest shrine, the Temple of the Emerald Buddha *(Phra Kaew Morakot)*. Rama I also wrote the *Unarat* in 1787, another of Thai literature's essential works. Again derived from Hindu mythology, the story is about a demon that appears as the god Indra to have sex with his wife, Nang Suchitra. Her revenge is to die and be reborn as a beautiful woman named Nang Usha in a lotus bud, who is then adopted by the demon and kept guarded in a magnificent palace. Unarat is the grandson of Krishna, a reincarnation of the god Vishnu, who is supposed the kill the demon. While

on a hunting trip he falls asleep in the forest after praying to the tree gods for success. A friendly tree god then takes him to Nang Usha, with whom he falls madly in love. When he awakes, however, Unarat is back in his real life—and angrily rejects his family and friends for Nang Usha. Equally upset, she uses magic to be reunited with her lost love, which infuriates the demon who watches over her. He sends out his armies to capture Unarat, but before the demon can kill him, Krishna comes to the rescue and fulfills Unarat's prophecy. Although complicated, the moral message in the story is simple in representing the triumph of good over evil. In particularly Thai fashion, however, the story is also a good romance. Rama I wrote many other love poems and stories, but also managed to edit the *Tipitaka* and even develop some of the famous *jataka* tales.

During the reign of Rama II between 1809 and 1824 Thai literature further expanded and influenced new drama and dance. As with so many of his predecessors, the king was himself a great writer and poet. However, without question the most famous literary figure from this era was Sunthorn Phu, a teacher to the king's children. Although a trusted member of Rama II's royal court, he was cast out by political intrigue during the reign of Rama III (Nangklao). After wandering as a monk for several years, he returned to the royal court and became its leading poet. His most famous contribution was the introduction of a poetic form called *sawatdee raksa,* which means "protecting one's welfare." The primary element of this form was the use of graceful language, often with stern practical and moral meanings:

> When you go to bed
> Don't forget to salute the pillow
> While saying your praise and gratitude
> To your parents and teachers.
> When you travel, or sit or sleep
> If you hear a strange noise at night
> The noise of ghosts, of spirits and demons
> Do not call out to it, for it will come to you.[17]

Sunthorn's most famous writing is the poem *Phra Abhai Manee,* which took over twenty years to write. Again mixing ancient mythology with romance and morality, the complex poem revolves around a man and his four women—one a sea serpent, one a mermaid, one the Eastern Princess Suwannamali, and one the Western Princess Laweng. Sunthorn is also famous for his proverbs, many of which are still used widely in Thailand today, such as "in times of love, even the soup from bitter vegetables tastes sweet, but when love dies, even sugar will taste bitter."[18]

### Siam

The nineteenth century is not as well known as others for its accomplishments, but there were developments that shaped the direction of Thai literature. The first Thai-character typeface was created in 1828, but it was not until 1835 that the printing press was introduced—brought by American missionary James Low. This led first to the mass production of books on Thai grammar and then, by 1844, to the first Thai-language newspaper. In 1862 the first literary book in Thai was published, *Nirat London,* based on the travels of Siam's ambassador to England. Another significant development was the work of King Rama IV (Mongkut), who had spent 27 years in a monastery before taking the throne, and brought to the court a working knowledge of several different languages, including English. He was among the first people to write about Siam and its traditions in foreign languages. The circulation of ideas, prayers, sermons, books, and stories had a great impact upon the future direction of Thai literature and Thai society.

Not all the changes were welcome. Influenced by the popular English literature of the Victorian era, some writers went too far for Thai sensibilities of the time. In 1885 Luang Phichit Prichakon, a foreign-educated nobleman, penned the short story *Sanuk Nuk* (Fun Thinking), which featured four young monks contemplating their futures. While the others discuss the virtues of business or government service, one character elects to remain in the priesthood, where he can have economic security and peace of mind. Set at Bangkok's famous Wat Bowonniwet, the story utilizes the common Western literary device of realism. To many foreigners *Sanuk Nuk* would appear lighthearted, if not satirical. However, to the Buddhist *sangha* the story was offensive in its depiction of a materialistic monk. Under pressure from the order, King Chulalongkorn (Rama V) banned its further publication.[19]

## MODERN LITERATURE

### Early Twentieth Century

The early twentieth century also brought rapid change to Thailand and Thai literature. King Vajiravudh (Rama VI) continued in the traditions of the royal court and was a prolific writer, both in Thai and Western languages. He embraced not only poetry, but also plays, songs, and historical and fictional prose.[20] Reflecting political change in Thailand and internationally, Rama VI was best known for his nationalistic writings, many of which employed graphic humor, sarcasm, and even controversial ideas about race and ideology. A number of court and government officials also contributed to Thai literature, many bringing in the influences of their Western education or travel.

Prince Nara, who served as the minister of finance in the late nineteenth century, wrote plays and operas. Prince Bidhya, who also served as minister of finance in the 1920s, was well known for his short stories and poems like "Nala" and "Kanok Nakorn." Kukrit Pramoj—journalist, actor, and prime minister—wrote several popular books such as *Phai Daeng* (1961; Red Bamboo) and *Si Phaen Din* (1953; The Four Reigns). Luang Vichit Vadakarn, a career diplomat and long-serving minister of foreign affairs, wrote 24 plays and 36 musicals in addition to 537 books and articles on various aspects of Thai history.[21]

As prolific as the royal court and upper classes were, Thai literature in the 1920s and 1930s also signaled the end of the absolute monarchy and the domination of the arts by the social elite. Three of the most important works of the period were all written shortly before the 1932 coup: *Lakhon Haeng Chiwat* (Life is a Play) by Akat Damkoeng in 1929; *Khwan Phit Khrang* (The First Mistake) by Buppha Kunchon (writing under the alias of Dok Mai Sot) in 1930; and *Songkhram Chiwat* (The War of Life) by Kulap Saypradit in 1932. Akat and Buppha were from aristocratic backgrounds, but Kulap was a commoner. Despite their different social standings, and although they used different styles, these three all focused on class consciousness, discrimination, and the virtues of democracy.[22] In their advocacy of social justice, these works in many ways foreshadowed the revolution.

Changing times were also reflected in the work of Kanha Watanaphat, who wrote under the pen name K. Surangkhanang. Her best-known book, *Ying Khon Chua* (1937; *The Prostitute*), tells the story of a young girl from the country who is tricked into coming to Bangkok and then forced into prostitution. She becomes pregnant by a young aristocrat and struggles to raise the child away from the dark world of Bangkok's streets. Both a love story and a tragedy, the book was initially rejected by Thai publishers because of its sympathetic portrayal of prostitutes, whom they considered immoral. At the time, many Thais also viewed the discussion of sexual relations as pornographic. However, with the help of influential Thais, such as Prince Chula Chakrabongse, the book was published to wide acclaim. It has subsequently been reprinted in several editions and even been made into a movie—becoming one of modern Thai literature's most famous works.[23] K. Surangkhanang went on to write over 40 novels and nearly 100 short stories and was honored in 1986 as one of Thailand's greatest authors.

### Post–Word War II Literature

Similarly, the tremendous changes in Thailand after World War II ushered in another period of social commentary through literature. The massive eco-

nomic and military presence of American forces in Thailand during the Vietnam War era had a pronounced effect on Thai society and culture. Dramatic increases in prostitution, narcotics, and corruption were associated with American servicemen. The very close relationship between the Thai and U. S. governments alarmed many Thais who feared that American ideas and customs were polluting their culture. Intellectuals like Sulak Siwarak launched serious criticisms against the Thai government, warning about the dangers of American influence. Poets such as Angkhan Kalayanaphong and writers such as Rong Wongsawan joined in. Through short stories and novellas Rong pointed to the degradation of Thai culture, and the crass materialism of the Americans. Ironically, many Thai writers drew from the same impulses shared by American youth in their campaigns against materialism, the Vietnam War, and the domination of their parents' generation.

By the late 1960s and early 1970s, Thai literature again reflected the coming revolution. Short stories such as Sujit Wongthet's *Kamon Lasandran* (1967; Second Nature) and *Muan Yang Mai Khoey* (1974; As if It Had Never Happened) by Witthayakon Chiangkun highlighted the clash of American modernism with rural life and traditional Thai values. Wanit Jarungkit-anan's "Michigan Test" (1974) parodied the middle-class Thai obsession with learning English and studying or working in the United States. In order to get his American visa, the main character must first pass an examination in English. A friend advises him to ask for help by worshipping before Brahma at the Erawan shrine, to which he replies: "He's been standing there with his four arms in the air for God knows how many years, and he still can't even wiggle them. How could he possibly be any help...old Brummer-Brahma?"[24]

## Contemporary Literature

Other contemporary writers include S. P. Somtow, a master of both Thai- and English-language supernatural and science fiction stories, including "The Vampire's Beautiful Daughter" (1997), "Darker Angels" (1998), and "Jasmine Nights" (1994)—the latter a curious blend of fantasy and autobiography. His 2003 work "Do Comets Dream?" is part of a book series derived from the popular television show *Star Trek: The Next Generation*. More controversial is the poet-painter Vasan Sitthiket, whose powerful, often profane, poetry addresses a range of political and social issues. His "Fate of the Urbanites" (1984) described the many contrasts of modern Bangkok:

A city with many faiths
A city where monks speak Pali
A city where Dharma is reciting by heart

A city which is advised by Brahmins
A city where law is written by criminals
A city which is full of beggars
A city where people only work to survive
A city which is full of beautiful people
A city where women show their upper leg
A city where the aged are forgotten
A city where art belongs to the genius
A city where garbage covers the footpaths
A city which is full of impossible dreams
A city where deception flourishes
A city where truth is a lie.[25]

Like Vasan, other prominent figures in the Thai literary world have also become powerful social critics. Poet and artist Angkarn Kalyanapong focuses much of his work on environmental degradation, political corruption, and the erosion of Buddhist values in modern Thailand. Internationally re-nowned author and Buddhist scholar Sulak Sivaraska is a leading human-rights and antiglobalization activist. He has twice been nominated for a Nobel Prize for his work on social justice in Thailand. In 1963, he was named the editor of *Sangkhomsat Parithat* (Social Science Review), a quarterly jour-nal that quickly became the major forum for artists and academics discussing social, political, and economic problems in Thailand. Sulak has been openly critical of the Thai government and, on several occasions, even slighted the monarchy. For the latter, he has faced numerous criminal charges and court hearings, but he has always managed an acquittal—on at least one occasion due to intervention by the king.

The infusion of foreign ideas, and particularly Western influence, into Thai literature has clearly been the most important development of the mod-ern era. Technology, political, economic and social change, and particularly reforms in education have also had great impact, by making literature acces-sible to many more Thai people. Equally vital, however, is the fact that liter-ature has moved beyond the exclusive domain of royal courts, monks, and government officials.[26] In this way the content and style of modern writing has significantly changed. It is now much more realistic and immediate. Although it still deals with moral and ethical questions, modern Thai literature is less confined to Buddhist philosophy, mythology, and folklore. Political reforms have dramatically reduced, if not eliminated, censorship, producing a very active literary scene and a diverse range of writings. Among the most important contemporary contributors are short-story writers Kham-sing Srinawk and Kampoon Boonthavi; novelists Seni Saowaphong (or Sakdichai Bamrungphong) and Suwat Woradilok (or Rapeeporn); and poets

Angkarn Kalayanaphong and Naowarat Phongpaiboon. Collectively these writers and others now address issues such as class conflict, discrimination, the transformation of nature, technology and globalization, and the struggle in beliefs between generations. Born into a poor farming family from the Northeast, Pira Sudham has become one of Thailand's best-known English-language authors with books such as *The Monsoon Country* (2001)—a fictional account that deals with the alienation of rural, traditional culture in the modern age—and its sequel *The Force of Karma* (2002), which examines developments in post-1992 Thailand through an elaborate tapestry of individual lives.

It should also be noted that a great deal of foreign-language literature has been translated into Thai and is widely available throughout the country. King Bhumipol has himself translated two major English-language works into Thai: in 1993, *Nai In Phu Pit Thong Lang Phra* (1976; *A Man Called Intrepid*) by William Stevenson, about the Canadian-born World War II spymaster (also named William Stephenson), and *Tito* (1972; by Phyllis Auty), about the Yugoslavian dictator. The king has also written, in both English and Thai, the *Mahajanaka* (1996)—an interpretation of one of the *jataka* tales from the *Tipitaka*.[27]

### Women and Literature

Another aspect of change is that Thai literature is no longer dominated by men. Women have become increasingly influential in Thai literature, especially in the second half of the twentieth century. Writing under the pseudonym Dokmaisod, M. L. Busba-Nimmanheimindra, probably the most influential Thai woman writer of the twentieth century, penned short stories in the 1940s and 1950s such as "Nung Nai Roi" (One in a Hundred) and *Nij,* both of which dealt with growing up in a rapidly changing Thai society. Kanchana Nakananta wrote "Look Kwaang" (1968; The Wide World), dealing with the struggles of four parentless children, and "Yawdrak Puu Gawng" (1972; My Beloved Captain), a romantic comedy turned into a popular Thai film. Another famous female writer, Suwanee Sukhontha, wrote prize-winning short stories "Khao Chu Karn" (1972; His Name Was Karn), "Talee Reu Im" (1973; Will the Sea be Full), and "Luuk Rak" (1973; My Beloved Son); the first of which deals with the clash between modernity and tradition, while the latter two confront problems facing Thai youth. Novelist Sukanya Cholasueks, better known by her pen-name Krisna Asokesin, wrote *Rua Manut* (1968; The Human Boat) and *Tawan Tokdin* (1973; The Sunset). Both described the life journeys of individuals and their contrast with family values. In the short story "Sa Nee Plaai Ja Wak" (1987; The Enchanting Cook-

ing Spoon), M.L. Boonlue Kunjara Debyasuvan portrayed the conflict between the demands of tradition and more contemporary society on the Thai woman. It also pointed to the hypocrisy of men who want the idealized traditional Thai female, but at the same time want her to be sophisticated and modern.[28] On still another level, the story plays with the concept of class, intellectual elitism, and even Buddhist morality.

Although writings by women form a more recent contribution, it is important to point out that women have always played a central role in Thai literature. Even in traditional tales written centuries ago, women characters are prominent. In the epic poem *Chanthakhorop* from the Ayutthaya period, women are portrayed as evil. In other works they are seen as subservient to men, even fragile and mindless—in sharp contrast to Thai society, where women have traditionally been the real head of the household. Yet because of the influence of folktales and local traditions, in which women are generally seen as stronger figures, Thai literature also portrays more redeeming female characters.[29] The *Tribhumikatha* from the Sukhothai era depicts the heroine "mounted upon her war elephant, the proud queen rides forward into battle beside her king."[30] In many epic poems of the Ayutthaya period, such as *Khlong Kamsuan* and *Lilit Phra Law,* women are idealized as symbols of virtue and pure love.

Despite the many advances of Thai women in modern times, these divergent characterizations still pervade the literature, often intentionally. The portrayal of women is becoming more realistic, however, addressing issues of sexuality, personal relationships, and the conflicting requirements of career and the traditional family. For example, recent work such as "Maw thii Khut may awk" (1987; A Pot That Scouring Will Not Save) by Anchalee Vivathanachai (writing under the pen name Anchan) deals with spousal abuse. The book *Puu Ying Kon Nan Chuu Boonrawd* (That Woman's Name Is Boonrawd), by Supa Sirising (Botan) addresses poverty and discrimination, while the short story *Matsii* by Wanna Sawadsee (Sri Dao Ruang) deals with a dark side of parenthood.[31] Although some Thais find the subject matter too controversial, such work demonstrates the dynamic nature of Thai literature.

## NOTES

1. Klaus Wenk, *Thai Literature: An Introduction* (Bangkok: White Lotus, 1995), chapter 1, passim.

2. Santi Leksukhum, *Temples of Gold: Seven Centuries of Thai Buddhist Paintings* (New York: George Braziller, 2000), pp. 129–36.

3. Siraporn Nathalang, "Different Family Roles, Different Interpretations of Thai Folktales" in Siraporn Nathalang, ed., *Thai Folklore: Insights into Thai Culture* (Bangkok: Chulalongkorn University Press, 2000), pp. 3–9.

4. William Klausner, "Siang Miang: Folk Hero" in ibid., p. 64.

5. Siraporn Nathalang, "Tai Creation Myths: Reflections of Tai Relations and Tai Cultures" in ibid., p. 87.

6. Ka F. Wong, "Nang Naak: The Cult and Myth of a Popular Ghost in Thailand" in ibid., pp. 123–36.

7. Foreign News Division, *Facets of Thai Cultural Life* (Bangkok: Government Public Relations Department, Office of the Prime Minister, 1984), pp. 55–56.

8. Robert J. Bickner, *An Introduction to the Thai Poem "Lilit Phra Law" (The Story of King Law* (Dekalb: Northern Illinois University Press, 1991), pp. 1–38.

9. Jeannette Faurot, ed., *Asian-Pacific Folktales and Legends* (New York: Simon and Shuster, 1995), pp. 201–206.

10. M.L. Jumsai Manich, *History of Thai Literature,* 3rd edition (Bangkok: Chalermnit Press, 2000), pp. 95–101.

11. Foreign News Division, *Facets of Thai Cultural Life* (Bangkok: Government Public Relations Department, Office of the Prime Minister, 1984), pp. 40–41.

12. Jumsai, *History of Thai Literature,* pp. 111–112.

13. J.M. Cadet, *The Ramakien: The Thai Epic* (Tokyo: Kodansha International, 1971), pp. 30–44.

14. Theodora Helen Bofman, *The Poetics of the Ramakian* (Dekalb: Northern Illinois University Press, 1984), p. 124.

15. Center for Southeast Asia Studies, Northern Illinois University, Thai Studies at *www.seasite.niu.edu/Thai/literature/ramakian/introduction.htm.*

16. Srisurang Poolthupya, "Thai Customs and Social Values in the Ramakien," paper no. 11, Thai Khadi Research Institute (Bangkok: Thammasat University, 1981), pp. 1–15.

17. Foreign News Division, *Facets of Thai Cultural Life,* pp. 27–29.

18. Jumsai, *History of Thai Literature,* p. 137.

19. Benedict R.O'G. Anderson, *In the Mirror: Literature and Politics in Siam in the American Era* (Bangkok: Editions Duang Kamol, 1985), pp. 12–13.

20. Wyatt, *Thailand: A Short History,* pp. 224–34.

21. Jumsai, *History of Thai Literature,* pp. 170–74.

22. Anderson, *In the Mirror,* pp. 14–16.

23. David Smyth, ed., *The Prostitute* (Kuala Lumpur: Oxford University Press, 1994), pp. vi–ix.

24. Ibid., pp. 40–55.

25. Apinan Poshyananda, *Modern Art in Thailand: Nineteenth and Twentieth Centuries* (Singapore: Oxford University Press, 1992), p. 226.

26. Herbert P. Phillips, *Modern Thai Literature* (Honolulu: University of Hawaii Press, 1987), pp. 9–26.

27. His Majesty King Bhumipol Adulyadej, *The Story of Mahajanaka* (Bangkok: Amarin, 1996), passim.

28. Ibid., pp. 152–57. See also Jumsai, *History of Thai Literature,* pp. 174–78.

29. National Identity Board, Office of the Prime Minister, *Women in Thai Literature,* book 1 (Bangkok: Office of the Prime Minister, 1992), passim. See also Hong Lysa, "Of Consorts and Harlots in Thai Popular History," *Journal of Asian Studies* 57/2 (May 1998): pp. 333–53.

30. Susan Fulop Kepner, ed., *The Lioness in Bloom: Modern Thai Fiction about Women* (Berkeley: University of California Press, 1996), p. 1.

31. Ibid., passim.

# 4

# Theater, Dance, Music, and Film

## TRADITIONAL THEATER AND DANCE

### Khon Dance-Drama

In the traditional sense, drama and dance are inseparable in Thailand. The dance-drama emerged from the *Ramakian* during the Ayutthaya period, and remains the most important dimension of Thai theatrical arts. The best-known Thai dance-drama is called *Khon*. It was derived from Hindu temple rituals and dancing, but like Thai literature, quickly took on influences from Thai folklore and mythology. *Khon* was originally performed only within the royal court, and only by men, including the female roles. By the mid-nineteenth century, however, women joined the theater too. *Khon* is characterized by very vigorous and formalized movement with precise musical accompaniment. The acting and dancing parts are inseparable. Nonspeaking characters dance out their lines while a chorus sings along. Training for *khon* is extremely demanding and difficult, and usually starts in childhood.[1]

*Khon* is also famous for its colorful and elaborate costuming, especially the masks. Made from paper and decorated with gold, lacquer, and imitation jewels, the masks are designed to represent the traditional monsters, demons, and gods from the *Ramakian*. Costumes are equally colorful, and resemble the traditional clothing of royalty. Characters are identified by the colors they wear; for example, one of the heroes, Phra Ram, always wears deep green, while Hanuman wears white. Traditional *Khon* productions were nearly 24 hours long in total, and usually spread over several days. To produce the entire original *Ramakian,* with all 311 characters, would take more than a month of

*Lakhon,* a Thai classical dance (courtesy of Tourism
Authority of Thailand).

continuous performance.[2] King Rama II's shorter version is now used for the
theater, with most performances lasting only a few hours.

### Lakhon

A less formal type of dance-drama in Thailand is the *Lakhon.* It too is based
on the *Ramakian,* but also draws from the *jataka* tales and local folklore.
Although *Khon* and *Lakhon* costumes are almost identical, only a few characters in the latter wear the masks. Moreover, the dance movements in *Lakhon*
are more graceful and fluid, famous for the delicate expressions of the hands
and upper torso, which are designed to communicate emotions. *Lakhon* has
many variations throughout the country, but there are primarily three differ-

ent types. The *Lakhon Chatri* is probably the best known, and can often be seen at popular shrines or temples. *Lakhon Nai* tends to be more formal, and is performed only by women, while *Lakhon Nok* is performed only by men.

Probably the best example of *Lakhon* is the *Sang Thong*. Based on the *jatakas,* this was written during the reign of Rama II and contains all the elements of a good Thai dance-drama: romance, love, war, revenge, the supernatural, and redemption. The story is about Phra Sang, the Prince of the Conch Shell. It begins with a king, Thao Yosawimon, who has no male heirs to succeed him. The King therefore tells all his wives that the first to bear him a son will be the number-one queen. Two of his wives become pregnant and go to see an astrologer to predict the sex of their children. One, Queen Chantha Thevi, is told she will bear a son, while the other—a scheming concubine—is told hers will be a girl. Unhappy with this, the concubine bribes the astrologer to reverse his predictions. When the Queen bears Phra Sang—in a conch shell, symbolizing his immortality—the astrologer convinces the king that the boy is evil. Both mother and son are banished, and end up in a forest working for their food. One day the rice that the queen has picked to eat is taken by angels posing as birds. In her efforts to shoo the birds away, the queen breaks the conch shell, condemning Phra Sang to life as a mortal.

Fearing the boy's return to the kingdom, the concubine casts a spell on the king to kill Phra Sang. After numerous failed attempts to kill the boy, the king orders his son to be drowned with a heavy stone, but Phra Sang is saved by a magical serpent—who then gives him to a friendly ogress for safekeeping. As an ogress she must eat animals and humans, and when Phra Sang learns this he flees from her, although not before stealing some of her magical powers and dipping himself in her special gold. The ogress tries to follow him, but soon dies of a broken heart. In thanks to her, Phra Sang prays and is rewarded by being sent to another kingdom where he can choose a bride from among seven beautiful daughters. Wearing the mask of the ogress (which is of an ugly, "kinky-haired" man), Phra Sang hopes to attract a true love. When one daughter, Rotchana, sees through the mask and falls in love, her father becomes angry and banishes the two to the forest, where he plans to kill Phra Sang on a hunting trip. The god Indra stops the king, and gives Phra Sang all his lands. Indra also visits Thao Yosawimon and makes him beg Queen Chantha Thevi for forgiveness. The story ends with a tearful family reunion, and the defeat of the evil concubine.[3]

## Likay

Another type of dance-theater is called *Likay.* This is the most popular form among Thais because it weaves together elements of the *Lakhon* with

comedy, satire, pantomime, and opera. *Likay* is almost always set in a fictitious ancient royal court, but uses contemporary and local references. Actors
sing their lines, and are accompanied by an orchestra. They wear bright, often
outrageous costumes, and heavy, colorful makeup. *Likay* performances may
occasionally be partly ad-lib, drawing on the audience for its content. At their
center, *Likay* stories almost always deal with romance and a good sense of
humor. Because of its bawdiness and informal nature, Westerners often consider *Likay* a form of burlesque.[4] To the Thais, *Likay* is folk-theater, and it is
a particularly popular form of entertainment in rural areas. In the South, a
very similar dance-comedy is popular. This is the *Manohraa*, or *nora*, which is
again based on the *Ramakian*, but features a half-woman, half-bird creature
(the *kinnarii*) as the captured princess.

### Puppetry

A less well known form of traditional theater in Thailand is puppetry. The
*Nang Yai* shadow play involves intricately detailed marionettes, often 6.5 feet
(2 meters) tall, held against a backlit white screen. Originally from the Ayutthaya period, this ancient practice predates any of the dance-dramas. In fact
the elaborate, delicate movements of the puppets gave rise to the *Khon* and
*Lakhon*. In southern Thailand another form of puppetry is called *Nang
Talung*. In this, the marionettes are smaller and usually do not have as many
moveable parts. The puppet masters often ad-lib their performance through
songs and jokes. Rarely seen today, *Hun Krabok* puppetry involves intricately
detailed marionettes—often based on characters from the *Ramakian*—which
are moved from beneath.

### Folk Dances and Chinese Opera

Throughout Thailand there are also many local folk dances. Most famous
are the North's *Xoe* and *Sap*, in which agile dancers perform between bamboo
sticks moved quickly to the beat of music, or the Northeast's *Fon Phu Thai*
with its graceful sweeping steps. There is also the candle dance *(For Thien)* in
Chiang Mai, which involves a kind of *lakhon* with elegant lit candles. It originated from the animist belief that candles could beckon the souls of children
haunted by evil spirits. The Northeast is also famous for the circle dance *(ram
wong)*, in which couples create three layers of circles—one danced by the
individual, one by the couple, and one by the entire crowd of dancers.

Chinese opera has also been an important form of traditional theater in
Thailand. Famous for its colorful costuming, distinctive singing style, and
strange noises, Chinese opera was extremely popular, not just among those of

Chinese descent but also Thais—despite the fact that few could understand it. In ancient Chinese tradition, the operas were considered offerings to the gods. Today, they are a regular feature in festivals, usually alongside *Likay* performances. Although decreasing in popularity, Chinese operas can still be found in Thailand, especially in the South and Northeast.

## TRADITIONAL MUSIC

Music is an important part of Thai culture. Anthropological evidence suggests that the Tai people were fairly active makers of musical instruments even before the development of Indic cultures in Southeast Asia. Through the Khmer and Burmese, Tai people probably absorbed music and musical

*Fon Phu Thai* dance and musicians (courtesy of Tourism Authority of Thailand).

instruments originally from India. Chinese, Malay, and later Western influences have also played a critical role. However, little is really known about the evolution of music in Thailand. Until the twentieth century there was no Thai notation system, and therefore no way to write music down. With no written records most music was passed from generation to generation orally. The destruction of Ayutthaya also compounded the problem, destroying any records and many of the artistic depictions of musicians. Stone inscriptions dating back to thirteenth-century Sukhothai mention the accomplishments of Tai musicians, and suggest that music was very much part of that kingdom's many artistic interests. The *Tribhumikatha* mentions "heavenly musicians" *(Gandharavas)* living with the Four Great Kings of the East and other wise beings half-way up Mount Meru.[5] However, for the most part scholars of Thai music are limited to the study of the nineteenth and twentieth centuries only.

Much of the understanding of Thai musical heritage comes from the study of instruments. It is likely that during the Sukhothai period Tai people developed their own music based on the traditions of other cultures, primarily Indian, Khmer, and Chinese. This belief is supported by the similarities between instruments like the Thai *chakhe* (a three-stringed floor zither) and Indian models dating back to ancient times. There are also similarities between smaller *chakhe* and the ancient Chinese *yang-chin,* and between the barrel-shaped *khlong that* Thai drum and the Chinese *tang ku.* Records from ancient China refer to drums shaped like the *khlong that* as "belonging to the southern people"—perhaps a reference to the Tai. Moreover, Thai dance and dance music shares a great deal with Khmer traditions, right down to the costuming.[6]

### Sukhothai

However it evolved, Thai music began to exhibit distinctive attributes during the Sukhothai period. This is best illustrated in the development of instruments unique to Thailand such as the *ranaat ek* (a bamboo xylophone), the *phin* (a small guitar), the *pii* (a woodwind instrument like a clarinet), and the *khaen* (an elaborate cross between a large bamboo flute and a harmonica). Many of these instruments are mentioned in the earliest written records of the Tai people, and even some songs from the Sukhothai era are still sung in Thailand. Music also took on its characteristic institutional structure and social standing during this period. Technically servants, musicians were very highly regarded members of the royal court, and were even fought over by nobles who wanted to have the best ensemble as a mark of prestige. Training began at a very young age and lasted through a lifetime under the patronage

of court officials. Some of the practices of the Sukhothai era remain part of the formal study of Thai classical music today. There is a special relationship between student and master governed principally by the *thaang*, or school of thought that is followed. Given the largely oral traditions of Thai music, teaching is as much a matter of passing on a performing tradition as knowledge of a certain repertory of compositions. In this way students followed closely the musical interpretations of their teachers. The Sukhothai period also gave rise to the *wai khruu*, a special ceremony that must be performed by all students to honor their mentors.[7] Such traditions are designed to impress upon the student the value of music, as well as reinforcing Thai concepts of social status.

### Ayutthaya

During the Ayutthaya period instrumental ensembles were even more vital members of the royal court. Competitions to demonstrate musical skill were a regular feature, and as a result compositions became much longer and more complicated. New singing techniques were also introduced. The Ayutthaya period is most famous for the *phleng raung*, a kind of musical suite. Songs in the *phleng raung* were based on short stories, many from the *Ramakian*. These songs were then used in *khon* dance dramas, and remain part of classical performances today. There are only 29 known *phleng raung*, distinguished by their tempo and meter: *phleng reo* (fast), *song mai* (medium), and *prop kai* (slow). The longest of these, *tao kin phak bung*, is 684 measures plus repeats, which requires very great stamina to perform.

### Bangkok Period

The literature of the Bangkok period provided much new material for songs and dance dramas, and many masterpieces were put to music. During the nineteenth century expanding contact with Western nations brought new instruments and musical influences to Thailand. Fearing the extinction of their native music, Thai musicians created a unique scale, differentiating it from any other system. However, Western classical music was also welcomed. Largely due to the efforts of composer and teacher Phra Chen Duriyang, Western classical music took root in Thailand through the establishment of orchestras and education programs. Almost immediately, young gifted Thais were sent overseas to study, and Western traditions became mandatory for music students in Thailand. There was also a proliferation of government and private agencies dedicated to the study and promotion of Western classical music.

### The Fundamentals of Thai Music

Unlike most Western music, traditional Thai music is nonharmonic and has a melodic or linear progression. The main melody is played simultaneously in variations that are divided into faster and slower rhythmic units and usually played by different instruments. There is generally not great complexity of rhythm, but rather a straightforward division of the main beat. Rhythm and meter are based on the cymbals and drums. Cymbals set the pace on pieces in quadruple time, while drums do so in pieces in triple time. There is also little syncopation in the main melody, and few dynamic changes within a piece, in part owing to the relatively limited dynamic ranges of most Thai instruments. To the average Westerner the music may seem disorganized, like unrelated pieces being played in different registers. In reality several registers are being used at once to develop a very complex sound texture. To make matters more intricate, the precise pitches are determined almost exclusively by "feel." During the performance, musicians make microtonal adjustments to the melody, which give it particular inflections. There is no formal precision to tuning instruments, and instead it is all done by ear.[8] The result is that there is no standard pitch, which means that often ensembles perform with no close agreement on this between instruments.

### Thai Instruments

There are about 50 different Thai instruments, many in the percussion section alone. Almost all ensembles include a *khawng wong.* This is a set of tuned gongs arranged horizontally in a semicircle, ordered according to pitch and set over a rattan frame. The size depends on the number of gongs: a *khwang wong yai,* or large circle, has 16, while the *klang* (medium) and *lek* (small) versions have fewer. The player sits in the middle and plays the gongs with mallets traditionally covered in buffalo hide. The *khwang wong* carries the main melody in any piece, and may be accompanied by a *khong mon*—a similar array of gongs arranged on a curved row and played vertically. Another regular feature is the *ta-phon,* or two-headed hand drum. The *ta-phon* sets the beat for the ensemble, and demands special recognition. Traditionally made from a single piece of teak or jack-fruit wood, it is has two heads of unequal size, which are then entirely covered over with leather and twisted sugar cane. The rims and heads of the instrument are painted with a black sap. The *ta-phon* is tuned with a special paste made from cooked rice and ash, smeared on the centre of the drum head; the heavier the mix, the lower the sound. Prior to a performance, musicians make offerings of flowers and incense to the *ta-phon,* which they consider to be the "conductor." Women are prohibited from playing the *ta-phon,* owing to an ancient association between the drum and male virility.

The *thon* is a single-head drum shaped like a goblet and played with a pair of alternating buffalo-hide mallets. There are also a series of other drums called *khlongs,* which are named for the country from which they are believed to have come. For example, the *khlong khaek* is known as the Indian drum, while the *khlong marigan* is from the United States. Also very important are the *ching,* small metal hand cymbals that help set the rhythm and meter. *Chap lek* are bigger versions. *Khong rao* are cymbals played on a rack, while the *mong* is played on a stand, like a more basic gong. Rounding out the percussion section is the *rammana,* a shallow pie-shaped drum that looks like a tambourine without the jangles.

A number of flutes can be found in an average ensemble. The *khlui* comes in four different sizes based on length. The *pii,* more like an oboe, also comes in a range of sizes. The *pii-nai,* about 16 inches (40 centimeters) long, is often made of marble, or covered in mother-of-pearl inlay. Made from wood or ivory, the *pii-chawai* is about 10 inches (25 centimeters) long with a bell-shaped end that provides a unique wailing sound. The *pii-mon* is about 20 inches (50 centimeters) long with a metal bell and a deeper sound. Among the more unusual Thai instruments are the *phin,* or plucked group. This category contains a variety of zithers, but also the *krajappi* (which is becoming rare), a lute up to 6 feet (1.8 meters) long with double courses of strings, played with a plectrum made of horn. Bowed instruments include the *so sam sai,* made of a special coconut shell with three lobes, which act as resonators. About 50 inches (125 centimeters) tall with a long neck, the *so sam sai* is often decorated with elaborate lacquer designs.[9]

## Musical Compositions

There are three types of ensembles in classical Thai music: the *pii-phat,* the *mahori,* and the *khraung sai.* The *pii-phat* contains two types of xylophones, two gong circles, a quadruple reed *pii,* drums, and cymbals. The *mahori* has a three-string fiddle, both varieties of two-string fiddles, a zither, a flute, both xylophones, gong circles, *ching* cymbals, and a drum pairing of *thon, rammana,* or *klong khaek.* The *khraung sai* involves a fuller orchestra with almost all Thai instruments represented. The type and size of the ensemble depends on the circumstances and audience. For example, originally only the *pii-phat* could perform at cremation ceremonies. Generally there are seven major repertoires of compositions that ensembles play. The *naa phat* are melodies from the late Ayutthaya period used primarily in *khon* dances. They are formal pieces that depict emotion in the dancers and are never improvised or altered. Similarly, there are the *lakhon* compositions used for those dances. The *seephaa mahori* are much less formal and are widely used in all forms of

entertainment. The *phleng diaw* are instrument solos, while the *phleng ryang* are ensemble pieces used more for rituals. The remaining two categories of compositions are rarely heard in Thailand: *naang hong,* which were for traditional funerals, and "floating lotus" *(bua lauj)* pieces, which are restricted for the cremation ceremonies of royalty.[10] Classical Thai singers use a complex system based on tonal inflection to pronounce each syllable of the lyrics. This comes from intuition and experience, and is regarded as a very difficult skill. By design, most lyrical musical compositions are written around only one emotion to allow the singer to fully express the feeling. For example, the *maun raung haj,* a composition style that accompanies traditional cremation ceremonies, is sung to imitate the sound of crying.

Folksongs have remained a constant influence in Thai music. Many are based on the worship of nature and spirits and stem from ancient ceremonies designed to ensure good harvests of rice, such as the *phleng hae nang maeo,* which welcomes the rain. Similarly, the *phleng anchoen,* or "invitation song," is sung to invite good spirits into the home or fields, while the *phleng hae nak* is often sung as part of a monk's ordination rituals.[11]

Thai nursery rhymes developed from the same oral tradition and involve a host of spirits usually represented by natural elements. As is true of many other countries, lullabies are among the best-known of songs in Thailand. In the Buddhist tale extolling the virtue of giving *(wessandon jataka),* an angel sings soothing songs to the children of the Buddha-to-be. Therefore, although most Thai lullabies developed first as folksongs, many make reference to Buddhism—like "Khun Thalay Ralok" (The Child of the Seawaves), which reminds children to make merit by having pity and being kind. Many children's songs are funny and playful as well as instructive. "Nok Kratung" (The Stork) is a humorous pun about childbirth, while the "Moyay" (Drunken Boat) encourages children to be modest and to help others in trouble. "Ri Ri Khao San " (The Long-Grained Rice) teaches the value of sharing as well as the importance of not wasting food, while "Ai Khay Ai Khong" (The Crocodile) pokes fun at arrogant people who have lost their power, beauty, or wealth—a reminder that such attributes are not important.[12]

Many classical Thai songs started first as poems, and then were set to music. These include works like the *Unarat* by King Rama I, and the works of famous early-nineteenth-century poet Sunthorn Phu. Some songs have been imported from other cultures, although their exact origins and meanings are not always clear. Others were created by Thais but drawn from foreign-language songs, such as "Ka Meen Sai Yok" (The Khmer of Sai Yok), composed by Prince Narai in 1888. King Chulalongkorn himself wrote the love song "Ka Meen Pii Gaao" (The Khmer With a Glass Pipe), based on an ancient Khmer tune. "Lao Damnoeun Sai" (The Lao Walks on the Sand) and "Lao Duang Duen" (The Lao and

the Moon) are also well-known Thai songs probably composed in the eighteenth or nineteenth century. Songs from the popular theatrical dance-drama *Khun Chang Khun Phaen* include "Paanaa Haateen" (The Burmese, in five sections), "Kneaek Lop Buri" (The Indian of Lop Buri), "Hoon Roong Jin" (A Chinese Overture), and "Ka Meen Yai" (The Big Khmer).[13]

Traditional Thai music varies to some degree from region to region, as do the instruments. For example, the *khaen* came originally from small villages of the North, while the *thon* is from the Northeast. The Northeast is famed for popular types of music like *molam* music, which involves songs that start very slowly and gradually intensify, eventually reaching a high-paced tempo. *Molam* also involves a unique dancing style, slow and graceful, without bodily contact. Traditionally, *molam* performances are very long, and involve a great number of dancers and singers. They also involved humor, impromptu theater, and often tricky verbal rhymes, all of which are very much part of Northeast tradition. For their efforts, *molam* performers are honored with flowers and money by the audience, who occasionally are drawn onto stage themselves. Music for the *khon, lakhon,* and *likay* dances also frequently take on regional characteristics.

### The Classical Style Today

Traditional music in Thailand suffered a decline throughout the twentieth century. With the end of the absolute monarchy in 1932 musicians lost their place at the royal courts, and the preservation and advancement of music gradually became the domain of government bureaucracy. The impact of Western culture has been far more damaging, drawing away many Thai youth to more modern music and generally diminishing the prestige of traditional musicians. Even instrument making suffered with the decline of craftsmanship and the transition to new materials. In recent years, however, there has been a resurgence of interest in the older ways. The Thai education system has expanded its curriculum to expose youth to traditional music. The study of classical dance has also expanded, with a corresponding effect on music. The Crown Princess Maha Chakri Sirindhorn, an accomplished classical musician in her own right, serves as an important advocate and patron, and has rekindled interest in the art.[14] Perhaps ironically, foreigners are also responsible for the popularity of traditional music in supplying the demand for a more authentic Thai experience.

## MODERN MUSIC

The Thais call all music *dontrii.* They use the phrase *dontrii Thai* to refer to traditional Thai classical music. More modern music is called Westernized

Thai music *(phleng Thai saakon),* while contemporary pop is known as *phleng luuk thung.* Making things yet more complicated, Thais will often refer to music by its country of origin regardless of the genre; so "Japanese music" becomes *phleen Jippun,* whether it was written yesterday or three centuries ago.[15] The labels can be confusing, as Thailand's modern-music scene is very diverse, much like that in any Western country. Pop, hard rock, alternative, country, and other musical styles can all be found. Modern Thai music also draws from the more classical custom of adapting poems and theatrical drama to song. King Vajiravudh (1910–1925) wrote a number of plays and songs set to more modern music from dance-dramas such as *Sang Thong* and literary masterpieces such as the *Unarat* and *Lilit Phra Law.* This tradition continued into the 1940s and 1950s when artists like Kaew Atchariyakul, better known as Kaew Fah, wrote popular songs based on classical poetry. Five of them, called the *Chula Trikun,* remain modern standards from which many new artists draw. Most, like "Chao Mai Mi San" (The Homeless Spirit), and the "Chao Phraya" (named after the river), deal with heartbreak and loss. Other modern artists in this tradition are Salai Krailert, who wrote over 50 songs such as "Petch" (The Diamond), "Duang Chai Nai Fun" (The Dreaming Heart), and "Kai Fah" (The Magic Rooster), based on the same literary works.[16]

### Western Influences

The Thai ability to imitate foreign influences is very much evident on the music scene. During the 1960s the popularity of rock and roll from the United States and Britain prompted a wave of Thai artists styled after Elvis Presley and the Beatles. Jazz made considerable inroads in Thailand during the 1920s and 1930s. Its popularity continued, and remains today, largely because King Bhumipol Adulyadej is a gifted and accomplished musician. He began composing in 1946 and since then has written about 50 jazz works, some of which have been played internationally. He also helped compose Thailand's current national anthem. Mahidol University now has a College of Music named after the king that offers degrees in jazz. Other Western music is also widely popular in Thailand. Bangkok is a major international venue for modern musicians of all different styles, and the city supports any number of clubs, bars, and concert venues covering the entire musical spectrum.

Thai musicians have also adopted Western ways. The most famous Thai rock group is Carabao, which has been recording for more than 20 years. Their music is a combination of Thai classical music with heavy metal—a unique sound. Banned for much of the 1970s, the songs of another Thai rock band, Caravan, continue to be popular. Adopting a Thai folk style for their

music, the group focused on political issues, upsetting the military governments of the time. Today's mainstream musical acts in Thailand include
Amita Tata Young, Loso, Siriporn Amphaiphong, Looknok Suphaphorn,
Labanoon, Kat, Beau, Pan, and Seven. Songs about love tend to be the most
popular in Thailand across a wide age range, although more varied themes—
as in the West—are increasingly popular among Thai youth.

Modern Thai music has also been shaped by the fusion of traditional music
with new influences. For example, artists like Tewan Sapsanyakorn have
mixed Thai folk music with modern jazz. The group Green Beans mixes Thai
classical music with Western-styled pop-rock. However, more traditional
Thai music is also increasingly popular. Artists like Sang Thammada and
Pungsit Campee continue to play folk songs, even retaining traditional
instruments. Singers like Mongsit Kamsoi are popular with their "up-
country" *(look thung)* music, while the *molam* style is still a favorite with performers such as Phimpha Phonsiri.[17]

## FILM

A European businessman, S.G. Marchovsky, brought the first motion pictures to Bangkok in June 1897, just 18 months after the first-ever world
showing in Paris. The films were simple street shots of the French capital, lasting only a few seconds. Still, they attracted large crowds of Siamese, who
called the pictures "Western shadow theater" *(nang farang)* because they were
shown against a white screen, like traditional shadow puppets. Later that year,
a brief film was released that captured the procession of King Chulalongkorn
in Geneva, during his trip to Europe. The king's younger brother, Prince
Sanbhassatra, brought back from the West movie cameras, projectors, and
film, and soon he began making the first Siamese motion pictures. Within a
few years, Bangkok boasted several cinemas. They showed whatever films
they could get—mostly short clips of foreign cities, everyday life in the kingdom, and occasionally, news events. Live bands often played musical accom-
paniments to the silent pictures. Handbills were given out, advertising the
films and describing the contents or actors. Food and other goods were sold
in the theater. The popularity of the new medium led to the establishment of
the first movie company in the country, the Siam Film Company, in 1918. It
secured contracts with European and American companies to distribute
Western movies, especially those made in the new capital of film—Hollywood. Cinemas in Siam provided live dialogue, in Thai, and even special
sound effects as a kind of soundtrack to accompany the pictures.[18]

In 1923, an American, Henry A. McRae, was the first to make a full-length
motion picture in Siam, which was called *Survana of Siam (Nangsao Suwan)*.

No known copy exists today. This, however, was the humble beginning of the film industry in Thailand. In 1926, *Double Luck (Chok Sorng Chan)* became the first movie made by Thais about Thais. Another movie, *Unexpected (Mai Khit Loei),* followed in 1927. The industry got a big boost from King Prajad-hipok, who was a movie fan and amateur filmmaker. He helped make the medium even more popular, and he even helped to finance the first talking-picture made in Siam, *Going Astray (LongThang),* in 1932—ironically, the same year that a revolution ended the absolute rule of the monarchy. A small office within the new government's Department of Public Information helped sustain the country's movie business through the Great Depression. The minister of finance, Pridi Phanomyong, even tried his own hand at directing and producing with *The King of the White Elephant (Phra Chao Chang Phu'ak)* in 1940—with an English soundtrack, no less. During World War II, the Thai government was even more active in the industry, turning out pro-Japanese and German propaganda films.

After the war, the movie business in Thailand was revived by American aid and investment, which began to flood the country in the 1950s, as Bangkok and Washington developed closer political ties. Hollywood films became extremely popular, even in remote parts of the kingdom. This was facilitated by the United States Information Service (USIS), which together with other American government agencies, delivered medicine, food, materials—and movies—to Thai villages in the North and Northeast as a means of combat-ing the spread of communism. By the mid-1970s, there were approximately 150 cinemas in Bangkok and another 700 elsewhere in the country. This did not include open-air cinemas—mainly places in rural areas where movies would be shown against large canvasses, cloths, and even corrugated iron-sheets—which numbered in the thousands. On average about 600 films were shown each year in Thailand; almost half were made in the U.S., 100 to 200 were from other countries, and roughly 60 to 80 were Thai movies.[19]

Political developments in Thailand during the mid-1970s led to a reduc-tion of American films coming into the country. The Thai industry compen-sated for this with increased production, turning out about 150 movies a year by 1978. Silent pictures were made in Thailand until the 1960s and were usu-ally still shown with narration live in the theater. However, until the 1980s, most Thai movies were undistinguished low-budget action, horror, or romance pictures. Since then the country's film industry has gone through a noticeable expansion. Not only have the quantity and quality of pictures increased, but so too has the variety of genres. Made in 2000, the comedy *Satri Lek* (Iron Women) was a surprise smash hit about the real-life adven-tures of a Thai volleyball team made up of transsexuals and transvestites who go on to win a national men's title. It was so well received that *Satri Lek 2* was

released in 2003. The action-comedy *Killer Tattoo* (2001) is about a hit man who is after the tattooed man who killed his mother, but also is layered with a dark humor. Historical pictures have recently drawn much attention in Thailand, with two blockbuster national epics. *Bang Rajan* (2000) is a patriotic action-war movie based on a village uprising against Burmese occupation during the Ayutthaya period, while *Suriyothai* (2001) is an action-romance dealing with a sixteenth-century queen whose heroism saved her kingdom. Based on chronicles from Ayutthaya, the movie centers on Queen Suriyothai, wife of King Mahachakkrapat (ruled 1548–1569), who dies saving her husband in battle during the Burmese attack on the kingdom. Costing about $15 million to make, *Suriyothai* is the most expensive Thai movie ever made. The cast included 70 major characters and approximately 5,000 extras, not to mention 700 elephants and 3,000 horses. Initially running over five hours long, the film was cut down to just over three hours for release in Thailand. For release in the West, it was further pared down to two and a half hours. *Suriyothai* was in part funded by the royal family and was in fact directed by a prince, Chatrichalerm Yuko, better known as Than Mui. The executive producer was American director Francis Ford Coppola, who as a student attended the University of California at Los Angeles (UCLA) with Chatrichalerm. Coppola was also instrumental in the film's release in the West through Sony Picture Classic. Although considered by some to be the "Thai Braveheart," reviews of the movie in both Thailand and the West were mixed. Still, it is clear that *Suriyothai* helped reinvigorate the Thai film industry, particularly with respect to historical epics.

However, horror, romance, and action movies are still the favorites, as they are in many countries. *Bangkok Dangerous* (1999) was a popular crime thriller–romance about a deaf-mute assassin and his partner, while *Krai Thong* (2001) is about a killer crocodile from Thai legends reeking havoc in modern times. Thais seem especially drawn to films about ghosts, which draw from folklore and mythology for their inspiration. The most successful Thai film in history is *Nang Naak* (1998), based on the famous tale (discussed in chapter 3) about a woman who dies in childbirth while her husband is away at war. He returns home to find his wife and child in the house, never realizing they are ghosts.[20] Recent films like *Jan Dara* (2001) seem to indicate that the Thai movie industry is willing to explore more complicated themes. This beautifully crafted movie, well received at international film festivals, details the tragedies of parental abuse and failed relationships. Similarly, *Satang* (2000) won much praise for its dramatic portrayal of life in Thailand during World War II.

Today, the Thai movie industry is rapidly expanding and gaining international notoriety. Film-maker Duangkamol Limcharoen, the managing director of Thai-based Cineasia, has linked with foreign investors such as Five-Star

Entertainment to significantly develop Thailand's movie production. Whereas in 1997 there were just 8 major movies made in Thailand, in 2003 there were over 40.[21] Moreover, Thai directors are becoming more prominent in the West, including Nonzee Nimibutr *(Nang Nak, Jan Dara),* Pen-ek Ratanaruang *(Mon-Rak Transistor,* 2000; *6ixtynin9,* 2001; *Last Life in the Universe,* 2003) and Oxide Pang *(The Eye,* 2002; *The Tesseract,* 2004). In 2003, the rights to *The Eye* (a suspense-horror film) were bought by American actor Tom Cruise for reproduction. Similarly, Wisit Sasanatieng's farcical *Tears of the Black Tiger* (2000), about 1950s Thai movies, was picked up for release by the American giant Cinemax.

### Films About Thailand

Foreign movies about Thailand have, on the whole, not found favor with Thais. Especially disliked are Hollywood adaptations of the life of Anna Leonowens, an English tutor at the court of King Mongkut who helped educate the future Rama V, Chulalongkorn. *Anna and the King of Siam* (1946) featured a King Mongkut played by a European actor (Rex Harrison) with unconvincing makeup and accent, while *The King and I* (1956) compounded these faults with being a musical, which was worst of all from the Thai point of view since it involved the king dancing, singing, and generally behaving in what was held to be a demeaning fashion. *Anna and the King* (1999, starring Jodie Foster) was considered less insulting, and at least managed to have an Asian actor (Chow Yun-Fat) play the king, but it is still not regarded highly by Thais. Other Hollywood films about the country, such as *Brokedown Palace* (1999) and *The Beach* (2000), were deemed offensive for their portrayals of Thailand as being run by drug lords, or dominated by a corrupt, brutally harsh judicial system. The latter movie also caused controversy by allegedly destroying pristine beaches during filming in the South. Thailand has also been active as the filming location for Hollywood movies such as *The Deer Hunter* (1978), *The Killing Fields* (1984), and *The Ugly American* (1963), which featured then future Thai Prime Minister Kukrit Pramoj as the fictional prime minister of a troubled fictitious country, Sarkan, clearly intended to represent Vietnam.

### Notes

1. William Warren, *Images of Thailand* (Hong Kong: Hong Kong Publishing, 1981), pp. 50–60.

2. Mattana Rutnin, *Dance, Drama, and Theatre in Thailand: The Process of Development and Modernization* (Chiang Mai: Silkworm Books, 1996), pp. 12–20.

3. Fern S. Ingersoll (translator), *Sang Thong: A Dance-Drama from Thailand* (Rutland, VT: Charles E. Tuttle, 1973), pp. 19–158 passim.

4. Margaret J. Kartomi, " 'Traditional Music Weeps' and Other Themes in the Discourse of Music, Dance and Theatre of Indonesia, Malaysia, and Thailand," *Journal of Southeast Asian Studies* 26 (September 1995): pp. 366–400.

5. Santi, *Temples of Gold,* pp. 129–30.

6. David Morton, *The Traditional Music of Thailand* (Berkeley: University of California Press, 1976), pp. 3–12.

7. Pamela Myers-Moro, *Thai Music and Musicians in Contemporary Bangkok* (Berkeley: University of California Press, 1993), pp. 236–55.

8. Morton, *The Traditional Music of Thailand,* pp. 24–43. See also Terry E. Miller and Sam-Ang Sam, "The Classical Musics of Cambodia and Thailand: A Study of Distinctions," *Ethnomusicology* 39 (Spring/Summer 1995): pp. 233–34.

9. Morton, *The Traditional Music of Thailand,* pp. 40–102.

10. Myers-Moro, *Thai Music and Musicians in Contemporary Bangkok,* pp. 30–58.

11. Suvanna Kriengkraipetch, "Folksong and Socio-Cultural Change in Village Life," in Siraporn Nathalang, ed., *Thai Folklore: Insights into Thai Culture,* pp. 143–66.

12. Foreign News Division, *Facets of Thai Cultural Life,* pp. 137–52.

13. Ibid., pp. 110–29.

14. Patricia Myers-Moro, "Thai Music and Attitudes towards the Past," *Journal of American Folklore* 102/404 (Spring 1989): pp. 190–94.

15. Myers-Moro, *Thai Music and Musicians in Contemporary Bangkok,* pp. 4–9.

16. Foreign News Division, *Facets of Thai Cultural Life,* pp. 130–36.

17. Thai World View, at *www.thaiworldview.com.*

18. Dome Sukwong and Sawasdi Suwannapak, *A Century of Thai Cinema* (London: Thames Hudson, 2001), pp. 8–9.

19. Ibid., pp. 9–13.

20. Ibid. See also Cummings and Martin, *Lonely Planet: Thailand,* pp. 45–46.

21. *Far Eastern Economic Review,* January 23, 2003, pp. 50–53.

$$5$$

# Art

## TRADITIONAL ART

Traditional art in Thailand is defined chiefly by Buddhist art, as seen in religious architecture, murals, decorative techniques, and images of the Buddha. Nearly all art and architecture prior to the twentieth century is categorized as "classical" for its Buddhist symbolism. Almost all classical Thai art originated from the royal courts. Like religion and literature in Thailand, fine arts have been greatly influenced by other cultures—chiefly Indian. Up until the thirteenth century most artistic traditions in Thailand were incorporated from neighboring Indic kingdoms, such as the Khmer and the Burmese. However, with the emergence of Sukhothai, distinctively Tai arts were born. Each of the major Tai kingdoms cultivated a wide variety of the arts, but experts believe that each also had a noticeable specialization. The Sukhothai period is best remembered for its sculpture, while the Ayutthaya period is recognized more for its architecture, and the Bangkok period for its painting.

### Artistic Periods

Art historians have developed numerous categories to define various styles of Thai art. They are generally named for the city or region in which artifacts were found. The most recent system categorizes Thai art into 11 major historical periods (though with rather fluid boundaries), some with further subdivisions. Most of the categories are not unique to the Tai peoples, but rather reflect the dominant artistic traditions of the region. The first, known as the Mon (or Dvaravati), extends from the sixth through the thirteenth centuries

C.E., covering much of what is now Central, Northern, and Northeastern Thailand. Overlapping this is the Khmer period from the seventh through thirteenth centuries, found mostly in the Northeast and Central regions. Peninsular (or Srivijaya) art is an even broader classification, referring to a civilization based in present-day Indonesia that extended its influence across much of Southeast Asia. This art is characterized by Indian, Mon, and Khmer influences found in the Central and Northeastern regions from the third to the fourteenth centuries.[1] Lanna Thai refers to art from the North, influenced by the Burmese, Shan, and Lao, between the thirteenth and fifteenth centuries. Lopburi art, found from the tenth through thirteenth centuries, and Suphanburi-Sangkhlaburi (or U-Thong) art, from the thirteenth to the fifteenth centuries, both reflected mixes of later Mon, Khmer, and local traditions.

The Sukhothai period, between the thirteenth and fifteenth centuries, represents the first uniquely Thai artistic tradition. The Ayutthaya period is divided into three categories: the first, or "A" era, from 1350 through 1488; the second, or "B" period, from 1488 to 1630; and the third, "C" phase, from 1630 to 1767. While the first is characterized by Khmer and Sukhothai traditions, the second and third represent unique styles. The final category, Ratanakosin, or Bangkok, shaped chiefly by European influences, covers art from the eighteenth century to the present.[2] Some art historians also refer to this as the "Burmese" period.

### Sculpture

Historically, sculpture is the principal form of art in Thailand. The earliest evidence of permanent settlements in the country comes from carvings at Ban Chiang, dating back over 4,000 years. Imprinted coins and certain Vishnu statues date from the fifth and sixth centuries, suggesting a fairly advanced artistic community during the Dvaravati era. Images of Ganesha and Vishnu from the eighth century have been found in Northeastern Thailand. There is substantial evidence of sculpting in the Mahayana Buddhist tradition from the eighth and ninth centuries, as well as pieces—clearly inspired by Vietnamese and Chinese influences—which probably came through trade.

Since the Sukhothai period, sculpture has been almost always dedicated to Buddhism, and to a lesser degree, Hinduism. In part this fixation comes from Buddha himself, who was asked before dying what could be done by disciples to honor him. He replied that they could take something from his body and set it in a mound of dirt. This was later interpreted to be a request to make symbols, and especially sculptures, of the Buddha.[3] Buddha figures are considered sacred, as is the act of creating one. Sculpting one earns great merit,

and requires blessing from a monk—as does moving or replacing one. In fact, Thai law does not allow Buddha figures to be destroyed. They are instead repaired, reshaped, or used in other sacred forms. For example, fragments of destroyed Buddhas at Ayutthaya in 1767 were incorporated into temples in Bangkok.

The different images of the Buddha, or *lakshanas,* are taken from ancient texts and from Sanskrit poetry. The Pali language texts mention 32 major and 38 minor *lakshanas,* with 108 characteristics of his feet alone. From these metaphoric descriptions, sculptors of the Sukhothai era crafted much-idealized portraits. His head was to be shaped like an egg. His nose was to look like a parrot's beak, and his arms were to be smooth and round like a young elephant's trunk. To these the Thais added their own interpretations: arching his nose and eyebrows more, increasing the fullness of his chest and thighs, and adding a rippling frock across his shoulder.[4] Generally, classic Sukhothai Buddha images are distinguished by a lack of definition, smooth surfaces, continuous curves, an oval head with elongated features, and a crown of flames (the *ushnisha*) symbolizing enlightenment. Sukhothai's sculptors also began the tradition of carving Buddhas in an enormous variety of sizes, from miniatures to the massive figures nearly 160 feet (50 meters) tall. The position of the Buddha was also carefully planned according to religious script. There are three types of sitting, or *maravijaya* Buddhas: one with both soles of the feet upward (*vajrasena*); one with one leg on top of the sole of the other foot (*virasana*). There is also one standard position of Buddha sitting on a throne with both feet on the ground (the so-called European style, originally Buddhist in tradition but later thought to be similar to European forms). There is a walking Buddha—an image almost entirely restricted to the Sukhothai era—and a reclining Buddha, capturing his last moments on earth before dying. The different hand gestures of Buddha sculptures are called *mudras,* and again have various meanings. There are officially 40 acceptable hand gestures, but six are most commonly seen. These are the gestures of preaching, bestowing charity, being called to earth, symbolically setting in motion the Buddhist religion, meditating, and calming fear.[5] Among Hindu images, sculptures of Brahma (the Creator), Siva (the Destroyer), and especially Vishnu (the Preserver), were the most common in the Sukhothai period.

Commonly such sculptures were made of stone, wood, ivory, stucco, terracotta, ceramic, and especially bronze. In fact, there are more bronze statues of Buddha in Thailand than anywhere else in the world. During the Sukhothai period, these bronze images were cast solid. Since then, however, most have been hollow. The sculpting process for a bronze Buddha begins with a core of sand and clay shaped into an image. Shellac and beeswax are then applied as a covering, into which features are carved. Traditionally, cow dung or mud

Buddha statue at Sukhothai Historical Park (courtesy of Jonathan Wong).

was used to fill all crevices. Then the entire image is covered in thick clay and baked, melting the wax, which then flows out, leaving a space between the clay core and the outer clay covering. When cooled, this mold is then filled with bronze, which occupies the space left by the wax.[6] The best images from this period can be seen at the magnificent Sukhothai Historical Park, a UNESCO World Heritage Site sprawled over an area of some 28 square miles (72 square kilometers). A number of the stone and terracotta Buddha statues in the park are nearly 65 feet (20 meters) tall. In contrast to Sukhothai, the Ayutthaya period is not known for its sculpture. Although the art continued, the attentions of the kingdom were directed more toward architecture and literature. Buddhas from the Ayutthaya period are characterized by more detail, less graceful design, and a more "human" portrayal.

Not all images of the Buddha are huge or incredibly detailed. There are also very small ones, carved into votive tablets or on amulets *(khruang lang khong khlang)*. Many Thais carry with them a small amulet bearing the Buddha's image *(phra khruang)* for luck, and the merit in making one of these small ones is still believed to count for the artist. They come in thousands of designs and sizes and range widely in price. There are five particularly revered *phra khruang,* which together are worth nearly $250,000. They are all owned by Payap Khampan, a highly respected collector of and authority on amulets. The most precious is commonly known as *Phra Somdej,* named after the ven-

Standing Buddha at Sukhothai Historical Park (courtesy of Jonathan Wong).

erable monk Somdej Phra Buddacharn Toh of Wat Rakang, who blessed it 150 years ago. Because it has been blessed, it is believed to have special power. The powder used to create the image was a special concoction made from flower seeds and the dried leaves of 108 plants, all considered holy. Delicately crafted, the *Phra Somdej* fits easily in the palm of the hand, while the Buddha image itself is only slighter bigger than a thumbnail. The *Tiratana* proclaimed: "Even if a man makes an image as small as a grain of barley...placing it on a round figure or staff like a small pin, a special cause for good birth is obtained thereby, and will be as limitless as the seven seas, and rewards will last as long as the coming four births."[7] There are also other amulets containing sculpted images of Buddhist scrolls or symbols from mythology.

*Kinnari* statue at the Grand Palace, Bangkok (courtesy of Arne Kislenko).

## Painting

Because of the tropical climate, paintings in Thailand did not survive well prior to the development of modern conservation techniques. Few works predate the late Ayutthaya period, but cave paintings from around 500 B.C.E. demonstrate that the art has long been a tradition in the region. The best-known and best-preserved paintings in Thailand are from the Bangkok era, after 1767. Most focus on religious subject matter, often supplemented with mythology and folklore. The classical Thai tradition is characterized by an emphasis on perspective and atmosphere, particularly with regard to the environment of the subject. Almost all traditional paintings have deliberate meanings based on Buddhist literature and mythology, many taken from the *Ramakian* or the *jataka* tales of Buddha's past lives. Foreign influences have also played an important

role over time, and experts point to attributes of Hindu, Chinese, and even Arabian or Persian culture in the subject matter of Thai paintings.[8]

Many classical painters focused on murals at the temples. Most of these are incredibly detailed depictions of the *jatakas, Tribhumikatha,* or later the *Ramakian,* although often they also incorporate Thai folktales, narrative scenes, local historical events, and even nursery rhymes. Especially popular were the "ten great" *jatakas* of the *Tosachat,* and in particular scenes from Buddha's "great birth," which recaps his previous nine lives. Traditionally, the upper portion of the wall was reserved for depictions of Buddhas of the past, who are always shown aligned in rows, while the lower portions were used for the *jatakas.* In *jataka* tales the *Bodhisattva* is always the central figure, around whom the rest of the story is painted.[9] During the Sukhothai period, *jataka* were shown in single scenes, but by the Ayutthaya era they had become more complex. Stories and scenes were separated by saw-tooth jagged lines, or the addition of natural scenery as background. The process in painting these murals was extremely laborious, and required great skill. Walls were first cleaned with a mix of fine sand, sugar, leaves, and lime water. Pigments for the paint were taken from cinnamon, charcoal, turmeric, and fruits such as the mangosteen. They also used red and yellow ochre, ground minerals, and the dye from vegetable greens bound together with gum-tree resin. Brushes were made from animal hairs, or fibers and roots from trees.

Few murals survive from the Sukhothai period, but fragmentary evidence suggests that the tradition was extremely important early on. A mural at Wat Sri Chum contains 64 ornately decorated tiles in a variety of dimensions depicting the *jatakas,* many packed into just one square. Murals from Ayutthaya are far more common and even more elaborate. The ones at Wat Chong Nonsi date to the late seventeenth century, and depict an unusual scene from the victory over *Mara* in Buddhist cosmology. Here *Mara* has among his army foreigners, like the Japanese and Persians, as well as the usual ranks of demons. The murals of Wat Mahathat in Ayutthaya show episodes from the life of Buddha and portraits of 24 past Buddhas, each meditating under a different species of tree. The Bangkok period also claims some impressive murals. One depicting the *Ramakian* at the library of Wat Rakhang is painted on wood, making it rather unusual. The scriptorium of the Suan Pakkad palace in Bangkok has lacquered walls showing the famous story, but with the unique addition of French soldiers from the time of King Louis XIV. The *Ramakian* portrayed on the walls of the Buddhaisawan Chapel in the National Museum of Thailand is one of the most famous illustrations of the tale. At Wat Yai Suwannaram in Phetchaburi there is an enormous depiction of Mount Meru and the heavens, created by two of the greatest painters of the mid-nineteenth century, Thong Yu and Khong Pe.[10]

Murals are not the extent of classical Thai painting. Other popular mediums were furniture, shutters and door frames, and banners of cloth *(pra bot)* used to depict religious scenes. Some painters also created illustrations *(nangsu khien)* for books, either on paper or palm leaves.

The earliest-known example of books comes from the sixteenth century. Palm-leaf books were made from long thin leaves that were cut and dried, and then incised with a tool to write or draw in inks. To finish it was then rubbed with a smooth paste that darkened the lines without affecting the leaves. The leaves almost always were used for Buddhist texts in the original Pali language. Special ones were then adorned with decorations and a special wrap. Paper was created from the bark of the *khoi* bush. It was mashed into a paste that was then spread on poles to dry. Inks and chalks were used to color it or write on it. Most books depicted the *jatakas* or the *Tribhumikatha,* but some were used to record poems and lyrics. Some manuscript paintings were used for astrological books and divination or fortune telling. Others had a more practical purpose, and served as a sort of early medical text on which the important points of the human body were detailed. One traditional manuscript from the early nineteenth century recounts the *Ramakian* in 3,000 pages.[11] Unfortunately, few examples of palm-leaf or paper books made prior to the seventeenth century have survived, because of the degradation of materials in the humid climate, and the destruction of Ayutthaya. Perhaps ironically, the best examples are overseas, taken home by early travelers and preserved much better in the colder, drier climates of Europe and Japan.

Classical painting on all mediums flourished most during the early stages of the Bangkok period, beginning in the late eighteenth century. Although religious subject matter still dominated, painters began to experiment with different topics. Many paintings from this time emphasize nature and more everyday life events. They also often depict humor, use stronger colors, and show definitive signs of Western influence. The murals at Wat Phra Singh in Chiang Mai, dating from the early nineteenth century, show lovers hiding in the bushes, fantastic costumes, people with tattoos and odd expressions, old ladies gossiping, and common things like eating utensils. These paintings also reflect regional variations in form. The tradition in Northern Thailand has always been toward brighter colors, vibrant black outlines, and a simpler, "everyday" subject matter.[12]

However, the Bangkok kingdom also witnessed significant departures from classical form in painting. King Rama IV (Mongkut) was a patron of several "radical" artists who rejected traditional style. The most famous was Khrua In Khong, who preferred surreal images and often mystical settings. Despite the fact that he never left Thailand, Khrua in Khong also incorporated Western

influences into typical Buddhist religious and morality motifs. The murals at Wat Bowonniwet in Bangkok depict Thais dressed in European-styled clothes, against a backdrop of steam boats and clipper ships. Similarly, paintings at Wat Benchamabopit (better known as the "Marble Temple") show King Rama V during his European travels.

## Ceramics

Pottery in Thailand dates back to the earliest recorded settlement at Ban Chiang. Today, it continues to be an important artistic medium. Of course pottery can also have a functional as well as a decorative purpose, and in Thailand ceramics serve both ends well. The North is famous for its terracotta water jars, which are traditionally placed outside temples and homes so that passersby can refresh themselves. The Northeast is known best for its dark-brown flower pots and its beautifully decorated yellow-green storage jars, usually boasting dragon or floral designs. Blue-green celadon stoneware dates back to the Sukhothai period, but is now one of Chiang Mai's many exports. Using a clear glaze made from limestone, ash, and clay, the same techniques for making celadon centuries ago remain largely unchanged today.

## Lacquerware

Anyone who has been to Thailand will probably be familiar with Thai lacquerware. It is one of the country's most famous artistic creations, and has a high profile throughout the country. Although the tradition probably originated in China, the Thais have made it their own over the centuries, and now produce the finest examples in the world. Lacquerware begins with finely woven baskets or dry wood carved into a shape. A coating called *samuk,* made up of ashes from burnt rice husks and ground clay, is then mixed with the latex of the *rak yai* tree, which is boiled and cooled until it forms a workable black lacquer. When this coat hardens, the object is then repeatedly sanded and polished until smooth. The entire process is repeated—often more than a dozen times—before the final few coats of pure black lacquer are applied. The object is then polished with water and powdered clay to make it shine. Finally, designs are etched on. One process using gold designs is called *lai rot nam.* The other, using colors, is called *lai kud.* The entire process is very time-consuming and labor-intensive. Bowls, boxes, cups, vases, trays, and tables are generally the focus of this art. High-quality lacquerware is judged by the intricacies of the design and flexibility of the finished material. Lacquer decoration can also adorn walls, doors, and window shutters.

### Mother-of-Pearl Inlay

The use of shells in decoration dates back to between the sixth and eleventh centuries. However, during the Ayutthaya and early Bangkok periods of Thai history, shell decoration became an important artistic form. Temple doors, window shutters, and a host of other objects were decorated through the difficult process of inlay, which the Thais call *khruang muk.* This begins with the cutting of the flame snail *(muk fai)* native to the Gulf of Thailand. The outer shell is removed and the inner shell is cut into small flat pieces. These are then sanded and glued to wooden surfaces to make patterns, which are in turn used in designs on a wide variety of materials. In fact, mother-of-pearl inlay was used to decorate the soles of the Reclining Buddha's feet at Wat Po, one of Thailand's holiest shrines. Today inlay is seen on a wide variety of artistic products.

### Silk and Cloths

Thailand is famous for its beautiful silk and cloths. Many traders and explorers first came to the country primarily for these goods. After several centuries of prosperity, by the early twentieth century Thai markets were undermined by cheaper Chinese and Japanese products. However, after World War II an American trader, Jim Thompson, helped to rebuild the Thai silk industry, which still boasts the largest hand-weaving production in the world. Today, silk is by far Thailand's best-known handicraft. Queen Sirikit has done much to promote the silk industry. Silk is made into a huge array of shirts, dresses, sarongs, scarves, shawls, and robes. Many tailors can craft entire suits on demand in just a couple of days. Thai silk is also sold "raw" in sheets. There are almost endless color and print variations, as well as several weight categories. The same goes for Thai cotton cloth, which is famed for its high quality and fine embroidery. Particularly popular are designs created by Northern hill tribes, found on bags, clothes, wall hangings, and quilts.

### Nielloware and Silverware

The Thai tradition of nielloware (or *khruang thom*) originated during the Ayutthaya period. Some experts believe that it was introduced by the Portuguese, while others trace its origins in Thailand back to traders from Persia and India. Essentially a kind of silverware, nielloware involves a special craft that dates back at least to the reign of King Narai (ruled 1656–1688), when it was given as a gift of state to foreign dignitaries. The best nielloware is 92.5 percent pure silver, cut into thin sheets and formed into three-dimensional

objects such as goblets or pieces of jewelry. The objects are then covered in an oxidizing agent such as borax before designs are etched into the silver. Then an amalgam (or niello) of copper, lead, sulfur, and not more than 8 percent silver is applied as a kind of inlay by burning it into the object. The niello turns a distinctive blue-black color that is then highlighted by repeated polishing and sanding. Additional designs are then incised, or additional burning is applied aimed at changing the hues of certain colors. Artists use their own measurements for the niello composition and apply different techniques in order to create unique, signature pieces. Lesser-quality nielloware contains only about 50 percent silver, which makes it more difficult for the amalgam to adhere, resulting in a noticeably inferior product. The detail in design and color are also trademarks of quality.

The entire process of making nielloware is complex and time-consuming. It is labor-intensive, and involves a great deal of training and expertise. The tradition died off in the beginning of the twentieth century, largely due to a slackening of standards in government regulation of the arts and the importation of foreign crafts. Today, however, the art form is enjoying a revival, primarily because of tourism. Many foreigners seek it out as a distinctive Thai product. The best nielloware in Thailand comes from the southern city of Nakhon Sri Thammarat and is therefore often called "Nakhon niello." An almost identical process—minus the application of niello—is used to make traditional silverware. Both forms are seen on a range of handicrafts widely available in Thailand today.[13]

## Basketry and Furniture

Baskets in Thailand have likely been around since the very beginnings of history. They were and remain, of course, a functional tool in everyday life, particularly in rural areas. However, the unique designs of Thai basketry have also spawned a considerable artistic trade. In most areas of the country baskets are made by weaving strips of bamboo or rattan. Specific designs differ from region to region, and even town to town, based primarily on the quality of materials used and the specific function intended for the basket. Bamboo and rattan furniture pieces are also created in much the same way, although obviously on a larger scale and with the addition of wood, metal brackets, and often elaborate designs. The variations in size and style of basketry and furniture are enormous, from large chests to small fruit baskets and placemats. The bamboo and rattan designs are now used more commercially to adorn everything from lamps to dining tables. Many communities in Thailand also produce wooden furniture. Traditionally teak was used for the finest pieces, but with the depletion of most Thai forests the trade in that wood is now strictly

regulated. Antique teak furniture is available for sale, including export, with the appropriate permits. Other woods are now more commonly used to reproduce older designs.

## MODERN ART

The modern period in Thailand is not as easily defined as it is in the West. In part this is because the traditional artistic heritage is so mixed with other cultural influences, making it difficult to demarcate artistic periods on a chronological basis. As in architecture and design, Chinese and Western influences are the most recent additions to this collage, and are usually used to mark the beginning of "modern" art in Thailand. The late nineteenth and early twentieth centuries witnessed a fusion of Chinese, Western, and Thai artistic styles, particularly in painting. To a large degree this was overseen by Prince Naris, the sixty-second child of King Mongkut, who headed the Thai Department of Fine Arts. He was very interested in the merging of Thai mythology with Western ideas. It was his designs that served as the basis for Bangkok's Wat Benchamabopit with its "European" murals. Although there is no definitive beginning to the modern period, many experts agree that the 1930s represents the start of a new era in Thai artistic expression. During that decade, Thailand underwent dramatic political and social upheaval with the end of absolute monarchy and the development of militant nationalism. This was a period significantly influenced by foreign ideas and artists. For the most part, however, this time frame is seen as the beginning of the modern era because of the work of one man in particular, Corrado Feroci (also known by his Thai name, Silpa Bhirasri), an Italian who came to Thailand in 1924 and over the next four decades became the country's father of modern art. He helped introduce impressionism, postimpressionism, and cubism to Thai art.

Even in the early twentieth century most artists in Thailand were still working under the patronage of the royal court and wealthy Thais. Because of this fact, most artistic expression was confined to religious works, in order to help earn the patron and artist good merit. Feroci helped make art more accessible to the people and less uniform in its focus. He also introduced new artistic ideas and techniques, which affected almost all mediums. Feroci contributed his own work to the country's artistic heritage, casting the statue of Rama I at the foot of the Memorial Bridge in Bangkok. He also designed the capital's famous Democracy Monument in 1939 (though ironically with clearly fascist overtones), and the Victory Monument two years later. Between 1950 and 1953 Feroci created the bronze and metal sculpture of Taksin the Great, which has served as a model for all Thai sculptors since. Most of all, Feroci helped to develop Thailand's first Academy of Fine Arts in

1933, and taught there until his death in 1962. It remains today as the country's premiere art school, part of Silpakorn University. Over such a long career he taught several generations of Thai artists. He also helped organize and finance them through groups like the League of Artists, and the Society of Painters and Sculptors.

Some of Feroci's disciples include sculptors like Pimarn Mulapramuk (who created *Warrior* in 1938–40), Cham Khaomeecheu (*The Archer,* 1935–38), and Khien Yimsiri (*Vanity,* 1959; *Children's Game,* 1962), all well known for their modernist form. Significantly, Feroci did not teach surrealism or abstract art to his students. As a result, those artistic schools did not make a substantial impact in Thailand. However, he did teach artists like Fua Haribhitak, who went on to become Thailand's most famous impressionist and abstract painter with works like *Japanese Prison Camp* (1943–45), *Fraglioni Rocks, Capri* (1955), and *Composition* (1955). Fua styled himself after Pablo Picasso, even naming his *Blue Green* (1956) in the tradition of Picasso's "color" phases, such as his "blue" and "rose" periods. Feroci also taught Sompot Upa-In, who became a leading futurist painter with *Bangkok 2500: The Age of Dictatorship* (1957).

Although Feroci did not teach his students traditional Thai arts, they learned the skills to rediscover them later. Many of his students fused modernism with dimensions of the classical form, in the process creating a new and unique Thai contemporary art. The 1970s and 1980s were especially important in this process, ushering in dramatic social and political changes that further influenced Thai artists. Painter Thammasak Booncherd's *Imperialism* was finished in 1976 at the height of Thailand's student revolution. Similarly, the *Fasting Buddha* (1976) by Prateung Emjaroen caused controversy for its depiction of an emaciated, nearly transparent, Buddha surrounded by skulls and demons. By the early 1980s the painter Thawan Duchanee tried to reinterpret Buddhist iconography for modern times, and pioneered a controversial new representational art called Visual Dhamma, graphically depicting men acting with animal instincts. Panya Vijinthanasarn (*Struggle,* 1981) painted more serene, detailed, and symmetrical works, but often mixed in fantastic monsters or symbols from Thai folklore. Artists such as Panya and Paiboon Suwannakut also recreated the magnificent murals of Ayutthaya. Prasong Luemuang (*Festival,* 1989) favored dreamlike paintings with bright colors, but usually with Buddhist imagery intertwined, while Preecha Thaothong (*The Temptation of Mara,* 1981) used visual metaphors of Buddhist teachings.

Social and political issues were the major inspiration for many Thai artists through the 1980s. Kamin Lertchaiprasert's photo etching self-portrait *Suffering No. 7* (1986) is seen as a commentary on the rapid modernization of

Thailand and its effects on the Thai identity. Pinaree Santipak became the most recognized female painter of her generation through her treatment of sexuality and motherhood in *The Egg That Wouldn't Hatch* (1990). Another woman, Somboon Phuangdorkmai, drew attention with her controversial *Dinner for Men, Tears for Women* (1991), which shows a nude female form reclining on a plate, about to be devoured by men. Equally jarring is her *The Faith We Share* (1991), which depicts a mother and her children begging in a modern, Westernized Bangkok. More subtly Therdkiat Wangwarcharakul comments on loneliness and routine in everyday life with *Tuk-Tuk Life* (2003) and *Life Must Go On* (2001). Jiripat Tasanasonboom has merged the world of Thai folklore with American pop culture. His *Darth Maul with a Headdress* (2002) shows the evil character from the Hollywood movie *Star Wars Episode I* wearing the traditional Thai *chada*. His *Superman and Rama's Struggle over Sita* (2002) has the famed superhero fighting with *Rama* over Queen *Sita* in a scene from the *Ramakian,* while Mickey Mouse and other cartoon figures look on. Meanwhile, Jintana Piamsiri has returned to a more traditional style, painting scenes from Thai village life. The artist and poet Vasan Sitthiket has caused considerable debate with his expressionistic paintings, many with overt political and religious commentary. *In God We Trust* (1997) shows hungry dogs representing various nations, including Thailand, licking a fat, naked man representing America, who offers them money and weapons. *Rape of Mother Earth* (1999) depicts a woman, symbolizing nature, being horribly violated by businessmen from oil and gas companies, as well as an atomic warhead. *Love You—Thailand* (2001) shows a nude woman being sexually assaulted by a number of men—including Uncle Sam, military men looking like wolves, and even a Buddhist monk. He has also painted himself as a nude female in *I Want to be a Model* (1996). Some consider his work to be powerful, while others consider the use of such graphic imagery to be offensive.[14]

## Materials and Mediums

The use of materials and mediums in Thai arts has also changed significantly. In *Buddha Footprint* (1982) Kamol Tassananchalee used handmade paper, acrylic, gold leaf, thread, and wood to produce his work. Pichai Nirand's early work of the same name (1968) was a mix of sand, glue, and oil paint. Montien Boonma used soil, mashed paper, charcoal, rice flour, and various pigments to create his *Black Stupa* (1989). Rice, sacks, straw, horns, and stools went into Montien's *A Pair of Water Buffalos* (1988), a piece of environmental art that makes a statement on the inequality between urban

and rural Thais. For many of his paintings Therdkiat Wangwarcharakul uses oils on recycled aluminum sheets. Jakraphun Thanateeranon is one of Thailand's leading photographic, installation, and performance artists. His work includes *Being* (2000) using tents, lamps, and transparent sheets, and *Creature and Destroyer* (1998) using photograms to construct a giant skeleton. Jarrasri Roopkamdee has created surreal images in woodcuts with *Thailand's Party* and *The Night Has a Thousand Eyes* (both 1995).

## Classifying Modern Art

Experts on Thai art identify three major contemporary schools. One belongs to an international community. Its members are generally not considered "Thai," but rather world artists. A second school has a more traditionally Thai approach to art. Its members continue to experiment by mixing classical and modern ideas. The third school also experiments between the traditions, but produces work designed more for commercial than artistic purposes.[15] Experts also identify four major genres of contemporary Thai art. The classical genre is for those who reproduce traditional Thai art largely for merit and money, but without significant innovation. The folk genre is for those who create handicrafts from Thailand's artistic traditions, but also for those whose main aim is to maintain the various traditional skills and techniques. The tourist genre is art generated as souvenirs and replicas of classic pieces. Lastly, the commercial genre is for those artists who work in decoration, creating Buddhas, cosmological patterns, and various other designs for Thai homes and workplaces. Regardless of their divisions or motivations Thai artists will undoubtedly continue the development of a unique and varied heritage.

## NOTES

1. Hiram Woodward, *The Art and Architecture of Thailand: From Prehistoric Times Through the Thirteenth Century* (Leiden: E.J. Brill, 2003), pp. 1–24, 51–55.

2. Philip Rawson, *The Art of Southeast Asia* (London: Thames and Hudson, 1967), pp. 137–53. See also, Cummings and Martin, *Lonely Planet: Thailand,* p. 211.

3. Steve Van Beek, *The Arts of Thailand* (London: Thames and Hudson, 1991), p. 26.

4. Carol Stratton and Miriam McNair Scott, *The Art of Sukhothai: Thailand's Golden Age* (Kuala Lumpur: Oxford University Press, 1981), pp. 58–67.

5. Robert E. Fisher, *Buddhist Art and Architecture* (London: Thames and Hudson, 1993), pp. 174–86. See also Rawson, *The Art of Southeast Asia,* pp. 145–53.

6. John Hoskin, "The Subtle Art of Casting Sacred Statues," *Sawasdee Magazine* 31/6 (June 2002): pp. 29–33.

7. Robert L. Brown (ed.), *Art from Thailand* (Mumbai: Marg Publications, 1999), p. 79. See also Rachada Rithdee, "Thai Talismans," *Sawasdee Magazine* 31/6 (June 2002): pp. 43–48.

8. Jean Boisseler, *Thai Painting* (Tokyo: Kodansha International, 1976), pp. 28–36, 172–73.

9. Rita Ringis, *Thai Temples and Temple Murals* (Singapore: Oxford University Press, 1990), pp. 90–152 passim.

10. K.I. Matics, *Introduction to the Thai Mural* (Bangkok: White Lotus Press, 1992), pp. 1–30. See also Santi, *Temples of Gold,* pp. 22–80.

11. Henry Ginsburg, *Thai Manuscript Painting* (London: British Library, 1989), pp. 2–28.

12. Van Beek, *The Arts of Thailand,* pp. 159–202.

13. Sukphisit Suthon, *Folk Arts and Folk Culture: The Vanishing Face of Thailand* (Bangkok: Post Books, 1997), pp. 45–48.

14. Apinan, *Modern Art in Thailand,* pp. 35–72, 201–226. For examples of some of the latest work by Thai painters, including Vasan, see Thavibu Gallery online at *www.thavibu.com.*

15. Herbert Phillips, *The Integrative Art of Modern Thailand* (Berkeley: University of California Press, 1992), pp. i–10. See also Van Beek, *The Arts of Thailand,* pp. 207–212.

# 6

# Architecture and Design

## Historical Architecture and Architectural Traditions

Thailand's architectural heritage has been shaped by a unique blend of diverse cultures. Indian, Sri Lankan, Cambodian, Burmese, Chinese, and European designs have all influenced traditional and modern Thai styles. Architectural historians point out that because of such a varied background, there is little agreement about what is absolutely "Thai." An old Thai saying echoes this in stressing that you must "build a house according to the heart of its dwellers."[1] In this regard, architecture serves as a particularly good representation of the Thai people and Thai culture—adaptive, open, and constantly changing. Long considered the highest form of the arts in traditional Thai society, in many ways architecture also demonstrates the importance and effect of Thai Buddhism. Much of the rich architectural heritage of the country is found in its palaces and temples, all designed and built in part to store up merit for the next life.

The earliest cultural site in Thailand at Ban Chiang dates from 3600 B.C.E. to around 300 C.E. Although no buildings survive, the artifacts found here suggest that some considerable architectural skills emerged over time. With its location at the center of Southeast Asia, what is today Central Thailand clearly served as a major crossroads in commerce and migration during the first millennium C.E. This explains why any native architecture was so greatly affected by successive waves of foreign influences. Over the centuries Indian traders brought to Southeast Asia new building designs and techniques. Chinese travelers may have brought others. The result is that the evolution of architecture in the region was very fluid. Some areas developed a succession

of skills and practices based on regular contact with outside influences, while more secluded areas often skipped stages. Of course shifting empires with their different political and religious organizations also affected architecture. Historical sites at Sathing Phra, Chaiya, and Nakorn Srithammaraj in Southern Thailand date from between the seventh and twelfth centuries, during the Srivijaya period. Dvaravati sites in the Northeast date from the eighth century, while Central Thailand cities like Lopburi have layers of remains dating back to the Dvaravati and Khmer, not to mention the ancient Tai. Artifacts found at Phimai in the Northeast are believed to have originated in the sixth century, making this among the oldest confirmed architectural sites in the country.[2] Inscriptions there date to 891 C.E., and suggest that it was originally a Khmer outpost, linked by roads, bridges, and rest houses all the way to the capital at Angkor Wat—roughly 250 miles (400 kilometers) away.

### The Thai House

Even the classic *ruan Thai,* or "Thai house" was probably derived from outside influences. Simple bamboo, teak, or thatched structures raised on stilts above ground were constructed to adapt to the seasonal rains and floods, which was especially important for communities congregating along riverbanks and canals. Adding to their functionality, the space underneath the structures was used for storage, cooking, or to house livestock. Originally these structures were very basic, usually consisting of only one room. Over time they became larger and more complex, incorporating open spaces or platforms for bathing and cooking. Still the basic style remained. Even in areas where monsoons and floods are less regular, this type of structure became the common architectural form for houses.[3] By the Ayutthaya period craftsmen made them more distinctively Thai by using prefabricated wood panels, which were then mounted on a frame of wooden posts. Wooden pegs, rather than nails, were used to hold everything together. Roofs were steeply curved—particularly in the Central Plains of Thailand—originally in order to accommodate torrential rain. Often the walls of a traditional building were also slightly inward-leaning—at least in Central Thailand—lending the inside space a greater sense of height. Unfortunately, given the rate at which organic building materials such as wood decay, no examples of the early Thai house remain. Ancient practice dictated that only religious buildings could be made of stone and brick, which means that temples and the accounts of early foreigner travelers offer the best historical evidence on the evolution of Thai architecture. The *ruan* style, however, did endure, and remains what many people consider to be "classically Thai."

Traditional house *(ruan Thai)* (courtesy of Carine Lindauer).

## Early Palaces

Early palaces were in effect extensions of this basic house-design, although much larger and more ornately decorated. The location and exact proportions of palaces were determined according to ancient laws of status within the royal family. Sons of kings born to royal mothers *(Chao fa)* were entitled to bigger and better palaces, complete with fortifications and closer to the main court. Sons born to the King by common mothers *(Phra ong chao)* enjoyed somewhat less spectacular housing further away and without any battlements. Another difference was in the roofs: *Chao fa* homes were two-tiered, while *Phra ong chao* homes had only one.[4] Again, time and war have long since destroyed virtually all of the early palaces.

### Indian Influences

Thai architects have been extremely adaptive not only with building techniques and materials, but also in design and decoration. Indian mythology and religion had a profound impact on the development of architecture in Thailand. Buildings became progressively influenced by religious principles, especially in the belief that there was a connection between physicality and spirituality. During the first millennium C.E. signs of Indian influence were already apparent, particularly in the style of roofs. Religious influences were incorporated into the steep design through decorations. Guarding the corners and summit of Thai roofs one can still see today figures from ancient Indian folklore. The most popular guardian is Naga (or Nak), the sea-serpent god of underwater kingdoms, who in Hindu mythology represents one of the essential elements of life. In Buddhist cosmology Naga represents the Serpent King Muchalinda, who protects the enlightened Buddha. There is also Garuda—a giant and fearsome bird ridden by Vishnu, the god of creation, and today the national and royal emblem of Thailand. Magical animal-like creatures called *kala* may also guard rooftops. In Hindu mythology they demanded a sacrifice from the god of destruction, Shiva, who became so enraged that he made the *kala* eat themselves and stand guard forever. In Thailand, the best known *kala* is Kirimukha (or Simhamukha), a fierce lion-faced beast with a human torso.[5] Indian influence is also seen through other symbols, such as the umbrella-like *chattra* (signifying the ascending realms of gods and their celestial power) and the wheel-like *chakra* (signifying the continuity of the universe). Thai folklore also has its own symbols and monsters, which feature prominently in architecture and design. Singha, a powerful lion creature, is so popular that Thailand's biggest beer company borrowed the name. Nak-Puggsee is part man, part bird, and part snake. Panorn Maruek is half-human and half-monkey, and occasionally part bird. There are also the flaming lion, Rajasi; the graceful bird Hong; the beautiful bird-woman Kinnari; and the ferocious *yakkhas*—monsters that stand guard at temples and palaces.

### Khmer Influences

Khmer architectural influence can also be seen throughout much of Thailand. The most recognizable features are the central towers, or *prang,* which guarded the main temple, or *prasat.* The *prang* are of cylindrical design—often looking like corncobs—and served as symbolic representations of Mount Meru, the heavenly city of the gods. The massive *prang* of Angkor in

Cambodia are the most famous example, but there are magnificent Khmer ruins in Thailand too; particularly in the Northeast at Prasat Muang Tam, Prasat Phanom Rung, and Prasat Phimai.

Khmer pyramidal designs are also seen widely in Thai *wat,* royal parasols, and even some *khon* masks. They represent the many different levels and tiers of Mount Meru. Khmer influences can be seen in the design of some Thai towns and cities, many of which were originally built around such *prang.* Urban planners of the Khmer empire were guided by cosmological references, and designed towns to conform to them. The Thais inherited from the Khmer a distaste for straight lines, favoring instead more complex and graceful forms. Many Khmer cultural traditions were of course retained and incorporated into those of the early Tai kingdoms, especially the emphasis placed on architecture. Designers, planners, and craftsmen of the Khmer and Mon empires were even considered part of the spoils of war, dragged off by the victor along with the defeated kingdom's portable riches.[6] Sukhothai-era architecture used sandstone and even brick for some parts of buildings, as was common in the Khmer empire. Vegetable-based glues held together the bricks, which were then covered in carved stone. By the Ayutthaya period some buildings incorporated a kind of stucco made from lime, sand, and vegetable glues and strengthened with a coat of hardened, unglazed clay—again based on Khmer adaptations.

### Chinese Influences

Chinese influence was also significant in the evolution of Thai style and design, gaining particular prominence in the eighteenth and nineteenth centuries. Trade between Siam and China flourished, and many Chinese artifacts made their way into the kingdom along with thousands of Chinese laborers and craftsmen. Stone sculptures and granite paving slabs were used in decorating Thai temples and palaces, and Chinese furniture became especially fashionable for Thai royalty and nobles. Ceramic tiles and porcelain were also heavily imported from China and can be seen in many pediments and other ornamentation. Chinese influence is also evident in the use of glass, mother of pearl, lacquer, and gold leaf. Likewise, decorated pillars and gables are a Chinese signature, and can be found throughout Thailand. So too can Chinese statues, some of which grace the most important Thai temples and palace complexes, including the Grand Palace. The Narai pavilion in front of the main audience hall in the Grand Palace is beautifully decorated with Chinese ceramics, while Chinese gates and stone warriors protect the Phra Thinang Amarin Winichai throne hall. There are also separate Chinese temples

Chinese statue at Wat Po (courtesy of Arne Kislenko).

in Thailand, distinguished by their colorful and sharply curved roofs and their different portrayals of Buddha.

### Western Influences

Western influences in architecture also gained currency in the nineteenth century as Siam opened up and began the process of modernization. Marble slabs, clear and colored glass, cast iron, and metal fixtures were all imported from Europe and incorporated into Thai design. Steel and cement were also brought into the kingdom to fulfill the role that would formerly have been taken by wood. Western labor-saving devices such as winches, pumps, and other tools revolutionized building practices in Thailand.[7] Western influences

shaped the construction of the Grand Palace in Bangkok and other, provincial palaces, as well as in a number of large mansions built for royalty and nobility during the reign of Rama IV.

## The Grand Palace

The Grand Palace was begun by King Rama I in 1785 as the official seat of government and the royal residence. Situated on the eastern bank of the Chao Phraya river between Wat Po and Wat Mahathat, the palace site was built around Thailand's most important temple, Wat Phra Kaew (discussed below). It consists of a number of building complexes, including a pavilion for royal elephants. Of the 24 major buildings in the central court of the Grand Palace, many have noticeable European designs. The Phra Thinang Dusit Maha Prasat, or throne hall, has a Greek-styled floor plan with Thai structure overtop. The Phra Thinang Boromphiman, a residence building used for dignitaries, is partly of French design, while even Phra Thinang Chakrapat Phiman, which contains the royal bedchambers, bears Roman columns. The most noticeable Western influences are in the Phra Thinang Chakri Maha Prasat, or "Great Hall," which was designed during the reign of Rama V by British architect John Clunish in the Italian Renaissance style. Distinctly Western in appearance, the building was given a Thai-styled roof to appease conservative voices at the court. Thais referred to the building as "the *farang* wearing the *chada*"—the foreigner wearing the Thai headdress.[8] In fact, some architectural experts point out that there is only one truly "Thai" building in the central court of the palace complex, the Sanam Chan pavilion, which was used as a place for the king to relax. The Grand Palace is now used only for important ceremonies, with the main royal family residing in the northern part of Bangkok at the Chitralada Palace, a beautiful but comparatively modest complex built in the early 1920s.

## Local Traditions

Local traditions and animistic beliefs have also shaped Thai style. Of course no Thai building is complete without its spirit house, which requires its own architectural considerations. In traditional homes, especially in Northern Thailand, gables and door lintels are usually carved with images and designs called magic testicles *(ham yon)*, supposed to ward off evil spirits and bring good luck.[9] The alignment of the house, and even the dates during which it is built, are of great concern to traditionalists. Astrologers are consulted to pick the best time to begin construction, while great care is taken to make sure the rooms of the home are properly fixed by direction. It is believed best to have the main entrance aligned so that people entering look North. The bedrooms should also

*Chakri Maha Prasat,* Grand Palace, Bangkok (courtesy of Brent Wardrop).

be in the North, with the kitchen and washing areas in the West. Toilet facilities in rural areas are very basic, often just a chamber pot. Where they do exist as part of the house, they must be lower than the rest of the rooms and again facing West. Doors and windows must open inward, and any image of the Buddha must face East. The size of the traditional home of course depends on the number of posts used to support it, but this again requires consultation with an astrologer. The main posts are then blessed by priests, or ceremonially named and honored with gifts of food to ensure that they will serve the house well. Buddhist monks also perform a ceremony blessing the house.

Even the garden area has design rules. Jasmine is a favorite plant because it brings good fortune, while jackfruit trees symbolize strength. Orchids are highly prized, and are a national symbol of the country. In water gardens the lotus is also very popular. Herbs and spices that can be used in the kitchen are very common, as are fruit trees. However, some plants cannot, by tradition, be grown in the home. The bodhi tree is regarded as sacred to Buddhism, and can only be grown in temples. Other trees with names that in Thai are associated with death or suffering are also considered bad gardening choices.

### Regional Variations

It is also important to note that there are some regional differentiations in classic Thai architecture, both in terms of design and the materials used. For

example, in the South homes were traditionally made of thatch and bamboo—not teak, which grew in the North. Similarly, European influences in the South are more prevalent, given its proximity to Malaysia. In the North, the best-known dwelling type is the "glancing crows" *(kalae)* house, with its unique V-shaped extended roof. Some experts believe that the *kalae* design originated to prevent birds from roosting, while others think it stems from an ancient practice of using buffalo horns as a symbol of wealth. Outward-leaning walls and a slightly more rectangular shape also distinguish the traditional Northern house from those in the Central region.[10] Floating homes, and even guesthouses, can be found in almost all rural areas of the country along major rivers and canals. Among the hill tribes, two basic architectural designs exist, one very similar to the traditional Thai design with homes of bamboo and thatch raised on poles, and one that favors building directly on the ground with earth floors. Given that most of the hill tribes live in remote, rural communities that are economically disadvantaged, architecture and design among them tends to be quite simple.

## THE THAI WAT

The best-known and probably most impressive examples of Thailand's classical architecture are its *wat*. Although the term is interpreted in English as "temple/s," *wat* can actually refer to a single structure or a complex. There are about 30,000 consecrated *wat* in Thailand, and they are an integral part of almost every town and city. In fact, in many ways the study of *wat* mirrors the historical development of Thailand itself through its various periods and influences.[11] Architecturally there are many different types of *wat* styles based on the time of construction, the geographical area, and the materials used. In this respect, the architectural heritage of *wat* in Thailand mirrors very closely the major periods of its art history.

### Basic Structure and Design

Most *wat* in Thailand are located in fenced-off areas central to the communities they serve, but their exact design and location is extremely varied. No two *wat* are the same. Most have developed over long periods of time and served a variety of functions, so their layout has changed. Some *wat* may even appear crowded and disorganized, but this is largely due to the rather *ad hoc* approach Thais have in adding to the complexes over time. It is important to keep in mind that building materials and techniques have also changed over time, leading to quite distinct differences between *wat*. Originally wood was the primary construction material, but few examples still exist today. Brick and plaster make up the majority of *wat* built since the Sukhothai period.

The majority of *wat* contain a consecrated chapel, a *bot* (or more formally known as *uposatha*), where prayers and religious ceremonies are held. They also usually have a *wihann* or *vihara*—rooms in which sacred images are kept. The *bot* is distinguished by eight boundary stones called *bai sema,* which lie at the corners to mark the sacred ground. Both the *bot* and the *wihann* may have small galleries, verandas, or gardens surrounding them on any or all sides. *Wat* also have one or more *chedi* or *stupa,* a solid cone, bell, or lotus-shaped tower, similar to a pagoda, and symbolizing the strength of Buddhism. The *chedi* at Phra Pathom in Nakhom Pathom is the world's tallest Buddhist monument at 417 ft (127 meters). These designs originally came from India and Sri Lanka, and are thought to have emerged from those used in burial grounds. There are many different shapes and sizes of *chedi,* again according to where and when they were built. The *chedi* are supposed to contain the relics of Buddha, and therefore are especially important structures. In fact the *wat* complex usually takes its name from the relic that its *chedi* holds. *Wat* that house relics associated with bodhisattvas can be identified by the words Buddhist Relic *(Phra That)* in their name. Sacred relics from Buddha himself earn the title Great Relic *(Mahathat).* Showing Pagan influences, some *wat* may also have a *mondop*—a cube-shaped building with a pyramidal roof where other sacred objects were kept. In addition, many *wat* in Thailand have a *saala*—shelters used for meetings and lectures—and *kuti,* or residences for the monks. Larger *wat* may also have a library for Buddhist scriptures *(haw trai)* and a bell tower *(has klawng).* Some compounds serve as funeral sites for worshippers, and may house their cremated remains in small *chedi* called *that kraduk. Wat* complexes often also have other, nonreligious buildings, serving as schools, community centers, or health clinics. Of course no *wat* in Thailand is without its own spirit house too.

The typical Thai *wat* also has a distinctive layered roof design in which the upper tiers are steeply pitched. This gives a very ornate and impressive curved look to the building. The roof gables are fashioned into the body of the Naga sea-serpent from Hindu mythology, so that his head sticks out and guards over the top of the complex. At the summit of the roof is another essential mystical symbol called the *chofa,* which may take the shape of a Naga. The origins and meaning of the *chofa* are unclear, but it has been referred to as a "bouquet in the sky."[12] The *chofa* is the finial ornament at the apex of the roof where the roof-boards come together. It is made to look like the Naga lying on top of the roof and jutting out over the edge. The high position of the *chofa* is consistent with the Thai hierarchy of body parts, and being at the top is considered to be the most sacred dwelling place of the soul of the *wat.* The roof is covered with tiles in a range of colors: green, blue, orange, brown, or yellow. Inside, the roof beams are frequently exposed, but the ceiling may also

Golden *chedi* at the Grand Palace, Bangkok (courtesy of Arne Kislenko).

be decorated with stars or the lotus motif. Intricate designs and symbols may decorate other parts of the roof, and especially the window shutters and doors of the *wihaan*. The walls of more simple *bot*s and *wihaan*s are usually white-washed. More elaborate ones may be highly decorated with murals, ceramic tiles, porcelain, marble, and even gold leaf. Paintings of the Buddha are especially common. Of course the centerpieces of the *bot* and *wihaan* are the Buddha images, which usually occupy the end of the buildings.

### A Quick Tour of Thailand's *Wat*

Among the many beautiful and important *wat* in Thailand, a few require special discussion. Chiang Mai, with only a fraction of Bangkok's popu-

lation, boasts nearly as many temples as the capital, lending weight to its claim to be the country's cultural and spiritual center. Wat Chiang Man is the oldest temple there—and one of the oldest in Thailand—built in 1296 by King Mangrai as the focus of his walled city. However, Chiang Mai's claim rests more on Wat Phra That Doi Suthep, built at an altitude of nearly 5,570 feet (1,700 meters) in the mountains overlooking the city. The first temple here was built in 1383 when the King of Lan Na wanted a place of honor for recently discovered relics of Buddha. According to legend he placed the relics on a white elephant, which was then set free to wander. The elephant climbed the mountain, trumpeted three times, knelt down and died. Now one of the most sacred sites in Thailand, the *wat* on Doi Suthep today was built largely in the sixteenth century. An enormous Naga-style staircase leads to the summit.

Sukhothai is now designated as a United Nations World Heritage site, with ruins, monuments, statues, and *wat* stretched over an area of some 28 square miles (72 square kilometers). The thirteenth-century Wat Mahathat there is surrounded by massive brick walls and guarded by a moat, accompanied by nearly 200 *chedi.* Its step pyramids and *mondop,* like those at Wat Phra Pai Luang, are excellent examples of Pagan influences, as are the lotus bud finials on the towers.[13]

Ayutthaya had nearly 400 *wat* within 150 years of its founding. Most were destroyed in the succession of wars the city fought, but some still remain. Now also classified as a World Heritage site, Ayutthaya has Wat Phra Mahathat, with its Khmer *prangs,* and the three magnificent *chedi* of Wat Phra Si Sanphet.

As the capital, Bangkok and its suburbs have over 100 palaces, including the Grand Palace complex. It also claims Thailand's most important *wat.* The holiest shrine in Thailand is in Wat Phra Kaew—that of the Emerald Buddha (Phra Kaew Morakot). Although its origins are murky, this image of the Buddha—actually made of a type of jade or quartz—has since the fifteenth century been well traveled in Thailand and Laos as part of the spoils of war. It was brought to Bangkok by the General Chakri, who later became Rama I. It is displayed on top of a magnificent array of other, golden Buddha images and is considered so sacred that photographs are not allowed by the general public. The *wat* itself was specially designed with three doors to face the sunrise and three to look toward the sunset. Wat Phra Kaew also houses the most important Buddhist library in the country, where the Thai *Tipitaka* is kept, as well as important statues of the first eight Chakri-dynasty kings. Nearby Wat Po is also one of Thailand's most sacred sites, with the world's largest reclining Buddha image.

## MODERN ARCHITECTURE

Modern architecture in Thailand has been most significantly affected by Western influence, which began to take shape during the mid-nineteenth century. Initially there was a concerted effort to blend traditional Thai style with European designs. A primary example is the Vimanmek teak mansion on the grounds of the Chitlada Palace. Built in 1868, it is the world's largest teak building with three stories and more than 80 rooms. Boasting the size and grandeur of European palaces of the time, it nonetheless remained essentially Thai in design. However, in more conventional architecture the traditional Thai style was largely displaced by Western influences during the early twentieth century. European functionalism became the dominant form, resulting in a considerable transformation of cities such as Bangkok. By the 1930s European influences were seen in the construction of most major hotels, railway stations, and even private homes. Some more elaborate Western-inspired designs of the time include the Thai Khu Fa, or Kraison building, originally begun as a villa during World War I in the Venetian Gothic style, and later finished in the 1930s, in part to a design by Corrado Feroci (see chapter 5). Urban planning ideas from the West also began to take root in Thailand. After World War II this trend continued, shaping newer parts of Bangkok in much the same fashion as other large urban centers throughout the world.

Traditional buildings have not been entirely abandoned or relegated to museums. Along Bangkok's *khlongs,* or canals, some more classical Thai homes remain. However, except for the extremely wealthy, the traditional teak design is now far too expensive. Due to over-logging of the wood in Thailand, strict controls are in place for its trade. Bamboo and thatch are, of course, not nearly as reliable or convenient for modern living styles. The result is that most buildings in Thailand are now built with brick and cement, very much as they are in Europe. Even the very wealthy now prefer Western-style homes and, again taking their cue from the West, city planners in Bangkok and other Thai urban centers are currently designing suburban developments to accommodate their expanding populations.

### The New Shape of Things

Progressively, more middle-class urban Thais are settling down in high-rise apartments and condominiums. Similarly, modern skyscrapers are becoming more and more familiar as the home of business and government. There has also been a drift toward shopping centers in the big cities. In this regard parts of Bangkok are almost indistinguishable from cities in the West. Another,

Village houses (courtesy of Tourism Authority of Thailand).

unfortunate, similarity is the congestion and pollution caused chiefly by automobiles. Thailand endures almost constant traffic jams throughout its major cities, to an extent that makes most Western cities look almost problem-free by comparison. The ongoing solution, which requires tremendous financial resources and political will, is to develop a comprehensive mass transit system. Here too the Thais have turned to the West in the hope of building better highways and cities. Yet as dire as things look for the preservation of a truly unique Thai style in architecture, there is hope. Recently some architects have returned to tradition in the hopes of incorporating it into modern designs, producing a "neoclassical" Thai style.

## NOTES

1. Piyalada Devakula, "A Tradition Rediscovered: Toward an Understanding of Experiential Characteristics and Meanings of the Traditional Thai House," Ph.D. dissertation, Faculty of Architecture, University of Michigan, 1999, p. 1.

2. Jacques Dumarcay and Michael Smithies, *Cultural Sites of Burma, Thailand, and Cambodia* (Kuala Lumpur: Oxford University Press, 1995), pp. 5–49.

3. Clarence T. Aasen, *Architecture of Siam: A Cultural History Interpretation* (Kuala Lumpur: Oxford University Press, 1998), pp. 1–20.

4. Naengnoi Suksri and Michael Freeman, *Palaces of Bangkok: Royal Residences of the Chakri Dynasty* (New York: River Books, 1996), pp. 11–16.

5. Smitthi and Moore, *Palaces of the Gods,* pp. 15–17. See also Sumset Jumsai, *Naga: Cultural Origins in Siam and the West Pacific* (Singapore: Oxford University Press, 1988), p. 31.

6. Anuvit Charernsupkul, *The Elements of Thai Architecture* (Bangkok: Karn Pim Satri Sarn, 1978), pp. 114–117. See also Smitthi and Moore, *Palaces of the Gods,* pp. 12–17.

7. Naengnoi and Freeman, *Palaces of Bangkok,* pp. 22–31.

8. Van Beek, *The Arts of Thailand,* pp. 170–79. See also Naengnoi and Freeman, *Palaces of Bangkok,* pp. 29–58.

9. Aasen, *Architecture of Siam,* pp. 70–74.

10. William Warren and Luca Invernizzi Tettoni, *Living in Thailand: Traditional and Modern Homes and Decoration* (London: Thames and Hudson, 1988), pp. 47–58.

11. Betty Gosling, *A Chronology of Religious Architecture at Sukhothai, Late Thirteenth to Early Fifteenth Century* (Ann Arbor, MI: Association for Asian Studies, 1996), pp. 4–20.

12. Michael Freeman, *The Temples of Thailand: Their Form and Function* (Bangkok: Asia Books, 1991), pp. 13–17.

13. Stratton and Scott, *The Art of Sukhothai,* pp. 32–49.

# 7

# Cuisine and Traditional Dress

## TRADITIONAL FOOD

No discussion of Thailand would be complete without mention of its food. In fact, when you mention Thailand, many people think first of the cuisine. Thai food is world famous, and remains one of the most popular international cuisines; a recent international poll surveying perceived excellence in cuisine ranked Thai food the fourth-best loved in the world. Almost every major European, Japanese, and North American city has at least a few Thai restaurants. Many Thai herbs and spices are also becoming increasingly available in Western countries, along with a noticeable expansion in the number of Thai cookbooks. The wide popularity of Thai food is even better demonstrated by the fact that there are few large Thai population centers outside Thailand. This means that most Thai restaurants in, for example, New York or Toronto, are run by non-Thais.

### Rice

Like most other Asian cuisines, the basic ingredient essential to all Thai meals is rice. So important is rice that in the Thai language "to eat" *(khin khao)* literally means "to eat rice." The expression, "have you eaten yet?" *(thaan khao laew reu yang?)*, is used in roughly the same way "how are you?" is in English—as a way of beginning a conversation. The word rice, or *khao,* is attached to the name of many dishes—making whatever you eat referred to as "with rice." No Thai meal is complete without generous servings of rice, and it is often eaten on its own, accompanied only by sauces or curries. Thai-

land is the world's largest exporter of rice, and it produces numerous varieties. Several different types are commonly used in traditional Thai cooking. Jasmine rice, for which Thailand is most famous, is the most common feature of Thai meals, particularly in the Central and Southern regions. Usually served plain and steamed *(khao plao* or *khao suay)*, this soft and fragrant long grain rice is washed several times, cooked without salt, and served fresh immediately. Sticky or sweet rice *(khao nio)* is also very common, particularly in the North and Northeast. This glutinous, shorter grain rice is often also found in desserts and sweets. It is never boiled, but rather soaked for long periods before being steamed. Unlike other grains, which turn white when cooked, sticky rice turns opaque and clumps together. Traditionally, it is eaten by hand—shaped into small balls that are then dipped in various condiments. Less commonly used and exported are Thai red and black rice. Both taste rather smoky and are more like wild rice in North America.

### Basic Ingredients

Beyond rice, Thai food is dominated by several key ingredients. Chilies, garlic, ginger, galangal (aromatic ginger), tamarind, lemon grass, coconut, limes, basil, and coriander (cilantro) are regular bases for almost every Thai meal. These ingredients reflect the historic influences of cuisines from India,

Traditional fishing (courtesy of Carine Lindauer).

China, Persia (Iran), Japan, and Europe. The chili, for example, is believed to have been brought to Thailand from its native South America by the Portuguese. Coriander, limes, and tomatoes are not native to Thailand, but came with Europeans as the Kingdom of Ayutthaya expanded its trade. Thai desserts, heavy on egg yolk and sugar, also illustrate European influence. Similarly, noodles probably came with trade caravans from China, while curries are trademarks of Indian cuisine. Fish and seafood are used widely, especially in coastal areas and in river deltas. Poultry and pork are highly favored staples throughout the country, and beef is also widely consumed, although generally less than other meats. An enormous array of fruits and vegetables, many unique to Southeast Asia, are also typical of Thai food. This abundance, and the refusal of the most devout Buddhists among the population to eat meat and fish, has given Thai cooks a wide range of vegetarian options. Like many other Southeast Asian cuisines, the complexity of Thai food lays not so much with *what* as *how*. Mastering the use of key ingredients, and an assortment of spices, sauces, and curries, is the main objective. Few Thai chefs follow recipes—instead the food becomes a matter of personal taste and expression. In this way, Thai cooking can be greatly varied.

### Regional Variation

With its mix of spicy, sour, and sweet tastes, Thai food can be quite distinct from other Southeast Asian fare. Moreover, it can be quite different from region to region within the country. There are four main culinary regions in the country, basically following geographic and climactic divisions. The North, with its cool winters and hot summers, has a varied cuisine. Being at the crossroads of historical trade and migration routes between India and China, Northern Thailand has been heavily influenced by other cultures and cuisines. Food tends to be spicier here than elsewhere in the country, in part owing to the impact of Indian and Chinese traders. As well, other ingredients very common in the rest of Thailand, such as coconuts, do not grow well in the mountainous North. The result is that the sweetness and smoothness familiar in the food of other regions is relatively absent in northern meals.[1] Far from the sea, the North's traditional cuisine is also less influenced by fish and seafood. Chicken, beef, and pork are far more the focus. The North is also famous for its wide array of condiments, sauces, and salsas—usually very spicy—that add much to any meal. The best known is *nam phrik pao,* with a base of roasted chillies, salt, shallots, and garlic. Probably the most distinct feature of Northern food is the use of sticky rice, which is widely favored over the Jasmine variety.

The Northeast of Thailand *(Issaan)* has Thailand's harshest climate, and the cuisine of the region very much reflects this. With relatively poor soil,

almost annual droughts, and cyclical floods, the area is the country's least fertile. Northeastern food is therefore characterized by more hardy vegetables and fruits, as well as a variety of roots and plants that grow easily. The region is famous for its chilies, which often dominate traditional dishes, such as vegetable or meat spicy salads *(yam* or *laap)* with mint and basil. Bordering the Mekong River, the Northeast also draws heavily upon fish. Salted and dried fish are very common, as is the fermented fish sauce *nam plaa.* Historically poorer and more rural than other regions of Thailand, the Northeast is generally seen as the country's "wild frontier." Still, the simplicity and spice of the area's cuisine are definitely unique and important contributions to Thai food.

The Central Plains of Thailand make up the country's chief rice-growing regions. There is also an enormous variety of fruits and vegetables, which influence many dishes. With the country's biggest city, Bangkok, as its focus, Central Thai cuisine is in many ways a hybrid of the other regions' food. There is also the noticeable influence of other countries in Central Thai cooking, owing to Bangkok's historic attraction for immigrants from elsewhere in Asia. Particularly important in this regard are the Chinese. Over the years Thai and Chinese—particularly Cantonese—cooking have fused in many Thai cities, but nowhere more than Bangkok, with its huge and vibrant Chinatown.

Lying on both the Andaman Sea and the Gulf of Thailand, the South is famed for its fish and seafood. Not surprisingly, they make the food of the region distinct. Southern cuisine is also known for its reliance on coconuts, peanuts, and fresh fruits. The area is best known for its rich, sweet curries *(kaeng),* and for its peanut sauce *(nam satay),* which usually accompanies grilled meats. With a fairly large Muslim population, pork is not as widely consumed in the South, but beef and especially chicken are. Although the heat and spice of Thai food can certainly be found in the South, traditionally it is less fiery than the North and Northeast. Southern food has also been more influenced by Chinese and Malay immigration.

### Markets

A true Thai culinary journey begins in the market. Almost every town and city in Thailand has one or more markets. They come in all sorts of different types and sizes, and in addition to a wide range of foodstuffs most markets also offer handicrafts, art, jewelry, clothing, and just about everything else any shopper could want. Although modern North-American-styled shopping centers and grocery stores are becoming more popular, the traditional market remains the choice of most Thais when it comes to food.

Probably the most famous, and photographed, type of market in Thailand is the floating market *(talaat naam),* which makes its way through Bangkok's

Floating food stall, Bangkok (courtesy of Jonathan Wong).

large canal, or *khlong,* system. These markets are made up of very lively and colorful wooden boats carrying fruits, vegetables, and even small grills or stoves offering up meals. Over a century old, Talaat Tom Khem is Bangkok's largest, drawing many shoppers. There are smaller floating markets on nearby canals, some designed with tourists in mind, and complete with boats for hire and boats packed with souvenirs.

On dry ground, Bangkok also boasts the enormous "weekend" or *chatuchak* market (Talaat Chatuchak), which draws an average of 200,000 visitors a day at weekends. It has more than 8,600 stalls selling everything imaginable, from vegetables, fruits, and flowers to household wares, opium pipes, live poultry, and even snakes.[2] Pak Khlong market is the city's best vegetable and fruit market, while Khlong Toey market, near Bangkok's port, has the advantage of offering a great variety of foodstuffs just offloaded from ships arriving from elsewhere in Asia.

Just as famous as Bangkok's markets is Chiang Mai's night bazaar. Really a collection of markets sprawled out across one of the city's main areas, the night bazaar operates every day of the year—rain or shine. In addition to the hundreds of stalls offering souvenirs, clothing, textiles, and antiques, there are many excellent eateries and a wide assortment of vegetable, fruit, and dry food vendors. During daytime hours Chiang Mai also has the massive Warowot market, with its fresh meats, seafood, and endless number of stalls teeming with fresh produce.

Chiang Mai streetscape (courtesy of Arne Kislenko).

Market stalls, Chiang Mai (courtesy of Jonathan Wong).

Man selling eggs, Chiang Mai (courtesy of Arne Kislenko).

## Meals

Throughout Thailand food and eating are matters of great importance. However, many meals are kept very simple. Breakfasts in Thailand may consist of rice porridge, or an omelet with vegetables. Lunch is usually kept to rice noodles or soups. Dinners tend to be more substantial. Supper for a family or for guests usually involves a soup, several curries or gravies, and any number of side dishes, dips, and sauces. Emphasis is always placed on the freshness of ingredients. With the exception of the rice, all dishes may be prepared in advance, and all are served at once. Traditional Thai meals do not have courses, and few dishes require being eaten immediately. This relaxed approach emphasizes the communal nature of Thai cuisine. Rather than individual portions, all dishes are shared, and dining is regarded as a social occasion to enjoy with family and friends. Thais eat mostly with forks and spoons, although some—especially those of Chinese origin—may eat with chopsticks. Noodles and spring rolls are most likely to be the targets of a Thai's chopsticks. The adoption of cutlery took place only in the twentieth century, and it still has not entirely caught on. Traditionally, some Thai food is eaten with the fingers, and this is still very common, particularly in rural areas. Salt and pepper are rarely seen on Thai tables; rather there will be *nam plaa,* soy sauce, and chilies. All meals are served with drinking water, although for Westerners anxious to cool down the heat of chilies, plain rice is a far better antidote. Other common beverages include Thai

coffee *(kaafae thom* or *kaafae thung),* both Indian and Chinese teas, and *naam manao*—iced lime juice mixed with sugar. Thai beer and rice whiskey are also widely consumed. For the very brave there is "white liquor" *(lao khao),* also sometimes known as "jungle liquor" *(lao theun).* The legal variety, sold in stores, is made from sticky rice and contains 35 percent alcohol like regular rice whiskey. Illegal, bootlegged versions are made from a variety of goods, including palm sap, sugarcane, coconut milk, and rice. These brews can contain up to 95 percent alcohol—making them very potent, and very dangerous, drinks. Liqueurs made from herbs, spices, roots, seeds, and fruits can also be found throughout the country, many homemade.[3]

As in many countries, Thailand's cuisine has two faces: one more formal and traditional, and one more everyday. Formal Thai cooking quite naturally involves more work. It is usually distinguished by the garnishes and presentation that accompany the dish. In upscale Thai restaurants and hotels, particularly those frequented by foreigners, Thai meals can be quite ornate—often accompanied by a performance of classical Thai music and served by staff wearing traditional, colorful dress. Emphasis is also placed on the artistic quality of the visual presentation of the meal, which may include elaborate carvings from exotic fruits, ice sculptures, and an endless variety of sweets. Of course most Thais do not eat this way every day and such presentations are reserved for guests and special occasions. In fact, although food and meals are very important to the culture, Thai cuisine need not be complicated and elaborate. At its best, it is usually quite basic, simple, and natural, emphasizing the openness and friendliness of the Thai people.

Whether it's in a formal or informal setting, traditional Thai food is both varied and delicious. Among the many classic dishes from the different regions are sour lime and lemongrass soup with shrimp *(tom yum goong);* thin rice noodles with vegetables, eggs, and peanuts *(pad thai);* green curry with chicken *(kaeng khieu wan kai);* green mango salad *(yam ma muang);* grilled fish, often in a peppercorn and coriander rub *(plaa pao);* barbecued chicken *(gai yang);* curry broth with egg noodles, meats, pickled cabbage, and lime *(khao soy);* pork curry made with ginger, turmeric, and tamarind *(Hang Le);* and morning glory vine fried in garlic *(phat phak bung).* For dessert, there's steamed coconut and egg custard *(sangkhaya);* bananas with palm sugar *(kluey buah chee);* sticky rice with coconut cream and mango *(khao nio ma muang);* or an assortment of tropical fruits such as rambutans, mangosteens, papaya, and pineapple.

### Dining Out

Cities such as Bangkok and Chiang Mai have many big hotels and fancy restaurants, which can be excellent places to eat. However, there are also

many good small dining establishments and food stalls in Thailand. Noodle shops *(raan kuaytlaw)* and night markets *(talaat toh rung)* are very economical places to eat, and usually represent more authentic and basic Thai cooking. Most cities and large towns have hundreds or thousands of stalls. They are even popular on major roads and highways in the countryside. Many small restaurants and stalls do not have menus, and are not usually set up to deal with foreigners who don't speak Thai. Still, most Thais, and budget-conscious tourists, frequent these smaller establishments as the best places to sample traditional, and inexpensive, cooking.

### Exotic Foods

It is possible to eat more unusual foods in many places in Thailand. Insects such as grasshoppers, beetles, ants, and various larvae are eaten by some Thais— and adventurous tourists. Often they are roasted, and accompanied by a sauce or coating. They are a good source of low-calorie protein and, despite Western attitudes, are considered quite tasty. Some bugs are even now available in Bangkok supermarkets. Dog meat is more commonly eaten in other Asian countries, but can be found in Thailand too—particularly in the Northeast.

### MODERN WAYS

Traditional Thai food has been significantly affected by changes in technology, agriculture, economics, and immigration. New technology has introduced refrigerators, microwave ovens, and electric rice cookers to many Thais, fundamentally changing the way in which they handle and prepare their foods. As Thailand has modernized since World War II, advances in farming, fishing, transportation, and land management have greatly increased food production. In addition to rice, Thailand is today one of the world's largest exporters of fish, fruits, and more recently, packaged foods.[4] Obviously this has helped the country feed its own people more effectively, but it is also one of the reasons Thai food has been so successfully promoted abroad. Conversely, economic development has also brought many international influences into Thailand, which have gradually made their way into Thai cuisine. This is especially true in Bangkok, with its large population of immigrants and foreigners. There are also considerable numbers of people from South and Southeast Asia in the capital, each with different culinary traditions that over time have influenced Thailand.

Even Westerners have made their impact. More and more, large cities in Thailand are reflecting Western influences in the range and type of foods made available. Fast food is especially popular, and in Bangkok there are many chain restaurants common in North America. Increased trade and

globalization have brought to Thailand Western foods and ideas, balancing the way that Thai cuisine has been exported. "Fusion" cooking, mixing different styles of cuisine, is more evident in some Thai restaurants catering to foreigners and tourists. At home, most urban Thais are turning increasingly to packaged and prepared foods, many imported from the West and other Asian countries. However, given the importance placed on food in Thai culture and the relatively low cost of dining out, many Thais continue to cherish more traditional foods and eateries. Open-air markets with fresh produce remain the preferred place to shop for most Thais. Moreover, despite considerable changes, the basics of traditional Thai cooking remain. It has always been highly adaptive, in many ways reflecting the Thai people's acceptance of different influences and their ability to cope with any circumstance.[5]

## TRADITIONAL THAI DRESS

There is no Thai official dress, although unofficial "national costumes" have been designated. These are based on traditional styles for both formal and informal occasions. For women this is a full-length dress called the *pasin.* Made of any color Thai silk, it is worn like a sarong with a long-sleeved silk blouse. On formal occasions this may also be accompanied by a colored silk sash worn from the left shoulder to the right side of the waist. Men wear a short- or (more formally) long-sleeved cotton or silk jacket with a very high neck and no collar, called a *sua phra ratchathan.* It can be any color but is traditionally white to contrast with black trousers. A colored silk cummerbund is added on formal occasions. Both the *pasin* and the *sua phra ratchathan* are derived from designs worn principally by the elite of Thai society long ago. The spectacular colored and embroidered costumes seen in the *khon* and *lakhon* dance dramas are also highly stylized versions of historical garments worn by royalty, and are seen today only on performing artists. This is also true of the traditional Thai headwear, the *chada,* with its unique pointed cone or pyramidal shape and bright, jewel-encrusted gold plating.

On a more everyday basis in rural areas men will generally wear shorts, plain shirts, and a rectangular piece of checkered cloth worn about the waist (the *phakaoma*), which serves as a towel, hammock, or headwear protection against the sun. Women traditionally wear a variation of the *pasin.*[6] In some areas, particularly the Northeast, men and women may wear clothes made from tie-dyed thick cotton or silk, known as *mawn khwaan.* The same fabrics are used in making the distinctive, triangular "axe-pillow" *(mon khwaan).* In the city most Thais wear Western-style clothes, which are widely available and even produced in the country. Businessmen wear suits and ties, school children wear uniforms, and jeans and t-shirts are a very common sight. The

Thais are, however, very concerned about appearances and do not wear tattered or revealing clothes. They consider these to be offensive, especially in areas that are sacred such as important temples and palaces. In such locations more formal wear is required, even for foreigners. This includes long-sleeved shirts, and long pants or sarongs. Thais dressed improperly will be turned away from these places. Whether in sacred places or not, Thais generally dress very modestly. Men tend to wear long trousers and buttoned shirts, while women wear blouses or pants and sarongs.

## DRESS OF THE HILL TRIBES

Each of the hill tribes produces an array of crafts, ranging from baskets to jewelry. However, they are perhaps best known for the colorful textiles they make and their beautiful traditional costumes. Every tribe has a different style and uses unique designs. Sometimes the differences extend down to villages and even families within the group. Each tribe also tends to specialize in some aspect of textile production, say weaving or embroidery, although cooperation between the groups is not very common. In fact, many of the ethnic minorities have a competitive approach to their traditional dress. They regard their clothing as symbols of status, wealth, and beauty. Within communities young women are encouraged to create the most intricate designs and best weaves possible in order to court possible suitors, help earn income, or maintain the reputation of the family. Tourist dollars have certainly become a major incentive in the production of hill-tribe textiles, but most groups do not continue the traditions solely for this reason. It is true that some groups wear their costumes primarily for Western tourists, but many more wear it on a regular basis, based on their customs and beliefs. Some tribes, and particularly the men within them, have abandoned their traditional dress in favor of more Thai and Western clothes. However most have not, and instead see their clothes as very much part of their culture.

### Karen

Karen women are renowned for their weaving skills, and boast some of the best and most colorful traditional dress. This includes bright red and blue colored cotton sarongs and blouses with a range of patterns and designs. Traditionally, unmarried women wear simple thick woven v-necked white blouses with vertical stripes, while married women can wear more colorful tops, often decorated with beads for trim. Karen women grow their hair long, wearing it tied back in a bun under white scarves. They also wear brass or bead bracelets. Men wear baggy blue or black pants with striped shirts similar in design to the women. In some groups of the Karen men wear black shirts with red or

orange cummerbunds and head scarves. The Karen are extremely self-sufficient. They grow their own cotton, then spin it into threads and dye it. Patterns are set while the cloth is still on the loom. Only special decorations are purchased. While Karen men have largely abandoned traditional dress, Karen women continue to wear it on a daily basis—not just for tourists. In fact the Karen believe that a woman's beauty is defined by how elaborate and detailed the designs of her clothes are. With this in mind, young girls begin weaving their own clothes at a very young age.

### Padaung

The Padaung Karen are perhaps best known for their "giraffe-necked" women. From a very early age—sometimes as young as two years old—girls wear heavy copper neck rings. By the time they are women their collar bones have been pushed several centimeters down, elongating the neck. The origins of the custom are not entirely clear, but it is believed to have started as a way of making women look unattractive to their enemies so that they would not carry them away as slaves or concubines. It may also be based on the fear of attacks by tigers, who grip their prey by the throats. A third explanation is from ancient tribal mythology, which celebrates the beauty of a long-necked dragon.[7] Whatever the origin, the custom is considered by the Padaung to be an essential rite, and a sign of great beauty. Traditionally the coils were worn only until marriage, but perhaps because of the weakening of their necks many women continue to wear them for the rest of their lives. In the past, old coins were melted down to form the rings, particularly in Burma where the majority of the tribe live. Today the coils are formed from copper sheets, and are even provided by some tour operators—eager to cash in on the crowds the women draw. Some women are even paid a regular wage to pose for photographs, and pass on the tradition to their children. In this respect, the custom has become exploitative, with some Padaung villages having the appearance of zoos.[8] Perhaps for this reason, or because of the pain the procedure inflicts on the women, the custom is dying out. Beyond the neck rings Padaung women wear very many colorful bands of cloth or silk in their hair, usually adorned with flowers or embroidered designs. They have white tunics with fine pink or red edging, which are usually accompanied by black shawls and blue or black cotton skirts. The men wear fairly basic loose pants and jackets.

### Hmong

The Hmong have two major tribal divisions, the "blue" and the "white." Hmong women wear elaborate dress made from cotton and hemp, decorated

with often intricate embroidery. Blue Hmong women are famed for their pleated skirts with red, blue, and white bands, as well as for their black satin jackets with orange, yellow, and red embroidered cuffs. White Hmong women wear a kind of baggy pants, tied off with wide bands or sashes. Their jackets tend to be simpler and usually have a blue cuff. Hmong women wear their hair in large buns. Both men and women traditionally wear plain blue or black caps. The men wear dark baggy pants and embroidered jackets that pull over the chest and close on the left shoulder. Many Hmong women wear ornate silver jewelry, which they make themselves. Silver coins and medallions are usually worn on their jackets. Hmong clothes are made chiefly from hemp, which they grow and weave themselves, but skirts are also made from cotton. The cloth is woven white and then dyed with indigo for the color. Hmong designs often incorporate batik as well as embroidery, and are considered among the more intricate of the hill-tribe costumes.

### Yao

Yao women wear distinctive long black jackets with fluffy red wool or dyed fur lapels. They are famed for their stitch-work and the elaborate designs they create on all clothing, especially their baggy trousers and distinctive head-wear—which for the women is a kind of blue or black turban. The Yao also wear and craft silver jewelry. Small children wear black caps with brightly colored pom-poms. Men wear blue and black jackets with diagonal silver buttons and embroidered cuffs and edges. Unlike the Karen and Hmong, the Yao do not grow their own cotton or hemp, and do not do their own weaving. They are, however, expert embroiders, and usually stitch from the back to show the design on both sides.[9]

### Lahu

There are four divisions to the Lahu tribe, two of which are well known for their weaving prowess. The "black" Lahu wear black capes covered in white stripes. The sleeves of the cape are decorated with bands of wool dyed orange, red, or blue. "Red" Lahu wear black trousers edged with white trim. Their shirts have colorful bands and intricate designs. Children wear similar shirts and trousers. Both groups of Lahu women also wear several distinctive black narrow skirts, colorful turbans, silver jewelry, and richly embroidered cloth or hemp shoulder-bags. Men in both groups wear black cotton shirts and baggy pants or sarongs. The Lahu do weave some components of their dress, especially the bands and trim. However, they usually buy, or trade for, most of the cloth used.

### Lisu

This is also true of the Lisu, who some regard as the best-costumed group. Lisu women prefer very bright clothing in a wide range of colors. They wear a kind of tunic, usually blue or green with multi-color strips woven in, which drops to the knee. The number and detail in the stripes is considered a mark of skill, and is the source of competition between women of the village. This is accompanied by black, blue, or green baggy pants into which bright bands of colors—particularly reds and yellows—are stitched. Sleeves and cuffs of all the garments tend to be elaborately designed. Lisu women also have unique headwear—a broad, flat black cap adorned with strips of multi-colored wool and special designs. By contrast, men usually have plain black jackets and baggy black pants, but at times of celebration will wear brighter-colored pants and a more stylish jacket. Both sexes wear silver jewelry on special occasions.

### Akha

The poorest of the hill tribes, the Akha are also one of the most distinctively dressed. The basis for almost all their clothes is black, but they are easily recognizable by their unique headwear, covered in white beads, aluminum balls, silver coins, and medallions, and topped off with colored strands of silk. Some women wear hats made out of colored bands rising up like a top hat. The women also sport rather different leggings, which are black with hori-

Hill-tribe woman, Chiang Mai (courtesy of Jonathan Wong).

zontal bands of various colors. On top of this they wear a short black skirt with a white or colored pouch tied around their waists. Men wear basic black pants and shirts. The Akha grow their own cotton and spin their own thread, weaving the cloth white and then applying dyes. They are also considered one of the best tribes at embroidery.

### Lawa

The Lawa wear knee-length tunics made of cotton or wool with a colorful band design and embroidered patches. Unmarried women then wear over this a loose white cotton blouse with fairly intricate designs on the edges, and tight

Hill-tribe girl at a flower festival, Chiang Mai (courtesy of Jonathan Wong).

skirts with colored horizontal bands. Married women wear a kind of long cotton dress. All women of the Lawa wear large necklaces of colored beads, and long cotton earrings that end in small brightly colored balls. Women tie their hair in large buns and may adorn it with colored cloth. The Lawa do not usually weave their own cloth, but are known instead for their design work.[10]

### Hill-Tribe Artisans and the Future

In all of the tribes, women do the work in making clothes. The process is very time-consuming and requires great dedication and precision. Embroidered pants or a fine jacket can take months of labor. Girls are put to the test at a very young age, often five or six years old, and learn from their elders how to work with needles, spindles, thread, dye, and designs. Most of the clothes produced today by the hill tribes are intended for retail in Thai cities, but being so poor most tribes also have to make their own garments. Despite the detail involved, most clothing is sold at prices Westerners consider very cheap. The skills and traditions in making these clothes have been passed down through the generations, but, like the hill tribes themselves, are now in danger. Increased demand for their clothing will of course bring pressure to change the nature of production, which will undoubtedly have serious implications for the societies themselves. More importantly, the lure of modern ways and big cities is drawing away many young people from the hill-tribe communities, which ultimately threatens their cultural survival—not just their fashion.

### NOTES

1. Jeffrey Alford and Naomi Duguid, *Hot Sour Salty Sweet: A Culinary Journey Through Southeast Asia* (New York: Artisan Publishing, 2000), p. 13.

2. Cummings and Martin, *Lonely Planet: Thailand,* pp. 269–70.

3. Ibid., p. 159.

4. National Identity Board, *Thailand into the 2000s,* pp. 258–59.

5. Charmaine Soloman, *The Complete Asian Cookbook* (Vancouver: Raincoast Books, 1992), pp. 292–93.

6. National Identity Board, *Thailand in the 2000s,* pp. 5, 85.

7. Foreign News Division, *Facets of Thai Cultural Life,* p. 131.

8. Hanks and Hanks, *Tribes of the North Thailand Frontier,* pp. 114–132. See also Richard West, *Thailand: The Last Domino* (London: Michael Joseph, 1991), pp. 13–14, 35–36.

9. Jim Goodman, "High Fashion, Hill Style," *Sawasdee Magazine* 26/8 (November 1996): pp. 32–35.

10. Thailand On-Line (Thailand Publications, Switzerland) at *www.thailine.com.* See also Cummings and Martin, *Lonely Planet: Thailand,* pp. 452–55, 516–517, 558–60.

# Gender, Courtship, and Marriage

## TRADITIONAL ROLES OF THE SEXES

It is often said that women in Thailand enjoy more freedom and have more rights than in any other country in Southeast Asia. In part this is due to the fact that Thai women have traditionally played a much greater role in economic and political affairs than their counterparts elsewhere. For example, in rural areas it has been common for women to inherit land as much as, or more than, men for almost two thousand years. It is also common throughout much of the country for women to control family-run businesses and household finances. This probably developed in part because of Buddhist practices, which gave men the predominant role in the priesthood *(sangha)*. Since only men could earn merit by joining the priesthood, women sought out other avenues. Moreover, since husbands and sons were often away for parts of the year studying as monks, it fell to women to manage more practical affairs. Travelers to Ayutthaya noted as early as the fifteenth century that women were responsible for all economic affairs of the home. This tradition was furthered in the nineteenth and twentieth centuries by the migration of men to work and study in urban centers or overseas. As of 1997, women constituted 45 percent of the paid workforce in Thailand—the highest percentage in all of Asia and fortieth in the world according to the United Nations Human Development Report—classifying it as a progressive country.[1]

### Issues and Problems

There are, however, considerable inequities between Thai men and women in some respects. As in many countries, including those of the West, women

generally earn lower incomes than men. They also often work longer hours, and with fewer avenues for promotion or advancement. Significant numbers of women work in family-run businesses but do not receive any direct wages. In manufacturing and service-industry jobs many women average 50–60 hour working weeks, but almost half earn incomes less than the average—a much higher proportion than men. Unlike in Western countries, it is quite common for women to work alongside men in construction jobs and other strenuous occupations, although they rarely receive the same wages for it. Nearly 40 percent of women are employed as private-sector service workers, whereas very few hold senior managerial or executive positions in businesses. The number of female lawyers, judges, doctors, and professors is very low compared to men. In agriculture, nearly one-third of Thai women earn income below basic subsistence levels. Compounding these problems is the fact that women remain the primary caregivers of children, and in addition are generally the main caregivers for elderly or sick parents and family members. Perhaps most significant of all is the fact that women still endure higher illiteracy rates and have lower educational qualifications than most men.

Women have had the right to vote in Thailand since 1932—the same time as men. However, by the late 1990s they made up less than 10 percent of elected officials, and only about 3 percent of members of parliament or the senate. The majority of government workers are women, but fewer than 10 percent occupy posts in the top three bureaucratic ranks. At local levels women were prohibited from becoming *phuyaiban,* or village leaders, until 1982. There are also persistent traditional beliefs in Thailand that undermine the status of women. One is the Buddhist concept that the greatest merit a woman could earn is in having her sons enter the priesthood. Another is the animist notion that women drain male power, which precluded them from working in politics and government.[2] Lastly, there is the question of legal rights. Although women have many of the same guarantees under law as men, there are still some areas in which their legal status is not equal. Until recently, men could divorce their wives on the grounds of adultery, but women could not do the same. Men who marry foreigners retain the right to buy and hold land in Thailand, but women do not.[3]

## Prostitution

Prostitution in Thailand is also symptomatic of the problems and inequities women face. Estimates on the number of sex workers in the country vary, but usually range from 200,000 to nearly 2 million. About 1 million people in Thailand are infected with AIDS, the majority of them women. Although prostitution is illegal, it is very common. In fact, it has made Thailand infamous as a major destination for Western and Japanese "sex tours."

Many foreigners come to Bangkok's Patpong district, or beach-resort towns such as Pattaya, especially to seek out the trade. There is a brisk business in teenage wives, and in girls "rented" for a few days or weeks. Prices are cheap, and the supply, sadly, is readily available.

Many young girls (and boys) in the business are from desperately poor homes. For them prostitution is an escape from poverty—no matter what the sacrifice. Many, especially from rural areas, are tricked by criminal organizations that run the trade into believing they can become famous singers or actresses in the big city. Some have also been fooled into going overseas with the expectation that they would become housekeepers or students. Occasionally girls, usually in remote villages, are even sold into the business by their parents in the hope of helping the family. Few women in the trade ever really escape it. Notwithstanding Thailand's recent efforts to combat prostitution, it remains a major social problem.

### Reform and Progress

Despite these inequities, the traditional roles of the sexes in Thailand are more equally balanced than in many countries. Moreover, there have been consistent and concerted efforts to improve the standing of women. Many of Thailand's modern kings have made this a priority. King Mongkut tried to give women greater freedom in marriage. King Vajiravudh promoted monogamy over traditional polygamy and supported educational reform in the hope of bettering the lives of his female subjects. King Bhumipol and Queen Sirikit today are also deeply committed to the process. Recently, successive Thai governments have done much to improve the situation. The country's new constitution, implemented in 1997, stated explicitly that men and women have equal rights—something very few Western countries have done. There have also been legal challenges to land ownership laws and other discriminatory practices. Cases that are testing the changes brought by the new constitution are now before the Thai courts. A number of important advocacy groups and organizations designed to promote the status of women have been created. Government policies with respect to healthcare, education, and labor have been enacted that will unquestionably help combat many problems women face.[4] Women are also becoming progressively more involved in Thai politics and government, and gradually breaking down the barriers that confront them.

### Changing Traditions

In addition to these developments Thai cultural practices with respect to the sexes are also noticeably changing. Arranged marriages are less and less

common in Thailand. Men are increasingly involved in childcare and household responsibilities. Whereas in the past Thai women did their best to ignore the adultery or violence of their male partners, today they often confront them personally and legally. Ancient practices, such as the traditional New Year's ceremony in which wives begged the forgiveness of their husbands, are rapidly fading. An old Thai saying notes that while men are the front legs of the elephant, women are the back, suggesting the dominant role of the men. This concept, however, is unlikely to have much of a place in the future of Thai relationships. Some experts think that the key to changing gender dynamics in Thai society is polygamy. Once widely accepted and practiced, polygamy has been slowly decreasing in Thailand. With the reforms of the early 1920s introduced by King Vajiravudh, polygamy came to be seen as a symbol of the country's backwardness and a violation of Buddhist precepts. It was also blamed for spreading venereal diseases and encouraging prostitution.[5] The practice of keeping "major" wives *(mia luang)* and "minor" wives *(mia noi)* stills exists today, and—when it comes to the wealthy, powerful, or famous—it is often the subject of much public attention. However, it is no longer as socially acceptable as it once was. Adultery is becoming far more clandestine in Thailand, as how it is usually conducted in the West.

## BUDDHISM AND WOMEN

Buddhism is often blamed for the inequalities women in Thailand endure. At the center of Thai culture, it is seen by some as a kind of moral framework for male domination. Thai activists such as Sukanya Huntrakul and Khin Thitsa argue that Buddhism gives women less status by implying in its doctrines and practice that they are inferior. However, some Western and Thai scholars have noted that Buddhist texts and rituals are, in fact, far more complicated and are often give paradoxical images of women. In some *jataka* tales, women are heroic, and often more moral and virtuous than men. Moreover, Buddhist scholars of both sexes argue that there is no differentiation between men and women on the path to enlightenment. They point out that according to Buddhist canons, women can reach *nibbana* without having first been born as males and that beliefs to the contrary have been inculcated from pre-Buddhist misogyny.[6] In early Buddhist texts, women are presented as full equals of men, a consideration reinforced by the concept of *karma*. Unlike the Judeo-Christian tradition, in Buddhism sexual identity is not fixed for eternity—the inference being that one can switch genders in different lives. Still, as many critics contend, in none of Buddha's past lives was he a woman. More important, as discussed in chapter 2, the Buddhist clergy *(sangha)* does not recognize the equality of women in the priesthood. The vast majority of

women ordained as monks follow the *Mahayana* tradition, not the Thai *Theravada* sect. Therefore, the role that religion plays in gender issues is not entirely clear. It is as difficult to blame Buddhism for the problems women face in Thai society as it is to blame Christianity for the inequalities women confront in the West.

## DATING AND MARRIAGE

For the most part dating and marriage in Thailand are undertaken by individual choice. In rural Thailand, where most of the population still lives, families often encourage relationships to develop as a means of strengthening communal bonds. However, binding arrangements without individual consent are increasingly rare. In more urban areas family control of relationships is even less evident. For most Thais, however, having the blessing or their parents and elders is very important and will usually be sought out before serious dating begins. In more traditional communities, it is not unusual for some family members to organize or chaperone the first few dates between a couple. At the very least, dates are expected to take place only in public areas.

With respect to affection and sexuality Thais are generally very reserved. Especially in most villages, premarital relations are extremely rare. People are far shyer about such matters than is usual in the West, and relationships develop much more slowly. Even holding hands is considered unacceptable in some communities. Instead conversation, poetry, and song are often the mediums through which couples court one another. Men usually initiate the process, but women take an equal part. It is traditionally assumed that women will remain virgins until marriage, but not necessarily men. When premarital sex between dating couples does occur and is made apparent to families and the community, both individuals are held responsible. They are usually given lectures by elders, but in some rural villages they may also face a kind of fine aimed at restoring their honor with local spirits.[7] With rapid urbanization and modernization some of these customs are being eroded. It is possible, in big cities especially, to see couples holding hands or kissing in public, and many social developments considered characteristic of Western societies have also made an appearance, including unwed mothers, negligent fathers, and teenage parents. However, for the most part the Thai remain very private and modest, and these matters are taken very seriously.

In rural Thailand the age of marriage for both sexes is lower than in the urban centers, owing mostly to different educational levels and labor priorities. By about age 15, young men and women in the country are considered essentially adult laborers, and set to work on the farms. Considerations of marriage and parenthood therefore tend to come earlier than for those Thai

who go on to university and other experiences in the cities. The average age of marrying in the countryside is about 20, while in the cities it is considerably higher for both sexes at about 28–35. Serious courtship in rural communities may involve a kind of dowry system, or at least a promise between households for economic exchange and support. However, in Thailand this involves the groom paying the family of the bride, as a way of thanking her parents for raising her. Even among more modernized and affluent Thais the practice of a monetary gift *(sin-sod)* from the groom continues. While there are few strict social prohibitions governing dating and marriage, most Thais tend to develop relationships with others of similar background and class. For more traditional Thais, astrological predictions and fortune-telling may influence decision making on marriage. Women also tend to avoid relationships with men who have not yet spent time in the priesthood, who they consider to be "unripe" *(khon dip)*.[8]

### Engagements and Weddings

Engagements in Thailand are marked much as they are in the West, with announcements and the offer of a ring to the bride-to-be. However, engagement parties are often held the same day of the wedding, to save money. Weddings in Thailand, as in many other countries, vary according to the wealth, status, and traditional beliefs of the couple and their families. Many Thais will, however, follow folk practices and Buddhist customs as part of their wedding celebrations. This involves first consulting an astrologer to pick a good date. August is generally considered the best month. The night before the wedding, the couple will attend a special Buddhist ceremony during which they thank their ancestors. In the morning of their wedding day the bride and groom first bring small gifts and food to monks to ensure that the marriage begins with merit. The monks in turn bless the couple with prayers, chants, and the sprinkling of holy water. Traditional ceremonies are presided over by nine monks (a lucky number). This begins with elders loosely binding the couple's wrists with string as a sign of their union and the continuity of the family. They may also wear a string over their heads that is tied together *(sai monkon)*, and wreaths of flowers. The strings are then placed in the monks' hands to signify that the marriage is now part of the Buddhist faith. There is no requirement to have a legal professional of any sort perform a ceremony, but the law does require that marriages be registered with the government.

The wedding ceremony also involves the offering of gifts to the couple *(khan mark)*, who then carry them to the house of the bride, accompanied by dancing and singing. The couple receives the ritual blessing of their families

and friends by sitting with their hands clasped together in prayer while guests pour water from a conch shell over them. Large celebrations, usually involving much food, drink, music, and dance, traditionally follow—and according to custom are paid for by the groom's family. A brief ceremony with more blessings ends the wedding and sends the couple off.[9] Recently, some urban Thais have become more familiar with Western-styled weddings—involving everything from invitations to the bride's white dress—and although some traditional Thais do not condone it, marriages to foreigners are not unheard of. It is customary in Thailand that immediately upon marriage the man moves into the home of the bride's parents. This practice originated as a means of guaranteeing the bride's family continued labor in the fields, but also stems in part from Thai folklore, which warns about the bad consequences of a wife and her mother-in-law living under the same roof.

## THE THAI FAMILY

Thais value family life very strongly, both for themselves and as an important part of Thai society as a whole. Typically Thais live with their extended family, which may include their parents and grandparents, and even sometime aunts and uncles. This stems from Thais' deep reverence toward their elders. "Old-age homes" as they are known in the West are considered highly disrespectful. Although this may give rise to what seems to most Westerners like an awkward or crowded household, Thais consider that extended families provide an important sense of community. They also reinforce concepts that the Thai consider essential, such as respect and compromise. Childcare becomes a more shared responsibility, and the arrangements may also be economically advantageous. However, the main motivation is to maintain strong family bonds.

### Raising Children

Thai children tend to be rather indulged by their parents and others in the family while they are very young, but strict discipline usually follows as they grow older.[10] Once they have reached an age of understanding, Thai children are taught about respect for their elders, Buddhist beliefs, and the rules of good behavior. They are also taught about duty and obligation, concepts that apply not just to the family but also the local village, their community, and in fact the country and its culture as well. Children who grow up on farms or in families with businesses will often be assigned small jobs at a very young age to reinforce these ideas. In most Thai homes children will also be given specific and regular chores, without the promise of allowances. The result is that

Village children (courtesy of Carine Lindauer).

later in life, children are accustomed to taking responsibility and will more naturally accept the obligation of taking care of their elders.

## NOTES

1. Philippe Doneys, "Political Reform through the Public Sphere: Women's Groups and the Fabric of Governance" in McCargo, *Reforming Thai Politics,* pp. 166–69.

2. Ghosh, *The World of Thai Women,* pp. 60–115.

3. Cummings and Martin, *Lonely Planet: Thailand,* p. 110.

4. Doneys in McCargo, *Reforming Thai Politics,* pp. 173–79. See also Ghosh, *The World of Thai Women,* chapter 6 passim, and Wyatt, *Thailand: A Short History,* pp. 4, 188, 228.

5. Scott Barmé, *Woman, Man, and Bangkok: Love, Sex, and Popular Culture in Thailand* (Lanham, MD: Rowman & Littlefield, 2002), pp. 157–66.

6. Penny Van Esterik, *Materializing Thailand* (Oxford: Berg, 2000), pp. 67–71. See also Kepner, *The Lioness in Bloom: Modern Thai Fiction about Women,* pp. 27–39.

7. Klausner, *Reflection on Thai Culture,* pp. 93–98, 283–85.

8. National Identity Board, *Thailand in the 2000s,* p. 84.

9. Thanapol, *Essays on Thailand,* pp. 108–9.

10. Klausner, *Reflections on Thai Culture,* pp. 310–11.

# 9

# Festivals and Fun

## TRADITIONAL CELEBRATIONS

Thailand is a country of great variety in its festivals, holidays, and celebrations. Every month of the year has at least one major occasion, while the months of May and October have four each. The majority are based on the lunar calendar, with December counted as the first month of the lunar year. Many festivals are designed to coincide with full moons, and some of them are centuries old, with uncertain origins. Some are based on a combination of Buddhist beliefs, Hindu mythology, and local traditions. Some are in keeping with ancient astrological configurations or agricultural cycles. Some have been abandoned over time, while others have been newly invented. However, all of them involve intriguing customs, and usually much food, dance, and fun. Traditional Thai celebrations can be divided into different categories based on the main focus or purpose of the events: Buddhist ceremonies, merit ceremonies, agricultural festivals, traditional events, sporting events, royal celebrations, local celebrations, and other events. Many of these overlap or take place simultaneously.

### Buddhist Ceremonies

There are six major Buddhist celebrations every year, all public holidays. *Maakha Buuchaa* (or *Magha Puja*) is marked on the full moon of the third lunar month, in February or March, and marks the gathering of Buddha's disciples. It involves hearing prayers and readings from scripture, as well as a communal candle ceremony. The first candle is lit by someone of high rank

within the *sangha* or royal family, traditionally on the *bai sema* or sacred boundary stones of the *wat*. That candle is then used to light other candles in the rest of the congregation. *Wisaakha Buuchaa* (or *Visakha Puja*) is held on the full moon of the sixth month, in May or June, and is regarded as the most important of religious holidays. It represents the birth, death, and enlightenment of Buddha. Prayers, sermons, and chants at the *wat* are accompanied by the *wien tien,* or circling of the temple three times with candles, lotus flowers, and incense—symbolizing the Triple Gems *(Tiratana)* of Buddhism.

The *Asaanha Buuchaa* (or *Asalaha Puja*) commemorates Buddha's first sermon and the delivery of his eight-fold path *(Atthangika-Magga or Magga)*. It is marked on the full moon of the eighth month, in July. *Khao Phansaa* (or *Khao Pansa*) follows *Asaanha Buuchaa* in July to coincide with the beginning of the rainy season. This is the time when monks are ordained and begin a three-month retreat for study and prayer, representing the period Buddha spent in *Tavatimsa* heaven preaching to his mother, who died when he was just seven days old. Sermons, chants, and prayers again mark the occasion. During *Khao Phansaa* the royal family also offers robes and small gifts to the priesthood, and the King changes the seasonal robes of Thailand's most revered symbol, the Emerald Buddha (Phra Kaew Morakot). A few days before *Khao Phansaa,* a special candle procession takes place, which over the years has become more of a festival. People make special beeswax candles that are supposed to remain lighted for the entire three month period of the rainy season. Many now craft elaborately designed candles, and carry them on floats in a large parade accompanied by food, drink, and dance. The last religious celebration, *Ohk Phansaa* (or *Ok Pansa*) marks the end of the rainy season in October with the regular sermons and prayers.

### Merit Ceremonies

Following *Ohk Phansaa* there is a merit ceremony known as *Thawt Kathin* (or *Thot Kathin*), which roughly translates as "making an offering to the monk of an embroidered frame," or "laying down the robes." People offer members of the *sangha* new robes, food, and other items that monks need. The robes include a shoulder shawl, loin cloth, and outer robe, which according to tradition must be made in one day. In Northern Thailand this is marked by a long procession of people who come down from the mountains led by a Buddha image, symbolizing the descent from the heavens. In Southern and Central Thailand *Thawt Kathin* is marked by the similar *Chak Phra,* or "pulling of the Buddha." This has turned into a colorful parade on land and water, with Buddha images being floated on specially designed barges, boats, and floats.

The most spectacular *Thawt Kathin* event is the Royal Barge Ceremony. The barges are long, wonderfully decorated traditional Thai boats made from elaborately crafted teak. From the Grand Palace members of the royal family travel in the boats about six-tenths of a mile (just over one kilometer) to Wat Arun (the "temple of dawn") across the Chao Phraya river to present new robes to the monks. The ceremony dates from the thirteenth century and reinforces the close bond between the king and the *sangha* as the keepers of the Buddhist religion. In total there are 51 barges, each with its own unique design, which travel in three parallel rows like a military procession. About 2,000 people are involved, most of them oarsmen dressed in traditional Thai costumes. Each of the boats is named for a creature from Thai mythology or a character from the *Ramakian.* The most important is the Golden Swan *(Suphanahong),* which in mythology was the steed of Brahma. This boat, nearly 165 feet (50 meters) long, carries the king. Immediately behind it is the *Anantanagaraj,* a barge designed to look like a fearsome Naga or sea-serpent, which carries the robes and gifts that the king will present. Other boats, in ceremonial order, carry other members of the royal family and high officials.[1]

Another merit-making event is "Season" or *Sart* day, which falls in the middle of the traditional Thai year, in September. It originated in ancient times, probably even before the spread of Buddhism, as a ritual offering of rice, fruits, and vegetables to holy spirits in order to secure their blessings for the harvest. *Sart* day was then adopted by Buddhists as a way of making merit and transformed into a ceremony that honored dead relatives by giving food to monks, who in turn led prayers aimed at making sure the dead were at peace. Traditionally, a sweet rice dish called *krayasart* is offered, made with red beans, sesame, and sugar, and wrapped in a banana leaf. It is usually served with ripe bananas as a dessert and passed among the congregation as well as the monks. This symbolizes both the strength of the community and the belief that with the *krayasart* goes the good name of the family who made it, thus ensuring that relatives—both living and dead—were honored by leaving "sweet tastes" with other people.[2] Today, *Sart* day has faded in importance, especially in Thai cities, but it remains important in some rural communities.

### Agricultural Festivals

Thailand's agricultural festivals are every bit as important, and just as colorful. Held in early May, the Royal Plowing Ceremony *(Raek Na)* marks the beginning of the rice-planting season. This is a multifaith event held in Bangkok at Sanam Luan field on the grounds of the Grand Palace, and it draws some of the biggest crowds in the country. The king presides in an

ancient ceremony dating back to the earliest origins of the Sukhothai era. It involves the blessing of sacred rice by Brahmin priests, which indicates that the ritual even predates Buddhism. A Lord of the Ceremony, appointed by the king and traditionally the minister of agriculture, then predicts the rainfall for the coming season by choosing one of three apparently identical cloths (called *panung*). The longest cloth means that little rain will fall and the harvest will be poor, while the shortest indicates good rainfall and a bountiful harvest. The Lord of the Ceremony then plows the field with a team of sacred white bulls, followed by four women, representing heavenly beings (called *nang thepi*), who scatter the rice while the Brahmins blow on conch shells. The bulls are then offered a choice of seven different types of food and drink—things such as rice seed, hay, sesame, and alcohol—and what they pick is supposed to be plentiful in the year ahead. The ceremony ends with the scattering of seeds to the crowd by the Lord of the Ceremony.

The Rocket Festival *(Boon Bang Fai)* also comes in May to welcome the rainy season. It symbolizes the prayer of farmers for a good harvest based on the legend that a Hindu rain god, Vassakan, loved being worshipped by fire. From this came the idea of sending rockets to him, which evolved over time into this festival. Today it is marked in typical Thai fashion with huge parades, colorful costumes, food, dance, and of course fireworks. The rockets are often enormous—some topping 33 feet (10 meters) tall—and they can pack a considerable punch. Many people see the festival as an opportunity to build the biggest, fastest, and most beautiful rocket possible—and the competition is fierce. The winner is the one that goes the highest, and the reward is the chance to lead in dance and song. Losers, especially those whose rockets blow up, earn a rather different prize, being thrown into the mud. The Rocket Festival is great fun, and one of the country's best-known celebrations.

The Ghost Festival *(Phii Ta Khon)* is also a wonderful community affair, originally from the Northeast. People dress as spirits, monsters, and demons with homemade costumes and masks. The celebration is a time for dancing and singing, as well as food and drink, but its origins have a more symbolic meaning too, based on the belief—probably taken from folklore and animism—that the dead that must be honored to keep them at peace. To begin the affair a local medium collects small pebbles to place around the temple in different directions, and then makes offerings to all the dead in the world. Symbolizing fertility, both agricultural and human, many of the men in costume carry phallic objects, usually made from papier-mâché, and then chase the women with them. The Buddhist content is based on one of the *jatakas,* when as a prince the Buddha-to-be came back from a long trip after everybody had thought he was dead. In surprise the people threw him a great party that awoke the dead, who then joined in too.

*Songkran* festival (courtesy of Tourism Authority of Thailand).

### Traditional Events

One of the best times to be in the country is during the Lunar New Year Festival *(Songkran)*. This begins on April 13th, which was made the New Year based on the Buddhist calendar during the reign of King Chulalongkorn (Rama V, 1868–1910). In 1941 Thailand officially adopted the Western practice of recognizing January 1 as the beginning of the New Year, but most Thais still consider *Songkran* as their "real" New Year celebration. *Songkran* involves a full week of almost constant celebration, during which three days—April 13 through April 15—are considered the most important. April 13 (called *Sang Karn Long Day* in some parts of the country) marks the day when the sun changes its position in the zodiac, and thus has come to represent a time to change or move on. In the morning, food and offerings are taken to the monks, followed by prayers. An important ritual then involves the honoring of ancestors and elders. Younger members of the family pour holy water over the hands of their seniors and receive blessings in return. April 14 (in some places called *Nao Day*, or *Da Day*) is a day reserved for food preparation and private meditation, while April 15 *(Phra Wan Day)* is for celebration. Traditionally, April 15 is a day to cleanse the soul through prayer, meditation, and the symbolic release of birds and fish. To symbolize the power of water as a universal element, Buddha images are then ritually

washed. The Thais, however, have interpreted these religious and astrological meanings in a uniquely fun way, too—as a massive, watery party. The entire community partakes in good-natured splashing—and everyone, young and old, gets wet. Unwary tourists are a prime target. The festival is accompanied with the usual food and dance, as well as spectacular parades, particularly in Chiang Mai, which is widely seen as the best—and wettest—place to be in the kingdom. Many Thais also celebrate two other New Years: December 31/January 1, as in the West, and the Chinese New Year *(Truut Jiin)*, which is usually in February, depending on a slightly different lunar calendar.

Another unique traditional event is *Loy Krathong*, which usually occurs in early November at the end of the rainy season. *Loy* means to float, and *krathong* refers to a boat made of banana leaves in the shape of a lotus. Thousands of these small craft are made by the people and are then adorned with offerings, usually incense sticks, candles, coins, and flowers. At night the boats are sent out on the water with wishes for good luck and prosperity.[3] The sight of so many *krathong* with candles alight is a moving and beautiful one. The festival is based on the Hindu goddess of water Kaileshvari (Chao Mae Kongkha in Thai) and signifies a "floating away" of old sins. Part of the celebration involves beauty contests, in which the winner is crowned queen of the festival—a tradition dating back to the Sukhothai era in honor of King Lithai's consort, who made the first ever *krathong*.

### Sporting Events

A number of celebrations and festivals involve things like boat races and kite-flying competitions, both of which are very popular in Thailand. Boat races differ across the country and accompany many events, with boats ranging in size, design, and decoration. One celebration especially devoted to the sport is the Long Boat Festival *(Pia Pee Nii Kaeaeng Rua Yaao)*, held annually at the end of the rainy season (September or October) in various locations throughout the country. The boats in these races are styled after the royal barges, and often have up to 60 oarsmen in double rows. Kite-flying competitions also accompany many festivals, and are a long-standing tradition in Thailand and other Asian countries. This stems from their use by ancient Chinese armies, who employed them to drop gunpowder bombs over their enemies. The Thais are accomplished kite-makers, by custom using bamboo and bark to craft unique designs such as the large star called a *chula*, the bird with a long tail called the *pakpao*, and the bird with bamboo pipes—making an eerie noise—called the *ngao*.

In Northeastern Thailand, every November there is the Surin Elephant Festival *(Ngaan Sa Daeaeng Chaang Jargwat Surin)*, or "roundup." Created in 1960

to attract tourists, this event is centered on demonstrations of elephants' tremendous strength, dexterity, grace, and intelligence. The culmination is a mock battle, styled after the ancient wars of the Tai kingdoms.[4] While some people may see this as abusing the elephants, others think it is the only way to generate money to pay for their care now that their traditional service in forestry and agriculture has been replaced by machines. Note that Thais consider the elephant an important national symbol. In addition to being used historically for work and war, in many Southeast Asian cultures elephants have been revered as symbols of power and prosperity—especially among royalty. White elephants—really a genetic variation of the species, marked by mottled pink or white skin and pearl-colored eyes—are especially prized as signs of good fortune. This stems from the belief that the night before giving birth to the Buddha, his mother had a dream in which a white elephant came bearing a lotus flower—the symbol of purity and knowledge. Long-standing Thai custom dictates that each white elephant discovered in the country must be given to the king to ensure the success of his reign. From 1812 until 1917, a white elephant adorned the country's national flag, and in 1996 two white elephants appeared on the Royal Ceremonial Emblem commemorating the 50th anniversary of King Bhumipol's coronation.[5] Today, March 13 has been set aside as Elephant Day in the hope of raising awareness about Thailand's declining elephant population. Sadly, some out-of-work elephants now live on the outskirts of major cities like Bangkok, venturing in for odd jobs or to ply tourists for handouts.

### Royal Celebrations

The Thais revere the royal family and take a number of occasions to mark their love and respect for them. Chakri Day, held on April 6th, commemorates the beginning of the Chakri dynasty, which began in 1782 with King Rama I. This event is chiefly acknowledged in a royal ceremony at the Grand Palace in Bangkok during which the king honors previous Thai rulers. A special ceremony is also held at the statue of King Rama I in the city. This is a time for the people to offer prayers for past kings. Special recognition is also given to a number of past monarchs on other occasions. Chulalongkorn Day, held on October 23rd, honors both the birth and death of this favorite king. January 25th commemorates the victory of King Naruesan over the Burmese in 1592, while December 28th marks the coronation of King Taksin in 1767.

King Bhumipol's birthday on December 5th is a major celebration and national holiday. This involves prayers, sermons, and offerings at the *wat*, with special attention to the *Tiratana*. To symbolize these Triple Gems, the birthday is actually marked over three days, during which Thais are expected to make merit. The celebration also involves making best wishes for the King.

A military parade and ceremony in which the armed forces swear allegiance to the monarchy are the highlight of the occasion. Similarly, coronation day, on May 5th, celebrates King Bhumipol's official installation with another three days of prayers and well-wishes to royals past and present. King Bhumipol has served on the Chakri throne since 1946, making him the longest-reigning monarch in the world today. The birthday of his wife, Queen Sirikit, on August 12th is also a national holiday marked in much the same fashion.

### Local Celebrations

Thailand has a number of festivals and celebrations unique to certain regions or populations of the country. Some, like the Moon Festival *(Yee Peng)* in September or October, involve ancient traditions. Held largely in areas with significant Chinese populations, this celebration revolves around the making, offering, and eating of moon cakes, made from red beans, nuts, durian, persimmons, egg yolks, and a variety of seeds. They symbolize a legendary Chinese heroine who became an immortal goddess, and now looks after farmers. The Moon Festival also symbolizes the Chinese rebellion against the Mongol Yuan dynasty in 1368. From Mon tradition comes the Honey Offering Ceremony *(Tak Bat Nam Phueng),* held chiefly in the North in September and October, during which people make special sweets with honey to offer the monks. The symbolism is that honey is rare at that time of the year, earning the makers more merit. The *Poi Sang Long* Festival, also in the North in April, originates from a mix of hill-tribe folklore and Buddhist rituals. Commemorating Prince Rahula, the son of the historical Buddha and his first novice, the festival centers around young boys who are shaved, blessed, and then outfitted in colorful robes and jewelry to resemble ancient crowned princes. They are carried around town by attendants to visit family and friends and receive blessings. Offerings to Buddha are also made, and the event ends with the boys being ordained as novice monks. *Sao Intakil,* an eight-day festival in some parts of the country, is held in late April or early May to commemorate Indra's Pillar. The high Hindu god is celebrated with parades, chariots, and huge decorated figures of Naga, along with the usual food, drink, and dance. A special ceremony honors Erawan, Indra's white elephant, with a type of rice liquor called *sura,* which he is believed to have enjoyed.[6]

The Vegetarian Festival *(Pra Pee Nii Gin Jee)* is held in October in the resort town of Phuket, and revolves around Southern Thailand's large ethnic Chinese population. In 1825, a traveling opera company brought to the area to entertain Chinese tin-mine workers fell mysteriously sick, probably with a jungle fever. To combat the malady, local doctors recommended a strict vegetarian diet, which was believed to honor Chinese emperor gods, Kiew Ong Tai Teh

and Yok Ong Sone Teh. When the troupe recovered, a celebration was held to further appease the gods, and the tradition began. Today the festival attracts much more than vegetarians. It also draws deeply pious people who believe that honoring the gods is still the main purpose of celebrations and who are willing to go to extreme lengths to do so. Among the many different processions and rituals associated with the festival, there is a welcoming of two other Chinese gods—Lam Tao, who cares for the living, and Pak Tao, who looks after the dead. Devotees demonstrate their commitment to the gods by undertaking various trials requiring considerable mental and physical strength. They call themselves *ma song* (entranced or possessed horses), and prove their spiritual convictions by bathing in hot oil, climbing ladders made from sharp blades, walking on hot coals, and piercing their bodies with swords, spikes, and nails.

The belief is that through torture *ma song* draw evil toward themselves, and away from the community. For this, *ma song* devotees are considered, especially by themselves, to be of the highest moral qualities—a sort of chosen people. Some *ma song* believe that the gods have spoken to them through visions and dreams, warning of impending doom if they do not make such sacrifices. The trials *ma song* endure are a public spectacle, and draw far more attention than the vegetarianism supposedly at the center of the festival. Huge crowds come to watch the *ma song* whip themselves into trances through meditation, dancing, or yelling and then perform self-tortures. The whole event lasts nine days: the length of time it took the opera troupe to recover and the number of gods honored by the Chinese community.[7] Each night of celebrations ends with loud parades and fireworks aimed at scaring off evil spirits still lurking about. Buddhist practices, such as offerings and prayers, are also part of the proceedings, but for the most part the Vegetarian Festival is a hybrid of Hinduism and Chinese religion.

Other celebrations, such as the Chiang Mai Flower Festival *(Thet Sakaan mai dek Mai Pradap)* held every February, were created only a few years ago as a means of attracting tourist money and just to have another reason to celebrate. There are also a host of other events held in the same tradition, such as the *Phanom Rung* Festival, held in March to showcase the historic park of that name. At the center of this Northeastern celebration is the *prasat* (temple sanctuary) at *Phanom Rung,* built between the tenth and thirteenth centuries. It is the best-preserved and largest example of Khmer architecture in the country, and sits on a "big hill" *(phanom rung* in Khmer) with spectacular views. It also contains a sacred replica of Buddha's footprint and a cherished lintel depicting a reclining Vishnu from the Hindu creation myth.

There are many more local and regional festivals in Thailand, covering every month of the calendar. Some are offshoots of the bigger celebrations discussed above, while others have been created as a means of generating

business and tourism. With such an extensive number of occasions and parties, it's hard to miss a reason to celebrate in Thailand.

### Other Events

In addition to this impressive list of festivals and celebrations, there are some other occasions that warrant attention in Thailand. Constitution Day *(Wan Rattana Tammanuun)*, held every December 10th, marks the 1932 coup and King Rama VII's decision to abolish the absolute monarchy in Thailand. January 16th honors educators, who are highly respected in the country, with Teacher's Day *(Wan Khruu)*. May 1 is marked as Labor Day *(Wan Raeaeng Ngaan)*, as it is in much of the world. Although they have comparatively few political celebrations, it should be noted that Thais are very patriotic, and it is not unusual to see many national flags out during the other festivals.

### FUN IN EVERYDAY LIFE

The Thai word for fun is *sanuk,* and it is a regular and important component of everyday life. The Thais believe strongly that everything in life should at least try to be fun. As a result, many Thais have a very noticeable sense of humor—indeed playfulness—to them. This applies to almost all circumstances, especially work. The Thais consider work important or valuable not so much as a measure of success as in the degree of *sanuk* that can be achieved. Some people familiar with Thai culture may also point out that the concept of fun has a deep-seated psychological meaning to it. By playing games, flirting, joking, and generally having fun, Thais are in fact demonstrating their sense of individualism in a society that otherwise expects a high degree of conformity with various expectations and rules of behavior. In part this would explain why Thais are so uncomfortable with confrontation, anger, and aggression, as discussed in chapter 10. *Sanuk* may in this way provide a kind of emotional buffer against the more difficult things in life. From a Buddhist perspective, having fun is entirely acceptable, especially if one keeps in mind the inevitably of suffering, as Buddha explained.[8] This does not mean that Thai people are carefree, or for that matter, careless. Rather, the concept of fun can be seen as a sort of philosophy: a distraction from, but also a reminder of, more serious things such as the impermanence of everything, and the world of responsibilities.

### Television, Radio, and Print Media

Thais, like many people, enjoy a variety of everyday leisure activities. Shopping, dining out with friends, going to the movies, or watching television at

home, are all regular activities. Television is extremely popular throughout the country, and can usually be found anywhere there is electricity. Thailand was the first country in Southeast Asia to begin regular, daily television service in 1955. Today, there are many local TV stations—both government-run and private. International cable and satellite channels are also accessed widely throughout the country. In a 1994 survey, it was estimated that among the Thai population of almost 60 million, there were almost 11 million TV sets—a number that has no doubt increased considerably in the past 10 years.[9] Thai TV mirrors the movie industry in many ways, especially with the focus on romance and comedy. Soap operas are especially popular. Most are based on the old *chakchak wongwong* folktales (see chapter 3). Just as in the West, a standard character is the bad girl *(nang itcha)* who complicates the life of the main stars of the show with her tricks and games. Many Thai shows feature at least some comedy, in keeping with the belief in *sanuk*. This is seen in the frequent addition to shows of a *ka-toi* character—a man dressed as a woman who provides comic relief. TV stars in Thailand are very famous and regularly appear on commercials, talk shows, and even game shows. Western, Chinese, Japanese, and Indian TV shows are watched and enjoyed, but Thai censors remove scenes with nudity, sexual contact, and extreme profanity. Depictions of drug use are also strictly regulated. Scenes showing gambling are usually allowed so long as they are accompanied by a warning reminding Thais that it is illegal. Violence is not generally censored, although some channels block out the pointing of a gun, particularly when aimed at the head, in deference to Buddhist sensibilities.

In 1984, nearly 70 percent of the Thai population listened to radio. Since then, the audience has decreased, mainly due to the popularity of television. By 1994, only about 44 percent of Thais listened to radio. Still, there are today over 500 radio stations, with nearly 40 in Bangkok alone. Many stations in the country are run by Radio Thailand, which is owned and operated by the government Public Relations Department. The armed services of Thailand each maintain their own radio services, as do the Thai National Police and some of the country's major universities. Most, however, are privately owned and operate on a commercial basis. As in many other countries, music, talk, and news shows are the most popular formats of radio in Thailand.[10]

Newspapers and magazines are also widely available in Thailand. There are today 38 daily newspapers throughout the country, with a combined readership of over 40 percent of the population—a figure that rises to over 68 percent in Bangkok. There are also four weekly, four monthly, four Chinese-language, and one Muslim newspaper. Among Thai-language dailies, the most popular are *Thai Rath, Khao Sod,* and *Matichon*—each with a reader-

ship of approximately 500,000. The two major English-language daily newspapers are the *Bangkok Post* and the *Nation,* both with circulations of about 60,000. There are over 50 major Thai-language magazines available, most of which focus on women.[11] As in many countries, entertainment, sports, and travel dominate the magazine business in Thailand.

Urban Thais are also very fond of nightclubs, bars, and discos. Sporting events, discussed below, are very popular attractions too.

## SPORTS AND HOBBIES

### Sports

The best-known sport in and from Thailand is *muay Thai,* or Thai kickboxing, which originated in the fifteenth century as a means of military mortal combat. Fighters (called *nak muay*) use their fists, elbows, shins, knees, and feet against their opponent in an effort to knock them down and out. Tripping with the feet and legs, and the forcing of one's body onto knees, are also permitted. However, blows to the head or struck while the opponent is not fully standing are prohibited. The fighters wear baggy, colorful shorts without shirts, and fight in a ring similar to those of regular boxing matches. Armbands with small amulets or talismans are also worn to bring luck. The entire sport is in fact highly ritualized. Apprentices learn from masters only after they have proven they are serious and committed to the sport. There are ceremonies to mark the maturing of a fighter, and to commemorate his first fight. Spirits are regularly consulted and worshipped. Before the fight begins both boxers perform a dance and ceremony *(wai khruu)* to thank their trainers and honor the spirits. The entire fight, or *khu ek,* is accompanied by music, which gets progressively louder and faster as the match goes along. Spectators shout and make bets, while in between rounds the referee wipes down both fighters.

This is a serious martial art, requiring great dexterity and strength. Despite that, some inexperienced, and foolish, foreigners can usually be found trying their luck in "all-comer" matches offered in many Thai towns. Few foreigners have actually mastered the skills required to become competitive enough to win on an international level, although that is starting to change as world interest in the sport increases. Many martial art experts consider *muay Thai* the deadliest of them all, as Thais are fond of pointing out. Famously, a Thai kickboxer once knocked out champions in five other martial arts in less than seven minutes. Because of the potential for serious injury, the government moved to regulate the sport in 1999 by prohibiting fighters younger than 18, but after a storm of protest from supporters they were obliged to back down. Thais consider this not just the national sport, but also a vital rite of passage

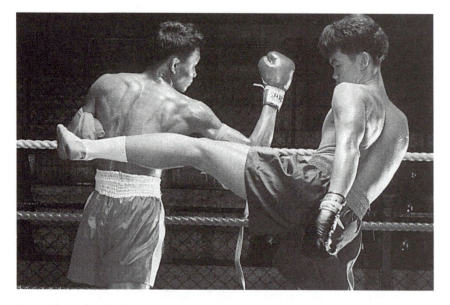

*Muay Thai* (Thai kickboxing) (courtesy of Tourism Authority of Thailand).

for those who take it up. As with boxing in the West, apologists often also defend it as the best means of allowing underprivileged youth a chance to succeed in life. Although it is not recognized as an Olympic sport, Thais take comfort in the fact that they are still generally the best in the world. Moreover, Thailand's first and second ever gold medals at the Olympics both came in regular or English style boxing (1996 and 2000).[12] *Muay Thai* is not only attended by sell-out crowds in big stadiums, but is also broadcast weekly on TV to large audiences. It may seem incongruous to Western observers that devout Buddhists can take pride in such a violent sport. However, the love for *muay Thai* is not much different than the love many devout Christians in the United States have for boxing or football.

*Krabi-krabong*, or sword-fighting, is another popular martial-art sport in Thailand. Considered by some to be the origin of *muay Thai*, *krabi-kabong* may be more than 500 years old. Like its better-known descendant, it was used by Tai soldiers in close combat. However, unlike kickboxing, this martial art is based on weapons: the sword *(krabi)*, the quarter-staff *(plawng)*, the halberd *(ngao*—a staff with a blade on the end), a pair of short-swords *(daap sawng meu)*, and a pair of clubs *(mai sun-sawk)*.[13] Fight rituals and training for *krabi-krabong* are almost exactly the same as in *muay Thai*, although obviously greater care is required to avoid killing or seriously wounding an opponent with the weapons. *Krabi-kabong* is mostly seen in tourist venues, such as festivals, although it does generate a serious, international martial-arts following.

Another popular Thai sport is *takraw,* which is played with a small rattan ball. Teams, which vary in size, form a circle and then try to keep the ball up in the air with their feet and heads only. Points are scored for both length of time the ball is kept aloft and the style of their acrobatic moves. Variations of the game also use a volleyball net and basketball hoop. Boat racing, especially in the old Thai style, remains another common sport. Increasingly Thais are also showing interest in other more international sports like football (soccer), golf, badminton, and tennis. Thailand was even represented at the 2002 Olympic Winter Games at Salt Lake City, with a modest team of one in men's cross-country skiing.

### Hobbies

Kite flying is one of Thailand's biggest hobbies, with regular and seriously regarded competitions for design and skill held throughout the country. Along with rocketry, it has many fans, in part because of their association with the many celebrations and festivals Thailand enjoys. Other popular hobbies include singing, dancing, and music, as well as card games, chess, playing the lottery, and travel. In some places more exotic pastimes exist, like cockfighting, and even fish- and beetle fighting.[14] In a more familiar pastime, in October 2003 a Thai student, Panupol Sujjayakorn, won the 7th World Scrabble Championship. Golf has also become increasingly popular in the country, in part because of tourism and in part because of the success of Tiger Woods—whose mother is Thai.

### NOTES

1. Ruth Gerson, *Traditional Festivals in Thailand* (Kuala Lumpur: Oxford University Press, 1996), pp. 1–20.

2. Tanapol, *Essays on Thailand,* pp. 146–47.

3. Ibid., pp. 8–20, 118–36.

4. William L. Warren, *The Thais at Leisure* (Bangkok: Department of Export Production, Ministry of Commerce, 1988), pp. 40–44.

5. Royal White Elephants at *www.21cep.com/thai/eleph.htm.*

6. Ouan Maitree, "The Sao Intakil Festival," *Guidelines Magazine* 9/5 (May 2002): p. 14. See also, J.M. Cadet, "Safeguarding the Northern Capital," *Chiang Mai City Guide* 4/5 (May 2002): pp. 18–20.

7. Grand Festival Thailand Web site at *www.thailandgrandfestival.com/festival. asp?festID=22.*

8. Klausner, *Reflections on Thai Culture,* pp. 280–82. See also William Warren, *Bangkok* (London: Reaktion Books, 2002), pp. 122–31.

9. National Identity Board, *Thailand in the 2000s,* p. 166.

10. Ibid., pp. 165–66.

11. Ibid.

12. Foreign News Division, *Facets of Thai Cultural Life,* pp. 23–25. See also Cummings and Martin, *Lonely Planet: Thailand,* pp. 138–41.

13. Cummings and Martin, *Lonely Planet: Thailand,* pp. 140–41. See also International Krabi-Krabong Association Web site at *www.geocities.com/Colosseum/Dugout/5001.*

14. National Identity Board, *Thailand in the 2000s,* p. 91.

# 10

# Social Customs

## THAI ATTITUDES

Thai culture has many social customs that govern behavior, particularly in public settings. Some are very common to Western cultures as well, but a good deal more are not, and illustrate a number of practices and beliefs discussed in previous chapters. For the most part Thais are extremely tolerant of foreigners who are unfamiliar with their customs, so much so that travelers often forget they are in another country whose people have different ideas about personal conduct. For those foreigners who take the time to learn and follow Thai customs, a greater insight into the culture is gained, and most Thais will respond with obvious appreciation.

### The Monarchy and Buddhist Religion

Not surprisingly, given its importance to Thai society, there are particularly strict rules and social customs when it comes to the royal family. Any negative comments about the monarchy, even in jest, are taken very seriously. In fact, they can—and often do—lead to long terms in jail. This even extends to images of the royals. Purposely defacing Thai money (the currency is called *baht*) is also an offence, as it bears the picture of the king. In 2001 a Scottish national made the nearly fatal mistake of urinating on a picture of the king, which under Thai law carries the death penalty. Instead, he was deported after a jail term and much international embarrassment.[1] Similarly, in 1995 a French national onboard a Thai Airways International flight made derogatory comments about one of the princesses, and was promptly arrested and jailed

upon arrival in Bangkok. He was released only after a personal apology to the king. These rules also apply to all members of the royal family, who in addition to their Majesties King Bhumipol and Queen Sirikit include their three children—their Royal Highnesses Crown Prince Maha Vajiralongkorn, Princess Maha Chakri Sirindhorn, and Professor Dr. Princess Chulabhorn—as well as the king's elder sister Princess Galayani Vadhana of Narathivas. The king and queen's eldest child, Thanpuying Ubolratana Rajakanya, relinquished her title as Princess when she married an American.

In addition to the reverence Thai people have for the monarchy as an institution, there is also genuine love and respect for the royal family. Although his power is more symbolic than real, King Bhumipol has been at the center of Thai politics for over five decades. His intervention in the political crises of both 1973 and 1992 saved Thailand from potentially bloodier conflict, and he still today occasionally makes statements that have significant bearing on the Thai government. Moreover, he has demonstrated a real commitment to improving the welfare of the Thai people through a host of projects and reforms. There have been over 2,000 royal initiatives dealing with agriculture, the environment, water management, healthcare, communications, and employment. Some programs, such as the Hilltribe Development Project, have received international recognition from the United Nations, foreign countries, and nongovernmental organizations. The king's flood-control plans in the Northeast have improved the economy of that impoverished region, while his watershed and wildlife conservation projects have helped stop environmental degradation in many places. Queen Sirikit is also highly regarded for her work with rural women in Thailand. In 1988, she was awarded the Ceres Medal by the Food and Agriculture Organization of the United Nations and an Honorary Fellowship in Great Britain's prestigious Royal College of Physicians—the highest honor the college confers.[2]

The Thai royalty is bound by the centuries-old "10 Kingly Virtues" (*Thammasat* in Thai, or *Dhammasattha* in Pali), which lays out the principles of monarchial rule based on the giving of alms, morality, liberality, honesty, gentleness, self-restraint, nonanger, nonviolence, forbearance, and rectitude. During the rule of divine kings, the monarchy was considered to be the center of the universe, a belief that is symbolized today by the king's crown—tall, pointed, and gold-plated, it represents Mount Meru, the apex of the Buddhist cosmos. The king's right eye symbolizes the sun, his left eye the moon, and his arms and legs signify the four cardinal points of the earth. Although few Thais today consider the king a god, the reverence he commands is very real and an integral aspect of Thai culture.

It is also a serious violation to in any way defame the national flag or to insult the country. Thais are very patriotic, and are required to stand every

day at 8 A.M. and 6 P.M. to hear the country's national anthem, played throughout the country in all public places and on radio and television. Movie theaters also play the national anthem before every film, while showing a picture of the king, for which everyone is expected to stand. Such reverence does not, however, apply to the government, which can be and is criticized quite often. These freedoms are the product of fairly consistent and considerable political and legal reforms since the mid-1970s. Criticisms of the Buddhist *sangha* are also allowed, but many Thais refrain from this with a similar reverence they show the royal family. There have, however, been recent political and legal arguments raised about the *sangha*—many by the monks or former monks themselves—and whether or not its power and influence allow for true religious freedom.[3]

The monarchy, the Buddhist religion, and the Thai nation are the pillars of Thai cultural identity. Thai history has, for the most part, been traced exclusively through kings—without whom, it is stressed, there would be no Thai nation. As defender of the religion, the king acquires even greater importance, and as many scholars point out, he in effect becomes the moral construct around which "everything Thai" is built.[4] The king is seen as the highest moral good in the world, and the embodiment of all Thai values.

### Power and Class

Some scholars believe that Thai society is in many ways driven by power, social status, and prestige. This may in part stem from a reverence for tradition, especially when it comes to the monarchy and the *sangha*, which have long served as the pillars of Thai culture. It may also be based on respect for elders, and the emphasis placed on masculinity in the traditional family and village unit. More than anything, however, scholars believe that the stress on power and class in Thai society is based in Buddhist thought—in which the sense of duty and morality are deeply ingrained. Moral goodness is seen as a means of spiritual growth, ultimately helping achieve wisdom, inner peace, and eventually liberation from the burden of *dukkha*.[5] To be morally good, one needs to follow the tenets of Buddhism, which in turn reinforces tradition. Added to this is an emphasis on education, which is regarded as a definitive measure of success in Thai society.

Taken together, these values maintain and promote societal structures based on respect, reverence, obedience, kinship, and community. People in positions of power are considered to have achieved a greater degree of "moral goodness" and thus to be wiser. Similarly, wealth is often seen as an extension of moral power. Although perhaps odd to many outsiders, the Thai way of viewing class and power is not so unique. Implicitly or explicitly, most soci-

eties in the world—including those in the West—have different societal "ranks," as well as the traditions and structures to reinforce them. Westerners might consider Thais to be submissive or passive toward authority. However, most Thais see this behavior as being part of the cosmic order. Power and rank are still subject to *karma,* so that the boss in this life may not be the boss in the next. Many believe that people who abuse their position will in turn be abused by others in another existence. Similarly, some Thais accept their lower position or rank in part with the belief that in a previous life they may have abused their power.[6]

### Status and Language

Thai society is very hierarchical. This is reflected in many customs and even the language. Personal pronouns, like "I" or "you," are governed not only by the gender of the speaker, but of the person being spoken to or about. For men the pronoun "I" or "me" is *phom,* while for women it is *dii-chan.* Between family or close friends, the word *chan* is often used by both sexes. With more traditional Thais *ku* may be used by either sex if they think they are of lower status than the person they are speaking to. *Rao* is usually used for "we" in all circumstances.

Even more gradations appear when talking in the second person. Between family and lovers, the word "you" is *thoe* (pronounced *theu*). Speaking to or about someone of higher status, "you" becomes *thaan.* This could include monks and the elderly, especially if they are strangers. *Khun* is more widely used for "you" where the status of people is equal or unclear, as well as when the conversation is between or about most friends. *Kae* can also be used for close friends, but is usually reserved for speaking to or about children or servants. *Meung* is derogatory and is not widely used except to insult, traditionally referring to people of the lowest class and rank.

When speaking to monks who are also family members, "you" becomes *luang phi* for brothers and *luang pho* for father. *Luang pu* could be used for monks who are well-known, while *luang thera* is used for a monk who has become an elder. Monks themselves will use similar distinctions based on age and their seniority in the *sangha.* If one ever addresses or discusses the king, "you" becomes much formalized as *kha* (or *khrap* for men) *Phra Phuta Chao*—meaning roughly "his holiness the king." In circumstances where the person is very highly respected, such as royalty or senior monks, the personal pronoun for "I" also changes to *khrapphom* or *khadii-chan.*

Within a family setting, children follow simplified rules: all persons older than them are addressed as *phi*; those younger as *nong.* Where ages of the people are the same only names are used. In families this takes on an added

dimension, since in addition to the pronoun conventions mentioned above, elder family members are assigned specific names younger family members use to refer to them. Maternal grandmothers are called *yai,* while maternal grandfathers are *ta.* Paternal grandmothers become *ya* while paternal grandfathers are *pu.* An aunt older than the father or mother is known as *bee-pa.* An uncle older than either is *lung.* Paternal aunts and uncles who are younger than the father of the speaker are *ah,* or *na* if a younger sibling of the mother.[7]

## The *Wai*

Status and class are also reflected in the traditional Thai gesture, the *wai.* This is often used as a greeting, and therefore is taken by many foreigners to simply mean "hello." However, the *wai* is more complicated than that, and is probably best described as a "social action." There are many factors governing the giving and receiving of the *wai* including rank, age, and sex, but also involving height, the bowing of the head, and the specific context in which it occurs. The hands are held together, palm to palm, as if in prayer and kept close to the body, held in front of the neck, chin, or nose. Between equals, or when given to strangers of unclear status, the *wai* is at neck level and the head is kept straight. When directing the *wai* at someone of lower status, the hands are held lower and the head kept straight. When addressing a superior, the *wai* reaches the nose and the head and neck are slightly bent. Before monks the traditional *wai* is given by dropping to one's knees, sitting on the heels, and putting the hands ahead as you lower your head to the floor. Before images of the Buddha this should be done three times. Before royalty, the same *wai* is given, but tradition requires that the person does not raise his or her head at all. One of the most memorable and revealing episodes in recent Thai history was during the 1992 election riots, when the king summoned top politicians in an attempt to end the crisis. They appeared on national television prostrate before the king delivering the very traditional *wai.* In keeping with Thai custom, the king did not (and, with the exception of monks, never does) respond.

Returning the *wai* is also complicated by rules of rank. As it is usual for someone who is inferior to be the first to give the *wai,* the receiver must be careful in gauging a response. It is not generally used to say " thank you," and therefore is not traditionally given to people in everyday affairs. The *wai* is not, therefore, given to servants, children, people who sell you something, or a bus driver. Giving a *wai* to these people can be seen as insulting—a reminder or taunt about their lower status. Similarly, when returning a *wai* from someone of an inferior rank the hands must be held lower than theirs have been. Delivering a *wai* to someone in a position of authority can be an effective way to address a difficult situation, or get something favorable from a particular con-

text.[8] This being said, the use of the *wai* by foreigners is generally appreciated by all Thais, and seen more as a greeting and respectful gesture than a suggestion of rank and class. The origins of the *wai* are not entirely clear and are likely not even Thai, but some suggest that, like the Western handshake, it evolved as a way of showing one's enemy that one was not carrying a weapon.

As well as the privileges associated with high rank, it also carries certain obligations in social settings. The superior is expected to pay for everyone in the party when dining out; to refuse, or for someone more junior to pay, would be considered rude. Likewise, dividing up shares of the bill, even between equals, is considered miserly—Thai friends traditionally do not do this, since it is considered disrespectful toward the friendship. Similarly, women generally do not pay, or contribute to, the bill if dining out with men. Within families and small communities, people of higher social rank are also expected to look after and sponsor some of their juniors as a kind of adoptive uncle or aunt.

### Welcomes

Thais are very hospitable, and it is not uncommon for foreigners visiting the country to be invited by strangers into their homes for food. Friends and strangers alike consider the welcoming of guests to be an important demonstration of Thai culture. In rural communities, some villages still perform the *bai sii su kwan,* or welcome ceremony. This involves a village elder blessing and welcoming someone who has returned from a long journey. Increasingly it is also performed for tourists who arrive in the community. Village elders symbolically welcome the traveler with garlands of flowers and the tying of a white thread around their wrists, both of which symbolically connect them to the place. Food and festivities usually follow.

### Smiles and Laughter

Thailand is known as "the Land of Smiles." Although stereotypical, the "Thai smile" is a real phenomenon with a genuine social purpose. It is used as a part of a greeting, but also to diffuse a potentially difficult circumstances. In the face of aggression and anger, particularly if they come from foreigners, a smile is the first defense in the hope of warding off further problems. It is also used to save someone embarrassment should they do something unintentional like tripping in public. The smile is a way to ask forgiveness or beg one's pardon, and in return to forgive the mistake. Where giving the *wai* might be misconstrued as insulting, a smile is a better means of saying "thank you." Laughter is used in much the same way, particularly in circumstances where the potential for unintentional embarrassment is greater. It can be quite effective and dis-

Welcome ceremony (courtesy of Tourism Authority of Thailand).

arming, although perhaps unusual, for a foreigner to see people around them laughing after they have walked into a pole or fallen into the river.

### Body Language

Some of the most important Thai social customs stem from body language. In part this has to do with the Buddhist concept that the head is sacred, being closest to the heavens. In part it also comes from the animist belief that the head is where the spirit of the body rested, and disturbing it would cause the spirit to flee, bringing bad health. The feet are considered the lowest part of the body— being the most distant from the heavens—and from a more practical perspective, because they walk through the dirt. Touching someone else's head or pointing to it is considered extremely impolite. The only exceptions are when an elder pats the head of a small child, or what couples might do in private. Touching or pointing to the head of a Buddha image is sacrilegious. Sticking out the feet is also very rude. Crossing one's legs, very common in the West, can be considered offensive in Thailand—especially in the presence of elders, monks, or someone of higher status—because it extends or points with the feet. Keeping the feet on the ground, sitting on one's heels, or putting the legs to the side are the preferred Thai styles. A major offence is using the feet to point in someone's direction, or worse yet, to point to their head. Aiming one's feet at an image of Buddha is strictly taboo, and even foreigners are expected not to do so.

It is expected that one removes his or her shoes when entering a temple and that he or she sits or kneels so that the legs and feet do not point at Buddha. Still, it is not uncommon to see tourists standing or sitting before the Emerald Buddha with their legs and feet stretched out, before they are told to position themselves properly.

When addressing people of higher status, Thais will also make sure they are on a lower plane. When they are walking with an elder or someone senior in rank they will stay slightly behind. In very traditional families this even applies to married couples, with the man taking the lead. Body language also applies to stepping, as one must avoid putting one's feet on the threshold of a *wat* (and instead, step over it), walking over food, or stretching over seated people. Pointing and waving are generally not done, based on reverence for the hand movements and gestures of Buddha. Some Thais even make sure to use only their right hands to pass something, with the left supporting it under the elbow. As in many traditional Eastern cultures, the left hand is considered "dirty" and used only to clean oneself after bodily functions. Eating with the left hand is viewed with great disgust in this context.

Physical acts are also considered in the context of modesty. As noted in chapter 8, courting couples holding hands and kissing in public is very un-Thai, as is hugging, touching, and even dancing too close. The exceptions, of course, are when holding a small child, or when dealing with close friends of the same sex. Seeing women or men hold hands in public is not taboo, therefore, nor is it considered sexually suggestive, but rather a common sign of friendship.

One of the most important cultural taboos with respect to bodily contact deals with monks. Having renounced their worldly senses, monks are strictly prohibited from coming into contact with women. This extends even to a handshake or tap or on the arm. To give to or receive something from a woman, the object must be passed through an intermediary. In the same context, monks are also prohibited from touching money.

One's grooming and appearance are also taken as a sign of one's respect, not just for oneself but for the society and culture as a whole. As discussed in chapter 7, this means that clothes must be worn with much greater discretion than in the West, particularly in the *wat* or royal palaces. In keeping with such modesty, nudity is considered very offensive. It is Westerners who have turned some of Thailand's beaches "topless," despite the fact that Thais won't appear that way themselves. Many Thais wear shirts and shorts even when swimming or working in the heat rather than exposing their bodies. In part this is in keeping with modesty, and in part it comes from the belief that dark skin is a sign of lower status—indicative of someone who works outside in the sun. With this in mind it is common to see women wearing a white protec-

tive cream on their faces, or carrying an umbrella to block out at the sun. This belief is related more to considerations of social class, not race as it is known in the West. Westerners may consider this attitude racist, and of course, like in any other country in the world, racism does exist in Thailand. However, for the most part, Thais are very tolerant of different races.

## The Darker Side

Against these conservative sensibilities, many Westerners are shocked and confused about Thailand's unfortunate reputation for prostitution, corruption, and drugs. These issues are a troubling fact of life for some Thais, but represent a relatively small proportion of the population. As discussed in chapter 8, Thailand does have a relatively large sex trade. Women, of course, make up the majority of sex workers, but not all. Young boys, transsexuals, and transvestites are also involved. Many Thais blame prostitution and drugs on American influence, particularly during the Vietnam War when so many of the brothels, massage parlors, nightclubs, and drug pens opened up. While partly true, this simplistic assumption ignores problems within Thai society. Many sex workers see prostitution as a means to escape poverty. Although foreigners come from all over the world to take advantage of this situation, Thai men also keep much of the prostitution racket alive. In the same way Thai drug addicts make up a significant portion of users in the narcotics trade.

However, it is essential to keep in mind that these social ills are not illustrative of Thai people or their culture as a whole. They are of course also problems common to many other countries in the world, including those in the West—some of which have sex trades as large or larger than Thailand's. Moreover, it is important to note that unlike many societies, which prefer to totally ignore such problems, the Thais have taken an increasingly proactive stance. Many political and legal reforms have been aimed against corrupt authorities. Recently, and amid much controversy over civil rights and police conduct, the Thai government has cracked down hard on criminal groups and the drug trade. More positive has been international response to Thailand's AIDS awareness campaign, which has been praised for efforts to encourage the use of condoms. Even Buddhist monks have become involved in advocating safe sex. There is clearly much work to be done, but stereotypes about Thailand's darker side can be misleading.

## Anger and Aggression

Thai society is not without violence. As with any people, it exists in many different forms. However, in accordance with Buddhist principles most Thais

avoid emotional extremes, especially when it comes to anger. This is reinforced by the belief in reincarnation and the concept of *karma,* as well as by other dimensions of Thai culture, such as a respect for elders and those of higher status. All these ideas put emphasis on maintaining social order, and avoiding confrontation—what the Thais refer to as *jai yen,* or a "cool heart." As a result, behavior that is common in Western and other cultures is not so readily accepted in Thailand. Shouting or raising one's voice when angry is considered very rude. It forces a confrontation and does not allow the person being shouted at to maintain their sense of dignity, or as it is often called, "keeping face." Of course this is an idealistic approach, and many commentators on Thai society note that instead of expressing anger people suppress it, with often worse results. The Thais call this *prachot,* or masking one's feelings. Sometimes this takes the form of talking about an issue indirectly, through imaginary references or by speaking about oneself in the third person. Much more seriously, it can lead to acts of revenge in violence against property and people.[9] However, many Thais do believe that the cool heart can and should be maintained, especially when it comes to relatively minor matters. Some of the most common expressions in Thai reflect this belief, including *chai yen yen* (roughly, "calm down") and *mai pen rai* ("no problem" or "it's nothing").

This easy-going attitude extends to virtually all social settings. Someone acting stupid while drunk, for example, would be largely ignored at a party or function. Whereas most Westerners would be angry, annoyed, or embarrassed, Thais will likely do nothing—in part to avoid confrontation and in part to avoid having the person lose his or her dignity even more. The Thai sense of time is also shaped by this approach. It is not unusual for some Thais to be late for social and business engagements. This may have to do with Buddhist perceptions of impermanence and the transitory nature of life.[10] It may also have to do with the hot climate, which slows everything down, as some have speculated about similar attitudes in other tropical countries. Whatever the reason, Westerners can often be perplexed and frustrated by this relaxed attitude. However, as Thailand undergoes rapid social and economic changes, the *mai pen rai* concept may be seriously threatened.

## HUMOR

Thai humor as it appears in movies and on TV is based on the *likay* dance-theater tradition. Many characters and routines are essentially modern adaptations of this traditional form of entertainment. Both in the media and in everyday life, wit and clever use of the language are the key elements of humor. Wordplay, puns, and physical comedy are very popular, but increas-

ingly, political satire and other humorous commentary are common. Often Thai jokes are quite bawdy and full of innuendo. Overall Thais have a very broad and well-developed sense of humor. This is very much part of *sanuk,* or fun, and in keeping with the *jai yen,* or cool heart.

## Notes

1. Thai World View at *www.thaiworldview.com/society/day4.htm* (accessed December 2003).

2. National Identity Board, *Thailand into the 2000s,* pp. 42–57.

3. David Streckfuss and Mark Templeton, "Human Rights and Political Reform in Thailand," in McCargo, *Reforming Thai Politics,* pp. 73–87. See also Mulder, *Inside Thai Society,* pp. 92–109.

4. See, for example, Mulder, *Thai Images: The Culture of the Public World,* pp. 50–58.

5. Mulder, *Inside Thai Society,* pp. 35–40.

6. Robert L. Mole, *Thai Values and Behaviour Patterns* (Rutland, VT: Charles E. Tuttle, 1973), pp. 68–70.

7. Thai World View, at *www.thaiworldview.com/family.htm* (accessed December 2003).

8. Cooper and Cooper, *Culture Shock!,* pp. 1–15.

9. Klausner, *Reflections on Thai Culture,* pp. 78–85, 245–49.

10. Ibid., pp. 322–27.

# Appendix:
# Thailand's Modern-Era Kings

**(Bangkok Kingdom, Chakri Dynasty only)**

| | |
|---|---|
| Phra Phutthayofta (Chaophraya Chakri or Rama I) | April 1782 to September 1809 |
| Phra Phuttaloetla (Rama II) | September 1809 to July 1824 |
| Phra Nangklao (Rama III) | July 1824 to April 1851 |
| Mongkut (Rama IV) | April 1851 to October 1868 |
| Chulalongkorn (Rama V) | October 1868 to October 1910 |
| Vajiravudh (Rama VI) | October 1910 to November 1925 |
| Prajadhipok (Rama VII) | November 1925 to March 1935* |
| Ananda (Rama VIII) | March 1935 to June 1946 |
| Bhumipol (Rama IX) | June 1946 to present** |

*abdicated the throne
**Coronation held May 1950
(Source: Wyatt, *Thailand: A Short History*, p. 313.)

# Glossary

**Anantanagaraj**  fearsome sea-serpent; name of royal barge
**anatta**  Buddhist concept of egolessness
**annica**  Buddhist concept of impermanence
**arupadhadtu**  world of absence of form in Buddhist cosmology
**Asaanha Buuchaa**  major Buddhist holiday
**Atthangika-Magga (or Magga)**  Buddhist concept of the Eight-Fold Path
**Ayutthaya**  Tai empire (14th–18th centuries)
**bai sii su kwan**  traditional welcome ceremony
**bhikkhuni**  an ancient order of female Buddhist monks
**Bodhisattvas**  Buddhist "beings of wisdom," and "Buddha-to-be"
**Boon Bang Fai**  Rocket Festival
**bot (or uposatha)**  consecrated chapel in Thai temple *(wat)*
**Brahma**  Hindu god of creation
**Brahmins**  Hindu priest caste
**bua laj**  type of Thai musical composition (for royalty)
**buat phra**  ordination ceremony
**bun**  merit
**chada**  traditional Thai headdress
**chakchak wongwong**  genre of Thai folklore
**Chak Phra**  Buddhist ceremony ("pulling of the Buddha")
**chakhe**  Thai floor zither
**chakra**  Indian symbol symbolizing the universe
**Chao fa**  princes born to royal mothers
**Chao**  princes
**chap-lek**  large Thai cymbals
**chattra**  an Indian symbol signifying the power of the heavens
**chedi (or stupa)**  towers symbolizing power at Thai *wat*

**ching**  Thai cymbals

**chofa**  architectural feature of a roof apex

**chula**  special kite (shaped like a large star)

**Chularajamontri**  the state counsellor for Muslim affairs in Thailand

**devaraja (or thammaraat)**  concept that kings are divine

**Dhamma**  Buddhist concept of truth

**dontrii Thai**  traditional Thai music (classical)

**dontrii**  music

**Dukkha**  Buddhist concept of pain and suffering

**Dvaravati**  ancient Southeast Asian civilization

**Erawan**  elephant of the god Indra in Hindu mythology

**Farang**  foreigners

**Farangset**  French

**Fon Phu Thai**  traditional dance of the Northeast

**Gandharavas**  "heavenly musicians" of Buddhist mythology

**Ganesha**  Hindu god of wisdom

**Garuda**  in Hindu and Buddhist mythology, a giant bird

**ham yon**  "magical testicles"—curved designs to ward off evil

**Hanuman**  monkey god hero of the *Ramakian*

**has klawng**  bell tower at Thai temple *(wat)*

**haw phii wat (or san phra phuum)**  spirit houses

**haw trai**  library at Thai temple *(wat)*

**Hinayana**  term for Theravada, meaning "lesser vehicle"

**hong**  in Thai mythology, a swan creature

**Hun Krabok**  Thai puppetry show

**Indra**  Hindu supreme god

**Issaan**  Northeastern Thailand

**Jataka (or chaa-dok)**  tales of Buddha's past lives

**kaafae thom (or kaafae thung)**  coffee

**kaeng khieu wan kai**  green chicken curry

**kaeng**  curry

**kala**  in Hindu and Buddhist mythology, demon-animals

**kalae**  Northern-styled house

**Kamadhatu**  "World of Desire" in Buddhist cosmology

**kha**  syllable used in polite speech (by women) designating respect for the person
  addressed

**khaen**  Thai instrument—a kind of harmonica/flute

**khao nio ma muang**  sticky rice with coconut cream

**khao nio**  sticky rice

**Khao Phansaa**  major Buddhist holiday

**khao plao (or khao suay)**  plain white (jasmine) rice

**khao**  rice

**Kharma**  concept that acts in life affect reincarnation

**khin khao**  expression, "to eat rice"

**khlong khaek**  Indian drums

**khlong Marigan**  American drums

**khlong that**  type of Thai drum

**khlong**  canal; also type of Thai drum

**khlui**  Thai flutes

**Khmer**  ancient Southeast Asian civilization

**khoi**  type of bush used in earlier times to make paper

**Khon**  Thai dance-drama and name of masks used

**khong mon**  type of Thai gong set

**khong rao**  cymbals played on a rack

**khrap**  syllable used in polite speech (by men) designating respect for the person addressed

**khraung sai**  type of Thai musical ensemble

**khruang lang khong khlang**  amulet

**khruang muk**  process of design in mother-of-pearl inlay

**khruang thom**  nielloware

**khu ek**  kickboxing match

**khunnang**  nobles

**khwan**  spirit or soul

**khwang wong**  type of Thai gong set

**kinnari**  half-woman and half-bird creature in Thai mythology

**kirimukha (or simhamukha)**  demon animal *(kala)* seen frequently in Thai art and architecture

**klang**  medium size

**kluey buah chee**  bananas and palm sugar dessert

**krajappi**  Thai lute-guitar

**Krathong**  boat made of banana leaves

**Krishna**  eighth reincarnation of god Vishnu in Hindu mythology

**kuti**  residences of the monks at Thai temple *(wat)*

**lai kud**  type of design style in lacquerware

**lai rot nam**  type of design style in lacquerware

**Lakhon**  Thai dance-drama

**lakshanas**  artistic images of the Buddha

**Lan Na**  northern Tai kingdom (13th–18th centuries)

**lek**  small size

**Likay**  Thai dance-comedy-opera

**look thung**  "up-country" Thai music

**Loy Krathong**  major festival

**Loy**  to float

**Maakha Buuchaa**  major Buddhist holiday

**mae chii**  female Buddhist monastic order

**Maha Jataka**  "Great Life" *jataka*

**Mahanikai**  sect of Thai Buddhist monks

**Mahathat**  designates a temple *(wat)* that holds relics of Buddha

**Mahathera Samakhom**    Supreme Council for the Buddhist order in Thailand

**Mahayana**    type of Buddhism

**mahori**    type of Thai musical ensemble

**Maitreya**    future Buddha

**Manohraa (or nora)**    Thai dance-drama

**mantras**    incantations

**Mara**    in Buddhism and Hinduism an evil god, like Satan

**maravijaya**    artistic depictions of Buddha sitting

**maun raung haj**    type of Thai singing (for funerals)

**mo phii**    ghost doctors

**molam**    musical genre from Northeastern Thailand

**Mon**    ancient peoples of Burma and Thailand

**mondop**    cube-shaped building with pyramidal top at a temple *(wat)*

**mong**    Thai gong

**Mt. Meru**    the center of Buddhist cosmology

**Muang Tai**    "Land of the Free"

**muay Thai**    kickboxing

**Muchalinda**    in Buddhist mythology, a serpent king

**mudras**    artistic depictions of Buddha's hand gestures

**muk fai**    type of snail

**naa phat**    type of Thai melody

**naam manao**    lime drink

**naang hong**    type of Thai musical composition (for funerals)

**Naga (or Nak)**    sea serpent in Hindu and Buddhist mythology

**nak muay**    kick-boxer

**nak-puggsee**    part-bird, part-snake creature in Thai mythology

**nam phrik pao**    spicy condiment made from chilies

**nam plaa**    fermented fish sauce

**nam satay**    peanut sauce

**Nan Talung**    Thai puppetry show

**Nan Yai**    Thai puppetry show

**Nan-Chao**    ancient kingdom, southwest China

**nang itcha**    female soap-opera character

**nang kwak**    female spirit of good fortune

**nang thepi**    in Buddhist mythology, heavenly beings (female)

**nangsu khien**    manuscript illustrations

**nen**    young apprentice Monk

**ngao**    special kite in the form of a bird with bamboo pipes

**Nirvana (or Nibbana)**    Buddhist concept of the state of absolute truth

**Ohk Phansaa**    Buddhist holiday

**pad thai**    rice noodle dish

**Pagan**    ancient Southeast Asian civilization

**pakpao**    special kite (a bird with long tails)

**Pali**    ancient Indic language used in Buddhist scriptures

**Panna**   Buddhist concept of wisdom

**panorn maruek**   half-human, half-monkey creature in Thai mythology

**panung**   cloths used in Royal Plowing Ceremony

**pasin**   Thai traditional dress (women)

**phakaoma**   traditional multi-purpose cloth worn by men

**phat phak bung**   stir-fried morning glory vines

**Phii Ta Khon**   Ghost Festival

**phii ton mai**   ghosts of the tree

**phii**   ghosts

**phin**   plucked instruments

**phin**   type of Thai guitar

**phleen Jippun**   Japanese music

**phleng anchoen**   invitation song sung in agricultural rituals

**phleng diaw**   instrumental solo in Thai musical composition

**phleng hae nak**   celebration song sung at ordination ceremonies

**phleng luuk thung**   pop music

**phleng raung**   Thai musical suites

**phleng reo**   fast-paced musical suites

**phleng ryang**   type of Thai musical composition

**phleng Thai saakon**   Western music with Thai lyrics

**Phra Kaew Morakot**   the Emerald Buddha

**phra khruang**   amulets with the Buddha's image

**Phra ong Chao**   princes born to common mothers

**Phra That**   designates a temple *(wat)* that holds Buddhist relics

**Phra**   honorary title used for monks

**phrai**   commoners

**phuyaiban**   village head or leader

**pii**   type of Thai woodwind instrument

**pii-phat**   type of Thai musical ensemble

**plaa pao**   grilled fish

**Poi Sang Long**   regional festival in Northern Thailand

**pra bot**   classical Thai paintings on banners of cloth

**prang**   Khmer tower

**prasat**   Khmer temple

**Prathet Thai**   "Country of the Free"

**prop kai**   slow-paced musical suites

**raan kuaytlaw**   noodle shops

**Raek Na**   Royal Plowing Ceremony

**Rahula**   the son and first disciple of the historical Buddha

**rajasi**   flaming lion-like creature in Thai mythology

**rak yai**   type of tree

**Rama**   title and name of Thai kings and figure from the *Ramakian*

*Ramakian*   Thai version of the *Ramayana*

*Ramayana*   ancient Hindu poetic drama

**rammana**   Thai instrument like a tambourine without jangles

**ranaat-ek**   type of Thai xylophone

**Ratanakosin**   modern Siamese empire based at Bangkok

**Ravana (or Tosakanth)**   evil demon-god of the *Ramakian*

**ruan**   house

**Rupadhatu**   world of form in Buddhist cosmology

**saala**   lecture halls at Thai temple *(wat)*

**sai monkon**   white thread used in wedding ceremony

**Sakyamuni**   Buddha's title as a historical figure

**Samadhi**   Buddhist concept of concentration

**samuk**   coating used in lacquerware

**sang chat**   "new nation"

**sangha**   Buddhist priesthood

**sangkhaya**   steamed coconut dessert

**Sanskrit**   ancient Indic language used in Buddhist scriptures

**sanuk**   the Thai concept of fun

**Sao Ching Cha**   giant swing of Brahman order in Bangkok

**Sao Intakil**   Hindu-Buddhist festival

**Sayam**   ancient Sanskrit word for Tai lands

**seepha mahori**   type of Thai musical composition

**Shiva**   Hindu god of destruction

**Sian (or Siao)**   early Portuguese term for Siam

**Sila**   five precepts of Buddhism

**Singha**   lion creature in Thai mythology

**sin-sod**   money given by the groom to the bride's parents

**Sita**   wife of Rama and a central figure from the *Ramakian*

**Skandhas**   Buddhist concept of dimensions to the human mind

**so sam sai**   Thai stringed instrument

**song mai**   medium-paced musical suites

**Songkran**   traditional Thai New Year

**Souvannaphoum**   "golden lands"

**Srivijaya**   ancient Southeast Asian civilization

**sua phra ratchathan**   traditional short- or long-sleeved shirt (men)

**Sukhavati**   Buddhist concept of "other worlds"

**Sukhothai**   central Tai kingdom (13th–15th centuries)

**Suphanahong**   golden swan ridden by the god Brahma in Hindu mythology

**sura**   kind of liquor

**Sutras**   Buddhist traditional texts

**takraw**   game played with a rattan ball

**talaat naam**   floating market

**talaat toh rung**   night markets

**talaat**   market

**Tanha**   Buddhist concept of want

**tao kin phak bung**   longest Thai musical suite

**ta-phon**   two-headed Thai drum

**Tavatsima**   Buddhist heaven with many Hindu gods

**thaan khao laew reu yang**   expression, "have you eaten rice yet?"

**thaang**   school of thought in Thai music

**tham khwan sam wan**   ceremony held at birth

**Thammayut**   sect of Thai Buddhist monks

**that kraduk**   small funeral tower (*chedi*) at temple (*wat*)

**Thawt Kathin**   Buddhist ceremony ("laying down the robes")

**thera**   Buddhist elders

**Theravada**   form of Buddhism that the majority of Thais follow

**thon**   single-headed Thai drum

*Tipitaka*   primary Buddhist canon, comprising the earliest-surviving Buddhist writings

**Tiratana**   the "Triple Gems" (or elements) of Thai Buddhism

**tom yum goong**   sour lime and seafood soup

**Tosachat**   "Ten Great *Jatakas*"

**Traibhumi Phra Ruang**   another name for the *Tribhumikatha*

*Tribhumikatha*   Thai Buddhist treatise on cosmology

**Trikaya**   Buddhist heaven

**Truut Jiin**   Chinese New Year (in Thai)

**tuk-tuk**   three-wheeled taxis famous in Thailand

**ushnisha**   in depictions of Buddha, the flame on top of his head

**vajrasena**   depictions of sitting Buddha with feet upward

**Vajrayana (or Tantric)**   type of Buddhism

**Vassakan**   Hindu god of rain

**Vinaya Pitaka**   vows of monastic service

**virasena**   depictions of sitting Buddha with legs crossed

**Vishnu**   Hindu god of preservation or creation

**wai khruu**   ceremony performed to honor teachers

**wai**   traditional greeting and sign of respect

**wan-nii**   today

**wat**   Buddhist temples in Thailand

**Wessandon Jataka**   one of the *jatakas,* about the virtue of giving

**wihaan (or vihara)**   building where sacred objects are kept at Thai temple (*wat*)

**Wisaakha Buuchaa**   major Buddhist holiday

**Xoe (or sap)**   Thai dance with bamboo sticks

**yai**   large size

**Yakkhas**   demons or monsters in Buddhist mythology

**yam (or laap)**   spicy meat salad

**yam ma muang**   green mango salad

# Suggested Reading

## GENERAL INFORMATION AND HISTORY

Cummings, Joe and Steve Martin. *Lonely Planet: Thailand,* 9th edition. Melbourne: Lonely Planet Publications, 2001.

Fineman, Daniel. *A Special Relationship: The United States and Military Government in Thailand, 1947–1958.* Honolulu: University of Hawaii Press, 1997.

Hewison, Kevin, ed. *Political Change in Thailand.* London: Routledge, 1997.

Keyes, Charles F. *Thailand: Buddhist Kingdom as Modern Nation-State.* Boulder, CO: Westview Press, 1987.

Keyes, Charles F. *The Golden Peninsula: Culture and Adaptation in Mainland Southeast Asia.* Honolulu: University of Hawaii Press, 1995.

McCargo, Duncan, ed. *Reforming Thai Politics.* Copenhagen: Nordic Institute of Asian Studies, 2002.

Pasuk Phongpaichit and Chris Baker. *Thailand: Economy and Politics.* Kuala Lumpur: Oxford University Press, 1995.

Randolph, R. Sean. *The United States and Thailand: Alliance Dynamics 1950–85.* Berkeley: Institute of East Asian Studies, University of California Berkeley, 1986.

Rong Syamananda. *A History of Thailand.* Bangkok: Chulalongkorn University, 1986.

Smithies, Michael, ed. *Descriptions of Old Siam.* Oxford: Oxford University Press, 1995.

Tongchai Winichakul. *Siam Mapped: A History of the Geo-Body of a Nation.* Honolulu: University of Hawaii Press, 1994.

Wyatt, David K. *Thailand: A Short History.* New Haven, CT: Yale University Press, 1982.

## THOUGHT AND RELIGION

Gehan Wijeyewardene and E.C. Chapman. *Patterns and Illusions: Thai History and Thought.* Canberra: Richard Davis Fund and Australian National University, 1993.

Hawkins, Bradley K. *Buddhism.* London: Routledge, 1999.

Hazra, Kanai Lai. *Thailand: Political History and Buddhist Cultural Influences,* vol. 2: *Buddhism and its Influence on Thai Culture.* New Delhi: Decent Nooks, 2000.

Ishii, Yoneo. *Sanga, State and Society: Thai Buddhism in History.* Honolulu: University of Hawaii Press, 1986.

Klausner, William J. *Reflections on Thai Culture.* Bangkok: Siam Society, 1981.

Lowenstein, Tom. *The Vision of the Buddha: Buddhism—the Path to Spiritual Enlightenment.* London: Duncan Baird, 2000.

Mulder, Niels. *Inside Thai Society: Religion, Everyday Life, Change.* Chiang Mai: Silkworm Books, 2000.

Reynolds, Craig J. *National Identity and Its Defenders: Thailand 1939–1989.* Clayton, Australia: Centre of Southeast Asian Studies, Monash University, 1991.


## LITERATURE

Kepner, Susan Fulop, ed. *The Lioness in Bloom: Modern Thai Fiction about Women.* Berkeley: University of California Press, 1996.

M.L. Jumsai Manich. *History of Thai Literature,* 3rd edition. Bangkok: Chalermnit Press, 2000.

Phillips, Herbert P. *Modern Thai Literature.* Honolulu: University of Hawaii Press, 1987.

Siraporn Nathalang, ed. *Thai Folklore: Insights into Thai Culture.* Bangkok: Chulalongkorn University Press, 2000.

Wenk, Klaus. *Thai Literature: An Introduction.* Bangkok: White Lotus Press, 1995.


## THEATER, DANCE, MUSIC, AND FILM

Mattani Rutnin. *Dance, Drama, and Theatre in Thailand: The Process of Development and Modernization.* Chiang Mai: Silkworm Books, 1996.

Morton, David. *The Traditional Music of Thailand.* Berkeley: University of California Press, 1976.

Myers-Moro, Pamela. *Thai Music and Musicians in Contemporary Bangkok.* Berkeley: University of California Press, 1993.


## ART

Apinan Poshyananda. *Modern Art in Thailand: Nineteenth and Twentieth Centuries.* Singapore: Oxford University Press, 1992.

Boisseler, Jean. *Thai Painting.* Tokyo: Kodansha International, 1976.

Fisher, Robert E. *Buddhist Art and Architecture*. London: Thames and Hudson, 1993.

No Nak Paknam. *Form and Continuity in Thai Art and Culture*. Bangkok: Muang Boran, 1987.

Phillips, Herbert P. *The Integrative Art of Modern Thailand*. Berkeley: Lowie Museum, University of California, Berkeley, 1992.

Santi Leksukhum. *Temples of Gold: Seven Centuries of Thai Buddhist Paintings*. New York: George Braziller, 2000.

Stratton, Carol, and Miriam McNair Scott, eds. *The Art of Sukhothai: Thailand's Golden Age*. Kuala Lumpur: Oxford University Press, 1981.

## ARCHITECTURE AND DESIGN

Aasen, Clarence T. *Architecture of Siam: A Cultural History Interpretation*. Kuala Lumpur: Oxford University Press, 1998.

Anuvit Charernsupkul. *The Elements of Thai Architecture*. Bangkok: Karn Pim Satri Sarn, 1978.

Ringis, Rita. *Thai Temples and Temple Murals*. Singapore: Oxford University Press, 1990.

Warren, William L and Luca Invernizzi Tettoni. *Living in Thailand: Traditional and Modern Homes and Decoration*. London: Thames and Hudson, 1988.

## CUISINE AND TRADITIONAL DRESS

Alford, Jeffrey, and Naomi Duguid. *Hot Sour Salty Sweet: A Culinary Journey Through Southeast Asia*. New York: Artisan, 2000.

Panurat Poladitmontri. *Thailand: The Beautiful Cookbook*. Toronto: HarperCollins Canada, 1992.

Soloman, Charmaine. *The Complete Asian Cookbook*. Vancouver: Raincoast Books, 1992.

Thompson, David. *Thai Food*. Toronto: Ten Speed Press, 2002.

## GENDER, COURTSHIP, AND MARRIAGE

Blackburn, Susan, ed. *Love, Sex and Power: Women in Southeast Asia*. Monash, Australia: Monash Asia Institute, 2001.

Ghosh, Chitra. *The World of Thai Women*. Calcutta: Best Books, 1990.

## FESTIVALS AND FUN

Gerson, Ruth. *Traditional Festivals in Thailand*. Kuala Lumpur: Oxford University Press, 1996.

Thanapol Chadchaidee. *Essays on Thailand*, 10th edition. Bangkok: Thanapol Vittayakarn, 1994.

## SOCIAL CUSTOMS

Amara Pongsapich, ed. *Traditional and Changing Thai World View.* Bangkok: Chula-
    longkorn University Press, 1998.
Mulder, Niels. *Inside Thai Society: Religion, Everyday Life, Change.* Chiang Mai: Silk-
    worm Books, 2000.
Sukphisit Suthon. *Folk Arts and Folk Culture: The Vanishing Face of Thailand.*
    Bangkok: Post Books, 1997.
Thanapol Chadchaidee. *Essays on Thailand,* 10th edition. Bangkok: Thanapol Vit-
    tayakarn, 1994.

# Bibliography

Aasen, Clarence T. *Architecture of Siam: A Cultural History Interpretation*. Kuala Lumpur: Oxford University Press, 1998.

Alford, Jeffrey, and Naomi Duguid. *Hot Sour Salty Sweet: A Culinary Journey Through Southeast Asia*. New York: Artisan, 2000.

Amara Pongsapich, ed. *Traditional and Changing Thai World View*. Bangkok: Chulalongkorn University Press, 1998.

Anderson, Benedict R. O'G, ed. *In the Mirror: Literature and Politics in Siam in the American Era*. Bangkok: Editions Duang Kamol, 1985.

Anuvit Charernsupkul. *The Elements of Thai Architecture*. Bangkok: Karn Pim Satri Sarn, 1978.

Apinan Poshyananda. *Modern Art in Thailand: Nineteenth and Twentieth Centuries*. Singapore: Oxford University Press, 1992.

*Bangkok Post*. Web site at *www.bangkokpost.com*.

Bickner, Robert J. *An Introduction to the Thai Poem "Lilit Phra Law" (The Story of King Law)*. Dekalb: Northern Illinois University, 1991.

Blackburn, Susan, ed. *Love, Sex and Power: Women in Southeast Asia*. Clayton, Australia: Monash Asia Institute, Monash University, 2001.

Bofman, Theodora Helene. *The Poetics of the Ramakian*. Dekalb: Northern Illinois University, 1984.

Boisseler, Jean. *Thai Painting*. Tokyo: Kodansha International, 1976.

Bowie, Theodore, ed. *The Arts of Thailand*. Indianapolis: Indiana University Press, 1960.

Brown, Robert L., ed. *Art From Thailand*. Mumbai: Marg Publications, 1999.

——— *The Dvaravati Wheels of Law and the Indianization of Southeast Asia*. Leiden: E.J. Brill, 1996.

Buddhist Studies Dharma Education Association, *Basic Buddhism Guide*, at *www.buddhanet.net/e-learning/basic-guide.htm*

Cadet, J.M. "Safeguarding the Northern Capital," *Chiang Mai City Guide* 4/5 (May 2002): pp. 18–20.

———. *The Ramakien: The Thai Epic.* Tokyo: Kodansha International, 1971.

Center for Southeast Asian Studies, Northern Illinois University, introduction to the *Ramakian* at *www.seasite.niu.edu/Thai/literature/ramakian/introduction.htm*

Chalk, Peter. "Separatism and Southeast Asia: The Islamic Factor in Southern Thailand, Mindanao, and Aceh," *Studies in Conflict and Terrorism* 24 (summer 2001), pp. 241–69.

Cooper, Robert and Nanthapa Cooper. *Culture Shock!: Thailand—and How to Survive It.* Singapore: Times Books International, 1982; revised as *Culture Shock!: Thailand,* Portland, OR: Graphic Arts Center, 1996.

Cummings, Joe and Steve Martin. *Lonely Planet: Thailand,* 9th edition. Melbourne: Lonely Planet Publications, 2001.

Cummings, Joe, *Thai Phrasebook.* Melbourne: Lonely Planet Publications, 1984.

Dixon, Chris. *The Thai Economy: Uneven Development and Internationalization.* London: Routledge, 1998.

Dumarcay, Jacques and Michael Smithies. *Cultural Sites of Burma, Thailand, and Cambodia.* Kuala Lumpur: Oxford University Press, 1995.

Durrenberger, Paul E., ed. *State Power and Culture in Thailand.* New Haven, CT: Yale University Press, 1996.

Englehart, Neil A. *Culture and Power in Traditional Siamese Government.* Ithaca, NY: Cornell University Press, 2001.

Faurot, Jeannette, ed. *Asian-Pacific Folktales and Legends.* New York: Simon and Schuster, 1995.

*Far Eastern Economic Review* (Hong Kong). Website at *www.feer.com*

Fineman, Daniel. *A Special Relationship: The United States and Military Government in Thailand, 1947–1958.* Honolulu: University of Hawaii Press, 1997.

Fisher, Robert E. *Buddhist Art and Architecture.* London: Thames and Hudson, 1993.

Foreign News Division. *Facets of Thai Cultural Life.* Bangkok: Government Public Relations Department, Office of the Prime Minister, 1984.

Freeman, Michael. *Temples of Thailand: Their Form and Function.* Bangkok: Asia Books, 1991.

Gehan Wijeyewardene and E.C. Chapman. *Patterns and Illusions: Thai History and Thought.* Canberra: Richard Davis Fund and Australian National University, 1993.

Gerson, Ruth. *Traditional Festivals in Thailand.* Kuala Lumpur: Oxford University Press, 1996.

Ghosh, Chitra. *The World of Thai Women.* Calcutta: Best Books, 1990.

Ginsburg, Henry. *Thai Art and Culture: Historic Manuscripts from Western Collections.* London: British Library, 2000.

———. *Thai Manuscript Painting.* London: British Library, 1989.

Goodman, Jim. "High Fashion, Hill Style," *Sawasdee Magazine* 26/8 (November 1996): pp. 32–35.

Gosling, Betty. *A Chronology of Religious Architecture at Sukhothai, Late Thirteenth to Early Fifteenth Century.* Ann Arbor, MI: Association for Asian Studies, 1996.

————. *Sukhothai: Its History, Culture, and Art.* Singapore: Oxford University Press, 1991.

*Guidelines Magazine* (Chiang Mai). Email *guidelin@loxinfo.co.th* for information.

Hanks, Jane Richardson and Lucien Mason Hanks. *Tribes of the North Thailand Frontier.* New Haven, CT: Southeast Asia Studies, Yale University, 2001.

Harvey, Peter, ed. *Buddhism.* London: Continuum, 2001.

Haseman, John B. *The Thai Resistance Movement During World War II.* Chiang Mai: Silkworm Books, 2002.

Hawkins, Bradley K. *Buddhism.* London: Routledge, 1999.

Hazra, Kanai Lai. *Thailand: Political History and Buddhist Cultural Influences,* vol. 2: *Buddhism and its Influence on Thai Culture.* New Delhi: Decent Nooks, 2000.

Hewison, Kevin, ed. *Political Change in Thailand.* London: Routledge, 1997.

Higham, Charles and Rachanie Thosarat. *Prehistoric Thailand: From Early Settlement to Sukhothai.* London: Thames and Hudson, 1998.

Hong, Lysa. "Of Consorts and Harlots in Thai Popular History," *Journal of Asian Studies* 57/2 (May 1998): pp. 333–53.

Hoskin, John, "The Subtle Art of Casting Sacred Statues," *Sawasdee Magazine* 31/6 (June 2002): pp. 29–33.

Ingersoll, Fern S. (translator). *Sang Thong: A Dance-Drama from Thailand.* Rutland, VT: Charles E. Tuttle, 1973.

Ishii, Yoneo. *Sanga, State and Society: Thai Buddhism in History.* Honolulu: University of Hawaii Press, 1986.

Kartomi, Margaret J. "'Traditional Music Weeps' and Other Themes in the Discourse of Music, Dance and Theatre of Indonesia, Malaysia, and Thailand," *Journal of Southeast Asian Studies* 26 (September 1995): pp. 366–400.

Kepner, Susan Fulop, ed. *The Lioness in Bloom: Modern Thai Fiction About Women.* Berkeley: University of California Press, 1996.

Keyes, Charles F. *Thailand: Buddhist Kingdom as Modern Nation-State.* Boulder, CO: Westview Press, 1987.

————. *The Golden Peninsula: Culture and Adaptation in Mainland Southeast Asia.* Honolulu: University of Hawaii Press, 1995.

Kislenko, Arne. "Bending With the Wind: The Continuity and Flexibility of Thai Foreign Policy," *International Journal* 17 (Autumn 2002): pp. 537–61.

————. "The Vietnam War, Thailand, and the United States," in Richard Jensen, Jon Davidann, and Yoneyuki Sugita, eds. *Trans-Pacific Relations: America, Europe, and Asia in the Twentieth Century,* Westport, CT: Praeger Publishers, 2003.

Klausner, William J. *Reflections on Thai Culture.* Bangkok: Siam Society, 1981.

Klima, Alan. *The Funeral Casino: Meditation, Massacre, and Exchange with the Dead in Thailand.* Princeton, NJ: Princeton University Press, 2002.

Kornfield, Jack, ed. *Buddha's Little Instruction Book.* New York: Bantam Books, 1994.

Levinson, David and Karen Christensen, eds. *Encyclopedia of Modern Asia.* New York: Charles Scribner's Sons, 2002.

Likhit Dhiravegin. *Demi-Democracy: The Evolution of the Thai Political System.* Singapore: Times Academic Press, 1992.

Lintner, Bertil. *Burma in Revolt: Opium and Insurgency Since 1948.* Chiang Mai: Silkworm Books, 1999.

Lowenstein, Tom. *The Vision of the Buddha: Buddhism—the Path to Spiritual Enlightenment.* London: Duncan Baird, 2000.

Matics, K.I. *Introduction to the Thai Mural.* Bangkok: White Lotus Press, 1992.

Mattani Rutnin. *Dance, Drama, and Theatre in Thailand: The Process of Development and Modernization.* Chiang Mai: Silkworm Books, 1996.

———, ed. *The Siamese Theatre.* Bangkok: The Siam Society, 1975.

McCargo, Duncan, ed. *Reforming Thai Politics.* Copenhagen: Nordic Institute of Asian Studies, 2002.

McCoy, Alfred. *The Politics of Heroin: CIA Complicity in the Global Drug Trade* (revised edition). Chicago: Lawrence Hill, 1992.

McVey, Ruth. *Money and Power in Provincial Thailand.* Honolulu: University of Hawaii Press, 2000.

Miller, Terry E. and Sam-Ang Sam. "The Classical Musics of Cambodia and Thailand: A Study of Distinctions," *Ethnomusicology* 39 (Spring/Summer 1995): pp. 229–43.

Mitchell, Donald W. *Buddhism: Introducing the Buddhist Experience.* New York: Oxford University Press, 2002.

M.L. Jumsai Manich. *History of Thai Literature,* 3rd edition. Bangkok: Chalermnit Press, 2000.

Moore, Elizabeth H. *Ancient Capitals of Thailand.* London: Thames and Hudson, 1996.

Morton, David. *The Traditional Music of Thailand.* Berkeley: University of California Press, 1976.

Mulder, Niels. *Everyday Life in Thailand.* Bangkok: Editions Duang Kamol, 1985.

———. *Inside Thai Society: Religion, Everyday Life, Change.* Chiang Mai: Silkworm Books, 2000.

———. *Thai Images: The Culture of the Public World.* Chiang Mai: Silkworm Books, 1997.

Myers-Moro, Pamela. "Thai Music and Attitudes Towards the Past," *Journal of American Folklore* 102/404 (Spring 1989): pp. 190–94.

———. *Thai Music and Musicians in Contemporary Bangkok.* Berkeley: University of California Press, 1993.

Naengnoi Suksri and Michael Freeman. *Palaces of Bangkok: Royal Residences of the Chakri Dynasty.* New York: River Books, 1996.

National Identity Board. *Thailand into the 2000s.* Bangkok: Office of the Prime Minister, 2000.

———. *Women in Thai Literature,* book 1. Bangkok: Office of the Prime Minister, 1992.

No Nak Paknam. *Form and Continuity in Thai Art and Culture.* Bangkok: Muang Boran, 1987.

Ouan Maitree, "The Sao Intakil Festival," *Guidelines Magazine* 9/5 (May 2002): p. 14.

Ockey, James. "God Mothers, Good Mothers, Good Lovers: Gender Images in Thailand," *Journal of Asian Studies* 58 (November 1999): pp. 1033–58.

Panurat Poladitmontri. *Thailand: The Beautiful Cookbook.* Toronto: HarperCollins Canada, 1992.

Pasuk Phongpaichit and Chris Baker. *Thailand: Economy and Politics.* Kuala Lumpur: Oxford University Press, 1995.

Peleggi, Maurizio. *Lords of Things: The Fashioning of the Siamese Monarchy's Modern Image.* Honolulu: University of Hawaii Press, 2002.

Penth, Hans. *A Brief History of Lan Na: Civilizations of Northern Thailand.* Chiang Mai: Silkworm Books, 1994.

Phillips, Herbert P. *Modern Thai Literature.* Honolulu: University of Hawaii Press, 1987.

———. *The Integrative Art of Modern Thailand.* Berkeley: Lowie Museum, University of California, Berkeley, 1992.

Piyalada Devakula, "A Tradition Rediscovered: Toward an Understanding of Experiential Characteristics and Meanings of the Traditional Thai House," Ph.D. dissertation, Faculty of Architecture, University of Michigan, 1999.

Phraya Anuman Rajadhon. *Some Traditions of the Thai.* Bangkok: Thai Inter-Religious Commission for Development and Sathirakoses Nagapradipa Foundation, 1987.

Rachada Rithdee, "Thai Talismans," *Sawasdee Magazine* 31/6 (June 2002): pp. 43–48.

Randolph, R. Sean. *The United States and Thailand: Alliance Dynamics 1950–85.* Berkeley: Institute of East Asian Studies, University of California, Berkeley, 1986.

Rawson, Philip. *The Art of Southeast Asia.* London: Thames and Hudson, 1967.

Reat, Noble Ross. *Buddhism: A History.* Berkeley, CA: Asian Humanities Press, 1994.

Renard, Ronald D. *Opium Reduction in Thailand 1970–2000: A Thirty Year Journey.* Chiang Mai: Silkworm Books, 2001.

Reynolds, Craig J. *National Identity and Its Defenders: Thailand 1939–1989.* Clayton, Australia: Centre of Southeast Asian Studies, Monash University, 1991.

Reynolds, E. Bruce. *Thailand and Japan's Southern Advance 1940–1945.* New York: St. Martin's Press, 1994.

Ringis, Rita. *Elephants of Thailand in Myth, Art, and Reality.* Kuala Lumpur: Oxford University Press, 1996.

———. *Thai Temples and Temple Murals.* Singapore: Oxford University Press, 1990.

Robertson, Richard G., ed., *Robertson's Practical English–Thai Dictionary,* 20th edition. Rutland, VT: Charles E. Tuttle, 1990.

Rong Syamananda, *A History of Thailand.* Bangkok: Thai Watana Panich, 1986.

Santi Leksukhum. *Temples of Gold: Seven Centuries of Thai Buddhist Paintings.* New York: George Braziller, 2000.

*Sawasdee Magazine.* Tourism Authority of Thailand, Bangkok.

Segaller, Denis. *More Thai Ways.* Bangkok: Post Publishing Company, 1987.

Shigeharu Tanabe and Keyes, Charles F., eds. *Cultural Crisis and Social Memory: Modernity and Identity in Thailand and Laos.* London: Routledge Curzon, 2002.

Siriporn Nathalang, ed. *Thai Folklore: Insights into Thai Culture.* Bangkok: Chulalong Korn University Press, 2000.

Smith, Malcolm. *A Physician at the Court of Siam.* Oxford: Oxford University Press, 1986.

Smithies, Michael, ed. *Descriptions of Old Siam.* Oxford: Oxford University Press, 1995.

Smitthi Siribhadra and Elizabeth Moore. *Palaces of the Gods: Khmer Art and Architecture in Thailand.* London: Thames and Hudson, 1992.

Soloman, Charmaine. *The Complete Asian Cookbook.* Vancouver: Raincoast Books, 1992.

Stratton, Carol and Miriam McNair Scott, eds. *The Art of Sukhothai: Thailand's Golden Age.* Kuala Lumpur: Oxford University Press, 1981.

Subhadradis Diskul. *Art in Thailand: A Brief History.* Bangkok: Krung Siam Press, 1971.

Suchit Bunbongkan. *Thailand.* Singapore: Institute of Southeast Asian Studies, 1996.

Sukphisit Suthon. *Folk Arts and Folk Culture: The Vanishing Face of Thailand.* Bangkok: Post Books, 1997.

Sumset Jumsai. *Naga: Cultural Origins in Siam and the West Pacific.* Singapore: Oxford University Press, 1988.

Surachart Bamrungsuk. *United States Foreign Policy and Thai Military Rule 1947–1977.* Bangkok: Editions Duang Kamol, 1988.

Tarling, Nicholas. *Nations and States in Southeast Asia.* Cambridge: Cambridge University Press, 1994.

———, ed. *The Cambridge History of Southeast Asia,* vols. 1 and 2. Cambridge: Cambridge University Press, 1992.

Taylor, Pamela York. *Beasts, Birds, and Blossoms in Thai Art.* Kuala Lumpur: Oxford University Press, 1994.

Terwiel, B.J. *Monks and Magic: An Analysis of Religious Ceremonies in Central Thailand.* London: Curzon Press, 1975.

Thai World View. Website at *www.thaiworldview.com*

Thailand On-Line. Thailand Publications, Switzerland, at *www.thailine.com*

Thanapol Chadchaidee. *Essays on Thailand,* 10th edition. Bangkok: Thanapol Vittayakarn, 1994.

Thavibu Gallery. Website at *www.thavibu.com*

Thompson, David. *Thai Food.* Toronto: Ten Speed Press, 2002.

Tongchai Winichakul. *Siam Mapped: A History of the Geo-Body of a Nation.* Honolulu: University of Hawaii Press, 1994.

Thorbek, Susanne. *Voices from the City: Women of Bangkok.* London: Zed Books, 1987.

University of British Columbia language library. Website at *www.library.ubc.ca/edlib/worldlang/thai/index.htm*

Van Beek, Steve. *The Arts of Thailand.* London: Thames and Hudson, 1991.

———. *The Chao Phya: River in Transition.* Kuala Lumpur, Oxford University Press, 1995.

Warren, William. *Bangkok.* London: Reaktion Books, 2002.

———. *Images of Thailand.* Hong Kong: Hong Kong Publishing, 1981.

———. *The Thais at Leisure.* Bangkok: Department of Export Production, Ministry of Commerce, 1988.

Warren, William and Luca Invernizzi Tettoni. *Arts and Crafts of Thailand.* San Francisco: San Francisco Chronicle of Books, 1996.

———. *Living in Thailand: Traditional and Modern Homes and Decoration.* London: Thames and Hudson, 1988.

Welcome to Chiang Mai and Chiangrai, *Comprehensive Consumer Travel Magazine* (Chiang Mai). Web site at *www.chiangmai.chiangrai.com*

Wenk, Klaus. *Thai Literature: An Introduction.* Bangkok: White Lotus Press, 1995.

West, Richard. *Thailand: The Last Domino.* London: Michael Joseph, 1991.

Woodward, Hiram. *The Art and Architecture of Thailand: From Prehistoric Times Through the 13th Century.* Leiden: E.J. Brill, 2003.

Wyatt, David K. *Thailand: A Short History.* New Haven, CT: Yale University Press, 1982.

# Index

**About the Author**

ARNE KISLENKO is Assistant Professor of History at Ryerson University, Toronto, and Adjunct Professor of International Relations at Trinity College, University of Toronto. He is the co-editor of *The Uneasy Century: International Relations in the Twentieth Century* (1996) and has written frequently on various dimensions of U.S.-Thai relations and Thai foreign policy.